Commercial Law Reports (Annotated): Being Reports of Important Decisions Relating to Companies, Banks and Banking, Insurance, Insolvency, and Similar Subjects in the Federal and Provincial Courts, Volume 1

Anonymous

COMMERCIAL LAW REPORTS.

(ANNOTATED.)

BEING REPORTS OF IMPORTANT DECISIONS
RELATING TO COMPANIES, BANKS AND
BANKING, INSURANCE, INSOLVENCY,
AND SIMILAR SUBJECTS IN THE
FEDERAL AND PROVINCIAL
COURTS;

TOGETHER WITH

ANNOTATIONS, A TABLE OF CASES CITED,
AND AN INDEX-DIGEST.

VOL. I.

TORONTO:
CANADA LAW BOOK COMPANY,
LAW PUBLISHERS,
32-34 TORONTO STREET,
1903.

279697

CASES REPORTED.

CASES CITED.

[IN THE SUPREME COURT OF CANADA.]

BEFORE SIR HENRY STRONG, C. J., AND TASCHEREAU, GWYNNE, SEDGEWICK AND KING, JJ.

HUGH P. KEEFER and the QUEBEC BANK (Plaintiffs) Appellants

AND

THE PHOENIX INSURANCE COMPANY OF HARTFORD (Defendant) Respondent.

(ON APPEAL FROM THE COURT OF APPEAL FOR ONTARIO.)

Insurance against fire—Insurable interest—Unpaid vendor.

1. An unpaid vendor, who by agreement with his vendee has insured the property sold, may recover its full value in case of loss, though his interest may be limited, if when he effected the insurance he intended to protect the interest of the vendee as well as his own.
2. The fact that the vendor is not the sole owner need not be stated in the policy, nor disclosed to the insurer.
3. Judgment of the Court of Appeal (26 Ont. App. R. 277) reversed, and that of the trial judge (29 O. R. 394) restored.

ARGUMENT: 20th April, 1900.

JUDGMENT: 19th February, 1901.

Appeal from a decision of the Court of Appeal for Ontario (26 Ont. App. R. 277) reversing the judgment at the trial (29 O. R. 394) in favour of the plaintiffs.

The plaintiff Keefer sold a piece of land to one Cloy for $2,000, payable by instalments, agreeing to keep it insured for the amount of the purchase money, which he did. A fire having occurred causing a loss of $1,740, when Keefer had been paid $800 by Cloy, the insurance company refused to pay more than the amount of Keefer's interest, and the latter brought an action to recover the full amount of the loss, the Quebec Bank, as assignee of Cloy's interest in the policy, joining him as plaintiff.

At the trial before Mr. Justice Ferguson, the plaintiff recovered the full sum claimed, but this judgment was reversed by the Court of Appeal. The plaintiffs then appealed to this court.

THE CHIEF JUSTICE.—

I concur in the judgment of Mr. Justice Sedgewick.

TASCHEREAU, J.—

I am of opinion that the appeal should be dismissed.

GWYNNE.—

I entirely concur in the judgment of the Court of Appeal for Ontario in this case. The policy of insurance sued upon is printed and is in the statutory form prescribed by ch. 167, R. S. O. 1887, and is one only of indemnity, expressed, I think, in very plain terms, whereby the defendant agreed,

" to indemnify and make good unto the said insured, his heirs or assigns, all such direct loss or damage (not exceeding in amount $2,000, nor the interests of the insured in the property herein described)."

At the trial the interest of the assured at the time of the policy being made, although then represented by him to be his own property, was in fact that of a vendor with a lien thereon for unpaid purchase money, amounting then to the sum of $1,200. Now that this policy so entered into operated solely as an insurance against loss of the insured's direct beneficial interest as such unpaid vendor cannot, I think, admit of a doubt.

The suggestion that the words " heirs or assigns " and " interests " (in the plural) as used in the above contract, which is in printed form, show that the assured intended to insure the interest of his vendee as well as his own, has been fully answered by the judgment of the Court of Appeal for Ontario, and nothing can in my opinion be usefully added thereto. As to the assured having had the intention suggested (assuming him to have entertained it), all that need be said is that such intention is not expressed in the contract, and it cannot be argued that a secret intention of the assured can be appealed to for the purpose of changing the terms of the contract, contrary to the intention of both parties to the contract as expressed therein. But this point also is fully dealt with by the judgment appealed against. The appeal, therefore, must in my opinion be dismissed with costs.

SEDGEWICK, J.—

The appellant Keefer, on the 25th July, 1893, being the owner of certain lands and premises in the town of Thorold, upon which the buildings covered by the policy in question were erected, entered into an agreement with one George C. Cloy to sell the property to him for $2,000, payable as follows : $300 in cash ; $500 in four months, and the balance, $1,200 in twelve months. At the same time Keefer verbally agreed with Cloy to keep the buildings insured to the extent of $2,000 until the purchase money should be fully paid. There was, at the date of the agreement, a policy in force covering the property for that amount, and this policy was allowed to remain until the 23rd of February, 1894, when the policy sued on was substituted for it, and issued to the appellant Keefer. Cloy at this time had paid Keefer $800 on account of the purchase money, and subsequently paid him $500. The policy was renewed from time to time, and on the 11th December, 1896, the frame building mentioned in the policy was destroyed by fire, and another building damaged to the extent of $40, making a loss of $1,740, the amount claimed in this action. At this date the purchase money payable to Keefer had been reduced by payments made by Cloy to $700. The interest which Cloy had, or claimed to have, under the policy was assigned to the Quebec Bank, and this action was brought by Keefer and the Quebec Bank to recover the total amount of loss, the bank claiming the interest of Cloy under its assignment, as well as that of Keefer.

The case was tried before Mr. Justice Ferguson, and judgment given in favor of the appellant. This judgment was reversed by the Court of Appeal, Mr. Justice Maclennan dissenting.

At the time of the fire, the appellant was the owner in fee of the whole property, but having only a beneficial interest to the extent of $1,200, and Cloy having a beneficial interest to the extent of $800, and the question in dispute here is whether an unpaid vendor can recover not only his beneficial interest but the beneficial interest of his vendee as well, as under the circumstances of the present case.

I am clearly of the opinion that he can. The learned Chief Justice of this court in *Caldwell* v. *Stadacona Fire and Life Ins. Co.* (11 S. C. R. 242) thus clearly lays down what I understand to be the law :

"Whatever doubt may be raised by text writers, it is clear, from the language of judges used in delivering judgments in cases of authority, that provided the assured had an interest at the time of the execution of the policy, and at the date of the loss, he is entitled to recover upon a fire policy the full value of the property destroyed, provided the whole interest in the property was insured, although his interest may have been a limited one merely."

He cites, among other cases, *Simpson* v. *Scottish Union Ins. Co.* (1 H. and M. 618), where Vice-Chancellor Wood says :

"I agree that a tenant from year to year, having insured, would have a right to say that the premises should be rebuilt for him to occupy, and that his insurable interest is not limited to the value of his tenancy from year to year."

And *Waters* v. *Monarch Assur. Co.* (5 E. and B. 870), where Lord Campbell says :

"The last point that arises is : To what extent does the policy protect those goods ? The defendants say that it was only the plaintiffs' personal interest. But the policies are in terms contracts to make good " all such damage and loss as may happen by fire to the property hereinbefore mentioned." That is a valid contract, and as the property is wholly destroyed, the value of the whole must be made good, not merely the particular interest of the plaintiffs. They will be entitled to apply so much to cover their own interest and will be trustees for the owners as to the rest. The authorities are clear that an assurance made without orders may be ratified by the owners of the property, and then the assurers become trustees for them."

My brother Gwynne at page 260, in the same case, expressed similar views.

Castellain v. *Preston.* (11 Q. B. D. 380), (a case very largely relied on by the majority of the court below), strongly supports the view just stated. Lord Bowen says :

"It is well known in marine and in fire insurance that a person who has a limited interest may insure nevertheless on the total value of the subject matter of the insurance, and he may recover the whole value, subject to these two provisions ; first of all, the form of his policy must be such as to enable him to recover the total value, because the assured may so limit himself by the way in which he insures as not really to insure the whole value of the subject-matter ; and secondly, he must intend to insure the whole value at the time. When the insurance is effected he cannot recover the entire value unless he has intended to insure the entire value. A person with a limited interest may insure either for himself and to cover his own interest only, or he may insure so as to cover not merely his own limited interest, but the interest of all others who are interested in

the property. It is a question of fact what is his intention
when he obtains the policy. But he can only hold for so
much as he has intended to insure. Then to take a case
which perhaps illustrates more exactly the argument, let
us turn to the case of a mortgagee. If he has the legal
ownership, he is entitled to insure for the whole value, but
even supposing he is not entitled to the legal ownership, he
is entitled to insure prima facie for all. If he intends to
cover only his mortgage and is only insuring his own
interest, he can only in the event of a loss hold the amount
to which he has been damnified. If he has intended to
cover other persons beside himself, he can hold the surplus
for those whom he has intended to cover.''

A case which I cite, not as authority, but as clearly
stating what I conceive to be the law, is that of *Insurance
Company* v. *Updegraff*. (21 Penn. 520.)

'' Although the vendor,'' (the court says), ''is not
bound to insure, or even to continue an insurance already
made, he may, like any other trustee having the legal title,
insure if he thinks proper to the full value of the property.
It is true that in the case of a mortgagee of a ship he can
only recover to the extent of his mortgage debt, unless it
appears that in effecting the insurance he intended to cover,
not his own interest only, but that of the mortgagor also.
If he intended to cover the whole interest, both legal and
equitable, he may recover the whole amount of the insurance, under a trust, as to the surplus, to hold it for the
mortgagor. The same rule applies to the case of an insurance by a vendor. There is this difference, however, that
as the whole estate is at law in the vendor, and the vendee
has only a title to go into equity, the insurance company
cannot assert the rights of the latter, or go into equity in
respect to them, except upon principles of equity and good
conscience. An insurance upon a house, effected by the
vendor, is prima facie an insurance upon the whole legal
and equitable estate, and not upon the balance of the purchase money. Where the form of the policy shows it to be
upon the house, and not upon the debt secured by it, the
burthen of showing that the insurance was upon the latter,
and not upon the former, rests upon the underwriters.
There is no hardship in this. The premium paid, as compared with that usually charged where the insurance is upon
houses, and not upon debts secured by them, is generally

decisive of the question, and the rates of insurance are peculiarly within the knowledge of the insurance company. If the insurance was upon the whole estate the premium would be according to the usual rates for houses of that description and location ; if it was only upon the debt due to the vendor, there would be a large reduction on account of the responsibility of the vendee, and the value of the lot of ground included in the sale, because both of these would, in that case, stand as indemnities to the underwriters. They would be entitled to a cession of the vendor's claims, from which an ample indemnity might be recovered.''

There cannot, I think, be any question but that in the present case the appellant intended to insure the whole property, and not merely his beneficial interest therein. The agreement between him and Cloy is clear evidence of this as well as the terms of the policy itself.   Nor in my view is there any doubt but that the company thought that it was insuring the whole property.   The premium is for an insurance not upon a partial but upon an absolute interest.   The terms of the policy show that the building itself was insured.   The company agreed to make good all such direct loss or damage not exceeding in amount the interests of the assured in the property described, and that word '' interests,'' I think clearly includes interests of all kinds, if insurable ; legal interests, equitable interests, and all other interests arising from any relationship between the assured and any one claiming under the assurance.

Some of the learned judges below seem to have thought the fact that Cloy's interest was not disclosed at the time of the insurance vitiated the policy.   The authorities are conclusively the other way.   Bowen L. J., in *Castellain* v. *Preston* (11 Q. B. D. 380) says two conditions only are necessary in order to entitle the assured to recover, '' first, the form of his policy must be such as to enable him to recover the total value ; and secondly, he must intend to insure the whole value at the time.''

It is nowhere a condition of his recovering the whole amount that he must disclose all the parties interested. The law, I think, is well laid down in Wood on Fire Insurance, sec. 151 :

'' Unless the policy requires that the interest of the insured shall be disclosed, a failure to disclose the nature of his interest or of the existence of a lien or encumbrance thereon, is not a fraudulent concealment, and the policy is operative if the assured in fact has an insurable interest therein.''

Lord Tenterden, in *Crowley* v. *Cohen* (3 B. & Ad. 478), says :

''Although the subject matter of the insurance must be properly described, the nature of the interest may in general be left at large.''

And see Arnold on Marine Ins., 6th ed. p. 51.

In arriving at the conclusion which I have done, I have been much influenced by the statement of the law in *Castellain* v. *Preston* (11 Q. B. D. 380). There is nothing inconsistent with our present judgment in that case. There it was practically admitted that the vendor insured only in his own interest, and the case proceeding upon that assumption merely held that the vendor having received the full amount of the purchase money the insurance company became subrogated to his rights against the vendee, and could recover from him, the vendor, any excess which he received beyond a proper indemnity. On the whole, I think, this appeal must be allowed, and the judgment of the trial judge restored.

KING, J.—

I agree with Osler J. that the case mainly turns upon the question :

''What is the proper construction of the policy of insurance? Is it limited by its terms to the plaintiff's interest which, though not disclosed to the company, was that of an unpaid vendor, or is it an insurance not only for himself but for others interested, as for example, the vendee, to the extent of the value insured ? ''

And again :

'' The question is whether the policy is apt for the purpose ? ''

The learned judge came to the conclusion that the words are not apt for such latter purpose, and that therefore the plaintiff's interest as unpaid vendor to the extent of the $700 remaining due at the time of the loss was alone at risk at that time.

The policy declares in the first place that the company
"in consideration of the stipulations herein named and of
$40 premium does insure H. F. Keefer for the term of one
year from the 23rd day of February, 1894, at noon, to the
23rd day of February, 1895, at noon, against all direct loss
or damage by fire except as hereinafter provided to an
amount not exceeding $2,000, to the following described
property, while located and contained as described herein
and not elsewhere, to wit : $1,700 on the frame building
(describing it) and $300 on his frame storehouse (describing
it)."

It subsequently goes on as follows :

"And the said Phœnix Insurance Company hereby agrees
to indemnify and make good unto the assured, his heirs
and assigns, all such direct loss or damage (not exceeding
in amount the sum or sums insured as above specified, nor
the interests of the assured in the property herein described), the amount of loss or damage to be estimated
according to the actual cash value of the property with
proper deduction for depreciation however caused."

I must admit to having been for some time of the
opinion that by the terms of the indemnity clause the insurer's liability was limited to an amount (within the sum
assured) not exceeding the assured's own interest at risk
and liable to be prejudiced by a loss.   Such seemed to me
the fair meaning and scope of the indemnity clause ; and it
appeared to be quite unnecessary to guard therein against
non-insurable claims or interests, as these would be excluded
by the implied terms of an insurance contract.   On fuller
consideration, however, I think that the policy has a different meaning.   By its opening clause, already recited, the
plaintiff is insured generally in respect of the property mentioned to the amount specified, that is to say, he is insured
generally in respect to his insurable interests in the property,
whatsoever they may be.   Then in the indemnifying
clause, the company undertakes in terms to indemnify and
make good unto the assured all such direct loss or damage ;
but that this may not appear to be a covenant to pay $2,000
in any event in case of loss, the words are added : " not exceeding in amount the sum or sums insured as above specified ; " and further, that it may not appear to be a covenant to pay the amount irrespective of the existence or continuance of the insurable interest of the assured, the further

words are added : "nor the interests (i.e., the insurable interests) of the assured in the property herein described," and then the clause goes on to provide for the mode in which the amount of loss or damage shall be estimated. Strictly, the saving clauses, both as to the sums specified as insured and to the insured's interests in the property, were not necessary ; nor were they more necessary in the one case than in the other, and in both cases appear to have been inserted by way of greater caution. The object of the clause of indemnity, so called, was not to limit or define the subject of insurance in any way. That had been sufficiently designated or described in the opening clause of the policy. As to the use of apt words to cover beneficial interests intended to be insured, it seems to me that these need not be specially descriptive of such other interests in the subject of the insurance. All that is meant is that the words shall be large enough to cover all that was in fact intended. If they are so, the insurer's concurrence in what the assured intended to be embraced in them is implied, and so the difficulty involved in his supposed non-concurrence is removed.

The next question is whether it is competent for an unpaid vendor retaining the legal title and having the right so to retain it, to insure and recover for the whole value of the property which he has bargained to sell, there being no question of his intention so to insure and no question of the use of apt words therefor in the policy.

It is not easy to see how such a case can be put lower than that of a mortgagee, as instanced by Bowen L. J. at p. 398 of *Castellain* v. *Preston* (11 Q. B. D. 380) where he says :

" If he has the legal ownership he is entitled to insure for the whole value. If he intends to cover only his mortgage, and is only insuring his own interest, he can only, in the event of a loss, hold the amount to which he has been damnified. If he has intended to cover other persons besides himself he can hold the surplus for those whom he has intended to cover. But one thing he cannot do, that is, having intended only to cover himself, and being a person whose interest is only limited, he cannot hold anything beyond the amount of the loss caused to his own particular interest."

I cannot concur with Mr. Justice Maclennan in regarding

what was said by Bowen, L. J., as "an authoritative statement of the law by the Court of Appeal in England." The
other members of that court had preceded him in the
delivery of separate opinions in which the several matters
arising in the case were fully considered, and we are not to
suppose that they adopted all the views and statements of
law expressed by Bowen, L. J., in his somewhat wide
incursion into the field of insurance law. To me it appears
that, in respect of what is said by him as bearing on this
appeal, his views mark a departure to some extent from
prior authority ; still we have in them the considered opinion
of a very high authority which, so far as I am able to
discover, appears also to have been adopted and established
as part of the law and practice of insurance, and which, as
limited by him, appears to be consistent with good sense.

The remaining and alternative part of the case relates to
the effect of the alleged agreement with the vendee for the
keeping alive of insurance on the premises. If that agreement were a valid one, I think that there could be no doubt
that under this policy the plaintiff could recover in respect
of the whole value of the property to the extent of the
insurance, for in such case the plaintiff, in addition to the
amount of his interest as unpaid vendor, would, in case of
loss, be prejudiced to the further amount to which he had
bound himself to keep up in the insurance.

The result is that I concur in allowing the appeal.

Appeal allowed with costs.

Solicitors for the Appellants : *Collier and Yale.*

Solicitors for the Respondent : *Smith, Rae and Greer.*

Notes :—

The case of *Castellain* v. *Preston* (1883) 11 Q. B. D. 380,
referred to in the above judgment, was one in which a
vendor, who had previously insured his house against loss
by fire, contracted for the sale thereof, no reference being
made to the policy of insurance. After the contract was
made, but before its competion, the house was damaged by
fire, and the vendor obtained the insurance money from the
company (the plaintiff). In an action subsequently brought
by the latter against the vendor it was held that they were
entitled to recover back the insurance money, either for their
own benefit, or as trustees for the purchaser. The principle

of subrogation laid down in this case was that, on payment of money due under a fire insurance policy, the insurers can enforce all the remedies of the insured, either in contract or in tort, as against third parties, in order to make good the loss.

And in *Aldridge* v. *G. W. Ry. Co.* (1841) 3 Man. & G. 515, it was decided that a contract of insurance was a contract of indemnity only, and that the insurer was put in the place of the insured as regards all his rights of action in respect of the cause of the loss ; the insurer thus having a right of action against the owner of property adjoining that of the insured, when the damage to the latter was caused by the negligence of the former in allowing the fire to spread.

If at some period subsequent to the fire the assured receives other compensation for his loss, the insurer can recover from him the amount which he has thus in all received in excess of his actual loss.

Darrell v. *Tibbits*, (1879) 5 Q. B. D. 560.

And see, *North British* v. *London, Liverpool & Globe*, (1877) 5 C. D. 569.

In *Rayner* v. *Preston* (1881) 18 C. D. 1, it was held that where a house was burned between the date of a contract for its sale and the date fixed for the completion of the contract, and the vendor had received the insurance money, the purchaser, as against the vendor, could not recover the insurance moneys either as an abatement of his purchase-money or for the repair of the premises.

As regards the effect of non-disclosure to the insurance company of the insured's exact interest in the property, contrary to a clause in the policy, the recent decision of the Supreme Court of Canada in the case of *Temple* v. *Western Assurance Co.* is in point. T. had insured his property against loss by fire, the policy containing a clause which stated that " if the insured is not the sole and unconditional owner of the property, or if any building intended to be assured stands on ground not owned in fee simple by the assured, or if the interest of the assured in the property, whether as owner, trustee, assignee, factor, agent, mortgagee, lessee, or otherwise, is not truly stated in this policy   .   .   .   .   . this policy shall become void, unless consent in writing by the company be endorsed thereon." At the date of the policy there was a small mortgage on the property then insured, but T., who insured as owner, did not communicate this fact to the company. It was held by the Supreme Court of Canada (judgment rendered June 5, 1901) that this mortgage did not, under the condition above quoted, avoid the policy.

———

[COURT OF KING'S BENCH, QUEBEC.]

(APPEAL SIDE.)

BEFORE SIR ALEXANDRE LACOSTE, C. J. AND BOSSÉ, BLANCHET, HALL AND OUIMET, J. J.

CAME (Defendant) Appellant.

v.

THE CONSOLIDATED CAR HEATING CO.
(Plaintiffs) Respondents.

Patent for a combination—Rules of construction—No infringement unless all the elements are used.

1. A patent is a contract between the government granting the same, or the public, and the patentee, and must be construed like all other contracts; but when there is any doubt as to the true meaning of the patent, which expresses the intentions of the parties to the contract, it must be interpreted against the patentee, as the latter is the stipulator.

2. Where a patentee, in one of his claims, describes the working of a locking and unlocking device, without any specific mention of a hinge joint (referred to in the other claims) which, in the opinion of the Court, is one of the elements co-operating in that process, and contributing to the firmness of the locking, such hinge joint will be held to form part of the locking device, and to be included in the claim of the same.

3. The true rule, both in Canada and in England, regarding the infringement of a patent for a combination is the same as that which has been firmly established in the United States, namely, that the patent is not infringed unless all the elements which go to make up the combination are used. In such cases it is impracticable to declare that there has been an infringement by the taking of the "pith and marrow," or "the substance and essence" of the patent, as it is generally impossible to arrive at the exact meaning of these terms with reference to a particular patent.

MONTREAL, May 29, 1901.

SIR ALEXANDRE LACOSTE, C. J. (*Translation.*)—

The action is for infringement of a patent and for an injunction.

The respondent is the assignee of Sewall, who obtained, on the 4th of May, 1887, a patent for what is known as the " Sewall Coupler."

The appellant is the agent of the Gold Car Heating Company, which manufactures a coupler known as the " Gold Coupler," claimed by the respondent as being an infringement of his patent.

The first judgment went against the appellant, granting an injunction, but as that was the real object of the suit, he was condemned only in the nominal sum of $25 as damages.

Sewall's invention consists in " certain new and useful improvements in hose couplings." Its object is " to construct a two part hose coupling, each half of which is alike, which may be used to couple together hose for the passage of steam, air, water, gas, etc."

The coupling hangs by gravity, and is provided with locking devices which keep the two halves locked together in all positions except when turned upwards at the centre. At the lower end of the meeting faces is what is called a hinge-joint, upon which the two halves of the coupler are turned to disengage them from each other.

Their combination is described as follows : " Each half of the coupling " is composed " of a body portion having an upwardly turned neck or extension, both of which are bored centrally to form with the hose to be coupled a continuous passage. The body portion is provided at one side with a broad flat extension projecting forward to overlap one side of the body portion of the companion half, and said extension has at one edge an overturned lip or flange. At that side of each half of the coupling opposite the broad extension a groove or passage is cut of suitable shape to receive the flange, and a shoulder is also provided which serves as a bearing. The meeting face of the body portion is provided at its lower end with a rib extending about one-half of the width of the coupling, and said face is cut away at the side of the rib to present a deep groove or recess, for the remaining distance, this recess or groove receiving the rib of the companion portion.''

Then the inventor shows how his combination will operate : '' The two halves of the coupling being placed opposite to each other it will be seen that the extension of one half overlaps the opposite side of the other half, the flange entering the groove and the rib entering a recess formed in the opposite half.''

A disclaimer is inserted which is in the following terms : '' I am aware that two parts hose couplings have been made, each part of which has a passage through it, but a valve has been employed at the junction of the two passages to close the passage when the two parts of the coupling are disengaged, and such a coupling having indirect obstructed passages I do not herein claim.''

And the claims read as follows : '' 1. A two-part hose coupling, composed of like halves or portions, each half consisting of a body portion, having a suitable passage therethrough, a broad extension, locking flange shaped as described and located at one side of the body portion, a groove or passage shaped as described upon the other side of the body portion and a joint connection at the lower side of the meeting face of the body portion upon which the two halves may be turned to disengage them one from the other substantially as described. 2. A two part hose coupling composed of two like halves or portions adapted to be locked together against lateral or downward pressure but to be disengaged by the upward movement only, each half of which consists of a body portion having a suitable passage through it, a broad extension located at one side of the body portion and having a locking flange upon the upper side of the broad extension and extending in a diagonal line, a groove or passage upon the other side of the body portion also extending in a diagonal line and having at the lower side of the meeting faces of the body portions a co-operative part of a separable connection, all substantially as and for the purpose set forth. 3. In a two part hose coupling composed of like halves or portions each of which has a free and unobstructed passage through it directly from end to end, which passages co-operate together to form a longitudinal unobstructed passage directly through the hose coupling, combined with locking devices, as described, upon each side to lock the said halves or portions together, as set forth.''

The Gold coupler is composed of two like halves consisting of a body portion having a free and unobstructed passage through it directly from end to end, which passages co-operate together to form a longitudinal unobstructed passage directly through the hose coupling combined with locking devices similar, practically, to those described in the Sewall patent, with the exception, nevertheless, of the hinge-joint, which is cut off in Gold's. There is in addition a rocking gasket at the end of each passage at the meeting faces, which ensures a steam tight joint.

The respondent urges that the Gold coupler is a piracy of his third claim, which does not include the hinge joint, and that the rocking gasket is an improvement upon his own combination, and cannot be used with his invention without a license.

He further says that even admitting that the hinge joint be included in every one of his claims it is not an essential part of his invention and that appellant in using the Gold coupler has taken the substance of his combination and has thus infringed his patent.

The question I now take up is not whether the hinge joint is an essential part of the patent but whether it is included in the third claim.

This patent, which is a contract between the government, or the public, and the patentee, must be interpreted like all other contracts. The intention of the parties must be found in the contract itself and the interpretation of its several clauses is a question of law which is left to the court. The rules of interpretation are those applied to other contracts.

The maxim, *ut res magis valeat quam pereat*, has really no application in this case, because, whatever interpretation we lay on the third claim, it will have an effect. But in case of doubt the contract is interpreted against him who has stipulated, that is to say, the patentee. It is in the light of these principles that we will examine the third claim of the patent.

The respondent contends that the third claim is a mere combination of the main portion of the two halves with the locking devices upon each side to lock said halves ; that the hinge joint is not part of the locking devices ; that its function, as stated in the patent, is not to help in the locking ; that at all events, it is not part of the locking devices which are on the sides of the coupler.

In deciding these propositions, reference must be made to the specifications where the invention is described and to the two first claims, being invited to do so by the words '' as described,'' and '' as set forth,'' contained in the third claim.

Does the hinge joint form part of the locking devices ?

Nowhere in the patent does Sewall say, in so many words, what he means by ''locking devices ;'' but no operation, whether of locking or unlocking, is described in which the hinge joint is not used.

After having described the several elements that compose his combination, that is to say, the body portion, the broad extension with its flange, the corresponding groove, and the hinge joint, he proceeds to show how the locking will be affected : '' The two halves of the coupling being placed opposite to each other, it will be seen that the extension of one-half overlaps the opposite side of the other half, the flange entering the groove and the rib entering the recess formed in the opposite half.''

So the rib and recess, that is to say, the hinge joint, is shown to be one of the elements co-operating in the locking of the couplers. And the inventor immediately adds : '' It will thus be seen that the two halves are firmly locked together,'' giving to understand that all the elements above named contribute to the firmness of the locking.

As to the unlocking, he says that the halves are '' capable of being disengaged only by moving them upward on the ribs turning in the grooves which serve as a hinge joint or connection.'' The important function of the hinge joint in the disengagement or unlocking of the coupler is thus clearly demonstrated.

In a lock every element used in unlocking forms part of the locking devices. I might add that in the first claim the hinge joint is described as a "joint connection upon which the two halves are turned to disengage," and in the second, "a co-operative part of a separable connection."

Our conclusion must, therefore, be that the hinge joint forms part of the locking devices.

But, says the respondent, the locking devices mentioned in the third claim, are limited to those "upon each side," and the hinge joint is not on the side, but at the lower end of the meeting face, as stated in the specifications.

This is true in one sense, but in the two first claims the hinge joint is mentioned as being at the lower side, while the flange and the corresponding groove are at the upper side.   There are four sides in the mind of the inventor.   To which side does he allude in the third claim?   It may be to the flange or groove only, but not necessarily so.   The third claim seems to have been put in to particularize a special passage through the main portion of the coupler which Sewall intended to cover by his patent.   A free and unobstructed passage—"direct from end to end"—"a longitudinal unobstructed passage directly through the hose coupling," and this seems to have been done as a precautionary measure in case his two first claims which apply to a suitable passage would be anticipated.

If the third claim had been the only one made, could it have been said that it did not cover the hinge joint?   Evidently not.   And why should we give a different interpretation because there are two other claims when the specifications disclose the evident intention of the inventor to include the hinge joint in every operation, and to make it the basis of the disengagement process.

If Sewall meant to include the flange and the corresponding groove only, why did he not say it clearly, as he did a few days previous to the fyling of his claim in the Canadian Patent Office, when he fyled his amended claim in the United States Patent Office?

No doubt, in interpreting a patent which is a contract between the patentee and the public, we must decide the question without any bias, but the public has a right to know what it is prohibited from doing.   It is upon the patentee, who is the stipulator, to prove the special restriction imposed upon the public by his third claim and in case of doubt the verdict of a court has to be "not proven." As Lord Cairns said in *Harrison* v. *Auderston Foundry Company*, 1, App., Cases, H. L., 574 : "In case a patentee claimed a subordinate or subsidiary part of the combination, it is necessary to see that the patentee has carefully distinguished those subordinate or subsidiary parts and has not left *in dubio* what claim to parts, in addition to the claim for combination, he meant to assert."

Again the question is not as to the validity of the patent, nor as to the validity of that one claim, but as to its extent.

We, therefore, come to the conclusion that the third claim is too vague and too ambiguous to enable us to say that the inventor contemplated a combination different from the one described in the two first claims, and that we must consider it as being the same combination which includes all the elements of the two others, and in particular the hinge joint.

Assuming now that the hinge joint is included in every one of the claims, is the Gold coupler an infringement of the Sewall patent? The Gold coupler has all the elements of the Sewall patent with the exception of the hinge joint, but it has another element, the rocking gasket, placed at the end of each of the passages that run through the coupler, and which, by its oscillating or rocking capacity, facilitates the adaptation of the two passages or tubes, so as to make a steam-tight joint, even in case the two faces would not meet squarely.

The respondent admitted that the Gold coupler would not be an infringement of its patent in the United States, where, according to the jurisprudence, in a patent for a combination, the patent is not infringed unless all its elements are used ; but it is claimed that the substance of Sewall's combination has been taken by the appellant, and that, according to the English and Canadian courts this constitutes an infringement.

I do not think that there is such a deep gulf between the English or Canadian jurisprudence and the American jurisprudence as respondent contends. To say with the American courts that in a patent for a combination of old elements the subject matter of the patent is the combination itself taken as a whole, which cannot be infringed unless the whole combination is taken, is clearer to my mind than the rule expressed by some of the English and Canadian courts that there is an infringement when the " pith and marrow," "substance and essence," of the combination have been taken. It is easy to find out the pith in a plant, the marrow in a bone, but it is often a heavy task to discover the pith and marrow of a combination.

I have looked at the precedents quoted by both parties, and nowhere could I find a definition of the words pith, marrow, or substance and essence, as applied to a combination, that would satisfy my mind and be a sure guide in the application of the law of this country.

It is understood by all that a patent is a contract between the patentee and the public by which certain privileges asked for by the patentee are granted to him.

The least the public can ask is that these privileges should be clearly defined, so that people acting in good faith may know without a metaphysical exertion of the mind what is left to them, and what they can use without incurring a penalty; it is for that reason that the law of patents has provided for an exact and complete description to be given by the inventor, and also for specific claims.

If the inventor claims a combination, that combination alone is covered, and the other inventors thus know upon what they can work. We find that rule laid down in many of the English cases. Take *Clark* v. *Adie*, 46 L. J., Ch. 185, which is a leading case. It was decided in that case that when a patent is taken out for a combination it will "protect the several subordinate parts, and all subordinate combinations of such parts, provided the subordinate parts or combinations be themselves properly subjects for a patent, and also provided that it is clearly and previously defined by the specifications what are the subordinate parts or combinations of parts in respect of which, as well as the entire combination, protection is claimed."

The Lord Chancellor said : " It must have been made plain that the inventor had it in his mind, and intended to claim protection for these subordinate integers."

Lord Hatherly said : "If you claim for a portion of the machine you must make it plain."

In *Harrison* v. *Anderston Foundry Co.*, 1, App. Cases, 574-578, Lord Cairns said : " If it is clear that the claim is for a combination, and nothing but a combination, there is no infringement unless the whole combination is used."

Lord Chelmsford : " If a patent is solely for a combination, nothing can be an infringement but the use of an entire combination."

Again, Lord Cairns, in *Dudgeon* v. *Thompson*, 3 App. Cases, 44 : " There is no such thing as the infringement of the equity of the patent, but that which is protected is that which is specified, and the infringement must be of what is specified."

That dictum of Lord Cairns was approved in the *Ticket Punch Register Company* v. *Colley's Patents*. In this case Smith, L. J. said : " Their (plaintiffs') complaint must be that the defendants have infringed the combination, for it is the combination, and nothing else which is protected.

These quotations show that the present rule in England is similar to that in the United States.

It is true that in some of the cases cited by the respondent, and by the learned judge who decided the case in the first court, and even in some of the cases above cited, the English judges put to themselves the question : " Has the combination in substance been taken ? "

Perhaps it is not easy to reconcile the dictum of some of the judges with the rule. Yet I think that we may safely say that the English courts never intended to go beyond the claims in the patent, and that if the claim is for a combination, the combination alone is protected ; also that the patent being a contract has to be interpreted like all other contracts.

Sewall claimed a combination of what is admitted by him to be all old elements to procure a coupling of hose having a steam tight joint, and disengaging automatically. According to his specification this coupling is done by the combination of the following elements : the body portion with its passage, the extension with its flange, and its corresponding groove, and the hinge joint. Every element has its special function or functions. The hinge joint forms part of the locking, and it helps in keeping the two halves firmly locked together ; it is a guide in coupling, and ensures the bringing of the two faces squarely together ; and it is the basis of the operation in the disengagement of the coupler.

Can it be said that the hinge joint is not a material part of the combination ? True, the coupler can be coupled and uncoupled without it, but the combination is destroyed, and the process is not as perfect, nor as safe, nor as practicable. This view is supported by the evidence which establishes that Sewall's coupler has never been put on the market without the hinge joint, and that the Safety and Martin Coupler, which have the elements of the Sewall without the hinge joint, could not compete with the Sewall.

It is true that the Gold has all the elements of the Sewall without the hinge joint, and it is a strong competitor of the Sewall on the market, but this is due to the addition of a new element, the rocking gasket, which obviates the inconveniences resulting from the absence of the hinge joint. The Gold does not couple so surely if the person who couples it is not in the practice of coupling hose, and the disengagement is not as perfect ; on the other hand, the rocking gasket secures in one way more safely a steam tight joint.   The Gold does not take from the Sewall Patent the advantage of always bringing squarely together the two faces, nor the firmness of the locking, nor so safe a disengagement so as to prevent a catching.

Under these circumstances can one say that the substance of Sewall's combination has been taken ? The substance of Sewall's is a special mode of coupling, by which he uses the flange already known, the groove already known, the gravity, also known, and the hinge joint, which is a new element.   If the patentee does not claim in his patent a subordinate combination of the body portion with the broad extension, with the flange and the groove, how can he reproach Gold for using this last combination with a new element, the rocking gasket? Patentees who are original inventors of devices are entitled to a broad construction, but a mere improver is confined to his particular device.

We must take into consideration the state of the art at the time the patent was taken. Car hose couplers and modes of couplings of many kinds had been invented and were then in use, all more or less perfect. Locking devices quite similar to the flange and groove in Sewall's, whether applied to side port or port end couplers were in use. The art was gradually advancing towards the thing desired, the field of invention was limited, Sewall discovered a particular device. Are we not to limit him to that particular device?

To take the substance of a combination does not mean merely taking some of the essential elements of the combination without which the combination could not subsist. If it was so, the body portion of the coupler could not be used without infringing.

To take the substance of a combination is to take the combination itself, the whole combination without omitting any material element which the inventor himself considered as material.

As I said, true it is that the coupling and uncoupling could be made without the hinge joint, but not so perfectly. Supposing that a medicine composed of five ingredients already known, should be patented for the cure of croup. Would the patent be infringed by another mixture, including three or four of these ingredients; and, more so, if it is established that this last remedy is less efficacious than the one patented?

Much stress has been laid on the wedging or folding action of Sewall's locking. I cannot see any other action than that of gravity. Gravity is the only acting agent that brings closer the two halves; the flange and the groove are passive, their function is to secure and maintain what gravity has done, and prevent the loosening of the tie.

I quite understand that equivalents or slight changes of no importance will not permit the infringer to escape. But I do not find in Gold's coupler the device as patented in Sewall's, and I am, therefore, to reverse, and this is the unanimous opinion of the Court.

The appeal is allowed.

Solicitors for the Appellant, *Robertson, Fleet & Falconer.*

Solicitors for the Respondents, *McGibbon, Casgrain, Ryan & Mitchell.*

[HIGH COURT OF JUSTICE FOR ONTARIO]

BEFORE MEREDITH, C. J.

Re ABBOTT—MITCHELL IRON AND STEEL CO.

Company—Petition for winding-up order—Service of demand for payment.

1. The demand for payment of a debt due, the neglect to comply with which is proof of insolvency, under R.S.C., cap. 129 (The Winding-up Act) sec. 6, is a formal demand in writing, duly served on the company. The service of a specially endorsed writ of summons does not meet these requirements, not being a " demand " but only a notice that certain proceedings will be taken if the amount thereby claimed is not paid within eight days.

2. It is a condition essential to the making of a winding-up order that the company shall have had the four days' notice of the application given by R.S.C., cap. 129, sec. 8.

TORONTO, July 18, 1901:

I held on the first argument that the case of the petitioners was not made out, but gave them leave to amend by setting up the demand in writing of payment, and the neglect for sixty days to comply with the demand, and the petition having been amended accordingly came on again to be heard on the 23rd of May last, when counsel for the petitioners contended that the service which had been effected on the respondent company of a specially endorsed writ in an action against it to recover the amount of the petitioners' claim was a sufficient demand in writing within the meaning of the Winding-up Act, R. S. C. 1886, cap. 129, sec. 6. Mr. Thompson, for the respondents, contended that it was not; and further argued that the case was not one in which a winding-up order should be made, because, as he contended, there remains practically nothing to be wound up. Contrary to the impression I had on the argument, I have come to the conclusion that the service of the writ was not a sufficient demand in writing requiring the respondent company to pay the amount due to the petitioners within the meaning of sec. 6. The writ is issued from the High Court in the name of the Sovereign, and requires the person summoned to enter an appearance within ten days, and informs him that in default of appearance the judgment may be signed. The endorsement gives the particulars of the claim, and contains a notification of the amount of the plaintiff's claim for debt and costs, and that if the amount be paid within eight days proceedings will be stayed. What the statute requires to be served is a demand in writing requiring the company to pay the sum due, that is, as I understand the language of sec. 6, to pay it at once. Now there is nothing of this nature in the writ or the endorsement upon it. There is in terms no such demand in writing, but only a notice of the effect of payment within eight days, and the claim is, having regard to the nature of the proceedings, not, I think, in the nature of a demand in writing requiring payment to be made. It is but reasonable where what is practically the bankruptcy of the Company is to follow the failure to comply with the demand served, or may do so, that the demand should be reasonably certain in terms, and at all events not calculated to mislead ; and I think that to treat the service of a specially endorsed writ as a sufficient demand in writing would be to sanction what would be calculated to mislead. There is a further objection to giving effect to this, as a ground for making the winding-up order. By sec. 8 of the Act, the petitioning creditor must give four days' notice of his application to the Company before applying by petition for the order, and it would, I think, be against the spirit as well as the letter of the Act if effect were given to a ground of which the Company had not that notice, and which was not put forward in the petition, notice of which was served upon it. Upon the whole, therefore, I conclude that the application should be refused, and I, therefore, dismiss the petition without costs.

Solicitor for the Petitioners, *L. M. Lyon.*

Solicitors for the Company, *Clute, Macdonald & McIntosh.*

Notes :—

It appears from this decision that in order to bring a company within the provisions of R. S. C., c. 129 (The Winding-up Act) sec. 6, (which defines when "a company is deemed to be unable to pay its debts as they become due,"—that being such insolvency as, according to sec. 5, s.s. (a), will justify the making of a winding-up order) it is necessary that a formal written demand for payment shall, for that purpose, have been duly served on the company on behalf of a creditor to the extent of $200 at least, and the company or bank (as the case may be) has failed to pay the debt within sixty or ninety days, respectively, after service of such demand.

And the service must, whenever possible, conform to any local statutes in force regarding the mode of serving process on corporations. *Re Qu'Appelle Valley Farming Co.*, (1888) 5 Man. L. R., 160.   *Re Rapid City Farmers' Elevator Co.*, 9 Man. L. R., (1894) 574.

In a Quebec case it was held that when a company is insolvent, and the insolvency is alleged in the petition, the creditor applying for the order is not obliged to allege and prove that he made the statutory demand. *Mackay* v. *L'Association Coloniale de Construction*, etc. (1884) 13 R. L., 383.

But this decision has not been adopted by the courts of other provinces. See *re Rapid City Farmers' Elevator Co.* (1894) 9 Man. L.R., 574.

But once the company has allowed the stated interval to elapse without complying with the statutory demand for payment, the court has no discretion, but must regard such " neglect " as conclusive evidence of insolvency under the Act. *In re Imperial Hydropathic Hotel Co.*, (1882) 49 L.T. 160.

The attitude of the company, however, must be that of " neglect." There may possibly be some reasonable cause for ·omitting to pay. *In re London & Paris Banking Corporation.* (1874) L.R. 19, Eq. 444.

The order may be obtained before the expiration of the sixty or ninety days after the service of the demand, if the company or bank is in fact insolvent ; but the burden of proving the insolvency then rests upon the petitioning creditor. *Eddy Mfg. Co.* v. *Henderson Lumber Co.* (1890) M.L.R. 6, S.C. 137.

The fact that the creditor is secured in respect of the debt upon which he bases his petition does not effect his right to obtain a winding-up order. *In re Chapel House Colliery.* (1883) L.R. 24 C.D. 259.   *Olathe Silver Mining Co.* (1884) L.R. 27 C.D. 278.

Section 8 uses the words " a creditor for the sum of at least two hundred dollars," omitting to state that the debt must be one which is then due. It has been held, however, that this omission is immaterial, and that it is only a creditor whose debt was actually due at the time of the service of the notice who is entitled to a winding-up order. *Re Atlas Canning Co.* (1897) 5 B. C. R. 661. *In re British Joint Stock Bank* (1890) L. R. 44 C. D. 703.

According to the decisions under the English Winding-Up Act it appears that while a shareholder is only entitled to an order upon proof that there will be some assets (see *re Rica Gold Washing Co.* (1879) L. R. 11 C. D. 36) or that there is a reasonable probability that there will be some (see *re Diamond Fuel Co.* (1879) L. R. 13, C. D. 400), a creditor is, upon proof of insolvency, entitled to one *ex debito justitiæ*, —whether or not there will be any assets for the creditors to divide. *In re Isle of Wight Ferry Co.*, 2 Hem. & R. 597.

And see also, *in re Professional, etc., Building Society*, (1871) L. R. 6, Ch. 856.

[COURT OF KING'S BENCH, MANITOBA.]

BEFORE KILLAM, C. J.

THE IMPERIAL BANK v. THE FARMERS TRADING CO.

Company — Managing director conducting all business — Liability of company for notes made by him.

When the directors of an incorporated company leave the conduct of the general business in the hands of a managing director or secretary, who accepts or makes or endorses such bills or notes as he sees fit, recording such transactions in the books of the company which are examined by its auditors, it will be inferred, (even when there is a by-law to the effect that promissory notes shall be signed by the president and the secretary or managing director) that such secretary or managing director was duly authorized to make promissory notes on behalf of the company ; and any such notes so made and used by him in the ordinary course of business will bind the company.

WINNIPEG, July 1901.

The plaintiff sued as endorsee of three promissory notes, alleging them to have been made by the defendant company in favor of A. J. Creighton and endorsed by the bank.

The Company was incorporated under the Manitoba Joint Stock Company's Act, R.S., M. c. 25, for the purpose of carrying on a trading business. It deals chiefly in agricultural instruments, vehicles, binder-twine and tea. Its place of business is in the town of Portage La Prairie. There are four directors, three of whom are farmers residing at some distance from the town. The fourth is Mr. G. A. J. A. Marshall, who personally conducted and managed the business. In July, 1897, Mr. Marshall was appointed secretary of the company, and in January, 1898, the directors passed a resolution "that Mr. Marshall's position be defined as Managing Director of the Company."

A by-law provided for the secretary keeping minutes of the meetings and having the custody of the corporate seal, books, and papers of the Company. There was no by-law, resolution or other act expressly defining the powers or duties of the managing director.

A by-law provided that cheques were to be signed by the president or vice-president and countersigned by the managing director or secretary.

Another by-law authorized the directors to borrow money from a bank, and empowered the president and the managing director or secretary to sign promissory notes therefor on behalf of the Company.

There was no by-law or other act authorizing the making, acceptance, or endorsement of notes, bills, or cheques, except as just mentioned.

On the 2nd January, 1900, an agreement was made between one Arthur J. Creighton and Marshall, acting for the Company, by which the Company ordered of Creighton certain specified quantities of tea of different kinds at specified prices for future delivery, and Creighton agreed to accept the Company's promissory notes, for the aggregate amount of the order, less ten per cent. thereof, payable in three months from the 2nd January, 1900. The notes were given signed "For the Farmer's Trading Company, Ltd.,

G. A. J. A. Marshall, managing director." The notes sued on are part renewals of these, and are signed in the same way. No tea was ever delivered under the order, and the Company never received any consideration for the notes except Creighton's acceptance of the order of the tea.

On account of the distance at which the three directors resided it was impossible for them to oversee or be consulted about the details of the business, and the specific transactions Marshall managed, both buying and selling. He states that he never told them of the course of business, and that they left it all to him.

From the year 1895 the Company was in the habit of buying tea from Creighton, and from the time of Marshall's appointment as managing director he was accustomed to give Creighton promissory notes, similarly signed, for tea, and also to make notes and accept bills in the same form on behalf of the Company for goods purchased. Many of these were retired by the Company's cheques.

The words " For the Farmer's Trading Company, Ltd.," and " managing director" were impressed on such notes and bills by one rubber stamp, kept in the office of the Company, which was used also for the purpose of endorsements. Different stamps were used for signing cheques.

The cheques were usually signed by the president in blank and left for Marshall to fill up and sign. Counterfoils showed what they were given for.

Notes made and bills accepted were usually entered in a book kept in the Company's office for the purpose of showing bills payable by the Company.

According to Marshall's evidence auditors were from time to time appointed by the directors, and these or any other person examining the books would see that Marshall was in the habit of giving notes for the Company.

There was no direct evidence of knowledge on the part of the shareholders or directors, other than Marshall, of his course in these matters. Marshall professed himself unable to say whether they had such knowledge or not.

The question is whether under these circumstances the Company can be held liable upon these notes.

By section 62 of the Manitoba Joint Stock Companies Act, R. S. M., c. 25, a promissory note made by an agent or officer of a company '' in general accordance with his powers as such officer under the by-law of the Company or otherwise '' is binding upon the Company.

It is clear then that the power may be conferred without by-law.

The powers and duties of the managing director were not expressly defined in any way, but it is evident that he was to exercise large and important functions, otherwise the business of the Company could not go on. His powers, whatever they were, can be gathered only by inference from the nature and course of the business.

It is unnecessary to cite authority to show that the powers of officers or agents of corporations can be inferred. The books are full of cases in which the courts have drawn inferences as to the extent of their powers for the purpose of rendering corporations liable in contract or on tort.

In Lord Justice Lindley's work on Partnership, 6th ed., p. 135, referring to the case of *Hawtayne* v. *Bourne*, 7 M. & W. 595, it is said : '' It will be observed that what is necessary to carry on the partnership business in the ordinary way, is made the test of authority where an actual authority or ratification can be proved. . . . . What is necessary for carrying on the business of the firm under ordinary circumstances and in the usual way is the test . . . The question whether a given act can or cannot be said to be necessary to the transaction of a business in the way in which it is usually carried on must evidently be determined by the nature of the business and by the practice of persons engaged in it. Evidence on both of these points is therefore necessarily admissible, and as may readily be conceived, an act which is necessary for the prosecution of one kind of business may be wholly unnecessary for carrying on another in the ordinary way.''

Of course there are many powers which a partner has to bind his firm that are not presumed in an agent or manager of an incorporated firm. But *in re Cunningham & Co., Limited*, 36 C. D. 532, North, J., adopted the principles there laid down as applicable for determining the authority of a manager of a branch of the business of a Joint Stock Company.   And in considering the authority of the manager in that case to make a prmissory note for the Company, he referred to the fact that it was not in the ordinary course of the business of that Company because it was a newly formed Company and had not yet any ordinary course of business.

In the present case there is no evidence of the ordinary practice of persons engaged in the particular kinds of business in which the defendant Company engaged.   It is, however, well known that it is very common for dealers buying from larger dealers or from manufacturers to give promissory notes or accept bills of exchange for the goods purchased, and I think that very slight evidence should be required to prove such a practice as would involve the inference that this course was necessary for carrying on the business of this Company under ordinary circumstances and in the usual way.

Here the manager made notes and accepted bills for goods purchased, and he did so in the most open way.   The transactions appeared in the books of the Company, its cheques were used—and this, too, appeared on the books—to retire such bills and notes, and the Company's books were audited and the transactions passed.   This course extended over a period of more than two years.   I think that it may properly be inferred from this that the manager was intended to have this among his other powers.

If he had the power to give the Company's notes at all, it is unnecessary to inquire into his authority to enter into the particular transaction out of which the notes in question arose.   Creighton was a dealer in tea from whom the Company was accustomed to buy, and there does not appear to have been anything to indicate to the Bank that the transaction was anything out of the ordinary course.   See *Bryant, Powis and Bryant, Limited*, v. *Quebec Bank*, (1893) A. C. 179.

There will be judgment for the plaintiff for the full amount of the notes, interest and charges, with costs.

Solicitors for the Plaintiffs, *Anderson and Ormond.*

Solicitors for the Defendents, *Cooper and Taylor.*

Notes :—

In the case of *Bryant, Powis and Bryant, Limited,* v. *Quebec Bank*, (1893) A. C. 179, referred to in the foregoing judgment, the Judicial Committee of the Privy Council held that the appellant company was liable to the bank on two bills of exchange indorsed in the name of the company, " per pro C. G. Davies," and discounted by the bank in the ordinary course of business.   In giving judgment their Lordships said that the law on the subject appeared to be "very well stated" in the following extract from the decision rendered by the Court of Appeal for the State of New York in *President, etc., of the Westfield Bank* v. *Cormen*, (1867) 37 N. Y. R., 320 at p. 322.

(The passage is an excerpt from a quotation in the judgment in *North River Bank* v. *Aymar* (1842) 3 Hili, 262 at p. 270, and was only cited as such in the New York case above mentioned):—

" Whenever the very act of the agent is authorized by the terms of the power, that is, whenever by comparing the act done by the agent with the words of the power, the act is in itself warranted by the terms used, such act is binding on the constituent, as to all persons dealing in good faith with the agent ; such persons are not bound to inquire into facts aliunde. The apparent authority is the real authority." See also *Bryant, Powis and Bryant, Limited,* v. *Le Banque du People*, (1893) A. C. 170.

[IN THE HIGH COURT OF JUSTICE FOR ONTARIO]

Before FERGUSON, J.

THE DONNELLY SALVAGE AND WRECKING CO.
v. TURNER

Towing Contract—Vis major—quantum meruit.

When a tug contracts to tow a stranded vessel, but is prevented from
actually doing so by stress of weather and by ice, nothing will be
allowed for the work done in attempting to reach the vessel, when
the evidence shows that by the exercise of due diligence the master
of the tug might have informed himself that it would be impossible
to effect a passage by the route attempted.

TORONTO, June 25, 1901.

The Donnelly Salvage and Wrecking Company are the
plaintiffs, and they carry on business in the city of Kingston. The defendant was the owner of the schooner
"Wave Crest," and on the 7th day of December, 1899, this
vessel being loaded with stock, went ashore off Point
Breeze, in the state of New York, on the south side of
Lake Ontario, and thereby became and was in a position of
danger and peril. It was necessary to have the vessel
relieved immediately if that were possible. The defendant,
having his vessel in this position, communicated by telegraph with the plaintiffs, and several telegrams passed
between the parties. The first of these dated 8th December
from defendant asked the plaintiffs what they would take to
pull the vessel off. The answer was: "Don't wish to
contract. Will send Donnelly, one hundred and fifty
dollars per day. Will you want steam pump also?" The
reply to this was: "Accept terms. Vessel close to harbor.
Weather fine. Send tug and pump immediately. Want
schooner towed Toronto. Wire reply." It was contended
that adding to this acceptance "Want schooner towed to
Toronto" prevented if from being such an acceptance as
completed a contract. This question, I think it not necessary to determine, because I am of the opinion that the
response, "Will leave with steamer Donnelly as soon as we
get outfit on board," and the fact that the plaintiffs did so
leave, show a complete contract. I think there was then a
consensus and that the parties were *ad idem*. Each of the
first two of these telegrams was dated on the 8th of
December, and each of the last two on the 9th of December.

The plaintiffs say that the defendant on or about the 9th day of December, 1899, engaged the steamer and pump at the sum of $150 per day for the steamer, and a reasonable sum, which would be $45 per day, for the steam pump, together with the services of their wrecker, engineer, and diver, whose services were worth $14 per day, and that they continued in the employment of the defendants for the ensuing six and a half days, whereby the defendant became indebted to the plaintiffs in the sum of $1358.50, which sum is wholly due and unpaid.

The defendant denies that he is indebted to the plaintiffs, and denies that the plaintiffs rendered any service whatever to the defendant in respect to which the plaintiffs are entitled to any compensation from the defendant, and submits that the plaintiffs' action should be dismissed with costs.   The plaintiffs' tug " Donnelly " did start on the trip or voyage to the place where the defendant's vessel was in difficulty.   It started about eleven on the night of Saturday the 9th of December.   It appears that there are two routes from Kingston to the place where the defendant's vessel lay.   One of these was through what is called the " Gap," and then in a somewhat oblique direction across the lake, which was, or may be called, the outside route. The other route was through the Bay of Quinte and through the Murray Canal, and then almost directly across the lake. This was, or may be called, the inside route.   The plaintiffs' tug proceeded on the Saturday night through the Gap and some 15 miles out into the lake, when, in the opinion of her seamen, as they said, they found the weather so stormy and the sea so rough that they could not safely go any further, when they turned back and took shelter.   After this they proceeded westward into the bay, taking the inside route, in which they found ice to such an extent that they turned back to the eastward again.   It then occurred to them that a wind that they observed might have removed the ice that had stopped them in the Bay, when they communicated by telegraph and were informed that the ice had gone.   They then turned and went westward again in the Bay, and upon their arrival at Murray Canal found the gate locked and the keeper absent, which caused further delay.   Having found the keeper of the canal and got the tug through, the mariners on board were advised by telegram that the defendant's vessel had " gone to pieces."   Upon receiving this advice the tug went home to Kingston.   The six and one-half days for which the plaintiffs charge wages were spent chiefly if not almost altogether, in the Bay of Quinte going one way and another, taking on coal, etc. The plaintiffs do not profess to have performed any service actually useful to the defendant, but say and contend that they did the best that they could, or that could be done in the circumstances, and that they were prevented from serving the defendant in the manner anticipated and contracted for by reason of the inclemency of the weather and the consequent roughness of the water, the act of God, *vis major*, and they, the plaintiffs, claim the reward the same as if they had actually performed the services for the defendant as intended by the contract.

It is, I think, not needful that I should here state with particularity what the plaintiffs' tug and men were doing during the time spent in the Bay of Quinte, during nearly if not quite the whole of the six and one-half days. There is in the evidence a sort of written history of this and a chart showing where the tug went and where she was during the period. The evidence shows, however, that during parts of the time neither the plaintiffs nor the defendant knew where she was or what the tug was doing.

The plaintiffs, claiming wages for the time spent to no purpose, should at least show reasonable diligence on their part, and that they were prevented from doing what was intended by the contract by the act of God, the superior power. In the view that I have taken of the case I need not say that these would entitle the plaintiffs to recover the wages, but I think that before the plaintiffs can be permitted to recover they must at least show these things.

When on the night of the 9th December the plaintiffs' tug went through what was called the Gap, and some fifteen miles out became discouraged by reason of the weather, the sea, etc., turned back to shelter, and the men concluded to take the inside route, it seems plain to me that they should have ascertained whether this inside route was clear for them to go through, and that if they had made the effort they would have discovered that it was not, that ice was there to block their way. That this discovery could have been made appears by the ease with which they afterwards discovered that the same ice had been taken away by the wind.

Then, if the plaintiffs' men had made this discovery, it

seems plain that they would not have attempted to go by the inside route at that time, but, on the contrary, would either have remained in their place of shelter or gone back to Kingston to await better weather to enable them to go by the outside route.   I cannot see that the plaintiffs' men were at all right or prudent or diligent in the position in which they were, and knowing the urgency of their mission, in blindly locking themselves and the tug up in the bay for the space of about or nearly a week, when they might have ascertained the condition of the passage before going in. If the plaintiffs' men had been diligent and ascertained that they could not go by the inside route, their plain duty was to go by the outside route as soon as possible. In such circumstances, and upon the contention of the plaintiffs (the pleadings are not full), the burden rested upon them, the plaintiffs, of showing that they were always ready and willing and that during this period the time for which they claim the wages, there was owing to stress of weather, &c., no reasonable opportunity of their getting with their tug out into and crossing the lake.   The evidence is that the weather on the American side was during the period generally good.

Much evidence of various kinds was given respecting the weather on this side at or about the place through which the tug would have to go from the Gap.   This evidence I do not write out here in detail.   My opinion and finding upon it is that it does not show that during the period the weather was always such that there was no reasonable opportunity for the plaintiffs' tug to go through the Gap and across the lake to or towards the relief of the defendant's vessel.   I am of the opinion that the plaintiffs have failed to satisfy the onus that thus rested upon them.

It was not contended that, as the hiring was by the day, the plaintiffs are entitled to pay for the time that elapsed before their negligence in going blindly into the Bay in their effort to take the inside route.   I think I need not consider this or whether or not their negligence would disentitle the plaintiffs to such pay.   The amount would be small in any view of this, only for a few hours, the fractional part of a day.

I do not think, on the whole case made, that the plaintiffs are entitled to recover, and the action should, I think, be dismissed with costs.

Then, as to the counter claim, I am of the opinion that in the way above stated there was a breach by the plaintiffs of their contract with the defendant. But, as I freely stated to counsel at the argument, I am not given any means of measuring the damages, if any, arising from that breach. The vessel was in fact lost. There is some evidence that the value of her before she went upon the rocks was $3,000 or $4,000. But from all that appeared I would be disposed to discount such opinion evidence largely. The evidence contained in the examination of the defendant's husband and agent, read to him at the trial when in the witness box, was that the value of the vessel when upon the rocks was about $500, and he said he had an offer for the vessel lying upon the rocks of $500. This, I understood, was to include the sails and gear, which were sold for $237.50. I am not given any skilled evidence as to the possibility of saving the vessel, or the probability of her being saved, and if so in what condition, by the most expert craftsmen. All is left in uncertainty and gloom, and still, and after calling attention to this, I am asked to measure damages. All I can in the circumstances say is that the defendant has not proved any damages in the way that a suitor should prove damages for the payment of which he expects an order against his opponent.

Then, assuming that the defendant does not prove any damages, there arises no mischief from a dismissal of the counter claim, which dismissal should I think be without costs.

The action will be dismissed with costs and the counter claim will be dismissed without costs.

Judgment accordingly.

Notes :—

TOWAGE :—In a recent English case it was held that a contract to tow a vessel from one port to another, for a certain fixed sum, was indivisible; and that, therefore, if the complete performance of the contract was prevented by circumstances beyond the control of either party, the tug cannot recover on a quantum meruit for so much work as was actually done with a view to fulfilling the contract.

In that particular case a fog coming up, the towed vessel became stranded on a rock, (no one being in fault), thus rendering impossible the completion of the towage contract. *The Madras* (1898) Probate, 90.

See also, *Appleby* v. *Myers* (1867) L. R., 2 C. P. 651.

A contract which is originally one for towage may become a matter of salvage. In such a case, however, the burden is upon the owners or navigators of the tug to prove clearly that such unforeseen dangers arose that their obligations under the contract of towage were extinguished by *vis major*, and that, so far as that contract was concerned, they might have abandoned the tug. *The I. C. Potter* (1870) L. R., 3 Ad. & Ec. 272.

But in a later case it was laid down that the danger need not be such as would put an end to the towage contract,—but that it is sufficient if these unforeseen perils are of such a nature that they cannot be inferred to have been within the contemplation of the parties at the time the contract was made. *Five Steel Barges* (1890) L. R. 15 P. D. 142.

In *The Westburn* (1896), 74 L. T. 130, the facts were that a tug had contracted to take a ship into a certain harbour. At the entrance, however, a fog came on, and before the tug could anchor the ship went ashore, and was then rescued by the tug from what was a dangerous situation. It was held that the tug was entitled to salvage.

But if the tug, through negligence, gets its tow into a dangerous position, it is not entitled to salvage for subsequently rescuing her therefrom. *The Robert Dixon* (1879) L. R. 5 P. D. 54.

If those making the contract on behalf of the vessel which is to be towed conceal facts regarding the danger of the proposed service which are of such a nature that it may reasonably be inferred that, had they been disclosed, the tug would never have undertaken the work upon ordinary towage terms, the contract is inoperative, and the work done will be considered a salvage service. *The Kingalock* (1854) 1 Sp. Eccl. and Adm. 264.

Every contract of towage contains the implied undertaking that the tug is suitable and is properly equipped for the kind of service required by the terms of the contract. *The Undaunted* (1886) L. R. 11 P. D. 46.

Moreover, those in charge of the tug are bound to use all proper skill and diligence, and the owners are not released from their liability under this obligation by a provision in the contract to the effect that the captain and crew of the tug shall, during the continuance of the contract, be considered to be the employees of the owner of the vessel which is being towed. *The Ratata* (1897) Probate 117.

As evidence of the vital distinction which the law makes between salvage and towage services, it may be noted that there is no maritime lien on a ship for towage services as there is for salvage. See *Westrup* v. *Great Yarmouth Steam Carrying Co.* (1889) L. R. 43 C. D. 241.

———

[IN THE SUPERIOR COURT, QUEBEC.]

Before DAVIDSON, J.

THE PABST BREWING CO.
v.
H. A. EKERS and THE CANADIAN BREWERIES, Limited

Trade name—Place of manufacture—Common law right.

1. A manufacturer, whose goods are generally known to the public by a certain name, has a common law right, apart from the Trade Mark Act, for protection against a competitor who uses the same or some similar name in such a manner that the ordinary purchaser is liable to think that his goods are made by the manufacturer to whose goods the word or words composing the name originally applied.

2. This right extends to the use of the name of the place where the goods are made when the same has always been used in connection with them. The beer manufactured by the plaintiff company was always known as "Milwaukee" beer, and an injunction was therefore granted restraining the defendants from advertising their beer (which was made elsewhere) as "Milwaukee" beer.

MONTREAL., June 13, 1901.

The plaintiffs pray that the defendants may be severally condemned in the sum of $5,000 by way of damages, and further, that they be "enjoined from using the word 'Milwaukee' in connection with the brewing, bottling, sale, purchase and advertising of beer not brewed in the city of Milwaukee in the state of Wisconsin. . ."

In support of the suit plaintiffs allege that they are an incorporated company, and that for fifty years past they and their predecessors have been engaged in the business of brewing lager beer and malt extract at Milwaukee; that the beer brewed by them and by other brewers in Milwaukee has become well known in the United States and Canada as the product of Milwaukee, and has acquired a reputation which is of great value to the plaintiffs; that plaintiffs have for upwards of eleven years marketed its products in Montreal and in this province, and have had an office and bottling establishment in this city. The complaint made against defendant Ekers is in the following words :—

"5. On the 1st of March, 1898, and at divers times thereafter, known to the defendant Ekers, but unknown to the plaintiff, the said defendant Ekers, in bad faith and with the unlawful and fraudulent intent of appropriating the reputation of the breweries of the said city of Milwaukee, and of causing his goods to be sold as the product of the said breweries in Milwaukee, to the detriment of the plaintiff, has continuously made use of the words "Milwaukee Lager," and has used the word "Milwaukee" to designate lager beer which is not the product of the said city of Milwaukee, but which as the plaintiff believes, was, in fact, brewed in the city of Montreal."

The other defendants, the Canadian Breweries Company, are complained of in identical terms. It is further alleged that :

"7. The said illegal and unauthorized use of the name of the said city of Milwaukee has had the effect of deceiving buyers and the public generally, and has caused damage to the plaintiff in a sum which the plaintiff fixes at five thousand dollars in the case of the defendant Ekers, and at a like amount in the case of the other defendant. . ."

And lastly that : " The plaintiff has protested against the said illegal use of the word ' Milwaukee ' by the defendants, and has requested the defendants to discontinue the use thereof ; but the defendants have refused and neglected so to do, and have continued and are now continuing such illegal use of the said word."

The defendants plead that plaintiffs have no exclusive right to use the word " Milwaukee ; " that Milwaukee is merely the name of the place at which plaintiffs carry on their business, and is without special significance, and any person is entitled to use it, provided he does so in good faith, as defendants have done ; that with respect to the sale by them of "Milwaukee lager beer," defendants marked the same as made by them at Montreal, and never pretended that it was made at Milwaukee, and still less that it was made by plaintiffs ; that the word Milwaukee has never been registered by plaintiffs in accordance with the laws in force in Canada, and is not their exclusive property, and is not a trade mark or trade name."

The writ issued in February, 1900. Defendant Ekers sold out his business to the other defendants in June, 1899, and has never since manufactured, advertised or sold the lager beer complained of. While in business he was never protested nor sued, nor have any damages been liquidated in regard to his use of the word. The action in so far as directed against him is dismissed with costs.

Since their assumption of the business the Canadian Breweries have made use by labels and advertisements of several different descriptions of their labels. Thus :—" The Canadian Breweries, Limited, Ekers' Milwaukee Lager, Montreal ;" " Ekers' Milwaukee Lager, Montreal Special Brew," " Ekers' Milwaukee Lager ;" " Ekers' Brewery, Milwaukee Lager, 409 St. Lawrence Main street."

Defendant Ekers began to use the word Milwaukee in 1885, and adopted it (p. 11). " I suppose Milwaukee was a lager beer place."

Milwaukee has for a great many years been famous for the lager beer brewed there by plaintiffs and others, whose efforts have given it, in this respect, a reputation unsurpassed on the continent. The product is commonly identified and sold as "Milwaukee beer." Plaintiffs have for a long time past spent large sums of money in advertising their beer throughout Canada. It was always identified with the name of Milwaukee. Four years ago they established an agency in Montreal. That, of course, did not mark their earliest sales.

A common law right exists to prevent a manufacturer or trader from making and selling goods by names, words or marks which may mislead or confuse the public by creating the belief that they are those of a competitor.

This right exists independently of the possession of a registered trade mark. The object of the Trade Mark Act is to relieve traders from the necessity of proving their course of business for a number of years in order to show their exclusive right to sell goods by a particular description. The probability of misleading not experts or persons who know, but ordinary or unwary customers is the mischief to be guarded against. Although the first purchaser is not deceived, nevertheless, if the article is so delivered to him as to be calculated to deceive a purchaser from him that is illegal.

It is not only names or marks in which particular individuals have acquired a personal property that the law protects. An exclusive right is not essential to the maintenance of the action. It is sufficient if the right asserted is exclusive as against the defendant. If by long continued industry, skill and generous use of capital or by the possession of some local advantage in the way of springs, peculiar quality of water, material or otherwise, a place has achieved a reputation for great excellence in some particular article, its name cannot be usurped by competitors in other localities. Right of redress is common to all whose interests are invaded by an unlawful appropriation of the name of a locality.

The many authorities cited by plaintiff, which include a number of well known cases, support these principles :

In *Southorn* v. *Reynolds*, (1865), 12 *Law Times*, *N.S.*, 75, plaintiff made pipes at Broseley, in Shropshire, and they were known as " Southorn Broseley Pipes." His brother carried on another establishment there and also sold pipes under that name. The defendant had no establishment there, but sold pipes called " Reynolds' Purified Clay Pipes, made by Southorn from Broseley," the Southorn being a workman who had once been employed at Broseley. Injunction granted to restrain the use of "Southorn" and "Broseley."

In *Braham* v. *Beachim* (1878), L.R., 7 Ch. D., 848, "Radstock Coal" case.—The principal plaintiff, Countess Waldegrave, was the owner or lessee of all the collieries in the parish of Radstock except one small piece, and had sold the coal under the names "The Radstock Coal Company," and "The Countess Waldegrave,s Radstock Collieries." The defendants, also in the coal business, adopted the style first, of "The Radstock Colliery Proprietors,"and, later, of "The Radstock Coal Company, Colliery Proprietors." although they were never entitled to raise coal in the parish of Radstock, nor until after the commencement of the action, within any part of the district through which the seams of Radstock coal extended. The Court granted an injunction on the ground that the defendants' conduct was calculated to deceive ; and that they were not entitled to continue to use either of the names adopted by them. I cite these two cases as examples of English jurisprudence. Sebastian and other text books discuss many others.

In the Scotch case of *Dunnachie* v. *Young*, 10 Scot. Sess. Cas., (4th series), 874 ("Glenboig Bricks"), the plaintiffs at Glenboig made bricks (which became known by the name of the place), from a seam of clay, which extended to Heathfield, where the defendants were in the same business and used clay from the same seam. The defendants called their bricks "Young's Glenboig." An injunction was granted against the use of the word "Glenboig."

Decisions in the United States are emphatic on the point. In the *City of Carlsbad* v. *Kutnow*, 68 Fed. Rep. 794, the use of the word "Carlsbad" was restrained at the suit of the plaintiff, the German City, which had for years evaporated the salts of Carlsbad springs and sold them under the name of "Carlsbad Sprudel Salz." The defendants, a firm of New York druggists, put up similar salts and called them : "Improved Effervescent Carlsbad Powder." Although the genuine Carlsbad salts are not effervescent, and the word "improved" was relied upon as implying that the salts were different from those sold under the name of "Carlsbad" alone, the defendants were enjoined from using the word "Carlsbad" in any form.   This decision was confirmed by the Circuit Court of Appeals, 71 Fed. Rep. 167.

In Pillsbury-Washburn Flour Mills Company v. *Eagle,* 86 Fed. Rep. 608 (1898), an injunction was granted at the suit of companies engaged in the milling business at Minneapolis, restraining a firm of flour dealers in Chicago from using the words "Minneapolis" and "Minnesota" to designate flour not milled in Minneapolis, but purchased from millers in Milwaukee, Wis.

Plaintiff cites the unreported cases of *Pabst Brewing Company* v. *Hanley Brewing Company* (Mass., April, 1899), and *Schiltz Brewing Comqany* and *Pabst Brewing Company* v. *Fred Hollander Company* (N.Y., September, 1900), in which Boston and New York brewing companies were prohibited from using the word Milwaukee.

The French authorities are of the same tenor.   "La loi protège non seulement les noms de fabricants, mais encore les noms de lieux.   Cela est juste." Pouillet, "Traité de Marques de Fabrique," Nos. 394, 395.

"Le mon d'une ville appartient exclusivement aux industriels qui y possèdent des fabriques ; eux seuls peuvent, à l'exclusion des étrangers, en revêtir leurs produits et profiter ainsi de la réputation acquise par une fabrication spéciale." Fuzier-Herman, Rep., "Concurrence déloyale, No. 245.

I grant the injunction asked for.   As to damages, they were not seriously pressed for and, under the circumstances of the case, would not in any event have been granted. Costs to plaintiff as in an action of the first class.

McGibbon, Casgrain, Ryan & Mitchell, solicitors for the Plaintiffs.

Hall, Cross, Brown & Sharpe, solicitors for the Defendants.

Notes :—

A trade name and a trade mark are essentially different. The latter is something invented by the user for the purpose of distinguishing his goods in a particular manner.   *Turton* v. *Turton* (1888) 42 C. D. 128.

But a trade name is someting which, though perhaps only the name of the first maker of the article in question, or the name of the place where it is made, may in time become a mere designation of the article itself. *Hall* v. *Barrows* (1864) 33 L. J. Ch. 204.

And when a name has, by usage, become such a designation, the original user will be granted an injunction restraining others from using the name, and thus leading the public to suppose that their goods are those of the first user. *Wotherspoon* v. *Currie* (1872) 42 L. J. Ch. 130. *Bouluois* v. *Peake* (1868) 13 C. D. 513n.

And it has been held that a manufacturer has not the right to call his goods by a name which would be a fair and accurate description of them when the goods of another manufacturer are already so well known by that name that the public would be misled. *Reddaway* v. *Banham* (1896) A. C. 199. But see, *Burgess* v. *Burgess* (1858) 22 L. J., Ch. 675.

In *Tussaud* v. *Tussaud* (1890) 44 C. D. 678, Madame Tussaud & Sons, Limited, which had been so registered, and which had for many years carried on business under that name, obtained an injunction restraining a company promoted by Louis J. Tussaud and others from carrying on a similar business under the name of "Louis Tussaud, Limited."

But a company cannot acquire any title to the exclusive use of a name which merely describes the nature of its business. *Colonial Life Insurance Co.* v. *Home & Colonial Insurance Co.*, (1864) 33 L. J., Ch. 741.

The Sun Life Assurance Co. of Canada opened an office in London, after it had for many years carried on business elsewhere under that name. The Sun Life Assurance Co., which had done business since 1810, having its head office in London, applied for an injunction to restrain the former company from doing business under that name anywhere in Great Britain. It was held that as the use of the full name "The Sun Life Assurance Co. of Canada" was neither a misstatement of fact, or in any respect fraudulent, the defendant company had a right to use it in England, but that it would not be entitled to denominate itself "The Sun," or "The Sun Life" simply, without the addition of the words "of Canada." *Saunders* v. *Sun Life Assurance Co. of Canada* (1894), 1, Ch. 537.

In the very recent case of La Societié Anonyme des Anciens Etablissements Pauliard et Lavessor v. The Pauliard-Lavassor Motor Co. (Limited), (1901) 17 T. L. R. 680, it was held that the plaintiff company, which was a foreign one, having an English market for its output, was entitled to an injunction restraining not only the defendant company, but also its individual incorporators, from further infringing their trade name in that country.

In *Rose* v. *McLean Publishing Co.* (1896) 24 Ont. A. R. 240, it was held that the use of a geographical name in a secondary sense, as part of the title identifying a mercantile journal, and not as merely descriptive of the place where the journal is published, will be protected. The company publishing ''The Canada Bookseller and Stationer'' were therefore restrained from using that title, on the ground that it conflicted with ''The Canadian Bookseller and Library.''

See also *Robinson* v. *Bogle* (1889), 18 O. R. 387.

Wilson v. *Lyman* (1898), 25 Ont. A. R. 303.

[IN THE COURT OF QUEEN'S BENCH, QUEBEC.]

(APPEAL SIDE.)

GOLDBERG v. THE DOMINION WOOLLEN CO.

BEFORE SIR ALEXANDRE LACOSTE, C.J. AND BOSSÉ, BLANCHET, WURTELE AND OUIMET, J.J.

Commercial contract—Sale of goods—Implied cancellation of first agreement—Mise en demeure.

1. Where a contract for the sale of goods stipulated that on one part the delivery thereof, and on the other the payment therefor, should be made at certain specified dates, and it appeared that the vendor had not been ready to deliver at the time agreed upon, that the vendee had then taken no action but had subsequently demanded and received delivery of smaller orders, and that the vendor had treated this, in his books, as a cancellation of the original contract, it was held on the evidence (there being no allegation that the vendee had tendered, or even that he had been able to pay the amount due on the first contract at the time named) that the contract had been rescinded by the conduct and acts of the parties.

2. The fact that a contract is of a commercial nature only avoids the necessity for a *mise en demeure* (i.e., the making of a demand for the fulfilment of the obligation) when the date for the doing of the act in question is stated in the contract.   Moreover, since, where a *mise en demeure* is necessary, damages only run from the time that the same is given, the mere bringing of an action for damages for the non-delivery of goods some time previous thereto is not such a *mise en demeure* as will entitle the vendee to damages, as, in such a case, whatever loss there may have been has been suffered before the date of the *mise en demeure*.

Appeal from a judgment of the Superior Court.   The facts of the case are set forth in the present judgment.

M. Goldberg and S. W. Jacob, for Appellant.

S. Beaudin, K.C., and J. G. Martin, for Respondent.

MONTREAL, December 27, 1900.

The judgment of the Court was delivered by

BLANCHET, J.—(*Translation.*)

The Appellant, a wholesale clothier of ready-made goods, claims from Respondents, who are manufacturers, the sum of $10,000, for failure to deliver goods sold.

The facts which have given rise to this action, are as follows :

During the months of January and February, 1898, Vineberg, who was manager of his wife's (the Appellant's) business establishment, placed two orders with the Respondents for the manufacture of 42,100 yds of cloth of a special color and weight, known as *frieze*, and various other brands to be used in Appellant's business.   The conditions of said orders were that the goods were to be paid for on the 1st of June following, and that they should be paid for in "spot cash."   It was also agreed that samples of these goods would be delivered on the 15th and on the 30th (sic) February.

From the outset, the conditions agreed upon by the parties were not followed ; the samples were not delivered upon the dates fixed, only a part being delivered during the month of March ; and they were not paid for "spot cash," but by notes.

During the month of April there was no delivery made, nor on the 1st of June, the date fixed for the complete delivery ; but on the 25th of May, six days before, Vineberg had placed an order with the Respondents for the manufacture of a certain number of yards of the same cloth, of which he requested the delivery at the earliest possible date, and at the same time a delay of 60 days was given him for payment.

On the 2nd of June, the day after that fixed for the delivery of the goods, the directors of the Company Respondents, met and decided that Vineberg was to pay according to the conditions agreed upon, that is "spot cash," and that no delay was to be given him. The question then arose as to giving sureties. The Company was disposed to accept a party by the name of Westgate, but Vineberg stated that that would cost him too much, and he offered other sureties, who were refused.

The matter remained thus until the 22nd of June. On that day 325 yards of cloth were delivered. During July and August nothing was delivered. On the 10th of September Appellant had a letter sent by her husband to the Company, complaining that no goods had been delivered. The next day the Company answered that they were sending a certain quantity of cloth, and that they expected to ship the same by boat. This was followed by three unimportant deliveries of goods, (a few hundred yards), which were also paid for by notes, of which one was kept over at the bank for some days on account of want of funds, while the other was only paid subsequently as it was not collected by the Company.

On the 9th of October, Appellant wrote a letter to the Company complaining that she had not received the goods mentioned in the orders, and stating that she would hold the Company responsible for all damage resulting from the delay in filling such orders.

The Company having failed to comply with said request, the Appellant instituted an action for damages to the extent of $4,000; and subsequently, on discovering that $4,000 did not cover all the damage suffered, she desisted from this action and took out a second one, (the present suit), claiming $10,000 as damages.

This action has been met by a plea in which Defendants state :—The order given by you (the Appellant) on May 25th constitutes a revocation or abandonment of your original contract. At that date you found out that you

did not need such a large quantity of goods; you found
out that you could not pay us, at the time fixed, the
price due on said contract, i.e., $25,500; and you therefore
gave another order, which we accepted, for a certain and
much smaller quantity of cloth, and it is in fulfillment of
this latter order that subsequent deliveries were made.

Vineberg, on the contrary, contends in his plea, that the
Company, seeing that they were not in a position to deliver
the goods ordered at the date fixed, the 2nd June, solicited
additional delay from him, saying :—Give us a statement
of what you need at once for your business, and we will do
our best to deliver that quantity, and, to return one kindness
by another, instead of paying us cash, we will give you
delay to pay.

One of these two versions is supported by the testimony
of Robert, who is the Company's manager.   Robert swears
positively that it was perfectly well understood and agreed
between the parties that the two first orders were cancelled,
and that the order of May 25th was substituted in their
stead ; that Vineberg had admitted he was unable to find
the money wherewith to pay for the first order, and that
the subsequent deliveries of goods were made by virtue of
the second order.

This evidence is very plausible, and is supported by the
testimony of the other employees of the Company's business
establishment.   Thus, it is proved in a satisfactory manner
that immediately after the demand of credit contained in
the order of May 25th was refused, the two first orders were
erased from the books and were replaced by the second
order.   It is proved that, at that date, there was a certain
quantity of goods ready for delivery, and even addressed to
Appellant, and that at once these goods were unpacked, put
back on the shelves, and sold at a loss, because, as I have
said, this cloth was of a special weight and brand which
probably would have been of no use to other commercial
firms ; the Company was therefore forced to sell it at a loss.

This would prove at least the good faith of Robert and
of the other employees, and that they really believed that
the order of May 25th was a revocation of the first two
orders.

Vineberg's version has also something to commend it.   It is evident that the Company was not ready to deliver the 42,000 yards of cloth on the 2nd of June, and it is therefore manifest that it needed delay.   His assertion that the Company demanded from him additional delay is very plausible.   On the other hand it is inconceivable that Vineberg, knowing that in five days he could have exacted the complete delivery of the goods ordered, and knowing also that in default of such delivery he could have claimed the damages he now seeks to recover, should have abandoned such an advantageous position for the purpose of substituing another order, an order of two thousand seven hundred yards, and should have asked delay to pay for the latter.   This does not appear to be very probable.

But another fact confirms me in this opinion.   It is that during the three or four months that followed, nothing in the record shows that any reference was ever made to these two orders, but all Vineberg asked for was "the goods." Verbal demands were made, which were followed by deliveries of small quantities of goods, but nothing in the record shows in any way that a special demand was ever made for those particular goods.

Nevertheless, whatever may be our opinion on this point, we do not think that the case should be decided on this question.   The Respondent has raised two other contentions which are mentioned in the judgment, and which are sufficient to do justice to the parties in this case.

It is evident, taking Vineberg's pretension that it was agreed the goods should not be delivered on June 2nd, that it was understood and agreed between the parties that the goods were to be delivered later on.

The Appellant says : This is a commercial contract, and in contracts of this kind there is no necessity for a *mise en demeure*, because the contract itself is a *mise en demeure*.

That is true, but on one condition, and this condition is very important : the date of the delivery must be stated in the contract.   Here the date is mentioned in the two first orders, but the negotiations that took place between the parties show in the clearest possible manner that this date was changed, that an additional delay was granted, and no limit to this delay fixed.   Therefore a new *mise en demeure* was necessary, and it was necessary at an opportune time. Not only was this necessary, but, further, the Appellant should have shown or indicated that she was ready to pay the price for the goods.

There is no proof on this point; there is not even any allegation that the Plaintiff was ever able to pay the $25,000. There are many affirmations on the part of Vineberg, who says: I could easily have found the money; I could have secured it from certain banks on ordinary paper, the paper of my clients. But this is no proof that he had the control of $25,000, that he could tender that amount, and that he could pay it cash; and it is evident that under these circumstances the Appellant's demand is not well founded.

We may say that the record contains a letter of the 9th October demanding the delivery. That letter is not clear. As I said a moment ago, in the first line of it reference is made to "orders," and in the last line there is a claim of damages for failure to deliver the goods mentioned "in the order." It is doubtful to which order this refers, and under such circumstances this letter cannot be considered a regular *mise en demeure*.

The *mise en demeure* has therefore been made only by the institution of the action. When the action was instituted all the damages had been suffered; and the law on this point is clear and positive. If a *mise en demeure* is necessary, damages begin to run solely from the date of the *mise en demeure*.

In this instance damages can certainly not be awarded; and, as I have stated, the Appellant has not even alleged that she could have fulfilled her contract in due time.

When two parties are bound under a contract, it is not sufficient that the purchaser should say to the seller: You have not made the delivery in due time. He must show that he was ready and able to pay. It would be absurd to award damages to a person who could not have paid the price of the things bought.

For these reasons we believe that the two grounds mentioned in the judgment of the Superior Court are sufficient to confirm the same.

Judgment confirmed and appeal dismissed with costs.

Solicitor for the Appellant: *S. W. Jacobs.*

Solicitors for the Respondents: *Foster & Martin.*

[IN THE HIGH COURT OF JUSTICE FOR ONTARIO.]

BEFORE MEREDITH, C.J.

BENNETT v. WORTMAN.

Infringement of Patent—Assignee selling article after reassignment to Patentee—R.S.C. cap. 61, secs. 28 and 31.

1. The words "puts in practice any invention" as used is R.S.C. cap. 61, sec 28, (which defines the acts which give a right of action for the infringement of a patent) should be construed so as to include the act of selling "the subject matter of the patent," authority to restrain which by injunction is conferred by sec. 31 ; and, in any event, the Court has always power under such latter section to restrain the sale of a patented article by one who has no legal right to sell it.

2. B, having obtained a patent for a certain invention, assigned the same to W for the term of four months, with the option of purchasing the same at the end of that period. At the expiration of the time so fixed, W elected not to buy the patent, and reassigned the same to B ; but he continued to sell the patented articles which he had manufactured during the four months in which he had been the assignee of the patent. B having brought action to restrain such sales, it was held that, while the making of the articles in question during the four months was a lawful act on the part of W, yet the latter, on and by the reassignment of the patent to B, had divested himself as to the future of all rights (including the right to sell the patented articles then manufactured) which he had acquired under the previous assignment, and that these rights were thereby again exclusively vested in B.

The facts of the case are fully set forth in the head note.

JULY 20, 1901 :—

MEREDITH, C. J.:—

This action was tried before me without a jury at London, on the 12th April, last and at the close of the argument I decided all the questions in dispute except the one as to the right of the Defendant to sell the sad irons which were manufactured by him in the four months during which he was assignee of the patent granted to the Plaintiff in accordance with which they were made, after the expiration of the four months, and after he had in pursuance of his agreement with Plaintiff having elected not to purchase the patent re-assigned it to the Plaintiff—as to which I reserved judgment.

It was argued on behalf of the Defendant that a patentee
has no remedy against one who sells the patented article or
thing without the authority of the patentee, and in support
of this argument section 28 of the Patent Act, R.S.C. cap.
61, which gives right of action for an infringement was
appealed to.

It is true that the section does not use the word sell in
defining the acts which are to give the right of action, the
language of it being '' Every person who... makes, constructs
or puts in practice any invention..., or who procures such
invention from any person not authorized... to make or use
it and who uses it shall be liable...'' but section 31 authorizes the Court or a Judge in an action for the infringement
of a patent to make an order on the application of the Plaintiff
or Defendant for an injunction restraining the opposite
party from further use, manufacture or sale of the subject
matter of the patent, and reading the two sections together,
the proper conclusion is, I think, that the legislature
intended that the words '' puts in practice '' in section 28
should include selling the '' subject matter of the patent,''
authority to restrain which is given by section 31 ; but,
however that may be, there is, I think, no doubt whatever
that the Court has jurisdiction under section 31 to restrain
the sale of the patented article by one who has no legal
right to sell it, and that is the remedy which the Plaintiff
in this action seeks.

Would, then, a sale by the Defendant of the sad irons
which he manufactured under the authority of the assignment to him of the patent, after he had reassigned it to the
Plaintiff, be an infringement of the patentee's rights and an
act that at the instance of the patentee should be enforced ?
The answer to this question must, I think, be in the affirmative.   The assignment of the patent to the Defendant no
doubt conferred on him the exclusive right, privilege and
liberty of making, constructing and using and vending to
others to be used the patented invention.   The making by
him of the irons which are in question was, therefore, a
lawful act, but when he re-assigned to the Plaintiff the
patent, he divested himself as to the future of all the rights
which he had acquired under the previous assignment and
thereafter the exclusive right which I have mentioned became revested in the Plaintiff.   It is, of course, clear that,
after the reassignment to the Plaintiff, the Defendant had

no longer any right to make or construct the patented article
or thing and in my opinion he had not thereafter the right
of vending it to others to be used. The exclusive right of
vending it to others was, as I have said, vested in the
Plaintiff and the right being an exclusive one, it follows
that it could not exist in any one else.   This observation
does not, of course, apply to articles lawfully sold to a purchaser, for by the sale they are withdrawn indefinitely from
the operation of the franchise secured by the patent.

The language of Chief Justice Taney in delivering the
judgment of the Supreme Court of the United States in
Bloomer v. *The Onewan* (1852) 14 Howard at p. 549, is
apposite.   In pointing out the distinction between the grant
of the right to make and vend a patented machine and the
grant of the right to use it, referring to the right of a
grantee of the latter nature, he says: ''When the machine
passes to the hands of the purchaser it is no longer within
the limits of the monopoly, but in the case of a grant by
the patentee of the right to make and vend, (he is speaking
of a sale of the exclusive privilege of making and vending
it for use in a particular place) the interest acquired necessarily terminates at the time limited for its continuance by
the law which created it.''   Applying this to the facts of
the case I am dealing with, it leads to the conclusion that
every right granted by the Plaintiff to the Defendant terminated at the time limited by the contract for the continuance of the right: see also *Bloomer* v. *Millinger* (1863)
1 Wallace 340 ; *Brooks* v. *Bicknell* (1845) 4 McLean at p. 67.

If I am right in this view I have expressed, this is an *a
fortiori* case, for the application of the principle of these
decisions, for the sale of the patent to the Defendant was a
conditional one, and whether it was to be absolutely depended upon the election which he should make at the
expiration of the four months, and if the Defendant's contention as to the extent of his right were well founded it follows that it was open to him during the four months to make
enough of the patented articles to answer the requirements of the market for them for the whole term of the
patent and to deal with them as free from the monopoly of
the patent after the four months, and so in effect to appropriate to himself the whole value of the patent, for which if
he elected to purchase according to his agreement he was to
pay in addition to what he had paid $920, without paying

anything. It is, in my opinion, impossible to interpret the instrument on which the rights of the parties depend so as to produce such a result.

I come, therefore, to the conclusion that the Plaintiff is entitled to an injunction restraining the Defendant from vending to others the sad irons in his possession at the time of the re-assignment of the patent to the Plaintiff and there will be judgment accordingly.

The Defendant must pay the costs of the action except as to the matters as to which he has succeeded and the costs of these the Plaintiff must pay.

Solicitor for the Plaintiff : *U. A. Buchner.*

Solicitor for the Defendant : *T. H. Luscombe.*

[IN THE HIGH COURT OF JUSTICE FOR ONTARIO.]

Before a DIVISIONAL COURT :—ARMOUR, C.J.O., AND FALCONBRIDGE, C.J., K.B.

HARDING et al

v.

THE METROPOLITAN LIFE INSURANCE CO.

Life insurance policy—Action to recover premiums paid—Insurable interest of the insurer in the life of the insured—14 Geo. III, cap. 48.

When an insurance is effected on the life of C by his wife (who is named as the beneficiary), the mere fact that the premiums are subsequently paid by H (a person not having an insurable interest in the life of C) will not of itself render the policy void as being in contravention of 14 Geo. III, cap. 48, unless it is also proved that the real transaction was the insurance by H of the life of C for her own (H's) benefit.

Appeal by the Plaintiffs from the judgment of a Judge of the County Court for the County of York, dismissing an action brought to recover the amount of premiums alleged to have been paid by the Plaintiff, Laura Harding, in respect of an insurance claimed to have been effected by her on the life of her father, Robert Clark.   The Plaintiff, Jane Clark, wife of Robert Clark, died during the continuance of the action.

The judgment appealed from held that there was no evidence to shew that the Plaintiff Harding had effected the insurance; but that, on the contrary, it appeared that it had been effected by the deceased Jane Clark, and that Laura Harding had merely promised to pay the premiums if her mother did not do so.

JUNE 24, 1901.

The judgment of the learned Judge of the County Court is right and must be affirmed.

No cause of any action was established by either of the Plaintiffs at the trial.

The contention made before us was that the policy in respect of which the Plaintiff Harding had paid the premiums which she sought to recover back was a void policy as made in contravention of the Act 14 Geo. III, c. 48.

But the evidence in my opinion wholly failed to establish this.

The policy was produced and as far as it showed was a policy upon the life of the Plaintiff Clark payable to his executor, administrator, wife, relative by blood or lawful beneficiary.

The application was not produced although expressly made by the policy a part of it and the Plaintiff's counsel refused to consent to its being put in evidence, and evidence therefore of its contents was inadmissible, and I think that proof of this application was a necessary part of the Plaintiff's case in order to establish the illegality of the insurance.

The insurance appeared to have been effected by the wife of the Plaintiff Clark upon the life of her husband, and as far as one can conjecture from the evidence the wife was named as the beneficiary in the application and so far the insurance was a valid one, the wife having an insurable interest in the life of the husband.

The mere fact that the Plaintiff Harding paid the premiums would not of itself show that the transaction was in contravention of the statute unless it were also shown that the real transaction was the insurance by the Plaintiff Harding of the life of the Plaintiff Clark for her own benefit, but this the evidence, in my opinion, failed to establish.

The evidence failed also to establish any knowledge in the Defendants that the transaction was other than it appeared to be by the application.

The appeal must be dismissed with costs.

Solicitor for the Plaintiffs : *T. Hislop*.

Solicitor for the Defendants : *F. S. Mearns*.

Note :—

See also the recent decision of the Court of Appeal for Ontario in *North American, etc.* v. *Brophy*, (a case dealing with the application of 14 Geo. III., cap. 48), and not yet officially reported.

[IN THE HIGH COURT OF JUSTICE FOR ONTARIO.]

Before FERGUSON, J.

SAUNDERS v. THE ONTARIO BANK.

Contract—Sale of goods by sample— Warranty—Warehouse receipts—Agency.

1. A bank advanced money upon the promissory notes of a cold storage firm, endorsed by M, one of the members of the firm, warehouse receipts for goods deposited by M with his firm being taken as security for his endorsations. The cold storage company bought eggs with the monies so obtained, and warehoused them in the name of M, receipts being issued to him. The firm becoming financially embarrassed, the manager of the bank checked over the goods then in the warehouse, and instructed O'R, the other partner, to sell them and to pay the proceeds of such sales into the bank, which was duly done. One of the purchasers having brought an action for damages caused by breach of warranty regarding the condition of the eggs, the bank contended that it had not been the vendor. Held, that since the bank had, in fact, had the control

over the goods, their title not being disputed, it was immaterial whether or not the the warehouse receipts upon which the title was based were such as would have proved good against all comers.

Held, further, that the arrangement between the local manager of the bank and O'R virtually constituted the latter the agent of the bank for the sale of the goods, no ratification by the head office being necessary ; and that, therefore, the bank was liable for the breach of the implied warranty which, it appeared, was given by O'R, so acting as its agent.

The facts of this case are fully set forth in the head note and in the judgment.

FERGUSON, J.:—

AUGUST 2nd, 1901.

The Plaintiffs in the statement of claim allege that on or about the 9th day of February, 1901, the Defendants sold to them 4500 dozens of eggs f.o.b. cars at the city of Ottawa, at the price of thirteen cents per dozen, and say that at the time of such sale the Defendants warranted such eggs to be in good condition and of good quality, and equal in quality and condition to a certain sample box or case of eggs produced by the Defendants for examination by the Plaintiffs about the time of such sale and upon the faith of which the sale was made and that they, the Plaintiffs, paid the Defendants the sum of $585.00, the amount of the purchase price ; that the Defendants delivered to the Plaintiffs the said quantity of eggs, but that a large portion thereof was damaged by frost, and therefore not in a good condition for sale or use, and that on account of the eggs being so frozen and not in a good condition they, the Plaintiffs, were forced to sell the eggs without delay, at and for the sum of $270.00, being six cents per dozen, that being the best price that could be obtained for them, and that they, the Plaintiffs, sustained loss or damage amounting to the sum of $315.00 by reason of the eggs being so frozen and not in good condition.

The Defendants deny that they sold these eggs or any other goods to the Plaintiffs, and also say that they did not nor did anyone on their behalf expressly or impliedly give to the Plaintiffs, or to any person on their behalf, the warranty referred to by the Plaintiffs, and that if any person or persons purported to make or give any warranty to the Plaintiffs, the same was not made or given by or on behalf

of the Defendants, and such person or persons had no authority from the Defendants to make or give any warranty,
and that no such warranty is binding upon them, the
Defendants.

The Defendants further say that the eggs referred to
were bought by the Plaintiffs from one Geo. A. O'Reilly,
and were of good quality and in good condition, and equal
to the sample in quality and condition and were so accepted
by the Plaintiffs, and that if the eggs were in any way
injured by freezing and otherwise such injury occurred after
delivery to and acceptance by the Plaintiffs.

The Defendants also say that the sum of $270.00 was
not the best price obtainable for the eggs, and that by the
exercise of reasonable diligence a larger price could have
been obtained.

The Plaintiffs claim as well for the loss of profits on a
re-sale of the eggs, and to this the Defendants say that no
such loss was suffered by the Plaintiffs.

A company known as " The Ottawa Cold Storage and
Freezing Company " was carrying on business in Ottawa,
which business seems to have been an extensive one. The
Company was composed of Geo. A. O'Reilly and James
McCullough.

This company obtained large credit of the Defendant
Bank. It appears that their method of doing business so
far as this has concern here, was that goods were purchased
in the name of McCullough as owner and for him warehoused by the Company, they, the Company, giving him,
McCullough, warehouse receipts in respect of the goods,
which McCullough endorsed to the Defendants as security
for the advances.

The Bank, the Defendants, appear to have advanced the
money upon the notes of the Company endorsed by
McCullough. The local manager of the Defendants Bank in
one part of his evidence says that he thought the warehouse receipts were taken from McCullough to secure his
endorsations of the notes, that the understanding was that
McCullough had the eggs warehoused with the Company.
But he says that the eggs were bought and paid for with
the proceeds of the notes of the Company on which

McCullough was endorser (that is money advanced by the Defendants). He says the Company was a wholesale purchaser of agricultural products and he might have taken the other kind of warehouse receipts, but he thought the way he did was the better way. He says the Company were also doing a warehousing business.

About the 1st of August, 1900, this Company were in financial difficulty. The Defendants' local manager, having learned this, went as he says and checked over the goods.

McCullough had gone away but O'Reilly was still there. The local manager says that if O'Reilly had gone as McCullough did, he would have appointed some other person to sell the goods. He says, however, that he left the goods in the hands of O'Reilly to dispose of them to the best advantage, that is to sell them as well as possible, and to pay the proceeds of the sale into the Bank, and that O'Reilly came to him from day to day and deposited the moneys received by him on such sales and finally reported to him that all the goods were sold. The sale to the Plaintiff took place as before stated on the 9th of July, 1901. It is, I think, most clearly proved that the identical moneys received by O'Reilly on that sale were paid by him into the Defendants Bank.

The Cold Storage and Freezing Company were also largely indebted to The Merchants Bank of Halifax, and about or shortly after the 17th of November, 1900, that Bank having sued, placed a writ of execution in the hands of the Sheriff against the goods and land of the Company, directing the levy of over $10.000. The Defendants having learned of this gave notice of their claim, the claim being founded on the warehouse receipts.

The Sheriff instituted interpleader proceedings and an order was made, but before the trial of any issue these Defendants satisfied the claim of the Merchants Bank. The Sheriff withdrew from possession of the goods under the seizure. The moneys paid by Defendants to the Merchants Bank were, according to the evidence, virtually charged against this Company, the Cold Storage and Freezing Company.

After the 1st of August, 1900, there was, as the local manager says, a change in the account of the Company in the Defendant Bank. The manager took supervision of it, and as I gather from the evidence the Company had no longer an account over which they had control.

Having considered the evidence as best I have been able with the view of ascertaining the real meaning of it, I have arrived at the conclusion that the sale of these goods (the eggs) to the Plaintiffs was a sale by the Defendants through their agent O'Reilly.

It does not seem to me material whether or not the warehouse receipts through which the Defendants claimed title to the goods were such as would technically prove a good title against all oncomers, or whether or not all the requirements of the 2nd sub-sec. of sec. 72 of the Act were strictly complied with. The Defendants really had control of the goods, no one after the settlement with the other Bank, so far as shewn, disputing their title, and no one complaining of any want of compliance with any of the requirements of the sub-sec. above referred to, and in any case these were not, as I think, things or matters to be looked after by the purchasers as between them and their vendors.

Although it was contended that there could be no good appointment of O'Reilly as agent for the sale of the goods, except by direction from the head office of the Defendants, I am of the opinion that the appointment shewn was sufficient for the purposes.

Then I think the sale made by the Defendants' agent, O'Reilly, to the Plaintiffs was a "Sale by Sample": It is said in Benjamin on Sales, 7th Am. ed., p. 685, that to constitute a "Sale by Sample" in the legal sense of that term, it must appear that the parties contracted solely in reference to the sample or article exhibited, and that both mutually understood they were dealing with the sample with the understanding that the bulk was like it. Or, as sometimes stated, to raise the implied warranty of conformity between sample and bulk it must appear that the alleged sale by sample was really such, that the portion shewn was intended and understood to be a standard of the quality, and not merely that it was in fact taken from the bulk.

It is shewn by the evidence that it is customary to buy and sell eggs by sample, and on the evidence of the witnesses Mills and Casselman, not in any way contradicted by O'Reilly or any other witness, I am of the opinion that this sale was really a sale by sample, and that the implied warranty as to conformity between sample and bulk was raised, or arose.

The evidence is that the eggs in the box, the sample, were good eggs and not frozen at all. On the evidence of Latorney, Champagne and Casselman, which seems to be uncontradicted, I find that at the time the sample was exhibited a large proportion of the bulk was frozen eggs. This, one would say, ought to have been known to Mr. O'Reilly, but he says he was not aware of it.

The evidence of the carters and railway men seems reasonably to show that the eggs were not frozen in transit, and the evidence of witnesses professing to be skilled or to have had large experience in the egg business goes, to shew that the freezing or some of it had taken place many days previous to the making of this contract, they, giving their reasons for knowing this, and the evidence of Latorney seems direct on this subject.

Then, if my view is right, there seems an implied warranty given by O'Reilly to the Plaintiffs when this sale by sample was made. There was a breach of this, or rather the warranty was untrue. By reason of this the Plaintiffs have suffered and lost and the Defendants have gained and profited. O'Reilly was acting, as I have already said, as the agent of the Defendants when he made this contract and when the warranty arose or was given.

The general rule is that the principal is answerable for every such wrong of the agent as is committed in the course of the agency or service and for the benefit of the principal, though no express command or priority of the principal is proved, and in this respect no sensible distinction can be drawn between the case of fraud and the case of any other wrong. *McKay* v. *Com. Bank of New Brunswick* L.R., 5 P.C. 411-412 and many other cases.

In was, however, contended that O'Reilly in doing what he did was acting in his own interest, and not in the interest and for the benefit of the Defendants. I have given attention to this argument and the assigned reasons on which it is bottomed, and my opinion is against it. I think he was acting in the interest and for the benefit of the Defendants, and I am of the opinion that Defendants are liable to the Plaintiffs for the loss that they sustained by reason of the eggs having been frozen, which on the evidence is $315.00.

The evidence as to this amount is all one way. As these damages were unascertained and unliquidated there will be no interest.

The Plaintiffs claim damages for loss of profits on a re-sale of the goods. The rule on this subject is laid down with clearness in the 6th ed. of Mayne on Damages at p. 55, and I think that in this case such damages must be considered too remote.

The Plaintiffs have not, as I think, proved enough to entitle them to succeed upon this claim.

There will be judgment for the Plaintiffs for the sum of $315.00 with costs of the action, which costs, if necessary to say so, will be on the High Court scale.

Order accordingly.

[IN THE HIGH COURT OF JUSTICE FOR ONTARIO.]

BEFORE MEREDITH, C.J.

PROVIDENT CHEMICAL WORKS

v.

CANADA CHEMICAL MANUFACTURING CO.

Trade-mark—Descriptive letters—Registration — Secondary meaning—Proof of acquisition—Fraud—Deception.

The letters C.A.P., standing for the words " cream acid phosphates," being descriptive merely, are not the proper subject of a trade-mark, and registration of them as a trade-mark, under the Trade-Mark and Design Act, will not give a right to the conclusive use of them.

Partlo v. *Todd* (1888), 17 S.C.R. 196, followed.

Words or letters which are primarily merely descriptive may come to have in the trade a secondary meaning signifying to persons dealing in the articles described that when branded with such words or letters the articles are of the manufacture of a particular person.

But where the Plaintiffs used the letters C.A.P., standing for " cream acid phosphates," in connection with acid phosphates manufactured by them, and the Defendants used the same letters, signifying "calcium acid phosphates," in connection with acid phosphates manu-factured by them and prominently stated thereon to be manufac-tured by them, and the evidence did not shew that there was on the part of the Defendants any fraud, or any intention of appropriat-ing any part of the Plaintiffs' trade, or that any purchaser or per-son invited to purchase was deceived or misled, or that the letters had come to mean in the trade, acid phosphates of the Plaintiffs' manufacture :—

Held, that the Plaintiffs could not complain of the use of the letters by the Defendants.

Reddaway v. *Banham*, (1896) A.C. 199, applied.

An action for an injunction and damages and other relief in respect of the alleged infringement by the Defendants of a trade-mark registered by the Plaintiffs. The facts and arguments are fully stated in the judgment.

July 24. (1901.)

MEREDITH, C.J. :—

The Plaintiffs are a manufacturing company having their head office and manufactory at St. Louis, in the State of Missouri, one of the United States of America.

Acid phosphates is one of the articles which the Plaintiffs manufacture, and it is manufactured in large quantities and a market for it is found both in the United States and in Canada, as well as elsewhere.

The Plaintiffs have for many years manufactured acid phosphates which they designate "cream acid phosphates," and upon the packages in which it is put up for sale and sold are stamped the letters C.A.P., which are said to have been used as the initial letters of the words "cream acid phosphates."

These letters the Plaintiffs have registered as their trademark, in the United States on the 21st September, 1886, and in Canada on the 24th July, 1900. Their name and place of business also formed part of the trade-mark so registered.

The Defendants are a manufacturing company, and have for many years carried on business at London, in this Province; about nine years ago they commenced the manufacture of acid phosphates as a branch of their business for the purpose of utilizing one of the bi-products in the manufacture of sulphuric acid, the manufacture of which forms their principal business.

Calcium is, as I understand, one of the ingredients of the acid phosphates manufactured by the Plaintiffs and by the Defendants.

The Defendants for several years have used in connection with the acid phosphates manufactured by them the letters C.A.P., branding them upon the packages in which it is put up for sale, and advertising it under those letters; the letters being intended to signify calcium acid phosphates.

Calcium acid phosphates is a proper as well as a scientifically correct designation for the acid phosphates manufactured by the Defendants, though the word "calcium" is used perhaps more frequently after than before the other two words—acid phosphates of calcium.

It was not contended that the Defendants in adopting and applying to the product of their manufacture the letters C. A. P. had in fact any intention to put off their goods as the goods manufactured and sold by the Plaintiffs under that brand ; had it been so contended, the contention would not have been supported by the evidence, for the contrary is satisfactorily shown.

The Plaintiffs' case is, however, that the letters C.A.P., though primarily, perhaps, descriptive of the article to which they were applied, have acquired a secondary meaning, and have come to be known and recognized in the trade as indicating the specific article manufactured by them and sold under that brand—cream acid phosphates— and that the Defendants have no right to apply those letters to the acid phosphates which they manufacture, because, as they contend, the result of their so doing is, that those dealing in the article are likely to be misled into thinking that the goods of the Defendants so branded are the specific article manufactured by the Plaintiffs and sold under the same brand ; and they also claim that they are proprietors of the registered trade-mark to which I have referred, and therefore entitled to the exclusive use of the letters C.A.P. as applied to the article of acid phosphates.

The relief claimed by the Plaintiffs based on these alleged rights is an injunction restraining the Defendants from using the letters C.A.P. in connection with any baking powder material not manufactured by the Plaintiffs, and from using them so as to induce the belief that the material manufactured or sold by the Defendants is the same as that manufactured and sold by the Plaintiffs, and from in any way infringing the Plaintiffs' alleged trade-mark ; they also claim damages and an order for the obliteration of the letters C.A.P. wherever they are used by the Defendants in connection with their acid phosphates, and for the destruction of any dies or other instruments for stamping or marking those letters, in the possession of the Defendants.

I purpose dealing first with the claim as far as it is based on the Plaintiffs' rights as owners of the trade-mark and therefore to the exclusive use of the letters C.A.P. when applied to any material for making baking powder.

It is clear, I think, that primarily the letters C.A.P., standing as they do for the words "cream acid phosphates" or "calcium acid phosphates," are descriptive merely, and are not therefore the proper subject of a trade-mark.

As Mr. Justice Burton pointed out in *Partlo* v. *Todd*, 14 A.R. 444, at p. 452, a word or name which is merely descriptive of an article, or which is indicative merely of its quality or composition, cannot properly be the subject of a trade-mark. That, I take it, is a correct statement of the law, and it is conclusive against the Plaintiffs' on this branch of the case, unless by the registration of the letters under the Trade-Mark and Design Act as a trade-mark they have acquired a right to the use of them which the Defendants are not entitled to question in this action. If the decision of the Supreme Court in *Partlo* v. *Todd*, 17 S. C.R. 196, is still the law, the registration does not help the Plaintiffs. That was conceded by Mr. Cassels, but he contended that the decision proceeded upon the ground that there was no machinery provided by the Act for expunging from the register a trade-mark improperly admitted to registration, and no longer governed because, by subsequent legislation, jurisdiction is given to the Exchequer Court, at the suit of anyone aggrieved by an entry in the register of trade-marks without sufficient cause, to make an order expunging or varying the entry as the Court thinks fit.

This contention is not, I think, well founded, for, as I read the report of the case, the judgment of the Court did not proceed upon the ground upon which Mr. Cassels argued that it was rested, but upon broader grounds. The head-note to the report lends colour to the argument, but it is not warranted by anything which is found in the judgment, and I must, therefore, follow *Partlo* v. *Todd*, and, following it, hold that it is open to the Defendants in this action to raise and rely on the objection to the Plaintiffs' claim which is, in my opinion, fatal to it, that at the time of the registration the Plaintiffs were not proprietors of the trade-mark because the letters C.A.P. were not, for the reasons I have already mentioned, the subject of a trade-mark.

I come now to the other branch of the case.

In *Reddaway* v. *Banham* [1896] A.C. 199, the House of Lords, after a full review of the authorities, laid down the law which is to be applied in determining as to the right of one who is not the owner of a trade-mark in respect of them to restrain another from using names, marks, letters, or other indicia which the former has applied to articles put upon the market by him.

As put by the Lord Chancellor (p. 204) the principle of law to be applied is, that nobody has any right to represent his goods as the goods of somebody else, and, as said by Lord Herschell (p. 209)), it is that stated by Lord Kingsdown in these words : ''The fundamental rule is, that one man has no right to put off his goods for sale as the goods of a rival trader, and he cannot therefore (in the language of Lord Langdale in *Perry* v. *Truefitt* (1842), 6 Beav. 66) be allowed to use names, marks, letters, or other indicia, by which he may induce purchasers to believe that the goods which he is selling are the manufacture of another person.''

It seems to have been conceded on all hands that that principle has no application where the names, marks, letters or other indicia are descriptive of the material of which the article is composed or of its quality or nature—as if in that case the words ''camel hair'' conveyed to persons dealing in belting the idea that it was made of camel hair—but that it was to be applied where the names, marks, letters or other indicia, though primarily they conveyed that meaning, had come to have a secondary meaning and to be understood in the trade to mean, when applied to an article, that it was one manufactured by the person who was known to have applied them to such an article of his manufacture.

To apply, then, the principle of that case to the facts of this. There can, I think, be no question, as I have said already, that the letters C.A.P. as used by the Plaintiffs were merely descriptive of the article phosphates, and unless, therefore, they had come to have in the trade a secondary meaning and to be no longer merely descriptive, but to signify to persons dealing in acid phosphates that acid phosphates so branded were of the Plaintiffs' manufacture, there was nothing to prevent the Defendants from applying to acid phosphates manufactured by them the name of '' calcium acid phosphates '' or the letters C.A.P. as being the initial letters of those three words and standing in place of them.

As I have said, there is no case made on the evidence of fraud on the Defendants' part, and no ground for thinking that in using the letters C.A.P. they did not do so simply because they stood for the words "calcium acid phosphates," and without any idea or intention of appropriating to themselves any part of the Plaintiffs' trade. Nor is there any pretence for saying that any one who has purchased their goods bearing the brand C.A.P., or any one who was invited by advertisement or otherwise to do so, was deceived or led by the use of the letters to believe that what he was purchasing or invited to purchase was the article which the Plaintiffs manufactured and sold under that brand.

The evidence does not satisfy me that the letters C.A.P. used by the Plaintiffs in connection with acid phosphates manufactured by them have acquired a secondary meaning, or have come to mean in the trade acid phosphates of the Plaintiffs' manufacture, or that those words were understood in the trade otherwise than as descriptive of the article simply.

Acid phosphates are not sold either by the Plaintiffs or the Defendants by retail, but only, as I understand the evidence, to manufacturers of baking powder, who in ordering it are in the habit of doing so calling the article "acid phosphates," and not by the name either of "cream acid phosphates" or of "calcium acid phosphates." Mr. Fullerton, one of the witnesses examined on behalf of the Plaintiffs, who had purchased both from them and from the Defendants, testified that he called the article indifferently by the two names "C.A.P." and "phosphates" simply. The evidence also shews that it was customary in the trade to designate other articles used in the manufacture of baking powder by the initial letters of the words descriptive of them, as B.C.T. to signify baker's cream of tartar, and C.T.S., cream of tartar substitute, and the like. This is important, I think, as indicating that persons in the trade would understand the letters C.A.P. to mean cream acid phosphates or calcium acid phosphates according as they purchased from the Plaintiffs or from the Defendants; in other words, they would know, if they were buying acid phosphates from the Plaintiffs, that it was of the grade called by them cream acid phosphates, and if from the Defendants, that called by them calcium acid phosphates.

But, even if the letters C.A.P have acquired the secondary meaning I have spoken of, something more is required to be shown by the Plaintiffs to entitle them to the relief they seek. It is only—even in that case—if the use which the Defendants make of the letters is calculated to deceive persons in the trade into the belief that the article purchased from the Defendants under that brand is the article manufactured and sold by the Plaintiffs under the same brand, that the acts of the Defendants are a violation of the rights of the Plaintiffs.

I quote from the speech of Lord Morris in the *Reddaway* case. After expressing his concurrence with the judgment of the House, he proceeds—referring to the finding of the jury that camel hair belting had become so identified with the name of the Plaintiff that camel hair belting had in the market obtained the meaning of Reddaway's (the Plaintiff's) belting—as follows: "That finding establishes as a fact that the use of the words 'camel hair belting' *simpliciter* deceives purchasers, and it becomes necessary for the Respondents to remove that false impression so made on the public. That, to my mind, is obviously done when the Respondents put prominently and in a conspicuous place on the article the statement that it was camel hair belting manufactured by themselves. Having done so, they would, as it appears to me, fully apprise purchasers that it was not Reddaway's make, by stating that it was their own. A representation deceiving the public is and must be the foundation of the Appellants' right to recover ; they are not entitled to any monopoly of the name 'camel hair belting' irrespective of its deceiving the public, and everyone has a right to describe truly his article by that name, provided he distinguishes it from the Appellants' make. In this case the Respondents did not so distinguish it because they ommitted to state that it was their own make:" [1896] A.C. pp. 221-2.

That statement of Lord Morris, if I may venture to say so, appears to me to crystallize into a few words the whole case, and to properly state the rule to be applied and the limits of its application.

If, then, it was open to the Respondents in that case— what they had done having been fraudulently designed with intent to deceive, and having had that effect—to set themselves right by adopting the course pointed out by Lord Morris, it is an *a fortiori* case that these Respondents, who have not acted fraudulently—have not intended to deceive, and have not in fact deceived any one into the belief that in buying goods of their manufacture he was buying the Plaintiffs' goods—and have taken care to put prominently on the articles of their manufacture the statement that they were manufactured by them—have not represented their goods as the goods of the Plaintiffs, nor by the use of the letters C.A.P. put off their goods for sale as the goods of the Plaintifs—have committed no wrong for which the Plaintiffs are entitled to call them to account.

Had I been of a different opinion, it would have been necessary to consider the effect of the laches and delay of the Plaintiffs in taking proceedings to assert their rights against the Defendants, but, as it is, I need not consider that question.

I have not referred to any of the cases cited upon the argument but the two I have dealt with, because the general question with which I have had to deal is so fully dealt with in the *Reddaway* case, and because the American cases cited by Mr. Shepley are not altogether in accord with the view taken by the English Courts as to the application of the rule laid down in *Re Reddaway* to cases where the names, words, letters, or other indicia used are descriptive merely of the article or indicative merely of its quality or composition.

The result is that, in my opinion, the Plaintiffs' case fails, and their action must be dismissed with costs.

Solicitor for the Plaintiffs : *H. Cronyn.*

Solicitor for the Defendants : *E. W. M. Flock.*

Note:—

See in connection with this case the notes upon the decision in *Pabst, etc.* v. *Ekers et al.*, reported *ante* p. 38.

[IN THE SUPREME COURT OF CANADA.]

Before TASCHEREAU, GWYNNE, SEDGWICK, KING AND GIROUARD, JJ.

MAGANN (Defendant), Appellant

v.

AUGER et al (Plaintiffs), Respondents.

(31 S.C.R. 186.)

(On appeal from the Court of Queen's Bench, of the Province of Quebec, Appeal Side.)

Contract by correspondence—Mailing letter of acceptance— Place where contract made—Indication of place of payment— Jurisdiction — Declinatory exception— Waiver— Procedure.

C.P.Q. Articles 85, 94, 129, 1164, 1173, 1175, 1176.—C.C. P.Q. Articles 85-86.

An offer was made by the plaintiff by letter dated and posted at Quebec, and was accepted by defendant by a letter dated and posted at Toronto. An action having been brought upon the contract in the Superior Court for the District of Quebec, the defendant, who had been served substitutionally, petitioned in revocation of a judgment which had been entered by default, first taking exception to the jurisdiction of the Court, and then constituting himself incidental plaintiff, and, as such, making a cross-demand for damages to be set off against the plaintiff's claim.

Held, that in the Province of Quebec, as in the rest of Canada, in negotiations carried on by correspondence, it is not necessary for the completion of the contract that the letter accepting an offer should have actually reached the party making it, but the mailing in the general post-office of such letter completes the contract. (*Underwood v. Maguire*, R.J.Q., 6 Q.B., 237, overruled.)

Article 85 of the Civil Code, as amended by 52 Vict., ch. 48, (P.Q.) providing that the indication of a place of payment in any note or writing should be equivalent to election of domicile at the place so indicated, requires that such place should be actually designated in the contract.

In forming an opposition or petition in revocation of judgment the defendant, in order to comply with Art. 1164 C.P., P.Q., is obliged to include therein any cross-demand he may have by way of set-off or in compensation of the plaintiff's claim and, unless he does so, he cannot afterwards file it as of right.

A cross-demand so filed with a petition for revocation of judgment is not a waiver of a declinatory exception previously pleaded, nor an acceptance of the jurisdiction of the court.

In order to take advantage of waiver of a preliminary exception to the
competence of the tribunal over the cause of action on account of
subsequent incompatible pleadings, the plaintiff must invoke the
alleged waiver of the objection in his answers.

The judgment appealed from, affirming the decision of the Superior
Court, District of Quebec (Q.R., 16 S.C. 22), was reversed.

Appeal from a judgment of the Court of Queen's Bench
(Province of Quebec), Appeal Side, affirming the judgment of the Superior Court for the District of Qubec, dismissing the defendant's declinatory exception, and, on the
merits, maintaining the plaintiff's action with costs.

The facts of the case are set forth in the head note and
in the judgment.

The judgment of the Court was delivered by :

TASCHEREAU, J.

The judgment of the Superior Court, confirmed by the
Court of Appeal for the same reasons, as appears by the
printed case, dismissed the appellant's exception to the
jurisdiction on the sole ground that by constituting himself
incidental plaintiff he had submitted to the jurisdiction of
the Court, and waived his said exception. We think that
judgment untenable. The appellant's incidental demand,
though not so in express terms as it was for instance in
Peale v. *Phipps*, (14 How. 368) was of its nature merely
alternative, in the event of his exception to the jurisdiction
not prevailing. If any part of the appellant's petition was
illegal it was the incidental demand, not the declinatory
plea. It is that demand that should have been objected to
by the respondents, as incompatible with the exception to
the jurisdiction. The respondents replied to the petition
and declinatory plea and proceeded to trial and judgment
upon the declinatory plea as a separate issue, and it was
the court *ex proprio motu* which suggested the question
of waiver. Now, it it a well settled rule that waiver must
be pleaded or invoked by the party who relies upon it. In
this case, if there had been a waiver at all, it was on the
part of the respondents who asked the Court for a judgment on the merits of the appellant's declinatory exception
without invoking waiver of it by the appellant. Then,
were it necessary to determine the point, it would seem
that appellant is right in his contention that under articles
1164, 1173, 1175, 1176 C.C.P., (new), his incidental or

cross-demand was rightly filed with his petition. Arts. 217, 218, 219, C.C.P., *Turcotte* v. *Dansereau* (27 Can. S.C.R. 583), *Brunet* v. *Colfer* (11 Q.L.R. 208), 5 Boncenne-Bourbeau, 100 et seq. Though not a plea, in the ordinary sense of the word, the cross-demand was in the nature of a set-off, or compensation against the respondent's claim. Had he not filed it with his petition, he could not later have been allowed to file it, as of right.

Having come to the conclusion that the appellant had not waived his declinatory exception, we have to pass upon its merits, and determine whether or not the whole cause of respondent's action has arisen in the District of Quebec. If not, it is conceded, the Court had no jurisdiction. This brings up the controverted question raised in *Underwood* v. *Maguire* (R.J.Q., 6 Q.B. 237), and noticed in Sirey, Code Civil annoté, under art. 1101, no. 32, under art. 1583, no. 40; Code de Procéd., under art. 420, no. 78, and in Pandectes Françaises vo. "Obligations'" no. 7054. In negotiations carried on by correspondence is the contract entered into only when the letter containing the acceptance has reached the party who has made the offer? Or, as put in Sirey, loc. cit. "Est-il nécessaire pour la perfection du contrat que l'acceptation soit parvenue à la connaissance de celui qui a fait l'offre?" The jurisprudence and commentators' opinions in France on the question are fully cited and collected in Sirey and the Pandectes, loc. cit.

If counted merely, the respondent's contention that the question should be answered in the affirmative would seem to have a majority in its favour. But if the reasoning is weighed, the question should, we think, be answered in the negative, and we adopt the view taken by Pothier, Vente, no. 32 ; 24 Demol. Ier, des Contr. No. 72 ; by Marcade, vol. 4, under art. 1108, no. 395 ; by Lyon-Caen, Dr. Commercial, vol. 3, nos. 25 et seq.; by the annotator to the arret of the 21st Jan., 1891, in Pand. Franç. 92, 2, 163 ; by the annotator to the same arret in Dalloz, 92, 2, 249 ; by Guillouard, Vente, vol. Ier, no. 15 ; by Vigié, Dr. Civ. Fr., vol. 2, no. 1112 ; and by Hudelot, Obligations, no. 37. It would appear useless to repeat here the argumentation upon which these commentators have reached their conclusions upon the question. A simple reference to them is sufficient. They completely refute the reasoning upon which the contrary doctrine is based.

If it were required for the *aggregatio mentium* necessary
to create mutuality of obligations in a contract made by
correspondence that the party who has made the offer has
received the acceptance of his offer, it would follow that the
party accepting should himself not be bound till he is
informed that his acceptance has reached the party offering.
It is obviously of the greatest importance to the commercial
community that such a doctrine should not prevail.

By the conclusion we have reached upon the question,
we declare the law to be in the Province of Quebec upon the
same footing as it stands in England, and in the rest of this
Dominion, a fact rightly alluded to by Mr. Justice Bossé in
Underwood v. *Maguire* (R.J.Q., 6 Q. B. 237), as of great
importance specially in commercial matters.

It had previously in France been said by a learned writer
that this view of the question "est celle qui présenterait le
plus de chances de succès devant la juridiction commer-
ciale." Boncenne-Bourbeau, vol. 6, p. 163.

It has been argued for the respondents that as under arts.
1152 and 1533 of the Civil Code the payment by the appellants under this contract had by law to be made to them in
the District of Quebec, where delivery of the ties sold to
them had to take place, they had the right to bring the
action there under the provisions of art. 85. In France, no
doubt, the action is rightly brought where the payment
has to be made, But that is so only in virtue of art. 420 of
their Code of procedure, which is treated by the commentators and the jurisprudence as an exception in the *tribunaux
de commerce* to the ordinary rules in the matter. Dalloz,
63, 1, 176; Pand. Fr., 99, 1, 22. At common law, the
indication of a place of payment does not confer jurisdiction
upon the tribunals of that place. I refer to Demol. vol.
Ier, no. 374 ; Sirey Cod. Civ. Ann., under art. 111, no. 52 ;
12 Duranton, no. 99 ; 27 Demolombe, vol. 4, des contrats,
no. 274 ; 6 Boncenne-Bourbeau, 210 et seq.; *Wurtele* v.
Lengham, (1 Q.L.R., 61); *Tourigny* v. *Wheeler*, (9 Q.L.R.,
198); *Cloutier* v. *Lapierre*, (4 Q.L.R., 321); *Clark* v.
Ritchey, (9 L. C. Jur. 234). By the act 52 Vict., ch. 48,
amending article 85 of the Civil Code, the indication of a
special place of payment in any note or writing, wherever it
is dated, now confers jurisdiction over any action relating
to such note or writing upon the tribunals of the place so

indicated.   But here, in the written agreement sued upon there is no such indication of a place of payment and the declaration does not allege any. *Bent* v. *Lauve*, (3 La. An. 88); *Vidal* v. *Thompson*, (11 Mart. La. 23); *Morris* v. *Eves*, (11 Mart. La. 730.)   The place of payment designated by the law alone is not the indication required by art. 85 of the Code as it now reads.   It is a stipulated domicile, one expressly contracted for by the parties not the place indicated by the law that this article provides for.

When article 94 of the Code of Procedure read with art. 86 of the Civil Code says that a defendant may be summoned in the case of an election of domicile for the execution of an act, before the Court of the domicile so elected, it means clearly a conventional domicile, not a legal domicile, not the place that the law alone designates as the place of payment.

It would seem, moreover, that article 85 C.P.Q. requires that the election of domicile and the indication of a place of payment equivalent thereto under its provisions, be made at such a designated place in a locality that the notifications, demands and suits relating thereto may be made and served thereat :· art. 129 C.P.Q.   For instance, if a note says " payable at Quebec," that is not an election of domicile under this article.

We hold therefore that the contract between the parties in this case having been made in Toronto where the appellant accepted the respondent's offer and mailed his letter of acceptance, the whole cause of action did not arise at Quebec, and the indication of a place of payment as required to give jurisdiction over the matter to the Superior Court at Quebec not having been alleged nor proved, the action not having been personally served upon the appellant must be dismissed.

Appeal allowed with costs, declinatory plea maintained and action dismissed with cost.

Solicitors for the Appellant : *Dandurand, Brodeur & Boyer.*

Solicitors for the Respondents : *Taschereau, Pacaud & Smith.*

Notes :—

The rule of private international law, that the law governing the obligations arising out of a contract is that of the country where the contract is made, (*lex loci contractus*), is equally applicable in Ontario and in Quebec ; and, in each of these provinces, the qualifications to which it is subject are similarly recognized. These modifications were briefly summed up by Mr. Justice Willes in the case of *Lloyd* v. *Guibert* (1865) 35 L.J., N.S. 74, in the following words : " It is generally agreed that the law of the place where the contract is made is *prima facie* that which the parties intended, or ought to be presumed to have adopted, as the footing upon which they dealt, and that such law ought, therefore, to prevail in the absence of circumstances indicating a different intention, as, for instance, that the contract is to be entirely performed elsewhere, or that the subject-matter is immoveable property, situate in another country, and so forth."

As an example of one of the various kinds of exceptions to the general rule alluded to in the above statement of the law, reference may be made to the case of *The Queen* v. *Doutre*, (1884), L. R., 9 Ap. Ca. 745, where it was held that a contract made with a member of the Bar of the Province of Quebec for his professional services, was governed by the laws of that province (as being the professional domicile of the advocate) irrespective of where the contract was made.

And see, also, *Chamberlain* v. *Napier*, (1880), L.R. 15 C.D. 614.

In the Province of Quebec the law on this point is contained in article 8, of the Civil Code, which reads as follows : " Deeds are construed according to the laws of the country where they are passed, unless there is some law to the contrary, or the parties have agreed otherwise, or by the nature of the deed or from other circumstances, it appears that the intention of the parties was to be governed by the law of another place ; in any of which cases, effect is given to such law, or such intention express, or presumed."

And see, *Moore* v. *Harris*, (1876), L. R., 1 Ap. Ca. 318.

Vennor v. *Life Association of Scotland*, (1886), 30 L. C. J. 303.

Rogers v. *Mississippi & Dominion S.S. Co.*, (1888), 14 Q. L. R. 99.

In the case of contracts by correspondence, however, the question when and where the contract is actually made is one which has given rise to much controversy, especially amongst continental jurists. Several works have been published upon the debated point,—whether at the place and moment when, in the ordinary course of despatch, the acceptance passess out of the possession and control of the offeree, the contract is so completed as to debar the offeror from thereafter withdrawing his proposal,—or whether it is only concluded when and where such communication is actually received by the offeror.

As regards contracts made by letter, the English rule is that which was laid down in the well known case of *Bryne* v. *Van Tienhoven*, (1880), L. R., 5 C. P. D. 344, namely that the contract is completed at the time and place when and where the offeree posts the letter accepting the proposition of the other party. A letter revoking the offer will not avail against such an acceptance unless it has been received before the latter is mailed ; the fact that it was written and posted before the letter of the offeree was sent is immaterial.

In other cases it has been held that an acceptance by letter completes the contract from the date of the posting of the same, even though its delivery in due course is accidentally delayed.

See, *Adams* v. *Lindsell*, (1818); 1 Barn. & Ald. 681 ; *Dunlop* v. *Higgins*, (1848), 1 H. L. 381 ; or even when it s not delivered at all.

See, *Household Fire Insurance Co.* v. *Grant*, (1879), L.R., 4 Ex. D. 216.

And a letter withdrawing the offer, which is only received by the offeree after he has posted his letter of acceptance, is inoperative, as the contract is completed from the date of the mailing of such latter letter.

In re Imperial Land Co., Harris's Case, (1872) L.R.7, Ch. 587.

In re Scottish Petroleum Co., Maclagan's Case, 51 L.J., Ch., 841.

And see, also, *Henthorn* v. *Fraser* (1892) Ch. 27.

It is submitted, therefore, that the headnote of *Magann*
v. *Auger*, (as reported in 31 S.C.R. at p. 186.) which states
"that in the Province of Quebec, *as in the rest of Canada,*
....the mailing in the general post-office of such letter (of
acceptance) completes the contract, *subject, however, to
revocation of the offer by the party making it before receipt by
him of such letter of acceptance*" is incorrect.

There is, apparently, nothing in the judgment of Mr.
Justice Taschereau to indicate that that was the conclusion
arrived at by His Lordship.   On the other hand, Mr. Justice
Taschereau says (at p. 193): "By the conclusion we have
reached upon the question, *we declare the law to be in the
Province of Quebec upon the same footing as it stands in
England, and in the rest of the Dominion?*"—a result
which would not be arrived at if the proviso contained in
the headnote was included in his judicial ruling on the
point.

Amongst French jurists there has always existed a
difference of opinion as to whether or not it is necessary to
the completion of a contract that the acceptance should
have actually been made known to the person who made the
offer.   The majority of the authors who have dealt with
the question, (as is mentioned in the judgment of Mr.
Justice Taschereau, at p. 193), have maintained that it is ;
and that view of the question was adopted by the majority
of the Court of Queen's Bench in *Underwood* v. *Maguire*,
(1895), R. J. Q., 6 Q. B. 237, which was the ruling authority on the point in the Province of Quebec, until it was put
aside by the Supreme Court in *Magann* v. *Auger.*

As shewing the present tendency of the French Jurists
upon this point, however, it may be said that Mr. Mignault
(Le Droit Civil Canadien, vol. 5, p. 198, note b), draws
attention to the fact that whereas Beaudry-Lacantinerie in
his Précis (No. 797 *bis*) expressed the opinion that the
contract was only completed when the offeror was actually
made aware of the acceptance of his offer, he has since come
to the conclusion (vide his work Des obligations, Nos. 37
et seq.) that the contract is a perfect one from the very
moment that the offeree has expressed his acceptance in the
proper way, it being unnecessary for that purpose that such
acceptance should, at the time, be within the knowledge of
the offeror.

[IN THE COURT OF APPEAL FOR ONTARIO.]

Before ARMOUR, C. J. O., AND OSLER AND LISTER, J. J. A.

BROPHY (Defendant), Appellant.

v.

THE NORTH AMERICAN LIFE INSURANCE CO.
(Plaintiffs) Respondents,

Policy of life insurance—Lack of insurable interest—14 Geo. III., Cap. 48—Form of decree.

A policy of insurance was issued by an insurance company upon the life of C., the premiums being paid by B, who, at the same time, bought from the same company an annuity, the entire proceeds of which were to be and were devoted to that purpose, and the whole transaction being made with the intention of benefiting B, to whom the policy was subsequently assigned by C. The latter, having died, the company brought an action for the cancellation and delivery of the policy.

1. Held, that the policy was void as being in contravention of 14 Geo. III., cap. 48, the Defendant B not having had any insurable interest in the life of C.

2. Held, further, that, the trial judge having determined that the company had no knowledge of the true nature of the transactions, the latter was entitled to ask for the cancellation of the policy, but that in so seeking the intervention of the Court the company itself was bound to do equity, and should therefore return the Defendant B the balance of the total amount of all premiums paid on the policy, with interest, after having set off against this sum the costs of the action.

Appeal from a judgment of STREET, J.

The facts of the case are fully set forth in the head note, and in the judgments.

TORONTO, SEPTEMBER 21st, 1901.

ARMOUR, C. J. O. :—

The evidence in respect of the impeached policy of insurance is very plain and simple.

One Richard Alexander Cromar, a broker and insurance expert, as he called himself, on the 27th October, 1885, wrote to the defendant Brophy as follows : " *Re* the pleasant intercourse we have had in business matters lately.—On the condition of your making me, A. C., your referee, adviser and broker in any transaction relating to insurance, real estate or monetary investments, I agree and hereby promise to allow you the following rebate or commission on all premiums or amounts paid to any company or institution transacting business in Canada as follows, viz. :—Annuity bonds, one-half of one per cent. ; endowment policies, single premiums, one per cent. ; endowment policies, annual premiums, ten per cent. On all other transactions the half of commission given me as a general broker. Advice in any matter I will be pleased to give you to the best of my knowledge and ability gratis."

This proposed arrangement was apparently agreed to by the defendant Brophy, and continued in force until after the impeached policy was effected.

The defendant Brophy deposed as follows :—" I wanted to know from him the different kinds of insurance, and we had a talk about it two or three times, and he was telling me the different plans, and they did not suit me altogether, and I was thinking over that thing one night and I wanted to have as little trouble with the business as possible myself, and I was thinking over it one night after we had talked the second or third day, and the next morning I told him what I had been thinking of during the night, that there seemed to be a convenient and easy way for me, and that would be to buy the annuities and let the annuities go for insurance on my life, and he struck the table and said that is the best idea I ever heard. I have been a long time doing insurance business and that never came into my mind before; so he went out of the room where we were and told the manager then what he proposed and that he approved of so much, and that is the first insurance he did for me." The insurance here referred to was an endowment policy in the New York Life upon the life of the defendant Brophy effected in 1885. Shortly before the effecting of the impeached policy the defendant Brophy had an interview with Cromar, and this is the account he gave of it :—" I said I had some more money to put into insurance, and he said, wouldn't it be much better for you to have a young life. How would it be if I put it on my life, and he drew out the figures and showed me the difference in the insurance that I would get on his life and on my life, and showed me the advantage of putting it on his life, and that is the way he came to put the insurance on his life."

The defendant Brophy thereupon, through Cromar, applied to the plaintiffs for an annuity bond for $300, and Cromar applied for an insurance on his life for an amount, the annual premium for which would be met by the annuity bond, which amount was ascertained to be the sum of $6,025.

The annuity bond was issued by the plaintiffs for the annual sum of $300, payable to the Defendant Brophy on the fifth day of March, in each year, and the policy of insurance on the life of Cromar for $6,025, in consideration of the annual premium of $300, was issued by the plaintiffs, payable to Cromar on the fifth day of March, 1917, if living ; if not, his executors, administrators or assigns. This policy was originally written with premiums payable annually, 20th February, but was altered, making the premiums payable on the 5th day of March in each year, the same day on which the annuity of $300 was payable.

The amount charged for the annuity was......$2,546.70
and for the premium of insurance.................300.00
                                               ─────────
                                               $2,846.70

and from this was deducted one-half of one
    per cent. on the sum paid for the an-
    nuity bond $12.73
and ten per cent. on the premium of insur-
    ance 30.00
                                     ─────   42.73
                                               ─────────
                                               $2,803.97

these deductions being made in pursuance of the arrangement contained in the letter of Cromar of the 27th October, 1885. And for this balance of $2,803.97 the defendant Brophy sent his cheque to the plaintiffs.

Thereafter, until the death of Cromar, who died on the 24th April, 1900, the money payable by the annuity bond was applied in payment of the premiums payable by the policy of insurance.

On the 13th of March, 1897, Cromar, by assignment under his hand and seal, assigned, transferred and set over unto the defendant Brophy, and for his sole use and benefit, all his right, title and interest in and to the said policy of insurance, subject to all its terms and conditions, expressly reserving to the insured, however, sole right and power to make choice of any investment, option or options granted under the conditions of said policy, and personally to receive the full benefit thereof without the consent of any person or persons named therein as assignee or assignees, and that in the event of the death of the said assignee or assignees before the policy became due, then and in that case the proceeds thereof should be payable when due to the insured, his executors, administrators or assigns.

The defendant Brophy said that this assignment was not according to his agreement with Cromar; that by it he was entitled to an absolute assignment, but that he submitted to taking it rather than have any trouble.

The defendant Brophy had no insurable interest in the life of Cromar, and the policy of insurance, effected as it is shown by the above evidence it was, was clearly a wagering policy within the Statute, 14 Geo. III., ch. 48, and I do not think that the provisions of the assignment made it any less so, for the insurance was an entire contract, and being void in part, was void altogether. I have no doubt that, so far as the defendant Brophy was concerned, he acted in ignorance of the law, and with no intention to do anything unlawful.

If the plaintiffs were aware, at the time of this transaction, of its nature, and there is a good deal in the evidence tending to this conclusion, they would have no right to come to a Court seeking relief, for they would be in *pari delicto* with the defendant Brophy. The, learned trial judge, however, found that they were not aware of it, and I am not prepared to dissent from his finding. I at first thought that to entitle the plaintiffs to come to the Court, seeking the relief they here seek, they ought to have tendered or offered to return the premiums they had received, with interest; but I find several cases in which such relief has been given without any such tender or offer.

The proper form of decree to be made herein will be that the policy be delivered up to be cancelled; that the premiums of insurance received by the plaintiffs be paid to the defendant Brophy with interest thereon from the date of their receipt ; that the plaintiffs do have their costs of this action; that the counterclaim be dismissed with costs, and that this appeal be dismissed with costs, and that all the costs when taxed be set off against the premiums and interest payable by the plaintiffs to the defendant Brophy.

I refer to the following authorities in support of this decree.

Whittingham v. *Thornborough*, (*Finch Case 31*. 2 Equity Abridg. 635. 2 Vernon 206.) *De Costa* v. *Scandrett*, 2 Equity Abridg. 636. 2 P. Wms. 170. *Desborough* v. *Curlewis*, 3 Equity Ex. 175. *India & London Life Assce. Co.* v. *Dalby*, 4 De G. & S. 462 ; *Prince of Wales, &c., Assn.* v. *Palmer*, 25 Beav. 605 ; *The British Equitable Insce. Co.* v. *G. W. Railway Co.*, 38 L. J. Chy. 132. And the decree made by V. C. Strong in the *National Life Insurance Co.* v. *Egan*, reported on motion for injunction, 20 Grant 469.

OSLER, J. A. :—

The policy in question, though valid upon its face as being a policy in favor of Cromar upon his own life for a sum payable to him on the 20th February, 1917, should he then be living, or to his executors in case of his death before that time, was an illegal, void and invalid instrument under section 1 of 14 Geo. III., chap. 48, because Cromar was not at its inception the person really interested therein. The insurance was effected by and for the benefit of the defendant, who was to pay the first and subsequent premiums thereon under an agreement between Cromar and himself, by which Cromar was to make the application and obtain the policy and then to assign it to the defendant. The defendant's own evidence appears to me to establish this beyond any question, and the case is thus distinguished from that of these plaintiffs v. *Craigen* reported in 13 S. C. R. 278, where the facts showed that the application was really made by the person whose life was insured, though for the benefit of persons named in the application and policy, and to whom on the death of the insured the policy was to be payable. There the premiums were payable and were paid by the insured. The insurance was in its inception one really obtained by the applicant himself on his own life, though by the terms of the policy the money was directed to be paid to persons whom he intended to benefit. As is pointed out in the judgment of the present Chief Justice of the Supreme Court, no rule of law or statute prevents insurance of that kind : "It is not one which the statute, 14 Geo. III., was intended to prevent. . . . . Of course, if it is made to appear by the evidence that the undertaking of the person whose life is assured to pay the premiums is colourable and the premiums are in reality to be paid by a third person who has no insurable interest in the life and who is to have the benefit of the insurance, the policy will be a wager policy and so within the statute and void."

The evidence so plainly establishes all this in the present case that I think it unnecessary to say more than that I agree with the findings of the learned trial Judge thereon. The case of *Vezina* v. *The New York Life*, 6 S. C. R. 30, was much relied upon by the defendants. But that case turns altogether upon the facts which were held by the majority of the Court to prove that the insurance was valid in its inception as a bona-fide insurance for his own benefit by the person whose life was insured without collusion between himself and the person who had paid the premiums and to whom he afterwards assigned the policy. I refer also to the case of *Evans* v. *Reynolds*, L. R. 4 Q. B. 622.

An important question, however, bearing upon the proper disposition of the plaintiff's action remains to be considered. It is clear that where a policy is not void upon its face and of which the illegality is made to appear only by evidence dehors the instrument itself, the insurers are not bound to wait until an action has been brought against them by the insured, but may, just as in the case of a policy which has been obtained by fraud, (*National Life Ins. Co.* v. *Evans*, 20 Gr. 469) themselves actively seek the intervention of the Court to relieve them from liability by cancelling the policy upon proper terms. *North America Life Assurance Co.* v. *Craigen*, 13 S. C. R. 273, 293 ; *Desborough* v. *Curlewis*, 3 Y. & C. 175. The action, therefore, may

well lie in the present case as the policy is not on its face
open to the objection relied on.   The plaintiffs, however,
do not appear to have tendered repayment of the premiums
received by them thereon before action, nor do they by
their pleadings, as they did in the Craigen case, submit to
such order being made in respect thereof as the Court may
think proper.   In the present state of the practice I am not
prepared to hold that a tender of the premiums before
action was necessary.   It is true that the defendant could
not maintain an action to recover them, cognizant as he
must be held to have been of the illegal nature of his agreement with Cromar and of the illegality of the policy
obtained in pursuance thereof.   When the policy is avoided
for actual fraud on the part of the insured he cannot recover
back the premiums: *Feise* v. *Parker*, 4 Taunt 640 ; *Anderson* v. *Thornton*, 6 Exch. 425 ; *Howard* v. *Refuge Friendly
Society*, 54 L. T. N. S. 644 ; and, except where the insured
renounces the contract before the termination of the risk,
the rule is the same when it is avoided for illegality, as for
want of interest or otherwise where the facts were known
to him : *Lowry* v. *Bourdieu*, Dougl. 468 ; *Park on Insurance*, vol. 1, p. 456 ; *Campbell* v. *Allen*, (1808) 12 Fac.
Dec. 853 ; *Patterson* v. *Powell* (1832) 2 L. J. N. S. C. P. 13 ;
Dawker v. *The Canada Life Assurance Co.*, 24 U.C.R. 591.
Fraud, or illegality, is an answer to an action by the
insured "not from any merit in the defendants which justifies them in retaining money which *ex aequo et bono* is not
theirs, but from the demerit of the plaintiff which excludes
him from the aid of a Court to draw it out of the defendants' hands."   But where the insurers are unwilling
to await the result of an action upon the policy and
themselves seek the intervention of the Court to relieve
them by cancelling it, a different principle applies.   The
money they receive for premiums is not theirs, as the risk
never attached, and therefore in seeking equitable relief
they must themselves do equity by returning the premiums
or submitting to any order the Court may think proper to
make.   The distinction is well stated in *Schwartz* v. *The
United States Insurance Co.*, 3 Wash. C. C. Rep. (1812)
170, 175.   That was an action by the insured for a return
of the premiums on a policy avoided for fraud.   WASHING-
TON, J., said : " The cases of *Willingham* v. *Thornborough*,
2 Vern. 206 ; *DaCosta* v. *Scandrett*, 2 P. Wms. 170, and
Wilson v. *Duckett*, 3 Burr. 1361, in which the premium was

decreed to be refunded notwithstanding the fraud of the insured in obtaining the insurance, fall short of establishing the point for which the plaintiffs' counsel contends. In the two former the insurers were plaintiffs in Equity seeking to set aside the policy on the ground of fraud, and since the insurers could not in conscience retain these premiums, no matter how great the demerit of the insured might be, a Court of Equity, governed by its own principles, could not relieve the insurers on other terms than compelling them to discharge that to which they had no equitable right, and placing the parties in the situation they were in when the contract was entered into. The other case, though tried at law, was made under a decree of the Court of Chancery in which the insurers were complainants, and offered in the bill to repay the premiums.''

The same rule prevails in more modern cases.

In *The Prince of Wales Assurance Co.* v. *Palmer* (1858), 25 Beav. 605, the policy was avoided in Equity at the instance of the Company for the fraud of the person who had procured it. The premium was ordered to be applied so far as would be necessary in payment of the costs, and the residue to be paid into Court, with liberty to apply.

In *London Assurance Co.* v. *Mansell*, 11 Ch. D. 363, the Company procured the contract for insurance to be rescinded on the ground of the fraudulent misrepresentations of the applicant. They had tendered back the premium, and it was ordered to be repaid by them. '' Where equity relieves in ordering the insurance to be cancelled, the general rule is that the party in whose favour the decree is made shall do equity by returning the consideration.'' *Bunyon on Life Assurance* (1891), pp. 120, 121 ; *Barker* v. *Walters* (1844), 8 Beav. 96 ; *Anderson* v. *Fitzgerald*, 4 H. L. Cas. 484.

The only hesitation I have had as to the jurisdiction of the Court to deal with the premiums in this case arises from the fact that the plaintiffs have not in their pleadings or at the trial expressly submitted themselves thereto. It was certainly usual under the former practice to make such a submission in the pleadings, either expressly or by the general prayer for ''such further and other relief as the case might require or the Court might think fit.'' And if it is really essential, the only consequence would be that the plaintiff's action must be dismissed with costs.   Dealing with this point, in *Barker* v. *Walters* (1844), 8 Beav. 92, the Master of the Rolls said :—"If it were necessary to make the offer, this, I own (*i. e.*, the prayer for general relief), seems to me to be sufficient." The report does not indicate that any such offer was made in *The Prince of Wales Assurance Co.* v. *Palmer, supra*. And an examination of the pleadings in the *Egan* case, *supra*, discloses that there was neither tender nor offer to return the premium, nor anything beyond the prayer for general relief. That case was tried before STRONG, J., and the decree ordered the policy to be cancelled and the premiums to be set off as far as might be necessary in payment of the plaintiffs' costs, the balance to be repaid to the defendant.

The plaintiffs, no doubt, have strenuously opposed any order to repay the premiums, but I think that when they bring their action to trial, move for the judgment of the Court and having obtained it insist upon retaining it, they have made a sufficient submission of all their equitable obligations as to the premiums to enable the Court to make the proper order in respect thereof.. They are not now in a position to ask for a dismissal of their action and, therefore, the judgment at the trial must be amended by directing a reference, if necessary, to ascertain the amount which has been paid to the plaintiffs on account of premiums, and the payment of that amount to the defendant or so much thereof as may remain after deducting the plaintiffs' costs of suit. There should be no costs in respect of the appeal as to the judgment in the action, success being divided. The appeal as to the counterclaim should be dismissed with costs.

LISTER, J. A.:—

The plaintiffs ask to have a policy of life insurance issued by them on the life of one Alexander Cromar, now deceased, for the sum of $6025.00 delivered up to be cancelled upon the ground that it is a wager policy within the meaning of 14 Geo. III., and, therefore, void, under section 1 of that Act.

The defendant resists upon the ground that the policy was issued to Cromar upon his own application and for his own benefit, and that it was by him duly assigned to the defendant by an assignment executed on the 13th of March,

1897; and by way of counterclaim he seeks to recover from the claintiffs the amount of the assurance with interest and posts, and he also asks for such further and other relief as may be deemed necessary and proper.

The facts, as they are succinctly stated in the opinion of my brother Street, were these : '' The defendant Brophy was an elderly man and a priest ; Cromar was an insurance agent canvassing for one Company, and perhaps for more, and in 1885 he began to do some insurance business for Brophy. At that time Brophy was in the habit of buying annuities from insurance companies, insuring his own life and allowing the annuity payments to go in payment of the premiums on the policies on his life. Cromar did all his business in insuring his life ; and an arrangement was made between them by which Brophy in effect received the benefit of part of the commissions which Cromar got from the insurance companies to whom he took Brophy's application for insurance. Then in the year 1896 or the beginning of 1897, a new system was adopted upon Cromar's suggestion, and Brophy took out eleven policies of insurance in different companies which are mentioned in the schedule which has been put in, amounting in all to upwards of seventy thousand dollars. That system was this : Brophy purchased an annuity upon his own life in the company in which he was insured ; in the case of the North American Life, which is typical of this, he purchased an annuity upon his own life for three hundred dollars. Then, instead of insuring his own life, he insured Cromar's, that being part of the arrangement between him and Cromar —for an amount the premiums upon which would be equal to the amount of the annuity which Brophy had purchased. Then there was a further agreement, as Brophy, who is the defendant in this action, tells us, under which the policies were at once assigned to him, Brophy. The advantage which Cromar was to get from this was the commissions on the premiums payable to the insurance company and on the original insurance. This arrangement was carried out with regard to policies in eleven companies ; and in ten companies Cromar carried out the arrangement to the letter. That is to say, contemporaneously with and as a part of the insurance and of the annuity transaction, Cromar made an absolute assignment to Brophy of the policies : but he began to think apparently before he had completed the assignment of the North American policy that he was not getting enough out of it, that he was allowing Brophy to insure his

(Cromar's) life, and that Brophy was going to make a good deal of money out of it, while he (Cromar) was making nothing but his own commissions out of the company ; and when he came to assign the North American policy, instead of assigning the policy absolutely, as he assigned the other ten policies, he assigned it in such a way that if he should survive Brophy, then he (Cromar) should get the benefit of the insurance. Brophy said that at the time he got the assignment he did not like it, that it was contrary to the agreement under which this insurance had been effected, but that he was afraid that Cromar might make trouble in the transaction between them. He did not want it too public, and so he said nothing about it. In other words, the defendant himself, through his fear of publicity being given to this large business that he had been carrying on— an illegal business, I may say, in insurance—and believing himself to be under Cromar's thumb, rather than make matters unpleasant, submitted to the breach of his agreement which Cromar had committed by assigning this policy not absolutely, but in the way in which I have stated it."

The learned trial judge found that the arrangement between the defendant and Cromar was one by which the defendant having no interest in Cromar's life should be permitted to insure it for his (Brophy's) benefit, and that the plaintiffs had no knowledge of such arrangement, and he held that the plaintiffs were entitled to the relief asked for, and that the defendant was not entitled to recover back the premiums paid, and he accordingly gave judgment for the plaintiffs with costs and dismissed the defendant's counter-claim with costs.

The plaintiffs have not, by their statement of claim or otherwise, offered to return to the defendant the premiums which they received from him on the policy in question. Upon these facts I concur in the conclusion arrived at by the learned trial judge that the policy in question is, as being contrary to or in evasion of the provisions of 14 Geo. III., cap. 48, sec 1, void. That section is in these words : " Whereas it has been found by experience that the making insurance on lives and other events wherein the assured shall have no interest hath introduced a mischievous kind of gambling, that from and after the passing of this Act, no insurance shall be made by any person or persons, bodies politic, or corporate on the life or lives of any person or persons, or on any other event whatsoever, wherein the person or persons for whose use benefits or on whose account such policies shall be made shall have no interest or by way of gaming or wagering, and that every assurance made contrary to the true intent and meaning hereof shall be null and void to all intents and purposes whatsoever."

It has no application to an assurance bona-fide effected by a person on his own life, and who, without consideration, valuable or otherwise, by will or assignment, directs payment of the sum assured to be made at his death to a third person:—*Ashley* v. *Ashley*, 3 Sim. 149; *North Am. Life Ass. Co.* v. *Craigen*, 13 S. C. R. 278. But an assurance effected by one on his own life, not for his own use and benefit, but really for the use and benefit of another, who has no insurable interest in his life, and who pays the premiums and takes an assignment of the policy, is void. The law looks upon such a transaction as a mere evasion of the provisions of the Statute.—*Shilling* v. *Accidental*, 27 L. J. Ex. 12; 2 H. & N. 43; *Vezina* v. *The New York Life*, 6 S. C. R. 30. In this case the evidence of the defendant himself makes it plain that he had no insurable interest in the life of Cromar; that the assurance was effected by Cromar under an arrangement with the defendant, by the terms of which it was to be effected, not for Cromar's use or benefit, but for the use and benefit of the defendant, who, under the arrangement, was to pay and did pay the premiums, and to whom the policy was to be assigned. Clearly, under these circumstances, the transaction, from its inception to its completion, by the assignment of the policy to the defendant, was illegal and void, as contravening the provisions of section 1 of the Statute; in other words, it is a wager policy within the Statute, and therefore void; and so far as this action is concerned, it is, I think, immaterial that Cromar did not fully carry out his arrangement with the defendant by an absolute assignment of the policy.

As to the premiums the question arises, are the plaintiffs in consequence of not having offered by their statement of claim either to repay the premiums paid, or to submit to such terms as the Court might think fit to impose entitled in this action to the relief which they seek? I think they are. Mr. Porter, in the third edition of his work on the Law of Insurance, at p. 95, states both the rule and the reason for the rule in these words: "Equity, however, will only decree the delivery up of a fraudulent and, therefore, void policy, when the insurer seeking relief offers either to repay the premiums paid or to submit to any terms which the Court may think proper to impose in granting such relief, which will include the re-payment of premiums. To hold otherwise would be to let the insurer affirm and deny the contract in one breath.''

While the earlier cases seem to support the rule, as Mr. Porter states it, it has not been applied in the more modern cases. In *Prince of Wales Co.* v. *Palmer*, 25 Beav. 605, where the plaintiffs sought a cancellation of a life assurance policy on the ground of fraud, no such offer was made, and yet the Court decreed its cancellation and ordered that the premiums received by the plaintiffs should be applied in payment of the costs of the parties ; and in the case in our Courts of *The National Insurance Co.* v. *Egan* — unreported as regards the hearing and final judgment—which was also an action for the cancellation of a policy for fraud in which no offer was made by the bill to repay the premiums or to submit to such terms as the Court might think fit to impose, in granting the relief there sought, the present Chief Justice of the Supreme Court, then Vice-Chancellor, decreed the relief prayed for, with costs to be paid out of the premiums, and the surplus, if any, to be paid to the defendant. It would seem to follow from these cases that whatever the rule may have been, it is not now necessary that an insurer before he can successfully invoke the aid of the Court to relieve him from a policy which he alleges to be illegal, must, by his statement of claim, offer to repay the premiums paid or to submit to such terms as the Court may think fit to impose in granting relief. In such cases the Court will assume that the person seeking relief is willing to submit to any terms which it thinks fit to impose.

I think the judgment appealed from should be varied by ordering that the premiums paid by the defendant with interest thereon be applied in payment of the plaintiffs' costs, and the residue, if any, paid to the defendant, (see *The British Equitable Insurance Co.* v. *G. W.R.*, 38 L.J. Ch. 132), and that the judgment as varied should be affirmed with costs.

Judgment affirmed as varied.

Solicitor for the Appellant : *D. O'Connell.*

Solicitors for the Respondents : *Kerr, Davidson, Patterson & Grant.*

[IN THE SUPREME COURT OF CANADA.]

BEFORE TASCHEREAU, GWYNNE, SEDGWICK, KING AND
GIROUARD, JJ.

MAGANN (Defendant) Appellant

v.

AUGER (Plaintiffs) Respondents

(31 S.C.R. 186.)

(On appeal from the Court of Queen's Bench, of the Province of Quebec.)

Contract by correspondence—Mailing letter of acceptance—Place where contract made—Indication of place of payment—Jurisdiction —Declinatory exception—Waiver—Procedure.

Editor's Note :—

Since the publication of the report of this case in the last number (p. 71) the editor has had the advantage of seeing an opinion given on the point in question by the eminent French jurist, M. Edouard Clunet, editor of the Journal du Droit International Privé. M. Clunet states that he considers the judgment of the Supreme Court as delivered by Mr. Justice Taschereau a correct exposition of the law ; that is, that according to the prevailing French decisions regarding contracts in which the offer and acceptance is communicated in writing, it is not necessary to the completion of the contract that the acceptance of the offeree should be communicated to the offeror,—the contract being concluded by the very acceptance itself.

[IN THE JUDICIAL COMMITTEE OF THE PRIVY COUNCIL.]

BEFORE LORD HOBHOUSE, LORD DAVEY, LORD ROBERTSON
AND SIR RICHARD COUCH

BURLAND et al

v.

EARLE et al

(AND CROSS APPEAL.)

*Management of Company—Power of majority to accumulate
profits as reserved funds—Sale by director to Company—
Salary of director.*

The majority of the shareholders of an incorporated joint stock
company have the power, even against the wishes of the minority, to
set aside as a reserve fund whatever proportion they deem fit of the
annual profits of the company, and there is no jurisdiction in the
court to compel such company, so long as it is a going concern, to
divide the whole of these profits amongst its shareholders. The
question as to what proportion should be so divided is entirely a matter
of internal management, which the shareholders must decide for themselves, the court having no jurisdiction to control the decision so
arrived at, or to say what is a "fair" or "reasonable" sum to retain
undivided. And since the company thus has power to retain a balance
of undivided profits, it follows that it may invest the moneys so
retained in such securities as the directors may select, subject to the
control of a general meeting of the shareholders.

The president of an incorporated joint stock company bought the
plant of an insolvent concern, which he shortly afterwards sold to the
company of which he was president at a considerable profit. There
was no evidence that the president was authorized by his own
company to purchase these assets, or that he was in any way a trustee
for his company of the property so bought. Held, that though, upon
these facts, the company might, perhaps, have at one time obtained
a decree of rescission of the contract, yet the court had no power to
compel the vendor to accept another contract whereby he would be
disposing of the assets at a less price.

Hon. EDWARD BLAKE, K.C., and MR. R. C. SMITH,
K.C., for the Appellants.

MR. HALDANE, K. C., and MR. F. H. CHRYSLER,
K.C., for the Respondents.

The facts of the case are fully set forth in the judgment.

November 9th, 1901.

Lord Davey, in now delivering their Lordships' judgment, said : The appellants and respondents were shareholders in the British American Bank Note Company, which was
incorporated in 1866, under an Act (27 and 28 Vic., c. 23)
of the old Province of Canada.   The objects for which the
company was formed were "to engrave and print bank
notes, debentures, bonds, postage and bill stamps and bills
of exchange, and to carry on all other branches incidental
thereto."   The capital was originally $100,000, divided
into shares of $100 each, but was subsequently increased to
$200,000, of which $170,000 only had been issued.   By
section 1 of the Act provision was made for the incorporation
by Letters Patent of joint stock companies for the purpose,
inter alia, of carrying on any kind of manufacturing
business, and by section 5 it was declared that every company incorporated under the authority of the act should be
subject to the general provisions set out in sub-sections 1 to
34 thereof.   Sub-section 7, so far as material, was as follows :

"7.   The directors of the company shall have full
power in all things to administer the affairs of the company,
and may make or cause to be made for the company any
description of contract which the company may by law
enter into ; and may from time to time make by-laws not
contrary to law, to regulate, *inter alia*, the declaration and
payment of dividends, the number of directors, their term
of service, the amount of their stock qualification, the
appointment, functions, duties, and removal of all agents,
officers and servants of the company, the security to be
given by them to the company, their remuneration and that
(if any) of the directors, the time at which, and the place
or places where the annual meetings of the company shall
be held, and where the business of the company shall be
conducted."

The act contained no express provisions as to the formation of a reserve fund or as to the investment or application
of the undivided profits of the company.   Shortly after the
formation of the company the shareholders made a number
of by-laws, of which the following are material for the
purpose of this litigation :—

"9.   The shareholders of the company may at any
general meeting of the company vote and award to the
directors of the company such compensation as they may

think proper.   10. At all meetings of the company every shareholder shall be entitled to as many votes as he may own shares in the company, and may vote by proxy; but no shareholder shall be entitled to vote unless he has paid all calls in respect of his shares.   11. The directors shall have the management of the affairs of the company, the appointment, control, and removal of all the officers and employees of the company, and shall from time to time regulate their several duties and remuneration.   12. At every annual general meeting the directors shall present a report and abstract of the accounts of the company, a concise statement of their affairs, and a true and succinct statement of their assets and liabilities and if they deem fit shall recommend the declaration of a dividend of so much per cent. on the stock out of the earned profits of the company; and in the interval between the annual general meetings of the company the directors may at any regular meeting declare a dividend whenever an actual cash balance in the hands of the secretary-treasurer from the earned profits of the company shall, in their judgment, warrant the payment of such dividend.   13. The directors may set apart any portion of the profits for a reserve fund, subject to the approval of a general meeting, or to the appropriation of such sum by such meeting to any other purpose.   14. The number of directors shall never be less than three, nor more than six.   Every new board of directors as soon as elected shall elect a president and a vice-president; they shall also elect the president or vice-president, or any director, to be at the same time manager, and if any of the places of these officers become vacant they may be filled by the board electing others in their place. 16. At every board meeting three directors shall constitute a quorum.   The president shall preside, in his absence the vice-president, and failing both any director.   The president or chairman, as a director, shall have one vote.''

The company was formed by the union of two groups—one represented by the appellant, G. E. Burland, and the other by a Mr. Smillie, and the respondent Earle.   Mr. Smillie was the first president, and Burland and Earle were first directors.   Mr. Smillie retired from the company in 1881, and sold his shares.   Burland from time to time increased his holdings, and at the date of the action he held 1,077 shares and was president and manager of the company.   The respondents held between them 433 shares.

Earle continued on the board until 1900, when he resigned.
Mrs. Cunningham, one of the respondents, sued as the
administratrix of James Cunningham, deceased, who was at
one time the auditor, and from 1887 until 1892, when he
died, a director. Mr. Gillilan, another respondent, was a
director from 1892. The company's business was extra-
ordinarily successful. In some years it paid to its shareholders a dividend exceeding 100 per cent., and the average
of the dividends paid during the thirty years of its existence
prior to the commencement of the action was said to exceed
40 per cent. per annum. In addition to the dividends so
paid the company had accumulated undivided profits to the
amount (at the commencement of the action), of $264,167.
That sum was not formally carried to the credit of a rest or
reserve fund, but stood to the credit of the profit and loss
account of the company. Shortly before the commencement
of the action the company lost a valuable contract with the
Dominion Government. The result was a serious diminution
of the profits of its business.

The action was commenced by the respondents on
December 7, 1897. By their amended statement of claim
they prayed for a declaration that the accumulation by the
defendants of a surplus or reserve fund was *ultra vires* and
for an immediate division and distribution amongst the shareholders of all sums of money accumulated and retained as a
reserve fund over and above the authorized capital stock of
the company, and various other items of relief.

Their Lordships would confine their attention to the
points which have been discussed on these appeals. Those
were—(1) the formation of the rest or reserve fund;
(2) the investment of it ; (3) a claim by the respondents to treat Burland as a trustee of the plant
and material of a certain insolvent company called the
Burland Lithographic Company, which he purchased at
a sale by auction and resold at an enhanced price to the
company, and to make him account to the company accordingly for the profit made by the resale ; and (4) a question
as to certain sums drawn as salaries by Burland and J. H.
Burland. It was an elementary principle of the law relating
to joint stock companies that the court would not interfere
with the internal management of companies acting within
their powers, and, in fact, had no jurisdiction to do so.
Again, it was clear law that, in order to redress a wrong done

to the company or to recover moneys or damages alleged to be due to the company, the action should *prima facie* be brought by the company itself (*vide Foss* v. *Harbottle*, 2 Hare 461 ; *Mozley* v. *Alston*, 1 Ph. 790, and other later cases).   An exception was made to the second rule where the persons against whom the relief was sought themselves held and controlled the majority of the shares in the company, and would not permit an action to be brought in the name of the company.   In that case the courts allowed the shareholders complaining to bring an action in their own names.   That, however, was mere matter of procedure in order to give a remedy for a wrong which would otherwise escape redress, and it was obvious that in such an action, the plaintiffs could not have a larger right to relief than the company itself would have if it were plaintiff, and could not complain of acts which were valid if done with the approval of the majority of the shareholders, or were capable of being confirmed by the majority.   The cases in which the minority could maintain such an action were, therefore, confined to those in which the acts complained of were of a fraudulent character or beyond the powers of the company.   A familiar example was where the majority were endeavoring, directly or indirectly, to appropriate to themselves money, property or advantages which belonged to the company, or in which the other shareholders were entitled to participate, as was alleged in Menier's case (L.R., 9 Ch., 350).   It should be added that no mere informality or irregularity which could be remedied by the majority would entitle the minority to sue if the act when done regularly would be within the powers of the company and the intention of the majority of the shareholders was clear.   That might be illustrated by the judgment of Lord Justice Mellish in *Macdougall* v. *Gardiner* (1 Ch. D., 13, at p, 25).   There was yet a third principle which was important for the decision of this case.   Unless otherwise provided by the regulations of the company, a shareholder was not debarred from voting or using his voting power to carry a resolution by the circumstance of his having a particular interest in the subject matter of the vote.   That was shown by the case before the Board of the *Northwest Transportation Company (Limited)* v. *Beatty* (12 A.C., 589).   In that case the resolution of a general meeting to purchase a vessel at the vendor's price was held to be valid, notwithstanding that

That was for obvious reasons unwise and imprudent, but it must have been within the knowledge of Earle, Cunningham and Gillilan, and no complaint or remonstrance seemed to have been made until the institution of the present suit. Burland was, of course, bound to account for all the moneys of the company which came into his hands. Very full accounts were directed by the Court of Appeal, including special directions as to a loan made to one Bennett, with respect to which Burland was charged with foisting upon the company a bad debt of his own. There was no appeal from that portion of the judgment, and the accounts and enquiries would be prosecuted accordingly.

Mr. Haldane asked for some injunction with respect to those matters, but did not make clear to their Lordships the form or extent of the injunction to which he considered his clients were entitled. The Court of Appeal granted an injunction to restrain the appellants and the company from employing the net profits and earnings of the company already, or which might hereafter be earned, in the purchase of shares of the capital stocks of banks or other companies and from using any portion of the net earnings and profits for the purpose of making loans to persons or corporations, and also an injunction to restrain the appellant Burland from investing in his own name or "personally controlling" any portion of the earnings or moneys of the company or from dealing with the same otherwise than in accordance with the judgment. For the reasons which had already been given it was clear that so sweeping an injunction against the directors and the company could not be maintained. And it was equally clear that the injunction against Burland could not be maintained. It was not *ultra vires* for the company, if it thought fit to do so, to invest in the name of a sole trustee, however imprudent and undesirable such a course might be. Nor could Burland, as shareholder, manager and president of the company, be restrained from exercising any personal control over any portion of the company's earnings, in which, indeed, he had the largest interest. If it appeared that under the guise of investing undivided profits, or the reserve fund the directors were, in fact, embarking the moneys of the company in speculative transactions or otherwise abusing the powers vested in them for the management of the company's business, different considerations would of course arise. But it did not appear to their Lordships that the investment of the surplus profits

in bank shares or bonds of trading companies really bore
that character, or was intended to be or was otherwise than
a *bona fide* exercise of the powers of the company and the
directors.   The temporary investment of $50,000 in the
Lachine Rapids Company was more open to criticism, but
on objection being made Burland took that investment to
his own account, and it was a little remarkable that his
having done so was now made a topic of complaint against
him.

The next matter was the sale to the company by Burland
of the lithographic plant, etc., of the Burland Lithographic
Company.   That company had been carrying on business at
Montreal, and, having become insolvent, was wound up.
Burland was a stockholder and creditor, and bought all the
assets for $21,564.   He shortly afterwards sold the property
to the appellant company for $60,000.   The property,
together with some other plant purchased from another
company, was subsequently sold to a company formed for the
purpose at an enhanced price, payable in shares, which were
distributed as a bonus among the shareholders of the company.   Burland had been ordered to pay the company
$38,436, the amount of the profit realized by him on the
resale.   Both courts had held that the resale was by Burland's advice and influence and was made without disclosing
to the company the price at which he had purchased.   It
was also held in the Court of Appeal that Burland bought
the property with the intention of reselling it to the company.   The respondent Earle was present at the sale and
knew all about the transaction, and Gillilan knew what Burland had paid very shortly afterwards.   Their Lordships
thought the relief granted by the courts altogether misconceived.   There was no evidence whatever of any commission
or mandate to Burland to purchase on behalf of the company or that he was in any sense a trustee for the company
of the purchased property.   It might be that he had an
intention in his own mind to resell it to the company, but it
was an intention which he was at liberty to carry out or
abandon at his own will.   It might be also that a person of
more refined self-respect and a more generous regard for the
company of which he was president would have been
disposed to give the company the benefit of his purchase.
But their Lordships had not to decide questions of that
character.   The sole question was whether he was under
any legal obligation to do so.   Let it be assumed that the

company or the dissentient shareholders might by appropriate proceedings have at one time obtained a decree of rescission of the contract. But that was not the relief they asked or could in the circumstances obtain in this suit. The case seemed to their Lordships to be exactly that put by Lord Cairns in *Erlanger* v. *New Sombrero Phosphate Company* (3 A. C., 1218). In that case the bill prayed for rescission or alternatively for the profit made by Erlanger and his syndicate on the resale to the company. Lord Cairns said at p. 1235 : '' It may well be that the prevailing idea in their mind was not to retain or work the island, but to sell it again at an increase of price, and very possibly to promote or get up a company to purchase the island from them, but they were, as it seems to me, after their purchase was made, perfectly free to do with the island whatever they liked, to use it as they liked and to sell it how and to whom and for what price they liked. The part of the case of the respondents, which, as an alternative, sought to make the appellants account for the profit which they made on the resale of the property to the respondents on an allegation that the appellants acted in a fiduciary position at the time they made the contract of August 30, 1871, is not, as I think, capable of being supported, and this, I understand, was the view of all the judges in the courts below.'' See also *In re Cape Breton Company* (26 Ch. D., 221, and 29 Ch. D., 795). To rescind the sale was one thing, but to force on the vendor a contract to sell at another price was a totally different thing.

The question of salaries stood in this wise. Burland's salary as manager was fixed in 1879 at $5,000 per annum, which was increased from time to time to $12,000. In addition he had since 1888 drawn a further sum of large amount, to which he claimed to be entitled, under the terms of a resolution of the board of directors. The Chief Justice held that the title to that increment as well as to the fixed salary was a question of internal management and dismissed that part of the respondent's claim. The Court of Appeal, holding that Burland was not entitled to the increment under the terms of the resolution, ordered him to repay the amount drawn by him since the date of the resolution. The amount which he was directed to pay on that account was $53,000, or thereabouts. Their Lordships agreed with the Court of Appeal that Burland's right to retain that sum depended on the construction of the resolution, and it was so put by his counsel, Mr. Blake. On the whole, their Lordships were not prepared to differ from the Court of Appeal on the point. In regard to J. H. Burland, they thought he was entitled to retain his salary although there had been a shifting of his office.

The appellants (defendants) had succeeded on all questions relating to the accumulated fund and as to the sale of the lithographic plant. They had failed as to Burland's salary and succeeded as to J. H. Burland's salary. It would be almost impossible to do justice by a strict apportionment of the costs of the action up to trial, and to endeavor to do so would lead to certain inconvenience and consequent expense to taxation. In all the circumstances their Lordships thought that justice would be met by (1) discharging all orders as to costs made in the courts below; (2) directing the plaintiffs to pay to the defendants two-thirds of their costs of the action up to and including the trial; (3) directing the defendants to pay to the plaintiffs two-thirds of the costs of plaintiffs' appeal to the Court of Appeal, which rightly succeeded as to Burland, but ought to have failed as to J. H. Burland, and the plaintiffs to pay to the defendants two-thirds of the costs of the defendants' appeal to the Court of Appeal, which ought to have succeeded except as to the directions for Burland accounting.

Their Lordships would humbly advise His Majesty that the order of the Court of Appeal be varied in the manner above stated as to substance and costs. The respondents in the principal appeal would pay to the appellants two-thirds of their costs of that appeal and the appellants would pay to the respondents one-third of their costs of the same appeal. The costs of the cross-appeal would be paid by the appellants therein. In the court below the greater part of the plaintiffs' costs up to trial and the costs of the defendants' appeal were ordered to be paid out of the accumulated fund. If the parties agreed their Lordships thought it would be a proper case in which to make that order as to all the costs in the courts below and of the principal appeal to the Board.

Appeal allowed in part.

[IN THE COURT OF KING'S BENCH.]

(APPEAL SIDE.)

BEFORE SIR ALEXANDRE LACOSTE, C.J., AND BOSSE, BLANCHET, HALL AND WURTELE, J.J.

THE BANK OF TORONTO (Plaintiff) Appellant

AND

THE ST. LAWRENCE FIRE INSURANCE COMPANY
(Defendant) Respondent.

Fire Insurance—Transfer of Rights under Policy—Significa-
tion—Art. 1571 Quebec Civil Code—Interprovincial Rights
of Fire Insurance Companies.

The stock of a commercial firm, which was insured, having been destroyed by fire, the firm transferred by private writing all its rights under the policy to a bank. The solicitors of the bank then wrote the insurance company that such transfer had been made; and subseqnently the solicitors of the bank at Montreal again notified the insurance company of this transfer by a letter, the bearer of which also handed the agent of the company a copy of such transfer, the original being open to inspection at the office of the solicitors.

Held, (Hall and Wurtele, J. J., dissenting) that this signification of the sale or transfer was not sufficient to satisfy Article 1571 of the Civil Code, and that the signification should have been made by a ministerial officer (i. e. in notarial form) in order that the insurance company might have been fully assured that it should pay to the bank the moneys due under the policy.

Held, further, (by the full Court), that a fire insurance company, incorporated by the Legislature of the Province of Quebec to carry on business therein, might effect in the Province of Quebec an insurance on goods or premises situated in another Province.

The appeal was from a judgment of the Superior Court which dismissed an action brought by the Bank of Toronto, to recover the sum of $2,500, amount of an insurance effected with the company respondent, on the 6th April, 1897, by the John Eaton Company, Limited, and transferred to the Bank on the 22nd May, 1897, on merchandise which had been destroyed by fire on the 20th May, 1897. The action was dismissed by Mr. Justice Langelier, on the 18th June, 1901, on the ground that the signification of the transfer was not made in accordance with the formalities prescribed by law. This judgment was confirmed by the majority of the Court of Appeal, Hall and Wurtele, J.J. dissenting. The dissentient judgment of Mr. Justice Wurtele, in which Mr. Justice Hall concurred, is as follows :—

WURTELE, J. (dissenting)—

The John Eaton Company, Limited, carried on a large wholesale business in dry goods in the city of Toronto, and for the prosecution of its business obtained large advances from the Bank of Toronto. The company's stock was insured by it in a large number of insurance companies, and it was agreed between the company and the bank, by an agreement bearing date at Toronto, the 17th June, 1896, that in the event of any loss by fire the company would hold the insurances in trust for the bank, to the amount of its claim, and pay over to it to that extent any sums which might be awarded as indemnity for the loss, and that in the event of such loss by fire, the company would, if the bank should require it, assign and transfer the insurances to it to the extent of the company's indebtedness. It was also agreed that this undertaking would apply to any insurances which might be subsequently effected upon the stock held at any time by the company, and that the company would not transfer any of the policies of insurance on their goods to any other persons so long as it was indebted to the bank.

On the 6th April, 1897, the company insured its stock in the St. Lawrence Fire Insurance Company, to the extent of $2,500. The policy was issued and the premium was paid in Montreal.

On the 20th May, 1897, the stock of the company was totally destroyed by fire, and on the 22nd of the same month the company transferred all the insurances, which had been effected by it on its stock to the bank, to be applied to the payment of its indebtedness.

On the 20th May, 1897, being the day on which the fire had occurred, the insurance company was notified on behalf of the company, by the firm of Beatty, Blackstock, Nesbitt, Chadwick & Riddell, solicitors practising in Toronto, that a fire had occurred on the morning of that day, whereby the goods insured by it had been totally destroyed. All the insurance companies which had insured the company's stock and which had representatives in Toronto, appointed a committee to represent them, and Mr. Edwards was appointed by this committee, with the concurrence of the insured, to adjust the loss. This fact was communicated to the St. Lawrence Fire Insurance Company by the firm of solicitors above mentioned, and it was requested either to send a representative to act with Mr. Edwards, or to agree that this gentleman should represent it in so far only as the amount of the loss was concerned.

On the 1st June, 1897, the firm of solicitors above mentioned, who were then acting for the bank, wrote to the St. Lawrence Fire Insurance Company that they had prepared the proofs of loss on behalf and in the name of the insured, and they enclosed a duplicate of the document and requested the company to acknowledge its receipt.

Mr. Charles Wm. Beatty, one of the firm of solicitors, when examined as a witness, swore that he had assisted in the preparation of the proofs of loss, and that a duplicate of them had been enclosed in a letter which had been duly mailed in Toronto, to the address of the insurance company in the city of Montreal. The other duplicate has been produced as an exhibit in this case.

On the 28th June, 1897, the Bank of Toronto, acting by their solicitors, above mentioned, notified the insurance company by a letter mailed at Toronto, that the John Eaton Company, Limited, had assigned to the Bank all its right, title and interest in the moneys payable by virtue of the policy issued by it to the company, and required it not to pay the same to any other person.

On the 11th October, 1897, the Bank of Toronto, acting through their solicitors, proposed by a letter to the insurance company, an arrangement for the purpose of saving unnecessary litigation ; and after an interview between the solicitors and the officers of the insurance company, other letters were written to the insurance company on the 20th and 28th of the same month on the same subject.

The insurance company never acknowledged the receipt of the letters notifying it of the occurrence of the fire and of the transfer which had been made by the John Eaton Company, Limited, to the Bank, nor of the letter transmitting the proofs of loss, nor, in fact, any of the letters which had been written to it concerning the fire and the insurance granted by it. Its conduct in this matter was, therefore, to say the least, rather devious.

By the conditions of the policy, in order to recover the insurance it was necessary to commence a suit for that purpose within six months after the fire had occurred, and the bank was, therefore, obliged to bring a suit against the insurance company for the recovery of the amount of the policy, and it instructed Messrs. Macmaster & Maclennan to institute an action with that view.

When the insurance company was notified on the 28th June, 1897, of the transfer of the insurance to the Bank, no copy of the transfer was sent or delivered to the insurance company; but on the 6th November, 1897, Messrs. Macmaster & Maclennan, acting on behalf of the Bank of Toronto, wrote to the St. Lawrence Fire Insurance Company, demanding payment of the sum of $2,500, being the amount of the policy issued to the John Eaton Company, Limited, and transferred to the bank, giving the number of the policy, the date of the fire, and the place of the execution, and the date of the transfer of the amount of the insurance, and notifying the insurance company, in order that there might be no misunderstanding about the matter, that the bearer of the letter would hand and deliver to it with the letter a copy of the formal transfer and assignment which had been executed at Toronto on the 22nd May, 1897, and that the original was in their office where the officers of the insurance company would be given communication of it. This letter was delivered to Mr. Francis Gauthier, the manager of the St. Lawrence Fire Insurance Company, together with a copy of the transfer, by Mr. Boileau Drolet, who is an advocate practicing in Montreal, but who was then a student in the office of Messrs. Macmaster & Maclennan. Immediately after this delivery of a copy of the transfer, the action in the present case was instituted for the recovery of the amount of the insurance.

The St. Lawrence Fire Insurance Company contested the action on the following grounds :—

1st. That it was incorporated by the Legislature of the province of Quebec to carry on the business of insurance in this province; that the goods insured under the policy mentioned in the action were in the province of Ontario; that the insurance company had no right to effect this insurance ; and that it was without effect and did not bind it.

2nd. That the John Eaton Company, Limited, had fraudulently concealed from the insurance company the fact that it was not the absolute owner of the property insured, as it had assigned its interest in the goods and in the policy of insurance to the bank on the 17th June, 1896, which were facts material to the risk ; and that such concealment vitiated the policy.

3rd. That notice of the fire had not been given and that sworn proofs of loss had not been furnished as required by the conditions of the policy.

4th. That the bank had not made a proper signification of the transfer upon the insurance company prior to the institution of the action.

The appellant joined issue upon these pleas.

Judgment was rendered on the 18th June last (1901), rejecting the contentions of the insurance company with regard to the two first grounds of defence, but dismissing the action upon the grounds that the sworn proofs of loss, although they had been prepared and completed, did not appear, from the evidence, to have been received by the insurance company, and that the signification made upon it of the transfer to the Bank was insufficient.

The bank has appealed from this judgment. Our enquiry will be directed principally to the questions raised by the two last grounds of defence, and a brief reference to the two first grounds will suffice.

The first ground of defence is, in short, that the St. Lawrence Fire Insurance Company was incorporated by the Legislature of Quebec to carry on the business of insurance in the province of Quebec, and that it had neither right nor power to insure property within the province of Ontario. The company was incorporated by the Legislature of Quebec, and was authorized "to transact and carry on, in the province of Quebec, the business of insurance." (49-50 Vict., cap. 71, sec. 2.) A trading corporation is an association of persons which, in the contemplation of law, form an entity, and is authorized by the legislative power to carry on a particular business, and it has the right to prosecute its legitimate business in the same manner as an individual engaged in a similar enterprise, but it cannot, however, perform any act that is prohibited by its charter or the general law, which is unauthorized, and is therefore illegal and without effect. A trading corporation may, in general, enter into any contract which can further the business for which it has been chartered unless restricted by its charter or by a general law. (Morawetz, Nos. 320, 326 and 336.) In this case the charter gives power to the company to transact and carry on, in the province of Quebec, the business of insurance ; it empowers it to make contracts of insurance within the province of Quebec, but the company is not restrained as to the objects of the insurance being property which is within this province. An individual domiciled within the province of Quebec has the right to underwrite a policy of insurance on property within another province, and so also has the company respondent. While, however, a trading corporation is permitted in general to exercise within another province the general powers of transacting business given to it by the Legislature of its own province, it cannot do so when such action is prohibited by law of the other province (Morawetz, Nos. 960 and 961) ; but, in the present case, no such prohibition exists. The company respondent therefore had the right to make a contract at Montreal, in the province of Quebec, to insure goods at Toronto, in the province of Ontario, and the first ground of defence was properly rejected by the Superior Court.

The second ground of defence is that the John Eaton Company, Limited, had fraudulently concealed from the company respondent the fact that it was not the absolute owner of the goods insured, and that such concealment annulled the policy. The Bank appellant in making advances to the John Eaton Company, Limited, exacted no lien on its stock of goods, nor any transfer to it as collateral security of such stock of goods, and it was satisfied with the moral guarantee which the possession of such stock of goods, by its debtor, gave to it. The goods remained the absolute and full property of the John Eaton Company, Limited,—formed its stock in trade, and could be and were disposed of by it in the prosecution of its business. But the destruction by fire of the stock of goods would have the effect of depriving the Bank appellant of its faculty of obtaining payment of its advances, and to guard against this eventuality it was stipulated that the goods should be insured ; that the insurance should be kept by the John Eaton Company, Limited, and that in the event of a loss by fire the insurance should be held in trust by it for or transferred to its creditor. The bank appellant had no right of property or ownership in the goods, which, on the contrary, had always belonged in full ownership to the John Eaton Company, Limited, and the insurance was only transferred to the bank appellant after the fire and the loss of the goods. The company respondent had no interest to be informed of the agreement between the Bank appellant and the insured, and there was no fraudulent concealment of a material fact which could increase, or in any way affect the risk. The second ground of defence is therefore unfounded, and it was properly rejected by the Superior Court.

The third ground of defence,—that notice of the fire had not been given, and that proofs of loss had not been furnished, is purely a question of fact.

With respect to the notice of fire, Mr. Gauthier, the manager of the company respondent, acknowledged that his company had received the letter of the 20th May, 1897, from the firm of Beatty, Blackstock, Nesbitt, Chadwick & Riddell on behalf of the John Eaton Company, Limited, notifying the company respondent of the occurrence of the fire ; and he, in fact, produced at the trial the letter itself.

With respect to the proofs of loss, he admitted that the company respondent had received the letter of the 1st June, 1897, which stated that the proofs of loss were enclosed, and requested that their receipt should be acknowledged, and he also produced this letter at the trial, but he stated that he could not find the proofs of loss in the office of the company respondent, that he did not remember having seen them, that all the papers had been given to Mr. Languedoc, who was the secretary of the company respondent, and that, if the proofs of loss were transmitted to the company respondent in a registered letter, the chances were that they had been received. Mr. Languedoc swore that he did not remember ever having received or seen them. Mr. Chas. Beatty, on the other hand, swore that the proofs of loss were enclosed in the letter of 1st June, 1897, which was received by the company respondent.

A list of all the insurances effected on the stock of goods held by the John Eaton Company, Limited, was attached to the proofs of loss which Mr. Beatty swore had been prepared and sent to the company respondent, and a similar statement was attached to and formed part of the transfer, of which a copy was delivered to the company by Mr. Drolet.   Mr. Gauthier in his evidence speaks of having seen in the office of the company respondent, two lists of insurances.   Here is what he says :—

Q. And you are not prepared to swear that a sworn claim was not also delivered to your company within the delay fixed by the policy?

A. No ; the reason why I cannot trace that paper. . . .

Q. And you cannot recollect it ?

A. No ; in the two lists of insurances, it puzzled us.

Q. So it is quite possible that you may have received it ?

A. Yes.

Now only two lists of the insurances were delivered to the company, one attached to the proofs of loss and the other attached to and forming part of the transfer, and consequently the presumption is that the proofs of loss had been received.

Upon the whole evidence their Lordships are of the opinion that the weight of evidence is in favor of the appellant, and that it has been established that the proofs of loss were delivered in due time.   This ground of defence is therefore unfounded and must be rejected.

Now we come to the last ground of defence, that a proper signification of the transfer of the amount of the insurance by the John Eaton Company, Limited, to the Bank appellant, was not made upon the company respondent prior to the institution of the action.

The contention of the company respondent, under this head, is that the signification of the transfer of a debt must be made by a notary and that the copy delivered to the debtor must be authenticated or certified, and that, for want of these formalities in the present case the signification is without any legal effect.

The principle of our law, as formulated by the Civil Code in article 1472, is that the contract of sale is perfected in general by the consent alone of the parties, although the thing sold be not then delivered ; and this principle applies as well to the parties to the contract as to third persons. But to this general rule there is an exception in the case of the sale of debts against third persons, which by article 1570, is only perfected by the contract between the seller and the buyer, and which, under article 1571, gives no possession available against third persons until " signification of the act of sale has been made and a copy of it delivered to the debtor." The buyer may, however, be put in possession by the acceptance of the transfer by the debtor.

There is a difference between article 1571, of our Code and article 1690, of the French Code, which reads as follows :—

" Le cessionnaire n'est saisi à l'égard des tiers que par la signification du transport fait au débiteur. Néanmoins le cessionnaire peut être légalement saisi par l'acceptation du transport fait par le débiteur dans un acte authentique."

Under the provisions of our Code, in order to vest the buyer as against third parties, it is necessary that a copy of the act of sale or transfer be delivered to the debtor, while by the provisions of the French Code the delivery of a copy is not required ; then by the provisions of the French code the acceptance by the debtor of a transfer must be contained in an authentic title, while our Code does not require that the acceptance be in authentic form. Under the terms of the article of the French Code, it may be inferred that the signification as well as an acceptance should be made in an authentic form, but the terms of the article of our Code require neither signification nor acceptance to be in authentic form.

The old French law, as contained in the Coutume de Paris, required the delivery of a copy of the transfer to the debtor in order to seize the buyer with respect to third parties, and under the definition of third parties the debtor is included. Article 108 of the Coutume de Paris said :—

" Un simple transportation ne saisit point ; il faut signifier le transport à la partie et en donner copie." Therefore, the old law required, in the first place, a signification of the transfer, and, in the second place, a delivery of the copy.

Signification is synonymous to notification, and in the case of the transfer of a debt, means the action of giving notice of the transfer to the debtor.   In the old edition of Denisart, vol. 4, Verbo "Signification," we read : " Le mot signification est synonyme à notification ; ainsi signifier un acte, un jugement, un arrêt, etc., c'est en donner connaissance par exhibition de l'original dont on laisse copie.   Le mot signification est aussi quelquefois synonyme à avertissement."

In Rolland de Villergues, Vol. 6, Verbo "Notification," we see : "C'est l'acte par lequel on donne connaissance de quelque chose dans une forme juridique."

Then again in the old edition of Denisart, verbo "Transport," we read : "La signification n'est pas seulement nécessaire pour dépouiller le cédant, elle l'est encore pour notifier au débiteur le droit du cessionnaire ; et la coutume ne permet pas à celui-ci de le poursuivre avant la signification, parce que sans cela il ne peut connaître la cession."

In Huc, Cession des Créances, Vol. 2, No. 324, we read :—" La signification, en soi, n'est rien autre chose qu'un acte officiel par lequel le débiteur est informé que la créance dont il est tenu d'acquitter le paiement entre les mains du créancier originaire, est passée dans le patrimoine d'un autre qu'il devra désormais considérer comme son seul créancier."

In the Century Dictionary, under the word "Signification:" we find :—"In French-Canadian law, the fact of giving notice; notification," and under the same word we find in the Standard Dictionary :   " In French Canadian law, notification."   The essence of a signification is, therefore, the making known to a third party the existence of a legal fact, and in the case of the transfer of a debt, the signification is the service on the debtor of a notice mentioning and describing such transfer, together with the delivery to him of a copy of the transfer.   When notice is given, and when at the time of the service of the notice a copy of the transfer is delivered to the debtor, the signification, in my opinion, is made in a legal and official form, no matter by whom the service has been effected, as the law prescribes nothing in that respect.   The signification has, however, to be made in writing, and, in order that due proof of it may be made, there should be a duplicate or copy of the notice ; when the notification is thus made, and a copy of the transfer is delivered to the debtor, the signification, in my opinion, becomes and is an official act. A simple verbal intimation to the debtor would not be an official act and is, therefore, ineffective to vest the transferree. Under the old law of France there was no enactment regulating the manner in which the signification had to be made, but under the jurisprudence of the time it was made by a bailiff, and under the present jurisprudence of France and not under any text of law, it is also made by a bailiff.

Our law does not specify by whom the signification of a transfer has to be made to the debtor, and it, therefore, resolves itself into a matter of proof. To have the signification made by a person whose writings or certificates and returns are authentic is, of course, advantageous, but it is not essential that it should be made by such a functionary. All that is essential is that legal proof be furnished of the signification. In France the acts of a bailiff are authentic and, therefore, are a complete proof of the signification and establish its date, but here bailiffs are not authorized to signify transfers. Here a signification by a notary has the same effect as the signification by a bailiff in France, but the capacity conferred upon bailiffs here would not give to a signification made by one of them an authentic character.

Under article 5750, of the Revised Statutes of Quebec, the official functions of bailiffs are restricted to the service and execution of writs, orders and process, issuing from the courts in the province, which may be lawfully directed to one of them. The signification here by a notary is authentic and requires no other proof than the production of a copy of the act of notification, and of the certificates of the service ; but although this is the most convenient and advantageous form, it is not one which is absolutely and exclusively required by our law, and proof of the signification can, therefore, be made by any legal evidence. While the bailiff's return is no proof a bailiff may, himself, however, establish the service of the notification by his testimony. Article 1209 of the Civil Code provides that notifications may be made by a notary, but although this mode is certainly the most efficacious, it is not, under the terms of the article, an exclusive one. The words of the article are that notifications may be made by a notary and not that they shall be made by one, and article 15 explicitly declares that the word " shall " is imperative, but that the word " may " is only permissive.

The signification of a transfer cannot be made by a bailiff, and the law does not make it obligatory that it should be made by a notary ; it can, therefore, be made in any manner which is susceptible of being legally proved. Ferrière in the second volume of the Grand Coutumier, at page 132, No. 28, in stating that transfer need not be executed before notaries, observes : " Notre coutume ne le requiert point et il n'y a aucune raison qui y oblige," and I can say in like manner that our law does not require the signification to be made by a notary, and that there is no more reason for it than that deeds of sale of movables which have legal effect against third parties, should be executed before a notary. The signification in one case, and the execution of the sale in the other case, are matters of proof, and both may be voided by the proof of fraud ; but until fraud has been proved they should have their full effect. In this connection it must not be forgotten that a vital difference exists between the old law in France and the law here with respect to the effect of the contract of sale. In France under the old rule a sale was only consummated by delivery, while here it now is perfected by the consent alone of the contracting parties. In France the signification of the transfer of a debt replaced the delivery, and was, therefore, made in a solemn form, but here the signification does not replace the delivery, and it is only required as a notification to the debtor of the change of his creditor, and, therefore, it is not necessary to use a solemn form. If the signification can be proved, it is effective.

In the case of *St. Jean* v. *Delisle* (2, L. C. R., p. 152), in which judgment was rendered on the 30th December, 1851, by the Superior Court, presided over by Justices Day, Smith and Mondelet,—it was held that a bailiff's certificate of the signification of a transfer could not be taken as authentic ; and in the case of *McCorkill* v. *Barrabe* (M. L. R. L., S. C., p. 321), in which judgment was rendered on the 31st January, 1885, by the Court of Review, presided over by Justices Johnson, Papineau and Mathieu, Mr. Justice Papineau, speaking for the court, said : " It·was pretended at the argument that the transfer and the signification thereof should have been by notarial act. It is unquestionable that transfers and significations in authentic form offer advantages over those made by private writing, which are not to be ignored. They make proof of themselves. Those by private writings must be proved and are without date in law, though they bear one upon their face, till such proof is made. Notwithstanding this, there is no law which requires that such transfers and significations should be made by notarial acts. In the present case the two transfers were made *sous seing privé*, and they were proved, but the signification thereof was made by a bailiff of the Superior Court. Such a signification, not coming within the official powers and duties of a bailiff, had to be proved also. It was proved. Proof was also made that defendant was signified with a copy of the note with the endorsation thereon, previous to the institution of the action."

In the absence of an express enactment requiring the signification of a transfer to be made by a notarial act, such signification falls under the ordinary rule of law, which only requires deeds of gift *inter vivos*, contracts of marriage, and deeds conferring hypothec to be executed in notarial form and allows all other acts to be executed by private writing. Significations may consequently be made by a private writing, and under the provisions of article 1225, of the Civil Code, their date may be established against third persons in the several ways which it indicates.

Besides deeds which have to be in notarial form under the general law, certain other deeds have also under special statutes to be made in that form; for instance, under the statute 10-11, Vict., cap. 111, deeds of commutation of the tenure in Crown seigniories and under the statute 38 Vic., cap. 26, transfers of seigniorial dues. The last mentioned statute also enacts that the signification of a transfer of seigniorial dues is to be made by a notary, but the enactment is special and for a special and particular case and establishes an exception to the general rule, which does not require by any text of law a notarial signification. If the rule of law required in all cases of the transfer of debts a notarial signification, this special enactment would not have been required; and its enactment confirms the general rule.

Until the date is proved a private writing has no certain date against a third party; but article 1225 provides that the date may be established against him by legal proof. To prove the date of a private writing by testimony, is no violation of the principle contained in article 1234, that testimony cannot be received to contradict or vary the terms of a written document, inasmuch as to prove the date of the execution of a deed by private writing is only the establishing of one of the circumstances under which it was made. It is, therefore, allowable to establish the date of such a deed by witnesses or by any other legal mode of proof. It is also permissible to prove in the same way the day and hour of the signification of extra-judical acts, such as the signification of a transfer (8, Aubry and Rau, 323.)

In this case the signification of the transfer is proved by Mr. Drolet. Pothier says, in his Treatise on Obligations, that deeds by private writing make proof of their contents against the parties to them and third persons, but that they have no certain date against third persons until the date is established by legal proof, and that they must be held to have a certain date against third persons from at least the day on which they are produced and delivered to such third person. (Pothier. Obligations, No. 749, and 1 Rolland de Villargues, verbo, acte sous seing privé, No. 68.)

In the present case the copy of the transfer was delivered to the company respondent, on the 6th November, 1897, and consequently it has, as regards the company respondent, a certain date as of that day.

In the present case the company respondent was notified, in the first place, of the transfer by a letter dated 28th June, 1897, from the solicitors of the bank appellant, which specifically mentioned and described the transfer, but no copy of the transfer was transmitted with this letter, and then the company respondent, was again notified of the transfer by the letter dated 6th November, 1897, from the solicitors of the bank at Montreal, which also mentioned and described the transfer. This last letter of notification was delivered to the company respondent, by Mr. Drolet, who delivered with it to the company respondent, a copy of the transfer. Mr. Drolet proved the delivery of both the letter of notification and the copy of the transfer to the company respondent. The original of the transfer was produced, and Mr. Beatty proved its execution. A form of notice of transfer is given in the Civil Code in connection with article 1571a, and the notice of transfer given by the bank's solicitors at Toronto, and also that given by the bank's solicitors in Montreal, comply with this form and contain all that was required for a proper signification. The notification under this form is not required to be authenticated by a notary. Our law requires the delivery of a copy of the transfer to the debtor when signification of it is made. In the present case a copy was delivered to the manager of the company respondent, by Mr. Drolet. The manager, Mr. Gauthier, admitted this fact, and, moreover, the company respondent produced the copy delivered to the company respondent, with an amendment which was made to its plea, and fyled it in the case. The company respondent, however, complains that this copy was not certified, but there is no law which specifies in what manner the copy of a transfer contained in a private writing is to be certified, or even that it has to be certified. Our law allows transfers to be made by private writings and it leaves copies of such deeds to be proved in the same way as the originals. This was decided in the case of *Guerin* v. *Craig* by the Court of Review in Quebec in 1892 (2 Q.L.R., 168), which also held that the deposit of a deed by private writing with a notary is only for the purpose of security and does not give to copies thereof made by the notary the effect of an authentic deed.

There is no pretence that the copy delivered is not a true copy, and, as a matter of fact, it is a correct and accurate copy of the original transfer, as is established by a comparison of the copy with the original, which are both in the record. The signification of the transfer and the delivery of a copy, therefore, in my opinion, comply with the requirments of our law.

At the argument it was contended that the fact that the copy of the transfer, which was delivered to the debtor, was not certified, imposed an undue obligation upon him and necessitated going to the place of business of the transferee to examine the original transfer and verify its validity ; but this is the position in which a debtor in France is always placed, as there, although the signification is made in authentic form, no copy of the transfer is given to him, and it is only summarily described in the notification.

In the present case no third party has set up any claim to the amount of the insurance, either by transfer or by attachment, and the company respondent, can, therefore, only be called upon to pay it either to the John Eaton Company, Limited, or to the bank appellant. The John Eaton

Company, Limited, cannot claim it, as the transfer of all its rights has been produced—is admitted by it and stands unchallenged ; and under the transfer, even without a signification, the company respondent could safely have paid the amount of the insurance to the bank appellant. (4 Aubry and Rue, page 434.)

On the whole, I am of the opinion that the bank appellant, is entitled to recover the amount of the insurance, which was transferred to it, and for the recovery of which the present suit was instituted.

At the argument, the fact whether or not the signification had been made before the institution of the action, was raised, but in the plea this contention is not raised. The bank appellant, in its delaration alleges that the transfer had been duly signified and served upon the company respondent. It is true that the company respondent denies that allegation, but in its special pleading it is not contended that the transfer was not signified before the suit was instituted and served, but merely that the copy of the transfer had not been signed by the parties and had not been authenticated in any manner, and that the bank appellant had no right to institute the action before a valid copy of the transfer had been served. No special complaint is made that the signification was not anterior to the institution of the action, and the only complaint is that the copy of the transfer was not authentic and valid. The copy served, although not certified, was, in my opinion, sufficient for the purpose of the signification. In France, under the modern jurisprudence, all that is required is to describe in a summary way the transfer in the notification, leaving the debtor to verify its correctness, as I have already stated.

The judgment appealed from does not allege that the signification was not anterior to the institution of the action, and under the pleadings and the facts of the case, I hold that it was anterior, and that the suit was, therefore, properly brought.

It has been contended that as the copy of the transfer, which was delivered to the company respondent, was neither authentic nor certified, it could not safely pay the amount of the insurance to the bank appellant. The company respondent really owes the amount of the insurance granted by it, and does not deny or repudiate its contract, and if it was doubtful as to whom the payment was to be made, it had the means in two ways to protect itself and pay the amount of insurance with perfect safety to the bank appellant.   The insurance is payable at the company's office in Montreal, and before handing over the money it had the right, not only to ask for a proper release, but also to exact surrender of the policy and due exhibition of the original transfer.   The payment, therefore, could have been made with perfect safety, and whether the copy served was authentic and certified or not, is consequently immaterial. All the company respondent, had to do was to notify the bank appellant, and the latter had to go to the company respondent's office and to produce all the documents necessary to prove its rights and to be the basis of a valid release. Then again, if the company respondent had doubts as to the validity of the transfer, it had the right, as mentioned by Huc, Cession des Créances, Vol. 2, No 336, to bring the transferror into the case, and to have the matter adjudicated upon.   "Le cèdé, qui a des doutes sur la sincérité de la cession et qui ne voudra pas s'exposer à payer deux fois, devra faire juger la difficulté en mettant en cause le cédant."

Not only legally, but equitably, the bank appellant, to my mind, is entitled to recover the insurance, and the dismissal of the suit on a technicality, from which the company respondent has suffered and can suffer no injustice, will cause the bank appellant to lose a debt justly due to it, as it would then be prescribed, and will allow the company respondent to avoid the payment of a debt for which it is legitimately liable.

I would, therefore, maintain the appeal with costs :   set aside and annul the judgment appealed from, and condemn the company respondent to pay to the bank appellant the amount of the policy granted to the John Eaton Company, Limited, with interest and costs of suit.

Mr. Justice Hall concurs with me, but the majority of the court is of opinion that the judgment dismissing the action for the want of a signification in notarial form should be confirmed, and it, therefore, now only remains for us to enter our dissent.

Bosse, J., for the majority of the court, agreed with the other members of the Court of Appeal, that the three grounds first pleaded were not sufficient to dismiss the action, but on the question of signification they concurred with the judge of the court below that the signification was insufficient. Article 1571 of the Civil Code says that the buyer of a debt has no possession available against third persons until signification of the act of sale has been made, and a copy of it delivered to the debtor. The transfer here was made by a private writing, and the signification was made by a letter from the solicitors of the bank to the insurance company, informing the company that the policy had been transferred to the bank, and that the original (of which a copy was sent to the company) was in their hands, and might be seen by the company. The majority of the court considered that this did not fulfil the requirements of the law, and that the signification should have been made by a ministerial officer, in order that there might be no doubt in the mind of the debtor that the transferee had become the creditor, and that the debt might be paid to him with safety. The judgment of the court below was therefore confirmed, Justices Hall and Wurtele dissenting.

———

[IN THE COURT OF APPEAL FOR ONTARIO.]

ERNEST ARNOLDI et al (Defendants) Appellants

v.

LA BANQUE PROVINCIALE (Plaintiff) Respondent.

Promissory notes —Material alteration by holder—Subsequent cancellation thereof—Effect on renewal note—Sureties.

When the holder of a promissory note (some of the makers of which are sureties for the others) inserts the words " jointly and severally," in order to establish a liability of that nature, such addition is a material alteration which avoids the note : And the fact that the holder subsequently strikes out the words so inserted will not render the note enforceable against the makers, even though they did not know of the addition until after the same has been struck out.

A note given in renewal of one which has been dealt with as above mentioned cannot be enforced, since, as the original note is avoided, there is no consideration for the one given in renewal thereof.

When the holder of a promissory note is aware that some of the makers thereof are sureties for the others, his acceptance of a renewal note not signed by one of the sureties discharges the other sureties.

When judgment has been taken against partners in their firm name,
subsequent judgments may be taken against them individually on
a promissory note which they gave as collateral security for the
same debt.

Action on promissory notes, the first of which (so far
as material hereto) was for $5,000, and was given to the
plaintiff bank on 7th November, 1898, while the second for
$4,800, was given as a renewal on 10th May, 1899.

A number of the appellants were sureties on the first
note for the principal debtors. The agent of the bank had,
therefore, been instructed by the head office to procure a
joint and several note, but he omitted to do so, and
advanced the money on a joint note merely, not discovering
his error until some days later. He then drew the attention
of one of the principal debtors to this fact, and the latter
replied that it was an oversight which would be remedied.
The agent, with the consent of that debtor, then inserted
the words necessary to ensure a joint and several liability,
and it was arranged that the approval of the other parties
should be procured. This was not done, however, and a
few days later the agent drew his pen through the words
which he had put in. Subsequently the renewal note for
$4,800 above referred to was given by the makers (other
than King Arnoldi) of the original note, all of whom, with
the exception of the defendants E. C. Arnoldi and Bowie,
were then ignorant both of the alteration and of the later
cancellation thereof, which had been made in the original
note by the agent of the holder.

Moreover, the agent of the plaintiff bank, although
aware that some of the makers of the original note for
$5,000 were sureties for the others, accepted as renewal
thereof the note for $4,800 upon which the name of one of
the sureties, King Arnoldi, did not appear.

The other facts, and the contentions of the parties, are
set forth in the judgment.

6th November, 1901 :—

ARMOUR, C. J., O :—

I am unable to agree with the finding of the learned-trial
Judge that the Manager of the Bank at the time he took the
note dated the 10th May, 1899, made by all the defendants
but the defendant King Arnoldi, did not observe the absence

of the defendant King Arnoldi's name from it, and that such absence was not called to his attention by the defendant E. C. Arnoldi from whom he received it, for I think that the weight of evidence is the other way, and I think the proper conclusion of fact to be that he was told by the defendant E. C. Arnoldi that the defendant King Arnoldi had not signed it, and that he was induced to take it by the assurance of the defendant E. C. Arnoldi that the defendant King Arnoldi would subsequently sign it. Whatever may be thought of the evidence of the defendant E. C. Arnoldi in this regard standing alone, I cannot ignore the corroboration of it by the defendants H. W. Bowie and Kirby, more especially as the evidence of the defendant Kirby was not contradicted by the Manager, and to this must be added the fact that the Manager was taking this note as a renewal of the note dated the 7th November, 1898, which it would not have been without the signature of the defendant King Arnoldi. This note, therefore, when given to the Manager was to his knowledge an incomplete instrument, and being such no recovery could be had upon it by the Bank, the defendant E. C. Arnoldi having no authority to deliver it to the Bank until it was signed by the defendant King Arnoldi, it having been signed by the parties who signed it upon the distinct understanding that it was not to be used until all the defendants had signed it, and having been handed after it was so signed to the defendant E. C. Arnoldi upon that understanding. (*Aude* v. *Dixon*, 6 Exch. 869.)

But even if this finding of fact by the learned Judge is to stand, there could be no recovery upon this note against the defendants, who were sureties, for the manager of the Bank when he took this note took it not as an original note but as a renewal of the note dated the 7th November, 1898, made by all the defendants of whom the defendants E. C. Arnoldi, E. D. Arnoldi and H. L. Bowie, were under the name of the Citizens' Exchange and Loan Agency, the principal debtors, and the other defendants were their sureties, as the manager of the bank well knew, and in taking this note as a renewal of the original note the manager of the Bank was bound to see that it was in truth a renewal of it, and that it had the signature to it of the defendant King Arnoldi, and having taken and used it as he did without his signature, the bank must suffer for his neglect, and not the co-sureties of the defendant King Arnoldi, and it must be held that such his act and neglect released such co-sureties from their liability upon this note. It is also clear that the bank cannot fall back upon the note of the 7th November, 1898, and recover against the defendants upon it, for this among other reasons, that the action upon it has been dismissed as against the defendant King Arnoldi, a joint maker of it, on a ground common to all the joint makers of it, and there is no appeal against such dismissal. (*Phillips* v. *Ward*, 2 H. &. C. 717.) And it cannot fall back and recover against the defendants for the consideration, for the reasons given by the learned trial Judge.

In my opinion, therefore, the appeal must be allowed with costs and the action dismissed with costs.

OSLER, J. A. :—

The plaintiffs cannot maintain their action against the defendants King Arnoldi, Kirby, H. W. Bowie and St. Jacques in respect of the $5,000 note because, as to them, it was certainly avoided by the alteration made therein, with however innocent intention, by their manager. (*Carrique* v. *Beaty*, 24 A. R. 302, and cases there cited.) As to this I agree with the learned trial judge. I am, however, unable to follow him in holding that the defendants Bowie, Kirby and St. Jacques are liable upon the other note sued on—the note for $4,800 of the 10th May, 1899. That note was intended to be given solely as a renewal of the former note, but when they signed it and parted with it to the bank, assuming for the moment that it was then as to them a completed instrument, they had ceased to be liable upon the original note by reason of the alteration which had been made therein by the holders, an alteration of which they were ignorant and to which they never assented. Therefore, there was no consideration to them for making the second note, and the plaintiffs being holders with notice cannot recover against them thereon. I am also of opinion that these appellants are entitled to succeed upon another ground. They, together with the defendant King Arnoldi, were parties to the original note as sureties for their co-defendants Ernest D. Arnoldi, E. C. Arnoldi and H. L. Bowie, who composed the partnership firm of the Citizens' Exchange & Loan Company, as the plaintiffs' manager knew, and they undoubtedly signed the renewal upon the express condition that all the parties to the former note should sign it, and that it should not be made use of in any way as a security until this was done. I think the evidence of the defendant E. C. Arnoldi, that the manager knew this when it was handed to him in its incomplete state, wanting the signature of King Arnoldi, which had not been in fact obtained, is amply corroborated. As regards these three parties, therefore, the bank never acquired or held it as a complete instrument and cannot maintain any action upon it. (*Foster* v. *Mackinnon*, L. R. 4. C. P. 704 ; *Lewis* v. *Clay*, 67 L. J., Q. B. 224 ; *Brown* v. *Howland*, 9 O. R. 43, and cases there cited ; affirmed 15 A. R. 750.)

The only remaining question is as to the liability of the other three defendants, E. C. Arnoldi, Mrs. Arnoldi and Mrs. Bowie, which is of little importance except as regards the costs of the action, as the bank has already recovered judgment against their firm on the last of the series of the monthly notes for which the note of the 10th May, 1899, was supposed to be held as collateral.

These defendants by their partner, E. C. Arnoldi, put forward this note as a complete note for the purpose of inducing the manager to discount their firm's note at one month, and as a security on the faith of which the manager did in fact discount the latter note, the proceeds of which they received and applied by means of their firm's cheque. I do not think they can now be heard to say that, as to them, the $4,800 note was not a valid instrument and, therefore, as to them the judgment should be affirmed and their appeal dismissed.

MacLENNAN, J. A. :—

I think the appeal should be allowed. The action was dismissed as against King Arnoldi, and there is no appeal against that judgment. The formal judgment is against all the other defendants, but it is not stated upon which of the notes sued upon it has been granted. This is explained in the reasons for judgment of the learned Judge wherein he expresses the opinion that the first note, namely, that for $5,000, was avoided by the alteration made by the plaintiffs' agent without the knowledge or consent of the parties thereto. The recovery, therefore, must be taken to be upon the note of the 10th May, 1899, for $4,800.

I am of opinion that the learned Judge was right in holding that the first note was avoided by the alteration, although it was not made with any wrongful or fraudulent intention. Mr. Charbonneau's instructions from the head office were to procure a joint and several note from the parties who were offered as sureties (letter, 12th Oct., '98). Unfortunately the note was drawn as a joint note merely, and not joint and several, was signed by all the parties, was brought to the agent, who accepted it and advanced the money upon it without observing that it was not joint and several. This he discovered a few days afterwards and sent for Mr. E. C. Arnoldi and drew his attention to it. Mr. Arnoldi said the omission was an oversight ; that he intended to make it joint and several. Thereupon the words jointly and severally were inserted by the agent with Mr. Arnoldi's concurrence, and it was arranged that they should go together to the parties to get them to approve of the change. This was never done, Mr. Arnoldi and Mr. Bowie, the only other persons aware of the alteration, not caring to go round to get the approval of the other signers. Some days afterwards the agent struck his pen through the words which he had interlined. I think we must hold that the alteration avoided the note, and that its validity was not restored by the subsequent cancellation. (The Bills of Exchange Act, 1890, Sec. 63 ; Maclaren on Bills and Notes, 345,-6,-7 ; Chalmers on Bills, 5th Ed., 213-14 ; *Master* v. *Miller*, 1 Sm. L. C. 871.) The first note having been thus avoided shortly after its date in November, 1898, that circumstance has an important bearing upon the question of the liability of the appellants other than Arnoldi and his wife and Mrs. Bowie, who are the principal debtors. There is no doubt whatever that the only consideration to these appellants for giving the note of the 10th of May, 1899, was their supposed liability upon the note for $5,000 which became due upon that day. The new note was signed solely for the purpose of renewing *pro tanto* the old one. That being so, and there being no liability on the old note, there was no consideration for the new one as between these appellants and the bank, and they are entitled to succeed in their appeal on that ground.

I am also of opinion that it is proved that the appellants Kirby and St. Jacques signed the new note upon the express condition that it should also be signed by King Arnoldi, who had signed the old note with them, and that not having been signed by him it never became, in the hands of the payees, an obligation binding upon those appellants. I agree with the Chief Justice that the weight of the evidence is in favour of the view that the want of King Arnoldi's name was observed by Mr. Charbonneau at the first, and was regarded by him as a defect which ought to be remedied to make it the instrument intended by all the parties. But even if it were otherwise, the contract was one between the makers and the bank, and unless it was completed in the manner intended it never became binding. I therefore think that those two appellants are entitled to succeed on this ground also. (*Lewis* v. *Clay*, 67 L. J., Q. B. 224).

There are also other grounds on which perhaps our judgment in favour of the appellants, the sureties, might be rested, but I think the foregoing are quite sufficient. The case is different as regards the appellants E. C. Arnoldi and his wife and Mrs. Bowie, who were the principal debtors. The note for $4,800 represented a real debt due by them to the bank, and they received the benefit of it. By means of it they paid off the $5,000 note on which they were undoubtedly liable, for the alteration was made with the concurrence of a member of the firm. There is, therefore, no reason why they should not be held liable or why the judgment against them should not be allowed to stand. It was contended that a judgment for the same debt on another note dated the 19th September, 1899, at one month's date, recovered against them by their partnership name of the Citizens' Exchange & Loan Co., was a bar to the present action, but the answer to that is that the present action is upon a different contract and there is no reason why there should not be a judgment upon it although it be for the same debt. The appeal of the defendants Kirby, St. Jacques and H. W. Bowie should be allowed with costs, and the action against them should be dismissed with costs, and the appeal of the other defendants should be dismissed with costs.

Solicitors for the Appellants Kirby *et al*: *Gormully and Orde*.

Solicitors for the Appellants Arnoldi *et al*: *Code and Burritt*.

Solicitor for the Respondent: *W. H. Barry*.

[IN THE SUPREME COURT OF CANADA.]

BEFORE SIR HENRY STRONG, C. J., AND TASCHEREAU,
SEDGWICK, GIROUARD AND
SIR L. H. DAVIES, J.J.

(APPEAL FROM THE COURT OF APPEAL FOR ONTARIO.)

ALFRED ROBINSON (Plaintiff) Appellant,

v.

GEORGE T. MANN (Defendant) Respondent.

*Promissory note—Liability of stranger endorsing—Bills of
Exchange Act, 1890 (45-46 Vict., Cap. 61), Sec. 56.—
" Aval"—Chattel mortgage—Consideration—R. S. O.
(1897), Cap. 148, Secs. 2, 4, 5, 8 and 38.*

W. M. requested G. M. to endorse his (W. M.'s.) note, which G. M.
did, being given as security for such endorsement a chattel mortgage on W. M.'s stock in trade. The note was signed by W.M. and
was made payable to the order of the Molsons Bank ; G. M. then
endorsed it, and W. M. got it discounted at the Molsons Bank, at
whose instance it was subsequently protested for non-payment. A
few days after protest G. M. paid the amount due on the note, and
took possession under his mortgage, and about two weeks later
W. M. assigned for the general benefit of his creditors. Upon action
being brought by the assignee to set aside the chattel mortgage as
fraudulent and void, it was contended, *inter alia*, that G. M. had
never incurred any liability by endorsing the note in question because
it was not made payable to him but to the Molsons Bank, and was
never endorsed by the payee.

Held, that G. M. was liable on the note as an endorser by virtue of
the Bills of Exchange Act, 1890, (45-61 Vic., Cap. 46), Sec. 56.

Held, further, that the requirement of R. S. O., (1897) Cap. 148, Sec.
8, that a chattel mortgage shall set forth the consideration, had been
sufficiently satisfied by setting out therein the note itself, and
declaring that the endorsement thereof was the consideration,—it
not being necessary to state in the mortgage the legal effect of the
facts set out.

In September, 1897, Walter Mann requested his brother,
the respondent, George Mann, to endorse his note for
$1200.00. The respondent did so upon being secured by a
chattel mortgage on Walter Mann's stock in trade, executed
on the same day as the note was made. The note was
signed by Walter Mann as "W. Mann & Co." (of which
firm he was the sole member), and was made payable to the
order of the Molsons Bank, three months after date.

The respondent then put his name on the back of the note, and Walter Mann had it discounted at the Molsons Bank. The note was subsequently protested for non-payment, and a few days later the respondent paid the amount due thereon, and then took possession under his chattel mortgage of the goods covered thereby. About two weeks later Walter Mann made an assignment for the general benefit of his creditors.

This action was subsequently brought by the appellant as assignee of Walter Mann under R. S. O. (1897), Cap. 147,—but was so brought for the exclusive benefit of the Dunlop Tire Co., Limited, that company having obtained an order from a judge of the High Court of Justice for Ontario under Sec. 9, s.s. 2 of the above Act. The action was tried at London before the Honourable Mr. Justice Meredith, who dismissed the same with costs. The plaintiff then appealed to the Court of Appeal for Ontario, which confirmed the judgment of the trial judge. A further appeal was then taken by the plaintiff to this court.

31st OCTOBER, 1901 :—

The judgment of the court was delivered by :

SIR HENRY SRONG, C. J. (oral) :—

We all think this appeal must be dismissed. The questions to be decided are : First : Did the respondent incur any liability by endorsing a note not made payable to him but to the Molsons Bank, and not endorsed by the payee? Secondly : Were the recitals in the chattel mortgage of the consideration for which it was made sufficient?

As to the first point it appears that the note in question was in form as follows :

"London, Sept. 25th, 1899.

" $1200.00.

" Three months after date I promise to pay to the order of the Molsons Bank, at the Molsons Bank here, twelve hundred dollars for value received.

"W. MANN & CO."

Endorsed on the back was the name

"GEORGE T. MANN."'

- Then the position was this, George T. Mann, the present respondent, endorsed a note signed by W. Mann & Co. and payable to the Molsons Bank. It is contended that he was not an endorser, and as such liable to the bank to whom the note so endorsed was delivered and by it discounted, Walter Mann receiving the proceeds.

Next, what was the legal effect of this endorsement? Section 56 of the Bills of Exchange Act, 1890, provides that "where a person signs a bill otherwise than as a drawer or "acceptor he thereby incurs the liability of an endorser to a "holder in due course and is subject to all the provisions of "this Act respecting endorsers."

Then, when the bank took the note was it not entitled to the benefit of the respondent's liability as endorser? Certainly it was, for the endorsement by force of the statute operated as what has long been known in the French commercial law as an "aval," a form of liability which is now by the statute adopted in English law.

The argument for the appellant, as I understand it, is that this endorsement at most amounted only to a guarantee, and that there being no consideration expressed in writing the Statute of Frauds would have been an answer if the bank had sued the respondent. Some colour is given to this argument by the case of *Singer* v. *Elliott*, as reported in 4 T. L. R., p. 524, but there the Bills of Exchange Act was not referred to, and it appeared that the bill had not been negotiated. It is to be remarked that that case is not to be found in the regular series of reports. Here, however, the note was negotiated and the 56th section of the Act applies and creates a liability as endorser, independently altogether of the principle of guarantee. If the section referred to is to have any effect it must apply in a case like this.

Then as to the recital in the chattel mortgage : It declares the endorsement of the note to be the consideration, and sets out the note itself, which is surely a sufficient compliance with the requirement of the Act that the consideration should be recited. It is not necessary that the mortgage should state the legal effect of the facts set out as forming the consideration. It is sufficient to state the facts and leave the legal effect to be inferred.

I agree with the reasons given by their Lordships in the Court of Appeal for deciding this case in favour of the respondent, but I do not go so far as Mr. Justice Osler who, I think, puts the case too favourably for the appellant when he says that the bank would have found it difficult to enforce the liability on the note against the respondent. In my opinion the respondent was clearly liable as coming within the 56th section of the Bills of Exchange Act already referred to.

The appeal fails and must be dismissed with costs.

Appeal dismissed with costs.

Solicitors for the Appellant : *Ryckman, Kirkpatrick & Kerr.*

Solicitors for the Respondent : *Hellmuth & Ivey.*

Editor's Notes :—

The doctrine of "aval" has (as is stated in the foregoing judgment) long been known to French jurists, but it is only by statutory enactment that it has, to a certain extent, become part of the English law.

Nougier, Vol. I., No. 822, says :—(Translation)—"Aval is an agreement by means of which a person who is a stranger to a bill of exchange makes himself liable jointly and severally for its payment at maturity in favour of the drawer, of one of the endorsers, or of the acceptor. This act has received the name of *aval* because, the commentators say, it signifies *to make good.*"

It may here be mentioned that, according to French jurisprudence, some of the attributes of aval are that it is presumed to be, and generally is, gratuitous ; that it cannot be given after the maturity of the bill of exchange ; that it always involves joint and several liability, but that joint and several liability does not exist between two givers of aval.

In the case of *Steele* v. *McKinlay* (1880) 5 A.C. 754, it was held by the House of Lords that in order to constitute acceptance of a bill of exchange there must be a signature by the drawee, showing his assent to the order of the drawer and that no other person writing his name on the bill can thereby render himself liable to the drawer on the bill ; but that where a person signs a bill otherwise than as drawer or acceptor he thereby incurs the liabilities of an indorser to a holder in due course.

In giving judgment in *Steele* v. *McKinlay*, Lord Blackburn (at p. 772) said : " An indorsement in general is a transfer in writing by the holder of the bill to a new holder on whom the property is thereby conferred ; and it is clear that J. McKinlay was not such an indorser. But I quite agree that by the custom of merchants, as modified by English law, there may also be an indorsement by a person, not a holder of the bill, who puts his name on the bill to facilitate the transfer to a holder. By the old foreign law, not in this respect entirely adopted by the English law, this might be done by what was termed an *aval* (said to be an antiquated word signifying underwriting), either on the bill itself or on a separate paper ; and if such an *aval* was given by any one, his obligation to all subsequent holders of the bill was precisely the same as that of the person to facilitate whose transfer the *aval* was made."

And in further stating the law on the point Lord Blackburn added : " Such an indorsement creates no obligation to those who previously were parties to the bill, it is solely for the benefit of those who take subsequently. It is not a collateral engagement but one on the bill, and it is for that reason and because the original bill has incident to it the capacity of an indorsement in the nature of an 'aval' that such an indorsement requires no new stamp."

In the earlier case of *ex parte Yates*, (1858) 2 De G. & J. 191, it was held that when, some time after the issue of a note, a person added his signature to accommodate the maker, he was liable not as a new maker, but as an indorser, even when the name was written on the face of the note.

The principle of the decision in *Steele* v. *McKinlay*, *supra*, to the effect that the backing of a bill by one who is a stranger to it renders him liable as an indorser to a subsequent holder was adopted by the Imperial Bills of Exchange Act, (see 45-46 Vic., Cap. 61, Sec. 56), which was followed, in that respect, in the drafting of our Bills of Exchange Act, Sec. 56 of which reads as follows : "Where a person signs a bill otherwise than as a drawer or acceptor, be thereby incurs the liabilities of an indorser to a holder in due course, and is subject to all the provisions of this Act respecting indorsers."

In *Jenkins* v. *Comber* (1898), 2 Q. B. 168, it was held that a stranger to a bill who writes his name across the back of it before it has passed out of the hands of the drawer does not, by reason of the Bills of Exchange Act, thereby become liable to the drawer upon failure of the acceptor to pay the bill at maturity,—the provisions of sec. 56 regarding the liability of a person who signs otherwise than as drawer or acceptor only being satisfied when the bill is complete on its face when it is signed by such person.

And see also *Singer* v. *Elliott* (1888) 4 T. L. R., 524 ; *Stagg* v. *Brodrick* (1895) 12 T. L. R. 12.

In the Province of Quebec a person who put his signature on the back of a note before its indorsement by the payee, was an indorser *pour aval*, and was liable as such without notice of dishonour or protest.

See Civil Code, Art 2311. *Merritt* v. *Lynch* (1859) 3 L. C. J. 276. *Pariseau* v. *Ouellet* (1850) M. C. R. 69. *Fyfe* v. *Boyce* (1891) 21 R. L. 4. *Coutu* v. *Rafferty* (1891) M. L. R. 7 S. C. 41.

But since the enactment of the Bills of Exchange Act, 1890, an indorser *pour aval* is, like an ordinary indorser, discharged by the failure to protest.

Emard v. *Marcille* (1892) R. J. Q. 2 S. C. 525. *Banque Jacques Cartier* v. *Gagnon*, R. J. Q. (1894) 5 S. C. 500.

But the Bills of Exchange Act, 1890, does not render notice of protest or dishonour necessary in order to hold indorsers *pour aval* liable on bills or notes made before that statute became operative. *Fyfe* v. *Boyce*, supra. *Coutu* v. *Rafferty*, supra.

———

[IN THE SUPREME COURT OF BRITISH COLUMBIA.]

BEFORE DRAKE, J.

THE BRITISH COLUMBIA STOCK EXCHANGE, LIMITED,

v.

IRVING.

Gaming contract—Dealing in differences—Illegality of the transaction.

In an action brought by brokers against a customer to recover money alleged to have been paid to satisfy the latter's liability on an order given to the brokers to sell a number of shares of a certain stock, it appeared in evidence that no scrip of shares ever passed, and that the brokers, according to their own admissions, would have closed the transaction at any time upon the payment of the difference in the price of the stock at that time and when they were directed to sell the same. Held, that the contract was illegal, and that the court would therefore leave the parties to it in the position they then were.

VICTORIA, 21st October, 1901.

The facts of the case are fully set forth in the judgment.

DRAKE, J. :

This action is brought by the plaintiffs to recover $637, money alleged to have been paid by the plaintiffs at the defendant's request to Downing, Hopkins & Co., Seattle, brokers, in respect of the purchase of 300 Continental Tobacco shares at 62⅝. The plaintiffs are a company incorporated in this province.

The defendant instructed them to sell 300 shares of the Continental Tobacco Company. The plaintiffs asked for cover, and the defendant paid them $600, that is $2 a share. No time was fixed for the delivery of the shares or closing the transaction. The plaintiffs called upon the defendant from time to time for more money, as the shares were steadily rising, and on or about the 29th day of May they called for $2,400, which the defendant refused to pay. They thereupon alleged that they purchased 300 shares in the market at 62⅝ a share, in order to satisfy the defendant's liability. The defendant when he sold the shares sold 100 at 52, and 200 at 51⅝. The plaintiffs never asked the defendant for the scrip which he sold, and they purchased without notifying him of their intention to do so, and without asking him to deliver the scrip.

The mode of business as alleged by the plaintiffs was that on receipt of an order from clients they instructed their agents in Seattle, Messrs. Downing & Hopkins, to buy or sell as the case might be, and that the prices of the New York market were the governing prices for all transactions.

A good deal of evidence was given about the commission which they alleged they charged for transacting business in order to substantiate the fact that they were not principals in the business transacted.

They have made no claim for any commission, and have not sued for it, but merely for money alleged to be paid on the purchase of 300 Continental Tobacco Company's shares at $62.87 per share.

From the evidence of Mr. Jno. Nicholles for the plaintiffs it appears that the rule is that if the margin is exhausted the trade is closed. "We have," he says, "to close the trade on the exhausted margin to protect ourselves from loss—unless the trader remargins—this is continually repeated, and it is difficult to see what claim he can have for further funds, when the margin is exhausted." And he further says : "We never have any scrip delivered to us to sell. We settle the differences according to the fluctuations of the market." And he further says : "We would have closed the transaction on his (the defendant's) account at any time by his paying us the difference, or a receipt by him of the difference according to the rise or fall of the market without handling the shares at all." This evidence clearly indicates the nature of the business transacted, and that it was dealing with differences only.

The plaintiffs produce a sold note, which is as follows :

B. C. Stock Exchange, Ltd.,

Correspondents, Downing, Hopkins & Company,

Victoria, B. C., May 6, 1901.

Mr. Irving :

Dear Sir,—We have this day sold for your account 200 Con. Tobacco 51⅝, exhausts at 54⅜, stop loss 56⅜.

J. N.

All sales are made in accordance with market prices of the property at the time of the order on the New York Stock Exchange, and quotations thereof authorized by said Exchange.

Yours respectfully,

B. C. STOCK EXCHANGE, LIMITED,

Per J. N.

No evidence was given to show what was the market price at New York on the day they alleged they bought 300 shares, viz., 25th May. The plaintiffs claim that they actually sold the 300 shares as instructed by the defendant; how, when, or to whom, is not disclosed. If they in fact sold, the purchasers would be entitled to demand delivery of the stock, but here the time is left open and no day fixed for a settlement, and from the continual demand for cover made by the plaintiffs it is evident that they treated the sale not as an actual one, but as one for which the defendant might be responsible to pay if the shares rose in the market, until the margin was exhausted, and that closed the deal. The contract says " stop loss at 56⅜," but instead of doing so they continued until the shares rose to 62⅝. This case, as far as the facts are concerned, is on all fours with *Thacker* v. *Hardy* (1878), 4, Q. B. D., 685. Lord Justice Lindley in his judgment says the plaintiff was employed to buy and sell on the stock exchange, and everything he did was perfectly legal, unless it was rendered illegal by reason of the object they had in view. If gaming and wagering was illegal I should be of opinion that the illegality of the transactions in which the plaintiff and defendant were engaged would have tainted as between themselves whatever the plaintiffs had done in furtherance of their illegal designs, and would have precluded him from claiming in a court of law any indemnity from the defendant in respect of the liabilities he had incurred. Gaming and wagering contracts, under the English law, cannot be enforced, but they are not illegal, *Fitch* v. *Jones* (1855) 5 E. & B., 238.

This is the point in this case. Are gaming and wagering contracts under the Dominion law illegal? Section 1 of 51 Vic., C. 42 says that everyone who, with intent to make, gain, or profit by the rise or fall in price of any stock of any incorporated or unincorporated company, makes any contract, oral or written, purporting to be for the sale or purchase of any such shares or stock, in respect of which no delivery of thing sold or purchased is made or received, and without the bona fide intention to make or receive such delivery, and every one who acts, aids, or abets in the making or signing of any such contract or agreement is guilty of a misdemeanor. And that is followed by a protecting clause for the broker, that if the broker received the delivery of the thing sold there is no offence, although he retains or pledges the same as security for the advance of the purchase money. This act is aimed at the exact contract which was made in this case. The law has made gaming and, wagering contracts illegal, and the evidence of the plaintiffs discloses that no stock was ever delivered or intended to be delivered, and that the intent was to make a profit from the fluctuations of the stock market. The Privy Council in *Forget* v. *Ostigny* (1895) A. C., at p. 325, points out that the decisions of the English courts are not authorities upon the construction of the Canadian code, but throw light on what constitutes a gaming contract, and cite Lord Justice Cotton's view of what a gaming contract is. He says the essence of gaming and wagering is that one party is to gain and the other to lose upon a particular event which at the time of the contract is of an uncertain nature. That is to say, if the event turns out in one way A will lose, if it turns out the other way, he will win.

That is the fact here. As far as the defendant knew, he was dealing with these plaintiffs. He put up a margin to cover them from loss if the stock rose. If the stock had fallen they would have paid him the difference. The plaintiffs say they had no interest in the deal beyond their commission, but they have never asked for commission or charged commission, and no reference is made to it in their sold note. But even if they had, I think that the transaction is so tainted with illegality that they cannot recover. This court is not to be made use of for carrying out unlawful bargains, and as both parties are in the wrong, I give judgment for the defendant, but without costs.

Action dismissed without costs.

Solicitor for the Plaintiffs, *J. M. Bradburn.*

Solicitor for the Defendant, *W. J. Taylor, K. C.*

Editor's Notes :—

In England wagering and gaming contracts are dealt with by two enactments—8-9 Vic., cap. 109, and 55-56 Vic., cap. 4.

In the well known case of *Thacker* v. *Hardy* (1879) 4 Q. B. D., 685 (referred to in the foregoing judgment) it was held that, where a customer employed a member of the London Stock Exchange to buy and sell shares for him, knowing that, according to the rules of that Exchange, the broker would be obliged to enter into other contracts entailing the responsibility of accepting or delivering shares on the next settling day, such a contract did not come within the provisions of the Gaming Act, 1845, even though the broker knew that his principal never intended to accept or make actual delivery ; and that the broker was therefore entitled both to recover his commission on the transactions, and to be indemnified against all loss on the contracts into which he had thus been compelled to enter in order to carry out the instructions of the customer.

And see also, *Ex-parte Pyke, In re Lister* (1878) 38 L. T. 923.

The decision in *Thacker* v. *Hardy, supra,* has not been materially affected by 55-56 Vic., cap. 4.

See Stutfield on Betting, 3rd Ed., 96.

But contracts to speculate in differences in the prices of stocks, where there is no intention to really buy or sell, are void under 8-9 Vic., cap. 109, sec. 18, even when there are written agreements stating that shares are in fact to be bought and sold.

Universal Stock Exchange v. *Strachan* (1896) 74 L. T., 468, *In re Gieve* (1899) 1 Q. B., 509.

Forget v. *Ostigny* (1895) A. C., 318, was a case in which the facts were similar to those of *Thacker* v. *Hardy ;* and the Judicial Committee of the Privy Council (to which an appeal was taken from the Court of Queen's Bench, Quebec), followed the decision rendered in that case.

It may be mentioned that the law on this subject in the Province of Quebec is contained in Article 1927 of the Civil Code, which reads as follows :—" There is no right of action for the recovery of money or any other thing claimed under a gaming contract or bet.   But if the money or thing have been paid by the losing party he cannot recover it back unless fraud be proved."

The section of 51 Vic., cap. 42, referred to in the above judgment, is now incorporated in sec. 201 of the Criminal Code, 1892 (55-56 Vic., cap. 29).   *In re Dowd* (1899) R. J. Q., 17 S. C., 67, it was held that a broker who merely acts as such for two parties, one a buyer and the other a seller, without having any pecuniary interest in the transaction, apart from his fixed commission, and without having any knowledge of the intention of the contracting parties to gamble in stocks or merchandise, is not guilty of any offence under this section of the Code.

[IN THE SUPREME COURT OF CANADA.]

(APPEAL FROM THE COURT OF APPEAL FOR ONTARIO.)

BEFORE SIR HENRY STRONG, C. J., AND TASCHEREAU,
SEDGWICK, GIROUARD AND
DAVIES, J.J.

THE OTTAWA ELECTRIC CO. (Plaintiffs) Appellants

v.

ST. JACQUES (Defendant) Respondent

*Contract—Construction of apparently contradictory clauses—
Principle of giving effect, if possible, to every stipulation.*

Plaintiffs agreed to light a certain hotel leased by defendant, and the
latter agreed to pay for the light so supplied. The written contract
between the parties contained the two following clauses :—"This
contract is to continue in force for not less than thirty-six months
from the date of first burning, and thereafter until cancelled in
writing by one of the parties thereto ;" and—"This contract to
remain in force after the expiration of the said thirty-six months
for the term that the party of the second part renews his lease for
the Russell House. . . . ." The defendant's lease having
expired at the end of the thirty-six months he renewed it for a period
of five years. Held, that he could not, during that time, cancel the
contract by a notice in writing, as, if so, the second clause above
quoted would be nugatory.

Judgment of the Court of Appeal for Ontario reversed, Girouard, J.,
dissenting.

The facts are fully set forth in the judgment.

Nov. 16, 1901 :—The judgment of the majority of the
Court was delivered by

SEDGWICK, J.—

The Standard Electric Company of Ottawa, to whose
rights in the premises the appellant company has succeeded,
entered into a contract with the respondent on the fifth of
November, 1891, to supply the Russell House, of which the
latter was lessee, with electric light. The period during
which this supply was to, or might continue, was fixed by
two clauses, the interpretation of which is the question
involved here.

The first clause is as follows :

" This contract is to continue in force for not less than thirty-six months from the date of first burning, and thereafter until cancelled in writing by one of the parties thereto."

There is no dispute about this clause. The light was furnished and paid for during the three years therein specified. It so happened that the lease under which Mr. St. Jacques held the Russell House had, at the time of the agreement, three years to run, and it is conceded that the period of supply fixed upon was mainly influenced by that consideration, and that the clause itself had reference only to their present conditions.

The second clause reads :—

" Special conditions, if any..............This contract to remain in force after the expiration of the said thirty-six months for the term that the party of the second part renews his lease for the Russell House, and should he fail to renew his lease, the parties of the first part will not remove their wires from the Russell House, providing the new tenant does not wish to use electric incandescent lights, but if the new tenant does wish to use electric incandescent lights and not take them from the parties of the first part, they will expect to be paid for the wiring the sum of five hundred dollars, and if this contract is renewed for five years, the wiring is to belong to the Russell House."

About the period of the expiration of the lease under which the property was held in 1892, a renewal was entered into at a higher rental and for additional property, the term therein specified being for the period of five years to be computed from the first of November, 1895. On the first of December, 1897, the defendant, St. Jacques, gave notice of cancellation of the contract, to take effect from the date of notice, and required the company to disconnect the wires connecting the Russell House with the main line.

The question is, Was this cancellation effective for the purposes of putting an end to the agreement between the parties?

The learned Chancellor, before whom the case was tried, in attempting to give effect to both clauses, and having stated that they were not repugnant or contradictory, thus interprets the contract :

It is to be enforced for thirty-six months, and thereafter for the term that St. Jacques renews his lease until cancelled in writing by one of the parties.   And this construction was adopted by the Court of Appeal.   In my view, however, but with the greatest deference, this is not the proper construction.

Both of the learned judges who dealt with the case below, admit the principle that effect must, if possible, be given to every stipulation of a contract, no one part being rejected unless absolutely repugnant to some other part. And they were apparently of opinion that there was no repugnancy between the two clauses or any difficulty in giving them both a clear and definite meaning.

I agree with this, but the effect which they gave to the second clause had the effect of eliminating it altogether from the agreement.   If, as the learned Chancellor says, it was to be in force for thirty-six months and thereafter for the term that St. Jacques renewed his lease until cancelled in writing by one of the parties, then he could have cancelled it immediately upon the expiration of the thirty-six months, independently of the fact whether he renewed or did not renew his lease, so that the insertion of the clause respecting the rights and obligations of the parties upon a renewal of the lease was rendered absolutely futile and unnecessary.

The agreement, so far as its duration was concerned, had reference first, to the existing term ; and, secondly, in respect to a non-existing but contingent term to be determined by the parties subsequently.   The second clause had relation to rights of the parties only upon and in the event of the contingency happening, in which case certain new rights and liabilities would arise.   Mr. St. Jacques was under no obligation to renew the lease, but we must assume that the provision was as much in his interest as in the interest of the appellant.   He would appear to have been anxious to secure lights for his hotel should he remain its tenant after its termination, and it was, I imagine, with that end in view that this special provision was inserted.   It had no reference whatever to the condition of affairs during the first three years, but it was a definite and unambiguous arrangement securing his supply of light for a definite period of time thereafter should he in future elect to renew his lease. In other words, the appellant company undertook to deliver to him, and he undertook to pay for, during the period of five years from the commencement of the term created by the new lease, all such light as he might require for the purposes of his hotel.

I have not been able to appreciate any argument which justifies the respondent in attempting behind the company's back, and without its consent, to put an end to the agreement at the time and in the manner which he did. The moment that Mr. St. Jacques became a tenant for the renewed term of the Russell House property, then, for the first time, the second clause took effect, and, in so far as the duration of that extended lease was concerned, the time was a part of the contract between the lighting company and the lessee of the hotel. It rendered certain the duration of the contract which, up till then, had been uncertain as depending upon the contingency as to whether a renewed term would ever be created, and its effect was to give to the lessee an absolute right to have five years' supply of light at contract prices, and to the company, payment therefor for the same period.

If the new lease had itself contained any provisions for shortening the term from five years to a lesser period, or had given an option to the lessee to terminate it at any time, or had stipulated for a forfeiture, of which there is nothing of the kind here, I am not prepared to say that such provisions would not have to be read into the contract, but I repudiate the idea that in circumstances like the present any one party to a contract can annihilate or even prejudice the rights of another party by some secret or voluntary agreement which the former may make with a third party. *Lord Dynevor* v. *Tennant.* (L. R. 13 App. Cas. 279.)

The respondent's counsel endeavoured to make a point under the Statute of Frauds. We disposed of that at the argument, it appearing that there was no change made in the agreement sued upon, either verbally or in writing, the alleged change in the method of computing the price being for convenience only, and legally subject to alteration or to a return at any time to the original manner of ascertaining the monthly consumption.

The appeal, in my judgment, should be allowed with costs in all the courts, and judgment entered for the plaintiff with the usual reference to the Master to ascertain the damages sustained by the plaintiff between the first day of December, 1897, and the thirty-first day of October, 1900. Upon payment of these damages, the Russell House will be entitled to retain possession of the electric fixtures in the pleadings mentioned, and the money paid into court either returned to the defendant or credited upon any judgment which may be recovered against him, as the Master may determine.

GIROUARD, J. (dissenting)—

I agree with the court below. I believe we should give effect to the two clauses, and that we do so by holding that during the first thirty-six months no cancellation of the lease can take place, but that it may be done after by either of the parties.

Appeal allowed with costs.

Solicitors for the Appellants : *MacCracken, Henderson and McDougal.*

Solicitors for the Respondent : *O'Connor, Hogg and Magee.*

[IN THE SUPREME COURT OF CANADA.]

(APPEAL FROM THE COURT OF APPEAL FOR ONTARIO.)

BEFORE SIR HENRY STRONG, C.J., GWYNNE, SEDGWICK, GIROUARD AND DAVIES, J.J.

C. S. HOTCHKISS et al. (Defendants) Appellants

v.

WILLIAM ARTHUR WILSON (Plaintiff) et al. (Defendants) Respondents

Company promoting—Fraud in obtaining stock subscriptions —Liability of directors for acts done by agent for their benefit.

H., who was managing director of an incorporated company, was authorized by his board to secure the services of McK. to solicit stock subscriptions for the company. H. subsequently interviewed W. for that purpose, gave him a prospectus of the company and stated that he himself as well as each of the various directors had subscribed and actually paid for a large amount of stock. McK. also made similar statements to W., who subsequently gave his cheque $1,000 in payment for certain shares. This cheque, endorsed by H. as managing director and by E. as president of the company, was then deposited to the credit of the company, and the proceeds eventually used to pay certain salaries which had been voted by the directors to certain of the promoters as officials of the company. W. having become aware that nothing had ever actually been paid in, brought action to recover the money he had thus paid on the ground that he had been induced to subscribe by false representations regarding the financial standing of the company.

Held, that since E. and the other directors had authorized H. and McK. to act for them in obtaining W.'s subscription, and had received W.'s money, and had derived a profit from the fraud practised upon him, they were liable for the acts of H. and McK.

JUDGMENT OF THE COURT OF APPEAL FOR ONTARIO CONFIRMED.

The defendants (other than the defendant company) were a syndicate formed for the purpose of purchasing a certain patent for advertising boards from the defendant Hotchkiss, and with the object of obtaining incorporation as a joint stock company in order to exploit this patent. Pending the receipt of Letters Patent, the defendants organized themselves into a provisional board of directors, and Hotchkiss was appointed managing director. At a subsequent meeting of the board held in April, 1898, Hotchkiss was authorized "to secure the services of Mr. J. T. McKay and such other persons as may be necessary to solicit stock subscriptions for this and local companies and for advertisements, subject to the approval of the board."

On 10 June, 1898, Hotchkiss saw the plaintiff, gave him a prospectus of the company, and suggested to him that he should subscribe for a number of shares, stating that the defendants other than himself had subscribed and paid for $5,000 worth of stock each, that he himself had paid in $25,000 for stock, that one Willoughby had paid $5,000 for a like purpose, and that there was then standing to the credit of the company in the Toronto branch of the Bank of Nova Scotia the sum of $50,000. The same day the defendant McKay spoke to the plaintiff about subscribing for stock, and made the same statements as had Hotchkiss regarding the affairs of the company, except that he did not mention the name of the bank in which the $50,000 was supposed to be deposited.

On 26 July, 1898, (a few days before the Letters Patent were obtained) Hotchkiss had another interview with the plaintiff, who then (relying, as he swore, upon the statements that $50,000 had actually been paid in cash for shares subscribed for by the directors), took ten shares, and paid therefor $1,000 by cheque payable to the order of the company. This cheque was endorsed by Hotchkiss as managing director, and Ellis as president, and was then deposited to the credit of the company. As a matter of fact nothing had previously been paid in for shares, and all that remained to the credit of the company at its bank was the balance of the money advanced by three of the directors for the expenses of obtaining incorporation. The company received its charter in August, 1898, and the salaries, which it had previously been decided should be given to some of its officers, were then paid, the plaintiff's $1,000 being, in part, used for that purpose.

Subsequently plaintiff learned that no money had, in fact, been paid for the shares subscribed for at the time that he had paid $1,000, and he therefore brought action to recover that amount, alleging that he had been induced to subscribe by false representations regarding the financial position of the company.

At the trial, judgment was given for the plaintiff, Armour, C. J., holding that the defendants Hotchkiss and McKay were acting as the authorized agents of their principals, the other individual defendants, when they made the misrepresentations in question. This judgment was confirmed by the Court of Appeal for Ontario, and the present appeal was taken from the judgment of that court.

11 NOVEMBER, 1901 :—

The judgment of the court was delivered by

SIR HENRY STRONG, C. J. (oral) :—

We do not think that we should withhold our judgment in this case. It is to be regretted that an appeal was taken to this court considering the amount involved, the nature of the questions raised and the unanimity of opinions in the courts below, especially in the Court of Appeal.

I have no hesitation in saying that I am quite prepared to adopt the principle of law laid down by Mr. Justice Lindley (Lindley on Partnership. 6th ed. p. 161), namely, that where false representations have been made by an agent in executing his mandate, though the principal has not directly authorized such representations, yet the rule of *respondeat superior* applies as in other cases, and it is not essential that the principal should have ratified or derived benefit from the act of his agent.

I am not sure that all my learned brothers will concur in this, but I am sure they will agree as to what Mr. Justice Moss finds to be the effect of the evidence, namely, that it is patent from the depositions that the principals, if they did not expressly authorize the statement made by their agents, did receive benefit from it in getting the money sought to be recovered by this action. I cannot do better than read an extract from the judgment of Mr. Justice Moss who says :

" It was essential to the plaintiff's case that he should establish either that the appellants themselves were knowingly guilty of actual misrepresentations, on the faith of which he acted, or that they authorized Hotchkiss and McKay, or one of them, to act for them in obtaining the plaintiff's subscription, or that they received the plaintiff's money or some of it ; or that in some way they derived a profit or benefit from the fraud practised upon the plaintiff. I think upon the testimony the plaintiff has succeeded in establishing the three latter propositions."

For myself I go further than this and say that neither express authority to make the representations, nor subsequent ratification nor participation in the benefits were necessary ingredients to make the appellants liable, though I agree with Mr. Justice Moss in his conclusion from the evidence that the latter element was in fact present here.

The appeal is dismissed with costs.

Editor's Notes :—

The judgment in this case rests upon the well established rule that a principal is liable for the fraudulent act of his agent, acting in the course of his business.

Barwick v. *English Joint Stock Bank* (1867) L. R. 2 Ex. 259.

Blake v. *Albion Life Assurance Society* (1878) 4 C. P. D. 94.

It is not necessary to prove that the fraudulent act was done at the instance or with the privity of the principal.

Mackay v. *Commercial Bank of New Brunswick*, (1874) L. R. 5 P. C. 394

And an action will in like manner lie against a company for the fraud of its agent, acting as such.

Mackay v. *Commercial Bank of New Brunswick*, supra.

But the principal is not liable when his agent, without his command or knowledge, commits a fraudulent act for his own personal benefit, and not for the purpose of advancing the interests of his principal.

Thorne v. *Heard* (1895) App. Cas. 495.

British Mutual Bank v. *Charnwood Forest Ry. Co.* (1887) 18 Q. B. D. 714.

Weir v. *Bell* (1878) 3 Ex. D. 238.

And in such a case it is immaterial whether or not the person to whom (for instance) the fraudulent representation is made, believed that the agent was authorized to make the same.

Richards v. *Bank of Nova Scotia* (1896) 26 S. C. R. 381.

The principal is not liable when the agent is not acting within the scope of his authority. Thus a company is not liable for the fraudulent misrepresentations of its secretary, it not being within the ordinary course of the duties of the secretary of a company to make any representations whatever on its behalf.

Newlands v. *National Employers' Accident Association* (1885), 53 L. T. 242.

Barnett v. *South London Tramways Co.* (1887), 18 Q. B. D. 815.

When the principal is responsible for the wrongful acts of his agent, the liability is a joint and several one with the agent, and either or both may be sued. But if a judgment is obtained in an action taken against the agent alone, it will (even though it remains unsatisfied) be a bar to any action against the principal.

Brinsmead v. *Harrison* (1872) 7 C. P. 547.

APPEAL DISMISSED WITH COSTS.

Solicitors for the Appellants : *Kilmar, Irving and Porter*.

Solicitors for the Respondent Wilson : *McEvoy, Pope and Perrin*.

Solicitors for the Respondents, The Highway Advertising Company of Canada : *Hanna and Burnham*.

[IN THE COURT OF APPEAL FOR ONTARIO.]

BEFORE ARMOUR, C.J.O., OSLER, MACLENNAN AND LISTER, J.A., AND LOUNT, J.

In re ARMY & NAVY CLOTHING CO.

Winding up—Assignee becoming liquidator—Bond for performance of duties—Liability thereunder.

H. was the assignee of the estate of an incorporated company under an assignment made by virtue of the Assignments and Preferences Act (Ontario). Winding-up proceedings were subsequently taken, and H. was then appointed liquidator, and the appellants in this case entered into a bond conditioned on the due performance by H. of his duties of liquidator. H. misappropriated certain monies which were in his hands as assignee at the date of the winding-up order, and which, by the terms of such order, he should have paid over to the liquidator. Held, that those executing the bond were liable for such monies.

Held, further, that the appellants could not now object to the jurisdiction of the court to make the various orders in the winding-up proceedings (which were recited in the bond itself) or to question the validity of the appointment of H as liquidator.

Held, further, that the appellants were entitled to bring this appeal from the order of the Master, fixing the amount of their liability under the bond.

APPEAL DISMISSED WITH COSTS.

The facts are fully set forth in the head note, and in the judgment of Osler, J.A.

6 Nov., 1901.

ARMOUR, C.J.O. :—

The appellants were, in my opinion, entitled to appeal from the report of the Master fixing the amount of their liability under the bond given by them, and consequently this appeal is properly before us for adjudication.

The bond executed by the appellants contained recitals of all the orders made by the Court, and of the appointment of Henderson as permanent liquidator of the property, assets and effects, and the appellants executed the bond as security for the proper performance by Henderson of his duties as such liquidator and cannot now be heard to object to the jurisdiction of the Court to make these orders or to the validity of the appointment of Henderson as such liquidator. The condition of the bond was "that if the said Edward James Henderson, his executors, or administrators, or any of them do and shall obey all lawful orders of the said Court in respect of the winding up of the said company and shall duly account for what he, the said Edward James Henderson, shall receive or become liable to pay as liquidator of the property, estate and effects of the said company, at such period and in such manner as the Court, or the said Master-in-Ordinary shall direct," then the obligation should be void, otherwise to remain in full force and virtue.

The effect of the several orders above referred to and of the appointment of Henderson as permanent liquidator, and the approval of the said bond, was that the property, estate and effects of the said company, theretofore in his hands as assignee of the said company, became the property, estate and effects of the said company in his hands as liquidator, and were property, estate and effects of the said company received by him as such liquidator within the condition of the bond, and which by the terms of the condition he was bound to duly account for at such period and in such manner as the Court, or the said Master-in-Ordinary should direct. *Middleton* v. *Chichester*, L.R. 6, Ch. 152.

I do not think that the mode adopted by him of keeping his bank account, or whether he kept the money realized from the property, estate and effects of the said company in his private account in the bank, or in an account opened in the bank in his name as liquidator, or whether he kept the money in his own possession, at all affected his liability for it as liquidator.

The appeal should, therefore, be dismissed with costs.

OSLER, J.A. :—

The first question is, What is the extent of the appellants' obligation under their bond ?

The bond was given as the security on the appointment of one Henderson as permanent liquidator of the Army & Navy Clothing Co. of Toronto (Limited). He was appointed by order of the 4th April, 1898, subject to his giving security as required by the Act. The bond appears to have been executed on the 7th April, and it was approved by the Master-in-Ordinary on the 13th April, 1898. Henderson had been assignee of the estate of the company under an assignment made in pursuance of the Assignments & Preferences Act of Ontario, and as such had acted in administering the estate, the assets of which had come into his hands. Then proceedings for winding up the company, under the Winding-Up Act of Canada, were taken, the result of which, so far as Henderson and these appellants are concerned, must be taken to be that from the date of the order of the 16th March, 1898, hereafter referred to, the assignment under the Provincial Act was superseded. Henderson's powers as assignee were at an end, and from the time his appointment as liquidator took effect his relation to the estate was in the quality of liquidator only, and the appellants were security for him as such. The terms of their obligation are :—That if Henderson do and shall obey all lawful orders of the Court in respect of the winding up of the company, and shall duly account for *what he shall receive or shall become liable to pay as liquidator* of the property, estate and effects of the company at such period and in such manner as the Court, or the Master-in-Ordinary shall direct, then the obligation shall be void.

Henderson thereafter actually transferred to his account as liquidator in the bank a sum of $7752.31, part of the assets of the estate in his hands, and for this sum, which he afterwards appropriated to his own use, the appellants are undoubtedly liable under their bond, unless some objection other than that which I am now dealing with is entitled to prevail. He had also received as assignee, and had in his hands when his appointment as liquidator took effect, the further sum of $1794 which, if the $1400 afterwards transferred to his account as liquidator on the 28th May, 1898, be not part of it, he never transferred to that account, although he was and still is debtor to the estate in respect of it, and the question is whether under the terms of their bond the appellants are liable in respect of this sum.

The respondents rely upon the order of the Divisional Court made on the 16th March, 1898, which is recited in the bond, by which, among other things, it was ordered that the winding-up of the company should be proceeded with under a former order of the 11th January, 1898, proceedings under which had been stayed until further order. Following this is the further direction that ''the said E. J. Henderson, as assignee for the benefit of creditors of, &c., do forthwith, on the appointment of an interim or permanent liquidator of the said company, deliver over to the interim or permanent liquidator of the said company all the assets and effects, books of accounts, papers and documents of the said company now in his possession, and do account to the liquidator of the company for all the assets and effects which may have come into his possession as assignee of the company.''

Henderson was a party to the action and matter in which this order was made. It was made on notice to him, and, as I have said, is recited in the appellants' bond.

The $1794 in question was actually in his hands as assignee when his appointment as liquidator took effect, and the Master-in-Ordinary, on taking his accounts as such, charged him therewith with the other moneys which he had also misappropriated after they had been transferred to his liquidator's account, and ordered him to pay it over to his successor in the office. The appellants' contention is that Henderson never received this sum as liquidator but always held it as assignee of the estate, and was a mere debtor or defaulter in the latter capacity for whose omissions, debts or defaults the appellants are not liable. With this contention I cannot agree. Whatever merit there might have been in it, if Henderson had been a defaulter in respect of this fund when the appellants' bond took effect, it is devoid of force as applied to the facts. The fund was in existence then and afterwards, though it may have been standing in the bank at Henderson's credit as assignee, or simply at the credit of his private account, and in either case it became his property as liquidator of the estate on the completion of his appointment as such and he was liable as liquidator under the terms of the bond to pay it when ordered to do so. And whatever may have been the account to the credit of which it was standing when he became liquidator, the moment he drew it out of that account he also received it as liquidator within the terms of the bond. It could not be otherwise. His breach of duty in not depositing it to the credit of the liquidator's account could not absolve the defendants or entitle them to say, as they attempt to say, that until he did so he did not receive it as liquidator. Security given on behalf of a liquidator is not of so illusory a character as this contention, if well founded, would make it out to be. The liability of a surety is doubtless not to be extended by implication or construction, but in the present case I think that which is sought to be impressed upon the appellants comes within the very terms of their obligation.

I refer to *Meyers* v. *The United States* (1839), 1 McLean 493 ; *Farrar* v. *United States* (1831), 5 Peters 372 ; *United States* v. *Boyd* (1841), 15 Peters 187.

The remaining objections to the judgment amount only to this, that the Court had no jurisdiction to make the winding-up order so as to affect the administration of the trusts of the assignment. I do not assent to the soundness of this objection, but I think it is not open to the appellants. The orders made stand unreversed, and they entered into their bond on the footing of their being valid orders. And the winding-up proceedings have been carried on by the liquidator on that footing, and the liquidator's appointment was confirmed on the faith of the security offered by the appellants.

I think the appeal was competent, disagreeing with the respondents' contention in that respect, but I think that it must be dismissed with costs.

APPEAL DISMISSED WITH COSTS.

Solicitors for the Appellants : *Laidlaw, Kappelle and Bicknell.*

Solicitors for the Liquidator : *Clute, Macdonald and Mcintosh.*

[IN THE SUPREME COURT OF BRITISH COLUMBIA.]

BEFORE McCOLL, C.J., AND WALKEM AND MARTIN, J.J.

DRYSDALE (Plaintiff) Appellant

v.

THE UNION STEAMSHIP CO. (Defendants) Respondents.

Carriers—Bill of Lading—Time limited for notice of loss— Implied warranty of seaworthiness.

A bill of lading contained certain provisions limiting the liability of the carriers, and concluded with a clause to the effect that the owners would not be liable for any loss or damage to merchandise shipped on the vessel in question unless the claim on account of the same was made within one month from the date of the bill of lading. D's goods were damaged, the injury being occasioned by the unseaworthiness of the vessel, but the demand for compensation was not made within the stipulated period. Held, that the condition as to time in the bill of lading only referred to the other matters and exceptions referred to therein ; and that, as the implied warranty of seaworthiness was both outside and antecedent to the bill of lading, a claim for damages for breach of that warranty was not affected by the provision in the bill of lading that all claims should be made within one month.

Tattersall v. *National Steamship Co. (1884) 12 Q. B. D. 297,* and *Maori King v. Hughes (1895) 65 L. J. Q. B. 168,* followed.

Judgment of IRVING, J., reversed, McCOLL, C. J., dissenting.

Appeal from judgment of IRVING, J., delivered 24th April, 1901. The plaintiff, on 5th June, 1899, shipped on defendants' steamer, The Cutch, six cases of dry goods to be carried from Vancouver to Skagway. The bill of lading contained the following conditions :

" The within goods are shipped and received subject to the following conditions :

" If the consignee is not on hand to receive the goods, package by package as discharged, then the master may deliver them to the wharfinger or other party or person believed by said master to be responsible, and who will take charge of said goods and pay the frieght on the same, or deposit them on the bank of the river, or other usual place for delivering the goods. The responsibility of said master shall cease immediately on the delivery of said goods from the ship's tackles.

" The steamer on which the within goods are carried shall have leave to tow and assist vessels ; to sail with or without pilots ; to tranship to any other steamer or steamers ; to lighter from steamer to steamer or from steamer to shore ; to deliver to other steamers, companies, persons or forwarding agents any of the within goods destined for ports or places at which the vessel on which they are carried does not call. The master and owners shall not be held responsible for any damage or loss resulting from fire at sea, in the river or in port ; accident to or from machinery, boilers or steam, or any other accident or dangers of the seas, rivers, roadsteads, harbors, or of sail or steam navigation of what nature or kind soever.

" It is expressly understood that the master and owners shall not be liable or accountable for weight, leakage, breakage, shrinkage, rust, loss or damage arising from insecurity of package, or damage to cargo by vermin, burning or explosion of articles or freight or otherwise, or loss or damage on account of inaccuracy or omissions in marks or descriptions, effects of climate, or from unavoidable detention or delay, nor for the loss of specie, bullion, bank notes, government notes, bonds or consols, jewellery, or any property of special value, unless shipped under proper title or name and extra freight paid thereon.   ●

" Live stock, trees, shrubbery, and all kinds of perishable property at owner's risk. Oils and all other liquids at owner's risk of leakage, unless caused by improper stowage.

" It is hereby understood that wool in bales, dried hides, butter and egg boxes, and all other packages, must be, each and every package, marked with full address of consignee ; and if NOT so marked it is agreed that the delivery of the full number of packages as within mentioned without regard to quality, shall be deemed a correct delivery, and in full satisfaction of this receipt.

" It is agreed that in settlement of any claim for loss or damage to any of the within mentioned goods, said claim shall be restricted to the cash value of such goods at the port of shipment at the date of shipment.

" It is agreed that the person or party delivering any goods to the said steamer for shipment is authorized to sign the shipping receipt for the shipper.

" On delivery of the goods within enumerated as provided herein, this receipt shall stand cancelled, whether surrendered or not.

" In consideration of the goods being carried by the company at a reduced rate, it is expressly agreed and declared that the shipper waives and abandons any right accorded by Statute or otherwise, to hold the company responsible in any manner for the keeping, or safe or prompt carriage of the goods, and waives and abandons all advantage and benefit accorded by the Statute 37 Vic., c. 25 to the shipper, and himself accepts all responsibility for the safe keeping and carriage of the goods, and agrees to hold the company absolved and discharged from delays, damages, or losses from whatever cause arising including delay, loss or damage arising through from negligence or carelessness, or want of skill of the company's officers, servants, or workmen, but which shall have occurred without the actual fault or privity of the company.

" It is expressly agreed that all claims against the said steamer or her owners for damage to or loss of any of the within merchandise must be presented to the master or owners thereof within one month from date hereof ; and that after one month from date hereof no action, suit or proceeding in any court of justice shall be brought against the said steamer or the owners thereof for any damage to or loss of said merchandise ; and the lapse of said one month shall be deemed a conclusive bar and release of all right to recover against said steamer or the owners hereof for any such damage or loss."

The goods were damaged and plaintiff commenced an action but not within a month. The following is the judgment of

IRVING, J. [who after setting out the facts proceeded :]

The goods were damaged on the voyage by salt water : and I think there can be no reasonable doubt but that the salt water reached the goods by reason of the packing under the plate which covered the manhole in the top of the ballast tank blowing out. Having regard to the condition above set out it seems to me unnecessary to decide the point whether this leakage was unseaworthiness (which the defendants are supposed to warrant) or negligence against which they have provided by other conditions in their bill of lading.

It was argued (1.) that the plaintiffs were outside the bill of lading altogether ; (2) that the words of exemption were not sufficiently clear and explicit ; and (3.) that the bill of lading being in derogation of the provisions of Cap. 82 of the Revised Statutes of Canada could not be invoked, that is to say, that it was contrary to public policy.

With regard to the third point, I think the answer is to be found in the maxim of *cuilibet licet renuntiare jure pro se introducto* and the case of *The Glengoil Steamship Co.* v. *Pilkington* (1897), 28 S.C.R. 146 ; and as to the first and second grounds I can only refer to the language of the condition, that it was expressly agreed that all claims for damages which would include as well those arising from a breach of the fundamental warranty of seaworthiness as those specifically mentioned in the exceptions, should be presented within one month and suit brought thereon within that period. Stringent as this condition is, it must prevail because the parties so agreed. Judgment for defendants with costs.

The plaintiff appealed and the appeal came on for argument at Vancouver on 8th June, 1901, before McCOLL, C. J., WALKEM and MARTIN, J.J.

Cur. adv. vult.

Sir C. H. Tupper, K.C., and *Gilmour,* for Appellant.

Davis, K.C., for Respondent.

7TH NOVEMBER, 1901.

McCOLL, C. J. :—I think the appeal should be dismissed.

WALKEM, J. :—On the 5th of June, 1899, the plaintiff shipped several packages of goods, under a bill of lading of that date, on board the defendant company's steamer Cutch for carriage from Vancouver to Skagway, and thence, by the usual available means, to Dawson, there to be delivered to one Fraser, his agent. On their delivery, the packages were found to be badly damaged by salt water. The plaintiff has, therefore, brought this action to recover his consequent loss, as it was due, as he alleges, to the unseaworthiness of the steamer.

In addition to the ordinary exemptions as to liability for loss that are inserted in bills of lading in favor of shipowners, the bill of lading in this case contains a special stipulation to the effect that the company is not to be liable for any loss unless the claim for it is presented within a month from the date of that document. As a matter of fact, the present claim was not presented within that period.

On behalf of the company, unseaworthiness is denied and the above stipulation pleaded as a bar to the action. Two issues are thus raised—one of fact, and one of law. But unseaworthiness being at the very root of the plaintiff's case, it follows that if, in our opinion, it has not been proved, the legal question need not be considered ; and, *e converso,* if our opinion should be to the contrary.

The case was tried without a jury ; and the court found as a fact " that the goods were damaged on the voyage by salt water," and " that there could be no reasonable doubt but that the salt water reached the goods by reason of the packing under the plate which covered the man-hole in the top of the ballast-tank blowing out." I agree with this finding as far as it goes ; but as it is not a direct finding of unseaworthiness, I must deal with that question and the evidence relating to it.

With respect to unseaworthiness the following extract from Lord Blackburn's judgment in *Steel* v. *State Line Steamship Co.* (1877,), 3 App. Cas. 72, at p. 86, serves, amongst other purposes, to indicate the real issue of fact involved in this case, and, consequently, the evidence applicable to it. It is " quite clear," his Lordship observes, " that where there is a contract to carry goods in a ship, whether that contract is in the shape of a bill of lading, or any other form, there is a duty on the part of the person who furnishes or supplies that ship, or that ship's room, unless something be stipulated which would prevent it, that the ship shall be fit for its purpose. That is generally expressed by saying that it shall be seaworthy ; and I think also in . . . . contracts for sea carriage, that is what is properly called a 'warranty,' not merely that they should do their best to make the ship fit, but that the ship should really be fit." Consequently, the only issue of fact is— Was The Cutch fit, on the 5th of June, 1899, for the purpose for which the plaintiff then engaged room in her ? Hence, much, if not all, of the evidence given at the trial as to antecedent fitness, or efforts to ensure fitness, for instance, in 1898, is irrelevant.

The captain states that the steamer left Vancouver for Skagway on the 5th of June, and had fine weather throughout the voyage. This at once disposes of the suggestion made by another witness that a rough sea, or unusual wash, might have forced the sea-cock, or the tank of the vessel, to leak. After a run of seventeen or eighteen hours, she reached Alert Bay and discharged some cargo, which, it is said, was in good condition. Before leaving the bay, the water ballast-tank was re-filled, by direction of the captain, with salt water from the sea-cock, after which the sea-cock was, apparently, but, as it turned out, not completely, closed, as he states, and as appears by the following entry in the log, on the 6th of June :—" Cargo damaged in afterhold by salt water. Opened Egg Island 11.04. Upon examining into the same, the chief engineer told us that while pumping into the ballast-tank, some sea-weed got into the valve of the sea-cock causing it to leak after it was apparently shut off, and the consequence of which was the ballast-tank overflowed and a large quantity of sea water got into the hold. The pumps were started going, immediately, to clear the hold ;" and, as further evidence shews, were kept going until the steamer reached Skagway.

When the quantity of water was sufficiently reduced to permit of its being done, the leakage in the sea-cock was stopped ; but as to when this happened there is no evidence. From the fact that it was found necessary to keep the pumps going throughout the voyage, it is reasonable to infer that it happened when the steamer was well on her way, or near Skagway. The tank, I might state, could not be reached at any time during the voyage for the purpose of being pumped out, as it lay in the bottom of the after-hold of the ship, and beneath its floor, on which all the cargo was stowed. A correct conception of what is meant by the sea-cock, and of its position and purpose, is necessary to properly appreciate the charge of unseaworthiness. According to the evidence, there is a permanent hole in the hull of the steamer, about four feet below its water-line, large enough to admit of an inflow of salt water sufficient to fill the tank, if needed. This hole is covered on the outside of the hull by an iron grating of half-inch mesh, and is connected inside by a pipe, or tube, with the tank which is near by. In this pipe, the sea-cock, or, as it is termed by some of the witnesses, a "valve," is placed for the purpose, when necessary, of either letting the salt water into the tank, or shutting it off. An every-day example of the principle of its construction is that of the ordinary water tap.

Now, it is beyond question, in view of the hull inspector's statement that the express purpose of the grating was " to keep any dirt out—sea-weed, or anything else," that, as sea-weed entered the pipe and clogged the sea-cock, thereby causing it to leak, the grating was radically defective inasmuch as its half-inch mesh was, obviously, too large for its purpose. Hence, the inspector's opinion to the contrary, when certifying, in 1898, that the ship was, in effect, seaworthy is of no value on this point. The leak was a serious one, for, according to the captain's evidence and the log, it resulted in the overflowing of the tank and the mischievous and, naturally, incursive flow of " a large quantity of water into the hold." The correctness of the statements of some of the witnesses to the effect that even if the sea-cock had leaked no damage could have been done if the tank were full, or partially so, must be admitted, as, at best, the water in the tank would naturally have neutralized, in proportion to its quantity, the pressure of the in-coming leak. But this evidence was given on the assumption that the tank itself was sound, which was not the case. I, therefore, consider that the defective character of the grating is, in itself, clear evidence of unseaworthiness.

I shall now deal with the condition of the tank, as the damage to the goods is mainly attributed to its having been materially defective from the outset. From the evidence it appears that it is on the bottom of the ship in the after-hold. It conforms to the shape of the ship, and is fourteen feet wide forward, and thence tapers aft for about sixteen feet to a point. It is three feet deep, and of twenty-five or thirty tons capacity. It is made of steel, and is flat on the top. In the top there is an oval man-hole twelve by sixteen inches, sufficiently large to admit of a man passing through it. The cover of the man-hole is a flat plate of the same oval shape, but two inches wider in circumference. Without going into further details, the plate is fastened down by stud-bolts, that is to say, by bolts four and a half or five inches long, with screw threads at each end. These bolts, which are eight or ten in number, pass through the holes in the plate and corresponding holes in the top of the tank, and are secured inside the tank by being " headed," and above the covering plate by ordinary nuts. Between the plate and the top of the tank, an endless oval piece of rubber, about two inches broad and three-sixteenths of an inch thick, is placed. This is called a rubber joint. Before the rubber is placed in its position, holes are punched in it to correspond with the holes in the plate and top of the tank. It is then slipped down on the stud-bolts before the plate is placed over it; and the plate is then tightened to the requisite degree by the upper nuts on the bolts. When the tank was examined in Skagway it was found that a portion of this rubber had been " blown out ;" in other words, the rubber was not sufficiently strong to resist the upward pressure of the sea water in the tank. There is evidence to the effect that the best quality of rubber available was selected when the vessel was " re-modelled " in June, 1898; but there is also evidence, for instance, of Mr. Hardie, a witness called for the defence, to the effect that the quality, or durability, of such rubber can only be ascertained by using it, and that what may appear to be a good article as sent out by the manufacturer may turn out to be otherwise. This is common sense. Either he, or another witness, states that rubber is liable to become hard and brittle after more or less use, and that in such case it becomes useless. There is a diversity of opinion as to the durability of rubber, some witnesses stating that it ought to last at least two years, while others take a different view of it, but this is neither here nor there in view of the actual fact that the rubber in question was forced away from the stud-holes under a pressure of salt water which, it is almost needless to say, it was expected to more than withstand. A witness, who was employed about two years and a half in the engine room of the Empress of India, a steamship of about 6000 tons, states that while so employed he never knew of any trouble having occurred with respect to the tanks, which were from 70 to 100 tons capacity, as the man-holes and sea-cocks were well looked after. It would appear that the rubber in question was never examined from the time it was placed in position, in June, 1898, until it was blown out twelve months afterwards. It seems to be a rule that before a steamship leaves port her tank, if she has one, must be carefully examined. In this case, the examination was farcical, for the second mate states, with respect to his examination of the man-hole of the tank, that he lifted the hatch above it and took a "glance" at it, and this, to my mind, is all that he actually did. He says he "kicked" some of the nuts to see if they moved, and on further cross-examination is not sure how many he kicked, or whether he kicked any of them. A reference to his evidence will shew that from first to last it is, to say the least of it, most discreditable; for, although he was present at the examination of the tank at Skagway, his memory is a blank with respect to its condition: and it is also a blank in respect to any facts that could possibly militate against his employers' interests. At all events, the fact remains that the rubber in question was blown out by an ordinary pressure of the sea-water in the tank; hence, it matters not whether the fresh water tests which were applied to the tank before the steamer left Vancouver were satisfactory or not. This disposes of a lengthy discussion before us as to the effect of the difference between the static pressure of fresh and salt water with different heads or levels. The fact that the tank was inaccessible from the time the steamer started until she reached Skagway, owing to the stowage of the cargo above it, tends to shew that the cover of the man-hole could not have been tampered with at any time during the voyage, and, consequently, that it was defective when the steamer sailed. On this ground, as well as on the former ground with relation to the grating, I am of the opinion that the ship was unseaworthy. In other words, the defect in the grating, as well as in the rubber joint in the man-hole, contributed, so to speak, to the mischief complained of.

Now, the implied warranty of seaworthiness was, as Lord Blackburn points out in the case I have referred to, a warranty, for instance, in the case of The Cutch, that she was seaworthy, or, in other words, not a " rotten ' ship when the plaintiff engaged room in her. This engagement was, obviously, a matter antecedent to the delivery and stowage of the plaintiff's goods on board, and also to the signing of the bill of lading, which, with its specific exemptions, constituted the contract between the parties. It follows that as there is no exemption, as might have been the case, as to unseaworthiness, the plaintiff's charge of unseaworthiness is in no way affected by the terms of the bill of lading, as the special stipulation at the end of it, to which I have referred, can only be read, as having relation to the previous matters contained in it. It seems to me that the decision in the case of *Tattersall* v. *National Steamship Co.* (1884), 12 Q.B.D. 297, puts an end to discussion on this point. In that case there was a contract for the carriage of cattle from London to New York to the effect that the shippers should, amongst other things, be in no way responsible " for escape, disease or mortality, and that, under no circumstances, should they be liable for more than five pounds a head." Several of the animals contracted a foot and mouth disease owing to the uncleanly condition of the ship before she started, and died from the effects of it ; and it was held that the provision in the bill of lading limiting the defendants' liability to £5 a head did not apply to the implied warranty of seaworthiness, as the warranty was outside of the bill of lading, and antecedent to it.

In view of this decision, let us suppose that the special stipulation in the last clause of The Cutch's bill of lading were worded in the more comprehensive language of the stipulation in the *Tattersall* case, that is to say, that " under no circumstances " should the defendant company be liable ; could the result have differed from the opinion expressed on the point in that case ? There is, therefore, only one inference to be drawn from it, and that is, that the defendant company, notwithstanding the special stipulation I have referred to, is legally liable for the damage that occurred.

As the question of damages was not dealt with by the Court below, the case would, necessarily, have to be sent for a new trial; but, as counsel for both parties have agreed that, in the event of our finding that the steamship was unseaworthy, the amount of damages should be $1,476.18, judgment is to be entered for that amount, and the costs of this action and of this appeal.

MARTIN, J. :—

It is established by the evidence that the sea water flooded the ship by coming into the ballast-tank through a leaky sea-cock in the bottom of the ship, and, because of the man-hole of the tank not being properly secured (packed) escaped from the ballast-tank into the hold. The inflow of water was kept down by pumping and the sea-cock was finally properly closed, but in the meantime the water could not be prevented from flowing into the hold from the tank since it was impossible to get at the man-hole because of the cargo.

Now this was something not "easily curable by those on board," to quote the language of Lord Lindley in *Ajum Goolam Hossen & Co.* v. *Union Marine Insurance Co.* (1901), A.C. 362 at p. 371, a case reported since the argument, and after considering the evidence in the manner directed by that case, I am satisfied as a matter of fact that The Cutch was unseaworthy when she sailed.

The question of law then arises—is the last exception in the bill of lading a bar to this action?

It is admitted that liability for unseaworthiness may be excepted in a bill of lading—an example of a partial exception will be found in *The Cargo ex Laertes* (1887), 12 P.D. 187.

It is contended by the appellant's counsel that this exception must be by express terms, and the respondents' counsel takes the ground that if that be the case the question of whether there has been such an exception becomes one of construction of the language used in the bill of lading, and contends that the exception here is wide enough to cover everything.

It will be noted that this exception is one as to time, and it is urged that not the liability itself but the result of it is what is excepted, and that after the loss has occurred and the liability has arisen from such loss, it does not matter how that liability arose—whether by negligence after sailing or unseaworthiness on or before sailing—that the two sources of liability are merged and no cause of action thereon can be enforced after the expiration of the time limit. It is admitted that there is an implied warranty of seaworthiness, but it is contended that the appellant cannot be in a better position than if there were an express exception of unseaworthiness, and it is submitted that if there were such an exception nevertheless the time limit is a bar, because the clause invoked deals only with what results from that liability which has arisen.

The contention is certainly ingenious and plausible, and our attention has been called to an expression used by Lord Justice Collins in *Queensland National Bank* v. *Peninsula and Oriental Steam Navigation Co.* (1898), 1 Q.B. 567 at p. 571, wherein he said that in that case there was no "magic" in the word "unseaworthiness." But nevertheless it is clear from the judgments in *Steel* v. *State Line Steamship Co.* (1877), 3 App. Cas. 72, 4 R.C.., 717 ; *The Cargo ex Laertes, supra ; Gilroy, Sons & Co.* v. *Price & Co.* (1893), A.C. 56 ; *Maori King* v. *Hughes* (1895), 65 L.J., Q.B. 168, and others, that in those cases at least there is something akin to "magic" in the sense that term is used by the Lord Justice, because, as Lord Justice Smith says in *The Maori King*, p. 172, different considerations apply to a contract to carry goods by sea from those which apply to one to carry by land. What we have to do, as the last mentioned learned Judge also said in *Tattersall* v. *National Steamship Co.* (1884), 12 Q.B.D. 297 at p. 301, is to ascertain "the true meaning of a very special bill of lading ; " and how can that true meaning be ascertained unless the question of seaworthiness was fairly presented to the minds of the consignor and owner ?

If this were an ordinary contract, it might very well be that, because the penultimate clause takes away any right of action for loss or damage by the shipowners' officers and servants occurring without said owners' actual fault, therefore the last clause must apply to liability of all other kinds, otherwise the clause itself would have nothing to take effect on. But that does not dispose of the matter because the further question arises—admitting the exceptions, to what

period of time do they relate?   The respondent contends to
"all times," just as it was similarly contended in *Tattersall's*
case to apply to all "circumstances."   After a full consideration of this bill of lading, and of the cases cited, I
have come to the conclusion that Lord Justice Smith
supplies the answer in *The Maori King* at p. 172:

"In my opinion, there is the implied warranty, which
I have mentioned, and I think that the exceptions all apply
after the ship sets sail.   They are exceptions during the
voyage, when, if any of the matters mentioned take place,
the shipowner is not to be liable.   But if there is, as I think
there is, an implied warranty that the machinery shall be
fit for its purpose when the ship sets sail, then the exceptions do not apply, and are no answer to a claim by the
owner of the goods founded on the original unfitness of the
machinery"—in the present case—unseaworthiness.

Taking this view, the case of *Moore* v. *Harris* (1876), 1
App. Cas. 318, particularly relied on by the respondent, does
not afford us much assistance, though it is otherwise a decision of much commercial value.   In my opinion the appeal
should be allowed with costs.

Appeal allowed, McColl, C.J., dissenting.

Solicitors for the Appellants: *Tupper, Peters & Gilmour.*

Solicitors for the Respondents: *Davis, Marshall &
Macneill.*

Editor's Notes :—

There is always the implied warranty on the part of the
owner that his ship is seaworthy,—that it is in a proper
condition to take the cargo in question on the voyage contracted for.

Steel v. *State Line Steamship Co.* (1877) 3 A. C. 72.

Thus where the cargo is one of frozen meat there is an
implied warranty that the refrigerators are capable of doing
what will reasonably be required.

The Maori King v. *Hughes*, (1895) 2 Q. B. 550.   See
also, *Tattersall* v. *National Steamship Co.* (1884) 12
Q. B. D., 297.

Moreover this implied warranty of seaworthiness is an absolute warranty, and therefore the owner is liable if the ship is not seaworthy at the commencement of the voyage, even if he has done his best to make her so, and the defect is latent.

The Glenfruin (1885) 10 P.D. 103.

And a clause in the bill of lading excepting the owner from liability for "defects latent on beginning the voyage or otherwise" does not relieve him from liability for a defect patent to himself at the commencement of the voyage.

Cargo Waikato v. *New Zealand Shipping Co.* (1899) 1 Q. B. 56.

And when the voyage is in stages the implied warranty is that the ship shall be seaworthy at the commencement of each stage.

Thin v. *Richards & Co.* (1892) 2 Q. B. 41.

And this warranty, in such a case, includes a condition that at the commencement of each stage of the voyage the vessel shall be supplied with the amount of coal necessary for the completion of that stage.

The Vortigern (1899) 80 L. T. 382.

But after the commencement of the voyage the implied warranty does not extend to latent defects.

The Rona (1884) 51 L. T. 28.

In the American case of *Bowring* v. *Thebaud*, 56 Federal Rep. 520, it was held that an exception in a bill of lading as to the perils of the sea and navigation did not affect the owner's liability for damages caused by a breach of the implied warranty of seaworthiness.

[IN THE COURT OF KING'S BENCH FOR MANITOBA].

BEFORE KILLAM, C.J.

THE GLOBE SAVINGS AND LOAN COMPANY

v.

THE EMPLOYERS' LIABILITY ASSURANCE CORPORATION.

Policy of guarantee insurance— Condition that insured should furnish proof of loss satisfactory to insurer—Expense of insured (the employer) prosecuting employee at request of insurer.

Where a condition in a policy of guarantee insurance required the employers to give the insurers immediate notice in writing of the discovery of any fraud on the part of the employee, and the employers did immediately communicate such information to the insurers, but did not give any formal notice of same, and the insurers then took steps themselves to find out the exact facts, it was held that the insurers had thereby waived their right to the strict performance of this condition.

Held, further, that a condition requiring the furnishing of proof of loss to the satisfaction of the insurers did not compel the employers to establish to the satisfaction of the insurers themselves their absolute liability under the policy.

Where in the application for the policy the insured had stated that the pass-books and bank-books in which the employee made entries would be checked by the head office every month, it was held that the insurers had a right to rely upon such statements, and that if the course thus indicated was not in fact followed, the insurers would, on equitable grounds, thereby be discharged from liability,— apart altogether from the question whether or not the incorporation of the application in the policy effected a warranty that the employers would have such examination made.

When the informal communication of loss was made, the insurers, under a term in the policy, required the employers to prosecute the employee. The employee was convicted for various offences ; some of which were committed after the first communication by the insured to the insurers. Held, that independently of the condition in the policy, the insurers were bound to reimburse the employers for all reasonable expenses incurred in connection with the prosecution of the employee for fraudulent acts done prior to the date when the insured first gave the insurers information of the loss.

ARGUED: 10th November, 1900.

DECIDED: 24th April, 1901.

The facts are fully set forth in the judgment.

Action upon a guarantee policy by which the defendants engaged, subject to certain conditions, to reimburse the plaintiffs for any pecuniary loss, to the amount of $3,000, sustained by the plaintiffs by any fraud or dishonesty of one Young, a local agent of the plaintiffs, which should amount to larceny or embezzlement. The main defences were that some of the conditions precedent to the liability of the defendants had not been fulfilled, or were not proved to have been fulfilled, and that by certain acts and omissions on the part of the plaintiffs, or their officers, the policy became void as against the defendants.

KILLAM, C. J. :—

This is an action upon a guarantee policy of the Employers' Liability Assurance Corporation (Limited), to which I shall refer as "the corporation," agreeing, subject to certain conditions, to reimburse the Globe Savings and Loan Company, of which I shall speak as "the company," for any pecuniary loss to the amount of $3,000, sustained by the company by the fraud or dishonesty of one Young as local agent of the company at Winnipeg, which should amount to embezzlement or larceny.

The policy was put in evidence without proof and without objection ; it has been treated throughout the trial as a valid agreement binding, according to its terms, upon the corporation, and I assume it to be so. It is upon a printed form which I think I am justified in inferring to have been furnished by the corporation. The printed form sets out that the corporation has caused the agreement to be signed by the Canadian Manager and Attorney, acting under power of attorney, and purports to be signed by " F. Stancliffe, Manager and Attorney for Canada," and by "C. W. I. Woodland, Chief Agent for Ontario." The latter description appears not to have formed part of the original form, but to have been stamped upon it subsequently, and one can hardly infer from it any particular authority in Mr. Woodland or any recognition of him by the corporation in any capacity. On the face and on the back of the policy F. Stancliffe's name is given as that of the Manager and Attorney for Canada. It is shown that, during the period of the events affecting this action, he acted as such manager for Canada, and his signature to the policy is proved. There is no evidence of the contents of the power of attorney appointing him.

The principal office of the corporation is in London, England. The principal office for Canada is in Montreal, in the province of Quebec. Mr. Woodland acted as agent of the corporation in Toronto, in the province of Ontario, but the extent of his powers and authority does not appear.

Young was engaged as agent of the company at Winnipeg, in this province, in March or April, 1896. He was formally appointed by a written document, dated the 22nd April, 1896. The head office of the company is at Toronto, in the province of Ontario, and the general manager of the company is Mr. Day, who, prior to Young's appointment, had been the company's agent in Winnipeg, where Young had been in some way associated with him in the real estate business. As local agent of the company, it was Young's duty, *inter alia*, to collect moneys payable to the company upon mortgages, taxes and insurance premiums unpaid by mortgagors, rents or purchase money of property mortgaged to the company and leased or sold by it, and instalments payable by shareholders of the company upon its capital stock, and to deposit such moneys to the company's credit in a local bank. He did collect large sums, and is clearly shown to have committed in reference thereto acts of fraud and dishonesty amounting to embezzlement or larceny. There is *prima facie* evidence that the company sustained loss thereby.

The main defences are that some of the conditions precedent to the liability of the corporation were not fulfilled, or were not proved to have been fulfilled ; and that facts existed under which the policy became void as against the corporation.

One condition precedent was that "on the discovery of such fraud or dishonesty the employer shall immediately give notice thereof in writing to the corporation at its chief office in Montreal, stating the number of policy, cause, nature and extent of loss, and the address, if known, of the employed."

For the company it is claimed that the first discovery on its part of any act of fraud or dishonesty on the part of Young arose out of information acquired by Day on the 9th February, 1898, that Young had not made a satisfactory adjustment of his accounts for the previous month. This information he gave to Woodland verbally on the 10th

February, and by letter dated 11th February. Woodland transmitted it to Stancliffe by letter dated 12th February, giving the name of Young and the number of policy. Apparently no formal notice, fully complying with the condition, was ever sent by the company to the head office of the corporation at Montreal.

It is evident that the company had not the information which would enable it to give such a notice at once upon making the initial discovery. It could not be aware of the cause, nature or extent of the loss without considerable investigation. The parties must be taken to have contemplated the probability of such a case, and the word "immediately" must be construed accordingly. Correspondence ensued. A statement of sums claimed to have been appropriated by Young and the names of parties from whom various of these sums were said to have been collected was forwarded by the company to the Montreal office of the corporation. Agents and solicitors of the corporation investigated the books and papers of the company and asked for and obtained various proofs. The corporation did get immediate notice of the fact of loss, and was evidently satisfied to waive exact compliance with the condition as to notice, obtaining the information in these various ways. I think that I may properly infer that the chief officer of the corporation in Canada, in charge of the office where the notice was to be given, had power to waive, and that he did waive, any further performance of the condition.

The question of the fulfilment of the conditions as to proof of the claim is one of greater difficulty. The main provision is that the employer is to "furnish his claim, with such full particulars thereof as shall prove to the satisfaction of the corporation the cause, nature and extent of the loss he has sustained and the correctness of his claim." To this is added the following clause :—

"On condition, also, that the particulars furnished by the employer in proof of his claim shall include all reasonable verification of the statements made in his written proposal or statement above mentioned, and of the compliance therewith, and shall be all or any of them verified by affidavits duly certified if required by the corporation."

Now, the onus is certainly upon the company to show performance of these conditions. But it must be borne

in mind that the language is that of the corporation particularly, and that, where the guarantor has taken up a
hostile attitude, the onus is a very heavy one.   The conditions should be construed as strictly as their language
reasonably permits, and the court must be very astute to
draw inferences in favor of a party who has to prove the
opinion of his opponent under such circumstances.

As early as was reasonably possible the company did
furnish its claim, with considerable details.   After some
correspondence on the subject, in which the burden of doing
so was thrown upon the company, the latter procured the
prosecution of Young to conviction for the theft of moneys
collected and appropriated by him in the course of his employment.   Agents and solicitors of the corporation were
given the opportunity to examine the books, accounts and
other records of the company, and they made requisitions
for proof upon certain points.   The evidence was there to
satisfy them, and I consider that I may properly infer from
the circumstances and the requisitions made that they were
satisfied that the cause of the loss was Young's wrongful
and fraudulent appropriation of the moneys of the company, and that the nature of the loss was a loss of money
collected by the company's agent for it.   As to the extent
of loss, from the fact that no further proof was asked upon
this point I infer that they were satisfied of the extent of
the loss.   And I infer that they were satisfied of the correctness of the claim in the sense that they were satisfied
that the company had sustained loss by the fraud and dishonesty of Young in the course of the employment in
which the corporation was guarantor for him and amounting
to embezzlement.

There is in the policy a condition that, if any difference
shall arise in the adjustment of a loss, the amount to be
paid by the corporation shall be ascertained by arbitration.
This indicates that there can be a liability under the policy
without the correctness of the claim in amount being established to the satisfaction of the corporation otherwise than
by the award of arbitrators.   The parties have agreed to
waive the condition as to arbitration and to have the question of the amount of liability (if any) determined by the
Court.   This involves a concession of the right of action
without proof that the corporation was satisfied of the
correctness of the claim in respect of amount.

It does not appear to me that the condition should be so construed as to require the employer to establish to the satisfaction of the guarantor the absolute liability of the latter and the absence of any defence. This would be to make the guarantor almost an absolute judge in his own cause on all points, a position which cannot be considered as intended to any greater extent than the language of the contract distinctly calls for.

In pursuance of some arrangement or understanding between Woodland and a former manager of the plaintiff company, Day applied to Woodland, after Young's appointment, for a policy of guaranty. The result was the filling up of a printed form of the defendant corporation, styled "Employer's Proposal." This began with a communication, dated April 28th, 1896, addressed in the name of Stancliffe to Day as manager of the Globe Company, as follows :—

"Mr. Frederick S. Young, of Winnipeg, having applied to this corporation for a guarantee in your favor of $3,000, I have to request that you will be good enough to reply as fully as possible to the questions below, as your answers and the declaration appended will form the basis of the contract between you and the corporation."

Then followed a series of questions, answers to which were filled up in Day's office by Woodland upon information from Day. At the bottom was the following :—

"I declare that the above statements are true and I consent that the above replies shall be taken as the basis of the contract between us and the above named corporation," which was signed "Globe Savings & Loan Co., E. W. Day, Man.," with the date "28, 4, '96."

Among the questions and answers were the following :—

"2. Is the applicant at present in your employment, and, if so, how long and in what capacity have you employed him?" Ans. "Just engaged as agent."

"3. Have you always been satisfied with his conduct and honesty, and have his accounts always been correct?" Ans. "Yes, so far as I know."

"7. With respect to the duties and responsibilities of the applicant, please reply as fully as possible to the following questions :—

"(c.) What is the largest sum which he will have in his hands at any one time, and for how long?" Ans. "$300 to $1,000, two or three days."

"(d.) Is he required to give printed receipts from a book with counterfoil? If so, how often will the counterfoils be examined and checked?" Ans. "Receipt pass book when money is paid him, checked monthly by head office list."

"(e.) How often will you require him to render an account of cash received and pay the same to you?" Ans. "Monthly."

"(f.) Are moneys to be paid into the bank by applicant? If so, how often will the bank book be inspected and checked?" Ans. "Yes. Monthly by head office."

"(g.) How often will you balance his cash accounts, and how will you check their accuracy? Please explain fully." Ans. "Monthly by office records."

"(h.) Will the balance in his hands, if any, be counted and paid over, or how dealt with?" Ans. "No balance."

"14. Are you aware of any reason why this guarantee for applicant's honesty should not be granted?" Ans. "No."

This is evidently the employer's "written proposal or statement" referred to in the second condition respecting proofs and in the policy generally.

The policy is expressed in its body to have been granted in consideration of a certain payment of money and "of the statements, representations and agreements made by the employer in his written proposal or statement which is hereby made a part of this agreement."

One of the conditions of the policy is as follows: "And this agreement is entered into on the further condition that, if during the continuance of this agreement . . . . any change shall be made in the said employment which shall have the effect of making the actual facts differ from the written proposal or statement hereinbefore referred to, in any respect, without notice thereof being given to the corporation at its chief office in Montreal, and the consent and approval, in writing, of the Canadian manager and attorney obtained thereto, or if any suppression, mis-statement or material omission shall have been made by the employer in his proposal, or at any other time whatever, of any fact affecting the risk of the corporation, or in any claim, made under this agreement, or if the employer has entrusted, or shall continue to entrust, the employed with money, securities, or other evidences of value, after having discovered any act of dishonesty or fraud, this agreement shall be null and void, and all premiums paid thereon forfeited to the corporation.''

It would seem convenient to discuss somewhat the effect of the "proposal" and the interpretation of the other provisions of the policy relating thereto in connection with the condition requiring certain proofs with reference to it.

In the absence of special stipulations or special circumstances, the following principles are applied in equity to contracts of suretyship or guarantee for the honesty of an employee :—

Misrepresentation by the employer of material facts inducing the contract entitles the surety to avoid the contract ; but mere non-communication of fact, prior to the making of the contract. does not vitiate it unless occurring under such circumstances as to be fraudulent towards the surety : *Hamilton* v. *Watson*, 12 Cl. & F. 109 ; *North British Insurance Co.* v. *Lloyd*, 10 Ex. 523 ; *Owen* v. *Homan*, 3 Mac. & G. 378, 4. H. L. C. 997 ; *Blest* v. *Brown*, 4 DeG. F. & J. 367 ; *Greenfield* v. *Edwards*, 11 L. T. 663. Any alteration, without the surety's consent, of the contract or terms of employment, affecting materially the situation of the surety, discharges him : *McTaggart* v. *Watson*, 3 Cl. & F. 525 ; *Watts* v. *Shuttleworth*, 5 H. & N. 235, 7 H. & N. 353 ; *Calvert* v. *London Docks Co.*, 2 Keen, 638 ; *Owen* v. *Homan, supra ; Small* v. *Currie*, 23 L. J., Ch. 746. *Blest* v. *Brown, supra.*

Where the contract of suretyship is entered into in consideration of an agreement by the employer with the surety to perform some act material to the protection of the surety, performance of this agreement is a condition of the

liability of the surety: *Watts* v. *Shuttleworth, supra ;
Watson* v. *Alcock*, 22 L. J. Ch. 858 ; *Lawrence* v. *Walmsley,*
12 C. B., N. S. 799.

Otherwise, the mere passive inactivity of the employer,
his neglect to examine or check the employee's accounts or
to enforce payment by him, does not discharge the surety ;
there must be some positive act done by the employer to the
prejudice of the surety, or such degree of negligence as to
imply connivance and amount to fraud : *McTaggart* v.
Watson, 3 Cl. & F. 525 ; *Creighton* v. *Rankin*, 7 Cl. & F.
325 ; *Dawson* v. *Lawes*, Kay, 280 ; *Black* v. *The Ottoman
Bank*, 15 Moore P. C. 472.

Benham v. *The United Guarantee and Life Ass. Co.*
7 Ex. 744, was an action at law upon a policy of guarantee
in favor of the treasurer of a literary institute, agreeing to
reimburse the treasurer for any loss to be sustained through
want of honesty of the secretary of the institute. The
declaration alleged that the policy recited that, as a basis of
the contract of guarantee, the plaintiff had lodged at the
defendant's office a certain statement or document in writing,
described as Employer's Guarantee Proposal, containing,
among other things, a declaration, signed by the plaintiff,
of the truth of the answers thereby given to the
questions therein contained, and that the policy witnessed
that, relying on the truth of the declaration contained in
said statement or document, the defendants agreed, &c. It
was also alleged that, by the terms of the policy, it was to be
subject to the rules of the company, one of which was that
" Any *fraudulent* mistatement or suppression in any
declaration in consequence of which a policy of guarantee is
granted by the company renders such policy void from the
beginning." One of the questions was, " The checks which
will be used to secure accuracy in his accounts, and when
and how often will they be balanced and closed?" The
answer was, "Examined by finance committee every fort-
night." The declaration alleged the truth of all the
answers. There was a plea setting up the answer which I
have stated, and alleging that the finance committee had
neglected for twenty-six fortnights to examine the accounts.
On demurrer, the plea was held bad. By analogy to statements on which policies of insurance are issued, the Court
considered that the answers in such a collateral document
were representations and not warranties.

In *Towle* v. *The National Guardian Assurance Society*, 3 Giff. 42, 30 L. J, Ch. 900, a policy of guarantee for a collector of taxes had been issued after another officer of the employing body had stated, in answer to questions proposed by the company, that the largest sum to be held by the collector would be from £100 to £200 not longer than a week, and that the collector's accounts were checked weekly by the surveyor of taxes and the balance then agreed on would be paid over. The policy contained a condition that misrepresentation, whether from false statement or suppression of truth or any other cause, in consequence of which the policy was granted, would render the policy void from the beginning.

Sir John Stuart, V. C., held that the answers were merely representations by a third party, and not warranties, and, considering them as given *bona fide*, and to indicate merely the intention when they were given, he held the policy binding. On appeal, Sir J. L. Knight Bruce, L. J., considered the policy void, both because the answers were not true when made and also because the course of business indicated by them was subsequently disregarded. Sir George Turner, L. J., agreed with him as to the answers being untrue, but expressed no opinon as to the effect of the neglect to comply with them subsequently.

In the case of *The Harbour Commissioners of Montreal* v. *The Guarantee Co. of North America*, 22 S. C. R. 542, it was held that the neglect of the employing body to check the accounts of the employee as indicated in the answers to preliminary questions discharged the surety from liability. It appears more particularly from the report of the case in the lower Court, Q. R. 2 Q. B. 6, that the policies were subject to special conditions requiring the business to be conducted as the answers indicated.

The present case differs from all of these. In *Benham* v. *The United, etc., Co.*, there was merely a demurrer to a plea at law. No equitable principle was involved. The court was oppressed by the idea that to hold that the answers amounted to warranties would require the application of the doctrine of the insurance cases, under which the warranties must be strictly and absolutely complied with. The company's rule, incorporated in the policy, applied, in its terms, to a fraudulent mis-statement or suppression only. Having to ascertain the intention of the parties—and not to apply any equitable principles arising out of their relations—the Court might well hold as it did.

In *Towle* v. *The National, etc., Society*, Sir John Stuart followed the Benham case in holding the answers to be representations, and not warranties. He considered them to be but representations made by a third party, and not by the employers ; they were, therefore, in his view, not a part of the contract or of the consideration.

On the other hand, the *Montreal Harbour Commissioners'* case turned on express provisions not found in the policy now in question. Here the proposal was signed in the name of the company by its manager. In accepting and suing upon the policy, the company acknowledges the manager's authority to make the proposal for it. The policy was granted in consideration, partly, of the statements, representations and agreements contained in the proposal, which was declared to be a part of the agreement.

The questions and answers may be divided into three classes, as relating to (1) Existing facts, (2) Young's future duties, (3) Company's future course.

Mis-statements and omissions of existing facts are specifically dealt with in an express condition. So, also, is a change of employment having the effect of making the actual facts differ from the written proposal. It may be possible to treat the expression "change of employment" as covering a change in the duties of the employee, not involving his employment in a different capacity or an alteration in his contract with the company. Even so, the company cannot be treated as having contracted for his strict performance of his duties. The utmost obligation that could be laid upon the company, whether by virtue of contract or in equity, would be that it should not expressly or by tacit concurrence assent to an alteration in the duties set out in the proposal. I doubt if even knowledge and passive endurance of his breach of those duties, not evidencing such concurrence therein as to effect an alteration and not amounting to notice of an act of fraud or dishonesty, would relieve the surety.

But when we come to the course indicated as that to be followed by the company, it seems to me to be but an

inadequate protection of the surety if the court holds that
the proposal indicated only the intentions of the company
and its officers at the time of making the proposal. Whether
we are or are not to construe the incorporation of the
proposal in the policy as constituting a warranty by the
company that it will adhere to the course indicated by the
answers, it appears to me, that, upon principles of equity,
the surety should be considered as discharged by a departure
from that course materially contributing to a loss insured
against. Such a case would seem to come within the
principle of *Lawrence* v. *Walmesley*, 12 C. B. N. S. 799. A
failure to use the checks and safeguards set out as intended
to be used would seem as injurious as parting with a more
definite security. I am strengthened in this opinion by the
view which Lord Justice Knight Bruce took of *Towle* v.
The National, etc., Society.

Having indicated these opinions, I turn back to the
second condition respecting proofs of loss. That required
" all reasonable verification of the statements " in the proposal and of " the compliance therewith." The particulars
in proof of loss were to include such verification, and were
to be " verified by affidavit if required by the corporation."
Several questions seem to arise upon the interpretation of
this provision. It appears to me that the latter portion,
" if required by the corporation," relates only to the affidavit. Some verification of the statements in the proposal
and of the compliance therewith is absolutely required.

Then there is a question whether the second condition
as to proofs is separate or is a modification of the first, so
as to require that specific evidence as part of the evidence
of the " cause " of the loss or of the " correctness of the
claim." This is a material question since the latter construction would require not only such verification as the
court considers reasonable, but such as satisfies the corporation.

I incline to the view that it should be considered as
separate and independent, requiring something additional.
It is to be " all reasonable verification ; " that is all that it
is in fact reasonable to require. Proof to the satisfaction
of the corporation should not be exacted unless clearly
stipulated for. Where the construction is doubtful, it
should be against the alternative requiring such proof.

Something more than proof of facts and intention exist-ing when the proposal was made is necessary. "Com-pliance therewith" must mean subsequent compliance with the indicated future course. What is meant by "the com-pliance therewith?" Is it that the employer must prove that there has been in fact compliance in every respect? Or must he prove merely to what extent there has been actual compliance? I incline to the latter view. It cannot be that the employer must have proved, in order to recover on the policy, that the employee has complied in all respects with the course indicated as that to be followed by him, when his departure from that course may be a part of the very acts of fraud or dishonesty sued for, or the means whereby it has been committed or concealed. And it does not seem that one can divide up the proposal and prove only compliance by the employer.

After an examination of the books and papers of the company, the solicitors for the corporation wrote to Mr. Day for further proofs. They asked for "your statutory decla-ration verifying the statements contained in the company's proposal for the guarantee bond herein." They stated that they desired "such statutory declaration to have special reference to your knowledge or the knowledge of any of the officers of the company," respecting certain matters. The first two of these were alleged irregular or fraudulent acts of Young prior to his employment by the company. The third was an alleged practice on Young's part of depositing the company's moneys in another bank than the one in which he was directed to deposit. The fourth was an alleged practice of Young to make deposits in the com-pany's bank by his own cheques on another bank for which there were no funds and which were subsequently charged back. The others were certain specific instances of the last mentioned practice.

They also asked for certain specified statements of account alleged to have been forwarded by the company's bank to Day and all vouchers sent down by the bank with these statements, particularizing debit slips charging up Young's dishonored cheques.

Day sent to the solicitors a statutory declaration deny-ing knowledge of the alleged irregularities, denying the authority of Young to make deposits in another bank and all knowledge and approval of or consent to it by himself or any other officer of the company. He then went on to trace somewhat in detail his acquisitions of knowledge of Young's dishonored cheques and course in connection therewith leading up to the final discovery of his defaults in February, 1898. He annexed and verified a copy of the bank statements from the 2nd August, 1897, to 31st March, 1898, covering the whole period for which statements were asked. He did not attempt to verify generally the statements in the proposal.

· The solicitors then wrote Day calling his attention to the fact that he had not verified the statements in the declaration, asking for further explanation of one item and repeating the request for the debit slips, avowedly for the purpose of inquiring into the company's knowledge of the dishonored cheques. In reply Day asked to be allowed to inspect the proposal, and said that as to "deposit slips" he would positively declare that, with the exception of one which he particularized, no such notices or slips were received at his office, and made a further statement as to the other item of which explanation had been asked. The solicitors then wrote pointing out circumstances claimed to be inconsistent with the declaration as to the particular item. Day then forwarded to them his statutory declaration stating, in general terms that the answers given by him in the proposal were true to the best of his knowledge and belief. The solicitors replied that the declaration did not yet cover the points asked for by previous letters.

Shortly afterward the company's solicitors wrote those of the corporation demanding payment. In reply the latter stated that they had notified Mr. Day that the evidence furnished was not satisfactory; they called attention to the condition requiring verification of the statements in the proposal and of the compliance therewith. referred particularly to the questions about payment into the bank, the inspection and checking of the bank book, the balancing of the cash accounts and checking their accuracy, and the answers thereto; they claimed that their requisition to Day "included a verification that these provisions of the proposal for the insurance had been carried out," and that he had overlooked this; they called attention again to their request for debit slips.

The result was that Mr. Day furnished another statutory declaration, made on the 21st November, 1898, in which he stated that, shortly after the end of every month, the company's office in Toronto received a statement from the bank at Winnipeg showing all deposits by Young, that these monthly statements were transcripts or exact copies of the company's bank account for any named month and were duly examined, and that Young forwarded at the close of every month his cash account "and the same would be checked with the bank statement." He declared, further, that the company did not receive any of the debit slips except one of January or February, 1898, which reached them after they had begun proceedings against Young.

It appears to me that Mr. Day's second declaration contained reasonable verification of the statements of existing facts and of the existing course of business at the date of the proposal, except in so far as those statements were incorrect, a matter to which I will presently refer.

The company furnished the particulars in proof of its claim principally by giving the corporation access to its books and papers. To some extent we can now see what was thus learned as to the course of business, and we can make some inferences from the letters of the solicitors. I infer that they learned, in a general way, the extent to which Young was accustomed to have money in hand and the length of time he usually held it before .depositing ; that they learned the facts about the receipt pass-books, the practice in depositing and the balances in Young's hands. They evidently learned that, in practice, the bank book itself was not directly inspected, but that statements, which were copies of the entries, were forwarded by the bank to the company from time to time. Mr. Day's third declaration stated that this was done shortly after the end of every month. I cannot infer that they learned whether or how often they were inspected and checked. Mr. Day declares only that they were " duly examined."

Then, upon the point of checking the accuracy of Young's accounts, I cannot infer that the agents of the corporation learned whether or when or how often this was done. Day declares only that " the same would be checked with the bank statement." His declaration showed on its face that the company did not receive the debit slips.

So far I have been dealing with the form of the proofs‚ and not with their accuracy.

Without intending to be exhaustive I will say that I find them to be inaccurate and untrue in the following respects. In so far as the second declaration is to be deemed to verify the course of business in respect to receipt pass-books, it was untrue. There was no such existing or intended course of business as the proposal represented in this regard. The third declaration was inaccurate in alleging that the bank statements were forwarded monthly.

And just here I think that I should say that I strongly suspect that the company did receive a number of the debit slips showing charges of Young's dishonored cheques. Where the receipts are signed by one of the Toronto officials I find that the paid cheques and other vouchers were received there. It is true that the apparent course of business was to transmit these receipts before getting the vouchers ; but, in the absence of any evidence of efforts to get them or complaints of not receiving them, I should infer that they were forwarded. In some cases Young signed the receipts for such vouchers and in those instances, notwithstanding the general evidence of the bank's practice, I cannot infer that the vouchers were forwarded to the bank. I have not compared the receipts with the accounts sufficiently to ascertain positively whether such debit slips were among the vouchers which I thus find to have been forwarded to the Toronto office.

It appears that, in some cases, parties who were liable to make periodical payments to the company were furnished with what were called pass-books in which it was Young's duty to enter payments as they were made. But such pass-books were not furnished to all who were so liable, and Young received many exceptional payments which could not well be entered in any such books. And where such pass-books were used there was no attempt to inspect and check them oftener than once a year. The answer in the declaration with reference to these pass-books was wholly inaccurate as a statement both of the existing and of the intended course of business. There was no attempt to comply with it. We cannot assume that the officers of the corporation had such a knowledge of the company's business that they would see the impracticability of the indicated course of business. They were entitled to rely on the answer as indicating the existence of a safeguard which, in fact, never existed. This safeguard would have been very material and, if it had existed, it seems almost certain that Young's defalcations could not have been continued so long or have been as extensive as they were.

The bank pass-book was not itself inspected at the head office, but the inspection and checking of copies of the entries in it, furnished by the bank independently of Young, would seem to me a substantial compliance with the answer in the proposal upon this point. These copies were not always furnished monthly. In some instances several months elapsed without their being furnished or checked. I have not examined the entries with sufficient care to form an opinon whether, if these had been furnished and checked monthly, the officers of the company would have acquired sooner than they actually did knowledge of any material facts.

Upon the question of the proofs I find that, within a reasonable time after the 9th February, 1898, the company did furnish its claim with such full particulars in proof thereof, as proved to the satisfaction of the corporation the cause, nature and extent of the loss which the company had sustained, within the meaning of the condition relating thereto.

On the other hand, I find that the company did not furnish reasonable verification of the statements made in the written proposal or of the compliance therewith. A declaration untrue in fact does not seem to me reasonable verification. In respect of the receipt pass-books the statement in the proposal was incapable of verification and Day's declaration to the truth of the answers cannot in this respect be deemed reasonable verification. While I assume that the agents of the corporation learned of the actual course pursued upon this point, and also of the fact that copies of the entries in the bank pass-book instead of the book itself, were inspected and checked, there was no evidence given to officials or agents of the corporation of the fact that this was not done monthly. In this latter particular I think that there was not reasonable verification of the extent of compliance with the answer relating to the bank pass-book.

These findings seem to me sufficient to defeat the claim on the policy.

Further, both the absolute untruth of the answer relating to the receipt pass-books, even though given, as it probably was, carelessly and without intention to misrepresent, and the failure to pursue the course of business indicated by the answer upon this point seem to me fatal to the right to recover. I express no opinion upon the effect of failure to procure and inspect the bank statements monthly.

While the grounds thus indicated are the only ones upon which I intend to dispose of the main claim, there are some other points upon which I think that I should make some finding of facts for the information of the Court upon any appeal that may be taken.

While some attempt was made to show some dishonest conduct of Young's prior to his becoming agent for the company, the evidence seems to me wholly insufficient for the purpose or to show that Day or the company was aware, when the application for the guarantee was made, of any reason why it should not be granted.

For the defence it was claimed that the company, through Day and one Kilgore, another employee, obtained knowledge of Young's defalcations prior to February, 1898. The evidence chiefly relied on for this purpose is documentary. I should have no difficulty in concluding that Kilgore knew of some as early as the 8th November, 1897, and there is much reason to suppose that he had the knowledge some months earlier. But unless, in the midst of the mass of material, I have overlooked something or have failed to give due weight to some written evidence, I cannot find that it is sufficiently proved that Day had such knowledge, though there may be room to suspect it. I must confess that I have not considered the effect upon this point of the evidence respecting the Cleland transaction. If necessary for the purpose, I should not be satisfied that Day was not aware of the contents of the letters of 23rd December, 1896, and 10th May, 1897, signed by him, and, taking the onus to be on him to show the contrary, I should find that he was so aware. But while these letters complain of cheques having been dishonored after deposit and credit taken therefor by Young, it is not a necessary inference that the writer understood that Young had appropriated the moneys and put in bad cheques for them. Even the fact that one cheque appears to have been drawn by one Young does not indicate that the drawer was Young, the company's agent. Payments might be made to him by cheques of third parties, and the name Young is not an uncommon one.

It clearly appears that the company continued Young in its employment and entrusted him with moneys after having discovered acts of dishonesty and fraud. There is an important question as to whether a distinction can be drawn between defalcations committed before and those committed after the discovery in regard to the liability of the corporation. For the company it is claimed that the corporation assented to the subsequent employment and waived the condition of the policy relating thereto. I cannot find any sufficient evidence of such consent or waiver. There seems to be no evidence of Woodland's authority to so consent or to waive the condition, and I cannot find as a fact that he assumed to do so. I do not feel that I can place sufficient reliance upon Day's evidence of any such consent. Counsel for the plaintiff endeavored to get Day to qualify or explain his statements upon this point in his examination for discovery, but the attempted explanation was dragged from him in such a way that I could not accept it. Certainly there is no evidence whatever that Woodland consented to Young's being entrusted with moneys after his default was known.

There are some further questions arising out of the company's claim to be paid for expense incurred in prosecuting Young.

One of the conditions of the policy was, " That the employer, when required by the corporation, shall at the corporation's expense, use all diligence in prosecuting the employed to a conviction for any criminal act which he shall have committed, and in consequence of which a claim shall have been made under this agreement."

I find that, after an informal claim had been made, but before the details or any proof had been furnished, the corporation required the company to prosecute Young, and that the company procured information to be laid and a prosecution conducted to conviction. Some of the offences of which Young was thus convicted were committed after the 10th February, 1898, when Day first gave notice of the shortage. The detailed claim was partly for subsequent defaults.

I cannot find that the corporation knew of the subsequent defaults until the details were furnished or intended to require prosecution for these.

If the corporation chose to demand prosecution before a formal notice was given or a detailed claim made, and without ascertaining the facts, still the company had a right to assume that the request was made upon the terms of the policy and that the prosecution was to be conducted at the expense of the corporation. I do not think that the liability for this expense was dependent upon the liability under the policy.

There will be judgment declaring that the defendant corporation is not liable to reimburse the plaintiff company for any pecuniary loss sustained by the plaintiff through the fraud or dishonesty of Frederick Smith Young, and dismissing the action so far as it relates to a claim therefor.

The judgment will further declare that the defendant corporation is liable to repay to the plaintiff company all sums paid by the plaintiff for expenses reasonably and properly incurred in and about the prosecution of Young for acts of fraud or dishonesty amounting to embezzlement or larceny committed by Young prior to the 10th day of February, 1898. There will be a reference to ascertain the amount and an order to pay. The defendant must pay the costs of the action, so far as it relates to a claim for these expenses, and the plaintiff must pay all costs occasioned by the addition of claims upon which it does not recover and incurred in the defence against the last mentioned claims.

H. M. Howell, K. C., and *W. R. Mulock, K. C.*, for the Plaintiffs.

C. P. Wilson, and *C. W. Bradshaw*, for the Defendants.

[IN THE COURT OF APPEAL FOR ONTARIO].

BEFORE ARMOUR, C.J.O., OSLER, MACLENNAN, MOSS
AND LISTER, J.J.A.

THE AGRICULTURAL SAVINGS & LOAN COMPANY

(Plaintiffs) Appellants.

v.

THE LIVERPOOL, LONDON & GLOBE INS. CO.

(Defendants) Respondents.

*Fire insurance—Effect of renewal of contract—Non-disclosure
of prior insurance—Rights of mortgagees.*

The "renewal" of a contract of fire insurance is really the formation
of a new contract between the parties, and therefore, the fact that
there was prior insurance not disclosed at the date of the making of
the original contract, does not affect the validity of the subsequent
contract (known as the "renewal"), when no such prior insurance
is then in force.

A mortgagee who, by the terms of a policy, is entitled to payment
according to his interest, may sue the insurers in his own name for
the amount thus due him.

Judgment of Rose, J., reversed.

The facts are set forth in the judgment.

5TH NOVEMBER, 1901.

The judgment of the Court was delivered by

ARMOUR, C. J., O. :—

By a policy in the defendant company, under the hand
and seal of one of its directors, it was witnessed that one
Calvin Randolph Arnott, Esq., of the village of Watford,
having paid to the defendant company, the sum of $26.25
for the insurance against loss or damage by fire (subject
to the conditions and stipulations endorsed thereon which
constituted the basis of the insurance) of the property
thereinafter described to the amount thereinafter mentioned
not exceeding upon any one article the sum specified on such
article, namely,—"$300, on the building only of his brick
galvanized iron roofed building, 24 x 45, occupied by the
assured as a cold storage building, situate and being on a
part of lot No. 27, west side of Main Street, village of

Watford, Ont., marked No. 1 on diagram endorsed on assured's application No. 140312, which form part hereof, and are his warranty." "$1200 on his machinery and fixtures therein attached and affixed thereto." "$1500. Fifteen hundred dollars loss, if any, under this policy payable to Agricultural Savings and Loan Company, London, Ont." " Other concurrent insurance, $600 on first item and $700 on second item in Alliance." "Subject to mortgage clause hereto attached." And the defendant company did thereby agree that from the 9th day of May, 1898, until 12 o'clock noon of the 9th day of May, A. D. 1899, and for so long afterwards as the said insured, his or her or their heirs, executors or administrators, should from time to time pay or cause to be paid the sum of $26.25 to the defendant company, or to the known agents thereof, on or before the commencement of each and every succeeding 12 months, and the Board of Directors should agree thereto by accepting the same ; the funds and property of the defendant company should (subject to the conditions and stipulations endorsed thereon which constituted the basis of that insurance) be subject and liable to pay, reinstate or make good to the said insured, his or her or their heirs, executors or administrators, such loss or damage as should be occasioned by fire to the property therein above mentioned and thereby insured, not exceeding in each case respectively the sum or sums therein before severally specified and stated against each property.

The " conditions and stipulations" endorsed on the policy were not the conditions prescribed by the Statute, and this policy must be held to be subject not to the conditions and stipulations endorsed thereon but to the statutory stipulations.

The mortgage clause to which this policy was made subject was as follows : " It is hereby provided and agreed that this insurance as to the interest of the mortgagees only therein shall not be invalidated by any act or neglect of the mortgagor or owner of the property insured nor by the occupation of the premises for purposes more hazardous than are permitted by this policy. It is further provided and agreed that the mortgagees shall at once notify said company of non-occupation or vacancy for over thirty days or of any change of ownership or increased hazard that shall come to their knowledge, and that every increase of hazard not permitted by the policy to the mortgagor or owner shall be paid for by the mortgagee on reasonable demand from the date such hazard existed, according to the established scale of rates for the use of such increased hazard during the continuance of this insurance. It is also further provided and agreed that whenever the company shall pay the mortgagees any sum for loss under this policy, and shall claim that as to the mortgagor or owner no liability therefore existed, it shall at once be legally subrogated to all rights of the mortgagees under all the securities held as collateral to the mortgage debt, to the extent of such payment, or at its option the company may pay to the mortgagees the whole principal due or to grow due on the mortgage, with interest, and shall thereupon receive a full assignment and transfer of the mortgage and all other securities held as collateral to the mortgage debt, but no such subrogation shall impair the rights of. the mortgagees to recover the full amount of their claim. It is also further provided and agreed that in the event of this property being further insured with this or any other office on behalf of the owner or mortgagee the company, except such other insurance when made by the mortgagor or owner shall prove invalid, shall only be liable for a rateable proportion of any loss or damage sustained. At the request of the assured the loss, if any, under this policy is hereby made payable to the Agricultural Savings & Loan Company, as their interest may appear, subject to the conditions of the above mortgage clause.''

The plaintiffs were the mortgagees of the insured property by virtue of a mortgage bearing date the 7th day of May, 1898, made by Calvin Randolph Arnott and one James Arnott, who executed the same as surety for the payment of the mortgage money in pursuance of the Act respecting short forms of mortgages, securing payment to them of the sum of $3000 and interest, as therein set forth, which said mortgage contained the following covenant : "And that the said mortgagors will insure the buildings on the said lands to the amount of not less than three thousand dollars currency.''

C. R. Arnott in his application for this policy in answer to the question, " What other insurance and where ? Name companies and amounts,'' said $1500 on above property just being taken to-day in the Alliance Assurance Company, and by this application the applicant agreed with the defendant company "that the foregoing is a just, full and true exposition of all the facts and circumstances in regard to the condition, situation, value and risk of the property to be insured so far as the same are known to the applicant and are material to the risk, and agrees and consents that the same be held to form the basis of the liability of the said company, and shall form a part and be a condition of this insurance contract," and on the margin of the application appears these words: "Loss, if any, payable to the Agricultural Savings & Loan Co., London, Out., as their interest may appear."

Prior to the date of this policy, and on the 25th day of April, 1898, C. R. Arnott had insured the property covered by this policy in the Perth Mutual Fire Insurance Company, for three years from that date, in the sum of $4,000, which insurance was on the 14th April, 1899, cancelled by that company.

The insurance effected by this policy was renewed by the following renewal receipt :—

The Liverpool & London & Globe Insurance Company.

Receipt	Renewing Policy
No. 160389	No. 3732312
Sum insured, $1500	Premium, $26.25

Received the 9th day of May, 1899, from C. R. Arnott, Esq., the sum of twenty-six 25/100 dollars, being the premium for the renewal of policy above named to the ninth day of May, nineteen hundred.

Not valid until countersigned by the Company's authorized agent at Watford.

Countersigned at Watford.   G. F. C. Smith,

W. E. Fitzgerald, Agent.   Recordant Secretary,

Canada Branch.

C. R. Arnott left the country on the 2nd February, 1900, and on the 5th February, 1900, G. F. C. Smith, the chief agent of the defendant company, wrote to W. E. Fitzgerald, its agent at Watford, as follows :—" Your favour of the 29th ult. came duly to hand and we showed your

letter to the Alliance as requested.   They also advised us of
their inspector's report of the premises insured.   It would
appear that the refrigerating plant is of no value and that
the property does not warrant the present amount of
insurance.   We would prefer under the circumstances not
to continue on the risk and would ask you to obtain the
surrender of the policy, allowing a rebate of $5.75 for the
unexpired term, which you will please pay and take credit
for in your account less commission.''

On the 8th February, 1900, G. F. C. Smith, chief agent
of the defendant company, wrote to the plaintiffs as
follows :—

''Re policy No. 3732312, J. R. Arnott, of Watford.   In the
absence of J. R. Arnott from Watford we write you direct to
advise you that on account of the cold storage building
insured under the above policy being unoccupied we do not
care to continue on the risk.   Will you, therefore, please
return us the above policy with your release in cancellation
thereof.   Our agent, Mr. Fitzgerald, of Watford, will pay Mr.
Arnott the amount of unearned premium $5.75 and obtain
his discharge.''

On the 9th February, 1900, the plaintiffs' manager wrote
to James Arnott a letter, on the margin of which there was
this memo. :—'' Have just received notification from
Insurance Co., cancelling their policy.''

On the 12th February, 1900, G. F. C. Smith, chief
agent of the defendants, wrote to W. E. Fitzgerald, their
agent at Watford, as follows :—

'' Re Policy 3732312, Arnott.—In reply to your post card
of the 7th inst. we would say that we had already written
to the Agricultural Savings & Loan Company, of London,
calling for the cancellation of the above policy ; we would
prefer to go off the risk at once.''

On the 13th February, 1900, Mr. Fitzgerald wrote to the
plaintiffs as follows :—'' To-day I received by book-post, and
I suppose it was from you, two insurance policies issued to
C. R. Arnott, one policy being number 3732312 in the
Liverpool & London & Globe Insurance Co., and the other
policy being 1572474 in the Alliance Assurance Co.   In
your letter that you wrote me the other day you stated that
these policies had been cancelled.   The company have so

written me also and . therefore, since these policies are cancelled it may be necessary for you to effect insurance in other companies. I have one other company that I do insurance business for, namely, The Wellington Mutual Fire Ins, Co., which is a stock company as well as mutual. I do not know whether I could get them to take a risk, say, of $2000 on this building or not. If you have already insured the building let me know. If not I can endeavor to place on an insurance for you in the Wellington Mutual. Arnott is not here at present. I have credited him with the rebate that is coming to him in respect of these policies. I may further say that I did all I could with the Alliance Assurance Co.. and the Liverpool & London & Globe Ins. Co.. to allow the said insurance to remain in force, but the Inspector of the Alliance Assurance Co., having a few weeks ago been here and made his report as to the building not being used for cold storage purposes now, etc., caused the companies to come to the decision they have and thus cancel the insurance. To-day both of said companies wrote me, their letters being dated yesterday. They positively refuse to reconsider the matter of cancellation and state they wish policies to remain cancelled or words to that effect." " P. S. Before Arnott's property mortgaged to you becomes less valuable, etc., would it not be well to sell and make what you can out of it. Nothing, I think, can be made by proceeding against James Arnott, whom his son has ruined financially, but he, James Arnott, says he will if given time pay you what you cannot get out of cold storage buildings some day if let alone." On the 14th February, 1900, the plaintiffs' manager wrote to Mr. Fitzgerald as follows :— " Re Arnott property.—If you can place $2000 insurance in any company you had better do so. The rebate of the insurance policies must be paid to us and not, as you suggest, credited to Arnott, so kindly send us cheque for same."

On the 15th February, 1900, Mr. Fitzgerald wrote to the defendant company as follows :—" Re Policy No. 3732312. The Agricultural Savings & Loan Company have sent me this policy and I wrote them I had credited rebate to Mr. Arnott which is $5.75. The Agricultural Loan Company want rebate themselves. The insured is, I think, entitled to rebate,and he being indebted to me I have surely a right, as in the past, to credit him with it in his account. What will I do with policy and what else do you wish me to do ?   How about rebate ?   I do not intend paying Loan Co., if not bound to."

On the 15th February, 1900, Mr. Fitzgerald wrote to the plaintiffs as follows :—" Your letter of yesterday's date received.   I will place $2000 insurance in Wellington subject to their approval on getting premium from you, say, $1.35 per $100 ins. for 12 months or $27.00.   Please reply by next mail.   The assured is party to get money and he has got it and is overpaid.   He is indebted to me and allows credit in this way."

On the 16th February, 1900, G. F. C. Smith, chief agent of the defendant company, wrote to Mr. Fitzgerald, their agent at Watford, as follows :—

" Re Policy No. 3732312, Arnott.—We have your post card of the 15th inst., advising that the mortgagees, the Agricultural Savings & Loan Co., have returned you the above policy for cancellation and that you advised them that you would credit Mr. Arnott with the rebate but that the Loan Company demand the rebate themselves.   If the premium was paid by Mr. Arnott you are entitled to retain it for him, but if it was paid by the Loan Company you will have to pay it to them.   Strictly speaking the only interest the Loan Company has in the policy is in the event of a loss by fire, they have no title to or in the policy except in such event.   You will please return us the policy and take credit for the rebate when you have received the discharges on the policy itself signed by both parties."

On the 16th February, 1900, the plaintiffs' manager wrote to Mr. Fitzgerald as follows : " You might make application to the Wellington Mutual and ascertain whether they will care to accept the risk.   If they do so I think there will be no difficulty in paying you the premium, though it is a very high one especially on that class of security, and if it was occupied it would be a very much less rate."

On the 17th February, 1900, Mr. Fitzgerald wrote to the plaintiffs as follows : "Your letter of February 16th received.   I have written the Wellington Mutual giving full particulars of risk and asking whether they will accept the offer of $2000 being $900 on the building, the same as the old policies, and $1100 on the fixtures and machinery attached and affixed thereto.   I will advise you whether they accept or not.   The rate quoted is not any higher than if building was occupied.   I have heard from both the Liverpool & London & Globe and the Alliance companies respecting cancellation of their respective policies and stating that when Arnott paid me the insurance premium he was the party to receive the rebate and not you, therefore I was correct in saying that he was entitled to get it.   Rate is only $1.35 per $100—total premium $27.00.''

On the 20th February, 1900, the plaintiffs telegraphed the manager of the defendant company as follows :—''Arnott policy No. 3732312.   Buildings destroyed by fire last night.'' And on the 20th February, 1900, the plaintiffs' manager wrote to the chief agent of the defendant company as follows :—

''Re policy 3732312, C. R. Arnott.—I yesterday wired you that the premises covered by above policy had been destroyed by fire.   We take position that the policy had never been cancelled, and we must ask you to return the policy to us, or if you do not hold it, to instruct your agent at Watford, Mr. W. E. Fitzgerald, to return it to us, and we can then make our claim in the usual manner.   Kindly also forward me a set of claim papers.''

This policy when produced at the trial had the following attached to it :—

''Re policy No. 3732312, C. R. Arnott.—In consideration of the sum of $5.75 return premium the above policy is cancelled and surrendered to the Liverpool & London & Globe Ins. Co.

'' C. R. ARNOTT,

'' per W. E. Fitzgerald,

'' Feby. 13th, 1900.   '' his Solicitor.''

The premises insured were used for the purpose of cold storage, the machinery being propelled by a gasolene engine, and when worked there was an engineer employed in the day time and one at night.   The business of cold storage ceased towards the end of September, 1899, owing to the machinery not working properly, and the premises were thereafter used for ordinary storage purposes for the business carried on by C. R. Arnott of buying and selling produce, and this business ceased about the 16th January, 1900, leaving about 1000 boxes which were all removed but about 75 at the time of the fire.

When C. R. Arnott went away he left the keys with his father, who left them with his son-in-law who had a shop in the village. On the day C. R. Arnott left the country a judgment was obtained against him for $2200. On the 1st May, 1900, there was due to the plaintiffs in respect of their mortgage the sum of $2052.56. The defendant company claiming the right to avoid the insurance offered to return the amount of the premiums received by them in respect thereof together with the interest thereon.

This action was, in my opinion, well brought by the plaintiffs. The policy is by deed, and it is not a deed *inter partes* but a deed poll.

If the policy had been by deed *inter partes* it might have been contended that no one could have sued on it but those between whom on the face of it the deed was made. But the policy is by deed poll and any one named or designated in it with whom a covenant is thereby made can sue upon it. *Green* v. *Home*, 1 Salk 197 ; Platt on Covenants, 5 ; Hamilton on Covenants, 6 ; *Mitchell* v. *City of London F. Ins. Co.*, 12 Ont. 706.

The stipulation in the policy " loss, if any, under this policy payable to the Agricultural Savings and Loan Company, London, Ont.," constituted a covenant on the part of the defendant company to pay to the plaintiffs the loss, if any, under the policy. *Bower* v. *Hodges*, 13 C. B. 765. It is not against this view that the defendant company covenanted " to pay, reinstate or make good to the said insured " such loss, for this covenant was subject to their covenant with the plaintiffs and payment to the plaintiffs of such loss as their interest might appear would be a discharge *pro tanto* of this covenant.

In this case the policy not being technically a deed *inter partes* the plaintiffs were as much parties to it as was C. R. Arnott.

By his mortgage he was bound to insure to the amount of $3,000, and in his application he set forth this mortgage and asked that the loss, if any, should be made payable to the plaintiffs, the mortgagees, as their interest might appear.

The defendant company were, therefore, aware that C. R. Arnott was the mortgagor and the plaintiffs were the mortgagees of the property to be insured, and that the loss, if any, was to be made payable to the plaintiffs as such mortgagees, and being so aware they issued this policy. *Hathaway* v. *Orient Ins. Co.*, 134, N. Y. 409 ; *The Watertown F. Ins. Co.* v. *The Grocers and Bakers Ins. Co.*, 41 Mich., 131.

And if anything were wanting to show that the plaintiffs were parties to this policy it is supplied by the mortgage clause to which the policy is made subject, which contains express agreements between the plaintiffs and defendant company. In taking the view which I have expressed I am not to be understood as at all dissenting from the decision of this court in *Mitchell* v. *The City of London Assurance Company*, 15 A. R. 162, which must be held to govern this case.

The non-communication to the defendant company by C. R. Arnott, in his application, of the fact of the existence of the prior insurance in the Perth Mutual Fire Insurance Company, is set up as an answer to the plaintiffs' claim, it being contended that although the insurance in that company was cancelled before the renewal of the policy sued on, the defendant company, notwithstanding their renewal of the policy, had the right as soon as they discovered the fact of its non-communication, which was shortly before the fire, to avoid the policy, and the learned trial Judge agreed with this contention, and on this ground dismissed the action. "As to the effect of a renewal of a policy there is some confusion if not disagreement amongst the authorities. It is generally held to be a new contract upon the terms and conditions stated in the policy expired—the old application in the absence of evidence to the contrary serving as the basis of the new contract and as if made at the date of the renewal." May, 4th Ed., Sec. 70 A.

I am of the opinion that the renewal of the policy sued on must be held to be a new contract upon the terms and conditions of that policy, for our law provides that " the insurance of mercantile and manufacturing risks shall, if on the cash system, be for terms not exceeding one year." R. S. O., cap. 203, sec. 167. And this was an insurance of a mercantile risk as understood by insurers, as was shown by the tariff of rates for such risks put in evidence at the trial, and was on the cash system. I am of the opinion, moreover, that apart from this statute the renewal of the policy sued on must be held to be a new contract upon the terms and conditions of that policy. *Long* v. *Ancient Order of United Workmen*, 25 A.R. 147 ; *Brady* v. *Northwestern Ins. Co.*, 11 Mich. 426.

If a new contract, it was entered into without any application such as was made for the former contract being required to be made, and if any effect is to be given to the old application as applied to the new contract it must be treated as practically a new application for the new contract made at the date of the new contract, and being so treated the contention of the defendant company must fail. The contention of the defendant company that the policy was cancelled must also fail. It was admitted that the proceedings prescribed by the 19th statutory condition for terminating the insurance had not been taken, but it was contended that the insurance was terminated in the only other way in which it could be terminated, namely, by the agreement of the parties, but C. R. Arnott never did agree nor did he ever authorize nor was any one ever authorized to agree for him. *Caldwell* v. *Stadacona F. & L. Ins. Co.*, 11 S.C.R. 212 ; *Morrow* v. *Lancashire Ins. Co.*, 29 O.R. 377, 26 A.R. 173.

I do not think that there was any change material to the risk within the terms of the 3rd statutory condition, as was contended by the defendant company, and that if there was the plaintiffs were protected against it by the provisions of the " mortgage clause."

The plaintiffs are in my opinion entitled to recover upon the policy, but only to the extent of the amount due upon their mortgage.

APPEAL ALLOWED WITH COSTS.

Solicitors for the Appellants : *Bayly and Bayly*.

Solicitors for the Respondents : *Hoskin, Ogden and Hoskin*.

Editor's Note :—

A similar judgment has since (30th December, 1901) been delivered by the Court of Appeal for Ontario in Agricultural Savings and Loan Co. v. The Alliance Assurance Co.,—the facts being almost precisely similar to those in the case reported above.

[IN THE SUPREME COURT OF BRITISH COLUMBIA.]

BEFORE MARTIN, J.

RICHARDS

v.

THE BANK OF BRITISH NORTH AMERICA.

Bank — Partnership — Two Accounts — Charging personal account with partnership overdraft.

R. and R. had a partnership account in a certain bank, and when the firm was dissolved the ledger-keeper gave it credit for a balance, for which the partners wrote cheques. About the same time one of the partners opened a personal account at the same bank, and when it was discovered that, through an error, the partnership account had been credited with about $200 too much, the bank, after notice, charged the partnership overdraft which had resulted from this mistake to the personal account of the partner above referred to.
Held, that the bank had no legal right to so charge such overdraft.

Action for damages tried at Vancouver on 22nd July, 1901.

In July, 1900, the plaintiff Richards and one Riley had a partnership account in the Bank of British North America. On July 21st, they sold out their hotel business to one Johnson, it being agreed that Johnson was to take over the business as it stood, pay all debts and get in any outstanding assets ; the balance in the bank standing to the credit of the firm to be applied to the payment of the debts of the hotel business.

On July 24th, the plaintiff Richards went to the ledger-keeper of the bank and asked for the firm's correct balance, stating that it was retiring from business and wished to close up the account, the pass-book then having been in the bank for some days and no cheques having been issued. The ledger-keeper wrote the balance in the bank-book in pencil as it was shown in his books. Richards then went back to the hotel and with his partner drew cheques to pay hotel debts to the full amount of the balance. All cheques on this partnership account had to be signed by both E. W. Richards and Molly Riley.

About this time Richards opened another account in his own name with the Bank of British North America. At the end of the month the bank found that the ledger-keeper had made a mistake in the books and had given Richards & Riley credit for a balance of $200 more than they were entitled to.   This was the balance which had been given to Richards. Richards was informed of this by the bank officials, and he told them if they would go to the hotel they could arrange the matter with the new proprietors.

About the end of August he was informed by the bank that as there had been an overdraft of $199.97 on the partnership account that amount had been charged to his private account ; he never acquiesced in this, but drew all the rest of the money out of his private account.

In December he issued a cheque to Carmichael & Dickie on his private account with the bank of British North America for $199.97 ; this cheque was duly presented for payment and refused.

Richards thereupon brought an action for damages against the bank for refusing to pay such cheque, and for the recovery of the amount of the same, which, he alleged, should stand to his credit in the books of the bank.

Pottenger and Kappele for Plaintiff.

Bowser, K.C., for Defendant.

JULY 30th, 1901.

MARTIN, J. :—

With some reluctance, and on the authority of *Watts* v. *Christie* (1849), 11 Beav. 546 ; *Wolstenholm* v. *The Sheffield Union Banking Company, Limited* (1886), 54 L. T. N. S. 746, and Lindley on Partnership (1893), 303–8, 676–7, I have come to the conclusion that the defendant bank was not legally justified in charging up against the plaintiff's account the overdraft of $199.97 of the partnership of Richards & Riley.   And, consequently, the defendant should have paid the plaintiff's cheque for $199.97 when it was presented on the 22nd December, 1900.   It follows that the plaintiff is entitled to recover that sum from the defendant.

As to damages, in my opinion all that the plaintiff is entitled to under the peculiar circumstances is interest at the legal rate from the time of such presentment.

In regard to costs, in view of the mean advantage the plaintiff has taken of the defendant's mistake, and the aggressive nature of this action, I feel that this is a case wherein, to mark the court's displeasure of such a line of conduct, the plaintiff should be deprived of costs.

JUDGMENT FOR PLAINTIFF, WITHOUT COSTS.

Editor's Notes :—

A bank has no lien on the separate, personal account of a customer for a balance due it by a firm of which he is a member.

Addis v. *Knight* (1818), 2 Mer. 117.

Watts v. *Christie* (1849), 11 Beaven 546.

See also *ex parte McKenna, In re Lawrence* (1862), 3 De G, F & J, 629.

A bank may regard several accounts kept by one customer as being the same account.

In re European Bank (1872), L. R. 8 Ch. 41.

And when a customer has different accounts at two branches of the same bank, the bank may treat the two accounts as one for the purpose of exercising its lien.

Garnett v. *McKewan* (1872), L. R. 8 Ex. 10.

Prince v. *Oriental Bank Corporation* (1878), 3 App. Cas. 325.

On the other hand, a bank may not apply the balance of an account, regarding which it has received notice that it is not a personal account, in order to repay an overdraft on a personal account which is in the name of the same person.

Ex parte Kingston (1871), L. R. 6 Ch. 632.

And see also, *Bradford Banking Co.* v. *Briggs* (1886), 12 App. Cas. 29.

But in a recent case it was held that where a customer of a bank opens a separate account for certain trust moneys, and it does not appear that the bank had notice that the moneys paid into this account were held on trust only, the bank has the right to treat such moneys as the property of the customer, and to apply them in settlement of an overdraft on his personal account.

Union Bank of Australia v. *Murray Aynsley* (1898), A. C. 693.

[IN THE COURT OF KING'S BENCH FOR QUEBEC.]
(APPEAL SIDE.)

BEFORE SIR ALEXANDRE LACOSTE, C.J., AND BOSSÉ, BLANCHET, HALL AND WURTELE, J.J.

THE MOLSONS BANK (creditor collocated) Appellant

v.

BEAUDRY et al. (creditors contesting) Respondents.

Advances by bank —Goods hypothecated— The Bank Act— Insolvent estate.

Sub-section 2 of section 74 of the Bank Act (53 Vic., c. 31, as amended) which authorizes banks to " lend money to any wholesale purchaser or shipper of or dealer in products of agriculture, the forest," etc., upon the security of such products, does not apply so as to cover an advance made by a bank upon the security of lumber which, at the date of such advance, has been through the saw mill,—the lumber, when converted into logs, being no longer the product of the forest within the meaning of that section. Judgment of the Superior Court affirmed.

Appeal from a judgment of the Superior Court, maintaining a contestation of a dividend sheet prepared in the matter of J. A Bulmer & Co., insolvents.

The contestants claimed that the curator to the above mentioned insolvent estate was not entitled to divide the assets into goods hypothecated to the Molsons Bank, and goods not so hypothecated ; that the goods thus classed as being hypothecated to the bank were under the privilege of lessors, and that the Molsons Bank had, therefore, been given a preference not maintainable in law. The appellant contended that as the goods in question, which consisted of certain lumber (which had passed through the saw mill), constituted its security for certain advances made under section 74 of the Bank Act (53 Vic. (D) c. 31, as amended), it had a right to the hypothecation of the security, and that the curator was warranted in making the division he had of the effects.

The Superior Court held that the lumber in question having, to a certain extent, been changed from its original condition was no longer the product of the forest at the time it was accepted as security for advances, and that therefore the transactions between the Molsons Bank and J. A. Bulmer & Co., in respect thereof, were not within section 74 of the Bank Act.

The Molsons Bank appealed from this judgment.

29 OCTOBER, 1901.

The judgment given by the majority of the Court of Appeal was in the following terms :—

(Translation.)

As regards the nature of the privilege claimed by the appellant, the Molsons Bank :—

Considering that the terms of section 74 of the Bank Act permit it to make loans to wholesale purchasers or shippers of products of agriculture, the forest or mines upon the security of such products ;

Considering that this privilege has been established for the purpose of aiding agriculture and the development of the forests, mines and fisheries, and that the security provided can be given to assure the repayment of the sums lent under the operation of that statute ;

Considering that this privilege cannot be granted to assure the payment of anterior debts or of those already existing.

Considering that it was incumbent upon the appellant to establish that the privilege which it had invoked had been created under the aforesaid conditions ;

Considering that the appellant has not established that the security claimed was granted at the moment of the creation of the debt, but that it appears to have been so as security for an anterior and pre-existing debt ;

Considering that the different lumber in question in this action, as detailed and declared in the record, are not the products of the forest nor their derivatives, in the sense of the said section 74 of the said statute ;

Considering that there is no error in the judgment appealed from, rendered by the Superior Court at Montreal, on 25 January, 1901,

The Court, for the reasons above given, doth confirm the said judgment with costs.

HALL, J. :—

Concurs in the judgment for the first five reasons, but differs from the majority of the court on the sixth reason, being of the opinion that the lumber in question comes within the terms of section 74 of the Bank Act, as being the product of the forest in the sense intended by that enactment.

WURTELE, J. :—

Concurs in the judgment on the ground that it has not been stated that the agreement establishing the privilege was made at the time the debt secured was created.

APPEAL DISMISSED WITH COSTS.

Solicitors for the Appellant : *Campbell, Meredith, Allan & Hague.*

Solicitors for the Respondents : *Lamothe and Trudel.*

Editor's Notes :—

Sub-section 2 of section 74 of The Bank Act, as amended by 63-64 Vic., c. 26, section 17, reads as follows :

" 2.—Loans to wholesale dealers, etc.—The bank may also lend money to any wholesale purchaser or shipper of or dealer in products of agriculture, the forest, quarry and mine, or the sea, lakes and rivers, or to any wholesale purchaser or shipper of or dealer in live stock or dead stock and the products thereof, upon the security of such products, or of such live stock or dead stock and the products thereof. The bank may allow the goods, wares and merchandise covered by such security to be removed and other goods, wares and merchandise mentioned in this sub-section to be substituted therefor, and those so substituted shall be covered by such security as if originally covered thereby : Provided always, that such goods, wares and merchandise so substituted are of substantially the same character and of substantially the same value as, or of less value than, those for which they have been so substituted.''

See also sec. 76.

The decision reported above is of interest as being the first judicial pronouncement upon what is or is not the product of the forest within the meaning of The Bank Act.

The security mentioned in and created by this sub-section is, in some respects, of the same nature as a warehouse receipt,—section 75 making it a condition precedent to the acquisition of either of these securities that the bill or debt for which they are taken as collateral security shall have been negotiated or contracted at the time they are so acquired, or that a written agreement for the future delivery of such security shall then have been made.

On the other hand, this security differs from a warehouse receipt inasmuch as the section creating it expressly states that the goods may be removed and others substituted therefor ; while a warehouse receipt will not apply to substituted goods unless there is a custom of trade to the effect that it does so.

See *Llado* v. *Morgan* (1874), 23 U. C., C. P. 517. *Wilmot* v. *Maitland* (1851), 3 Grant (Ont.) 107. *Bank of Hamilton* v. *Noye Manufacturing Co.* (1885), 9 O. R. 638.

[IN THE SUPREME COURT OF CANADA.]

BEFORE SIR HENRY STRONG, C.J., AND TASCHEREAU, GWYNNE, SEDGWICK AND DAVIES, J.J.

THE CANADIAN FIRE INS. CO.

(Defendants) Appellants,

v.

ROBINSON et al.,

(Plaintiffs) Respondents.

(ON APPEAL FROM THE COURT OF KING'S BENCH FOR LOWER CANADA, APPEAL SIDE).

Fire insurance—Agent delegating his authority—Lex loci and lex fori.

The local agent of a fire insurance company was empowered to make interim insurances by means of receipts countersigned by himself, provided that in all such cases the premiums for the insurances thus effected were paid in cash. The agent employed a canvasser, who assumed to make a contract of insurance for the company,—giving an interim receipt countersigned by himself as agent of the company, and taking in payment of the premium a promissory note payable to his own order three months from date.

Held, that the action of the person employed as canvasser did not bind the company, as he had assumed to make a contract of such a nature as the agent himself had no authority to make.

Held, further, that in any event the agent could not act through a sub-agent, the authority given to an agent of an insurance company invested with such powers as the one in question being such as involved and implied trust and confidence in the very person so chosen as original agent.

[*Summers* v. *The Commercial Union Insurance Co.,* 6 S. C. R., 19, *followed.*]

Held, further, that the *lex loci* of a contract must be presumed to be that of the *lex fori,* unless the former law is proved to be different.

Appeal allowed.

The agent of the Canadian Fire Insurance Company at Ottawa was one Smith, with whom one Healey shared an office. Smith represented various other insurance companies, and he made a verbal arrangement with Healey that the latter should be allowed a commission upon any fire risks which he obtained for him. Healey induced D'Amour and Charlebois, proprietors of a steam planing mill in the city of Hull, to take out a policy of insurance on their property for $5000.00, and he issued an interim receipt therefor, countersigned by himself as alleged agent of the Canadian Fire Insurance Co., and took in payment of the premium a promissory note payable to his own order three months after date. Smith himself had no authority to issue receipts for interim insurance unless the premium therefor was paid in cash. The evidence also showed (in the opinion of the court) that Smith never authorized Healey to effect the insurance in question.

A few days after this transaction the property in question was burned. The company refused to pay the insurance money, and action therefor was then brought by the Respondent Robinson, the assignee of D'Amour and Charlebois, of which firm he was a creditor. The Superior Court gave judgment in favour of the plaintiffs and this decision was confirmed by the Court of King's Bench for Lower Canada (Appeal Side), Hall and Bossé, J.J., dissenting.

The appellants then appealed to this court.

16TH NOVEMBER, 1901.

The judgment of the court was delivered by

THE CHIEF JUSTICE :—

There are, in my opinion, four distinct grounds for allowing this appeal.

First, Smith, if he did in fact delegate his authority as an agent for the appellants, for the purpose of effecting policies of assurance, to Healey, had no legal authority to do so. At the opening of the appeal there was some discussion as to whether the authority of Smith to appoint a sub-agent depended on the law of Ontario or Manitoba (the legal domicile of the company) or on that of Quebec, and my brother Taschereau remarked that the *lex loci* of the contract must be presumed to be that of the *lex fori* unless the former law was proved. I agree in this and consider that the question must be determined by the law of the Province of Quebec.

Article 1711 of the Civil Code is as follows :—

"The mandatary is answerable for the person whom he substitutes in the execution of the mandate, when he is not empowered to do so ; and if the mandator be injured by reason of the substitution he may repudiate the acts of the substitute.

This article 1711 deals only with the question of responsibility, and it does not define the cases in which the mandatary may appoint a sub-agent. The corresponding article of the French Code is 1994. These provisions appear to apply in cases where the mandatary is neither empowered nor prohibited by the contract of mandate to appoint a sub-agent.

There can be little doubt, although there is no express article to that effect, that the mandator may prohibit the delegation of his mandate by the mandatary to a third person provided the prohibition is express. Then, surely, when there is nothing requiring that the prohibition to delegate should be express in its terms, it may well be left to inference when the mandate necessarily implies trust and confidence in the person on whom it is conferred.

Then, in a case in this court, *Summers* v. *The Commercial Union Ins. Co.*, 6 S.C.R. 19, an appeal from Ontario, it was held that an agent of an insurance company such as Smith was in this case, could not act through the medium of a sub-agent, since the authority to the original agent involved trust and confidence in the nature of a *delectus personae*. It is therefore a case where the mandatary cannot legally discharge his duties by handing them over to another not selected by the mandator. There is an *arrêt* of a Belgian Court of Appeal to this effect. (Gand 26 May, 1851, Pasicrisie 1851 2–318.) For this reason I conclude that Smith had no legal power to substitute Healey for himself in making the contract of insurance with D'Amour and Charlebois.

Secondly, even if Smith had legal authority to substitute Healey, he, in point of fact, as appears from the depositions, never did so. Healey had apparently authority to get proposals for Smith, but Smith never empowered him to conclude contracts, to sign interim receipts or to receive premiums. It was incumbent on the plaintiff to establish this in proof by clear testimony, but he has failed to do so. It does not appear that Healey was authorized to conclude a contract and to sign an interim receipt with D'Amour and Charlebois or with any one else. This appears to have been his own view, for he erased Smith's counter-signature from the interim receipt thus indicating that he had not authority from the latter. The very way in which the interim receipt

he used came into the hands of Healey militates against the
pretension that he had in fact actual authority from Smith, for
Healey appears to have abstracted the receipt from a parcel
containing blanks sent by the company's agent at Toronto
addressed to Smith, and without having authority so to do
from the latter.   On the whole it is not proved that Healey
had *de facto* the authority he professed to exercise.   This is
further confirmed by the fact that he gave the interim
receipt without receiving payment of the premium, taking for
it a promissory note at three months, payable, not to Smith,
but to himself, which note he did not hand over to Smith at
once, although after some time he offered to deliver it to
latter, who refused to accept it.   There certainly never was
in fact any authority conferred by Smith to enter into a
contract of insurance to be binding on the appellants on the
terms and to be carried out in the manner this assumed
contract was.

Thirdly, even if it were granted that Smith could in law
substitute a sub-agent, and had in fact done so, there is a
clause in article 1711 (not to be found in the French Code)
which is conclusive as to the right of the appellants to
disavow Healey's acts.   The words of this clause are : " If
" the mandator be injured by reason of the substitution, he
" may repudiate the acts of the substitute."   If there could
be a case in which a principal would be entitled to say he
was injured by the acts of one who had assumed to act as
the sub-agent of his mandatary it is the present.   Here we
find this pretended sub-agent entering into a most
improvident contract of insurance as regards the risk taken,
not complying with the words of the mandate as regards
the interim receipt, and taking payment of the premium in
a manner not warranted by anything the appellants had
authorized, by a deferred promissory note payable, not to
the appellants, or their agent, but to the sub-agent himself.
It is impossible to say if there could be in law and was in
fact a substitution that the appellants were not grievously
injured by the way in which the substitute executed the
mandate, and this gives them a right to repudiate the
pretended contract.

Lastly, the powers of the sub-agent cannot exceed those
conferred on the principal agent.   Smith himself had no
power to enter into a contract in the terms of that which
Healey pretended to make, as his sub-agent, with D'Amour

and Charlebois.   He could only effect an interim insurance binding on the company by an interim receipt countersigned by himself and on receiving the premium in cash.   (*London & Lancashire Life Assurance Co.* v. *Fleming* (1897), A.C., p. 499 ; *Acey* v. *Fernie*, 7 M. & W., p. 150.) These terms were not complied with, and therefore on this last distinct ground, that on which Mr. Justice Hall's dissenting judgment proceeds, the respondents must fail.

The appeal is allowed and the action dismissed.   The appellants must have their costs here and in both courts below.

APPEAL ALLOWED WITH COSTS.

Solicitors for the Appellant : *Foran and Champagne.*

Solicitors for the Respondents : *Aylen and Duclos.*

[IN THE JUDICIAL COMMITTEE OF THE PRIVY COUNCIL.]

Before LORD HALSBURY, L.C., LORD MACNAGHTEN, LORD SHAND, LORD DAVEY, LORD ROBERTSON, LORD LINDLEY AND SIR FORD NORTH.

THE CANADIAN PACIFIC RAILWAY CO. (Defendant)

Appellant

v.

ROY (Plaintiff) Respondent.

Railway company—Sparks from locomotive—Liability for damage.

A railway company, authorized by statute to run locomotive engines along its line, is not, in the absence of proof of negligence, responsible for damage caused by sparks emitted from one of its locomotives which is properly managed and equipped, and is being used in the ordinary manner.

Judgment of the Court of Queen's Bench for Lower Canada (Appeal Side) reversed.

Hon. Edward Blake, K.C., for the Company Appellant.

Hon. Lomer Gouin, K.C., for the Respondent.

The facts are set forth in the judgment.

18TH DECEMBER, 1901 :—

The Lord Chancellor, in now giving their Lordships' judgment said : This is an appeal by the Canadian Pacific Railway Company against a judgment of the Court of Queen's Bench for Lower Canada affirming a judgment of the Superior Court of Quebec, whereby that company were held to be liable to damages to the extent of $300 for injuries to the plaintiff's property alleged to be caused, and now admitted to have been caused, by sparks escaping from one of their locomotive engines while employed in the ordinary use of their railway. Some questions were raised in the courts below, and to some extent referred to here, whether the judgment could be supported upon the ground of the appellants having been guilty of negligence in their management of the engine or its appliances being defective. No such question is now before their Lordships. By arrangement between the parties that question has been withdrawn, and their Lordships are not to be taken as giving any opinion whether there was any evidence of negligence, or, if there was, how that issue ought to be determined. The serious and important question sought to be raised in this appeal is whether the railway company, authorized by statute to carry on their railway undertaking in the place and by the means that they do carry it on, are responsible in damages for injury not caused by negligence, but by the ordinary and normal use of their railway. Both courts below have held that in the province of Quebec the railway company is so responsible ; and the question is whether that is the law. The argument appears to be founded on the suggestion that Quebec has a civil law of its own, and that in that province all corporations, like all other persons, are responsible for causing damage to their neighbours by a fault, that is to say, any actionable wrong, whether imprudence or want of skill ; and another article of the code provides that civil corporations, constituting by the fact of their incorporation ideal or artificial persons, are as such governed by the laws affecting individuals, saving the privileges they enjoy and the disabilities they are subject to. If the immunity claimed for the appellants were simply claimed upon the ground that they were a corporation, without reference to what they are authorized to do in that capacity, the argument would be well founded ; but the fallacy of the suggestion lies in supposing that that immunity is claimed because they are a corporation. If it were so there would be no difference between the law of England and the law as so expounded in the Province of Quebec. But the ground upon which the immunity of a railway company for injury caused by the normal use of their line is based is that the Legislature, which is supreme, has authorized the particular thing so done in the place and by the means contemplated by the Legislature, and that cannot constitute an actionable wrong in England any more than it can constitute a fault by the Quebec code. The principle has been lucidly expounded by Lord Hatherley in the case of *Geddis* v. *Proprietors of Bann Reservoir* (L. R., 3 App. Cas. 438) thus : "If a company in the position of the defendants there (*Cracknell* v. *Corporation of Thetford*, L. R., 4 C. P., 629) has done nothing but that which the Act authorized—nay, may in a sense be said to have directed—and if the damage which arises therefrom is not owing to any negligence on the part of the company in the mode of executing or carrying into effect the powers given by the Act, then the person who is injuriously affected by that which has been done must either find in the Act of Parliament something which gives him compensation, or he must be content to be deprived of that compensation because there has been nothing done which is inconsistent with the powers conferred by the Act and with the proper execution of those powers.   My Lords, I say the proper mode of executing those powers, because it appears to me that it is very neatly and appositely put by Mr. Baron Fitzgerald in giving his judgment in the Court of Exchequer Chamber in this form.   Mr. Baron Fitzgerald says:—" The substantial question raised on the pleadings to the first and second counts of the declaration appears to me to be whether these acts of the defendants were done in a due exercise of their authority under the local and personal statute, which has been mentioned, without negligence."   And Lord Cairns, in the case of the *The Hammersmith Railway Company* v. *Brand* (L. R., 4 H. L., 171, at page 215), points out that it would be a repugnant and absurd piece of legislation to authorize by statute a thing to be done, and at the same time leave it to be restrained by injunction from doing the very thing which the Legislature has expressly permitted to be done.   Lord Cairns said:—" It appears to me that the effect of the legislation on this subject is to take away any right of action on the part of the landowner against the railway company for damage that the landowner has sustained.   It must be taken, I think, from the statements in this case, that the railway could not be used for the purpose for which it was intended without vibration.   It is clear to demonstration that the intention of Parliament was that the railway should be used.   If, therefore, it could not be used without vibration, and if vibration necessarily caused damage to the adjacent landowner, and if it was intended to preserve to the adjacent landowner his right of action, the consequences would be that action after action would be maintainable against the railway company for the damage which the landowner sustained ; and after same actions had been brought, and had succeeded, the Court of Chancery would interfere by injunction, and would prevent the railway being worked—which, of course, is a *reductio ad absurdum* ; and would defeat the intention of the Legislature.   I have, therefore, no hesitation in arriving at the conclusion that no action would be maintainable against the railway company.'' This permission, of course, does not authorize the thing to be done negligently, or even unnecessarily to cause damage to others. Much was argued by the learned counsel for the respondent as to the peculiar jurisprudence of Quebec, but in truth there is no such difference in this respect as he seemed to suppose. The law of England, equally with the law of the province in question, affirms the maxim *Sic utere tuo ut alienum non laedas ;* but the previous state of the law, whether in Quebec, or France, or England, cannot render inoperative the postive enactment of a statute ; and the whole case turns not upon what was the common law of either country, but what is the true construction of plain words authorizing the doing of the very thing complained of. The Legislature is supreme, and if it has enacted that a thing is lawful, such a thing cannot be a fault or an actionable wrong. The thing to be done is a privilege as well as a right and duty, and it seems to their Lordships it comes within the express language of the code (article 356). But it is said that the Dominion Railway Act itself expressly maintains the liability of railway companies under provincial law for damages caused by their operation, and section 92 is referred to. This may be disposed of in a sentence. That section refers to compensation under the Act, and not to damages in an action at all, which is what the question is here. Section 288 is more plausibly argued to have maintained the liability of the company, notwithstanding the statutory permission to use the railway ; but if one looks at the heading under which that section is placed, and the great variety of provisions, which give ample materials for the operation of that section, it would be straining the words unduly to give it a construction which would make it repugnant, and authorize in one part of the statute what it made an actionable wrong in another. It would reduce the legislation to an absurdity, and their Lordships are of opinion that it cannot be so construed. They will, therefore, humbly advise His Majesty that the judgment of the Court of Queen's Bench affirming the judgment of the Superior Court ought to be reversed, except as to costs. In the exercise of the discretion expressly reserved to their Lordships by the order-in-council granting leave to appeal, their Lordships direct the appellants to pay the respondent's costs of this appeal.

APPEAL DISMISSED, WITHOUT COSTS.

Solicitors for Appellant : *S. V. Blake.*

Solicitors for Respondent : *Fox & Preece.*

Editor's Notes :—

The law on the point in question in this case was decided in England in *Vaughan* v. *Taff Vale Railway Co.* (1860) 5 H. & N. 679, where it was laid down that a railway company authorized by the Legislature to use locomotive engines was not responsible for damage caused by sparks from one of its engines, provided that the company had taken such precautions as it could, had adopted all appliances approved of by science, and had not been guilty of any act of negligence regarding the use of the engine.

This same principle was reaffirmed in the more recent case of *Port-Glasgow and Newark Sailcloth Co. v. Caledonian Railway Co.* (1893), 30 Scot. L.R. 587, where Herschell, L.C., enunciated the law in the following terms :—'' It is now well settled law that in order to establish a case of liability against a railway company under such circumstances, it is essential for the pursuers to establish negligence.   The railway having the statutory power of running along the line with locomotive engines, which in the course of their running are apt to discharge sparks, no liability rests upon the company merely because of sparks emitted having set fire to adjoining property.   But the defenders, although possessing this statutory power, are undoubtedly bound to exercise it reasonably and properly, and the test, whether they exercise this power reasonably and properly, appears to me to be this : They are aware that locomotive engines running along the line are apt to emit sparks.   Knowing this, they are bound to use the best practicable means, according to the then state of knowledge, to avoid the emission of sparks which may be dangerous to adjoining property ; and if they, knowing that the engines are thus liable to discharge sparks, do not adopt that reasonable precaution they are guilty of negligence, and cannot defend themselves by relying upon their statutory power. About the law, as I have expressed it, I do not think there is any controversy."

The Supreme Court of Canada has adhered to the English rule that, in the absence of proof of negligence, a railway company is not responsible for fire caused by sparks emitted from its properly equipped and managed engine. The various cases decided by that court, however, have generally gone into the question whether or not a certain act or omission on the part of the railway company constituted negligence. Thus, in *New Brunswick Ry. Co.* v. *Robinson* (1884) 11 S.C.R. 688, it was held that the use of wood as fuel was not in itself evidence of negligence ; whilst in *North Shore Ry. Co.* v. *McWillie* (1890) 17 S.C.R. 511, it was decided that running a too heavily laden train up grade in the face of a strong wind, which caused a great number of sparks to be sent out by the engine, was negligence such as would render the company liable in damages to owners of adjoining property injured thereby.

See also *Canada Southern Ry. Co.* v. *Phelps* (1884) 14 S.C.R. 132. *Canada Atlantic Ry. Co.* v. *Moxley* (1887) 15 S.C.R. 145.

In the Province of Quebec, however, a different rule has prevailed, and it has generally been held that, under Article 1053 of the Civil Code, a railway company is, apart from any proof of negligence, liable for damage caused by sparks emitted from its locomotives. That article reads as follows : "Every person capable of discerning right from wrong is responsible for the damage caused by his fault to another, whether by positive act, imprudence, neglect or want of skill."

The line of reasoning, followed in at least one case, was that one who carries on a hazardous undertaking is liable for all the consequences, and that neither the fact that the work in question is for the public good, or that every precaution was taken in the way of using the latest appliances known to science, will avoid that liability.

(*Grand Trunk Ry. Co.* v. *Meegan* (1885) M.L.R., 1 Q. B, 314.)

Jodoin v. *South Eastern Ry. Co.* (1882) M.L.R., 1 S.C. 316.

Leonard v. *Canadian Pacific Ry. Co.* (1889) 15 Q.L.R. 93.

Northwest Atlantic Ry. Co. v. *Betournay* (1891) 21 R.L. 190.

In the more recent case of *Senésac* v. *Central Vermont Ry. Co.* (1896) R.J.Q., 9 S.C. 319, it was held that the action should be dismissed because there was not sufficient proof that the sparks from the engine occasioned the fire.

(This decision was confirmed by the Supreme Court on the same ground as that tribunal had affirmed the previous decision, in the contrary sense, of *G.T. Ry. Co.* v. *Meegan,* —that a finding of fact, not manifestly wrong, would not be interfered with.)

Abbott's Railway Law cites with approval (p. 417) the judgment in *Senésac* v. *C.V. Ry. Co.* as being a correct exposition of the law, the decision in *Jodoin* v. *S.E. Ry. Co.,* supra, being condemned (see p. 415) as not even being in accord with article 1053. But it appears that *Senésac* v. *C.V. Ry. Co.* does not, in fact, weaken the decision in the latter case or in others similarly decided in the Province of Quebec,—the *ratio decidendi* simply being that it was necessary to prove that sparks caused the loss.

The effect of the judgment of the Judicial Committee of the Privy Council in the case above reported appears to be that the rule of law on the subject is declared to be the same in the Province of Quebec as it is elsewhere in Canada, and in England.

It may be added that probably the case of damage caused by sparks from a locomotive may be distinguished from some of the other cases considered (e.g., that of vibration) on the ground that the latter constitutes a continuing nuisance.

[IN THE EXCHEQUER COURT OF CANADA.]

BEFORE BURBIDGE, J.

THE BOSTON RUBBER SHOE COMPANY

v.

THE BOSTON RUBBER COMPANY OF MONTREAL, Ltd.

Infringement of trade mark—Use of corporate name—
Proof of intent.

" The Boston Rubber Shoe Company " registered its name as a trade
mark in Canada about a year after " The Boston Rubber Company
of Montreal, Ltd.," had obtained incorporation as such.   In an
action brought by the former company to restrain the latter from
using what was, in effect, its corporate name upon its goods (which
were of the same nature as those manufactured and sold by the
plaintiff company), it was held that no such injunction could be
granted, and that there was no infringement unless the evidence
satisfied the court that such name had been chosen by the defendant
company for the purpose of using it in order to obtain some
advantage from the reputation which the plaintiff company's goods
had acquired under a somewhat similar name, or that, subsequently,
defendant company had used its corporate name fraudulently or in
bad faith in connection with the sale of its goods.

BURBIDGE, J.:—

The action is brought to restrain the defendant company
from impressing or using upon rubber boots and shoes manufactured by it words that constitute in substance its corporate name, and for damages for an alleged infringement
by such use of its name of the plaintiff company's registered
trade mark.

The plaintiff company was, in 1853, incorporated under
the laws of the Commonwealth of Massachusetts, by the name
of " The Malden Manufacturing Company," for the purpose
of manufacturing cotton, silk, linen, flax, or india rubber
goods at the town of Malden.   In 1855 its name was, by an
Act of the Commonwealth, changed to " The Boston Rubber
Shoe Company."   Since that time it has continued to do
business by that name, and its business has prospered.   In
rubber boots and shoes it manufactures two grades or lines
of goods ; the one that which is spoken of as " the Boston
Rubber Shoe line " and the other " the Bay State line."
The former are known to the trade, and have been since as

early as 1865 at least, as "Boston." The other grade is
known as "Bay State." The company's annual output of
rubbers is about twelve million pairs. Mr. Sawyer puts it
at from ten to fifteen millions. Of this quantity about half
are "Bostons" and half "Bay State." These goods are
sold in the United States, in Europe and in Canada. But
the sale in Canada is not, I infer from the evidence, large.
Mr. Smith, of French & Smith, of Montreal, shoe merchants for some seven years prior to last year, sold from
fifteen hundred to two thousand dollars worth of these
goods per annum ; but not so many during the last year.
Mr. O'Brien, another Montreal boot and shoe merchant,
says that at present he sells a very small quantity of the
plaintiff's goods ; and he explains the reason to be that the
duty is too great ; that it kept out American rubber goods
for the last few years excepting job lots sold at a reduction
in price. The regular goods they do not buy because they
are too high. Mr. George H. Mayo, of William F. Mayo
& Company; Boston, who are wholesale dealers in rubber
shoes, and who sell all over the United States and in
Canada rubber shoes made by the plaintiff company, gives
from his books the sales in Canada in the year 1900 of such
goods at something less than five hundred dollars worth.

In April, 1897, the plaintiff obtained registration in the
United States Patent Office of the words "Boston Rubber
Shoe Company" as a trade mark for rubber boots and
shoes. And in October in the same year it obtained registration in Canada of the same words as a specific trade
mark to be applied to the sale of rubber boots and shoes.
In October, 1896, The Toronto Rubber Shoe Manufacturing
Company, Limited, had, upon the allegation that it had
been the first to use the same, registered as a specific trade
mark to be applied to the sale of rubber boots and shoes
the word "Boston," and on September 27th, 1897, the
latter company assigned all its right, title and interest in
such specific trade mark to the plaintiff ; but without, so
far as appears, any assignment of any interest in the
business in which The Toronto Company had used or
intended to use such trade mark.

In 1878, George H. Hood and others obtained, in
accordance with the laws of the Commonwealth of Massachusetts then in force, a certificate of incorporation as The
Boston Rubber Company, with power, among other things,

to manufacture and sell articles consisting wholly or in part of india-rubber. For some ten years this company confined its manufacture and business to articles other than rubber boots or shoes.   It then commenced to manufacture such articles, and in 1889, it registered in the United States Patent Office a trade mark for india-rubber boots and shoes consisting of a bell upon which appear the words " Boston Rubber Co., Boston, Mass."   The Boston Rubber Shoe Company, becoming aware of the intention of The Boston Rubber Company to engage in the manufacture of boots and shoes, applied, in the first instance, to the Attorney-General of the Commonwealth, praying him to file an information in the nature of a writ of *quo warranto* against The Boston Rubber Company to the end that the latter company might show by what warrant it used its name. The application being refused, a petition was presented to the Supreme Judicial Court of the Commonwealth for leave to The Boston Rubber Shoe Company to file such an information.   The petition was dismissed.

In 1896 The Boston Rubber Company appears to have gone out of the business of manufacturing rubber boots and shoes, and the promoter of the defendant company purchased for nine thousand dollars the portion of its tools, machinery and plant mentioned in the agreement, a copy of which is in evidence.   The purchase included, among other things, all callenders, blocks, dies, patterns, moulds, and all furniture and tools specifically adapted for the manufacture of rubber boots and shoes.   This sale was effected on the 30th of May, 1896.   On the 26th of August of that year an application was made by Charles L. Higgins, the purchaser of this plant, and others, for incorporation under *The Companies Act* (R.S.C., c 119) by the name of " The Boston Rubber Company of Montreal, Limited," for the purpose of carrying on the business of manufacturers of all kinds of rubber and gutta percha goods, and of all goods in the manufacture of which rubber or gutta percha is used, and for the purpose of dealing in such goods.   After publication of the notice of application letters patent were on the 27th day of November, 1896, issued under the Great Seal of Canada incorporating the company for the purposes mentioned.   In explanation of the choice of name Mr. Higgins says that " the town of St. Jerome had voted a bonus of fifty thousand dollars to the new company starting, and designated that company as The Boston Rubber Company. Consequently we would have had to have another vote taken in the town and at considerable cost, and we thought it best to go on with the same name under the circumstances." The Boston Rubber Company, like most rubber shoe companies, had made two grades of rubber boots and shoes; the better grade had impressed upon it the name of the company on the device of a bell (the company's trade mark to which reference has been made); and the other grade bore the name of the Neptune Rubber Company. The defendant company never used the device of the bell for the reason as stated by Mr. Higgins that he thought it was a trade mark belonging to The Boston Rubber Company, and because it was in use by the firm of J. & T. Bell, of Montreal. In using the moulds purchased from The Boston Rubber Company the words "Boston" and "Mass." were .dropped and the word "Montreal" substituted. The defendant company also manufacture two grades of rubber boots and shoes. On the better grade are impressed the words "The Boston Rubber Company, Montreal, Limited," and these goods in the company's catalogues, price lists and advertisements are referred to as "Boston." In the Illustrated Catalogue, Exhibit No. 15, will be found the following:—"Our Neptune brand is everything we claim for it—a high grade second, not so good as the Boston, but a good, clean, well-made, stylish rubber that will give excellent satisfaction for the money;" and in the same catalogue, as well as in the price list, Exhibit No. 16, the words "Boston Rubber Company" without any addition of the word "Montreal" frequently occur.

Now although the sales of the plaintiff's goods in Canada do not appear to be, or so far as the evidence goes, to have been, considerable, the term "Boston" or "Bostons" has, it seems to me, come in some way to have a commercial value as attached to rubber boots and shoes; and this value has, I think, been given to it by the plaintiff's enterprise and business. I come to that conclusion notwithstanding the fact that the plaintiff has seen fit to take from another company an assignment of a specific trade mark to be applied to the sale of rubber boots and shoes consisting of the word "Boston" and obtained by such company on the allegation that it was the first to use it. I express no opinion one way or the other as to the validity of that trade mark either as used by the company that registered it, or in the hands of the plaintiff under the circumstances existing in this case. But I am not prepared to accept the allegation mentioned as true. On the contrary, unless one splits hairs over the words " Boston " and " Bostons " as applied to rubber boots and shoes, it seems to me reasonably certain that the plaintiff company was the first to make use of the term in that connection ; and that any value it has acquired in that connection, any secondary meaning that it has come to have as denoting excellence in rubber boots and shoes, has been derived from its use in the plaintiff's business. And it seems to me that the defendant company, as honest manufacturers and traders, ought to discontinue its use, except so far as it forms part of the corporate name of the company. But this action is not brought to restrain the use of the word " Boston " or " Bostons " in the company's catalogues, price-lists and advertisements, but to restrain it from using upon goods of its own manufacture what in substance is its corporate name, the only difference being the omission of the preposition " of " before Montreal. But that does not appear to me of itself to be of great importance ; and I should not have thought anything of it but for the intentional dropping of the word " Montreal, " also in other connections to which reference has been made. As it is one cannot wholly lose sight of the incident in coming to a conclusion as to whether the defendant is honestly impressing its corporate name on its goods, or whether it is endeavouring to put thereon something that will give it the advantage of the reputation acquired by the plaintiff's goods. It would, I think, be much better and safer for the defendant to put on its goods its corporate name in the terms in which that occurs in its letters-patent. But for Mr. Higgins' explanation I should, I think, have come to the conclusion that the name of the defendant company had been chosen, and the form in which it is impressed upon the goods manufactured by the company had been adopted with a view to use and to get the advantage of using the word " Boston " or " Bostons " to which, as connected with the rubber boot and shoe business the plaintiff company's years of successful business had, especially in the United States, given a trade value and importance. However, in view of that explanation, which under all the circumstances I accept as a true explanation, I must, I think, acquit him and the company of any intentional or fraudulent adoption or adaptation of any part of the plaintiff company's corporate name, which subsequently to the incor-

poration of the defendant company it has registered as its
trade mark. The action is for the infringement of a registered
trade mark. The infringement alleged is the use, substantially, by the defendant of its own name upon its own goods.
The name had been chosen and given after notice, before the
plaintiff's trade mark was registered. It had been chosen
and the application for incorporation made before The
Toronto Rubber Shoe Manufacturing Company applied for
the registration of the trade mark "Boston," although the
letters-patent did not issue until about a month after the
latter mark was registered. There is no evidence of any
attempt by the defendant company to sell its goods as those
of the plaintiff. There is nothing to lead me to think that
the defendant company has in the use of its corporate name
or otherwise, acted in bad faith or fraudulently. At most
it has, I think, made the mistake—made it perhaps honestly
enough—of thinking that as it had bought out the Boston
Rubber Company it had as good a right to the use of the
word "Boston" as anyone else. In that view it may be
wrong; but that is not I think the question now before me.
What is to be now determined is whether the company
may or may not impress its corporate name upon goods of
its own manufacture, and that I think it may do in the
absence of any fraud or bad faith. Under ordinary circumstances it is not of, course, necessary to aver or to prove fraud
to obtain protection for a trade mark. But cases in which
that which is complained of is the use of one's own name or
the use of a company of its corporate name, stand in a somewhat different position. One may, if he does it honestly
and with no fraudulent intent, use his own name on his own
goods, although they may tend to some confusion; and the
same is I think true of the use by a company of its corporate
name.

In the present case the name was no doubt chosen by the
persons incorporated; and it was granted by the Crown upon
the declaration by Charles Higgins, one of such persons, for
himself and those associated with him, that the proposed
corporate name of the company was not the name of any
other known company incorporated, or unincorporated, or
liable to be fairly confounded therewith, or otherwise on
public grounds objectionable. If I thought that there had
been intentional deception in obtaining the name, that it had
been chosen with a view of reaping an advantage from the
reputation that the plaintiff's rubber boots and shoes had

acquired in the market I do not doubt that I ought to restrain the defendant company from using the name upon the rubber boots and shoes manufactured by it.   But I do not think it was selected with any such object or motive ; or that it is used (I speak now of the use of the corporate name) in bad faith or for any fraudulent or improper purpose.   Within those limits it has, I think, so long as it is allowed to retain it, a right to use its own name on its own goods.   If Higgins' declaration that the name proposed was not liable to be confounded with that of any other company, and that the name is not on public grounds objectionable is not true, if in making that allegation he was mistaken, there are appropriate remedies provided, but these are not in question here.

There will be judgment for the defendant company, and the costs will follow the event.

ACTION DISMISSED WITH COSTS.

Solicitor for the Plaintiff : *R. V. Sinclair.*

Solicitors for the Defendant : *McGown & England.*

Editor's Note :—

Since the above judgment has been set up, the appeal therefrom has been argued in the Supreme Court of Canada. The notes on the points in question will be given with the report of the decision of the latter tribunal.

[IN THE SUPREME COURT OF NOVA SCOTIA]

BEFORE McDONALD, C. J.

CAPSTICK et al

v.

HENDRY et al.

Insolvency — Assignment for benefit of creditors — Effect of provisions in the deed.

A deed of assignment for the benefit of creditors provided that after the satisfaction of certain specified liabilities, the creditors who signed the deed within sixty days from the date thereof should be paid *pari passu*, and without any preference; and that the residue of the estate should then go towards the payment, *pari passu* and without preference, of the claims of such creditors as did not become parties to the deed within sixty day—Held, that the creditors who executed the deed after the sixty days, but before any dividend had been paid, were entitled to rank *pari passu* with those who had executed it within that period; and that those who executed it after the payment of the first, but before the payment of the second dividend, were entitled to share equally with those who had executed before, except that they could not participate in the first dividend.

[*Whitmore* v. *Turquand*, 3 De G. F. & J., 107; *Haliburtou* v. *de Wolfe*, 1 N. S. D. 12 and *Douglas* v. *Sanson*, 1. N. B. Eq. 137, *followed*]

13th DECEMBER; 1901 :—

McDONALD, C. J., :—

This cause came before me on originating summons taken out on behalf of Edward A. Capstick, assignee and trustee under a certain deed of assignment made by one Mary E. Locke, as well individually as doing business at Lockeport under the name and style of C. Locke & Co., for the purpose of determining whether the unpreferred creditors thereunder who executed the assignment within 60 days from the date thereof are entitled to receive payment of their claims against the estate in preference to any or all of certain other creditors who did not execute the deed until after 60 days from the said date had elapsed.

The facts are substantially as follows :—

The assignment which bears date, the 31st December, 1897, and was made by Mary E. Locke as well individually as doing business under the name and style of C. Locke & Co., was duly executed by her as party of the first part, the plaintiff Capstick, the assignee. as party of the second part, and various other persons, firms and corporations, who claimed to be creditors of the assignee, as parties of the third part.   Out of the proceeds of the estate the assignee, under the terms of the deed of assignment, was to pay the creditors of the assignor in the following order :

1. Certain specified preferred creditors ;

2. The creditors referred to in the following paragraph of the assignment :—

" Fourthly in trust that the said trustee after the " payment and satisfaction of the said debts, hereinbefore " mentioned, shall apply the residue of the said trust monies " in and towards the payment and satisfaction of the several " debts and sums of money due and payable to the several " creditors of the said party of the first part who shall " become parties hereto within sixty days from the day of " the date of these presents, *pari passu*, and without any " preference or priority of payment."

3. The creditors referred to in the following :—" And " lastly, after the payment and satisfaction aforesaid, then " in trust that he, the said trustee or his executors or " assigns do and shall pay and apply the surplus of the. " trust monies, if any there shall be, in and towards the " payment of the several debts and sums of money due the " other creditors of the said party of the first part who may " not have executed this assignment within sixty days, *pari* " *passu*, and without any preference or priority of pay- " ments."

The deed was executed on or about the day of its date, 31st December, 1897, by the assignor and the assignee.

The deed contains no clause of release from the creditors to the assignor.

Notice of this assignment was advertised by publication in the " Morning Herald " and " Morning Chronicle " newspapers published at Halifax, in the " Shelborne Budget " newspaper, published at Shelborne, and in the " Royal Gazette." This notice was first published about the 10th January, 1893, and the publication thereof was continued from time to time for 30 days thereafter.

No notice was sent direct to any of the creditors, and there was no notice of any kind excepting such as was given by advertisement in the manner above indicated.

Certain creditors executed the deed of assignment, within the 60 days, and certain other creditors did not execute it until after the expiration of the 60 days.

Those who did not execute within the 60 days are as follows :—

1. Black Bros. & Co., of Halifax, N.S., who executed on 9th March 1898.

2. Wm. Muir Son & Co., of Halifax, N. S., who executed on 16th March, 1898.

3. DeLong & Seaman, of Boston, in the United States of America, in March, 1898.

4. E. K. Spinney, of Yarmouth, on 25th March, 1898.

5. Canadian Drug Co., of St. John, N.B., on 27th December, 1898.

On or about 9th April, 1901, the assignee paid a dividend of 20%, and on or about the 15th June, 1901, a second dividend of 20% of their claims, to each of the defendants who executed the assignment within 60 days from its date.

The assignee has now in his hands the sum of $2,232.63 belonging to the estate, which he estimates to be sufficient, together with the previous payments made by him, to pay a dividend of about 76% on the claims of those creditors who signed within 60 days, or about 45% upon the claims of all these creditors as well as of those who executed after the 60 days had expired.

The creditors who executed the deed of assignment after the time limited therein and thereby had expired, claim that they are entitled to rank equally with those who executed before the period of 60 days had expired, and that one of these classes should have no preference or priority over another. The question for me to determine is whether the claim can be allowed.

The first dividend declared by the assignee was paid after all the present claimants excepting the East Brook & Canadian Drug Company had executed the deed of assignment.

The second dividend was paid after all the claimants had signed.

Somewhat similar questions have arisen in England, as in New Brunswick and our own Courts.

In *Whitmore* vs. *Turquand* 1, J. & H. 444. and on appeal 3 De G. F. & J. 107, a case not altogether like the present, it was held by Wood, V. C., and in the higher Court by the Chancellor, that the plaintiffs who had neither assented to nor dissented from the provisions of the deed (the benefit of which was limited to creditors who executed it within three months) might, under the circumstances, execute it after a lapse of five years, and be admitted to share in the benefit thereof with those who executed within the prescribed time, no dividend having been declared and no rights or liabilities being affected by the delay. At p. 110 of that case the Chancellor says :—

" Since the case of *Dunch* vs. *Kent* 1 Vern. 260, the doctrine of this Court has been that the time limited for creditors to come in is not of the essence of the deed."

That being the case the late Chief Justice in *Haliburton* v. *De Wolfe* 1 N. S. D. 12 asks :

" What is to hinder the Court from doing that which right and justice may require? "

In the case last referred to it is pointed out by the Chief Justice that the English Courts have always claimed and exercised the right of dispensing with the strict observance and letter of the contract, and have given relief to non-executing creditors on equitable grounds. In concluding his judgment he says as follows :—

" It is apparent from the stream of decisions that a court of equity has the power of passing by the letter of the restriction and permitting a creditor to come in afterwards."

That, in my opinion, is the settled principle. The Court has the power, to be exercised or not according to circumstances, of allowing on equitable grounds, a creditor to come in and participate in the benefits of such a deed after the time limited for his doing so has expired. It is thus stated in Winslow on Private Relations between Debtor and Creditor, pp. 18-22 :—" It would seem, therefore, that unless the deed requires peremptory exclusion of all who do not accede within the time limited, the Court will not regard the accession within that time as essential, and that even where the deed required peremptory exclusion of those not acceding within the time the Court would relieve against accidental omission to do so."

In *Douglas* vs. *Sanson* 1 N. B. Eq. at p. 137 Barker, J. says:—"I think the weight of authority is altogether against regarding the time within which creditors are to come in under the deed as absolute." And at p. 138:— "But whether he (the creditor) is allowed to come in or not must be determined on the particular circumstances of each case."

In my opinion, therefore, influenced by these equitable considerations, which I think should guide me, I must, under the circumstances detailed in the statement of facts and in the various affidavits filed, allow the claiming creditors to come in and rank, as hereinafter indicated, with those who executed the deed within the required time.

The same considerations which induce me to allow them to come in at all, induce me also to allow them to participate (*pari passu* with the creditors who executed within the 60 days) in the division of the estate as and from the time when each creditor signed the deed.

Those creditors who signed before any distribution at all was made will share equally with the others in every respect. Those who executed after the payment of the first and before the payment of the second dividend will share equally with the others in every respect excepting that they will not be allowed to participate in the dividend paid before they signed the deed.

The assignee will be allowed his costs out of the estate. I will hear one counsel on behalf of all claiming creditors as to the costs of that class.

Solicitors for the Plaintiffs : *Harris, Henry & Cahan.*

Solicitors for the Defendants signing within the time limited : *Drysdale & McInnes.*

Solicitors for the other Defendants : *Borden, Ritchie & Chisholm.*

Editor's Note :—

In the number of The Law Quarterly Review published in January, 1902, will be found (at p. 94·5) an interesting note upon the gradual extension of the use of an originating summons in chancery matters. In its inception it was only applicable to an order for the administration of personal estate : " The originating summons first arose under 15 and 16 Vict. c. 86 s. 45, and was confined to the simple case of an order for the administration of the personal estate of a dead man " (per Chitty J. in re *Busfield* 32 C. D. 123 at p. 125.)

———

[IN THE SUPERIOR COURT OF THE PROVINCE OF QUEBEC.]

BEFORE LORANGER, J.

DAME AMANDA GIRARD, Plaintiff.

v.

THE METROPOLITAN LIFE INSURANCE COMPANY, Defendant.

Life Insurance ·— Policy — Delivery — Premium — Conditional Receipt.

HELD :—1. That the mailing by a company at New·York, to its Montreal superintendent, of a policy containing a condition that the company assumed no obligation until the policy was delivered and the premium paid when the proposed life was alive and in good health, did not constitute a delivery to the assured.

2. That although the application containing the above mentioned conditions had been signed on February 24th, 1900 ; the applicant had been medically examined on the 28th of February, 1900 ; the policy had been approved of by the defendant's chief medical examiner, at New York, on March 5th ; a policy had been prepared and signed on the 8th of March, and mailed at New York on the 9th, addressed to defendant's Montreal superintendent, where it arrived on the 10th of March, 1900, and although deceased had paid $4.00 as an advanced premium, receiving a receipt containing the condition that " no insurance is to be in force upon the application unless and until the policy be issued thereon and delivered in accordance with the terms of the application," yet as proposed life had become dangerously ill on the 8th March, 1900, and had died on the 10th of March, 1900, before the policy had arrived in Montreal ready to be delivered conditionally on his being alive and in good health, and his paying balance of premium, no obligation was incurred by the company.

MONTREAL, 25 November, 1901.

LORANGER, J. (translation) :—

"Inasmuch as the Plaintiff, widow of the late Josaphat Binnette claims $1,000 00 the amount of the life insurance policy upon the life of her husband, alleging that the latter on the 24th of February, 1900, made an application for insurance on his life, naming his wife beneficiary, and paid $4 00 to the Defendant on account of the first premium ; that after being medically examined, applicant was accepted, and on the 2nd of March following, the Defendant issued a policy of insurance which it transmitted to its Montreal agent to be delivered to the said Binnette ; that the deposit at the New York Post Office of this policy to be delivered to Binnette in Montreal, constituted a sufficient delivery ; that Defendant's agent here retained the policy in his possession for several days after·having received it and neglected to deliver it to the said Binnette ; that the latter died on the 10th of March, 1900, after two days of sickness of congestion of the brain ; that the Plaintiff after the death of her husband went to Defendant's agent to obtain a delivery of the said policy, and the Company refused to deliver it ; that she has also made a demand for death claim papers and at the same time offered to pay the balance on the premium, which demand and offer were also refused ; that Plaintiff reiterating her offer of payment, prays for judgment against the Company for the amount of the said policy less the amount of the balance on premium due.

"Inasmuch as the Defendant pleads that it had been agreed that the said policy could only come into force when the first premium should have been paid in its entirety and accepted by the Company during the lifetime and good health of the said Binnette ; that part only of said premium was paid, and a conditional receipt given for same.

"That when the policy was signed at New York, the said Binnette was no longer in good health, and when it arrived in Montreal to be delivered conditionally, he was dead ; that it was only towards the end of the following month, many weeks after Binnette's death, that the Plaintiff offered to pay the balance of the premium due, and that the actual payment of the entire premium to and its acceptance by the Company during the lifetime and good health of the Plaintiff's husband, are two warranties without the accomplishment of which the policy had no effect, nor could the Company incur any responsibility ; that the premium not having been paid during the lifetime of Binnette, the policy remains without effect ; that it had not been issued, but was in the possession of the Company's agent at the time of Binnette's death, and that in consequence Plaintiff had no action.

" Considering that the application signed by the Plaintiff and her husband contains the following condition : That the policy if issued would not come into force until the premium had been actually paid to the Company and accepted by it during the lifetime and good health of the party proposed for insurance.

" Considering that the receipt given for the $4.00 paid on account of the first premium mentioned in the application contained the following declaration : That the insurance does not take effect unless and until the policy be delivered in accordance with the terms of the application.

" Considering that the medical examination of the Plaintiff's husband having been judged satisfactory, the application which he made was duly transmitted to New York to Defendant's head office, where on the 8th of March the policy was prepared, made out and signed by the Company's officers in conformity with the conditions, warranties and declarations contained in the application which was a part of the contract of insurance ; notably that the policy contained the condition that no obligation was assumed by the Company prior to the date of its delivery to the " Insured," and unless on the said date the " Insured " was alive and in good health.

" Considering that it has been proved that the said policy of insurance was only posted at New York on the 9th day of March, addressed to Defendant's superintendent at Montreal, where it arrived the following day.

" Considering that it has also been proved that the Plaintiff's husband was suddenly taken ill on the afternoon of the 8th of March and that he died during the morning of the 10th between 9 and 10 o'clock, before the policy arrived at its destination ; that the Defendant's superintendent having been informed of the death of the Plaintiff's husband offered during the following week to return the $4.00 that had been paid, and that he refused to deliver the said policy, and returned it to the head office at New York.

"Considering that although the acceptance of a proposition of insurance, constitutes a valid agreement of insurance (Art. 2481, Civil Code, Quebec), in the present instance, the proposition of the Plaintiff's husband was subject to certain conditions which it was impossible for him to carry out owing to his sickness and death.

"Considering that the mailing at the New York Post Office of the policy of insurance addressed to Defendant's Montreal superintendent could not be considered under the circumstances to constitute a delivery of the said policy to the "Insured," being subordinated to the conditions precedent to which the "Insured" had agreed, to wit, that the policy could only be validly delivered if the balance of the premium due should be paid during the lifetime and good health of the proposed life.

"Considering that under these conditions, the Defendant after mailing the said policy to its Montreal superintendent to be delivered to the "Insured," did not disposses itself thereof, but on the contrary it was not permissible to the superintendent to give up the said policy before the conditions precedent relating to its delivery had been accomplished by the said Binnette.

"Considering that the warranties contained in the application of the Plaintiff's husband form part of the contract between him and the Defendant, and that the receipt given him for the payment of the said $4.00 was a conditional one.

"Considering that the conditions precedent to the delivery of the said policy were not accomplished, and that the said policy is without effect, grants Defendant's prayer and dismisses the action.

Solicitors for Plaintiff : *Hutchinson & Oughtred*.

Solicitors for Defendant : *Claxton & Kennedy*.

Editor's Notes :—

A contract of insurance becomes operative at the time when an agreement is arrived at by the insurer and the person to be insured. As a general rule it may be taken that such is the case when the premium is offered to and accepted by the insurer.

See *Canning* v. *Farquhar* (1886), 54 L. T. 350.

Policies are subject to the conditions they contain. Thus, in the American case of *McClave* v. *Mutual Reserve Fund Life Ass'n* (1892) 55 N. J. 187, (in which the facts were somewhat similar to those of the case reported above) it was held that where a policy contained a clause to the effect that no liability should arise unless the premium was paid and the policy was delivered in the lifetime of the insured, a delivery after the death of the insured would not render the insurer liable on the policy.

See also *Gallant* v. *Metropolitan Life Insurance Co.* (1896), 167 Mass, 79 :

Markey v. *Mutual Benefit Life Insurance Co.* (1879) 126 Mass, 158.

And in Porter on Insurance (Blackstone Edit.) it is stated at p. 46 ; " Insurers usually issue a policy even if the loss intervenes between the acceptance and the usual time for issuing. But it would appear that if the risk is changed before the premium is paid they will not be liable."

And at Porter, p. 75, it is said : " But it is the almost universal practice of insurers, other than marine, to stipulate that the contract shall not begin to take effect until the premium has been paid, and the Courts in the presence of such a stipulation will not, (unless the premium has been paid), give effect to the contract, where a loss has happened after an agreement to issue and accept a policy, but before the policy has been issued, or even when it has been delivered as an escrow."

In the case of *Buck* v. *Knowlton*, (1893) 21 S. C. R. 371, it appeared that K, the agent of a certain insurance company had sent his company an application, upon which the head office, issued a policy, which was mailed to K. After the policy had thus been sent to, but before it was received by K, the ship which was thereby insured was lost, and the company telegraphed K, not to deliver the policy, but to eturn it immediately. K did as he was directed, and the
r

Supreme Court of Canada held that "the property in the policy prepared at the head office and sent to K never passed out of the company, and was at the most no more than an escrow in the hands of the agent."

As to the delivery of the policy, without payment of the first premium, being insufficient to bind the insurance company ; see *Confederation Life Assurance* v. *O'Donnell* (1883) 10 S.C.R. 92 ; *Giles* v. *Jacques* (1885) 29 L. C. J. 138.

It is to be remembered, however, that the delivery of the policy is not essential to the completion of the contract unless there is a condition making it so.

Thus it is said in Porter on Insurance, (at p. 101) :—

"The commencement of the risk in the absence of a special stipulation is not conditional on the delivery to the assured of a policy, provided that the first premium is paid, and that the policy in all other respects is complete, and in such a case even death before complete delivery of the policy is no bar to recovery unless so stipulated."

In a recent English case the evidence shewed that an insurance policy against burglary had been made in accordance with the proposal, and had been duly signed and sealed, by the proper officer of the company. The policy contained a condition that no insurance should be held to be affected until the first premium due under the policy had been paid. The policy was kept by the company, and a loss occurred before the premium was paid. It appeared, however, that the insured had always been ready to pay the premium ; and it was therefore held that the company had waived that condition, and that (although the policy had not been delivered) the insured was entitled to recover on the policy.

Roberts v. *Security Co.* (1897) 1 Q. B. 111.

See also the very recent decision of a Divisional Court of the High Court of Justice for Ontario in *Armstrong* v. *Provident Saving Life Assurance Society*, reported in this number :

[IN THE HIGH COURT OF JUSTICE FOR ONTARIO.]

BEFORE FALCONBRIDGE C. J. K. B.

HALL v. HATCH.

BANK OF MONTREAL v. HATCH.

Execution — Money paid out by bank teller — Passing of property therein.

> H, a superannuated civil service employee, handed his superannuation declaration to the teller of the bank which was authorized to pay the superannuation allowance. The teller counted the money due under the certificate, and placed the bank-notes upon the ledge in the wicket between the teller's box and the outer office where H was standing; but before H touched the notes they were seized by a bailiff under an execution against H which had been placed in the hands of the sheriff. Held, that the property in the bank-notes passed to H as soon as they were placed on the ledge, and that, therefore, the seizure on behalf of the execution creditor was legal.

This was an appeal from a judgment of the local Master at Ottawa in an interpleader issue between the Bank of Montreal as claimant, against one Walter Hatch as execution creditor and the sheriff of the county of Carleton, directed in an action in the High Court of *Hall* v. *Hatch*, the defendant Hatch having recovered a judgment and issued execution against the plaintiff Hall.

The issue was directed at the instance of the sheriff, to try the right to a certain fund in his hands, which was claimed by the Bank of Montreal as well as by the execution creditor, the defendant Hatch. The plaintiff Hall claimed the same money from the bank, or alternatively, for the return of his pension certificate or cheque; and, by the consent of all parties, both the bank's claim to the money so seized and also Hall's claim over against the bank were disposed of summarily by the Master at Ottawa under Con. Rules 1110 and 1111.

The matter was argued before the Master at Ottawa, on the 27th of June, 1901.

The local Master gave the following judgment :—

July 15, 1901, W. L. SCOTT, L. M. :—This is an interpleader application made on behalf of the sheriff of the county of Carleton.   The facts are not in dispute, and are as follows :—

The plaintiff Hall is a superannuated civil servant entitled to receive the sum of sixty-three dollars per month from the Receiver-General of Canada, through the Bank of Montreal.

On the 27th of May, 1901, he went to the Ottawa office of the bank, and there presented to the paying teller the usual superannuation declaration for the purpose of drawing his allowance for the month of May.

The teller took up the declaration, counted out the sum of sixty-three dollars in notes and placed them upon the ledge in the wicket which communicates between the teller's box and the outer office of the bank, in front of Hall, for him to take up.   After the teller had removed his hand from the notes, and while they were still lying upon the ledge, but before they had been in any way touched or handled by Hall, they were seized by a sheriff's bailiff, under an execution issued at the suit of the execution creditor, Hatch.

Hall, through his solicitors, subsequently demanded payment of the sixty-three dollars from the bank, and the latter thereupon made a claim on the money in the sheriff's hands.

When the matter came before me the sheriff's right to interplead was not disputed, and all parties were agreed that instead of directing an issue, I should dispose summarily of the matters in dispute, under the provisions of Rules 1110 and 1111.   The plaintiff Hall also consented to come in and, in order to save expense, he and the bank agreed that their rights *inter se* should be determined here, without further litigation.

At common law the sheriff had no authority to seize money.   This right was first conferred in England by 1 and 2 Vict. ch. 110, sec. 12 ; and in Canada by the old Common Law Procedure Act of 1856, 20 Vict. ch. 57, sec. 22.   The legislation at present governing the matter is sec. 18 of the Execution Act, R. S. O. 1897 ch. 77, which reads .   " The sheriff or other officer having the execution of a writ against goods. . . shall seize any money or bank notes. . . belonging to the person against whose effects the writ of execution has issued, " etc.

The question on the answer to which the decision of this case depends, therefore, is, had the property in the notes passed to Hall at the moment when the sheriff's bailiff seized them ? If they were at that moment "belonging " to Hall they were liable to seizure, but not otherwise.

Among the numerous cases cited on the argument, the one which throws most light on that question is *Chambers* v. *Miller* (1862),13 C. B. N. S., 125, also reported 32 L. J. C. P. N. S. 30. The facts of the case were as follows. The plaintiff presented a cheque at the defendant's banking-house. The defendants' cashier counted out the amount in notes, gold, and silver, and placed it on the counter and went away. The plaintiff drew the money towards him, counted it over, and was in the act of counting it a second time, when the cashier (who had in the meantime ascertained of enquiry that the account of the drawer was overdrawn) returned and said that the cheque could not be paid. The plaintiff, however, having possession of the money, put it in his pocket, whereupon the cashier detained him until he returned the money, under a threat of giving him into custody on a charge of stealing it. Upon these facts it was held that the property in the notes had passed from the bankers to the bearer of the cheque, and that the payment was complete and could not be revoked. I shall quote some passages from the judgments, which I think will afford assistance in dealing with the present case.

Erle C. J., says, at pp. 132, 133 : " When a cheque is presented at the counter of a banker, the banker has authority on the part of his customer to pay the amount therein specified on his account. The money in the banker's hands is his own money. On presentment of the cheque, it is for the banker to consider whether the state of the account between him and his customer will justify him in passing the property in the money to the holder of the cheque. In this case, the banker's clerk had gone through that process, and so far as in him lay did that which would pass the property in the money to the plaintiff. He counted out the notes and gold and placed them on the counter for the plaintiff to take up. It no longer remained a matter of choice or discretion with him whether he would pay the cheque or not. The plaintiff had taken possession of the money, counted it once, and was in the act of counting it again, when the clerk, who had gone from the counter . . . returned and

claimed . . . to have the money back. Now, the bankers
had parted with the money, and the plaintiff had accepted
it. It is true he had not finished counting it, and that, if he
had found a note too much or a note short, there was still
time to rectify the mistake. But, according to the intention
of the parties; and the course of business, the money had
ceased to be the money of the bankers, and had become that
of the party presenting the cheque . . . The banker's clerk
chose to pay the cheque ; and the moment the person presenting the cheque put his hand upon the money, it became
irrevocably his ''

Williams, J., says, at pp. 134, 135 : " I see no ground
whatever for saying that the transaction was incomplete.
There was no evidence that anything further remained to
be done to complete it. The act of counting was no indication
on the part of the plaintiff that he had not accepted the
money. The argument was founded upon a mistaken view
of the mode in which the question arises. Where money is
paid, not in performance of a promise, at the precise day on
which it ought to have been paid, but in satisfaction of a
breach of promise, there must be not only payment, but
acceptance in satisfaction. That, however, is not so where
the payment is made in performance of an agreement on the
precise day, or where the creation of the right to receive the
money and the act of payment are simultaneous. In these
cases, where the money finds its way into the hands of the
person to whom the payment is to be made, the transaction
is complete.''

Byles, J., says, at p. 136 : "I must confess that I should
be inclined to hold, as a matter of law, that so soon as the
money was laid upon the counter for the holder of the
cheque to take, it became the money of the latter.''

Keating, J , says, at p. 137 : " The cashier counted out
the money, and placed it on the counter for the purpose and
with the clear intention of putting it under the control of
the person who presented the cheque. This was no conditional payment—as if the cashier had said to the party, ' I
hand you this money in payment of the cheque, on condition
of your counting it, and assenting to its correctness.' Suppose the plaintiff had been content to take up the money
without stopping to count it, could anybody doubt that the
property would have passed ? It does not the less pass

because the recipient chooses to count it before he puts it in his pocket.

Before applying the principles here enunciated to the present case, I shall examine some of the other authorities cited on the argument.   In Byles on Bills, 15th ed., p. 305, the law is stated to be as follows : '' Money laid down on the counter by a banker's cashier in payment of a cheque cannot be recovered back by action, though it were handed over under a misapprehension of the state of the drawer's account . . .A banker's counter is in the nature of a neutral table, provided for the use of both banker and customer. As soon as the money is laid down by the banker upon the counter to be taken up by the receiver, the payment is complete.''   The cases cited in support of this are *Chambers* v. *Miller*, and a case of *Pollard* v. *The Bank of England* (1871) L. R. 6 Q. B. 623.   In the latter case the circumstances were so different that it throws little, if any, light on the present case.

In Morse on Banks and Banking, 3rd ed., sec. 449, the principle is thus stated : ''From the moment that the act of transfer is completed, and the minds of the parties have met and agreed upon the thing transferred as constituting a payment, instantly the right to repudiate or annul the transaction ceases.   If the bank discovers at once that the drawer's account was overdrawn before the cheque was paid, it cannot recall the funds from the possession of the holder, not even if he be still at the counter, provided the act of transfer had been perfected by the intent and act of both parties, leaving nothing further to be done. ''

The American case of *Root* v. *Ross* (1857), 29 Ver. 483, decides that the fact that there is a dispute about the amount of money handed over does not make the transaction any less a complete payment.   In that case the defendant's agent handed a roll of bills to the plaintiff's attorney, stating that it contained sixty-three dollars.   The latter counted it and found only sixty-two.   It was then handed to a third party to count, who, being a sheriff, seized the money under an execution against the plaintiff.   It was held to be a complete payment, notwithstanding the dispute as to the amount.

In *Thompson* v. *Kellog* (1856), 23 Mo. 281, the head-note reads :   '' In order to constitute a transaction a payment, there must be both a delivery by the holder and an acceptance by the creditor, with the purpose on the former to part with, and of the latter to accept of, the immediate ownership of the thing passed from the one to the other. '' It was a suit by the plaintiff against his attorney to recover the amount of a bill on the ground that the acceptor, one De Baun, had paid the money to the attorney. The bill was presented at maturity by the Defendant to De Baun, who, when payment was demanded, uncovered a large quantity of dimes and half-dimes lying on a table and told the defendant that there was the money for him.   Defendant went up to the table, put his hand on the money, and in running his hand over it mixed it somewhat, and said, '' I suppose I shall have to take it, and I will go to my office to get bags for it '' : p. 282.   Defendant then went out and returned in three or four minutes. During this interval, a levy had been made upon the money as the property of De Baun under a judgment against him. Defendant again demanded payment of the bill.   De Baun told the defendant that there was the money ; that he had once paid it to defendant.   Defendant replied, '' I won't receive it ; it is in the hands of the sheriff.'' It was left to the jury to say whether or not the money had been paid to the defendant, under certain instructions from the Court which, in so far as they have any bearing on the present case, were as follows :— '' 1. If the jury believe from the evidence that . . . De Baun offered to the Defendant the amount . . . and the defendant received the same in immediate satisfaction of the draft ; . . . the jury should find for the plaintiff. 2. If the amount of the draft was tendered to the defendant by De Baun, as, aforesaid, and the same was not received by the defendant in immediate satisfaction of the draft ; or if anything remained to be done by the defendant, such as counting the money before the defendant would receive the same in satisfaction of the draft, then the jury should find for the Defendant. 3. A tender of the money to the defendant was not payment unless he received the same in immediate satisfaction of the draft ; . . . '' The jury found in favour of the defendant, and, an appeal from the finding was dismissed.

In delivering the judgment of the Court. Leonard, J., said : In order to constitute the transaction a payment, there must be both a delivery by the debtor and an acceptance by the creditor, with the purpose on the part of the former to part from, and of the latter to accept of, the immediate ownership of the thing passed from the one to the other . . . Admitting that the money, was within the physical control of the creditor, the question yet remained whether it was there with intent on his part to keep it as owner, which was necessary in order to make it presently his property ; or, in the words of the Court, whether he received it "in immediate satisfaction of the draft," or only with a view to count it over, reserving to himself, until after the examination and count were completed, the privilege of determining whether he would decline or accept the payment."

It will be noted that the question before the Court was not whether or not what took place was sufficient to pass the property in the coin to the defendant as agent for the plaintiff, but whether or not the jury who found that the property had not passed, were properly instructed by the Court. Unless the case of the presentment of a bill of exchange for payment at maturity can be distinguished from that of a cheque presented for payment at the office of a bank, the law as laid down in this case is slightly at variance with the statements of law to be found in the judgment in *Chambers* v. *Miller*.

In the latter case, as appears from the extracts already given. all of the four judges agree in saying that, under the circumstances, a payment is none the less complete merely because the payee has still to count the money.

Again, two at least of the judges, Williams and Byles, JJ., lay it down that no specific act of acceptance is in such a case necessary on the part of the payee, and there is nothing directly at variance with this view in either of the other judgments. What is actually decided by the case is, that were the holder of a cheque presents it to the teller of a bank for payment and the latter places the money on the counter for the former to take up, the property in the money passes from the bank to the holder of the cheque, at all events, the moment the latter places his hand on it, and that his not having yet counted it makes no difference.

I am asked here to carry the law one step further and say that the property passes even before the holder of the cheque, or in this case, the superannuation declaration, takes the money into his physical control. While this goes beyond the actual decision in *Chambers* v. *Miller*, it is not,

I think, contrary to it. It is, on the other hand, directly supported by the dictum already quoted of Mr. Justice Byles, and the statement in "Byles on Bills." Moreover, it is, I think, sound in principle. That, which, after all, must govern is the intention of the parties, to be gathered from their actions. Let us see then what takes place here.

Hall goes to the bank with his superannuation declaration, intending to draw the sixty-three dollars due to him. He presents the declaration to the paying teller, and the latter, acting for the bank, examines it, and finding it to be in proper form, decides to pay it. For this purpose he counts out sixty-three dollars in bills, and places them on the counter in front of Hall for him to take up. The teller has then, for the bank, done all in his power to pass the property in the bills to Hall. Hall has all along had the intention of receiving the money from the bank, since that was his very purpose in going there, and as he sees the teller count out and place on the counter certain bills, his intention evidently is to receive those very bills, subject, perhaps, to his counting them, but certainly subject to nothing else. Apart from the possibility of the amount being incorrect, or some of the bills not genuine, circumstances which it follows from *Chambers* v. *Miller* will not alone prevent the property in the money from passing, what conceivable reason could there be for Hall's not accepting the money he went to the bank to draw? At the moment, therefore, that the bills were placed on the bank counter, the minds of Hall and of the bank, represented by the teller, were at one. The latter intended to pass the property in those very bills to the former, and the former intended to receive them. The transaction would, therefore, appear to be complete.

I therefore hold that when the sheriff's officer seized the bills now in question, they were the property of the judgment debtor Hall.

It was argued on Hall's behalf, that his case was somewhat different from that of an ordinary customer of the bank, by reason of the bank's being the agent of the Government for the purpose of paying him the money. I do not see that this fact has any bearing on the case. The bank was paying its own money to Hall, in the expectation of being subsequently reimbursed by the Government; but even were it the very money of the

Government that was being paid out, the case would be in no respect different. Before the property in the bills passed, they were not seizable, whether they belonged to the bank or to the Government ; after the property passed, they were in either case Hall's bills, and so liable to seizure under the execution.

Counsel for the bank contended that even were the payment complete, as between the bank and Hall, at the moment of the seizure, yet the former had still an interest in the money, in the nature of a lien, sufficient to entitle it to prevent its seizure. No authority was cited in support of the existence of this supposed right, and I can see no reason for holding that it does exist. It was argued, that even if the money was Hall's money when seized, the bank had still a right to have it counted ; but it is plain from the language of the judges in *Chambers* v. *Miller*, and would seem to be clear law, apart from that decision, that the bank has no right whatever to compel the payee of a cheque to count money paid to him.

There will be judgment for the execution creditor with costs, and the claim of Hall against the bank will be dismissed with costs, payable by Hall to the bank. There will be the usual order as to the sheriff's costs.

From this judgment the plaintiff Hall and the claimant bank both appealed, and the appeals were argued together in Weekly Court at Ottawa, on the 6th of October, 1901, before FALCONBRIDGE, C.J.K.B.

DECEMBER 9, 1901. FALCONBRIDGE, C. J.:—I have consulted the authorities referred to in the extremely careful and elaborate judgment of the learned Master at Ottawa, and I have likewise perused and considered the additional citations and references on the argument before me : 11 Am. & Eng Ency. of Law, 2nd Ed., title "Estoppel," p. 385 et seq.; *Newington* v. *Levy* (1870) L. R. 6 C. P. 180 ; Holmested & Langton, 2nd Ed., 499, 500, 792, 794 ; Snow's Annual Practice, 1901, 355 ; *Ainsworth* v. *Wilding,* (1896) 1 Ch. 673 ; *Cropper* v. *Smith* (1884), 26 Ch. D. 700.

I see no reason to differ from the result of the Master's judgment, nor to add anything to what he has written on the subject.

Appeal dismissed with costs.

Solicitors for the Bank : *Gormully & Orde.*

Solicitors for the execution debtor : *Lewis & Smellie.*

Solicitor for the execution creditor : *R. V. Sinclair.*

Solicitor for the Sheriff : *MacCracken, Henderson & McDougall.*

[IN THE HIGH COURT OF JUSTICE FOR ONTARIO.]

BEFORE FALCONBRIDGE, C. J.

COUNSELL

v

LIVINGSTON et al.

Promissory Note — Sufficiency of — Notice of Dishonour — Husband and Wife.

On the day after a promissory note fell due, notice was sent to one of the indorsers thereof in the following terms :—" Dear Sir : I beg to advise you that Mr. T. C. L's note for $3,500 in your favour and indorsed by yourself and wife, and held by our estate, was due yesterday. As I have not received renewal, will you kindly see that same is forwarded with cheque for discount, as there is no surplus on hand." Held, that this letter was a sufficient notice of dishonour both to the indorser to whom it was addressed, and also to his wife, as the evidence shewed that he was her agent in the transaction.

Action (tried at Hamilton) by Charlotte F. Counsell, executrix of the will of C. M. Counsell, against T. C. Livingston, as the maker, and W. C. Livingston and Charlotte E. Livingston as the indorsers of a promissory note for $3,500.

The facts of the case are set forth in the judgment.

NOVEMBER 6. FALCONBRIDGE, C. J.:—The promissory note sued on was made by the Defendant Thomas C. Livingston, payable to the order of the defendant W. C. Livingston, (son of the maker), and indorsed by W. C. Livingston, and Charlotte Livingston, wife of the said W. C. Livingston.

It fell due on the 20th March, and was on that day presented by Mr. J. L. Counsell at the Bank of Montreal, the ledger-keeper replying, "No funds." In the course of the same day he (J. L. Counsell) saw the maker who said he had not the renewal, but would get it. Next morning the maker came into J L. Counsell's office, and said he had not the renewal yet. The note had been renewed many times, further renewals were in contemplation, and there were among the papers of the Plaintiff's testator blank notes signed by Thomas C. Livingston payable to the order of W. C. Livingston, but not indorsed by the latter.

I found at the trial that the defendant Thomas C. Livingston had no defence to the action, and I also found as a fact that J. L. Counsell on Tuesday, the 21st March did sign, enclose, stamp and mail in the general post-office at Hamilton the following letter :

HAMILTON, CANADA,

21st March, 1901.

Dear Sir,—I beg to advise you that Mr. T. C. Livingston's note for $3,500 in your favour and indorsed by yourself and wife, and held by our estate, was due yesterday.

"As I have not received renewal, will you kindly see that same is forwarded with cheque for discount, as there is no surplus on hand.

Yours truly,

J. L. COUNSELL.

W. C. LIVINGSTON, ESQ.,
  Brantford, Ont.

The two questions now to be decided are : (1) is the above a good notice of dishonour so as to hold W. C. Livingston? and further (2) if so, is the notice to W. C. Livingston a good and sufficient notice to his wife, the defendant Charlotte Livingston.

It was contended on behalf of the defendants W. C. Livingston and Charlotte Livingston that the letter in question was not a sufficient notice of dishonour, on the authority of *Solarte* v. *Palmer* (1834), 1 Bing, N. C. 194, and of *Furze* v. *Sharwood* (1841), 2 Q. B. 388. The first-named case was a judgment of the House of Lords (temp. Lord Brougham), and the opinion of the Judges was given by Park J.

As early as 1853 regret was confessed by Lord Campbell, C. J. at this decision. He said in *Everard* v. *Watson* (1853), 1 E. & B. 801, 804: "It has caused much confusion. It is, however, a decision which we cannot reverse; indeed, I fear the House of Lords could not do so. But I do wish that it were reversed by Act of Parliament. so as to relieve the commercial world from the risk of misconceiving the law." And he then proceeded to disregard the judgment on the ground that the words in the case which he was considering were not the same as those used in *Solarte* v. *Palmer*. In *Paul* v. *Joel* (1858), 27 L. J. N. S. Ex. 380, Pollock, C. B., again regretted (p. 383) the case of *Solarte* v. *Palmer*. "This inconvenient decision was eventually got rid of by considering it merely as a finding on the particular facts": see *Regina* v. *Bank of Montreal* (1886), 1 Ex. C. R. 154, at p. 171. It does not appear, as Judge Chalmers says in the 5th edition of his Digest of the Law of Bills of Exchange, at p. 158, that since 1841 any written notice of dishonour has been held bad on the ground of insufficiency of form. See also Byles on Bills, 16th edition, pp. 227-9; MacLaren on Bills and Notes, 2nd edition, p. 263; *Bailey* v. *Porter* (1845), 14 M. & W. 44.

For these reasons, I think that the notice was sufficient.

A perusal of the examination of Mrs. Livingston satisfies me that her husband is her agent in this behalf, and that notice of dishonour has been given to him for her under the Bills of Exchange Act, sec. 49, sub-sec. (h).

The plaintiff is therefore entitled to judgment against all the defendants for the amount of the note and interest, with full costs of suit.

Solicitors for the Plaintiff: *Martin & Martin.*

Solicitors for the Defendants, *T. C. Livingston: Herd and Livingston.*

Solicitors for the other Defendants: *Staunton & O'Heir.*

Editor's Notes:—

In Chalmers Bills of Exchange, 4th Edit., at p. 158, it is stated that "In 1834, the House of Lords, in *Solarte* v. *Palmer*, 1 Bing. N. C. 194, decided that the notice must inform the holder, either in terms or by necessary implication, that the bill had been presented and dishonoured: This inconvenient decision was frequently regretted, and was eventually got rid of by considering it merely as a finding on the particular facts (*Paul & Joel*, 27 L.J., Ex. at p. 384.) Since 1841 it does not appear that any written notice of dishonour has been held bad on the ground of insufficiency in form.''

The case decided in 1841, which is referred to in the above quotation, is that of *Furze v. Sharwood*, 2 Q. B. 388. In that case the following notice of dishonour was held to be insufficient: '' This is to give you notice that a bill drawn by you, and accepted by Josiah Bateman, for £47, 18s., 9 d., due July 19th, 1835, is unpaid, and lies due at Mr. Furze's, 65 Fleet Street.''

Chalmer's 4th Edit., says, at. p. 158, (note 6), that this notice ''would now probably be sufficient.''

In *Paul* v. *Joel*, (*supra*) the facts were that the holder of a bill of exchange called at the office of J., the drawer, on the day after its maturity. J. being then engaged he wrote on a piece of paper and sent in to him a notice in the following words: '' B's acceptance to J., £500, due 12th January is unpaid; payment to Roberts & Co. is requested before four o'clock.'' This notice was held to be sufficient.

In *King* v. *Bickley*, 2 Q. B. 419, a case decided at about the same time as *Furze* v. *Sharwood*, *supra*, it was held that following notice: '' I hereby give you notice that a bill of exchange for £50. at three months after date, by A. upon and accepted by B , and indorsed by you, lies at etc., dishonoured,'' sufficed, without any further statement to the effect that the defendant was looked to for payment.

The notice which was held to be sufficient in *Bailey* v. *Porter*, (1845) 14 M. & W., 44, was in the following terms: '' We beg to inform you that your indorsement of J. C's acceptance of £40, due the 17th June, 1842, remains due, with interest and expenses, as also other bills and to which we request your immediate attention, B. & Co.

· While the notice which the court considered sufficient in *Everard* v. *Watson* (1853) 1 E. & B. 801, reads thus: " We beg to acquaint you with the non-payment of W. M's acceptance to J. W's draft of 29th December last, at four months, £50, amounting with expenses to £50, 5s, 1 d., which remit us in course of post without fail, or pay to Messrs. E."

As to the sufficiency of notices of dishonour sent by post, even when the party to whom it is sent resides in the same town as the sender, see the decision of the Supreme Court in *Merchants Bank of Halifax* v. *McNutt* (1883) 11 S. C. R. 126.

———

[IN THE SUPREME COURT OF BRITISH COLUMBIA]

ADAMS AND BURNS

v.

BANK OF MONTREAL, THE KOOTENAY BREWING, MALTING AND DISTILLINC COMPANY, LIMITED LIABILITY, AND JOHN R. MYERS.

Debtor and Creditor — Preference — Collusion — Pressure — R.S.B.C. 1897, Caps. 86 and 87—Bank Act, Sec. 80.

Company — Mortgage by directors — Ratification by shareholders—The Companies Act, and amendments.

Where there is good consideration a mortgage comprising the whole of a debtor's property, will not be set aside even though the mortgagor is in insolvent circumstances to the knowledge of the mortgagee and the effect of the mortgage is to defeat, delay and prejudice the creditors, if pressure is proved.

A mortgage made by the directors of a company prior to the consent of its shareholders, without which consent there was no power to borrow, may be ratified by the shareholders.

Action to set aside (1.) a mortgage of real and personal property dated the 23rd day of September, A. D. 1897, given by the Kootenay Brewing, Malting and Distilling Company, Limited Liability, to the Bank of Montreal ; (2.) an assignment of book-debts by the Company to the Bank, dated October 2nd, 1897, and (3.) a judgment recovered by the Bank against the Company on December 1st, 1897, for $31,908.01.

The plaintiffs contended (1,) that the alleged mortgage was voluntary, fraudulent and void under the statute of Elizabeth ; (2.) that it was also void as a fraudulent preference ; (3) that is was also void as not having been executed in accordance with the provisions of the Companies Act, 1890, under which the defendant Company was incorporated; (4.) that the assignment of book-debts was void for the same reasons, and also for having been carried out in contravention of the Bank Act ; (5) that the said judgment was voluntary, fraudulent and void under the statute of Elizabeth, and (6.) that the money received by the Bank of Montreal from the sale of the said assets and from realization of the said book-debts, were exigible under the plaintiffs executions, and that the said Bank should be ordered to pay the same.

At the trial relief was not asked against defendant Myers, who had purchased the assets of the defendant Company from the Bank and had re-sold them, or the greater part thereof, before he was made a party to the action, and the action was dismissed as against him. The facts appear fully in the judgment of the trial Judge.

The trial took place at Rossland in February, 1899, before MARTIN, J.

GALT, for plaintiffs.

HAMILTON, for defendants, the Bank of Montreal.

NELSON, for the defendant Company.

CRONYN, for the defendant Myers.

17th APRIL, 1899, MARTIN, J. :—In this action the plaintiffs, on a variety of grounds, seek to set aside (1.) a mortgage of real and personal property dated the 23rd day of September, A. D. 1897, given by the Kootenay Brewing, Malting & Distilling Co., Ltd, Lty., to the Bank of Montreal, (2.) an assignment of book-debts by the Company to the Bank, dated October 2nd, 1897, and (3.) a judgment recovered by the Bank against the Company on December 1st, 1897, for $31,908.01.

On October 28th, 1897, the plaintiffs obtained judgment against the Company for the sum of $5,634.98, and issued execution therefor, and subsequently obtained other judgments and executions against the Company, the amount thereof at the date of the writ being $13,909.14. On or about December 22nd, 1897, the Bank took possession of the real and personal property and effects of the Company comprised in the mortgage and on February 15th, 1897, sold them by public auction to the defendant Myers for $25,000.00 and a month later assigned the book-debts to him also. At the time the directors of the Company authorized the giving of the mortgage to the Bank the Company's indebtedness to the Bank was about $40,000.00.

The plaintiffs allege that the Bank's judgment against the Company was obtained by collusion, and so should be set aside as fraudulent and void. I deal with this point shortly by saying that the slight evidence offered does not at all establish this allegation.

In the transaction attacked, the Bank charged the Company interest at the rate of 10 per cent. per annum, and it is contended that the mortgage and assignment are void on this account under section 80 of the Bank Act. But this section does not declare the note or other security void as was the case under the old Province of Canada Act. C.S.C. (1859), Cap. 58 Secs. 4 and 9, and the Bank Act of 1867,, 31 Vict. Cap. 11, abolished all penalties and forfeitures for usury— McLaren on Banks, 164-6. A consideration of the case of *La Banque de St-Hyacinthe* v. *Sarrazin* (1892), 2 Quebec S. C. 96, where the defendants were sued as indorsers, shews that a demand for payment of over 7 per cent. can be successfully resisted ; but from a careful perusal of the judgment I can find nothing to support the view that the transaction is void.

But the assignment of book-debts is also attacked under the last paragraph of section 64 of the Bank Act, which prohibits a Bank from lending money upon '' the security of any goods, wares and merchandise.'' Applying the case of *Humble* v. *Mitchell* (1839), 11 A. & E. 205 to the words, '' goods, wares and merchandise,'' I am of the opinion that they do not include choses in action : if the words were ''goods and chattels'' it might be different. It is alternatively argued that nevertheless the Bank had no power given it to loan on choses in action. That may be, but what has occur-

red here is that the Bank advanced a further sum of $4,000.
oo to the Company on the strength of the assignment of the
book-debts, and it has only been able to recoup itself out of
that security to the extent of $800.00.   Assuming that the
assignment will not stand, the case of *Rolland* v. *La Caisse
d'Economie Notre-Dame de Québec* (1895), 24 S. C. R. 405,
distinguishing *Bank of Toronto* v. *Perkins* (1883), 8 S.C.R.
603 shews that the Court will not allow the borrower to take
the money and refuse to do equity ; the Company here
could not obtain a direction that the Bank should hand it
over the amount collected from the book-debts so long as it
was still in the Bank's debt on that transaction, and if the
Company could not, its creditor cannot.

While on this question of book-debts I would further
point out that the plaintiff has no status, for it has been held
in this Court in *Hudson's Bay Company* v. *Haslett* (1896), 4
B. C. R. 450, that book-debts are not exigible under writs of
execution in the sheriff's hands ; and the late case of *Cum-
mings* v. *Taylor* (1898), 28 S. C. R. 337, shews that the proper proceeding under such circumstances is by garnishee
process.

Now, as to the mortgage alone. I find that at the time it
was given the Company was in insolvent circumstances to
the knowledge of the Bank.

So far as any argument directed to the effect of the statute of Elizabeth is concerned, I feel I can profitably add
nothing to the judgment of the Supreme Court of Canada in
Mulcahy v. *Archibald* (1898), 28 S C. R. 523, and the
plaintiff cannot succeed on that branch of the case.

But it is further contended that the mortgage is void as
being contrary to the Fraudulent Preference of Creditors
Act, R. S., B. C., 1897, Cap. 87, Sec. 3.   In answer to that
the Bank sets up "pressure," and submits that the evidence
brings the case within *The Molson Bank* v. *Halter* (1890),
18 S. C. R. 88, and *Stephens* v. *McArthur* (1891), 19 S.C.R.
446, which cases, as was said by the present Chief Justice of
Canada in *Gibbons* v. *McDonald* (1892), 20 S. C. R. at 589,
settle and conclude the law on this subject. See also *Beattie*
v. *Wenger* (1897), 24 A. R. 72 at pp. 76 and 81. I should
point out that the head-note in *Gibbons* v. *McDonald* goes
too far in inferring that *Stephens* v. *McArthur* requires a
want of notice of insolvency in order to uphold the mortgage.

Applying these cases to the present I am of the opinion that there was ample pressure here to rebut the presumption of a preference, and consequently the question of notice of the insolvency becomes immaterial. *Stephens* v. *McArthur*, pp. 451, 446 : '' When there is pressure on the part of a creditor seeking payment or security for a debt honestly due there can be no fraudulent preference,'' *Ib.* 452. These expressions are applicable to the present case. I cannot accede to the suggestion that the pressure here was a ''sham'' pressure, as in *Davies* v. *Gillard* (1891), 21 Ont. 431, for the circumstances here do not warrant my taking such a view. Counsel for the plaintiffs, on the authority of this last named case, argues that the doctrine of pressure does not apply where the debtor has transferred the whole of his property, or as the expression there is ''strips himself of everything in favour of one creditor.'' A perusal of *Davies* v. *Gillard* shews that it is an extreme case, and differs materially from the one under consideration. The mortgage here was authorized to be given at a board meeting on 13th September, and that the Company still had assets which were at least considered to be substantial is proved by the fact that on the 2nd of October following a considerable further advance, $4,000.00, was obtained from the Bank on the security of the book-debts. I have come to the conclusion that the officers of the Company at the time the mortgage was given believed that they might still tide over the difficulties which beset them : in *Davies* v. *Gillard* there could have been no such belief. I might further point out that the two learned Judges who decided that case put their decisions on different grounds, and Mr. Justice Falconbridge does not adopt the conclusions of Mr Justice Street on the point taken before me, nor did the trial Judge, Chief Justice Armour, take that view. But *Davies* v. *Gillard* is prior to *Stephens* v. *McArthur*, and in *Stephens* v *McArthur*, as I read it, the whole stock in trade of the partnership was covered by the mortgage which was upheld.

As to the contention that the mortgage was retained by Mr Nelson, the solicitor of the Company, who was also the Vice-President, for some days and not handed over to the Bank's solicitors till the same day the writ was issued, but before the Company had notice that the writ had been issued : the answer to this is, in my opinion, in view of all the circumstances, that Mr. Nelson had the custody and possession of that mortgage on behalf of the Bank's solicitors, and it was his duty morally and legally to them to act as he did : his evidence and his letter of the 23rd of September 1897, satisfy me that he held the mortgage for the purpose of protecting the interests of the Bank should that become necessary, as it did, though it was hoped to the last, however vainly, that disaster might be averted.

I do not attach much importance to the telegram* sent by Mr. Nelson in reply to one received from Mr. Galt after the writ had been issued : I regard the expressions therein as being more denunciatory than otherwise, even assuming that they were material in view of my opinion as above expressed.   And if Mr. Nelson's motives were what has been termed, " mixed motives," and I was entitled to disregard those of the President of the Company, still "it has been settled in the Exchequer Chamber by *Brown* v. *Kempton* (1850), 19 L. J., C.P. 169, that the intent to give a preference . . . . . must be the sole motive with which it is made, so that if the transfer be found to be the result of mixed motives, one of them only being the intention to prefer, it must be held good."—*Davies* v. *Gillard, supra.*

Transactions of this nature must, I think, be viewed and judged as a whole, and a circumstance here and there in the chain of events, which standing by itself might be of much weight, should not be singled out and magnified into undue importance.

Finally it is urged that the mortgage will not stand because the directors did not comply with the last clause of section 8 of the Companies Act of 1890, under which the Company was incorporated.   This section, after conferring

---

*NELSON, B. C., October 2nd, 1897.

To W. J. NELSON, Rossland : Writ issued against Kootenay Company and Bank for overdue account, and injunction against completing mortgage.   Have you any offer to make before we apply ? See Fraser and answer before noon.   A. C. Galt.

ROSSLAND, October 2nd, 1897.

To A. C. GALT, Nelson : Your conduct and proceedings are so completely in breach of faith that I decline to negotiate with you. Fortunately I knew of your contemplated action in time to frustrate it.   W. J. Nelson.

NELSON, B. C., October 2nd, 1897.

To W. J. NELSON, Rossland : Your telegram shews that the real breach of faith was by you.   A. C. Galt.

upon the Company power to mortgage, proceeds as follows :
" These powers shall not be exercised except with the
consent of the shareholders representing two-thirds of the
capital stock of the Company actually paid in,"

It is contended that this clause is imperative and not
directory, consequently the mortgage was *ultra vires*, wholly
void, and incapable of ratification. The steps taken to
ratify the mortgage appear from the minute-book of the
Company, put in by the plaintiffs, at a special meeting of
the shareholders held on the 25th of October, 1897. It
should be noted here that according to the evidence of
Deputy Sheriff Robinson the writs of *fi. fa.* were not placed
in his hands till the 1st of November. It appears that 485
shares of the Company had been issued and taken up, and
that shareholders representing 440 of these shares " approved,
ratified and confirmed " the action of the directors. It is
objected by the plaintiffs that this ratification took place at
a meeting called only to consider the question of issuing
debentures, and therefore is invalid ; and also that Mr. John
R. Myers, who acted as proxy for a large number of
shareholders, is not a shareholder and consequently could
not, under the Companies Act, represent the shareholders.
In answer to this the Bank and the defendant Company
contend that the clause relied on does not require a meeting
to be held at all, and that the consent of the shareholders is
sufficient, if I am satisfied from the evidence that such
consent was actually obtained, in whatever form. The
clause is certainly most unusual, the customary provision in
similar cases being that the consent of the shareholders shall
be obtained at a meeting called for that special purpose.
This is now required by our present Companies Act, sec.
122, sub-sec. (2) ; see also sec. 160 ; and compare the
Ontario Joint Stock Companies Act, Cap. 157, R. S. O.
1887, sec. 38 ; *Irvine* v. *Union Bank of Australia* (1877), 2
App. Cas. 366 at p. 373 ; *Merchants' Bank of Canada* v.
Hancock (1864), 6 Ont. 285 ; and *Sheppard* v. *Bonanza
Nickel Mining Co.* (1895), 25 Ont. 305. In Lindley on
Companies at p. 303 it is stated " The shareholders of a
Company cannot usually exercise any control over the
management of its affairs, except at meetings duly convened."
This is very far from saying that it can never be done in
any other way, and I feel that where the Legislature did
not in 1890 see fit to require the consent to be expressed at
a general meeting I would not be warranted in insisting

upon a requirement which by a subsequent statute has been made necessary. I am quite satisfied that these shareholders "consented" to this ratification through their representative, Mr. Myers ; and no objection was taken to his representation of them. My attention has been called to the form of the so-called proxies, which goes much further than is usual, the concluding words being—"the intention hereof being that my said proxy shall act in my place and stead in all affairs and at all meetings connected with the said Company." No authority having been quoted to me in opposition to the above view I must abide by it, and uphold the ratification.

Then as to the point that the mortgage being wholly void is incapable of ratification A mass of authorities has been quoted to me on both sides, and I have had the benefit of comprehensive arguments. As Lindley says, 173, "Statutes which are directory only are common enough, but it is not easy to recognize them with certainty before they have been judicially interpreted. There is, however, a natural tendency on the part of courts of justice to uphold an honest transaction although somewhat irregular, if to do so is consistent with the statute which is to be construed." Guided by these expressions I feel, after a careful perusal of all the cases cited, and others, that I am unable to distinguish this case in principle from a long line of authorities beginning with (for convenience) *Royal British Bank* v. *Turquand* (1855), 5 El. & Bl. 248 ; followed by *Fountaine* v. *Carmarthen Railway Co.* (1868), L. R. 5 Eq. 316 ; *Landowners West of England and South Wales Land*, &c., *Co.* v. *Ashford* (1880), 16 Ch. D. 411, 438 ; *McDougall* v. *Lindsay Paper Co.* (1884), 10 Pr. 252 ; *Purdom* v. *Ontario Loan and Debenture Co.* (1892), 22 Ont. R. 597 ; *Sheppard* v. *Bonanza Nickel Co.*, *supra* ; see also Brice on *Ultra Vires* (1893), 603, 631, 632, propositions 249, 250, 251, 252 ; Lindley, 176 and 177. There is no other course open to me than to construe this clause as directory and not imperative. I may add that I see no essential difference between this clause and section 38 of the Ontario Act above referred to, under which *Purdon* v. *Ontario Loan and Debenture Co.* and *Sheppard* v. *Bonanza Nickel Co.* were decided. Of course if no power to mortgage had been given the result would have been different.

But the plaintiffs' counsel urges that I should not apply the principle of ratification to this case because the Bank had

notice of the fact that there had been no consent of the
shareholders. It would appear that the Bank took the
mortgage either under the idea that no consent was necessary, or that the ratification could be obtained without
difficulty, it is not quite clear which. I do not see how the
question of notice affects this case, and no authority has
been cited to shew that notice prevents ratification under the
circumstances I have to deal with here. Notice would, of
course, be all important if the Bank were endeavouring to
hold the Company to a contract, but the Company is a co-
defendant here, and not only does not seek to set aside the
mortgage, but comes into Court and upholds it ; it is a creditor of the Company, not the Company itself that seeks to
set it aside. Now, if the Company is estopped by its acquiescence the creditor must be. Commenting on *Bargate* v.
Shortridge (1855), 5 H. L. Cas 297 ; 24 L. J., Ch. 457,
Brice says at p. 605. " This case goes farther than this, for it
was a creditor of the company who was attempting to get his
debt paid by process against a shareholder, and the decision
was that, as the company itself was estopped by its acquiescence, so also its creditors claiming through it were barred
by the same acquiescence." See also Lindley, p. 175, where it
is stated. "When a contract has been entered into on behalf
of a company informally, but has been acted upon and is
then disputed by the company, the question naturally arises
whether it has not been ratified or otherwise adopted by the
company, and so become binding on it." And here I call
attention to the language of Fry, J., in the analogous case
of *Landowners West of England and South Wales Land*, &c.,
Co. v. *Ashford, supra,* at p. 438, " The case I was referred
to before Lord Hatherly, of *Fountaine* v. *Carmarthen Railway Co.* (1868), L. R. 5 Eq. 316, does shew that the provision with regard to the general meeting is inserted in the Act
of Parliament for the benefit of the shareholders, and not of
the creditors. They could not stop the Company exercising
that power, and therefore it does not interest them." In a
similar case, *Greenstreet* v. *Paris* (1874), 21 Gr. at p. 234,
Vice-Chancellor Blake says : "It is clear that this mortgage
is a matter which might be confirmed by the shareholders,
and if, when the acts complained of are capable of confirmation a single shareholder cannot impeach them, I think it *a
fortiori* that an outsider should not have this right." There
the "outsider" was a subsequent incumbrancer. This ruling
has been repeatedly followed—*Bank of Toronto* v. *Cobourg,*

&c., *Railway Co.*, (1885), 10 Ont. R. 376 ; *Merchant's Bank*
v. *Hancock, supra.*, and the other Ontario cases above quoted.
In the last named case Chancellor Boyd lays it down. p.289.
"According to *Greenstreet* v. *Paris,* an outsider, such as an
execution creditor, could not be allowed to interfere in such
circumstances, and where there is no imputation of fraud or
illegality in its broad and culpable sense. " I have found
these elements are not present here.

The plaintiffs then are not in a position to attack the
ratification, or the means taken to bring it about.

In view of the conclusion I have thus arrived at it becomes
unnecessary for me to consider the point taken by the Bank
that the property having been sold too late for relief there is
no procedure or authority for making it accountable for the
proceeds.

I call attention to the somewhat peculiar form this action
takes. The plaintiffs, while complaining that the defendant
Bank has secured itself with intent to defeat and delay the
general body of creditors, do not ask that such creditors be
granted relief, but merely that they (the plaintiffs) be substituted for the Bank, in other words, put in the Bank's
shoes to the extent of their execution ; the statement of
claim asks that the Bank be ordered to pay the plaintiffs that
amount. The general body of creditors would probably not
like the plaintiffs to have priority over them any more than
the Bank, which certainly aided the Company generously in
its effort to establish itself ; but it is unnecessary to pursue
the point.

I have experienced not a little difficulty in coming to a
conclusion on some of the points in this complicated and
lengthy case (I may say the mere perusal of the evidence,
exhibits and cases cited occupied several days), and I think
the plaintiffs are not entitled to succeed. The action will
consequently be dismissed with costs.

17th August 1899.—Since writing the above I have learned that the cases of *Davies* v. *Gillard, supra,* on which the
plaintiffs' counsel placed not a little reliance, and which
consequently, I considered at some length, was reversed on
appeal—(1892), 19 A. R. 432. Of course I am quite satisfied that this fact escaped the attention of the learned counsel who cited the case, and my attention was not drawn to it

by the opposing counsel. Fortunately, no harm has arisen from the slip here as the case was distinguishable, but such an oversight might often have serious consequences, and the Court is entitled to assume as a matter of course that cases cited to it have not been reversed.

A. C. GALT, for the Plaintiffs.

C. R. HAMILTON, for the Defendants, the Bank of Montreal.

J. H. SENKLER, for the Defendant Company.

The plaintiffs appealed and the appeal was argued at Vancouver in September, 1899, before a full Court composed of Walkem, Drake, and Irving, JJ.

30th November, 1899 —DRAKE, J. : The Brewing Company are a Corporation incorporated under the Companies Act, 1890, as amended by Cap. 7 sec. 2 of 1892. That Act restricts the powers of the trustees in the management of the Company, and was intended to protect shareholders from liability beyond the amount of the calls that might be legally levied upon their shares. The Company under its provisions cannot borrow money or mortgage their property or sign bills or notes and other evidence of or securities for money borrowed, or to be borrowed, without the consent of the shareholders representing two thirds in value of the capital stock of the Company. This is a statutory addition to the memorandum of association, and the section is so framed that the consent of the shareholders is an imperative requirement to the exercise of the power of borrowing.

The defendants, the Bank of Montreal, had for some months been allowing the Company an overdraft, and an overdraft is borrowing ; and had advanced from time to time considerable sums of money to take up the Company's notes and bills. How far the directors were authorized to sign bills, notes or other evidence of debt, was not argued because these debts were swept into the mortgage which is questioned in this action. But this section indicates that the Act was not intended for the incorporation of purely industrial companies as it would fetter all commercial transactions. An inquiry into the origin of the Act shews that it was intended for mining partnerships, but as the Company have incorporated under it, they are bound by its provisions. On July 2nd, 1897, the Company, being heavily indebted to the Bank, the Bank applied for security, and the Bank's solicitors prepared a mortgage of the Company's real and personal property, which was not executed until the 23rd of September following. The Company appear to have hesitated about giving security, as they were in hopes of raising a sufficient sum by debentures to relieve the financial pressure they were suffering under.

The Company had invested all their capital in the brewery, buildings and plant, and had, in fact, no working capital, but relied on their profits to carry them on.

The evidence of the financial position of the Company is disclosed on p. 45. There Mr. Burritt, the President of the Company, states that in the early part of June they were crowded for funds, and he says that in August the Company could not meet their obligations as they became due, and they staved off the Bank as long as they could. The Bank was thoroughly conversant with the plaintiffs' claim before the mortgage was executed, and it was the desire of the Company to prevent the plaintiffs getting judgment. Mr. Nelson confirms the last witness as to the desire of the Bank for security; and after the mortgage was given it was arranged it should not be registered at once.

In June, 1897, the Company owed the Bank $11,901.00 on their own notes, and this indebtedness increased to $40,000.00. But the Bank, although not liking the transaction, apparently carried the Company on, and the Bank knew that a large proportion of the goods over which they required security was not paid for The mortgage deed purports to transfer the lands, buildings and assets of the Company, whether then in existence, or which might be subsequently brought on to the premises. It is in the ordinary form, and there is no ultimate trust for the mortgagors.

The plaintiffs contend that the mortgage deed was void under the statute of Elizabeth, as well as the assignment of book-debts which was subsequently executed, as having been given voluntarily and collusively for the purpose of defeating and delaying creditors. A deed may have that effect and yet not be void under the statute. This deed contains no ultimate trust for the benefit of the mortgagors except the clause that if after sale there should be a surplus that the same should be paid to the Company. This would be the right of the Company if such a clause were not

inserted. Every mortgage deed contains a clause authorizing the mortgagees in case they sell instead of foreclosing to
account to the mortgagor for any surplus. See *Boldoro* v.
London and Westminster Loan Co. (1879), 5 Ex. D. 47. No
benefit is required for the mortgagor. Further, under the
statute of Elizabeth it must be shewn that the deed was not
bona fide. It is not denied here that the Company were
indebted to the Bank in a large sum. The sole question on
this point of the case therefore is *bona fides*. Mr. Galt in
his able argument contended that the whole transaction was
fraudulent because there was an agreement not to register
at once ; and more or less false information was given to the
plaintiffs' agents as to the amount due to the Bank. The
security was kept secret, and was taken when it was clear
that the Company was insolvent ; but as Sir G. Jessel says
in *Middleton* v. *Pollock* (1876), 2 Ch. D. 108, there is no
law which prevents a man in insolvent circumstances from
preferring one creditor, except the bankruptcy law. Therefore, the mere fact of a deliberate intention of preferring, in
case of insolvency, will not be sufficient to avoid the claim,
assuming that it had been proved that the grantor was
insolvent and insolvent to his own knowledge, the security
being *bona fide*. The statute has no regard to the question
of preference or priority amongst the creditors of the debtor,
and pressure is an indication of *bona fides* ; and in *W. Morris*
v. *A. Morris* (1895), A. C. 625, the Lord Chancellor said it
was immaterial to inquire why the appellant refrained from
registering his security, he was under no obligation to do so :
no doubt he incurred the risk of losing his security.

The case of *Alton* v. *Harrison* (1869), 4 Chy. App. 622,
the debtor expecting an execution against him executed a
mortgage vesting his property in trustees for the benefit of
five creditors, and the deed contained a proviso that the debtor should remain in possession for six months, but so as not
to let in any execution, and in case any should be enforced
possession was to cease ; and it was there held that if the
deed was *bona fide*, and not a mere cloak for retaining a
benefit to the grantor, it was good under the statute of
Elizabeth, and the proviso as to retaining possession for six
months did not render the deed void. This case was followed
in *Ex parte Games* (1879), 12 Ch. D. 314.

The plaintiffs further contend that this deed was a collusive
deed, and therefore void, because under the primary mean-

ing of the term collusive '' it is acting in concert, '' and the
Bank and the Company were acting in concert in obtaining
the security. The term collusive in the preamble to the Act
of Elizabeth is used in connection with a fraudulent intention ; every agreement is in one sense an acting in concert,
but it is not therefore void. The intention in the Act is to
hinder, delay or defraud creditors, but a deed which is *bona
fide* and the result of pressure is held not to be within the
Act although it may have the effect of delaying or hindering
some creditors ; and it matters not if it affects all or only
part of the debtors' assets. Therefore, I am of the opinion
that under the statute of Elizabeth this mortgage cannot be
impeached.

The further question argued was that the deeds were
void under the Fraudulent Preference of Creditors Act. R.
S. B. C. 1897, Cap. 87, sec. 3. That section shortly says
·''in case any person being at the time in insolvent circumstances, or unable to pay his debts in full, makes any transfer
with intent to defeat or delay the creditors of such person,
or with intent to give one or more of the creditors of such
person a preference over his other creditors, such deed shall
be void as against the creditors of such person.''

It has been held in *McCrae* v. *White* (1883), 9 S. C. R.
22 ; *Long* v *Hancock* (1885). 12 S. C. R. 532 ; *Gibbons* v.
McDonald (1892). 20 S. C. R 587 ; *The Molson Bank* v.
Halter (1890), 18 S. C. R. 88, that where security has been
obtained as the result of pressure the Act does not apply.

But there is a further question here : Did the Bank know
that the Company was in insolvent circumstances ? Because
that is an ingredient in the question of *bona fides* where the
security is not obtained as the result of pressure. In *Gibbons*
v. *McDonald supra*, C J. Ritchie says that there was no concurrence of intent on one side to give, and on the other to
accept, a preference over other creditors, as there was nothing
to shew that the defendant was aware of the insolvency of
the debtor. That was a deed not given under pressure. The
cases of *Campbell v. Patterson* (1893), 21 S. C. R. 645 ; and
Stevenson v. *The Canadian Bank of Commerce* (1893), 23 S.
C. R. 350, both upheld the doctrine that the creditors'
knowledge of the insolvency of the debtor makes the security
fraudulent if it was given without pressure. The case of
Davies v. *Gillard* (1891). 21 Ont. R. 431 ; (1892), 19, Ont. A.
R. 432, was a case very much like this case on the facts.
and the deed was upheld.

The Company state that they were in hopes of getting financial assistance from the East, but it was only a hope that did not materialize. I think from a careful consideration of the evidence that when the mortgage was taken both the Bank and the Company knew that the Company was in insolvent circumstances, and had been for some time before.

In the case of *Colquhoun* v. *Seagram* (1896), 11 Man. R. 346, Killam, J., reviews the whole of the cases on the subject of pressure, and the effect of the judgment is that if there is pressure the knowledge of insolvency of the debtor, even if known to the creditor, will not vitiate the security.

A further objection taken by Mr. Galt is that both the mortgage and the assignment of book-debts are void on the ground that the sanction of the shareholders was not obtained in proper form, and prior to the execution of the deeds.

There is a distinction well recognized between cases which are *ultra vires* in their inception whether done by the directors or the Company and therefore void, and those cases where the directors of the Company have power to do the act provided certain prescribed formalities are complied with. On the first head it is only necessary to cite the case of *Baroness Wenlock* v. *River Dee Co.* (1887), 36 Ch. D. 684, where the power of borrowing was limited, and the directors exceeded this power, and their act was confirmed by the whole of the stockholders. It was held that the borrowing being unauthorized, no confirmation could render it valid.

In the second class of cases which concern the internal management and economy of the Company formalities may be waived, and irregular as distinguished from void transactions may be confirmed. There are, no doubt, cases in which the mere non-compliance with formalities has been held fatal, especially in cases between shareholders and the Company when the question has arisen as to the liability of a shareholder, such as *Sheffield Railway Co.* v. *Woodcock* (1841), 7 M. & W. 574, but in dealing with formalities where the members of the Company are concerned, if the act of the directors is one ordinarily within the scope of their powers, then the non-compliance with the prescribed formalities will not render the act void on the application of third parties : see *Ex parte Eagle Company* (1858), 4 K. & J. 549. Whatever rights the shareholders or the Company might have to effect this object, the evidence here shews that the Bank had notice that before the Company could borrow money under section 8 of the Companies Act, 1890, they were to obtain the consent of the shareholders representing two-thirds in value of the capital stock of the Company. The Bank's solicitors suggested or prepared a resolution to be submitted to the shareholders for the purpose of sanctioning the proposed mortgages, and this is clearly shewn by exhibit C. (2), a letter dated July 5th, 1897, to the President of the Company. The mortgage was executed on 23rd September, 1897. On 13th September, the directors passed a resolution sanctioning a mortgage to the Bank; but it was not until the 25th of October, that a special meeting of the shareholders was held when the directors' act was confirmed. At law a ratification is equivalent to a previous authority, and I think that if a ratification was given by the shareholders in proper form it would confirm the deed. In the case of *Agar* v. *Athenaeum Life Assurance Society* (1858), 3 C.B., N. S. 725, the directors had power to borrow, but only with the consent of an extraordinary general meeting. The directors did borrow without such consent : the debentures were held binding on the Company.

I think further, that the Bank were entitled to consider that after the care they had taken to prepare a resolution to be submitted to the shareholders for the purpose of confirming the proposed mortgage the necessary steps to obtain a confirmation had been complied with.

The appellants further contended that the assent of the shareholders was insufficient, because J. R. Myers, who held a large number of proxies, was not a shareholder ; and section 19 of the Companies Act says that no person shall be appointed a proxy who is not a shareholder in the Company. The same principle applies here. The Bank were entitled to consider that the statutory requirements which governed the Company had been complied with, and persons dealing with directors *bona fide*, and without notice of an irregular exercise of their powers are not affected by the irregularity : *Royal British Bank* v. *Turquand* (1855), 5 El. & Bl. 248. There the directors gave the Bank a bond which had not been authorized by a resolution of the Company. It was held that the Bank were not bound to ascertain whether the bond had been authorized   Chief Justice Jervis says, '' Finding that the authority might be made complete by a resolution the person dealing with the Company would have a right to infer

the fact of a resolution authorizing that which on the face of
of the document appeared to be legitimately done."

For these reasons I think the appeal should be dismissed
with costs.

WALKEM, J.—:I concur.

IRVING, J. :—The difficulties in this case are occasioned
by reason of a trading Company incorporating itself under a
statute inapplicable to trading companies. The case comes
before us on appeal from Martin, J., who dismissed the
plaintiffs' action as against the Bank and one John R Myers,
who was then, but is not now, a party to the action. The
Company was incorporated on the 19th of November, 1896,
under the B. C. Companies Act, 1890, and amending Acts,
with a capital of $50,000 00 ; $37,500 00 of which was
subscribed and paid up and immediately expended in plant,
etc. The first meeting of directors was held on 30th
November, 1896.

The defendants, the Bank of Montreal, were on and after
February, 1897, the Company's Bank. The plaintiffs were
simple contract creditors of the Company, and became
judgment creditors of the Company on the 28th of October,
1897. Their first judgment was for the sum of $5,634.98.
They subsequently obtained other judgments, amounting at
the date of the writ in this action, to $14,901.19.

Shortly after the Bank became the Company's bankers,
the directors, on 19th February, 1897, passed a resolution
that the Company should engage in the business of wines,
liquors, cigars, etc., and that the President and Secretary-
Treasurer be authorized to make purchases and such arrangements as they should deem advisable subject to the direction of the Board of Directors. At this time the Manager of
the Bank thought they were "all right," but that they
required more working capital to carry on their business.
The Company were selling on credit, taking notes from their
customers ; these were discounted by the Bank and if not
paid at maturity were charged up to the Company's account.
In addition the Bank advanced moneys to them for short
periods, pending the receipt by them of certain funds they
promised would be forthcoming. On the 18th of May, 1897,
the Bank began taking security. Owing to the depression
in trade in June and July, the Company's liabilities seemed

to have increased, and the Bank at this time began to press
for security, and in the latter month demanded a mortgage.
The Company on their side promised to put the account into
satisfactory shape by means of a mortgage debenture scheme
which its directors thought they could float. See exhibit 22,
dated 22nd July, 1897, meeting of directors held 9th August,
1897.

During the month of August the Bank continued to
carry the Company, and by the 13th of September, 1897, the
liabilities to the Bank amounted to about $40,000,00. On
the 23rd of September. 1897, the mortgage now sought to be
set aside was executed. By section 8 of the Companies Act.
1890, as amended in 1892 and 1894, it is provided as follows:

" All companies incorporated . . . . under this Act
shall have, in addition to the powers conferred on them by
section 5, the following powers, namely :

" (*a.*) The power, subject to the provisions of this Act,
to borrow money for the purpose of carrying out the objects
of their respective incorporations.

" (*b.*) The power, subject to the provisions of this Act,
to execute mortgages of their real and personal property, to
issue debentures secured by mortgage or otherwise, to sign
bills, notes, contracts and other evidences of, or securities
for money borrowed by them for the purpose aforesaid, etc.

" These powers shall not be exercised, except with the
consent of the shareholders representing two thirds in value
of the subscribed capital stock of the Company. ''

Now, Mr. Galt's main contention was that the directors
by virtue of this section had, in the absence of the consent
of the shareholders, no power to borrow any money, and as
there was no authority to borrow, there could be no debt.
and no liability on the part of the Company, citing *Cunliffe
Brooks & Co.* v. *Blackburn Benefit Society* (1884), 9 App.
Cas. 872 ; *Baroness Wenlock* v. *River Dee Co.* (1885), 10
App. Cas. 354, and *Ex parte Watson* (1888), 21 Q B. D.
301. This last case, in my opinion, is not in point, as in that
case there were two separate and distinct entities, and the
decision turned, not on a question of borrowing, because
there was no borrowing, but upon a gratuitous assumption
by the incorporated company of a liability incurred by the
unincorporated society. The two former cases do not bear

out his contention in its entirety. On the contrary both of these cases are authorities for this principle that a company may in some cases be equitably liable to re-pay money advanced beyond its borrowing powers where it can be shewn that the money so advanced has been properly applied to the re-payment of debts properly incurred by the company, and the question here is in which category does this case fall ? In *Cunliffe Brooks & Co.* v. *Blackburn Benefit Society* money was borrowed by the directors who were without borrowing powers, and with part of the money borrowed, certain payments were made to withdrawing members. These payments would have been proper enough if they had been made out of a special and definite fund as provided by the constitution for that purpose. But they were not, they were made out of a non-existing fund, and only supplied by means of a loan. "Therefore," said Lord Selborne, L C., in *Walton* v. *Edge* (1884), 10 App. Cas. 33 at p. 41, "in a case so arising (that is by the official liquidator representing all the contributories and also the creditors), all such payments were in a different category from those which might have been made in discharge of actual debts and liabilities of the society." In respect of moneys so applied it was held the Bank were entitled to recover.

In *Baroness Wenlock* v. *River Dee Co.*, *supra*, the plaintiffs in the Court of first instance obtained judgment for the whole amount claimed, Huddleston, B., being of the opinion that though the borrowing was *ultra vires* the Company had the benefit of the moneys and had applied them to the purpose of the Company. Before the Court of Appeal, the River Company admitted the plaintiff's claim (which according to the contention advanced by plaintiffs' counsel in this case was wholly bad) to the extent of $25,000.00 and to such further sums as the plaintiffs could shew had been applied in payment or in discharge of any debts or liabilities of the Company. Judgment was given accordingly, but the plaintiffs being dissatisfied appealed. The House of Lords affirmed the decision of the Court of Appeal.

In each of these cases then, and also in *Ex parte Watson*, per dictum of Wills. J., at p. 304, the principle of right of recoupment of moneys illegally borrowed, was, as to so much thereof as was applied in satisfaction of the Company's debts and liabilities, fully recognized.

In *In re Wrexham, Mold and Connah's Quay Railway Co.* (1899), 1 Ch. 440, Rigby, L. J., speaks of the recognition of that rule as being but "bare justice"; and Vaughan Williams, L. J., says, equity will treat such a borrowing, if borrowing it be, as *intra vires* if necessary. In the case before us the due application of the moneys to the Company's purposes was not called in question, and I therefore think that bare justice requires us to recognize this as a liability due from the Brewing Company to the Bank.

But regarding section 8 Mr. Galt says "section 8 requires the sanction of the shareholders." *The Royal British Bank* v. *Turquand* (1856), 6 El. & Bl. 327, and other authorities cited by the learned trial Judge, to which I would add *County of Gloucester Bank* v. *Rudry Merthyr Steam and House Coal Colliery Co.* (1895), 1 Ch. 629, and *Biggerstaff* v. *Rowatt's Wharf, Limited* (1896), 2 Ch. 93, and *In re Hampshire Land Co.* (1896), 2 Ch. 747, affirm the proposition that the Manager of the Bank. when he began to lend at the instance of the President in February, 1897, had a right to assume that all those essentials had been carried out by the directors and the Company, and in my opinion, as this went on for weeks and months, he had a right to assume that this exercise of power by the directors, if not originally sanctioned by the shareholders, had been acquiesced in by them ; *Evans* v. *Smallcombe* (1868), L. R. 3 H. L. 249. It is only in case the law imputes to the lender knowledge of these irregularities that the lender cannot recover. There is nothing so far as the borrowing of the money is concerned, to shew that the Bank had this knowledge. Messrs. Daly & Hamilton's letter written on 5th July, refers to the giving of the mortgage, and not in any way to the subject of the borrowing of this money. I arrive then at the conclusion that there was an advance of moneys which were properly, (I say properly because it is not questioned), applied to the Company's purposes for which the Company was equitably liable.

The Bank were not the only creditors who began pressing for payment ; several others were making inquiries. The plaintiffs, on the 28th of September, 1897, sent down Mr. Hearn to ascertain the condition of the Company's affairs. He was not told of the execution of a mortgage to the Bank, but whether intentionally or unintentionally, was given to understand that the directors by reason of section 8 found themselves unable to execute a mortgage. At this time the bill of sale and mortgage in favour of the Bank had been executed and at that time was being held, not as an escrow, but was being held by the Vice-President of the Company "pending the negotiations as to debentures." As to the sufficiency of the delivery by the Company notwithstanding the fact that it remained in the custody of the Vice-President of the Company, see *Zwicker* v. *Zwicker* (1899), 29 S. C. R. 527. The Vice-President on learning, on the 2nd of October, that the plaintiffs were about to take proceedings to restrain the Company from giving a mortgage, handed the bill of sale over to the Bank's solicitors. A good deal was made of this in the argument before us as to fraudulent conveyance, but the point is covered by the case of *W. A. Morris* v. *A. Morris* (1895), A. C. 625, where the respondent attacking a bill of sale as fraudulent, relied upon an alleged agreement by the bankrupt to inform the lender "if things were not looking so bright" so that he (the lender) could either register the bill of sale or take possession under it ; and the Judicial Committee held that, even if the bankrupt volunteered, as he alleged he did, to give the lender information if his circumstances should become precarious, it would not assist the respondent's case.

The letter from the Bank's solicitors when read in connection with Mr. Nelson's letters, shews what the mutual understanding was, namely, that Mr. Nelson should hold the bill of sale for ten days from the date of execution. This point too, is covered by the case I have just referred to, because as their Lordships remark, the question is not why the appellant, the lender, refrained from registering or postponed taking possession, but with what intent the assignment was made.

The next contention was that the mortgage was void under 13 Eliz., Cap. 5, sec. 1 ; R. S. B. C. 1897, Cap. 86, sec. 2, as being collusive within the meaning of that word as explained in *Edison General Electric Co.* v. *Westminster and Vancouver Tramway Co.* (1897), A. C. 193. I think this argument depends to a very great extent on the determination of the point I have just been dealing with. The statute was not intended to prevent any honest arrangement between debtor and creditor, though the result of that arrangement has been that creditors have been delayed or hindered. In all arrangements there must be a certain amount of negotiating, acting in concert, before the document embodying the arrangement is ready for execution.   This negotiation is not prohibited by the Act.   The Act strikes at collusion to the end, purpose and intent to defraud creditors.   I think it is quite possible to read all the portions of evidence to which we have been referred under this head, and feel that the negotiations were not collusive within the meaning of 13 Eliz , Cap. 5.

This brings me to the question of evidence. To establish charges of fraud there must be full and satisfactory proof. The fraud must be proved beyond all reasonable doubt, and where it is once shewn that there is a liability, that there is good consideration for the mortgage, those who attack that mortgage have a difficult task before them : *Hickerson* v. *Parrington* (1891), 18 A. R. 635.   And when the evidence is confined to the testimony of the persons who are, or are said to be, guilty of the alleged fraud, the task becomes more difficult.   In connection with the collusion, we are referred to the letters of the 2nd and 5th of July, written by the Bank's solicitors.   These letters are not, in my opinion, improper.   In these days of multi-copying, I do not attach to the enclosing to the procrastinating directors of a copy of the proposed minutes the importance which Mr. Galt attaches to that fact.

The statute of 13 Eliz., Cap. 5, requires that there should be a fraudulent intent on the part of the grantee as well as of the grantor.   It has, in my opinion, no appplication in this case unless it is shewn that the Bank, either directly or indirectly, made itself an instrument for the purpose of subsequently benefiting the Brewing Company.   I venture to think that a fair inference to be drawn is—the Manager of the Bank was concerned with securing his $40,000.00 rather than with benefiting the Brewing Company.   *Mulcahy* v. *Archibald* (1898), 28 S. C. R., 523, expresses all it is necessary to say on this point.

It was also argued that the mortgage was void under the B. C. Fraudulent Preference of Creditors Act, R. S. B. C. 1897, Cap. 87, sec. 2.   This section is a copy of the Revised Statutes of Ontario, 1877, Cap. 118.   There has been no subsequent legislation in this Province such as there was in Ontario by 47 Vict., Cap. 10, and 48 Vict., Cap. 26, and the amendments in Ontario and the decisions upon them shew that Cap. 118, our Cap. 87, is not as far reaching as creditors anxious to secure an even distribution of an insolvent

estate could wish for. This was owing to the decision that
the doctrine of pressure was to be regarded in interpreting
the statute. In the first reported decision under this Act,
Anderson v. *Shorey* (1885), 1 B. C., Pt. II., 327, McCreight,
J., declined to express any opinion on this point ; but in subsequent cases that doctrine has been recognized, and I think
that at this date what has been said by the Supreme Court
of Canada in *The Molson Bank* v. *Halter* (1890), 18 S. C. R.
88. *Stephens* v. *McArthur* (1891), 19 S. C. R., 446, in relation to the construction of the Ontario and Manitoba Statutes,
must be accepted as equally applicable to the British Columbia Act.

On the plaintiffs there is placed the onus of shewing a
fraudulent intent—a voluntary desire on the part of the
Company to prefer the Bank, and that that intent was
concurred in by the Bank. The evidence does not warrant
me in coming to that conclusion.

The Molson Bank v. *Halter, supra ; Stephens* v. *McArthur,
supra ; Gibbons* v. *McDonald* (1892), 20 S.C.R. 587 ; *Davies*
v. *Gillard* (1891), 21 Ont. R. 431 ; (1892), 19 Ont. A.R.
432, and *Colquhoun* v. *Seagram* (1896), 11 Man. R. 339
establish this, that where there is a good consideration, a
mortgage, comprising the whole of the debtor's property.
will not be set aside notwithstanding that the mortgagor is
in insolvent circumstances, to the knowledge of the mortgagee, and the effect of the mortgage is to defeat, delay and
prejudice the creditors, if there is pressure.

[The learned Judge here refers to the evidence and
proceeds.]

This establishes that the demand for security was made
by the Bank, that the Company postponed giving it for a
considerable period, and that when they did recognize that
"if the Bank left them they were gone beyond question"
they gave it.

Irvine v. *Union Bank of Australia* (1877), 2 App. Cas.
366, was cited as an authority for the proposition that
creditors are entitled to take advantage of the irregularities
in the management of their loans. In that case Irvine was
the purchaser of the interest of the Company in the land
then being made liable to a charge ; as such he could in an
action of foreclosure, raise any question as to the amount

chargeable that the mortgagors could. That is a different case from this where unsecured creditors are attempting to question the indebtedness of the Company. In the result I agree with the decision of the learned trial Judge that the action fails.

APPEAL DISMISSED.

Solicitor for the Appellants : *A. C. Galt.*

Solicitors for the Respondent, the Bank of Montreal, *Daly & Hamilton..*

Solicitors for the Respondent Company, *Wilson & Sempler.*

Note:—An appeal from this judgment was dismissed by the Supreme Court of Canada on 19th February, 1901, (See 31 S.C.R. 223) and the Judicial Committee of the Privy Council refused leave to appeal.

———

[IN THE COURT OF KING'S BENCH FOR MANITOBA.]

BEFORE KILLAM, C. J.

WHITLA
v.
THE ROYAL INSURANCE CO.

Fire Insurance — Abandonment of prior policy — Interim receipt — Authority of agent — Acceptance of note in payment of premium.

B. wrote to the agent of the defendant company, stating that he had a policy of insurance in another company which he was going to abandon and that he wished to obtain a policy from the defendant company. The agent, without B's knowledge, filled out the usual form of application for insurance on B's behalf, and forwarded the same to his head office : in answer to the question "What other insurance have you on the property now to be insured?" he wrote "None." The company issued a policy on this application and sent the same to the agent; the latter, who had previously given B an interim receipt, and who had received from B and had credited the company with the amount due on the first premium, kept the policy, and did not notify B of its receipt. Subsequently and before the maturity of a note which had been given in part payment of the premium, B's premises and property were destroyed by fire. He had not then abandoned the prior insurance. He paid the note when it fell due, put in his proof of loss, and his assignees subsequently sued the defendant company. Held, that the interim receipt only constituted an executory contract, it being a condition thereof that the prior insurance should be abandoned.

Held, further, that the fact that B had not paid the note given for the premium before the date of the loss would not have constituted a good defence to the action, since before that time the agent of the defendant company had negotiated the note, and had credited the company with the amount so realized and had accounted for the same.

The facts of the case are fully set forth in the head note and judgment.

10 January, 1902 :—

KILLAM, C. J.:—

This is an action to recover for damage by fire to a merchant's stock in trade under an insurance contract alleged to have been created by interim receipt.

The plaintiffs sue as assignees of Phileas E. Bourque, the merchant alleged to have been insured.

In the summer of the year 1900, Bourque purchased the stock in trade of Moise Landry at the Village of Altamont in this Province, and proceeded to carry on business in Landry's store.

On 12th July, 1900, Bourque obtained from The Manitoba Assurance Co. a policy of insurance against loss by fire to the amount of $2,500 ; divided as follows :—On household furniture, linen, beds, bedding, etc., $200 ; on wearing apparel $25 ; on watches, clocks, jewellery, and trinkets, $25 ; on a piano, $250 ; and on the stock in trade, $2,000.

On 1st January, 1901, Bourque wrote to Jos. T. Dumouchel, an agent of the defendant company, residing at St. Boniface, Man., a letter in the French language, which may be translated as follows :—

"Being urged to have myself insured against fire upon my stock here at Altamont when Mr. Landry begged me to write to you as being himself insured in your company. I took a little insurance last summer when I bought of Mr. Landry in the Manitoba Assurance Co. and as there are people who think that it is a weak company I am going to abandon. I had $2,000 upon stock, furniture, piano, etc. I have a stock of over $5,000 and I would desire to put on about $3,000 of insurance.

Awaiting your reply, I remain, etc."

Dumouchel replied that he would be glad to have his insurance, that he knew nothing about the standing of the other Company, but that his was a very strong one.

Bourque then wrote to him under date of January 5th that he desired to have only his stock and shop fixtures insured for $3,000, and giving some particulars not of present importance.

According to Bourque's evidence, Dumouchel replied, requesting him to send $75 for the premium, and he wrote Dumouchel that he could not pay the amount at once, but would do so later, in reply to which Dumouchel sent him a promissory note, payable to Dumouchel's order, for $51, and requested him to sign the note, and return it with a cheque for $25, stating that on receiving these he would put the insurance through for him.

Bourque signed the note and returned it with the cheque and a letter, dated 16th January, saying, that this suited him very well and excusing his delay.

Dumouchel's account is that, on receiving Bourque's letter of 5th of January, he sent him an interim receipt for the premium, and asked him to send his note for $50, and a cheque for $25 if it suited him.

The interim receipt was as follows :—

" ROYAL INSURANCE COMPANY.

ST. BONIFACE AGENCY,

No. 32,513.   7th January, 1901.

Mr. P. E. Bourque having this day applied for an insurance against loss or damage by fire to the extent of $3,000 on property described in application of this date for 12 months subject to the conditions as indorsed hereon of the company's policy, and having also paid the sum of $75 as the premium for the same, the property is hereby held insured for forty-five days from this date, or until a policy is sooner delivered or notice given that the application is declined.   If the application is declined the premium received will be refunded on this receipt being given up, less the proportion for the time the risk has been covered.

N.B. If a policy be not received before the expiration of the period above mentioned, and no intimation has been given that the application is declined, immediate notice thereof should be sent to the manager of the Company in Montreal.

On General Stock, Altamont, premium, $75.

(Signed)   JOS. T. DUMOUCHEL,

Agent."

On the back were indorsed the statutory conditions, without alteration or addition.

The receipt was on a printed form taken from a book of similar forms, with stubs for entering summaries of receipts issued.   The stubs are produced, and that corresponding to Bourque's receipt appears among them in regular course between one of 4th January and one of 9th January.

Dumouchel states that, on the 7th January he made an entry of the transaction in a book containing a record of business done, and this was intended as an entry of a credit to the Company of $75 ; also that he discounted the note with his Bank and had the proceeds and the amount of the cheque placed to his credit in the Bank in an account styled a "Trust account," that, "about the 1st of February" he sent to the Montreal office a report in the form generally used for the purpose in which, among other business, appeared entries of Bourque's insurance.

The report is on a form to show details of the business for a particular month and the agent's account with the company. By it the company was given credit for Bourque's premium of $75, less the agent's commission.   Dumouchel remitted to the Montreal office, about 15th Feb., the balance shown by this report to be due to the company.

Some time in January Dumouchel took a printed form of application for insurance and filled in it a number of particulars relating to Bourque's insurance, and in answering the question, "what other insurance have you on the property now to be insured ? " he wrote "None." He forwarded this application, unsigned, to the Montreal office.   He does not remember the date of forwarding it, but he says that it must have been the 7th or 8th of January.   It bears a stamp purporting to show that it was received at the Montreal office on the 19th January. Bourque never authorized the making of this application and knew nothing of it.

A policy was made out in pursuance of this application and signed by the assistant manager of the company for Canada, as attorney for the company, but not sealed. It bears date the 23rd January. It was forwarded to and received by Dumouchel who retained it and gave Bourque no notice of its issue. It is almost needless to say that no assent to the prior insurance appeared in the policy or was indorsed thereon

On the 10th February the store was destroyed by fire, and Bourque sustained a loss of stock, estimated at a little over $5000.

He claims that he did not know until after the fire of the arrival of the interim receipt, but that he found it afterwards in a desk that was saved, and explains this upon the hypothesis that the envelope containing it was opened by his wife, who assisted him in the business. His conduct immediately after the fire to some extent corraborates his claim in this respect.

Dumouchel's appointment as agent of the defendant company was made by instrument in writing signed by the Chief Agent of the company at Montreal, without seal. By this he was "authorized and empowered to receive proposals for insurance against loss or damage by fire. to sign interim and renewal receipts, to receive moneys and to do all lawful acts and business pertaining to said agency which may from time to time be given him in charge by said Chief Agent."

A condition of the Manitoba Assurance Co's policy was that " The Company is not liable for loss . . . . . if any subsequent insurance is effected in any other Company unless and until the Company assents thereto, or unless the Company does not dissent in writing within two weeks after receiving written notice of the intention or desire to effect the subsequent insurance. or does not dissent in writing after that time and before the subsequent or further insurance is effected."

The Manitoba Company was never notified of the subsequent insurance or of Bourque's intention to effect it, and never consented thereto in any way, and never learned of it until after the fire.

Bourque made claims and put in proofs of loss against both companies, and subsequently assigned his claims to the plaintiffs, who have sued both companies.

The promissory note for $51 was paid by Bourque at maturity, but after the fire.

The statement of claim in the present action is based upon the interim receipt alone, entirely ignoring the policy, and alleges that the insurance was subject to no conditions. The material defences are (1) that the premium was not paid before loss ; (2) that the contract of insurance was subject to the 8th statutory condition, namely, '' The Company is not liable for loss if there is any prior insurance in any other company, unless the Company's assent thereto appears herein or is indorsed hereon '' and that the Company gave no assent thereto, or no assent in manner required ; (3) misrepresentation that the insurance of $3,000 applied for was and was to be the only insurance upon the property ; and (4) breach of a warranty that the prior insurance would be abandoned.

I treat the statement of defence as amended in any respect necessary to give effect to these various defences, as I consider that the proper office of the Court is to ascertain the respective rights of the litigant parties without allowing itself to be hampered by forms of pleading to any greater extent than justice requires. There seems to me no doubt that the facts are now before the Court as fully and fairly as they could have been placed if the pleadings had been in any way differently worded.

Neither by the pleadings nor at the trial was the policy set up as superseding the interim receipt. It was not under seal. If the corporate seal was necessary in order to make it binding, there was no policy delivered. The cases in which the technical delivery of a sealed instrument, not delivered in fact, created an executed contract, so as to constitute performance of an executory one, have no application.

Without communication to Bourque there could be no delivery, actual or constructive, of this simple contract.

It is not denied that Dumouchel had power to grant the interim receipt according to its terms and to bind the company thereby, upon payment of the premium in cash. But, having regard to the terms of his appointment and to the decisions in *London and Lancashire Life Ass. Co.* v. *Fleming*, [1897] A.C. 499, and *The Canadian Fire Ins. Co.* v. *Robinson*, in the Supreme Court of Canada (not yet

reported *) it seems clear that Dumouchel's authority to issue
such a receipt was conditional upon payment of the premium
in cash, and that parties dealing with him had no right to
assume that he had any greater or other authority. The
very terms of the receipt imported that it was issued for a
payment in money and those accepting such a document on
other terms must do so at their own risk.

But Dumouchel having authority to enter into such a
temporary contract for the company, the knowledge acquired
by him in the negotiation must be imputed to the company ;
and if he assumed to contract for additional insurance to run
concurrently with that before existing, the company was
bound by his act : *Wing* v. *Harvey*, 5 D. M. & G. 265 ;
Bawden v. *London, &c. Ass. Co.* [1892] 2 Q. B. 534 ;
Watteau v. *Fenwick.*, [1893] 1 Q. B. 346 ; *The Liverpool,
&c. Ins. Co.* v. *Wyld*, 1 S.C.R. 604 ; *The Hastings Mut. F.
Ins. Co.* v. *Shannon*, 2 S R.C. 394 ; *Naughter* v. *The Ottawa
Agricultural Ins. Co.*, 43 U.C.R. 121.

In endeavoring to ascertain on what terms Dumouchel
intended to contract for the company, we must leave out of
consideration the language of the form of application which
he forwarded to Montreal, and confine ourselves to the
communications between him and Bourque, and the interim
receipt. The only application made by Bourque was such as
appeared in his letters, and it is to that application that the
interim receipt must be understood to refer. Such an
application, however, should be construed to be for insurance
upon the customary terms of the company. Dumouchel so
construed it, and expressed this in the receipt. And in
stating that "the property is hereby held insured" the
receipt must be taken as meaning insured upon the
conditions of the recited application.

The insurance purported to be contracted for was temporary, to continue only until a policy should be delivered or
the application declined—that is, a policy and an application
upon those conditions. In the natural course the policy
would cover the whole term, and express the conditions for
the whole term.

There can be no question of the application of section 3
of The Fire Insurance Policy Act, R S.M., C. 59. The only
conditions sought to be imposed were the statutory conditions,
without addition or variation.

———— (*) The case referred to by the Court was reported in Canadian
Commercial Cases p. 205.

It could be of no service to the plaintiffs upon this point to have it found that Bourque did not accept the receipt or know of its terms or its existence.   Dumouchel proposed to contract upon those terms and no others.   The Plaintiffs sue upon it as constituting the contract, though they wrongly allege it to constitute an unconditional contract.   They must be bound by it according to its true construction.

In *Parsons* v. *The Queen Insurance Co.* 43 U.C.R. 271 ; 4 A.R. 103 ; 4 S C.R. 215 ; 7 A.C. 96, the action was upon an interim receipt very similar to that. now in question. The material differences are that, in the former case, the receipt recited a proposal for insurance "subject to all the usual terms and conditions of the Company," which were not indorsed or otherwise directly specified, and the main statement was that "it is hereby held assured *uuder these conditions* until " etc.

The Court of Queen's Bench held that either the contract was unconditional, or the statutory conditions applied, but that in the latter case there was sufficient assent to the prior insurance, and that a court of equity would compel the issue of a policy with the requisite assent inserted or indorsed. Harrison, C.J. said "If there be prior insurances there must be the assent of the Company, and in the event of the issue of a policy that assent must appear in the policy or be indorsed thereon.   Where no policy is issued there cau be no assent to such insurance either appearing therein or indorsed thereon ; but it is only reasonable to hold that even an interim insurance is not binding in the face of such a condition unless there be not only notice of the prior insurance, but the assent of the Company thereto in aud by their agent authorized to effect interim insurances." And then, after discussing a question as to whether the agent had received a memorandum showing the prior insurances, he said, "The agent having received it, and afterwards accepted the premium and issued the interim receipt, must be taken to have assented to it, and his act under the circumstances must, so far as the interim receipt is concern-ed, and the rights of the plaintiff thereunder, be held to be the act and assent of the defendants.   It is true, as mentioned in *Hawke* v. *Niagara Dis. Mut Fire Ins. Co.* 23 Gr. 148, that the indorsement of consent might be made on the interim receipt instead of the policy, but to decide that the want of the indorsement on the interim receipt should vitiate

the claim thereunder, would, we think, be placing too rigor-
ous a construction on the interim contract."

The Court of Appeal held that the statute applied and
had the effect of making the contract one for unconditional
insurance, and in this view the majority of the Judges of the
Supreme Court of Canada concurred. Mr. Justice Gwynne,
however, was of the opinion that the statute did not wipe
out the conditions, and that it did not apply to interim
receipts, but that the contract was one for insurance upon
the conditions on which the policy should issue, which
would be the statutory conditions, with such variations as
would be effected by such of the conditions upon the policies
which had been in ordinary use with the defendants, as
would be good and valid under the statute if indorsed as
variations in the form prescribed by the statute; see 4
S C.R. at p. 328.

And this is the view which ultimately found acceptance
with the Judicial Committee of the Privy Council. Neither
Mr. Justice Gwynne nor the Judicial Committee expressed
any opinion upon the condition respecting prior insurance.

In the Court of Queen's Bench the interim receipt was
treated as evidencing only an executory contract, enforceable
in equity.

In the Court of Appeal, Moss, C. J. expressed the
opinion that it constituted an executed contract on which
the plaintiff could sue directly at law for the insurance
moneys. In the Supreme Court Mr. Justice Gwynne said
(p.p. 325,6). "The difference between an interim receipt
and a completed policy is well known, and must be deemed
to have been so to the Legislature . . . Although an action
may now, under the Administration of Justice Act, be
brought at law upon an interim receipt, whereas formerly it
only could be brought in equity, still the principle upon
which the action was sustained remains the same, namely,
that a contract involved in such a receipt was one which a
Court of Equity would enforce the specific performance of,
by decreeing the issue of a policy in accordance with the
terms of the agreement contained in the interim receipt."

In delivering the judgment of the Judicial Committee,
Sir Montagu E. Smith, after referring to the language that
"it is hereby held insured," etc., said (p. 124.) "No

doubt this last stipulation forms a contract of insurance
during this interval ; but the whole agreement is preliminary
only, and, in substance, the note contains a proposal for a
policy to be carried into effect, if accepted, by the delivery
of a policy as subsidiary thereto, and for the convenience of
the person proposing to insure immediate protection is
given to him . . . If in any case it should appear that any
interim note or any like instrument was intended by the
parties to be the complete and final contract of insurance,
and that this shape was given to the instrument for the
purpose of evading the Act, the present decision would not
be opposed to the instrument being treated as a policy of
insurance ; the ground of this present decision being that
the interim note in this case is what it professes to be
preliminary to the issuing of another instrument, viz : a
policy which the parties *bona fide* intended should be
issued . . . If the contract of the parties had come to be
executed, the company would perform it by issuing a
policy, subject to its own conditions if it could legally do so.
Indeed if the assured so required, it would be obligatory on
the company to perform it in this manner.''

I take the meaning of this to be that, while the language
of the receipt to some extent imported a present contract of
insurance, in reality it was an executory contract only.

In *Jones* v. *The Provincial Ins. Co.* 16 U.C.R. 477 the
plaintiff declared *in assumpsit* that, in consideration of
payment of a certain premium, the defendants promised and
agreed to insure him against loss by fire, and the breach
alleged was non-payment. There was a demurrer on the
ground that the contract was not under seal. Robinson, C.
J. pointed out that if the plaintiff intended to sue upon a
parol contract to insure the breach should be in not executing the policy. And the demurrer was allowed on the
ground that the company could not be liable on an agreement
by parol as an executed contract of insurance. But a Court
of Equity would interfere though the contract was not
under seal or executed with the formalities required by the
company's constitution   *In re Athenæum Soc.* 4 K. & J.
549 ; *Commercial Mut. Mar. Ins. Co.* v. *Union Mut. Ins. Co.*
19 How. 321 ; *Penley* v. *Beacon Ass. Co.* 7 Gr. 130.

While the formal contract assumed to be made on behalf
of the defendant company by the Montreal officials was not

under seal, I do not think that this affords sufficient evidence that the company could so contract without seal.

My own opinion is that which I understand to have been the opinion of the Court of Queen's Bench for Ontario and of Mr. Justice Gwynne in the Parsons case, that, under such a receipt there is not a contract which would have been enforceable by action at law under the former practice.

And in such a case, in ascertaining whether there was a contract completely made, cognizable at law or in equity, or what were its terms, we are not, in my opinion. to be confined to the interim receipt, or to the fact that it was issued and the premium received. The receipt is not to be taken as a formal document intended to embody the whole contract, and we are entitled to go back to the negotiations to ascertain, not only whether a contract was actually made, but also what it was that the parties intended to agree upon.

The transaction began with Bourque's letter of 1st January.

That and the other correspondence, as well as the interim receipt, must be looked at to ascertain what kind of a policy of insurance Bourque was applying for and which. after the making of a preliminary contract he could expect to compel the company to grant. And when granted it should cover the initial portion of the term and be the same for that as for the remaining portion.

And that letter was not a definite application, by a simple acceptance of which a contract would be created. It was only a tentative proposal, calculated to lead to negotiation and the settlement of terms. After a reply the letter of 5th January was sent, giving further particulars, and evidently intended to amount to a more definite application. Upon that Dumouchel made out the interim receipt and sent it to Bourque. either with a request for the $75, or with the note for signature and a request for $25.   In either case he promised that, on receiving what he asked for, he would put the insurance through for Bourque. He expressed no other condition.

Now, if the request had been for the insurance to the amount of $3000, and there had been no other insurance, then, upon payment of the premium there would have been a completed contract, enforceable in equity. And if there had been a true disclosure of the prior insurance, without the expression of intention to abandon, I think that there would have been a sufficient assent to the prior insurance.

If the receipt had expressly stated that the property was held insured upon the conditions indorsed upon it, then the words in the condition, " unless the Company's assent thereto appears herein or is indorsed hereon " would refer distinctly to the receipt itself. But the reference to the indorsed conditions is only for the purpose of identifying the conditions of the policy for which, as is recited, application has been made. The incorporation of these into the interim contract can only be made by inference, and, therefore, cannot be carried beyond the extent to which they are applicable pending the issue of the policy. The conditions are referred to only as the conditions of the company's policies, and the words "herein" and "hereon" do not relate to the receipt at all and are not made to do so.

I pass by the point that the amount of the prior insurance was not correctly stated in the letter of the 1st January, as it was not set up by the statement of defence or taken at the trial.

But the circumstances of this case differ materially from those of the Parsons case. There was not the bald application for insurance with notice of that before existing.

The first letter expressed an intention to abandon the prior insurance, and I can interpret it only as evincing a desire to have insurance to the amount of $3000 in all. This letter formed the basis of the whole transaction. When this and the second letter come to be consolidated into a definite application upon which the interim receipt was made out, it seems impossible to treat it as an application for a policy with assent to the prior insurance, and I do not think that one can infer from the sending out of the receipt and acceptance of the premium an assent by the agent to the prior insurance or a contract for insurance to the amount of $3000 in addition to that prior insurance. And for the purpose of inferring the intent of the agent and what Bourque should have interpreted it to be, I think that one may properly have regard to the fact that insurance to such an amount upon stock represented only as worth "over $5,000" would. from an insurer's point of view, be a most improvident transaction and one to which the company could not be expected to assent. In assuming this to be the character of such a contract, I do not rely upon the language of the printed application or the additional evidence given in the case against the Manitoba Assurance Co., but solely upon considerations of the nature of the contract of insurance and its consequences.

In my opinion the case should be treated upon the basis that, either there was not to be a contract concluded until the prior insurance had been abandoned, or it was a condition of the executory contract that it should be abandoned. And it does not appear to me material which is the proper view, though I prefer the latter.

It is true that Dumouchel did not expressly stipulate for any such condition, but promised, on the contrary, to put the insurance through on receiving the premium, or the note and a portion of the premium. But he had a right to rely on Bourque's representation of his intention, which there was ample time to carry out before the 16th of January, when the note and cheque were sent in. And if we are to take into consideration the facts that Dumouchel negotiated the note, credited up the premium to the company, reported it as paid, and finally remitted the amount, all without inquiring whether the other insurance had been abandoned or not, we are then surely entitled also to consider that he delayed about a week the forwarding of the application, and then represented that there was no other insurance.

But if it is to be considered that a contract was then made, then I would infer that a part of it was a promise by Bourque to abandon the prior insurance, and to do it within a reasonable time, and upon the ordinary rules for the construction of contracts I would take its performance to be a condition of the executory contract. And, further, I think that this action must be regarded as one for specific performance of the executory contract. As in case of other contracts, specific performance is in a measure discretionary.

Stipulations which might not be treated at law as warranties or conditions might be treated in equity as conditions to decreeing specific performance. It does not appear to me that, without having abandoned the prior insurance, Bourque would be granted specific performance by a Court of Equity.

Then can it be said that Bourque abandoned the prior insurance within the meaning of his letter? I think not. The policy of the Manitoba Assurance Co. remained a subsisting contract. It is true that it was subject to a condition preventing recovery upon it until that company should assent to the subsequent insurance and, also, that it was hardly conceivable that it would so assent. But it was open to the company to do so, and that assent could not properly be treated as creating subsequent insurance to the Royal's. It must be prior insurance or nothing.

It is true that Bourque took no steps to procure the assent, but it is also true that he made a claim and put in proofs of loss under the policy, and assigned the claim to the plaintiffs who are now suing upon it. I do not see how it can be said to have been abandoned.

I have discussed the matter as if the premium had been duly paid. I have done so for the reason that it would be most injust and inequitable that the defence should succeed on the ground of non-payment Dumouchel realized the amount by negotiation of the note, credited it to the company and accounted for it in due course. The position is entirely different from that in *London and Lancashire Life Ass. Co.* v. *Fleming;* [1897] A.C. 499. I do not overlook the necessity for authority from the applicant to the agent to so realize and pay over the money for him, or subsequent ratification of the acts, but it does not seem to me impossible to imply the necessary authority under the circumstances of this case. At any rate, Bourque could claim the proceeds of the note to have been his moneys in Dumouchel's hands, and I do not feel at all sure that, even after the loss, he might not adopt the application of the proceeds as amounting to payment of his premium in cash.

Upon the trial I was inclined to think that the plaintiffs must rely upon the remittance to Montreal as constituting the payment, and that, in adopting Dumouchel's payment, Bourque and they must adopt him as the agent to make the application sent to Montreal.

I think, however, that in this I did not give sufficient weight to Dumouchel's appropriation of the proceeds of the note by crediting up the money to the company and including it in his reported receipts, which, if he had sufficient authority from Bourque, operated as payment.

See *Eyles* v. *Ellis*, 4 Bing. 112; *Nightingale* v. *The City Bank of Montreal*, 26 U.C.C.P. 74.

But the defendant succeeds on what seems to me the much more equitable ground, that there never was any contract for additional insurance contemporaneous with that under the policy of the Manitoba Assurance Company, which was never abandoned.

I dismiss the action, with costs.

Solicitors for the Plaintiffs: *Macdonald, Haggart & Whitla.*

Solicitors for the Defendants: *Munson & Allan.*

[IN THE COURT OF KING'S BENCH FOR MANITOBA.]

Before KILLAM, C. J.

WHITLA

v.

THE MANITOBA ASSURANCE CO.

Fire Insurance — Policy — Conditions regarding subsequent insurance.

The Plaintiff, as assignee of B, sued the defendant company on a policy issued by it to B. One of the conditions indorsed upon the policy was as follows: " The Company is not liable for loss . . if any subsequent insurance is effected in any other company unless or until the Company assents hereto," etc., and the defence was based solely upon this clause. The other facts were the same as those in the preceding case of *Whitla* v. *The Royal Insurance Co.* Held, that as B and the Royal Insurance Co. had never entered into a contract for insurance to run concurrently with that effected by the prior contract with the present defendant, the condition above set forth had no application, and plaintiff was entitled to recover on the policy.

10TH JANUARY, 1902. KILLAM, C. J.:—While there was in this case some evidence not given in the case against The Royal Insurance Co. the material facts proved seem to be practically the same.

The only defence set up is under the 8th condition indorsed upon the policy: " The Company is not liable for loss . . . if any subsequent insurance is effected in any other Company, unless or until the Company assents thereto or unless,'' etc. The last part relates to a case in which previous notice of intention to effect further insurance is given, and has no application to the present case. There is an attempted variation as to which a question is raised, but it seems of no importance. I take the effect of the decision in *Parsons* v. *The Citizens' Ins. Co.* 7 A.C. 96, to be that if the conditions are not indorsed in manner required by the statute, then the policy is subject to the statutory conditions, and there is no attempt to vary the 8th condition in the portion applicable.

The ground upon which I have disposed of the case against the Royal Co. is that the contract of insurance (if any) with that company was at most an executory contract, subject to the condition that the insurance with the Manitoba Co. should be abandoned or to a stipulation which should be treated in a suit for specific performance as such a condition.

If it could be considered that in that case there was no completed contract as all was dependent upon the abandonment, then this case would come within the principle of *Commercial Union Assurance* v. *Temple*, 29 S. C. R. 206. But taking what seems to me the preferable view that it was but an executory contract subject to that condition, I do not think that it comes within the 8th condition of this policy.

It appears to me that an agreement to insure upon abandonment of the former policy amounts to no more than an agreement to insure upon the expiration of the former one. In either case it is not to be in force as an effective contract while the former one is, and it is only during the existence of the former contract that the first insurers should be required to assent. To an assurance which was not to be concurrent with the former one no assent should be deemed to be called for.

I do not overlook the fact that the term of the Royal Company was to begin with the 7th January, and that it was after that date when, if ever, there came to be a contract at all.

The real point is that Bourque and the Royal Co. never agreed upon an insurance which was to run concurrently with the Manitoba Co's policy, to which kind of insurance alone the 8th condition appears to me to be applicable, and if necessary to meet their real agreement, the abandonment could well be required to relate back to the 7th January.

This view does not seem to me in any way inconsistent with the principles of the decisions in *Jacobs* v. *The Equitable Ins. Co.* 19 U. C. R. 250 ; *Mason* v. *The Andes Ins. Co.* 23 U. C. C. P. 37, and *Gauthier* v. *The Waterloo Mnt. Ins. Co.* 6 A. R. 231.

I do not understand those decisions to proceed upon the ground that the making of claims for subsequent insurance, the putting in of proofs of loss thereunder on the bringing of actions thereon, creates any estoppel. Bourque and the plaintiffs were put in a very difficult position. If they elected to claim of one company only, they ran the risk of losing the one from which they could recover.

If my construction of the 8th condition is correct there arises the question of fact as to whether there was a subsequent contract for concurrent insurance. An erroneous claim that there was cannot change the facts.

I notice that proofs of loss under the Manitoba Co's policy do not state positively that there was other insurance. The statement is "There was no other insurance held by me upon the property at the time of the fire, excepting a policy in the Royal Insurance for $3000. "

As a matter of fact there was no such completed policy, and this statement does not directly assert that there was.

The exception may well have been intended to be one of an insurance which the claimant considered to be of doubtful existence.

There will be judgment for the plaintiffs for $2250, with interest from 27th, March, 1901, and costs of suit.

Solicitors for the Plaintiffs : *McDonald, Haggart & Whitla.*

Solicitors for the Defendants : *Tupper, Phippen & Tupper.*

[IN THE HIGH COURT OF JUSTICE FOR ONTARIO.]

(DIVISIONAL COURT)

BEFORE BOYD C. and FERGUSON, J.

ARMSTRONG

v.

THE PROVIDENT SAVINGS LIFE ASSURANCE SOCIETY.

Life Insurance — Initialling of application — Completion of contract—Due dates of premiums.

The mere initialling by the officers of an insurance company of an application for a policy of insurance, although it may shew that the company intend to issue the policy applied for therein, does not of itself constitute any contract with the applicant. But if a policy is subsequently made out and the applicant is told that it is ready for him, there will then be an acceptance of the original application, and the policy may be antedated to correspond with the date of the application.

When there is a provision in the policy that the same shall not go into effect until the first premium is paid, and the dates upon which the premiums are payable are also set forth in the policy, the fact that the first premium is paid to and accepted by the company after the date specified in the policy will not affect the time of payment of subsequent premiums, which will fall due on the dates stated in the policy.

PER BOYD, C. :—"The receipt of the policy after the first payment, accompanied by the silence implying the satisfaction of the applicant and the consequent payment of the second premium according to the terms of the policy, is cogent and, indeed, after his death conclusive evidence of his assent to the contract as expressed by the company in this policy."

This was a special case, heard, by agreement between the parties, before a Divisional Court, under Con. Rule of Practice (Ont.) 117. The facts are fully set forth in the judgment of FERGUSON, J.

NOVEMBER, 16, 1901, FERGUSON, J. :—Gamble D. S. Armstrong made an application to the defendants for a policy upon his life for the sum of $2,000, the same to be what was known as a twenty years renewable term policy. This was to be for the benefit of the applicant's mother, Sophia Amelia Armstrong, the present Plaintiff. The application was sent from Toronto, and appears to have been received at the head office of the defendants in New York as early as August 23rd. 1897. On that day certain officers of the company put initial letters upon the application, and from these it was contended that there had been an acceptance of the application and an insurance contract completed. This contention was for the purpose of claiming the issue of a policy in accordance with the terms of such supposed contract, it being contended that the policy that was issued by the defendants was not in accordance with the application. What appears may well indicate that the defendant's officers were satisfied with the application, but this was not at any time communicated to the plaintiff or the beneficiary, who acted in some of the matters at least appertaining to the proposed insurance as the agent of the applicant, and without such communication there could not be a completed contract : see *Equitable Life* v. *McElroy*, 83 Fed. R. 631 at p. 642 ; *Paine* v. *Pacific United Life*, 51 Fed. R. 689 at p. 693, and the cases there referred to ; also Pollock on Contracts, 6th ed., p. 31. This proposition is perhaps too plain for discussion.

The defendants had a policy prepared, and without any unreasonable delay forwarded it to their agents in Toronto, where the applicant and his mother, the beneficiary, resided, for delivery. This policy bears date the 23rd, of August, 1897. It was forwarded from New-York on the 26th of the same month and received by Mr. Hunter, the Canadian manager and agent of the defendants in Toronto, on the 28th, day of that month, when, as admitted by the case, the plaintiff was informed by him that he had the policy. It is also admitted by the case stated that no communication was made by the defendants or by any one on their behalf, to the applicant or the plaintiff, or to any person on behalf of either of them, relative to the acceptance of the application until after the issue of the policy and its receipt in Toronto when Mr. Hunter informed the plaintiff as aforesaid that he had the policy.

It is also admitted that the course of dealing adopted in this instance was the ordinary course, whereby the defendants considered and dealt with applications for insurances.

As already stated, it was contended that the policy was not drawn according to the application. I have read both documents and I am humbly of the opinion that the contention is not well founded. I think the policy does accord with the application, and is just such a policy as any reasonable person would expect to have in answer to such an application. The application does not state all that is set forth in the policy, but this, I apprehend, is never the case.

I do not think there is any material difference between the application and the policy as was the case in *Mowat* v. *Provident Savings Life Assurance Society*, 27 A. R. 675, and I think the sending of the policy was an acceptance of the application, the first and only acceptance of it, and cannot be considered to be a counter proposal as was intimated. These two documents, as I think, constituted the insurance contract between the parties.

As to the policy bearing a date as early as the 23rd. of August, I think the reasoning in the case of *McConnell* v. *Provident Savings*, 92 Fed. R. 769, is much in favour of the defendants, perhaps conclusively so, if the reasoning be adopted, as I think it should be. In the present case, as in that case, there was no agreement or instructions as to what the date of the policy should be.

This policy was not in fact delivered till the 4th day of October, 1897, the delays arising from two causes, both of which, as it seems to me from the evidence made part of the special case, were attributable to the plaintiff and the applicant. One of them was the neglect and delay in payment of the first premium. This the beneficiary, who was acting for the applicant, says in her evidence was partly owing to neglect and partly to sickness in her family. The other was difficulty in obtaining a further "health certificate" from the applicant, who had gone to British Columbia, and was there engaged, as I understand the evidence, with a railway surveying party. This difficulty seemed so great that the defendants finally consented to accept a certificate signed by the plaintiff as agent of the applicant, and on her own behalf as the beneficiary, instead of one signed by the applicant himself.

In the application there is a provision expressed in these words : "That the insurance hereby applied for shall not be binding on the society until the first premium due thereon has been actually received by the said society or its authorized agent during the life-time and good health " of the applicant. In the policy the provision is in these words : " This policy does not go into effect until the first premium thereon has been actually paid during the lifetime and good health of the assured. " These two provisions, are, as I think, to the same effect, the meaning being that should the death of the applicant occur before the payment of the first premium there would, in that case, be no insurance and the defendants should not be liable.

This, however, is not the view taken by the plaintiff, who contended that as the first premium was not in fact paid till the 4th of October 1897, that point of time must be considered the commencement, and that the half-yearly payments were to be made each half year after that day, that is to say, on the 4th, of April and October in each year instead of the 23rd of February and 23rd, of August in each year as provided in the policy. The plaintiff, acting for the applicant, paid, as before stated, the first premium on the 4th. of October, 1897, and received a receipt for it dated the 23rd of August 1897, which she retained and kept. This on its face states that the payment is up to the 23rd day of February, 1898. On the 26th day of February, 1898, she paid the second premium and was given a receipt stating that this was the amount required to cover the February premium, and another receipt (from the head office) stating that this was the premium due the 23rd February 1898. Both of those receipts she retained and kept. These, as well as the other receipt above mentioned, are parts of the case.

The third half-yearly premium was tendered on the 17th, day of October, 1898, and not before, and was refused by the defendants, their contention appearing to be that this premium should have been paid on the 23rd, day of August, 1898, or within the thirty days thereafter, the policy allowing 30 days' grace in the payment of premiums. The contention of the plaintiff is that this premium did not fall due till the 4th of October 1898, and that the tender of it was in good time, it being within the thirty days thereafter.

It is not disputed that if this tender was not in good time, or, in other words, there was default in payment of this premium, the defendants were not bound to continue or rather renew the insurance, and the defendants refused to continue or renew it.

On the case I am of the opinion that the third premium fell due on the 23rd day of August, 1898, and, as a consequence, the tender of it was too late, and the defendant's contention the right one.

The policy provides that the failure to pay any annual premium or instalment thereof as specified when due will terminate the policy.

The assured died on or about the 20th, day of October, 1898.

I am, for reasons that I have endeavoured to give, of the opinion that the plaintiff is not entitled to recover, and the consequence is that the action should be dismissed with costs.

I think the action should be dismissed with costs.

There is, however, another and separate reason which was urged for dismissing the action. The special case admits that the plaintiff, who is the administratrix of the estate of the insured as well as the beneficiary in the policy, did not furnish any proofs of the death of the insured till after the commencement of this action, viz., on the 19th day of April, 1899.

The agreement in the policy is to pay " within eighty days " after receipt of satisfactory proofs of the death of the assured. From this it would appear that the action was premature and should for this reason be dismissed, and, I suppose, with costs.

On the whole case I think the action should be dismissed with costs.

BOYD, C. :—My brother Ferguson has very fully set forth the facts of this case and his conclusions upon the law applicable thereto, and I agree generally in his results. The action, in my opinion, must fail on the merits.

I find no evidence of any prior agreement on which there might be based jurisdiction to reform the policy. The matters pertaining to the issue of the policy were by way of application, and the acceptance by the officers of the company was not for the purpose of informing the applicant, but for the guidance of their own sub-officials in preparing the proper policy.

This official acceptance was never made known to the applicant, nor was it ever intended that he should be informed of it. There is, in my opinion, no evidence of any concluded contract until the acceptance of the policy by the applicant. This was consequent upon the contemporaneous payment of the first premium and the delivery of the policy on the 4th of October, 1897. That policy bore date August 23rd, 1897, that being the date when the application was received at the head office in New York, at which time also some officers of the company marked it approved,—though the final act of acceptance was not till August 25th, 1897.

However, that policy as drawn up and issued signified this contract as understood by the company, and the receipt of the policy after the first payment, accompanied by the silence implying the satisfaction of the applicant and the consequent payment of the second premium according to the terms of the policy, is cogent and, indeed, after his death conclusive evidence of his assent to the contract as expressed by the company in this policy.

In England it appears to be usual after the directors have accepted the proposal to give notice of that to the applicant, and then call upon him for the payment of the premium. Hence it is said in *Collett* v. *Morrison*, 9 Ha. 173. if there is an agreement for a policy in a particular form and the policy be drawn up in the office in a different form, varying the right of the party assured, a court of equity will interfere and deal with the case on the footing of the agreement and not of the policy. Here, however, the difference is that there is no prior agreement to reform by.

Again, as said by Lord Cranworth in *Xenos* v. *Wickham* (1867), L.R. 2 H.L. 296 at p. 324: "It is not the practice that the assured should call for and examine the policy before he takes it away but that he should send for it evidently treating it as an instrument complete before it is taken away from the office. If when it has been sent to him, he should discover that it is not conformable to the slip, his only remedy would be a remedy in equity to get it corrected according to the real meaning of the parties."

Here, as I have said, the contemporaneous and the subsequent conduct of the insured indicates very clearly his acceptance of the policy, and his willingness to pay on the days therein provided for payment of later premiums. No case exists to reform.

It is admitted that the policy was issued according to the ordinary course of the company. I observe that in *Collett*

v. *Morrison* the same method was pursued as in this case. There the application was on September 9th, 1844, and the proposal was on September 16th, accepted by the directors and notice given to applicant. The premium for the year was paid on September 19th, and a policy signed bearing date September 9th, and it was expressed therein that the premium had been paid for twelve calendar months commencing on the day of the date of the policy: 9 Ha. p. 164.

I perceive no incongruity between the application and the policy if they be read together as one instrument. The application is for a 20 year's renewable term policy with premiums payable semi-annually. And the applicant therein agrees that the assurance applied for shall not become binding on the society until the first premium is actually paid. The policy is drawn up of date 23rd of August, 1897, and it is said to be granted in consideration of the payment in advance upon delivery of this policy of $13.38 and of the payment thereafter of $13.38 on or before the 23rd day of February and August in every year during the continuance of the policy. This is plainly and unambiguously expressed and accords with the application, and no one would misunderstand the obligation incurred.

All the American law is collected in the elaborate discussions upon this very controversy in the case of *New York Life Insurance Co.* v. *McMaster*, 87 Fed. R. 63; *McMaster* v. *New York Life Insurance Co.*, 99 Fed. R. 856; and *McConnell* v. *Provident Life*, 92 Fed. R. 769, in which the conclusions were conformable to that herein arrived at.

The action stands dismissed as agreed upon in the special case, with costs.

Solicitors for the Plaintiff: *Kerr, Davidson, Paterson & Grant.*

Solicitors for the Defendants: *Marsh & Cameron.*

[IN THE SUPERIOR COURT OF THE PROVINCE OF QUEBEC.]

(COURT OF REVIEW.)

BEFORE TAIT, A. C. J., PAGNUELO AND PARADIS, J. J.

THE PABST BREWING CO.

v.

H. A. EKERS and THE CANADIAN BREWERIES, Limited.

Trade name—Common Law Right—Proof of Deception.

A manufacturer, whose goods are generally known to the public by a certain name, has a common law right to protection against a competitor using the same or some similar name only upon making proof either of fraud or deception as regards such use, and of prejudice resulting therefrom.

Where the alleged infringement has extended over a number of years the fact that there is no proof of any one having been deceived during that period is very material.

Judgment of Davidson, J., reversed.

Action for damages for alleged wrongful use of a trade name, and for an injunction restraining the defendant, The Canadian Breweries Ltd., from making further use of such name. At the trial the action was maintained, as regards the injunction asked for, against the company defendant. (See 1 Can. Com. Cases, p. 39). The latter inscribed in review.

The judgment of the Court was given by Sir Melbourne Tait, A. C. J. : —

The plaintiff carries on a brewing business in Milwaukee, Wisconsin, U. S. A. The defendant Ekers, up to June, 1889, was engaged in a similar business in Montreal, when he sold out to the other defendant, the Canadian Breweries Limited, who now carry it on.

T

This action was instituted in February, 1900, to restrain the defendants from using the word " Milwaukee " in connection with the beer not brewed in that city, and to recover $5,000 damages from each of them for having used it.

The judgment under review dismissed plaintiff's action as against the defendant Ekers with costs, upon the ground that he had as already stated sold out his business to the other defendant before the institution of this action, and had never since personally manufactured, advertised, or sold the lager beer complained of, and that no damages had been liquidated in regard to the use of the word " Milwaukee " by Ekers, and no protest had been made while he was in business. But the judgment enjoined the other defendant as prayed for without awarding any damages against it, inasmuch as plaintiff had " not made proof in establishment of any sum certain for liquidated damages," and the defendant so enjoined now inscribes in review.

As the case is of importance it is perhaps desirable that the substance of the pleadings should be stated :—

The plaintiff alleges that it has been engaged in this business for more than fifty years, and that the beer brewed by it and other brewers in Milwaukee has become well known in the United States and Canada as the product of Milwaukee, and has acquired a reputation of great value to plaintiff; that it has for upwards of eleven years marketed its lager beer and malt extract in Montreal, and had an office and large bottling establishment there since the 13th of January, 1897; that on the 1st of March, 1898, and at divers times thereafter, Ekers, in bad faith and with the unlawful and fraudulent intent of appropriating the reputation of the breweries of Milwaukee, and of causing his goods to be sold as the product thereof, to the detriment of plaintiff, has continually made use of the words " Milwaukee lager," and has used the word " Milwaukee " to designate lager beer which is not the product of Milwaukee; that the other defendant has also since said date done the same thing; and that the illegal and unauthorized use of the name of the city of Milwaukee has had the effect of deceiving buyers and the public generally, and has caused damage to the plaintiff; that plaintiff has protested against the illegal use of the word " Milwaukee " by defendants and requested them to discontinue the use thereof, but they have refused and still continue to use said word.

The defendants plead together, alleging for defence in effect that they are ignorant as to the business carried on by plaintiff. They deny that the beer brewed by plaintiff has become well known in the United States and Canada as alleged, and that it has acquired the reputation alleged. They say that the name " Milwaukee " is merely accidental, being that of the place where plaintiff carries on its business, and has no special significance with regard to plaintiff's beer, or any special excellency in connection therewith, and that plaintiff has no exclusive right to make use of the word " Milwaukee " as pretended. They admit that Ekers for more than fifteen years sold lager beer styled " Ekers Milwaukee Lager," but clearly and plainly marked as made by him at Montreal, and the other defendant continued to do so; that they both had a perfect right to do this, and it was done openly without any protest or objection on the part of the plaintiff, who, on the contrary, acquiesced therein; that this was not done with any intention to deceive, and did not deceive the public in general, as falsely alleged by plaintiff; that the word " Milwaukee " has no generic or special character attached to it as connected with lager beer; that it is not a trade mark or trade name; that it does not in any way indicate any superior excellence of product and any person is entitled to use the same provided he does so in good faith, as defendants have done; that defendants never pretended that their beer was made at Milwaukee, and still less that it was made by plaintiff; that the word " Milwaukee " has never been registered by plaintiff in Canada as its property, and that it does not belong to plaintiff exclusively as against defendants.

The plaintiff, in answer to this plea, after denying certain allegations and praying acte of the admissions regarding the sale by defendants of the beer designated " Ekers' Milwaukee Lager," says that the word " Milwaukee " is of particular significance as bearing, according to the ordinary usage of trade, the exclusive meaning that such beer has been brewed at Milwaukee; that defendants can have no reason whatever, other than the desire to appropriate the reputation of the brewers of Milwaukee. for choosing that word in order to apply it to lager beer brewed in Montreal. Plaintiff also denies that defendants have made it clear that their beer was brewed at the City of Montreal, and allege that defendants adopted the form of words for the purpose of leading the public to believe that it was brewed at Milwaukee and was merely bottled or otherwise handled by defendants at Montreal. It further denies the alleged acquiescence: admits that it has never registered the word " Milwaukee " as a trade mark and does not pretend that the said word is its own property, but alleges that its action is based on its right to prevent unfair competition (*concurrence déloyable*), and injury to its business by the use of false. fraudulent. misleading and erroneous description of competing merchandise. which defendants are attempting to confuse in the eyes of the public with the products of plaintiff's breweries and other firms engaged in business in Milwaukee.

Defendant Ekers, as the proof establishes, began to use the word " Milwaukee " in connection with his own name, and the words " lager " and " Montreal," about the year 1885. The labels which were used on the bottles by the defendant company. when this action was taken, are produced as exhibits PP-1 & PP-2. The first has the words "The Canadian Breweries Limited," round the top of the outer circle ; the words "Ekers" at the top of the inner circle : the words " Milwaukee Lager," at the foot of the inner circle. with the words " Montreal " in the middle of it, and the words "Successors to Ekers' Brewery " at the top of the outer circle. The second contains the words " Ekers' Milwaukee Lager, Montreal," with the words "Special Brew. " written diagonally across them.

The placards used are marked PP-4 and PP-3. The former is marked " Ekers' Milwaukee Lager, Montreal," and the latter " Ekers' Brewery, India Pale Ale. Milwaukee Lager, Montreal, 409 St. Lawrence Street." Mr Scott, superintendent of company defendant, says this latter is out of date, and has not been used during his time.

The barrels are stamped simply with the word " Ekers," and the shipping tags or labels (D-2 and D-3) are marked respectively " Ekers' Brewery," with the word " Montreal " between, and " From Ekers Brewery, 409 St. Lawrence Main Street, Montreal." D-1 is not in use now.

A copy of an advertisement which the company defendant inserted in La Presse is also produced, and reads " The Canadian Breweries, Ltd., Montreal, Successeurs de H. A. Ekers, Bière. Porter et Lager, en bouteilles ou en futs." (Defendant's exhibit No. 6).

There is a photograph produced marked PP-7. That mark is evidently a mistake, as in the plaintiff's list of exhibits there is an exhibit entered as PP-8, which is said to be a copy of an advertisement at Sohmer Park. This photograph has not been produced or identified by any witness, so far as I have been able to find, as a photograph of such advertisement. Both Mr Ekers and Mr Scott, say that they know there is an advertisement at Sohmer Park advertising Mr Ekers' products, but neither of them can state how it reads.

The defendant Ekers being asked to explain why he used the word "Milwaukee " says :—"I suppose because Milwaukee was a lager beer place." He also says that at the time he commenced to use that word he knew very little about Milwaukee and had never heard of Milwaukee lager being sold in Canada, but had been told there were breweries there; that the name was suggested by a German named Knapp, whom he had then in his employ, and who was the first man to brew lager for him.

Plaintiff, as already pointed out, charges defendant Ekers with bad faith and fraud in using the word " Milwaukee "; that he did so with the unlawful and fraudulent intent of appropriating the reputation of the Milwaukee Breweries. and of leading the public to believe that his lager was brewed at Milwaukee; that the use of that name has had the effect of deceiving buyers and the public generally, and has caused damage to plaintiff; and he charges the other defendant with similar bad faith and fraudulent intent in continuing the use of said word.

The learned judge of the first court does not specially

say, either in his formal judgment or in his notes, reported
in 20 J. R. S. C., p. 20, that he finds these allegations of bad
faith and fraud proved. He alludes, however, to the reason
given by Ekers' for the word "Milwaukee" being used,
namely that he supposed it was because Milwaukee was a
lager beer place. He refers to the use of the word by Ekers
and the other defendant by means of labels and otherwise.
He also alludes to the efforts plaintiff has made to build up
its business, and the great reputation it has attained, and he
finds that this word, when connected with lager beer, is properly used to designate lager beer brewed in Milwaukee,
and that the word is of special significance and specially
valuable to plaintiff; that it has a lawful right to prevent
unfair competition and injury to its business by the use of
misleading descriptions of competing merchandise, and that
plaintiff is therefore entitled to an injunction, as against the
defendant "The Canadian Breweries, Ltd."

The learned judge has cited in his notes a number of English and American cases in support of the proposition of
law laid down by him. Perhaps the clearest and the most
comprehensive statement of the doctrine is found in the first
paragraph of the present Lord Chancellor's remarks in the
case of *Reddaway* v. *Banham* (L. R., [1896], A. C., 199),
known as the "Camel Hair Belting" case, where he says :—
"For myself, I believe the principle of law may be very
plainly stated, and that is, that nobody has any right to represent his goods as the goods of somebody else."

In the case of *Saxlehner* v. *Apollinaris Company*, Keke-
wich, (L. R., [1897] 1 Ch., Div.893), commenting on these
words of the Lord Chancellor, says: (P. 899)
"Observe that the propositionis perfectly general.
There is no limit as regards name, origin, honesty of
manufacture or sale, or otherwise; and although there
are elsewhere to be found learned and useful disqui-
sitions on the facts of the particular case, the application of the law to them and criticism of earlier authorities,
there is no departure from what the Lord Chancellor states
to be the principle of law. It matters not, therefore, how
a plaintiff's goods come to acquire a particular value, or
how the defendant's goods have come to adopt that value.
If, in fact, the defendant is selling his goods as those of the

plaintiff, he is doing what the law will not allow, and the plaintiff is entitled to relief against him."

It is most important, however, to remenber, as Lord Mc-Naghten stated, in this same " Camel Hair Belting," case, that " cases of this sort must depend upon their particular circumstances. The facts of one case are little or no guide to the determination of another." And in the " Stone Ale " case (*Montgomery* v. *Thompson*, L. R., [1891], A. C., 217), Lord Hannen remarked, " the principle contended for by the appellant may be admitted as correct, but in considering what might induce purchasers to believe that the appellant's goods are the goods of the respondents, all the circumstances of the case must be taken into account."

I have examined, with one exception, I think, the cases cited, and I have made some extracts from the remarks of the learned judges who took part in them which I attach to these notes. It appears to me that these decisions were based upon proof of either fraud or deception, and of damage and prejudice resulting therefrom, and that the facts are so different from those in the present case as to be, as Lord McNaghten says, little or no guide to the determination of it.

Milwaukee has, no doubt, for many years enjoyed a great reputation, both as respects the quantity and quality of the beer brewed there, but at the time Ekers commenced manufacturing lager and using that name it does not appear that beer manufactured in that place was well known or had been sold to any extent in Canada.

The Pabst Brewing Company dates from 1889, four years subsequent to defendant's use of the word " Milwaukee." The secretary of the Company says the name of the Philip Best Brewing Company, which was organized in 1873, was changed to the plaintiff's name in 1889.

There is no proof that beer brewed in Milwaukee was sold in Montreal prior to that sold by plaintiff's predecessors in 1887. In June, July, August and October of that year, and in April 1888, 235 casks of bottled beer were sold in Montreal. From that year to 1897,—a period of nine

years, — there seem to have been no sales in Montreal, but
from 1897 to 1899, they sold some 4,398 barrels, and 69
cases of bottled beer. Elsewhere there was sold in the province in 1894, 1895 and 1896, 598 barrels of beer and 235
casks of bottled beer, valued at $2,805. The quantities each
year are not stated. This renewal of sales after such a lapse
of time may be accounted for by the fact that about 1894 or
1895 there was a firm at Sherbrooke which carried on business under the name of the " Milwaukee Lager Beer Company," which bottled plaintiff's beer.   There was also a
grocer named Massé in Montreal, who did so for a while,
and then, in 1897, plaintiff opened a bottling establishment
in Montreal for selling Pabst Milwaukee Beer and Pabst
Malt Extract, so that plaintiff may be said to have been
doing business in this market for about six years prior to
the institution of this suit.

The name Ekers has been known and used in Montreal
in connection with the manufacture of beer there for about
fifty years. The defendant Ekers' father was a brewer, and
he succeeded to his business about fifteen or sixteen years
ago. Milwaukee was comparatively an unknown place in
Canada when the father of defendant commenced to brew
here, and as already pointed out, there is no evidence that
there was any Milwaukee beer in this market until some two
years after defendant Ekers had adopted the name " Ekers'
Milwaukee Lager." At that time there was really no Milwaukee brewed lager coming into competition with his. I
believe he took the name as a fancy one, as plaintiff has
taken the names of " Bohemian " and " Bavarian " in connection with its products, (see deposition of Mr. Brown,
plaintiff's representative, pp. 12 and 13, and plaintiff's exhibit, P. 3.) And he only took the word " Milwaukee " in connection with his own name which had been. for upwards of
thirty years previously known as that of a Montreal
brewer, and, so far as the labels and placards produced in
this cause show, with the word " Montreal," where it was
well known Ekers had a brewery, and also with the word
" lager," which latter word is not used by plaintiff, for it
appears that what we call " lager " is called " beer " in the
United States, and what we call " beer " is called " ale "
there.

I think the proof shows that Ekers had possession of the field here with the name of " Ekers' Milwaukee Lager " before any Milwaukee brewers came here.   The plaintiff corporation was not in existence until four years after Ekers commenced to use the word " Milwaukee."   During this time and for some nine years before the plaintiff opened business here, and for fifteen years before any objection was made the lager manufactured by Ekers had been sold on draught, probably in every bar room and restaurant of any importance in the city, and was well known as Montreal brewed.

Some nine witnesses, representing the principal bars and restaurants in the city, such as the Windsor Hotel, Freeman's Restaurant and the " Terrapin," and having an experience running from ten to twenty-four years in the business of retailing beer, say that they never knew of anyone being deceived by defendant's labels in supposing that they were buying beer brewed in Milwaukee; that Milwaukee lager is practically never asked for; that what is asked for is lager, and draught lager is given ; that if a Milwaukee or American lager is asked for the customer designates the name of the brewer.   These witnesses say that the labels are not calculated to deceive anyone ; that Ekers is a well known Montreal brewer, whose lager is known to be manufactured here, and that it is held in great reputation besides being half the price of American beer, and that the word " Montreal," which is prominently printed on the labels, indicates that the lager was brewed here.   This proof as to absence of deception has not been contradicted.

I may remark that plaintiff's beer does not appear to have been retailed on draught here, but only in bottles.

Mr Kerley, on Trade Marks, etc., at page 206, says :—" But where the marks have been circulating side by side in the market where deception is alleged to be probable, the fact that no one appears to have been misled is very material."

I believe that Eker's lager has acquired the reputation it now has on account of its intrinsic merit, and that it has always been well known that it was manufactured by him in Montreal, and that it does not come into competition with plaintiff's beer as being manufactured in Milwaukee, as plaintiff's is, or that plaintiff ever suffered any prejudice or loss by the use of the name complained of. So much is this the case that the first court could not find proof to justify a judgment for a cent of damage, although the name has been used for fifteen years, during six of which plaintiff was actually represented here by agents doing a bottling business for it, and therefore in competition with him.

At page 335 Mr Kerley says:—" But delay to pursue infringers, where the infringements are numerous and notorious, may amount to abandonment of the trade mark, and lead to its becoming *publici juris*. And, as already pointed out, it may have an important bearing on the weight of the evidence in the case, for if, in spite of long use by the defendant of the alleged infringing mark, no case of actual deception is proved, and the absence of this evidence is not altogether accounted for, it may be difficult for the court to believe that the defendant's mark is calculated to deceive. It has been suggested that, where the infringement has lasted a number of years, it is necessary for the plaintiff to prove that some persons have actually been deceived, but this is not, it is submitted, a rule of law."

As to the pretension that plaintiff suffers injury because of the quality of Ekers' lager being inferior to that manufactured by plaintiff, it is sufficient to say that there are at least ten or eleven breweries in Milwaukee, and it is not established that the beer manufactured by all of them is superior to Ekers'. If Ekers had used plaintiff's name this question of quality might come in, but with a dozen breweries in Milwaukee, some of them manufacturing, for aught we know, beer inferior to plaintiff's or Ekers', it does not seem to be a point of much weight. There are other places in the United States where beer is made equal to that made in Milwaukee, as for instance, St. Louis, New York and Rochester, so that the question of locality is not an all important question for people in Canada buying American-brewed beer.

I have come to the conclusion that plaintiff had no case against defendant Ekers, not only because he had sold out his business before any protest had been made by plaintiff against the use of the name " Milwaukee," but also because the facts proved do not bring him under the doctrine laid down in the cases cited. In my humble opinion he was not representing his goods as the goods of somebody else: he never intended to do so; and nobody has been deceived, and, judging from the proof made nobody is likely to be deceived. In other words, I do not think that Ekers has been guilty of any fault within the meaning of article 1053, C. C., upon which this action is based, and has not caused plaintiff any damage by using the word " Milwaukee " in the way he has used it.

The company defendant is certainly in no worse position. It knew Ekers had been using this word all those years without objection on the part of plaintiff or any other Milwaukee brewer, although plaintiff and another Milwaukee brewer named Schiltz had been selling beer in this market for a long time before its purchase of Ekers' business, in the case of plaintiff some six years. The company defendant is a Canadian brewing company, its advertisement and labels show it to be the successor of Ekers, whose rights it has acquired.

Considering the circumstances under which Ekers commenced to use and has used the name complained of, the business he has built up, and the absence of any proof of deception or damage, I think that the name of his lager deserved protection, and that it would be pushing the doctrine invoked in this case too far to enjoin the use of it.

I am therefore of opinion to reverse the judgment against the company defendant, and dismiss plaintiff's action against it, with costs, both of this court and of the court below, and in this view this court is unanimous.

Judgment of the Court below reversed, and action dismissed with costs.

Solicitors for the Plaintiffs: *McGibbon, Casgrain, Ryan & Mitchell.*

Solicitors for the Defendants: *Hall, Cross, Brown & Sharp.*

Editor's Notes:—

The judgment given at the trial in this case is reported at 1 Can. Com. Cases, p. 38,—where a note is also given of some of the various cases bearing on the subject. The judgment above reported appears to be based on the view that to give the right claimed by plaintiff it is necessary that there should be actual " proof of either fraud or deception, or of damage and prejudice resulting therefrom ;" and that, as a matter of evidence, such proof had not been made in the present case. In the former connection stress is laid upon the fact that the defendant Ekers had made use of the word in question, in Montreal, before the plaintiff company had made any sales in that city.

———

[IN THE SUPREME COURT OF BRITISH COLUMBIA.]

BEFORE HUNTER, C. J., AND DRAKE AND IRVING, JJ.

DOWLER

v.

UNION ASSURANCE SOCIETY OF LONDON

Fire Insurance Company—Agent of—Tax—Fire Companies Aid Ordinance, 1869 (*No.* 121), (*B.C.*) *and Fire Companies Aid Amendment Act,* 1871 (*No* 154), (*B. C.*).

In an action against defendant company under the Fire Companies' Aid Amendment Act of 1871, which applies only to city of Victoria, for taxes due by it as a company issuing policies within the city limits, it was held at the trial, that the plaintiff had failed to establish agency :

Held, by the Full Court, dismissing plaintiff's appeal, that the action was misconceived ; that the tax sought to be recovered was not on the company directly, but in respect of a special form of agency described in the statute ; and that the evidence negatived the existence of such an agency.

Appeal from the judgment of Martin, J., at the trial. The action was brought by the plaintiff, as Clerk of the Municipal Council of the Corporation of the City of Victoria, against the defendant as a Fire Insurance Company issuing policies of insurance against fires within the city limits upon properties situate within the city limits, between 1st July, 1897, and 31st December, 1898, for arrears of rates or taxes claimed to be due under the provisions of the Fire Companies' Aid Amendment Act, 1871. The facts appear in the following judgment of

MARTIN, J.: By Statute No. 82 of the Unconsolidated Acts of 1888, after reciting that " it is expedient that further provision should be made for the raising of funds for the support of the fire establishment," it is enacted that "in addition to the rates levied and collected, or hereafter to be levied and collected, upon and from all agents and* Fire Insurance Companies issuing policies of insurance against fires within the limits of the City of Victoria, upon property situate within such limits, there shall be payable to the Municipal Council thereof by the agent or agents of each and every such Fire Insurance Company so carrying on business within the said limits, the annual sum of three hundred dollars ; such sum to be payable by four quarterly payments..."

It is clear that this language only renders the agent liable for the tax—no additionnal obligation is so far imposed on the Company, and the section, which is inartistically drawn and awkwardly worded, is incomplete, assuming that it was aimed to make the Company primarily liable.

Then section 2 directs that " every such quarterly payment shall be made when due, as aforesaid, by the agent or agents of every such Fire Insurance Company, to the Clerk of the said Council, tac...... and if any such quarterly payments shall be in arrear for a period of thirty days, the same shall be recoverable by action, to be brought against

---

(*) The learned Judge was misled by a misprint of the word " and " for " of " in the second line of section 1 of No. 82, Unconsolidated Acts of 1888 : see Ordinance No. 154, R. R. L., 1871. Compare sections 1 and 4 of the Act respecting the Consolidation of the Statutes, assented to 6th February, 1889.

such agent or agents, or the Company which he or they represent, at the election of the said Clerk, as a debt due to
him in his name, in any Court of competent jurisdiction..."

In my opinon, the combined effect of the two sections is
that to bring a company within the scope of the enactment
it must have an agent in Victoria. It may be that the object
of the enactment was to make the companies primarily liable, in view of the benefits they would derive from the application, by section 2, of the proceeds of the tax to the preservation from fire of the risks they underwrote; but however laudable the intention, or however niggardly the spirit
of any company that would accept the benefit and refuse
contribution, yet if the language is, as here, so loose as to
be inoperative, or otherwise fail to positively fix the liability, the tax cannot be collected from it.

The next question, then, to be determined is—had the
Company an agent " so carrying on business " within the
meaning of section 1? If so, this action is maintainable under section 2, as a debt due to the plaintiff as Clerk of the
Council, from either the agent or the Company which he
represents.

In this case the circumstances are unusual, and the way
in which it came about that the defendant Company issued
policies upon property in Victoria is thus stated by the manager of the defendant Company at p. 8 of his evidence:

" The policies were issued under an arrangement between
the Union Assurance Society and the Law Union and
Crown Insurance Company. The Law Union and Crown Insurance Company were interested in various properties in
different cities of the Dominion, either as owners or mortgagees, and under the arrangement made between the two
companies the Union Assurance Society was to take over
the fire insurance on the properties that I have mentioned,
held by the Law Union and Crown as mortgagees, and issue
policies. The Law Union and Crown had agents at these
different points, and they stipulated that their agents should
be allowed the usual brokerage on such business, and, in
compliance with that arrangement, Robert Ward & Company, who were their agents in Victoria, forwarded the ap-

plications to us as the different risks expired, and remitted us the premiums, less the brokerage· "

" What was the brokerage? Fifteen per cent."

" Where was that arrangement made? The arrangement was discussed between the general manager of the Law Union Assurance Company at Montreal originally, and after, subsequently confirmed by the two head offices in London. England."

And at p. 10:

" After carrying it out, what was the practice between you and Robert Ward & Company? They were supplied with these application forms (indicating papers), and filled in the particulars on the form, which was simply a copy of the policies expiring in other companies, forwarding these forms to us in Montreal; the policies were issued in Montreal and sent to Robert Ward & Company, and the premiums were charged to their accounts—they remitted the premiums direct."

And at p. 13:

" The nine policies issued to Robert Ward & Company were in accordance with the arrangement made between the Law Union and Crown Insurance Company and ourselves, and there was no personal solicitation for these risks in Victoria, and in our dealings with Robert Ward & Company we treated them as agents of the assured, or the payees · under the policies."

And at p. 16:

" Had you not a person authorized to receive premiums for you in Victoria? No.

" Did not Robert Ward & Company collect premiums for you? I don't know ; they remitted premiums for us.

" Did they not collect premiums for you? No; according to my understanding of it, they were agents for the Law Union and Crown, and the Law Union and Crown were responsible to us for the premiums. If they paid premiums and collected from the property owners, it was to reimburse them for the premiums advanced.

" Were there not some premiums collected which were not anything to do with either of these two Companies, the Crown or the Union? No."

And at p. 32:

" Were not Robert Ward & Company made your agents because they were already insuring the property for the Law Union Company? I have already said they were not our agents."

" Were they not appointed for the purpose of collecting these premiums? I say Robert Ward & Company have never been appointed our agents for any purpose whatever."

" Were not Robert Ward & Company interested in the collection of these premiums because they had previously collected the premiums for some other office? Any collections of Robert Ward & Company in connection with these premiums they did on behalf of the Law Union Insurance Co., and I have no doubt they paid premiums before they were collected and then reimbursed the Law Union Insurance Company. "

" You cannot swear to that? I know from things we heard afterwards; I know in this Duck business; I know they paid premiums and never collected it; that was the reason for their repudiating. They paid that premium, paid it to us, and after some months they said, "We haven't been able to collect." I said, " That is a matter for the Law Union and Crown." They did not see it in that light; I wrote to the Law Union and Crown, and they did see it in that light—the Law Union and Crown were responsible to us."

And see also pp. 17, 19, 31, 37-8.

The witness further stated that the policies were issued in the names of the people who owned the property, but payable to the Law Union and Crown Insurance Co.

Reference was made to the fact that the words " Agency Victoria," or " Victoria Agency," appeared in the application forms and policy register of the defendant. The manager explains, p. 30, that this was simply a matter of convenience in keeping accounts:

" There was no objection from our point of view to the words ' Victoria Agency ' appearing on the application, or in the policy register, consequently I took no precautions to prevent the words appearing, but the word ' Victoria ' was put on or entered wherever it was necessary for the purpose of directing the account to which the premiums were to be charged."

And see also at p. 11:

" The words ' Victoria Agency ' is not written, but the word ' Victoria ' is filled in the policy column. This is a sheet from what we call our Policy Register, to bring out certain particulars with regard to the business to enable us to write out and keep track of it. From this column—the Agency column—the business is posted into the ledgers, and this would be into Robert Ward & Company's account. I did not know it was filled in to the Victoria Agency there, but the clerk who wrote it in followed the usual practice of filling in the Agency from which the business came, the source the business came from. I was going to say all the other policies were issued under similar circumstances. "

The evidence of the manager is corroborated by that of the managing partner of Robert Ward & Co., Ltd., Thomas R. Smith, who produced a letter of December 3rd, 1897, from the defendants to his firm, informing them of the fact that the Victoria Agency of Messrs. Munn, Holland & Co. had been withdrawn; it did not state that other agents had been appointed, but proceeded thus:

"To enable you to give effect to the wishes of the Law Union and Crown in regard to these insurances, we have decided to issue the policies from here, and we would thank you to let us have the particulars in good time so as to enable us to write the policies and have same in your hands before due time. We shall of course have pleasure in allowing you the usual 15 per cent. commission on this business.

We are sending you a supply of application forms, which
kindly complete for each risk as it comes round."

Robert Ward & Company had instructions from the Law
Union and Crown to place all their risks with the defendant
company; prior to that they had been placing them where
they thought fit; the risks were kept up by Robert Ward &
Company as agents for the Law Union and Crown, whether
the mortgagors paid the premiums or not. The premiums
they forwarded to the defendant company, and received
from it the policies which were placed with the Law Union
and Crown papers.

After a consideration of all the evidence, I find myself
unable to say that Robert Ward & Company were the agents
of the defendant. It is true that they rendered certain services for which they were remunerated by the defendant,
but those srvices were of a nature which could be and were,
rendered exclusive of any relationship of principal and
agent. While the remuneration was that usually paid to
agents, yet it was probably so allowed in view of the fact
that Robert Ward & Company had up to that time been in
the habit of placing these risks in their own companies, and
doubtless that was why the Law Union and Crown stipulated that the defendant was to allow Robert Ward & Company the same rate, since it would have been a harsh proceeding to have deprived them of business without cause
and made no compensation.

I find that the defendant company had no agent in Victoria, and therefore the statute does not apply to it. If it is
desired to extend the scope of the Act a very simple amendment will stop the loop-hole, but in the meantime the statute must be construed as it comes before the Court.

The action is dismissed with costs.

The plaintiff appealed, and the appeal was argued at Victoria on 16th June, 1902, before HUNTER, C. J., and DRAKE
and IRVING, J. J.

W. J. Taylor, K. C. (Bradburn, with him), for appellant.
Joseph Martin, K.C., for respondent.

On 29th July, 1902, the appeal was dismissed with costs, and the following judgments were handed down:

HUNTER, C. J.: In this case the facts appear *in extenso* in the judgment under appeal, so that I need not repeat them.

It may be noticed that section 1 of the statute, as it appears in the Unconsolidated Acts, being No. 82, contains a misprint in using the word " and " in the second line of the section, instead of the word " of," as will appear by reference to the original Act, R.L. 1871, No. 154, and also by reference to section 3, of No. 81, of the Unconsolidated Acts, being R.L. 1871, No. 121, of which statute the one under consideration is an amendment.

It is, therefore, plain, when the misprint is cleared up, that the tax is primarily imposed on the agent and not on the company, although section 2 gives a remedy for its collection against either agent or company.

Again, comparison of the provisions of section 3 of the principal Act, and of section 1 of the amending Act makes it clear that the tax is imposed only on those agents who issue policies within the city limits on property within the limits.

As pointed out by Mr. Justice Drake, the action is brought against the company as the issuer of the policies within the limits, whereas it is clear, as already stated, that the tax is imposed only on the agent. Therefore, in order to found an action against the company under section 3 of the Act, the statement of claim should have alleged that Ward & Co., were the agents of the company to issue fire policies in the city limits on property therein situate, that they had so issued such policies, and had not paid the tax. But, although the action is misconceived, and should in strictness be dismissed on this ground, I think that, even if it had been properly launched, it must have failed on the facts.

The evidence shews beyond doubt that the policies in question here were not issued in Victoria, but in Montreal, by agreement between the insurance society and the loan company, and were transmitted to and retained by Ward & Co., as agents for the loan company. The fact that Ward & Co., filled in the mortgagors' applications and forwarded them to Montreal does not make them the agents for the assurance society to issue their policies, and only those agents who issue policies are liable for the tax. Nor does the fact that by agreement made between the two companies at Montreal, Ward & Co., received a commission of 15 per cent, directly from the assurance society, instead of from their principals, the loan company, make them agents of the society. It is obvious that a request by A. to B. to pay C. does not, without more, make C. the agent of B.

The appeal should be dismissed.

DRAKE, J.: The question to be decided here is on the construction and meaning of the Fire Companies' Aid Amendment Act, 1871. This Act was an amendment to the Companies' Aid Ordinance, 1869. By that Act, Sec. 3, all agents of Fire Insurance Companies carrying on business in the City of Victoria were to pay a rate not exceeding one-eighth of one per cent, on the amount of insurance effected on property in Victoria insured by them. By the Act of 1871, in addition to the rates then levied and collected, it was enacted that there should be payable by the agents of each such Fire Insurance Company carrying on business in Victoria, the annual sum of $300.00, payable in quarterly payments; and by section 2, if any quarterly payment should be in arrears for thirty days, the same should be recoverable by action to be brought against such agent, or the Company, at the election of the Clerk of the Council.

The plaintiff's statement of claim alleges a claim against the defendants as a Fire Insurance Company, issuing policies against fire within the limits of Victoria, for arrears of rates or taxes payable to the plaintiff by virtue of the Act of 1871. No tax has been imposed on Fire Insurance Companies either by the Act of 1869 or 1871. What the Act of 1871 purports to do is to make the Company sueable for the amount of $300.00 due to the Corporation from persons acting as their agents in insuring property and issuing policies within the limits of the City of Victoria.

The Act of 1871 is wrongly printed in the volume of Unconsolidated Acts. Section 1 enacts, " In addition to the rates levied and collected upon all agents *of* Fire Insurance Companies," not "*and* Fire Insurance Companies," and this has doubtless misled the parties somewhat, as a considerable argument was addressed to the Court on the effect of the misprinted language.

Section 2 only gives the right to the Corporation to recover the $300.00 from the agent or the Company. Now, as this tax is not imposed on the Company, the sum to be recovered is the money due by the agent as such agent, and not due by the Company as taxee. All tax Acts are construed strictly, and nothing left to intendment: see *Oriental Bank Corporation* v. *Wright* (1880), 5 App. Cas. 842 at p. 856. The intention to impose a tax on the subject must be shewn in clear and unambiguous language; see *Cox* v. *Rabbits* (1878), 3 App. Cas. 473 and *Pryce* v. *Monmouthshire Canal and Railway Companies* (1879), 4 App. Cas. 203; in a taxing Act you must find words to impose the tax, and if they are not there no tax is imposed. I fail to find any words imposing this tax on the defendants, and therefore they are not liable on this statement of claim, which alleges that the Corporation claim $450.00 against the defendants as a Fire Insurance Company issuing policies within the limits of the city between 1st July, 1897, and 31st December, 1898, for arrears of rates or taxes which have become due and payable to the plaintiff as such Clerk, at the annual rate of $300.00, payable by the defendants to the plaintiff by virtue of the provisions of the Fire Amendment Act, 1871.

In the view I take it is not necessary to discuss the other point, whether or not Robert Ward & Co., were agents of the defendant Company as contemplated by the Acts in question, because they are not parties to this action. The action should be dismissed with costs.

Appeal dismissed.

Solicitors for the Appellants: *Taylor & Bradburn.*

Solicitors for the Respondents: *Marlin & Deacon.*

Editor's Note: —

In support of the statement of law that all enactments imposing a tax are to be construed strictly, see (in addition to the case cited in the above judgment):

Partington v. *Attorney-General,* (1869), L.R. 4 H.L. 100.

Hull Dock Co. v. *Lamarche,* (1828), 8 B. C. 42. *In re Thorley, Thorley* v. *Massa Co.* (1891), 60 L.J. Ch. 613.

And the intention of the legislature to impose the tax must be shewn by unambiguous language which places it beyond doubt.

Ingram v. *Drinkwater* (1875), 32 L. T. 746.

Shaw v. *Ruddin* 9 Ir. C.L.R. 214.

A recent case on the subject of fiscal statutes is of interest as illustrating the authority which the courts of one province should accord to the decision given by those of another upon such an act. In the case of *In re Studdert* (1900), 2 Ir. R. 400. It was held that in construing a fiscal statute applicable throughout the United Kingdom the court of one country should follow a conclusion previously arrived at by that of another country.

[IN THE SUPREME COURT OF CANADA.]

BEFORE SIR HENRY STRONG, C. J., AND SEDGWICK, GI-
ROUARD, DAVIES AND MILLS, J. J.

THE BOSTON RUBBER SHOE COMPANY (Plaintiffs) Appellants

v.

THE BOSTON RUBBER COMPANY OF MONTREAL,
(Defendants) Respondents

(ON APPEAL FROM THE EXCHEQUER COURT OF CANADA)

*Infringement of trade mark — Use of corporate name –
Deception of the public.*

"The Boston Rubber Shoe Company," registered its name as a trade
mark in Canada about a year after "The Boston Rubber Company
of Montreal, Ltd.", had obtained incorporation as such. An action
was brought by the former company for an injunction to restrain the latter from using what was, in effect, its corporate
name upon its goods (which were of the same nature as those
manufactured and sold by the plaintiff company) upon the ground
that such use was an infringement of the latter's registered trade-
mark.

Held, reversing the decision of the Exchequer Court (see 1 Can.
Com. Cases, 217, or 7 Ex. C. R. 187), that the use made by defendant company of its corporate name was an infringement of plaintiff
company's registered trade mark, and was such as would lead
purchasers of defendant's good to believe that they were buying
those made by plaintiffs, and that plaintiff company was therefore
entitled to the injunction demanded.

The facts are set forth in the judgment below, and in the
judgment rendered in the Exchequer Court. (see 1 Can.
Com. Cases 217).

R. V. Sinclair for the Appellants.

Beique K. C. and Mcgoun K. C. for the Respondents.

15 MAY, 1902:—

The judgment of the Court was delivered by:

Davies, J.:—The plaintiffs (appellants) brought their
actions in the Exchequer Court seeking to restrain the respondents (defendants) " from continuing to use the trade

mark of the plaintiffs," (the essential feature of which were alleged to consist of the words " Boston Rubber Shoe Company ") " or any other mark similar thereto upon rubber boots and shoes or any other goods made or sold by the defendants and from in any other way infringing the plaintiffs' registered marks or either of them. "

They also claimed damages and " such further or other relief as might be considered just. "

As regards the plaintiff company, the learned judge states the facts as follows : —

" The plaintiff company was, in 1853, incorporated under the laws of the Commonwealth of Massachusetts, by the name of ' The Malden Manufacturing Company ' for the purpose of manufacturing cotton silk, linen, flax or india-rubber goods at the Town of Malden. In 1855 its name was, by an Act of the Commonwealth, changed to ' The Boston Rubber Shoe Company '. Since that time it has continued to do business by that name, and its business has prospered. In rubber boots and shoes it manufactures two grades or lines of goods; the one that which is spoken of as ' The Boston Rubber Shoe Line ', and the other as ' The Bay State Line '. The former are known to the trade, and have been since as early as 1865 at least, as ' Bostons '. The other grade is known as 'Bay state'. The company's annual output of rubbers is about twelve million pairs· Mr Sawyer puts it at from ten to fifteen millions. Of this quantity about half are ' Bostons ' and half ' Bay State '. These goods are sold in the United States, in Europe and in Canada. But the sale in Canada is not, I infer from the evidence, large. "

In the year 1896, one Charles L. Higgins purchased from another company in the United States of America, called The Boston Rubber Company, all its calendars, blocks, dies, patterns, moulds and all furniture and tools specifically adapted for the manufacture of rubber boots and shoes.

This Boston Rubber Company had, at one time, included, in the goods they manufactured, rubber boots and shoes, but after some litigation with the plaintiffs connected with their right to use the name (but not, so far as it appears, in consequence of such litigation), had gone out of the business of manufacturing boots and shoes, and sold their blocks, dies, etc. to Higgins.

In 1896, Higgins applied for and obtained for himself and others incorporation under " The Companies Act ", (R.S.C. c. 119), by the name of "The Boston Rubber Company of Montreal Limited. " This company manufactures, amongst other goods, two grades of rubber boots and shoes at their works, in St. Jerome, in the Province of Quebec. On the better grade are impressed the words " The Boston Rubber Company, Montreal, Limited, " and these goods in the company's catalogues, price lists and advertisements, are referred to as " The Boston ".   In the illustrated catalogue, Exhibit No. 15, will be found the following :—

" Our Neptune brand is everything we claim for it—a high grade second, not so good as the Boston, but a clean well made, stylish rubber that will give excellent satisfaction for the money." And in the same catalogue, as well as in the price list, (Exhibit No. 16), the words " Boston Rubber Co. " without any addition of the word " Montreal " frequently occur.

The learned judge found as a fact, and the evidence fully justifies the finding, that although the sales of the plaintiffs' goods in Canada do not appear to be, or so far as the evidence goes, to have been considerable, the term " Boston " or " Bostons " has come in some way to have a commercial value as attached to rubber boots and shoes, and this value has been given to it by the plaintiffs' enterprise and business.

He further says with respect to the use of that term or terms that it seemed to him reasonably certain that the plaintiff company was the first to make use of the term in that connection, and that any value it had acquired in that connection, any secondary meaning that it has come to have as denoting excellence in rubber boots and shoes, has been derived from its use in the plaintiff's business ; and further, that the defendant company, as honest manufacturers and

traders, ought to discontinue its use except so far as it forms
part of the corporate name of the company.

Having reached these conclusions of fact and expressing
these opinions, however, the learned judge went on to say,
that this action was not brought to restrain the use of the
word " Boston " or " Bostons " in the company's catalogues, price lists and advertisements, but to restrain it from
using upon goods of its own manufacture what, in substance, is its corporate name, the only difference being the
omission of the preposition " of " before Montreal.

The learned judge accepted the explanation of Mr Higgins as to the circumstances under which the corporate
name of the defendants was adopted, and acquitted him and
the company of any intentional or fraudulent adaptation of
any part of the plaintiffs' corporate name. He further
says that there is no evidence of any attempt by the defendant company to sell their goods as those of the plaintiffs,
and that the question he had to determine was whether the
company might or might not impress their corporate name
upon goods of their own manufacture. He answered it in
the affirmative, in the absence of any fraud or bad faith.

It seems to me, with great respect, very difficult on the
evidence in this case to find that fraud and bad faith were
absent ; and, if I were compelled to find specifically on the
point, I would strongly incline to the opinion that the particular corporate name which Mr Higgins selected for his
company was selected by him because of the special value
which has attached to the term " Boston ", in connection
with rubber boots and shoes, by the enterprise, energy and
business of the plaintiffs. I can hardly conceive of any
legitimate use of the word "Boston" in the corporate name
of a Canadian company established to do a manufacturing
business in the Province of Quebec. The object of using
the name by stamping it upon each of the products of their
manufacture and offering them for sale so stamped may
not have been to deceive purchasers into the belief that they
were buying the goods of the Boston Shoe Co., but that
such would have been the result, I entertain no reasonable
doubt. If so, it would bring the case directly within the
rule laid down by Lord Kingsdown in Leather Cloth Co.,

v. American Leather Cloth Co., (11 H.L. 523 at p. 538),
quoted approvingly by Lord Herschell in Reddaway v.
Banham [1896] A.C. 199), viz:

" The fundamental rule is that one man has no right to
put off his goods for sale as the goods of a rival trader,
and he cannot therefore (in the language of Lord Langdale, in the case of Perry v. Truefitt, 6 Beav. 66, be allowed
to use names, marks, letters, or other indicia by which he
may induce purchasers to believe that the goods which he
is selling are the manufacture of another person. "
And entitles the person aggrieved to an injuction to restrain its use.

The term "Boston" or "Bostons" attached by the plaintiff company to their rubber boots and shoes was an "invented or fancy word" and not a descriptive one, and had
come in time, as found by the learned judge, to have a well
understood meaning in the trade, and to apply to a special
class of rubber boots and shoes which the plaintiffs manufactured and sold. Comparing the name and diagram
stamped by the defendant company on their boots and
shoes with the name and diagram stamped by the plaintiff
company on theirs, I can have no doubt that an ordinary
purchaser would be deceived. The deception would be
caused by the use of the term "Boston", and that this
would be so would seem to have been well known to the
defendants from the fact that the boots and shoes so
stamped by them are referred to in the company's catalogues, price lists and advertisements as "Bostons."

The distinction between an " invented or fancy word" as
a Trade Mark and a really descriptive one is of great importance in determining. where that is necessary, the presence or absence of fraud. But with all respect to the
learned judge I doubt very much that it is necessary to
find "fraud or fraudulent intent" on the defendants' part
in order to grant relief.

The general rule that a single manufacturer will not be
allowed to arrogate. to himself the exclusive use of a name
which he shares in common with many others. has of
course, been qualified in Holloway v. Holloway (13 Beav.

209), by the statement that the free use even of a man's own name will be hindered and restrained if it is shown that the person using it is doing so for the purpose of fraud. But I doubt much that such general rule, even without the qualification, could be invoked by the defendant company in a case such as this.

The whole question of the use of a name which had acquired a special meaning with respect to a special class of goods was exhaustively reviewed by the House of Lords in the late case of The Cellular Clothing Company, Limited, v. Maxton & Murray [1899] A. C. 326), where nearly all the leading cases on the subject are referred to. The distinction between an invented or a fancy name and a *bona fide* descriptive one is pointed out, and it was there held that the word "cellular" was an ordinary English word which appropriately described the cloth of which the goods sold by the respondents were manufactured, and that the term had not been proved to have acquired a secondary or special meaning so as to denote only the goods of the appellants.

In the case now under consideration by us, the term "Boston" or "Bostons" was a fancy word used with respect to a special class of goods manufactured by the plaintiffs in or near the City of Boston, and has come to have a special meaning in the trade as denoting only such goods. In giving judgment in the case just cited the Lord Chancellor says, on page 334, referring to the necessity for fraudulent intention being proved :—

"The only observation that I which to make upon that part of the argument is that it seemed to be assumed that a fraudulent intention is necessary on the part of the person who was using a name in selling his goods in such a way as to lead people to believe that they were the goods of another person. That seems to me to be inconsistent with a decision given something like sixty year ago, by Lord Cottenham, who goes out of his way to say very emphatically that that is not at all necessary in order to constitute a right to claim protection against the unlawful use of words or things—I say things because it is to be observed that not only words but things, such as the nature of the wrapper, the mode in which the goods are made up, and so on, may go to make up a false representation; but it is not necessary to establish fraudulent intention in order to claim the intervention of the court. Lord Cottenham says in that case, Millington v. Fox ; ' I see no reason to believe that there has, in this case, been a fraudulent use of the plaintiffs' marks. It is positively denied by the answer, and there is no evidence to shew that the defendants were even aware of the existence of the plaintiffs as a company manufacturing steel; for although there is no evidence to shew that the terms, ' Crowley ' and ' Crowley Millington ' were merely technical terms, yet there is sufficient to shew that they were very generally used, in conversation at least, as descriptive of particular qualities of steel. In short, it does not appear to me that there was any fraudulent intention in the use of the marks. That circumstance, however, does not deprive the plaintiffs of their right to the exclusive use of those names ; and therefore. I stated that the case is so made out as to entitle the plaintiffs to have the injunction made perpetual. ' That, my Lords, I believe to be the law. It was the law then, and it has not been qualified or altered by the fact that the Trade Marks Act has since been passed. which gives a feasible and perfectly facile mode of remedy in cases in which trade marks apply. "

And again, on page 336 :—

"There has not been any question, nor can there be any question as to what the state of the law is. It is laid down in Burgess's Case (3 De G. M. & G. 896), the Anchovy Sauce case, with great precision. The simple proposition is this :—That one man is not entitled to sell his goods under such circumstances, by the name, or the packet, or the mode of making up the article, or in such a way as to induce the public to believe that they are the manufacture of some one else. The proposition that has to be made out is that something amounting to this has been done by the defendant. and if that proposition is made out right to relief exists. "

And in the same case Lord Shand says, page 338 —

"There is a vital distinction in cases of this class between invented or fancy words or names, or the names of individuals such as ' Crowley ' or ' Crowley Millington, ' attached by a manufacturer to his goods and stamped on the articles manufactured, and words or names which are simply descriptive of the article manufactured, or sold. The idea of an invented or fancy word used as a name is that it has no relation, and at least no direct relation, to the character or quality of the goods which are to be sold under that name. There is no room whatever for what may be called a secondary meaning in regard to such words, as the Lord Advocate pointed out in the course of his argument. The word used and attached to the manufacture, being an invented or fancy name and not descriptive, it follows that, if any other person proceeds to use that name in the sale of his goods, it is almost, if not altogether impossible to avoid the inference that he is seeking to pass his goods off as the goods of the other manufacturer. A person invents or applies the term ' Eureka ' as the name of a shirt in his sales. If you buy a ' Eureka ' shirt, that seems at once to mean that you are buying a shirt made by the particular maker who is selling shirts under that fancy name. The public come to adopt the word ' Eureka ' as applicable to the manufacture of the particular person who began to use it, and as denoting the article he is selling, and if another person employs the word in the sale of the same or a similar article, it seems to follow that he is acting in direct violation of the law that no one, in selling his goods, shall make such representations as will enable him to pass them off as the goods of another so as to get the benefit of that other's reputation.

A totally different principle must apply in the case of goods which are sold under a merely descriptive name. "

He too states the question to be put as follows; page 340 : —

"It is true the question in issue in cases of this class may generally be broadly stated as : Did the defendants by their representations seek to induce purchasers to acquire their goods under the false belief that these goods were of the plaintiff's manufacture? "

I have no hesitation myself, in the case now before us, in answering the question put in that form in the affirmative. The word " Boston " which they used and put in their corporate name and stamped on the rubber boots and shoes they offered for sale and advertised in their circulars and advertisements, amounted to an emphatic representation under cover of which they sought to induce purchasers to acquire their goods under the false belief that they were the plaintiffs', and I agree with the learned Judge of the Exchequer Court that "as honest manufacturers and traders they ought to discontinue its use except so far as it forms part of their corporate name. "

I differ with him, however, as to their right under cover of their corporate name to stamp this invented or fancy word on the goods they offer for sale, unless it is so done as clearly to distinguish the goods from those of the plaintiffs, and also as to the power and duty of the Court to compel them to desist from their dishonesty. Lord Davey in the Cellular Clothing Case [1899] A. C., 326 from which I have been quoting, speaking of the logical foundation of this branch of the law, says at page 343 :—

" Shortly summed up, it is that a man shall not by misrepresentation pass off his own goods as those of his neighbour. "

"But there are two observations which must be made ; one is that a man who takes upon himself to prove that words, which are merely descriptive or expressive of the quality of the goods, have acquired the secondary sense to which I have referred, assumes a much greater burden — and, indeed, a burden which it is not impossible, but at the same time extremely difficult, to discharge — a much greater burden than that of a man who undertakes to prove the same thing of a word not significant and not descriptive, but what has been compendiously called a ' fancy ' word. "

The same doctrine is to be found in a leading case in the House of Lords known as The Camel Hair Belting Case, Reddaway v. Banham, [1896] A. C. 199), where it was held that the defendant should be restrained from using the words " Camel Hair " as descriptive of or in connection with belting made or sold by him and not manufactured by the plaintiff, without clearly distinguishing such belting from the plaintiff's. Lord Herschell in his judgment, at page 210, says :—

"Where the trade mark is a word or device never in use before, and meaningless, except as indicating by whom the goods in connection with which it is used were made, there could be no conceivable legitimate use of it by another person. His only object in employing it in connection with goods of his manufacture must be to deceive. In circumstances such as these, the mere proof that the trade mark of one manufacturer has been thus appropriated by another would be enough to bring the case within the rule, as laid down by Lord Kingsdown, and to entitle the person aggrieved to an injunction to restrain its use."

And again, as to the right of a man to use his own name, he says, page 211 :—

"The authority relied on was the case of Burgess v. Burgess (3 De G. M. & G. 896). When the judgments in that case are examined, it seems to me clear that no such point was decided. Turner, L. J. commences by saying: 'No man can have any right to represent his goods as the goods of another person; but in applications of this kind it must be made out that the defendant is selling his own goods as the goods of another.' He then points out that where a person is selling goods under a particular name, and a person not having that name is using it, it may be presumed that he so uses it to represent the goods sold by himself as the goods of the person whose names he uses; but where the defendant sells goods under his own name, and it happens that the plaintiff has the same name, it does not follow that the defendant is selling his goods as the goods of the plaintiff. He adds: 'It is a question of evidence in each case whether there is false representation or not.' This, I think, clearly recognizes that a man may so use even his own name in connection with the sale of goods as to make a false representation. In Massam v. Thorley's Cattle Food Company James L. J., said: 'Burgess vs Burgess (14 Ch. D. 748), has been very much misunderstood if it has been understood to decide that anybody can always use his own name as a description of an article, whatever may be the consequences of it, or whatever may be the motive for doing it, or whatever may be the result of it.' After quoting from the judgment of Turner, L. J. the passages to which I have just alluded, he said: 'That I take to be an accurate statement of the law, and to have been adopted by the House of Lords in Wotherspoon v. Currie (L. R. 5 H. L. 508), in which the House of Lords differed from the view which I had taken.'

Now it seems to me beyond doubt that Mr Higgins could not, either himself personally or in association or partnership with the others who applied for and obtained letters patent of incorporation under the defendants' name, have used the plaintiff company's trade mark, on rubber boots and shoes he might manufacture and offer for sale, without subjecting himself and themselves to the risk of an injunction. Nor am I able to see how he can, by obtaining for himself and his associates letters corporate under the statute, do under cover of the corporate name what he otherwise would be prevented from doing. The defendant company has the right to use its corporate name for all lawful and legitimate purposes. It has not the right to use it, however, by stamping it upon goods it has manufactured and offered for sale, if by so doing it causes the purchasing public to believe that the goods are those of the plaintiff company. The stamping of their corporate name, which embraces the plaintiffs' trade mark, upon the rubber boots and shoes manufactured by them would almost certainly lead purchasers to believe that the defendant company was a branch of the plaintiff company carrying on business in Montreal.

I think the prayer of the plaintiffs in the statement of claim sufficiently broad to cover the infringement charged of the plaintiffs' registered trade mark in the advertisements, circulars and price lists issued by the defendants, calling attention to their goods as " Boston " or "Bostons" and that the defendants should be restrained from the use of such words either by stamping them upon their goods or advertising them in circulars, price lists or otherwise.

I do not think the damages alleged to have been sustained thus far sufficient to justify the expense of a reference.

The appeal should be allowed with costs here and below. Judgment should be entered in the Exchequer Court for the plaintiffs for an injunction restraining the defendants from using the words " Boston " or " Bostons " as descriptive of or in connection with rubber boots or shoes manufactured by them, or rubber boots or shoes (not being of the plaintiffs' manufacture) sold or offered for sale by them, either by stamping upon such rubber boots and shoes, or by circular or advertisements or otherwise, without clearly distinguishing such rubber boots and shoes from the shoes of the plaintiffs.

Appeal allowed with costs.

Solicitor for the Appellants: *R. V. Sinclair.*

Solicitor for the Respondents: *McGoun and England.*

Editor's Notes:—

.When the first judgment given in this case was reported, the notes were held over because an appeal had then already been taken to the Supreme Court of Canada. (See 1 Can. Com. Cases, 223).

The judgment rendered in the Exchequer Court was to the effect that there had been no infringement of plaintiffs' trade mark; and that, moreover, since there was no evidence that defendants had chosen their name in order to sell their goods as those of plaintiffs, there could be no injunction upon that ground.

The judgment of the Supreme Court, besides finding that there was an infringement of plaintiffs' trade mark, lays down the rule that, in order to warrant the granting of an injunction, it is not necessary to prove a fraudulent intent on the part of the defendant, it being sufficient to shew that, as a matter of fact, the public, as a result of the latter's conduct, might be deceived regarding the indentity of the manufacturer of the goods.

Although a trade mark and a trade name are essentially different (see Turton v. Turton, 1888, L. R. 42 C. D. 128), yet it has been said that, when unchanged by legislation, the law applicable to each is the same (See per Lord Blackburn in Singer Manufacturing Co. vs Loog. (1882) 8 A. C. 15).

The case of Millington vs Fox (1838) 3 Hul· and Cr. 338, is authority, for the proposition that fraud on the part of the defendant need not be proved in order to entitle the plaintiff to an injunction restraining the defendant from further infringement of his trade mark.

And see also "Singer" Manufacturers vs Wilson, (1877) L. R. 3 A. C. 376.

In Singer Manufacturing Co. vs Wilson (1876) L. R. 2 C. D. 434, the Court of Appeal appeared to draw the distinction that it was necessary to prove fraud in the case of a trade name. (See remarks of Jessel, M. R. ib, p. 441-444). But in Singer Manufacturing Co. vs Loog, (1882) L. R. 8 A. C. 15, Lord Blackburn held that it was in no degree more necessary to prove fraud in an action to restrain the use of a trade name than in one to restrain the use of a trade mark.

To this rule, however, there appears to have existed, until very recently, the exception that a person could not be enjoined from using his own name unless fraud was made out.

Thus Sebastian in the fourth edition of his work on Trade Marks, referring to trade marks not coming under the Trade Mark Registration Act, and consisting of a name, says, (Ib. page 125) "that it is not necessary in order to obtain an injunction to prove the scienter where the infringer does not bear the name he has assumed, but that, on the other hand, where he does bear that name, such evidence must be produced."

See also Sebastian on Trade Marks, 4th Ed, page 261.

Turton vs Turton (1888) L. R. 42 C. D. 128.

But the chief authority in support of the above statement is the case of Burgess vs Burgess, (1858), 22 L. J. Ch. 675. There, where a father had for a number of years been the exclusive dealer in a sauce, known as "Burgess's Essences of Anchovies", an injunction to restrain the son from selling a somewhat similar article under that name was refused, no proof being made of any fraudulent intent.

In the later case of Reddaway vs Banham, 1896, A. C.
199, it was held that a person could not use words which
were properly descriptive of the goods he sold, if in the
trade they had already come to mean only the goods of
another manufacturer, — unless he qualified the same in
such a manner as to distinguish his article from that of
such other manufacturer.

In this case, the real effect of Burgess vs Burgess, *supra*,
was discussed at some length, and Lord Halsbury, L. C.
adopted the statement made therein by Turner L. J. that
" it is a question of evidence in each case whether there is
false representation or not ".

And in the same case Lord Macnaghten, cited with approval (page 215) the following statement of the law given
by James L. J. in Singer Manufacturing Co. vs Loog.
(1880) L. R. 18 C. D. 395, at p. 412 :

" That no man is entitled to represent his goods as being
the goods of another man ; and no man is permitted to use
any mark, sign, or symbol, device or other means whereby,
without making a false representation himself to a purchaser who purchases from him, he enables such purchaser to
tell a lie, or to make a false representation to somebody else,
who is the ultimate customer. "

It seems, however, that until recently, the rule that a
man will only be restrained from using his own name upon
clear proof of fraudulent intent has been recoognized both
by judges and text writers. But in the case of Valentine Meat
Juice Co. vs Valentine Extract Co. (1900) 83 L. T. 259,
it was held that there was no distinction in principle
between a case in which the name, the use of which was
complained of, was the name of a person who was carrying
on the business, and a case in which it was not the name of
such person. The use of the word " Valentine " or " Va-
lentines " in connection with the sale of any meat juice
preparation was, in this case, restrained by the Court of
Appeal, although the Court below had refused to grant an
injunction upon the ground that, in the absence of fraud,
a man would not be restrained from using his own name.

In that case Collins L. J. said (at p. 271) " it is immaterial whether deception arises from the use of a name which is. at it happens. the name of the defendant, or whether it arises from the use of any other descriptive words which in a sense may be accurate with what he sells. For, if the article which he sells has come to be known in the market as meaning something made by somebody other than himself, it is impossible for him to sell it *simpliciter* by that name. although it be his own, without misleading purchasers.

The " name " cases were thus put on exactly the same basis as the " descriptive words " cases, of which Reddaway vs Banham. *supra*. is the chief. — and the principle of that case was applied.

In the earlier case of Jamieson vs Jamieson (15 Reports of Patent Cases 169) Williams L. J. said (at p. 193) " that a plaintiff could never complain of the user by the defendant of either the plaintiff's personal name. or of any other name that he chooses to use for the purpose of denoting his goods. unless he first establishes that in the market. his goods have come to be known by that name ".

And in the case of Cash vs Cash (1900) 84 L. T. 349, and (1902) W. N. 32. the defendant was restrained from using his own name in connection with certain trimmings which he sold, because in the trade " Cash's Trimmings " were taken to be those of the plaintiff, unless he took proper precautions to distinguish them from those made by the latter.

The result of these recent decision. therefore. apparently is that it is no longer necessary to prove fraud in order to obtain an injunction restraining a man from using his own name ; the point now to be considered in such a case is only whether or not the person sought to be restrained is using his name in such a way that the public is likely to believe that his goods are those of some other person.

See also Grand Hotel Co. of Caledonia Springs, Ltd. vs Wilson. 3. O. R. 322.

The case. however. the facts of which most closely re-

semble the case reported above is Manchester Brewery
Co. vs. North Cheshire and Manchester Brewery
(1898) 78 L. T. 537. There the Manchester Brewery Co.
Lim. was carrying on business at Manchester, and the
North Cheshire Brewery Co. Lim. was carrying on business at Macclesfield, but the districts served by each
company to some extent overlapped. A new company was
formed to take over the business of the North Cheshire Co.
and was called "The North Cheshire and Manchester
Brewery Co. Lim." It was held that though it did not
appear that there way any fraudulent intention, yet the
name of the new company would suggest to any one who
knew the two old companies that they had been amalgamated, and that it so nearly resembled the name of the plaintiff
company as to be calculated to deceive. The injunction
asked for by the plaintiff company was therefore granted.

As to a corporate name being valid as a trade mark, see
Boston Rubber Shoe Co. vs Boston Rubber Co. 149 Mass.
436, at page 441.

[IN THE COURT OF KING'S BENCH FOR MANITOBA.]

BLACKWOOD

v.

PERCIVAL.

*Promissory note—Principal and surety—Effect of giving time
—King's Bench Act (Man., 58-59 Vict., cap. 6) sec. 39,
s. s 14.*

Defendant and G. H. C. made a promis-ory note for $3,500, payable
to the order of D. M. B., by whom it was indorsed over to the plaintiffs. who discounted the same at their bank, and gave the proceeds
to D. M. B., who used them as agreed. It had been arranged
between defendant, G. H. C., and D. M. B., that each should pay
one-third of the amount of the note, but this was unknown to plaintiffs until shortly before the note fell due. Defendant then paid
one-third by accepting a draft for that amount drawn on him by
plaintiffs who had refused to accept his cheque for the same sum
marked "in full of note $3,500." At the same time, D. M. B. gave
plaintiffs his note for $2,000, and money sufficient (with what
defendant had paid) to retire the original note. D. M. B's. note
for $2,000 was renewed several times, and was finally paid

by plaintiffs, who subsequently sued defendant for the balance due on his note for $3,500, which they had kept. Defendant set up the defence that he was only a surety, and that he was released by the fact that the plaintiffs had given time to G. H. C. and D. M. B.

Held, that even if defendant was a surety he would only be released from liability on the note upon proving that he had been prejudiced by the giving of time, and this he had failed to do.

The prejudice required to satisfy the King's Bench Act (Man., 58-59 Vic., cap. 6), sec. 39, s.s. 14, must be such pecuniary loss or damage as is the reasonably direct and natural result of the creditor having given the extension of time. The fact that defendant, relying upon D. M. B's. statement that he had paid the note paid him certain sums of money which he might otherwise have withheld, did not bring him within this rule.

Action upon a promissory note. The facts are fully set forth in the head note and in the judgments.

Trial before Bain J.

C. P. Wilson and G. A. Elliott for the plaintiffs.

H. R. Howell K. C. and J. S. Hough K. C. for the defendant.

12TH MAY 1902:—

Judgment was delivered by:—

BAIN, J.—

The plaintiffs sue in this action to recover a balance they allege to be due them on a joint and several promissory note for $3500, dated the 5th of August, 1897, made by the defendant Percival, under the name of George Percival and Co., and George H. Campbell, payable to the order of D. M. Blackwood three months after date.

It appears that on the 4th of August, 1897, the three parties named had entered into an agreement to become the joint owners of a hotel that was being built at Mine Centre, each taking a one third interest, and each of them becoming liable for a one third share of the indebtedness incurred in the erection and furnishing of the hotel.

Money being required to pay for the work that had been done on the building it was arranged that the defendant and Campbell should make a joint and several promissory note payable to the order of D. M. Blackwood, who undertook to get the note discounted through the plaintiffs, who are his brothers.

The note sued on was made accordingly, and the plaintiffs, at the request of D. M. Blackwood, indorsed it and had it discounted at the Bank of Ottawa in Winnipeg, and gave their cheque for the proceeds to D. M. Blackwood.

When the note was made it was agreed that each of the three parties to it would pay one third of the amount when it fell due. The plaintiffs had no knowledge of this agreement when they indorsed and discounted the note, but they were told of it by D. M. Blackwood about the time the note fell due.

On the 5th of November, 1897, the defendant sent the plaintiffs a cheque for $1166.67, to apply on account of the note and which the letter said, " must be understood to clear us. " As the cheque however, was noted to be " in full of note, $3500 ", the plaintiffs did not cash it, but they drew a sight draft on Percival for the $1166.67, attaching the cheque to the draft, and they discounted the draft at the Bank of Ottawa.

Then, according to the evidence of William Blackwood, one of the plaintiffs, D. M. Blackwood gave them his note payable to their order for $2000 and cash sufficient, with the proceeds of the discount of this note and the draft on Percival, to make up $3500; and the plaintiffs indorsed and discounted the note and they paid the Bank the $3500 and took up the note.

Percival paid the draft on him, but the $2,000 note of D. M. Blackwood was not paid by Blackwood when it came due, and after having renewed the note several times the plaintiffs paid the Bank the $2000 in October, 1898, and charged the amount to D. M. Blackwood in their books.

D. M. Blackwood has not paid the $2000 or any part of it, and on the 24th of February, 1900, the plaintiffs began

this action against the defendant to recover the balance of
the note for $3500, which in the statement of claim they
allege to be $2333.33 and they claim interest at 6 per cent
since the 8th of November, 1897.

The plaintiffs in their statement of claim have not taken
into account the money that D. M. Blackwood paid them on
account of the note; and if they are entitled to recover, it
will be for $2000 only and interest.

It was urged that the inference which should be drawn
from the evidence is, that it was D. M. Blackwood and not
the plaintiffs who paid the Bank and took up the note on
the 8th of November, and that the plaintiffs cannot therefore claim to be the holders of the note.

I am satisfied, however, that it was the plaintiffs who
paid the Bank and took up the note.

Sufficient funds to meet the note not having been provided by the parties liable, and the plaintiffs wishing to
avoid paying the $2000, and expecting probably that the
money would shortly be forth coming, it was reasonable
enough that they should take D. M. Blackwood's note for
the $2000 and indorse and discount it, and with the pro-
ceeds and the money they had in hand pay and take up the
note sued on. This is what William Blackwood says was
done, and I do not doubt his evidence.

Then, when it was seen that there was no likelihood of
the $2000 being paid, the plaintiffs paid the amount them-
selves, and charged it to D. M. Blackwood's account in
their ledger. The credit of $3000 that appears in this ac-
count represents nothing, and the entry was made in error
or by mistake, and D. M. Blackwood has paid nothing on
account of the $2000.

When the plaintiffs took up the $3500 note they retained
it; there was no agreement that the note for $2000 was to
be taken in discharge of the other note: And, if the liability
of the defendant to the plaintiffs is the ordinary liability of
the maker of a promissory note to the holder of it. I cannot see that anything that the plaintiffs have done has extinguished that liability.

The defence, however, is raised, that, as to the balance of the note which is unpaid, the liability of the defendant to the plaintiffs was that merely of a surety for the payment of the shares of the $3500 that Campbell and D. M. Blackwood should have paid, and that after the note came due the plaintiffs by giving time to D. M. Blackwood or Campbell discharged the defendant from further liability.

And to meet the provision in the Queen's Bench Act, 1895, sec. 39, s-s. 14, that while a surety shall be entitled to set up giving of time to the principal debtor as a defence "the same shall be allowed in so far only as it shall be shown that the surety has thereby been prejudiced," it is alleged that the defendants were thereby prejudiced to an amount greater than the plaintiffs' claim by being induced to alter their position with relation to the said D. M. Blackwood and George H. Campbell in that they paid to each thereof a large sum of money, and that they handed over and released to the said D. M. Blackwood a large quantity of goods, and in that they were induced to settle the accounts between them and the said D. M. Blackwood and George H. Campbell. The only evidence there is in support of this defence is that of Percival himself, and what he says is, that when he and D. M. Blackwood and Campbell met in Montreal in November, 1897, Blackwood and Campbell represented to him that the note in question and all other liabilities in connection with the building had been paid, and that he owed them $1630 on the settlement of the accounts, and that, having absolute confidence in them, he accepted their word and paid them that amount.

At this time, too, he and Blackwood agreed to release Campbell from "all obligations which may have been incurred and exist," in respect of the agreement of the 4th of August 1897; but it is not explained why, if all these obligations had been settled, a release was considered necessary.

When the plaintiffs indorsed the note, they had no knowledge, so far as is shewn, that the obligations of the several parties among themselves were otherwise than as they appeared on the face of the note; but shortly before, or at the time the note fell due, they were told by D. M. Blackwood that each of the three parties on the note had agreed to pay one third of its amount.

Whether the receipt of this information by the plaintiffs had the effect of changing the apparent liability of Percival on the note, and of making him, when he had paid his own share of it, only surety to the plaintiffs for the payment of the shares of the other two parties, and, if it had this effect, whether what took place between the plaintiffs and D. M. Blackwood amounted to a binding agreement to give him and Campbell, or either of them, time for the payment of their shares, are questions that I do not find it necessary to consider.

For, even if it were clear that the defendant was a surety, and that the plaintiffs gave time to Blackwood and Campbell, I think the defendant has not shewn that he has been prejudiced by the giving of time.

In Swire v. Redman, 1 Q. B. D. 536, Lord Cockburn spoke of the rule that the giving of time by the creditor to the principal debtor released the surety, as one that was not consistent either with justice or common sense, and in Oriental Financial Corporation v. Overend, L. R. 7 Ch. 142, Lord Hatherley spoke of the suggestion having been made that it would have been better if the Courts had decided *ab initio*, not that the surety should be absolutely released, but the be should be put to prove his injury, and be allowed damages for any injury he might have sustained by time having been given: and it is practically this suggestion that has now been embodied in the Queen's Bench Act.

In Samuel v. Howarth, 3 Mer. 272, Lord Eldon said that the reason of the rule that a surety is discharged when the creditor gives times to the debtor is "because the creditor by so giving time has put it out of the power of the surety to consider whether he will have recourse to his remedy against the principal or not, and because he in fact, cannot have the same remedy against the principal as he would have had under the original contract."

And he adds "The creditor has no right,—it is against the faith of his contract,—to give time to the principal, even though manifestly for the benefit of the surety, without the consent of the surety."

And if the creditor did violate the right of the surety the penalty was that he forfeited his whole remedy, without regard to the question whether the extension of time was for the benefit of the surety or not. But now, what would seem to be the just principle to prevail is that if the surety can shew that he has been prejudiced by the giving of time he is entitled to compensation from the creditor for his loss. The onus of proving that he has been prejudiced must rest on the surety, and, as I understand the Act, he must shew that he has suffered pecuniary loss or damage as the reasonably direct and natural result of the creditor having given the extension of time, and the defence will avail him to the extent of the loss or damage he can prove.

It will be found, I imagine, that few cases will occur in which sureties will be able to establish actual loss or damage under this defence, and I think the defendant has failed to establish any in the present case.

He paid the money to Blackwood and Campbell and executed the release, because, as he says, he believed their statement that they had paid the note and the other liabilities of the concern.

But how are the plaintiffs responsible for this mis-statement?

They were under no obligation to have notified him that the balance of the note had not been paid; and, as far as I can see, there was no connection whatever, direct or indirect, between the arrangement the plaintiffs made with D. M. Blackwood, and the loss or prejudice that the defendant complains of.

I think the plaintiffs are entitled to have judgment for $2000, interest and costs. Interest is claimed from the 8th of November, 1897, the due date of the note, but, it would seem that as long as D. M. Blackwood's note was carried in the Bank he paid the discount on it, and the plaintiffs are entitled to charge interest, therefore, only from the time they paid the Bank and took up this note, 21st of October, 1898.

The defendant appealed.

C. P. Wilson and G. A. Elliott for the plaintiffs.

H. M. Howell K. C. for the defendant.

5th July, 1902:

The judgment of the Full Court was delivered by: —

Killam, C. J. — The questions involved seem to be almost wholly questions of fact. But I agree with Mr Howell (counsel for defendant) that the case is one in which an appellate court has a very free opportunity to draw the necessary inferences unembarrassed by the opinion of the trial Judge. There is only one qualification to be made in this respect. Mr Justice Bain has indicated his view that the evidence of Mr William Blackwood is to be relied on and there is nothing in the case to warrant us in acting upon a different view.

The point that has been most strongly urged upon us now is that the note sued upon was satisfied as between the plaintiffs and the defendant when it was retired by the plaintiffs at maturity.

And upon this point the main question seems to be the question of fact, whether the note of $2000 made by D. M. Blackwood was furnished and received with the intent that it or its proceeds should go as a satisfaction of the note on behalf of himself or himself and his associates, or merely as a means of enabling Blackwood Bros. to raise the banker, and that he (William) could sue Geo. Percival as indorsers.

According to William Blackwood there was no understanding between him and D. M. Blackwood when he took the note except that "they" — presumably D. M. Blackwood, Campbell and Percival — would pay the banker and that he (William) could sue Geo. Percival and Co.

Apparently it was William Blackwood who retired the

$3500 note at the Bank, and he states that he was asked at the time if they should mark it paid, and that he said "No".

Prima facie this was not a payment or satisfaction by or on behalf of the makers, but by Blackwood Bros. on their own account, leaving them the holders of the note, and entitled to recover against the makers.

I do not overlook the various circumstances which Mr Howell has so fully pressed upon us as raising the inference that the $2000 note or its proceeds were received and used as payment by D. M. Blackwood for himself and his associates, but I cannot think them sufficient to warrant the inference.

I do not think that the letter of D. M. Blackwood to the defendant can be taken as evidence against the plaintiffs. Blackwood Bros. were dealing with D. M. Blackwood as representing himself and his associates, and in leaving it to him to explain the circumstances to his associates, and in expecting him to do it, they did not make him their agent for the purpose. His explanation was a matter between himself and his associates, and no part of the transaction between the plaintiffs and D. M. Blackwood.

Another important point is, whether the course of the plaintiffs, their drawing as they did for the defendant's third share without explanation, was calculated to induce the defendant to believe that the note had been paid and satisfied as between him and the plaintiffs, and to act upon that belief.

But I do not think that this was the case. At best the circumstances were equivocal, and the mere fact that the plaintiffs did not accept the cheque as it was, but sent back a draft, was calculated to make the defendant at least doub'-ful of their intention. Upon the defendant's evidence I think that he must be taken to have relied and acted on the representations of his own associates.

I agree so fully with what Mr Justice Bain has said upon the other points that I do not consider it necessary to add anything respecting them.

I would dismiss the appeal with costs.

Appeal dismissed into costs.

Solicitors for the Plaintiffs: Ewart, Fisher and Wilson.

Solicitors for the Defendant: Howell, Mathers and Howell.

———

[IN THE SUPREME COURT OF CANADA.]

BEFORE SIR HENRY STRONG, C.J., AND SEDGWICK, GIROUARD, DAVIES AND MILLS, J.J.

THE UNION STEAMSHIP COMPANY OF BRITISH COLUMBIA (Defendants) Appellants

v.

GORDON DRYSDALE (Plaintiff) Respondent

(ON APPEAL FROM THE SUPREME COURT OF BRITISH COLUMBIA)

Carrier—Bill of lading—Time limited for notice of loss—Implied warranty of seaworthiness—Construction of contract.

A bill of lading contained certain provisions limiting the liability of the carrier, and concluded with a clause to the effect that all claims for damage to or loss of goods should be made within one month from the date of the bill of lading. The goods were damaged, the injury being caused by the unseaworthiness of the vessel, but the demand for compensation was not made within the stipulated period.

Held, that the contract between the parties was such as to cover all the time from the hour of the delivery of the goods by the shipper to the shipowner, irrespective of the time when the goods were actually loaded on the vessel; that the implied warranty of seaworthiness was, therefore, not antecedent to the bill of lading, and that consequently the conditions contained in that instrument applied, and the claim for compensation should have been made within one month.

Judgment of the Supreme Court of British Columbia (see 1 Can. Com. Cases, 154 or 8 B. C. Rep. 228) reversed, Mills, J., dissenting.

The plaintiff on 5th June, 1899, shipped on defendans' steamer, The Cutch, six cases of dry goods, to be carried from Vancouver to Skagway. The bill of lading contained, in addition to various paragraphs limiting the owners' liability, the following clause:

"It is expressly agreed that all claims against the said steamer or her owners for damage to or loss of any of the within merchandise must be presented to the master or owners thereof within one month from date hereof; and that after one month from date hereof no action, suit or proceeding in any court of justice shall be brought against the said steamer or the owners thereof for any damage to or loss of said merchandise; and the lapse of said one month shall be deemed a conclusive bar and release of all right to recover against said steamer or the owners thereof for any such damage or loss."

The goods were damaged by reason of the unseawortheness of The Cutch, and plaintiff made a claim for compensation, but not withim the period of one month from the date of the bill of lading.

Plaintiff subsequently brought an action, which, at the trial before Irving J., was dismissed. On appeal to the Supreme Court of British Columbia this decision was reversed, and judgment was given in favour of the plaintiff. —McColl C. J. dissenting.

The defendant appealed.

7th and 8th March, 1902:—

Davis K. C. for the appellants.

Sir C. H. Tupper K. C. for the respondent.

15th May, 1902:—

The judgment of the majority of the Court was delivered by:

DAVIES J.—The sole question argued before us was whether the 10th clause of the Shipping Receipt which contained the contract between the parties applied so as to exempt the carriers from liability for having provided an unseaworthy ship in which to carry the plaintiff's goods. It is a pure question of construction. The learned counsel for the appellant, Mr Davis, based his argument upon the ground that if the warranty of seaworthiness had been expressly written in the contract the limitation of time within which suit was to be brought for damages sustained by the shipper would necessarily apply, and he argued that, *a fortiori*, the limitation must be held applicable to an implied warranty. Sir Hibbert Tupper, for the respondent, in whose favour the judgment of the court below was given, contended that the implied warranty of seaworthiness was a duty or obligation cast upon the shipowner outside of and independently of the contract and not affected or controlled by its provisions, the limitations of which only came into force when a seaworthy ship had been provided.

The learned judges of the court below felt themselves bound by what they held to be the decisions of the courts in England, specially in the cases of Steele v. The State Line Steamship Co. (3 A. C. 72), The "Maori King" v. Hughes ([1895], 2 Q. B. 550), and Tattersall v. National Steamship Co. (12 Q. B. D. 297). But with every deference to the opinion of these learned judges, I am of opinion that these cases are clearly distinguishable from the one now before us. In all those cases it will be found that the actions were brought upon bills of lading which began to operate when and after the cargo was placed on board; and as was said by Lord Justice Smith in the quotation from his judgment in the case of The "Maori King" made by Mr Justice Martin:

"The exceptions in the bill of lading will apply after the ship sets sail. There are exceptions during the voyage when, if any of the matters mentioned take place, the ship owner is not liable. But if there is, as I think there is, an implied warranty that the machinery shall be fit for its purpose when the ship sets sail, then the exceptions do not apply and are no answer to a claim by the owner of the goods founded on the original unfitness of the machinery."

4

Now I do not presume to question that the above extract contains a correct declaration of the law as applicable to the document the learned judge had before him. That law is too well settled by a long and well known line of cases beginning with Steele v. The State Line SS. Co. (3 A. C. 72), to permit of doubt being cast upon it. But does it apply to the contract we have before us? Is this shipping receipt which contains the contract between the parties on this appeal one which applies only when and after the ship sets sail? I think not. I think it was intended to cover and did cover all the period of time from and after the delivery of the goods by the shipper to the shipowner, even if that period should be partly anterior to the loading of the goods aboard the ship in which they might be placed. It reads as follows:

UNION STEAMSHIP COMPANY OF BRITISH COLUMBIA, LIMITED.

No.   Vancouver, B. C., June 5th, 1899.

From George V. Fraser, to be shipped on board the Union Steamship Co's (Ltd) steamer Cutch, whereof Capt. Newcombe is master, or on board any other steamer of the company, or on board of any steamer the company may employ, the following property in apparent good order, except as noted, (value, weight, contents and condition, being unknown to said master), marked as indicated below, to be delivered to S. P. Brown, in transit to Dawson. for George V. Fraser or assigns, care

subject to the conditions printed on back of this receipt. "

Here follows a description of the property.

The 10th clause of the conditions, printed on the back of this receipt and on the construction of which the dispute arises, reads:

"It is expressly agreed that all claims against the said steamer or her owners for damage to or loss of any of the within merchandise must be presented to the master or owners thereof within one month from date hereof: and that after one month from date hereof no action suit or proceeding in any court of justice shall be brought against the said steamer or the owners thereof for any damage to or loss of said merchandise; and the lapse of said one month shall be deemed a conclusive bar and release of all right to recover against the said steamer or the owners thereof for any such damage or loss. "

Now when does the liability of the steamship company arise under this receipt? Clearly not from the sailing of the ship on board of which the goods might be loaded, or from the loading of the cargo aboard, but from the receipt of the goods. They were received by the company to be shipped on board one or other of their ships as soon as reasonably possible. They might remain for sometime in the warehouse of the company before being shipped. Would not the liability of the company attach from the moment they received the goods? Clearly in my opinion it would. The cases, therefore, which were cited and relied upon by the respondent, and which were each and all bases, upon the proposition that the liability of the shipowner on the respective bills of lading, on which the several actions were brought, did not attach until after the loading of the goods aboard the ship, cannot apply to the case of this shipping receipt, where the liability began the moment the goods were received by the shipowner. The conditions limit the company's liability very much. The condition preceding the one as to the time within which any suit must be brought declares (*inter alia*) that, in consideration of the goods being carried at a reduced rate, the shipper himself accepts all responsibility for the safe keeping and carriage of the goods, and agrees to hold the company absolved and discharged from delays, damages or losses, from whatever cause arising, including delays, loss or damage arising through negligence or carelessness, or want of skill of the company's officers, servants or workmen, but which shall have occurred without the actual fault or privity of the company.

It was argued, with some force, that this exempts the company from all liability except that arising from their own actual fault or privity, and that they were practically

liable for little or nothing beyond their liability to provide
a seaworthy ship on which to load the goods, or a suitable
warehouse in which to keep the goods till shipment, and
that the next clause, limiting the time for bringing an
action, in cases where there was a liability, was practically
confined to just such a case as this is, viz. failure to provide
a seaworthy ship. But without placing too much reliance
on that argument, I desire to base my decision upon the
construction I give to the shipping receipt sued upon, and
holding, as I do, that the shipowner's liability under this
contract arises from the moment of the receipt by him of
the goods and that, if the goods were damaged though his
privity or default after such receipt and before they were
loaded he would be liable, it follows that his obligation or
duty, afterwards, to load the goods aboard of a seaworthy
ship is a subsequent and not an antecedent duty or obligation, that it is such arising out of the contract made and
not independently of it, and being so is within, and covered
by the limitation of the 10th clause as to the time within
which a suit may be brought.

Mills J. gave a dissenting judgment.

Appeal allowed into costs.

Solicitors for the Appellants: Davis, Marshall, and
Macneill.

Solicitors for the Respondent: Tupper, Peters and Gilmour.

Editor's Notes:—

The judgment given by the Supreme Court of British
Columbia in this case was reported at 1 Canadian Commercial Cases, 154, — a note being also given (ib. p. 165)
of the cases bearing on the point.

The judgment of the Supreme Court of Canada has
already been reported in the official reports of that court
(see, 32 S. C. R. 379.). But the head note appears to be
somewhat misleading . After setting forth that the bill of

lading in question provided that all claims for damage or loss would be barred if not made within one month from its date, it continues: "Held... that this limitation applied to a claim for damage caused by unseaworthiness of the steamer." From this it might well be inferred that the judgment of the Supreme Court was contrary to that rendered in Steel v. State Line Steamship Co. (1877) 3 A. C., 72, and subsequent English cases. From the judgment itself, however, it appears that what was really decided was that the particular facts of the present case did not bring it within the scope of those decisions, that in the present instance the terms of the contract were such that the liability of the carrier thereunder arose not upon the sailing of the vessel (as in the English cases referred to) but upon the delivery of the goods to him, — and that, therefore, the limitations contained in the contract took effect from that moment, — the implied warranty of seaworthiness thus being in no way antecedent to the bill of lading.

[IN THE EXCHEQUER COURT OF CANADA.]

BEFORE BURBIDGE, J.

HAMBLY

v.

ALBRIGHT & WILSON (Limited)

Patent for invention — Effect of importation and non — manufacture—Section 37 of The Patent Act as applied to a "process."

1.—The patentee of any invention is only in default for the non-manufacture of his invention when there is a demand for the same which he has not met, or when any person wishing to use the same has been unable to get it at a reasonable price.

2.—Where the invention is a process the patentee complies with the requirements of the Patent Act if he is prepared to permit the same to be used by anyone for a reasonable compensation.

3.—I the case of an article made according to the patented process being imported, section 37 of the Patent Act only renders the patent void as regards the interest of the person so importing the article or causing it to be imported; and importation by a licensee will not affect the interest of the owner.

Action for a declaration avoiding Canadian letters patent No 65698 (a process for the manufacture of phosphorus) upon the grounds that there had been an illegal re-issue, that there had been an importation contrary to the terms of section 37 of The Patent Act. and that the patentees had not manufactured in accordance with the provisions of that section.

After the first bearing (15 and 16 January, 1901) the Judge of the Exchequer Court, on 9 March, 1901, finding that there had been an importation, directed a reference to determine the interest in the patent of the person at whose instance such importantion had been made. The referee reported, (28 January, 1902), that at the date of the importation that person (Readman) had no interest whatever in the patent.

Upon motion to confirm the report of the referee, the merits of the case were again gone into by counsel.

Henry Aylen K. C. and A. W. Duclos for the plaintiff.

F. S. Maclennan K. C. and C. A. Duclos for the defendants.

20TH MARCH, 1902·

The Judge of the Exchequer Court gave the following judgment : —

The action is brought to obtain a declaration that letters-patent number 65,698 are null and void on the grounds (1) that the re-issue was made contrary to law and is bad ; (2) that there has been an importation of the invention contrary to the provisions of section 37 of the Patent Act ; and (3) that there has been a failure to manufacture in accordance with the terms of that section.

With regard to the first ground on which the declaration is asked, it appears to me that the commissioner had jurisdiction to grant the re-issue, and that his decision should be accepted as conclusive of the questions now raised as to the re-issue. — (The Auer Incandescent Light Manufacturing Co. vs. O'Brien, 5 Ex. C. R., 283).

With regard to the third ground on which it is sought to impeach the patent, it is certain that neither the patentee, nor his assignee, the Phosphorous Company, nor the defendants, its licensees, ever had any intention of manufacturing phosphorus in Canada in accordance with the process for which the patent was issued, or otherwise. This is clear from the evidence of Mr John William Wilson, a director of the defendant company, taken under commission. He states that from a manufacturer's point of view the consumption of phosphorus in Canada has never been sufficient to justify the defendants in putting up works to work the Readman patent for Canada alone; that they believed they were well enough placed by their own works not to do so, although they had been pressed once or twice by the Phosphorus Company to do so. By the expression, "our works", which Mr Wilson uses, I understand him to mean the defendants' works in England, and possibly also those that were put up in the United States at Niagara by the Oldbury Electro Chemical Company, to which the defendants in some of their letters refer as "their works". Mr Wilson also stated that obviously it would be no advantage to the defendants to manufacture in Canada unless there was a demand there; that they preferred to supply Canada from their other works; and that up to the end of 1896 they supplied the Canadian trade from England with phosphorus manufactured under their process chemically, which had nothing to do with the patent in question.

By the 37th section of the Patent Act, the provisions of which constituted one of the conditions on which the patent was granted, it is provided that the patent, and all the rights and privileges thereby granted, shall cease and determine, and the patent shall be null and void, at the end of two years from the date thereof, unless the patentee or his legal representatives or assignees, within that period, or any authorized extension thereof, commence, and after such commencement continuously carry on in Canada the construction or manufacture of the invention patented in such a manner that any person desiring to use it, may obtain it, or cause it to be made for him at a reasonable price at some manufactory or establishment for making or constructing it in Canada. Now this provision presents the difficulty that the language used is not apt or appropriate where the invention is an art or process, as it may be. One does not construct or manufacture a process, and no one can obtain a process or cause it to be made for him at a manufactory or establishment. In the present case the phosphorus made by the process for which the patent issued is the same as that made chemically. The invention is useful because phosphorus may be made more cheaply in the way discovered by the patentee. The only advantage that can possibly accrue to the people of Canada, for the grant given, is that, during its existence, they may get phosphorus cheaper than they otherwise would, and that after the grant has terminated the invention may be free to all. The only way that advantage could be secured in the present case, without allowing the importation of phosphorus made in accordance with the process protected by the patent, would be to impose upon the patentee or his assignees the obligation to make it, or cause it to be made in Canada, according to that process, so that anyone desiring to do so could obtain it at a reasonable price. But, as stated, there is the difficulty, and it it a real one, that Parliament has not so provided in apt and clear terms.

Then there is this further difficulty that in earlier cases arising upon this provision it has, in substance, been held by Dr Taché and others that a patentee is not in default for not manufacturing, his invention unless or until there is some demand for it with which he has failed to comply; unless some person has desired to use or to obtain it, and has been unable to do so at a reasonable price; and that where the invention is a process only, the patentee satisfies the statute and the condition of his patent by being ready to allow the process to be used by anyone for a reasonable sum — (Barter vs Smith, 2 Ex. C. R. 455; The Toronto Telephone Manufacturing Company vs The Bell Telephone Company of Canada. 2 Ex. C. R. 524). Now, Dr Taché's views are entitled to great consideration, and whether one agrees therewith or not, he cannot get away from the fact, on which Mr Maclennan relies, and to which I alluded in the Anderson Tyre Company, of Toronto, Limited vs The American Dunlop Tire Company (5 Ex. C. R. 100) that these provisions of the Patent Act have since his decisions been re-enacted on several occasions without anything to indicate any dissent by Parliament from the view that had been taken of such provisions. I do not myself profess to be satisfied with the result as illustrated by the present case, in which the only use made of the patent has been to aid the defendants in holding in their hands the trade in phosphorus within Canada, without any intention of manufacturing phosphorus here, or of giving the people of Canada the advantage of having it made by the cheaper process for which the patent was granted. But the construction put upon the provision in question has been received and acted upon for too long to be now disturbed, except by an amendment of the provision, if Parliament should deem any amendment necessary. Accepting the construction that has been put upon this provision imposing on a patentee the obligation to manufacture to be correct, the defendants here are not in default.

Then as to importation contrary to the statute, one case of the importation of phosphorus made by the process for which the patent was granted has been made out, with which the defendants were connected, I think, in such a way that it can with propriety be said that they caused the importation to be made. I am also of the opinion that the importation of phosphorus made according to the process mentioned is, within the meaning of the 37th section of the Patent Act, an importation of the invention. But that does not make the patent void; but void only as to the interest of the person importing or causing to be imported. At the time of the importation proved in this case the legal title to the patent was in Dr Readman, while the Phosphorus Company was the beneficial owner, subject to an exclusive license to the defendants to manufacture phosphorus in Canada upon, among other terms, one for the payment of a royalty of one penny per pound on all phosphorus so manufactured. Afterwards, and before this action was commenced, Dr Readman, at the request of the Phosphorous Company, assigned the patent to the defendants. By that assignment, which was made on the 26th of May, 1898, the legal title to the patent was vested in the defendants, and the license became merged therein. Apparently, this was done for the mutual convenience of the Phosphorus Company and the defendants, and without any intention by the former to give up its claim to the royalty on any phosphorus manufactured in Canada. This action is brought to have the patent declared null and void, which, under the circumstances, cannot be done, and even if it were thought that some other relief than that prayed for might be granted, nothing would be gained by declaring the patent void as to the defendants' interest at the time of the importation mentioned; for that would be to still leave them the owners of the patent either in their own right or in the right of the Phosphorus Company.

There will be judgment for the defendants, and they will be allowed their costs, except those of the reference to the registrar, in respect of which each party will bear his own costs.

Solicitors for the plaintiff: Aylen and Duclos.

Solicitors for the Defendants: MacMaster, Maclennan and Hickson.

Editor's Notes:—

According to section 23 of The Patent Act, the Commissioner of Patents may accept the surrender of a patent and cause a new one to be issued in accordance with an amended description and specification "whenever any patent is deemed defective or inoperative by reason of insufficient description or specification, or by reason of the patentee' claiming more than he had a right to claim as new", provided that such error arose from mistake or accident, without any fraudulent intention.

In the case of The Auer Incandescent Light Manufacturing Co. v. O'Brien (1897) 5 Ex. C. R., 243, the question came up whether the fact that the Commissioner made such re-issue was conclusive, or whether, after the same had been made, it was possible to contend that the case was not one falling within the purview of section 23. The point is dealt with at some length in the judgment (ib. p. 283 *et seq.*), and it was held that such action on the part of the Commissioner was conclusive,—such re-issue not being open to review.

The case here reported is of some importance as illustrating the difficulty of interpreting some of the provisions of The Patent Act when the invention in question is a process.

In the report of this case in the Exchequer Court Reports (7 Ex. C. R. 363), there is, apparently, a typographical error in the second paragraph of the head-note,—" section 31 " should be " section 37 ".

[IN THE SUPERIOR COURT OF THE PROVINCE OF QUEBEC].

Before CURRAN, J.

DUNENBERG ET AL.

v.

MENDELSOHN ET AL.

Promissory note—Insolvency of endorser—Right of Curator to waive protest.

An endorser of a promissory note who, before the maturity of the same becomes insolvent, is nevertheless entitled to protest as required by section 51 of the Bills of Exchange Act, 1890, and the curator to the insolvent estate has no power to waive protest, that being a right attaching to the insolvent personally. If, therefore, the curator undertakes to waive protest of his own accord, the holder of the note will lose his recourse against the endorser.

The facts of this case are set forth in the judgment.

S.-W. JACOBS, for the Plaintiffs.

R.-G. DE LORIMIER, for the Defendant.

1st. November, 1902.

Curran, J.

Defendants have been sued upon a promissory note dated at Montreal, 22nd August, 1901, payable on the 1st of January, 1902, at the Dominion Bank here, made by M. Mendelsohn and endorsed by the other defendant, Moses Mendelsohn, for a balance due of $291.64. Moses Mendelsohn, the endorser, went into insolvency, and Alexander Desmarteau was appointed curator; the latter waived protest, the note having been filed with him when it became due. Defendant, Moses Mendelsohn, met the action by two pleas, one an inscription-in-law, and the other a plea to the merits. Both issues were referred to the trial court. Defendant contends that he owes plaintiff nothing under the note, inasmuch as he was not duly protested, as required by section 51 of the Bills of Exchange Act of 1890, 53 Victoria, cap. 33. Further, that it does not appear that the curator Alexander Desmarteau was in any way authorized to waive protest, and that no order of a judge was obtained by him, upon advice of the creditors or the inspectors of the estate. He contends that this right of nomination is purely personal to the endorser, that he never gave his authorization to the curator to waive protest on his behalf. and that. as a consequence. he is discharged from all obligation to pay the note or any part of it.

Plaintiff replies that the curator was fully empowered in his quality to waive protest on defendant's behalf. This is a question of considerable importance. In support of this contention plaintiff cites the case of Bountin vs Cantin. R. J. Q.. 12 S. C., p. 186, in which we found the following statement : —

" In the present case the curator had given a waiver of protest which he had a right to give, it being a matter of pure administration. "

He also refers to the American and English Cyclopædia of Law, vol. 4. of second edition. page 454. but the quotation is against his pretension: " By whom waiver may be given. It has been stated as a general rule that the declaration which is to operate as a waiver of demand, protest, or notice. must be the act or declaration of the person entitled to take advantage of these formalities. since to permit the acts or statements of another to have this effect would be a solecism. "

Other authorities have been cited by plaintiff, but they do not seem to have any application to the point now in contestation. The question at issue is: Had the curator the right to waive protest on behalf of the insolvent endorser? The scope of the creditors' functions are defined, first, by article 870 of the Code of Procedure, which is invoked by both plaintiff and defendants: "The curator takes possession of all the property mentioned in the statement, as well as of the debtor's books of account and titles of debt, and administers the property until it is sold or realized in the manner hereinafter mentioned. He has in like manner a right to receive, collect and recover any other property belonging to the debtor, which the latter has failed to include in his statement, except such as is by law exempt from seizure." 2nd, by article 877: "The curator may, with the leave of the judge, upon advice of the creditors and inspectors, exercise all the rights of action of the debtor and all the actions possessed by the mass of the creditors." It appears to the court that the administration of the curator under article 870 is confined to that of the property, until it is sold and realized upon according to the rules laid down, whilst under article 877 there is no room for doubt that he needs the leave of the judge upon the advice of the creditors or inspectors. The right to waive protest on behalf of the creditors generally might, perhaps, be conceded to the curator, but the court cannot find authority anywhere enabling him to waive on behalf of the insolvent endorser. This view is borne out by Girouard on Bills and Notes, under section 49, at page 153, as follows:— "By the English Act it is provided that, where the drawer or endorser is bankrupt or insolvent, notice may be given either to the party himself or to the trustee. But as there is no insolvency law in Canada, that provision was left out by the Canadian Parliament. Notice of dishonor, in such a case, should always be given to the party himself, and if a trustee be appointed to his estate under the provincial laws, it would be prudent to repeat it to the trustee."

By section 51 of the Bills of Exchange Act, defendant, to be held responsible on this note in question as an endorser was entitled to a notarial protest. That right he admittedly did not waive; it is a right personal to himself, and whilst the curator to his estate has power to administer his property, under the terms of the

article cited, it cannot be contended validly that he has any
right to deprive defendant of any of the privileges conferred
upon him by a special statutory enactment.   The different
articles of the Code of Civil Procedure all tend to
establish that the curator is the representative of the mass
of the creditors. He administers the estate in their interests. When the insolvent debtor has rights they are
carefully safeguarded, and the curator is not allowed to
tamper with them of his own motion. Thus we find in article 879 of the Code of Civil Procedure that as regards the
sale of immoveables, the judge may order how the
same are to be sold, upon application made to him
by the curator authorized by the inspectors, or upon
petition of an hypothecary creditor, "after notice to
the debtor." The law foresees that the debtor may
have something to say on his own behalf, and, therefore, it provides that he shall have notice. In the present instance it is admitted that the insolvent endorser was
in no way consulted as to the waiver of a protest without
which his liability ceased. There was no order of any
judge, even if such order could avail for anything beyond
. the interest of the mass of the creditors, and under these
circumstances it appears to this court that plaintiff has lost
his recourse, and his action is dismissed with costs.

Solicitors for the Plaintiffs: JACOBS, PATTERSON & GAR-
NEAU.

Solicitors for the Defendant: DEMERS & DE LORIMIER.

Editor's Note:—

This case has now been taken to the Court of Review.
The notes will therefore be held over until judgment has
been given by that court.

[IN THE SUPREME COURT OF CANADA].

BEFORE TASCHEREAU, SEDGEWICK, GIROUARD, DAVIES AND MILLS, JJ.

BROPHY (Defendant) Appellant

v.

THE NORTH AMERICAN LIFE ASSURANCE CO. (Plaintiffs) Respondents

(ON APPEAL FROM THE COURT OF APPEAL FOR ONTARIO)

Policy of life insurance—Lack of insurable interest, 14 Geo., III cap., 48—Action for cancellation—Return of premium, paid.

A policy of insurance was issued by an insurance company upon the life of C, the premiums being paid by B, who, at the same time, bought from the same company an annuity, the entire proceeds of which were to be and were devoted to the payment of those premiums,—the whole transaction being made with the intention of benefiting B, to whom the policy was subsequently assigned by C. The latter having died, the company brought an action for the cancellation and delivery to it of the policy.

1.—Held, affirming the judgment of the Court of Appeal (1 Can. Com. Cases, 77, or 2. O. R. 559), that the policy was void as being in contravention of 14 Geo. III cap., 48, the defendant B not having had any insurable interest in the life of C.; and that, as the company had had no knowledge of the true nature of the transaction, it was entitled to obtain the cancellation of the policy.

2.—Held, further, reversing the judgment of the Court of Appeal (Davies and Mills, JJ., dissenting), that a return by the company of the premiums paid would not be made a condition of the cancellation.

Appeal dismissed and cross-appeal allowed.

Appeal and cross-appeal from a judgment rendered by the Court of Appeal for Ontario. The facts of the case are given in the following extract from the judgment of Armour, C. J. O. in that Court· (See 1 Can. Com. Cases, 79.)

"One Richard Alexander Cromar, a broker and insurance expert, as he called himself, on the 27th October, 1885, wrote to the defendant Brophy as follows: ' Re the pleasant intercourse we have had in business matters lately.—

On the condition of your making me, A. C. your referee, adviser, and broker in any transaction relating to insurance, real estate or monetary investments, I agree and hereby promise to allow you the following rebate or commission on all premiums or amounts paid to any company or institution transacting business in Canada as follows, viz :— Annuity bonds. one-half of one per cent ; endowment policies, single premiums, one per cent ; endowment policies, annual premiums,' ten per cent. On all other transactions the half of commission given me as a general broker. Advice in any matter I will be pleased to give you to the best of my knowledge and ability gratis.'

This proposed arrangement was apparently agreed to by the defendant Brophy, and continued in force until after the impeached policy was effected.

The defendant Brophy deposed as follows :—' I wanted to know from him the different kinds of insurance, and we had a talk about it two or three times, and he was telling me the different plans, and they did not suit me altogether, and I was thinking over that thing one night and I wanted to have as little trouble with the business as possible myself, and I was thinking over it one night after we had talked the second or third day, and the next morning I told him what I had been thinking of during the night, that there seemed to be a convenient and easy way for me, and that would be to buy the annuities and let the annuities go for insurance of my life, and he struck the table and said "that is the best idea I ever heard. I have been a long time doing insurance business, and that never came into my mind before : " so he went out of the room where we were and · told the manager then what he proposed, and that he approved of so much, and that is the first insurance he did for me. '

The insurance here referred to was an endowment policy in the New York Life upon the life of the defendant Brophy effected in 1885. Shortly before the effecting of the impeached policy the defendant Brophy had an interview with Cromar, and this is the account he gave of it :— " I said I had some more money to put into insurance, and he said, ' would'nt it be much better for you to have a young

life? How would it be if I put it on my life, and he drew
out the figures and showed me the difference in the insurance that I would get on his life and on my life, and
showed me the advantage of putting it on his life, and
that is the way he came to put the insurance on his life."

The defendant Brophy thereupon, through Cromar, applied to the plaintiffs for an annuity bond of $300, and
Cromar applied for an insurance on his life for an amount,
the annual premium for which would be met by the annuity bond, which amount was ascertained to be the sum
of $6,025.

The annuity bond was issued by the plaintiffs for the
annual sum of $300, payable to the Defendant Brophy on
the fifth day of March, in each year, and the policy of insurance on the life of Cromar for $6,025, in consideration
of the annual premium of $300, was issued by the plaintiffs,
payable to Cromar on the fifth day of March, 1917, if
living; if not, his executors, administrators or assigns.
This policy was originally written with premiums payable
annually, 20th February, but was altered, making the
premiums payable on the 5th day of March in each year,
the same day on which the annuity of $300, was payable.

The amount charged for the annuity was... $2,546.70
And for the premium of insurance.... .... ..   300.00
                                                 ─────────

And from this was deducted one-
    half of one per cent on the sum
    paid for the annuity bond.... ..... $12.73
And ten per cent on the premium of
    insurance.... .... 30.00   42.73
                                                 ─────────
                                               $2,803.97

These deductions being made in pursuance of the arrangement contained in the letter of Cromar of the 27th
October, 1885; and for this balance of $2,803.97 the
defendant Brophy sent his cheque to the plaintiffs.

Thereafter, until the death of Cromar, who died on the
24th April, 1900, the money payable by the annuity bond

5

was applied in payment of the premiums payable by the policy of insurance.

On the 13th of March, 1897, Cromar, by assignment under his hand and seal, assigned, transferred and set over unto the defendant Brophy, and for his sole use and benefit, all his right, title and interest in and to the said policy of insurance, subject to all its terms and conditions, expressly reserving to the insured, however, sole right and power to make choice of any investment, option or options granted under the conditions of said policy, and personally to receive the full benefit thereof without the consent of any person or persons named therein as assignee or assignees, and that in the event of the death of the said assignee or assignees before the policy became due, then and in that case the proceeds therof should be payable when due to the insured, his executors, administrators, or assigns.

The defendant Brophy said that this assignment was not according to his agreement with Cromar; that by it he was entitled to an absolute assignment, but that he submitted to taking it rather than have any trouble. "

At the trial judgment was given directing the cancellation of the policy. The Court of Appeal affirmed this decision, but directed that the company should return the amount paid to it as premiums on the policy.

D. O'CONNELL and E. J. BUTLER, for the Appellant.

J. K. KERR, K. C., and J.-A. PATERSON, for the Respondent.

6TH. MAY, 1902.

Taschereau, J. — This is an appeal and cross-appeal from the judgment of the Court of Appeal for Ontario, reported at page 559, vol. 2, of the Ontario Law Reports.

The Appellant, Brophy, appeals from that part of the judgment which decrees the cancellation of the policy and dismisses his counter-claim for the amount thereof, and the company appeal from that part of it which orders them to return the premiums they have received upon it.

I would dismiss the principal appeal. As held by this Court in *The North American Life Assurance Co.* v. *Craigen*, 13 S. C. R., 278, it is only when a person insures the life of another that the question of interest in that life becomes important, and any one may lawfully *bona fide* insure his own life and make the insurance payable to one who is totally without an insurable interest in his life. *Vezina* v. *The New York Life Insurance Co.*, 6 S. C. R., 30; *Stuart* v. *Sutcliffe*, 46 La. An., 240. Here, however, it is plain, by uncontroverted evidence, that the arrangement between the Appellant and Cromar was that he, the Appellant, who had no interest in Cromar's life, should insure it for his own benefit, he, the Appellant, paying the premiums. That it is consequently a wagering policy, immoral in its nature and tendency, and void, as found by the two courts below, is not, in my mind, susceptible of doubt. The evidence satisfies me that this transaction was only a part of a wide scheme between the Appellant and Cromar to engage in the wholesale business of speculating on wagering insurances. Counsel for Appellant strenuously relied upon the tontine feature of this insurance with the Respondents, and the fact that the tontine privileges accrued to Cromar. Some remarks in the opinion of Gwynne, J., in *The Manufacturers Life Insurance Co.* v. *Anctil*, 28 S. C. R., 103, would appear to give support to the contentions in favour of the appellant on that point, but, in the Privy Council, [1899] A. C., 604, in answer to the argument that as at the end of the endowment period the insured would have a proprietary interest, it was, therefore, not a gaming policy, Lord Watson said:

"That may be so, but his interest was contingent upon his surviving the date of the policy for a period of fifteen years. In the event of his death at any time during that period, the sole owner of the policy was the Appellant, Anctil."

And the judgment of this Court, declaring the policy there in question void as being a wagering policy, was affirmed.

I would dismiss Brophy's appeal, and we are all of that opinion.

Upon the company's appeal, I would allow it, and restore the decree of Street, J., at the trial.

The Court *a quo* orders the company to return the premiums *ex proprio motu*, without any plea by the Defendant to that effect, upon the ground that as they had fired the first shot and filed a bill to get the policy cancelled, before action by Brophy, they cannot get the relief asked for without returning the premiums, for the reason that where equity relieves in ordering an instrument to be cancelled, the general rule is that the party in whose favour the decree is made must do equity by returning the consideration. A question arose in the Court of Appeal as to the power to make such a decree in this case in the absence of a tender of the premiums, or of sufficient conclusions in the bill, but, in the view I take of the case, it is unnecessary for us to consider that point, which, I may say, however, would appear to be one upon which this court would probably not interfere with the judgment of the court of the province.

Then, had it been necessary to do so, this would most likely have been a case for us to exercise the power to amend given by sections 63 and 64 of the Supreme Court Act, by adding to the conclusions of the bill the words necessary to sustain the court's action in the matter. However, this is immaterial from my point of view, as I am of opinion, with deference, that there is error in the decree of the Court of Appeal, by whch the company are ordered to return the premiums. It cannot be controverted that the Appellant could not have maintained an action to recover them not from any merit of the company which justifies them, not from any merit of the company which justifies to them, but from the demerit of the Appellant, who, as a punishment for his illegal act, is denied a remedy to draw these moneys out of the company's hands.

Per Washington, J., of the United States Supreme Court, in *Schwartz* v. *The United States Insurance Co.*, 3 Wash. C. C. Rep., 170.

Upon this well established principle, it was held in *Taylor* v. *Chester*, L. R., 4 Q. B., 309, that a plaintiff cannot recover moneys paid out on an illegal consideration to which he himself was a party, where the illegality must appear by his own allegations, for the courts will not assist an illegal transaction in any respect.

See also *Lowry* v. *Bourdieu,* Doug., 468; *Palyart* v. *Leckie,* 6 M. & S., 290; *Paterson* v. *Fowell,* 2 L. R., C. P., 13; *Sykes* v. *Beadon,* 11 C. D., 170; *Begbie* v. *The Phosphate Sewage Co.,* L. R., 10 Q. B., 491; *Scott* v. *Brown,* [1892] 2 Q. B., 724. That decision rests upon the maxim "*in pari delicto melior est causa possidentis,*" which, however, does not apply, for here there is no "*delictum*" on the part of the company. The rule that governs in this case is "*cessat quidem condictio, quum turpiter datur.*" Pothier, Pand. lib. 12, tit. 5, art. 12, par. 8. The law is not so irrational as to make the *causa possidentis* less favourable when he is not *particeps criminis,* than when he is as guilty as the other party.

In *Howard* v. *The Refuge Friendly Society,* 54 L. T. 644, the plaintiff claimed the repayment of premiums upon a wagering policy which he had discontinued. "How can he bring an action upon such a transaction?" said Mathew, J., for the court, and the action was dismissed.

The case of *Dowker* v. *The Canada Life Assurance Co.,* 24 U. C., Q. B., 591, is not in a contrary sense. Draper, C. J., expressly says that if the plaintiff in that case was entitled to recover the premium it was because the policy in question, though null and void, was not a wagering policy nor one obtained by fraud.

The recent case of *The British Workman's and General Assurance Co.* v. *Cunliffe,* 18 T. L. R., 425, depended on its own special circumstances and has no application.

Nothing further need be added upon that point. There is no room for controversy upon it. So that, the conclusion of Brophy's counterclaim "for such further and other relief as may be deemed necessary and proper" (assuming it to be sufficient to include, alternatively, a claim for these premiums), must be dismissed. That being so, it would seem singular that, in the same case, a judgment would

dismiss his claim for the premiums, and at the same time
order the company to return them to him. It is upon a
broader ground, however, that I rest my opinion, that, in
this case, the want of equity is no bar to the company's
relief, leaving out of consideration altogether the appellant's
counter-claim.

Where a company asks the cancellation of a policy on
the ground of fraud and misrepresentation by the insured
the rule of the courts of equity, as laid down by the Court
of Appeal, has its full application. Such are the cases of
Barker v. *Walters*, 8 Beav., 92; *Whittingham* v. *Thorn-
burgh*, 2 Vern., 206; *DeCosta* v. *Scandret*, 2 P. Wms.,
170; *Wilson* v. *Ducket*, 3 Burr., 1361; *The Prince of
Wales etc. Association* v. *Palmer*, 25 Beav., 605; *The
British Equitable Assurance Co.* v. *The Great Western
Railway Co.*, 38 L. J. Ch., 132; *London Assurance* v. *Mansel*, 11 C. D., 363, wherein the premiums received by the
insurers, who were seeking to set aside the policies on the
ground of fraud, had to be returned to the insured as a
condition of their relief, though in the analogous cases of
Willyams v. *Bullmore*, 33 L. J. Eq., 461, and *W.* v. *B.*,
32 Beav., 574, that does not seem to have been required.

But where a policy is cancelled upon the ground that it
covers a wagering contract (especially without any guilty
participation by the company, as found in this case by the
two provincial courts), a distinction should be made, in
my opinion, and the company, in such a case, should not
be ordered to return the premiums. An insurance company is then acting in the public interest, as well as in its
own. It is as against public policy that such an instrument
is void, and in their endeavours to put a stop to acts which
the law reprobates it is a duty to the public that the company perform. It is an offence against the state, a fraud
against the law, that they ask the court to punish by the
cancellation of all the claims that the offender might otherwise have against them. They are allowed to waive all the
rights that fraud or misrepresentation by the insured would
have entitled them to, but the law denies them the right
to waive the nullities that it has enacted for the common
weal. Cf. *St. John* v. *St. John*, 11 Ves. Jr., 525. A court
of equity should, therefore, in such a case, relax its general rule, and consider it superseded, by refraining from im-

posing upon a relief which the public interest requires a condition which might have the effect of hindering and impeding a company in the performance of their duty to the state. An interference, in the name of equity, to alleviate the offender's punishment by ordering the return of the premiums into his guilty hands, would seem to me an inconsistency. The insured is not in a position to ask the assistance of the court, nor to invoke rules of equity the sole effect of which would be then to benefit the sole culprit. He has received no consideration from the company for the moneys he has paid, it is true, but he owes his loss to his own turpitude, and the court should have no pity upon him and no mercy for him, under any circumstances. I would apply to him the rule that he who has committed iniquity cannot claim equity.

We are in the matter unfettered by authority. Not a single case has been quoted at Bar, and after much labour I have not been able to find any, in which, where such a document has been cancelled at the suit of the company as being a wagering policy, it has been held contradictorily that a company are bound to return the premiums.

In *The Prince of Wales etc. Association* v. *Palmer*, 25 Beav., 605, though it would seem that the policy was of a wagering character, yet the suit seems to have been instituted and determined upon the ground of fraud, as the assignee of the policy had murdered the insured to get the insurance, a fact which would have had no importance, if the policy had been a wagering policy. And there, the company did not oppose the repayment of the premiums; they probably had tendered it by their bill. In the case of Desborough v. Curlewis, 2 Y. & C. Ex., 175, there are dicta that would seem to support the view that premiums have to be returned, but no direct decision upon the point.

Under these circumstances, in expounding the law for this Dominion this Court should, in my opinion, determine that an insurance company is not bound to tender before action, or to deposit in court, the premiums they have received on a policy the cancellation of which is asked upon the ground of its being a wagering contract, and void as against public interest and the positive enactments of the statute.

There is another ground taken at Bar on behalf of the company upon their contention that they should not, in this case, be liable for the repayment of the premiums.

The Appellant Brophy did not and could not, at the trial, consistently claim to be repaid these premiums, as he was throughout claiming the amount of the policy as a valid policy. If he had claimed the premiums, or if he may be now considered as claiming them, the respondent might invoke the express condition thereof that if any fraudulent or materially incorrect averment has been made, or any material information has been withheld by the insured, all sums which shall have been paid to the company on account of the insurance made in consequence thereof shall be forfeited.

The Appellant, Brophy, and the deceased, Cromar, undoubtedly made fraudulent and incorrect averments and withheld material information upon the initiation of this contract, in not informing the Respondents that the policy, from its very inception, was taken out by Cromar ostensibly on his own life, but really by the Appellant Brophy, for his own benefit, he agreeing to pay all premiums and contracting to get all the benefits; and in not fully disclosing to the Respondents all the facts and circumstances of the case which made the professed contract of insurance a gambling contract. The judgment of the court which absolves the Respondents of any guilt in the matter necessarily imports that they were deceived.

Upon the authority of *Duckett* v. *Williams*, 2 Cr. & M., 348, and *Venner* v. *The Sun Life Insurance Co.*, 17 S. C. R., 394, I would think that under this clause alone the company were not obliged to tender or pay into court premiums that were forfeited by an express stipulation of the contract, any more than if the forfeiture were decreed by a statutory enactment, as was the case, for instance, in *United States* v. *Minor*, 114 U. S. R., 233-238. However, as I think they were not obliged to do so under any circumstances, it is unnecessary for me to consider hypothetically what should be the result of the case if it depended upon that clause.

The appeal is dismissed with costs, the cross-appeal is allowed with costs, and the judgment of Street, J., is restored, the costs in the Court of Appeal to be against the Appellant.

Sedgewick, J:—

I entirely concur in the judgment of my brither Taschereau, but I wish to add a few words.

In Ontario, as in England, since the Judicature Acts, the filing of a bill in chancery, or the bringing of a suit to restrain an action at law in a Superior Court, is an impossibility. The jurisdiction formerly possessed by the Courts of Chancery, Queen's Bench, Common Pleas and Exchequer, (and other courts as well), has been fused, and is now exercisable not by a court of law or by a court of equity, but by the High Court of Justice alone. The machinery for enforcing civil rights and redressing civil wrongs is, in these acts, duly provided for, and a litigant, in pursuing his remedies (speaking generally), is not required to have recourse to the old common law or chancery rules of practice — different and repugnant as they usually were — but avails himself of the new procedure specially created for the amalgamated court.

In the case before us, we have the court in one breath declaring that Father Brophy is not entitled to receive back the insurance premiums, and in another breath that he is. It was for the purpose of abolishing this and other anomalies in the administration of justice that the Judicature Acts were passed, and, although the legislatures gave their confirmation and preference to equitable doctrines in regard to civil rights in preference to common law doctrines, where there was a difference, there was no similar declaration, either in favour of or against the old machinery and procedure, by the use of which these rights were thereafter to be determined and enforced.

The Chancellor had, from the first, claimed jurisdiction to set aside and cancel agreements upon the ground of fraud, forbidding, at the same time, the parties in fault from suing thereon. That claim was eventually, after much conflict, acquiesced in by the common law courts, and this jurisdiction, so established in Ontario, is now vested (the Court of Chancery, as such, having been abolished), in the High Court of Justice. It was in virtue of this specially transferred jurisdiction that the plaintiff company brought this suit, and asked, in effect, for a declaratory judgment as to the respective rights of Father Brophy and itself in regard to the policy in question. The assured was then dead. His assignee, Father Brophy, had, as I understand, delivered his proofs of loss and fulfilled all the conditions antecedently necessary to entitle him to payment. The only question in dispute was as to the company's liability for the full amount insured. Father Brophy had never asked for he repudiated as satisfaction of his claim, the payment to him of premiums paid to the company. The company likewise repudiated any obligation to do even that. The issue then was one which could only be adjudicated upon and determined by a judicial tribunal — in the present case, the High Court of Justice.

What then were the rights and liabilities of the disputants? That was the only question. Why the company began hostilities, instead of waiting for Father Brophy to make the first attack, has not been explained. Had the latter begun, making his counter-claim his statement of claim his action would have been dismissed, and no return of premiums would have been decreed. That, as I understand, is the opinion of the trial judge, and of every judge of the Court of Appeal and of this Court. But it was within the company's right to begin. The Chancery Court had given it, and the Judicature Acts had confirmed and ratified it. Nevertheless, the judgment of the court below has imposed upon the company, as a condition of success in its rightful claim, the payment of a sum of money which, in the same judgment, it has found the claimant not entitled to and that the company does not owe.

We have hitherto been taught that *vigilantibus non dormientibus equitas subvenit*, but the lesson now is that in litigation, the Fabian policy is the right one, and that he who, in the exercise of his rights has taken the opposite course, is to be punished for his vigilance.

There are, of course, many cases in which a plaintiff

may be ordered to pay money as a condition of relief. If in the present case, the ground upon which the cancellation is asked had been that there never was a real policy, owing to lack of the *consensus ad idem* at its inception, in such a case a refund of the premium might be ordered, these moneys never having been the company's property, and he that seeks equity must do equity.

Here, however, the money in question was the company's money validly received by it in consideration of a policy, lawfully issued and renewed by it. It was money held by the company, for the purposes of the company — for the benefit and security of and in trust for its shareholders and policy holders. It would, under such circumstances, have been a breach of trust upon the part of the company's executive had they made a present of it to Father Brophy, or to any one else. How can a court of justice order the violation of that trust by decreeing a refund?

I have gone over the cases referred to by Mr. Justice Osler. Most of the English cases were decided before the Judicature Act, the only one since being that of *London Assurance Co.* v. *Mansel,* 11 C. D., 363, before Sir George Jessel, M. R., where the question in controversy here was never argued and the refund was made by consent.

Girouard, J. I concur in the opinion of Mr. Justice Taschereau.

Davies, J. I concur in the judgment dismissing this appeal, but I am of opinion that the cross-appeal should be dismissed and the judgment of the Court of Appeal for Ontario sustained. I have nothing useful to add to the reasons given by the Court of Appeal for its judgment.

Mills, J. I concur in the opinion of my brother Davies.

Appeal dismissed with costs and cross-appeal allowed with costs.

Solicitor for the Appellant: Daniel O'CONNELL.

Solicitors for the Respondents: KERR, DAVIDSON, PATERSON & GRANT.

Editor's Note :—

The judgment given in this case by the Court of Appeal
for Ontario was reported at 1 Can. Com. Cases, 79.

[IN THE SUPERIOR COURT OF THE PROVINCE OF QUEBEC].

Before LAVERGNE, J.

ANGERS

v.

THE MUTUAL RESERVE FUND LIFE ASSOCIATION

*Life insurance—Contracts induced by false statements—Ariicle
1049, Civil Code of Lower Canada.*

In an action for resiliation of two contracts made with a mutual life
insurance company, and for the recovery of the moneys paid thereunder, it was proved to the satisfaction of the court, that the insured
had entered into the contracts in question relying on the truth
of certain false statements made by the company in circulars and
through its agents, the same including a table of the alleged
minimum and maximum rates of premiums which would ever
be charged ; that such statements were false to the knowledge of
the officials of the company ; that the insured paid certain premiums greater than the alleged maximum rate so long as the
same were covered by bonds placed to his credit by the company
as part profits,—but that, upon the rates being again raised considerably he paid one premium under written protest (so as not
to be without any insurance whatever) and then brought action ;

Held, that there had been no acquiesence on the part of the insured
who had acted in good faith throughout the transaction ; and that
(in accordance with article 1049 of the Civil Code), he was entitled
to recover all moneys paid under the contracts, with interest from
the date, of payment.

The facts are fully set forth in the head note and in the
judgment.

Hon. T. CHASE-CASGRAIN, K. C., and E. LAFLEUR, K. C.,
for the Plaintiff.

S. BEAUDIN, K. C., and AIMÉ GEOFFRION, for the Defendant.

LAVERGNE, J. :— (Translation.)

The court, after hearing the parties by their respective counsel, and part of the evidence, and after having read the other part of the evidence, examined the procedure and exhibits fyled, and upon the whole deliberated :

Whereas plaintiff has sued the defendants, and by his declaration complains that in 1885 he entered into a contract of life assurance with the defendants for the sum of $10,000; that in 1887 he entered into another contract of life assurance with the defendants for an additional sum of $10,000, and that he paid $4,932.20 in premiums thereunder; that he was induced to enter said association under false and fraudulent representations as to the amounts he would be called upon to pay; that without such false and fraudulent representations he would not have entered into such contracts, and that he is entitled, having been so deceived, to recover back the amount so paid in by him to the said company defendant, and interest thereon; and, further, that by reason of such fraudulent representations of defendants, plaintiff, who has now attained the age of 61 years, cannot get insured in another company without great loss and increase of premiums, and that under that head he is entitled, should his claim for reimbursement fail, to be paid damages at least to the sum of $6,509.50.

Whereas defendants plead that they are a mutual insurance company, duly incorporated; that they never deceived plaintiff by any false representations; that plaintiff entered into two policies of insurance in due conformity to written applications made by him, and upon different principles from those alleged in plaintiff's declaration; that defendants have adhered to all the conditions of said applications and policies; that even if such allegations of fraudulent misrepresentations as those made by plaintiff against defendants were true, that plaintiff acquiesced in the said policies, at different times; that plaintiff cannot now attack the said contracts that he has ratified, and that all the allegations of illegal conduct against the defendants are unfounded, as well as his claim for damages.

Whereas, plaintiff took a policy of life insurance for a sum of $10,00 in the company defendant in August, 1885, and another policy of life insurance for another similar amount of $10,000 in the said company in December, 1887.

Considering that in 1885, when plaintiff took his first policy of life insurance from said company defendant, and during several subsequent years, and especially when plaintiff took his second policy in said company, the said defendant, through its head office, was issuing and circulating throughout the United States of America and Canada, circulars and advertisements containing among others the following representations, offers and promises to people desirous of taking insurance:

" It has a reserve fund securely invested of $2,000 for every $1,000 liabilities that are likely to occur, thus making a guarantee for the payment of every claim.

" The expense of management limited to $2.00 on each $1,000.

" A reserve fund which provides against excessive assessments.

" The interest on the reserve fund is applied to the payment of death claims. This will be nearly quite sufficient to pay all claims caused by any increase in the death rate, by reason of the advancing age of the association.

" Its system provides through its reserve fund for the decrease of assessments and this lessens payments in after years.

" The assessments of persistent members will be greatly reduced in 15 years, and it is estimated that the certificate will be nearly if not quite self-sustaining.

" It furnishes greater benefits for the amount paid—from $3,000 to $4,000 insurance can be obtained at the cost of $1,000 in an old line company.

" You can by insuring in this association save from one-half to two-thirds the capital you take from your business, to pay old line companies for the same amount of insurance."

" THE RESERVE FUND."

" The treasurer is required to deposit 25 per cent. of the net assessment received with a trust company, &c., &c.

" By the constitution of the association it is provided that " the reserve fund " above $100,000 and in excess of sums represented by outstanding bonds, may be applied to the payment of claims in excess of the American experience table of mortality, and when any claim by death is due, to make up any deficiency that may then exist in the death fund.

" After the expiration of each period of five years during the continuance of a certificate of membership a bond shall be issued for an equitable proportion of the reserve fund, and the principal of said bond shall be available ten years from its date towards paying future dues and assessments under said certificate.

" Thus after fifteen years through the maturing of the bonds, the payment of future dues and assessments by our members will in a great measure be provided for, and the principal of the first bond will then be available to meet assessments, making this the most desirable plan ever presented to the American people.

" There are no stockholders to absorb profits and no surplus to be divided among trustees.

" Insurance actuaries calculate that should this association experience the same mortality and ratio of lapses as that experienced by the level premiums companies in the past decade, its certificates will be self-sustaining after fifteen years."

Considering that in 1887, company defendant through its head office in New York was issuing and circulating throughout the United States of America and Canada prospectuses, circulars and advertisements to the effect that by insuring in said company defendant would procure to the insured the following advantages:

" 1. Life insurance secured at half of the rates of ordinary companies.

" 2. The contribution, DOES NOT INCREASE WITH AGE, and may be less, but WILL NEVER EXCEED the maximum amount indicated by the tables — no dividends to be paid to stockholders; all profits accruing to policy-holders.

" 3. Profits will considerably reduce future payments of persistent members. In 1886, a dividend of $33\frac{1}{2}$ per cent. was declared upon all mortuary payments, and, in 1887, a dividend of 31 per cent. The reserve fund (Tontine) now exceeds $1,382,833, out of which $448,-804.87 were added this year, at the rate of $1,227.00 for each day of the year.

" 4. The security offered is greater than in any other company, &c., &c. It is the only company in which the funds deposited cannot be diverted or misappropriated by the functionaries.

" The payment of capitals due after death does not depend upon what can be collected from members. the association always having in hand values payable at sight sufficient to pay treble the amount of each policy after death."

Considering that the said circulars as well as the policies issued by the company defendant furnished tables of minimum and maximum rates of premium, which could be charged by said defendant for insurance.

Considering that said circulars, prospectuses, advertisements and tables of rates, as aforesaid, were published by the defendant at its head office in New York, and were under its authority published throughout the United States of America and Canada, and placed in the hands of its agents and sub-agents to be used in inducing people to take certificates of insurance from, and insure in, said company defendant.

Considering that plaintiff was shown the above circulars, prospectuses, offers, advertisements, representations and tables of minmum and maximum rates of premium, and by the same was induced to consent to the above mentioned contracts of insurance.

Considering that said representations, advertisements, circulars and tables of minimum and maximum rates of premiums were false, fraudulent and deceitful, and, that the company defendant, by its officers, knew them to be so false, fraudulent, deceitful and dishonest.

Considering that it is clearly proven that the rates based upon the age of entry of the insured were absolutely insufficient to maintain said policies in force, which defendant, by its officers, as experts in insurance, could not and did not ignore;

Considering, however, that defendant from 1885 up to 1895 did not charge plaintiff any larger premiums than the maximum rate at age of entry, and remained within the terms and limits which plaintiff was induced to believe would be carried out during the whole of his life-time.

Considering the fact that the representations and promises made to plaintiff were so carried out for ten years, that he had no reason to complain or to suspect fraud, and that he continued paying all claims made upon him promptly and faithfully.

Considering that on the 23rd. of January, 1889, a certain resolution was passed at a meeting of the said company, defendant, but at which plaintiff was not present, to the following effect :

" Whereas, the Mutual Reserve Fund Life Association was established upon the natural premium system of life assurance, which requires the members to pay simply their proportion of the death claims, with 33 per cent additional thereto, which additional sum has for its object the creation of a reasonable Surplus Reserve Emergency Fund to provide against unforeseen contingencies, its foundation principle being in opposition to accumulations of vast sums of money taken from the pockets of the policy holders, and

" Whereas the aforesaid Surplus Reserve Emergency Fund is rapidly increasing, and has already reached the enormous sum of one million eight hundred and eighty-five thousand dollars, therefore,

" Resolved, that in the event any sums are hereafter required for the payment of death claims in excess of the sums realized from current bi-monthly premium calls at the maximum rates at age of entry, as established by the Association, that are applicable to the death fund, the Board of Directors shall have power to pay such death claims in excess thereof from the current receipts that are applicable to the Surplus Reserve Emergency Fund provided that the same shall always be maintained at a sum of not less than two million dollars, but nothing in this resolution shall conflict with the provisions of the constitution and by-laws. "

Considering that the above resolution called " The Shields Resolution " was not of a nature to awaken the suspicious of a man inexperienced in insurance matters ; that on the contrary, said resolution was confirmatory of the representations made to plaintiff when he entered said company defendant, as it repeated that the calls were as at age of entry, and suggested the utilization of the Surplus Reserve Emergency Fund as provided in circulars and representations, and was passed in order to keep faith with the insured and not increase the premium rates, but in fact was not considered necessary afterwards, and was not so utilized.

6

Considering that in August, 1895, the company defendant suddenly increased the assessments payable by plaintiff about fifty per cent above the maximum mentioned in the tables of premium rates according to which plaintiff had been induced to insure, which maximum had never been exceeded before, and that the same increase was not applied to all the policy holders of said company, but discrimination was made against a certain class of policy holders of which plaintiff, forms part;

Considering that said call made in August, 1895, was accompanied with a letter of the President of the company defendant, F. A. Burnham, including a letter of the late President E.-B. Harper, explaining under what circumstances such increased call was made, and referring to a report of the Insurance Superintendent of New York, advising such a course;

Considering that even before the date of said letters and of said call in August, 1895, the plaintiff received from defendant, on the first of April, 1891, a bond for $218.98 to be credited to him as applicable to the payment of the future dues and assessments fifteen years after the date of his first policy (1885), which bond was to be followed by similar ones every five years on said policy;

Considering that said bond to be so placed to plaintiff's credit virtually, if not completely, covered the increase of $13.80 on every subsequent call, and covered said increase for over three years;

Considering that on the first day of June, 1893, plaintiff received from defendant another bond for $204.89 to be credited to him, applicable to the payment of the future dues and assessments fifteen years after the date of his second policy (1887), which bond was to be followed by similar ones every five years on said second policy;

Considering that said bond to be so placed to plaintiff's credit just about covered the increase of $14.70 on every subsequent call on his second policy for a period of three years;

Considering that plaintiff in 1895, when these increased calls were made upon him, had been paying premiums for over ten years upon one policy and for about eight years upon the other; that he had attained the age of nearly 58 years, being born in October, 1837, and had great interest in maintaining said policies in force;

Considering that in fact the bonds given plaintiff covered the increase in calls for several years, the defendant not having so far, nor in fact up to 1898, materially contravened nor violated the representations, promises and inducements upon which plaintiff insured with said company defendant;

Considering that until then, the plaintiff, who was a *bone fide* party to said contracts of insurance, and was not expert in insurance matters, had a right to still believe in the honesty of the insurers;

Considering that as company defendant were then still issuing hopeful as well as deceitful statements, showing the most favourable and flourishing state of affairs, and giving hopes of great profits to the insured in the near future, plaintiff continued to pay these increased calls, covered by the bonds in his hands, up to March, 1898;

Considering that in March, 1898, the company defendant again suddenly increased the assessments payable by plaintiff over one hundred and forty per cent above the maximum mentioned in the tables of premium rates according to which plaintiff had been induced to become insured, and that the same increase was not applied to all the class of the policy holders of which plaintiff forms part;

Considering that plaintiff, greatly alarmed by such a state of affairs, undertook to look closely into the matter, and decided drop his said policies of insurance with the company defendant and to insure with another company;

Considering, however, that a new insurance could not be easily secured, plaintiff being sixty-one years of age, and that it could not be done in a few days, plaintiff paid defendant such first increased call under written protest, in order not to be without insurance at all, whilst he was negotiating with another insurance company;

Considering that plaintiff after this, did not pay any more to said company defendant, but secured another insurance and brought his action to resiliate his contracts with company defendant and recover from them all the sums of money paid and interest thereon.

Considering that plaintiff then found out that he had been grossly deceived, and that insurance could not possibly be carried at the rates at which he had been induced to insure, and that this fact was afterwards fully substantiated by the defendant company's own expert witness and other experts;

Considering that the artifices practised by the defendant company and with its knowledge were such that plaintiff would not have contracted without them;

Considering that plaintiff has been decieved by the false representations made by means of divers written statements issued by defendant, and has been afterwards kept and maintained under such delusion and error by means of divers documents issued by the defendant company from its head office and sent to said plaintiff.

Considering that plaintiff, who was acting and dealing in good faith with said company, had a right to and was justified in believing and admitting that said company acted with the same good faith, and that said plaintiff's will and consent were only obtained by deceit and falsehood;

Considering that the duty of those issuing prospectuses and circulars holding out to the public the great advantages which will accrue to persons who will take shares in a proposed undertaking and inviting them to take shares on the faith of the representations therein contained, is to state everything with strict and scrupulous accuracy, and not only to abstain from stating as fact that which is not so, but to omit no one fact within their knowledge the existence of which might in any degree affect the nature or extent or quality of the privileges and advantages which the prospectuses hold out as inducements to take share;

Considering that defendant, as an insurer, has made repeatedly, and has maintained fraudulent misrepresentations and concealments, which are a cause of nullity of the contracts entered into the plaintiff who was an innocent party to said contracts;

Considering that like all other convenants, the Mutual Insurance contract is regularly formed only by the consent of the other party thereto, which to be valid, must not have been given by error or obtained by deceit and fraud;

Considering that the conditions of the association were concealed by the said defendant and its agents, and that the insured plaintiff entered into a company whose premiums were alleged to be fixed at a certain maximum rate, whilst as a fact it was not so, and that the subscriptions of the said plaintiff have been obtained only by means of false representations, deceit and fraud;

Considering that, under Article 1049, of the Civil Code, if the person receiving be in bad faith he is bound to restore the sum paid or received, with the interest and profits which it ought to have produced from the time of receiving it:

Considering that the plaintiff has paid defendant as premiums all the sums of money which he alleges to have so paid, and that defendant was always in bad faith when receiving them, and that said contracts of insurance were null *ab initio;*

Considering that the sums so paid by plaintiff to defendant for premiums on said policies amount to $4,932.20, and that the interest calculated thereon from the time of the payment of the various sums forming the above mentioned sum up to the second day of May, 1898, amount to $1,577.37, making in all the sum of $6,509.57.

Doth declare the said contracts of insurance entered into by plaintiff and defendant as aforesaid null and void *ab inito,* and each and all said payments made by plaintiff to defendant to have been so made by error and by reason of the false and fraudulent representations and concealments of defendant, and each and all said payments to have been received by defendant in bad faith, and doth condemn the said defendant to pay to the plaintiff the sum of $6,509.57, with interest theron from the date of service of summons, with costs distraits to Messrs. Angers, de Lorimier and Godin, attorneys for plaintiff.

Solicitors for Plaintiff: McGibbon, Casgrain, Ryan & Mitchell.

Solicitors for Defendant: Geoffrion, Geoffrion & Cusson.

Editor's Note: —

Article 1049 of the Civil Code of Lower Canada is as follows:

" If the person receiving be in bad faith he is bound to restore the sum paid or thing received with the interest and profits which it ought to have produced from the time of receiving it, or from the time that his bad faith began."

An appeal from the above judgment has been argued. and the case is now standing for judgment before the Court of King's Bench, Appeal Side.

[IN THE SUPERIOR COURT OF THE PROVINCE OF QUEBEC.]

BEFORE DOHERTY, J.

WESTERN ASSURANCE COMPANY

v.

BADEN MARINE INSURANCE COMPANY

Marine Insurance—Policy of re-insurance—Meaning of " special charges "—Effect of payment by first insurer as for a total loss.

Plaintiff insured a cargo, and re-insured part of the risk with defendant, the policy stating that the latter was to be liable for " special charges." The vessel carrying the cargo was wrecked, but some cattle were saved, and were taken to Halifax and elsewhere. It being found impossible to obtain another ship to take them to their destination they were finally sold, and the first insurer (the plaintiff) paid the principals who then abandoned), as for a total constructive loss. Plaintiff then claimed from defendant its proportion of the moneys spent for salvage of the cattle, for keeping them, and for the expenses in connection with their sale.

Held, that these expenses came within the meaning of the term " special charges."

Held, further, that the so called abandonment did not affect defendant's liability, as all the charges had then been incurred,—it being immaterial in the result whether the principals took the proceeds of the sale and were paid the balance due them by the first insurer, or whether the latter paid them in full, and then took the proceeds of the sale himself.

The facts of this case are set forth in the head note and in the judgment.

5th. November, 1902.

DOHERTY, J.:—

This is an action upon a marine re-insurance policy.

About the facts there is no dispute. Plaintiff had insured in favor of different persons a large number of cattle and sheep, shipped on the steamship Baltimore City from Montreal to Manchester, for sums amounting in the aggregate to $18,910. It re-insured this risk with defendant to the extent of $2,000. The re-insurance policy or certificate contained the following clause, " Insured against absolute total loss of vessel and animals, but to pay general average — and special charges."

The Baltimore City with the insured cattle on board sailed from Montreal on the 12th July, 1897. On the 17th she struck on a reef near Flat Island. After vain endeavors to get her off, the vessel was finally abandoned, a total wreck, on the 4th August. Meanwhile, some of the insured sheep and cattle had been jettisoned, and the remainder were landed on Flat Island. This island, it is admitted, was not a place of safety, and 163 head of cattle and 35 sheep were by the steamship Harlow City, taken from it, and transported to Halifax and Sydney; 148 sheep and 8 head of cattle were bought from Flat Island to Bonne Baie, apparently by one Harding. No special agreement was made by the master as to the charge to be made by the Harlow City for this transportation — it being merely agreed that terms of salvage should be arranged by the respective owners. It does not appear either that an agreement was made for the transportation to Bonne Baie, the captain merely stating that 132 sheep and 8 oxen were left in charge of the wreck commissioner to take to Bonne Baie. The amount payable for salvage on the live stock taken to Sydney and Halifax and Bonne Baie, was finally fixed at one-third of the gross proceeds of the sale thereof, less only auctioneer's commission and customs duty. The amounts which, by the admissions fyled, the parties give as being those paid for these salvage services are respectively :—$1,463.41, $1,178.22, and $203.79, forming a total of $2,845.22. The figures do not appear to me as regards the two first items to agree with those given by the adjuster in the exhibit fyled but I take them as accepted by the parties. The rate of salvage appears by the adjuster's statement to be as above stated. It further appears, also by the admissions of the parties, to have cost for legal and agents' expenses in arranging this rate of salvage $462.08, which added to the actual cost of salvage as admitted, makes a sum of $3,307.-50 for expenses in and about the salvaging of said cattle.

After arrival at Sydney, Halifax and Bonne Baie, endeavors were made to procure a vessel to forward the live stock to destination, but without success, and, consequently the stock was sold to the best possible advantage.

The admissions of the parties show that there were expended in caring for and maintaining the cattle, till they could be sold, and for expenses of sale, amounts aggregating a total sum of $1,760.71, and that there was paid for duties on the cattle landed at Bonne Baie, $113.41, making for charges apart from salvage expenses, a sum of $1,-874.12.

The principals insulted under these circumstances assigned all rights in the live stock to plaintiff, and were by plaintiff paid as for a constructive total loss.

Plaintiff claims that all the above mentioned expenditures constitute special charges, within the meaning of the reinsurance policy, and that inasmuch as it has been obliged to pay them by submitting to their being deducted from the proceeds of the cattle abandoned, it is entitled to recover from defendant a percentage thereof which shall bear the same proportion to the total of said charges, as the total amount of the reinsurance policy bears to the total of the re-insured policies. By its action it claimed that the expenditures aforesaid for what it contends to be special charges were larger than those above mentioned taken from the admissions fyled — and further claimed from defendant payment of a like proportion of certain general average charges to which the cattle were subject. For its proportion of the latter defendant has confessed judgment, and as regards the amounts of the former they are settled by the admissions above referred to.

Defendant denies liability for any proportion of the salvage and expenses of maintenance and sale of the cattle above referred to, upon two grounds, 1st. That they are not " special charges " within the meaning of the policy, or for which it is liable under the terms of said policy; and 2nd, That the principals insured having abandoned and plaintiff having paid them as for a constructive total loss, the latter has paid and can have no claim against defendant for any " special charges," — the expenses claimed as such having been incurred solely for the benefit of plaintiff, and after the cattle had ceased to be in any peril of absolute total loss which was the only species of loss which defendant was interested in having prevented.

Testimony has be⸱ n adduced by both parties for the purpose of throwing light upon what is understood in the business of marine insurance by the words " special charges." Defendant objected to the testimony tendered by plaintiff to that end, but upon the objection being reserved, examined a witness to rebut the testimony so taken under reserve. This testimony was, I think, admissible, (Kidston v. Emp. Marine Ins. Co. *infra cit.*).

Plaintiff's one witness is Mr. Boyd, an insurance adjuster of fifty years experience. He adjusted the loss in question, and prepared a statement showing all the items above mentioned as " special charges." He defines " special charges," in marine insurance, as any charges that would not have to be paid by the insurers except for an accident, charges resulting from some casualty before the insured effects have arrived at their destination, and been handed over to their owners, and distinguished from general average charges because, while the latter are charged to all the interests in the venture, " special charges " apply to a particular thing. They are, he adds, charges in relation to a particular interest. Under this definition he considers all the expenditures above mentioned "special charges," the salvage, in particular, because, in the present instance, it happened that the vessel and cargo were not salved as a whole, but piece-meal, in consequence of which each portion of the cargo has to pay its own salvage. To put it briefly, he treats the word " special " as equivalent to " particular, " and " special charges " as including every expense incurred in the salvage, keeping, preservation and disposal of any particular object insured, in ' this case of the live stock. In his deposition, though, he · does not speak of any custom attaching a particular meaning to the words; he gives us his own understanding of their meaning. upon which he has acted in his long experience as an adjuster, and which he tells us is the general understanding in the business.

Defendant's witness, Mr. Riley, was at the time of the issue of the policy of reinsurance, but is no longer, defendant's agent at Montreal. He, too, does not speak of any custom attaching a special or trade meaning to the words used, but tells us that, as he understands it, a " special

charge " is a special expense, as distinguished from the
general expense over a whole interest ; a special expense
on a special interest, of course, for the special purpose of
saving it from perils enumerated in the policy. Save that
he uses the word " special " where plaintiff's witness uses
" particular," this definition does not differ from that given
by Mr. Boyd. But the witness goes on to explain that his
view or contention is that once the cattle were in a position where they were no longer exposed to the perils insured against, the company defendant was not interested
in any subsequent operations on behalf of the cattle. In
cross-examination he says that his definition would include
in the " special charges " all the salvage items, but exclude
all expenses incurred for keep and sale of cattle, after arrival at Sydney, Halifax, and Bonne Baie. He further
concedes that if the cattle, after detention at these places,
had been — a vessel being found — carried on to their
destination, their keep during the detention would have
been a special charge. He says he never before had to
do with a case where cattle were sold before arriving at
their destination. In re-examination he distinguishes salvage from " special charges," and contends that it should
be adjusted as what he calls a " straight salvage settlement."

As a result of comparing the depositions of both these
witnesses, I find that they agree in treating the word
" special " as used merely to distinguish from an expense
incurred for the general interest of ship and cargo, one incurred for a particular interest ; that they differ as to what
expenditure, made in a particular interest, may be properly
treated as a special charge, in so far as Mr. Boyd thinks
salvage may be so treated, and Mr. Riley, on the other
hand, considers salvage as something to be treated apart
as a salvage charge. Mr. Riley further thinks that, under
its policy, the company defendant could be liable for no
charge whatever incurred after the cattle had reached a
place of safety. This, however, does not bear upon the
question we have first to determine, namely, " what is a
special charge " though we will, of course, have to decide
whether, for any charge, even if special, incurred after arrival of the cattle at a place of safety, defendant is liable.

In so far as both these witnesses agree in considering "special charges" as charges incurred in a particular and not in the general interest, I do not know that they add anything to what the policy itself tells us. By that instrument defendant undertook to pay general average — and special charges. As general average would include all extraordinary charges incurred for the common safety of ship and cargo (C. C., Art. 2552), the added undertaking to pay "special charges" must necessarily mean charges incurred in a particular interest. It did occur to me that there might perhaps be some question as to whether the word " special " was not used for the purposes of limiting the charges bearing upon the particular object insured, for which the re-insurer was to be liable to some special class of particular charges. Neither of the parties, however, suggesting any such restrictive effect or meaning as attaching to the word " special," their witnesses agreeing in treating it as synonymous with " particular," and there being nothing in the terms either of the re-insurance or insurance policy before the court — in both of which liability for " special charges," is undertaken — indicating to what — if to any — special class of particular charges that liability was intended to be limited, the conclusion, I think, imposes itself that the word "special" is used simply as distinguishing the charges so qualified from charges giving rise to general average contribution, which, in the immediately preceding words of the policies, both re-insurer and insurer have bound themselves to pay.

I take it, therefore, that " special charges, " and " particular charges " are convertible terms.

This being so we may dispense with the aid of testimony to tell us what they mean. We find that in England the words " particular charges " have a perfectly defined and well understood meaning: that they are used as covering all " expenses occasioned by a peril insured against, when they have been necessarily incurred in consequence of such peril, as for example, expenses of warehousing and forwarding cargo when a peril insured against has occasioned the necessity of such expenditure." (Arnould, 7th ed., 869). At No. 1008, the same author says: " Expenses incurred for preventing or mitigating a loss which would otherwise occur or increase, and would fall accordingly

upon the insurer, are called particular charges. " Kelly, C·
B., in *Kidston* v. *Empire Marine Insurance Company*
(L. R., 2 C. P., 357), discussing the question of the distinction to be made between "particular average" and
"particular charges," says: "The common law of England
itself defines the nature and character of these charges...
Forwarding of the cargo is a particular charge, not a
partial loss."

It may further be pointed out that the term "particular
charges," is there recognized as covering as well expenditures made for the purpose of forestalling or preventing
the occurrence of disaster to a particular interest, or dim-
inishing the loss therefrom resulting, which might not be
considered as incurred under what is called the "sue and
labour clause" of the ordinary maritime policy, as those
incurred under that clause; there being, however, this distinction to be made between particular charges of the first,
and those of the second class, that whereas the former
are treated as being claimable from the insurer under the
general terms of the policy, and may, therefore, form part
of a partial loss under it, for which responsibility would
be excluded under the usual stipulation "free of particular
average," and are never recoverable over and above the
amount of the policy itself, those incurred under the "sue
and labour clause," are treated as being expenditures made
in the interest of the insurer and under the authorization
by him given by the terms of that clause, and are recoverable by the insured over and above the amount insured.
(Arnould, sup. cit. — Kidston v. Emp. Marine Co., sup.
cit. — and L. R., 1 C. P., p. 532. — Great. Ind. Pen. Ry.
Co. v. Saunders, 30, L. J., Q. B., 218; 31 L. J., Q. B., 206;
Booth v. Gair, 33 L. J., C. P., 99; Aitchison v. Lohre, 4,
App. Cases, 755).

The last mentioned case (and indeed the others), we will
have occasion to advert to again. For the moment I desire
merely to point out that while it holds salvage charges not
to be recoverable under the "sue and labour clause," it does
not question their being "particular charges," where incurred in a particular interest.

Upon the whole, it would seem safe to say that in England
"particular charges" mean expenditures incurred in a par-

ticular interest. as distinguished on the one hand from general average charges, and, on the other, from actual damage sustained by a particular interest. And, in fact, the terms seem to have been adopted more particularly for the purpose of making the latter, than the former, distinction. In the cases of Great Indian Pen. Railway Company vs. Saunders; Booth vs. Gair; Kidston vs. Empire Marine Insurance Co., above cited, a distinction was sought to be made between expenditures called "particular charges," and "particular average," the endeavor being to limit the stipulation "free of particular average," to exempting the insurer from liability for partial damage to the thing insured, but not for expenses incurred for its preservation, styled "particular charges." In the result the distinction existing between the meaning of the two expressions was fully recognized, but it would appear to have been held that "particular average" included "particular charges," as well as partial damage, save only in the case of "particular charges" incurred under the "sue and labour clause," which would not be included in it.

Turning now from the English authorities to the dispositions of our own law, it may be said at once that in none of those dispositions do we find the words "special charges" or "particular charges" made use of. In but one article (art. 2512) is the word "charge" made use of, and that article has no bearing on our case.

On the other hand, we find liability for all the expenditures which in England would be called "particular charges," imposed upon the insurer by articles 2527, 2528, 2531, and 2537 of our code. The first of these articles declares "extraordinary expenses necessarily incurred for the sole benefit of some particular interest" to be (as well as damage sustained by ship alone or cargo alone) "particular average losses for which the insurer is liable to the insured, under the general terms of the policy, when the losses are caused by the perils of the sea." These "extraordinary expenses" are clearly the "particular charges" of the English law, and the article makes them equally clearly form part of a "particular average" loss. The next article, 2528, deals specially with the "salvage loss" ("frais de sauvetage" in the French version). and declares it also to be a loss by

perils of the sea. Article 2531 deals with certain particular expenditures in case of transhipment of goods, that is
" expenses of discharging, storage, reshipment, supplies,
freight, and all other costs not exceeding " the amount of
the policy, and imposes liability therefor on the insurer.
These are apparently only particular items inserted for
greater certainty, but which would, or at all events might
have been covered by the more general terms of article
2527. They are clearly among the particular charges of
the English law. Article 2537 in effect imposes upon the
insured the obligation which is in England held to be incumbent upon him under the " sue and labour clause " of
the policy, to do all in his power "between the time of loss
and abandonment to save the effects insured," and upon the
insurer the obligation by that clause by him undertaken to
indemnify the insured for all expense or charges by him
incurred in so doing. These latter charges or expenses, as
we have already seen, are among the " particular charges "
of the English law.

Of these four articles it may not be without interest to
mention that article 2531 reproduces article 393 of the
French Code de Commerce, as does our article 2537 substantially article 381 of that code, save that the latter article admits the right of recovery of expenses by the insured under it to the value of the goods by him saved;
and that our articles 2527 and 2528, so far as they determine the nature of the losses by them dealt with, contain
dispositions to be found in article 403 of that code. I
do not mention this because it seems to me that any question
arises herein making it necessary to go into any enquiry
concerning the source of our law, as to whether it be
French or English. In dealing, however, with the interpretation of terms used in the policy before me, which is in the
identical form of the English policy of marine insurance, I
have felt justified in seeking light upon the exact meaning of
these terms in the interpretation of the terms of the policy
in the country of its origin. In any case, as regards particular charges and the liability of the insured for them,
there does not appear to be any material difference between the law as it prevails in the three countries.

All the expenditures for which plaintiff claims under the name of " special charges " being charges which in England would come within what the parties treat as the equivalent designation of " particular charges," and being all charges for which by our law the insurer is declared to be liable under the policy, I feel justified in concluding that they are " special charges " within the meaning of the policy of insurance issued by plaintiff, and the certificate of re-insurance in its favor sued upon. Whether anything in the particular circumstances of the loss in this case relieves defendant of his responsibility, is a question to be considered later.

With regard to the salvage charges, and the expense of selling the cattle, I have had more difficulty in arriving at the conclusion above stated, than with regard to the cost of feeding and caring for the cattle during their detention, which is specially dealt with by article 2530.

As regards the salvage charges it appeared to me that the distinction sought to be made by defendant's witness, Mr. Riley, might find some support in the terms of article 2528, C. C., which deals with " loss by salvage," apparently avoiding the use of the word "charge" as applicable to expenditure for that purpose. But, apart from the fact that though between the assured and insurer an amount paid for salvage constitutes a loss, it nevertheless is essentially an expense incurred for the preservation of the thing insured. On turning to the French version of the article we find the salvage expenditure spoken of as " frais de sauvetage," the word " frais " being the equivalent of the English word " charge " and being in fact used in translating the last mentioned word in the only article of our code (2512) in which, as we have already remarked, it occurs. A further reason, which led me to hesitate with regard to treating salvage as a special or particular charge, I found in a first reading of the judgment of the House of Lords, in the case of Aitchison v. Lohre, above referred to (4 A. C. 755.) Their Lordships there refused to allow a claim for salvage arising under circumstances in many respects similar to those in this case, as a particular charge under the "sue and labour clause " and recoverable over and above the amount of the policy. In the course of their remarks they speak of it as being, and insist upon its being, a loss by perils of the sea recoverable under the general terms of the policy. At first glance this holding seemed to imply that, in the view of their Lordships, salvage, where earned by a salvor under the general maritime law was a loss and not a "charge." But a more careful examination of their language leaves no doubt in my mind, that by the use of the word "loss" they did not mean that because it was a loss it was not a charge or particular charge — but merely that they meant to make clear that it was that kind of a particular charge which would constitute a loss under the general terms of the policy, and not a charge incurred under the clause above-mentioned. That was the question before them. And, indeed, upon it they only arrived at the result they did, and which reversed the judgment of the Court of Appeal (3 Q. B. D., 558) by drawing a somewhat fine distinction between cost of salving, under a contract by the owner or master to salve at a fixed price, and the like cost when paid to salvors acting under the maritime law. The judgment — like many another — has not escaped criticism. (Maclachlan in 6th edition of Arnould on Marine Insurance.) But whether sound or not, it does not, as has been pointed out, hold that salvage expenses are not a "particular charge." Any doubt as to whether salvage charges come properly under the designation of "special charges," moreover, completely disappears, when we find this expression, used in the policy issued by plaintiff, in a clause stipulating that "no claim (except general average and special charges) shall attach in respect to any animal walking after being landed alive." To interpret the words in this clause as not covering salvage charges, would be to leave the insured without recourse, if the animals were once landed living as the result of salvage operations which might have cost the greater part of, or even their entire value. It seems impossible that this can have been intended, and the words cannot mean one thing in the insurance and another in the re-insurance policy.

As regards the expenses of the sale, the ground of my hesitation was that the actual selling of the cattle could perhaps hardly be strictly treated as an act for the preservation of the object insured, inasmuch as its result was to terminate all right in it, either of insured or insurer, and to put an end by one and the same act both to insured's ownership of and insurer's risk upon the property.

Under the circumstances, however, the sale having been made as the sole means of putting an end to daily increasing charges of maintenance of the cattle, which — once it was clear they could not advantageously be forwarded to their original destination, had ceased to be of any advantage, seems to me to have been a necessary step towards saving them for the insured, or for the insurer, should the former exercise the right the circumstances gave him of abandoning, from being entirely lost so far as value was concerned by the process of what is familiarly called "eating their heads off." This having become necessary in consequence of a peril insured against, the expense of doing it appears, therefore, justly enough to be treated as a particular or special charge, at all events as between the insured and the plaintiff as principal insurer.

Before leaving this question of what is to be understood by "specal charges," it may not be without purpose to point out that, although there is nothing before the court to indicate the object for which the clauses containing these words were inserted in the policy of insurance and certificate of re-insurance, the effect of interpreting them as we have done is to make these clauses tantamount to the stipulation "free of particular average" in the sense unsuccessfully sought to be attached to that stipulation in the cases above cited of the Great Ind. Pen. Ry. Co. v. Saunders, and Booth v. Gair, the insurers, from responsibility for damage to the object insured, but leaving them liable for total loss, general average and partial loss in so far as the same consists of particular charges. In the last mentioned of these two cases, in speaking of the clause "warranted free from particular average except general," Erle. C. J., said: "If the assured intended to confine the warranty to partial loss from damage to the cargo, and to leave the underwriter liable for expenses of transhipment, (the particular charge there in question), this policy does not express that intention."

It would appear to me not to be too hazardous a surmise, that the clause, as embodied in the policies now before the court, was desired for the purpose of attaining that result, and expressing that intention.

There remains for us to examine the grounds upon which defendant contends that even though the expenditure in dispute be special charges, the circumstances under which they were incurred and the fact of the abandonment by the principal insured relieve defendant of liability therefor.

If I have correctly apprehended defendant's contentions in this branch of the case they are two in number. He says, 1st, these charges were not incurred to forestall or prevent any loss for which I would have been liable, even had such loss occurred, and I had consequently no interest in their being made, and am not liable for them, and 2nd, my policy being one of re-insurance, and exempting me from liability for any total loss save absolute total loss of vessel and cattle, and you, plaintiff, having accepted the abandonment of the principals assured and paid them for a constructive total loss, have paid said principals assured no special charges, you have merely as owner of the cattle saved — as you were, in virtue of the abandonment, from the moment of the disaster — been obliged to submit to the diminution in their value resulting from the charge with which they were burdened. For this diminution I am in no way responsible to you.

As regards the first of these contentions, it is so far as regards the salvage charges unfounded in fact. Had the salvage not been effected the live stock would have remained on Flat Island — which it is admitted was not a place of safety, exposed to perish as the direct consequence of the perils insured against. Had they so perished, there would then have been an absolute total loss of both vessel and animals, for which defendant would have been liable. As for the not very seriously urged pretension of Mr. Riley in his testimony, that inasmuch as if but half a dozen or a dozen cattle or sheep had been saved there would have been no loss for which defendant could be responsible, the latter was interested only in and should be held liable only for the salvage of such dozen or half-dozen, it does not appear to me to deserve serious consideration.

As regards the other charges, more especially those incurred for the sale of the cattle, it is true that they were not incurred in defendant's interest, in the sense that they were not necessary to prevent an absolute total loss by perils of the sea. Once it had been decided to sell the cattle it became quite certain that there was no longer any danger of an absolute total loss by perils of the sea, and even before that decision had been arrived at the expenses incurred in feeding and caring for the cattle at the different places of detention, even if incurred with a view to their being forwarded, cannot be said to have been incurred for the purpose of preventing an absolute total loss by such perils. At Halifax, Sydney and Bonne Baie they were in no such peril.

Had defendant been the principal insurer, insuring only against absolute total loss, it might perhaps, in so far as these expenses are concerned, have found authority for the contention in the judgments in the cases above mentioned of Great Ind., Pen. Ry. Co· v. Saunders, and Booth v. Gair — though even then it would have had to face the difficulties which did not stand in the way of the insurers in those cases, namely, that the policies in these cases excluded liability for particular average generally, and made no mention of particular charges, whereas here liability for special charges is specially assumed; and that in those cases the insured had nothing whereon to base his claim, but the " sue and labour clause, " of the policies, whereas ,here we have, besides the disposition of article 2537, imposing upon defendant obligations analogous to those incumbent upon insurers under that clause, the express text of article 2530, making insurers by law liable for charges incurred during detention of cargo, at all events so long as there is hope of its being possible to forward it to its destination within a reasonable time.

But there is another, and it seems to me clearly peremptory answer to defendants contention now under examination, and one which applies as well to the salvage as to all the other charges. It is found in the fact that defendant is a re-insurer. As such it insured plaintiff's liability under its policies to the principals insured. So far as plaintiff's liability to such principals insured was for actual loss of the object insured, defendant limited its re-insurance to absolute total loss, but so far as that liability was for " special charges " defendant re-insured it without restriction of any kind. It seems, to me, therefore, that it is· quite immaterial in the present instance whether defendant was or was not interested in the incurring of all or any of the charges in question. It undertook unreservedly, in plaintiff's favor, to pay " special charges " (that is, of course, defendant's proportion of them), and having so unconditionally and unrestrictedly bound itself, it cannot now be heard in an endeavor to subject its obligation to conditions or restrictions not stipulated. The " special charges " which defendant undertook to pay, must, it seems to me be held to be, all those for which plaintiff might become liable under the policy, the risk wherein defendant partially re-insured.

The second ground on which defendant bases his pretension that he is relieved from liability for the special charges in question, does not seem to me to stand the test of careful examination better than the first.

There is no doubt that the result of the abandonment· made by the principal insured was to place plaintiff in the position of being owner of the property insured from the time of the abandonment, and· the plaintiff took what was abandoned with all the charges upon it. I say this, assuming the assignments made by the assured to plaintiff long after the objects insured had been sold and upon payment by plaintiff of the full amount of its policy, to amount to an abandonment properly speaking, as defendant contends they did, and, as plaintiff does not appear to question that they did. The latter by its answer to defendant's allegation of abandonment in the plea, says, it is true that one of the principals assured made an abandonment to the plaintiffs on terms of the assignment herewith fyled, and not otherwise, and denies the balance of the paragraph alleging that all the principals insured abandoned. But in the admissions fyled, it admits notice of abandonment was givent by all the insured, and that they were paid as for a constructive total loss.

Were it contended that these assignments did not amount

to abandonment properly so called, and did the question whether they did or not materially affect the result of the case, I confess it would seem to me, for reasons that need not be here gone into, to be, to say the least, open to very considerable doubt whether they did.

The abandonment, treating what was done as an abandonment, was made after all the special charges claimed had been incurred. The position then was that the insured were at liberty, had they so chosen, to make no assignment or abandonment, but take over themselves the balance of the proceeds of the cattle after payment out of them of all said special charges, and then claim from plaintiff, as a partial loss, the difference between the value of the cattle as established in the policy and the amount received by them out of the proceeds of the sale, which partial loss would be made up of the difference between the said value in the policy and the gross proceeds of sale, being the actual loss resulting from the perils of the sea, plus the amount of the special charges incurred to obtain those gross proceeds, and which the insured would have had to pay out of said gross proceeds. This would have amounted to exactly the full amount of plaintiff's policy, less the net proceeds of the sale of the cattle.

Had that course been adopted plaintiff would clearly, as part of such a loss, have paid the insured the full amount of the special charges herein in question. And that seems to me to be in reality and effect what was really done, only that instead of allowing the insured to draw the net proceeds of the sales of the live stock, and then paying them the full amount of its policies, less said net proceeds, plaintiff paid the full amount of its policies and took from the assured an assignment of said net proceeds.

But the position before the so-called abandonment being as above set forth, the special charges having then accrued, and plaintiff being liable therefor under its policy to the assured, and defendant in turn liable therefor to plaintiff, nothing that the principals assured might do thereafter, could affect the liability of defendant to plaintiff. The so-called abandonment could not, on the one hand, be invoked against defendant as rendering it liable for a total loss — under its policy of re-insurance there could be no such thing as a constructive total loss. But neither, on the other hand, can that "abandonment" be by defendant invoked as relieving it from an obligation which resulted from the express terms of its own policy, and which had become enforceable against it by plaintiff before such "abandonment" was made.

The position between plaintiff and defendant was fixed from the moment the cattle were sold. Special charges had then been incurred, and defendant, under its policy, was bound to pay its proportion thereof. Whether plaintiff paid them directly or indirectly seems to me quite immaterial to defendant's responsibility. The so-called abandonment, made long after said sale, seems to me to have been, as far as defendant was concerned, absolutely "*res inter alias acta*," and as such "*illa nec novet nec prodest.*"

Plaintiff has judgment for the sum of seven hundred and eighty-nine dollars and thirty-five cents ($789.35). This amount is less than that claimed by the action. It is the sum which bears the same proportion to the total amount of special charges admitted — (which is less than that alleged) — plus the general average charges admitted by the plea, as the amount of the re-insurance policy of defendant bears to the total amount of the policies issued by plaintiff.

As I make the calculation it is as follows: —

Total amount of plaintiff's policies....		$18,910.00
Total amount of special charges admitted.... ....:	$5,181.62	
General average charges....	2,281.63	
		7,463.25
Total amount of defendant's policy....		2,000.00

As $18,910.00 is to $2,000 so $7,463.25 is to $789.34

As I understood at the hearing that the parties would agree upon the amount, if the court settled the questions of principle invoked, I will, if they so desire, hear any observations they may have to make with regard to the correctness of the above figures and calculation.

I have formed the total amount of special charges by
adding together the amounts admitted specifically as having been expended for the different purposes above mentioned. They form an amount, as above stated, of $5,181.-
62. This is $191.83 less than the total of special charges
shown on exhibit P. 7. By the admissions fyled it appears
that in P. 7 there are items figuring as special charges,
amounting altogether to $137.97, which should not be so
charged. This accounts for so much of the difference between my figures and those of P. 7. There still remains
unaccounted for an amount of $51.86, which, if it should
be added to the total of special charges as I make it,
would increase by $5.49 the amount defendant ought to
pay. If the parties think it worth while to verify the figures I will make the correction, should it be found it
should be made, as I have power to do even after signing
the judgment under Article 546, C. C. P.

Solicitors for the Plaintiffs: LAFLEUR, MacDOUGALL &
MACKAY.

Solicitors for the Defendants: HALL, CROSS, BROWN &
SHARP.

Editor's Note:—

In the notes to Kidston v. Empire Marine Insurance Co.
in the Ruling Cases (14 R. C. at p. 268) it is said with
reference to the final judgment in Aitchison v. Lahore (4
A. C. 755).

" This judgment of the House of Lords is doubtless
binding on all inferior Courts in England, so that, *in the
case of salvage proper*, where no bargain is made for renumeration, and the right to renumeration for successful service defends merely upon the general maritime law, the
expense cannot be recovered under the suing and labouring
clause. It is, however, not beyond the competence of the
House of Lords to reconsider the principle of that decision,
having regard to the considerations brought to bear on the
question in the 6th edition (1887) of Arnould on Insurance
by David Maclachlan. See his note R. 807. "

This latter criticism is referred to in the judgment reported *supra*.

See, also, The Pomeranian [1895] Probate, 349.

Lysaght v. Coleman [1895] 1 Q. B. 49.

Alexandre v. Sun Marine Insurance Co. 51 N. Y. 253.

Cory v. Boylston Fire & Marine Insurance Co., 107 Mass. 140.

Buzby v. Phoenix Insurance Co. 31 Fed. R. 422.

[IN THE SUPREME COURT OF BRITISH COLUMBIA.]

BEFORE HUNTER, C. J., IRVING, AND MARTIN, J.

THE VICTORIA YUKON TRADING CO. (Defendants) Appellants,

v.

BOYLE (Plaintiff), Respondent.

Action on foreign judgment—Exemplification—Right to question judgment founded on void contract—Extra-territorial contract of company—B. N. A. Act, sections 91 and 92.

The province of British Columbia has the right to incorporate a company with power to enter into extra-territorial contracts of carriage, and it is therefore not *ultra vires* of a company which has been granted a charter by that province to contract to carry goods from British Columbia to the Yukon Territory.

In an action upon a foreign judgment the defendant may question the validity of such judgment on the ground that it is manifestly erroneous, as for instance, being founded on a contract void from its inception.

Although a foreign judgment obtained by default is liable to be set aside, yet so long as it stands it is "final and conclusive" within the meaning of that expression as applied to foreign judgments, and consequently an action may be brought upon it in another jurisdiction.

Per MARTIN, J. : —

Exemplification of judgment under the seal of the Court by which the judgment was pronounced is equivalent to the original judgment exemplified, and notice under The Evidence Act of an intention to produce it in evidence is unnecessary.

Appeal from the judgment of Drake, J.

The defendant company was incorporated under the Companies' Act of British Columbia, and during the season of 1899, operated as a transportation company between Bennett, in British Columbia, and Dawson, in the Yukon Territory, and undertook to carry for the plaintiff, who was a Dawson merchant, certain goods from Bennett to Dawson. The company failed to deliver, and the plaintiff commenced an action for damages in the Yukon Territorial Court, and the general agent for the company was served with the writ and statement of claim. which, although intended to be issued against the defendant company, did not contain the defendant's proper title; the writ and statement of claim were amended, and, under an order for substituted service, rendered necessary on account of the manager's absence out of the jurisdiction, were served on Messrs. Wade & Aikman, general solicitors for the defendant company at Dawson. Under the order, a copy of the writ and statement of claim was mailed to the company at Victoria, and a copy posted in the office of the Clerk of the Court at Dawson. A statement of defence was filed by Wade & Aikman, who also attended on behalf of the defendant company on an examination for discovery of an agent of the company. At the trial no one appeared for the company, and judgment went by default.

The plaintiff then commenced an action in the Supreme Court of British Columbia on the Yukon judgment, claiming $761.50, being the amount of the judgment. and $169.00, the taxed costs, or in all $930.50.

The action was set down for trial at the Civil Sittings commencing at Victoria on 4th March, 1902. and on 13th February the plaintiff gave defendant notice as follows:

" Take notice that the plaintiff intends at the trial of this action to give in evidence as proof of a certain record, proceedings and judgment in the Territorial Court of the Yukon Territory in an action wherein the present plaintiff was plaintiff and the present defendants were defendants an exemplification or certified copy thereof purporting to be under the seal of the said Territorial Court of the Yukon Territory. "

At the trial, which came on before Drake, J., on 17th March, 1902, counsel for defendant objected that the notice was not sufficient under the Evidence Act to permit the admission of the exemplification of judgment on the grounds that (1.) It did not specify the documents proposed to be used. (2.) The documents proposed to be given in evidence did not comply with the notice. (3.) Having regard to the fact that the documents proposed to be used were from the files of the Court of the Yukon Territory, the notice was not given within a reasonable time as required by the statute. (4.) All the other documents attached to the exemplification of judgment were not admissible in evidence in any event.

He also tendered evidence that in the ordinary course of post it would require at least eighteen days to communicate between Dawson and Victoria.

His Lordship held that the notice was insufficient in point of time, but overruled the other objections, and he granted an adjournment till 4th April. Later in the day the trial was proceeded with, both counsel agreeing that the hearing should be treated as if it had taken place on 4th April.

Counsel for defendant tendered in evidence the articles and memorandum of association of the company for the purpose of shewing its constitution and the method of the appointment of its officers, but His Lordship refused to receive them in evidence.

At the conclusion of the trial His Lordship stated: "There will be judgment for the plaintiff. The validity of a foreign judgment can only be disputed under certain circumstances, but in the face of Mr. Carmody's evidence, it is perfectly clear that the solicitors in this case in the Yukon were sufficiently appointed. Their solicitor was in a position to bind them, and has done so with reference to this claim. There was no objection taken then to the position he occupied. Judgment will go for the plaintiff for the amount of the claim and costs."

The company appealed, and the appeal was argued at Vancouver on 16th April, 1902, before Hunter, C.J., and Irving and Martin, JJ.

Duff, K. C., for the appellant.

Peters, K. C. and *Griffin* for the respondent.

29TH JULY, 1902.

Hunter, C.J.: This is an action on a foreign judgment which was recovered between the same parties in the Yukon Territory Court on a contract to carry the plaintiff's goods from Bennett to Dawson, the defendants having failed to deliver a portion of the said goods. The general agent for the company in the Territory was served with a writ of summons, which, although intended to be issued against the defendant company, was in error issued against a non-existent company with a similar name, and another writ was then served, owing to his absence, under an order for substituted service, upon Messrs, Wade & Aikman, general solicitors for the defendants at Dawson. They filed a statement of defence, and attended on the agent's examination for discovery, but no one appearing for the company at the trial, judgment went by default,

It has been assumed during the present proceedings, and I think properly so, that the company was within the clutch of the Yukon Court for the purpose of litigation in the Territory, and accordingly the plaintiff is suing on a *prima facie* valid foreign judgment.

Mr. Duff, however, on behalf of the company, contends that the judgment should not be enforced for several reasons. One reason is that the judgment has been recovered on an *ultra vires* contract; this being so, the judgment can be of no greater validity than the contract on which it is based, and for this he cites *Great North-West Central Railway Co.* v. *Charlebois* (1899), A.C. 114.

The first question then to be determined is, can the defendants allege that the judgment is void as being based on a manifestly *ultra vires* contract, or, in other words, can it be impeached for manifest error? No doubt we must be careful not to infringe the doctrine that we are not to act as a court of appeal to review a foreign judgment, but I think that neither the comity of the provinces, nor the canons of international law, require us to blindly enforce a default judgment obtained in a sister jurisdic-

tion. I think, on the contrary, that we are entitled to scru-
tinize all the proceedings (compare what was done in
Houstoun v. *Marquis of Sligo* (1885), 29 Ch. D. 448),
and if manifest error going to the root of the judgment
appears, that we may, and should, decline to perpetuate
and enforce the error. The case of *Castrique* v. *Imrie*
(1870), L.R. 4 H.L. 414, is not, I think, an authority
against this proposition. That was a case where the
French Courts, including the final Court of Appeal, after
a stoutly contested litigation, gave a decision *in rem,*
under which the property, an English ship, passed to a
purchaser by a judicial sale. The defeated party sought to
impeach the buyer's title in England on the ground that
the French Courts had erred in their application of English
law. He failed, and the case is really only an instance of
the inflexible adherence of the English Courts to the rule
of international law, that a foreign adjudication *in rem*
will be enforced even if it proceeds on a mistaken view of
English law, which *quoad* the foreign tribunal is merely a
mistake of fact. The case in hand is not that of a decision
in rem emanating from the Courts of another nation after
real litigation, but is a judgment taken by default in another Canadian jurisdiction, in disregard, as it is alleged, of
the paramount law of the land, which both the Yukon and
British Columbia Courts are bound to obey and properly
administer. Moreover, it does not require argument to
shew that there is a radical distinction between a judgment
thus obtained and one which is the result of real litigation.
In the case of a default judgment, the judicial mind is not
necessarily applied to the matters in issue, but the machinery of the Court is employed at the will of the plaintiff
to record a judgment in his favour which may or may not
be null and void; nor will it do to say that the default in-
variably creates an estoppel, for there may be void judgments as well as void contracts. If the contract was *ultra
vires* in any sense, it was so in the strict legal sense, that
is to say, it was, and is, beyond the power of the company
either to make it or to ratify it at any time or by any mode; and obviously a contract which cannot under any circumstances be *intra vires,* is void and incapable of ratification. Then, if void, and incapable of ratification, no question of estoppel can arise so as to prevent the company
from saying that the contract is void, as otherwise it would

come to pass that the Company might be able to do by estoppel what it could not do by law. Nor can a valid judgment, taken either by compromise or consent, or default, or *ininvitum,* spring from a void contract: *ex nihilo nihil fit.* No doubt a judgment may be got on a contract as to which there may be a doubt as to whether it is void or not, yet so long as such judgment stood it would ordinarily be presumed that the judgment was valid; but I think this presumption cannot apply to a default judgment which purports to enforce a contract *ex facie* void by the paramount law of the land.

I think, then, that the defendants are entitled to challenge the validity of the judgment on the ground that it is manifestly erroneous, as being recovered on an *ex facie* void contract, and if they were right in this contention, then the judgment, in my opinion, should not be enforced. But I think that Mr Duff's contention that this judgment is based on an *ultra vires* contract, and that therefore it is void, must be rejected. If I caught his argument rightly, it was that the Province could not create a corporation with power to undertake contracts of carriage beyond the limits of the Province, or, at any rate, that if it was able to do so that it had not done so, and, therefore, that the company was not liable; but I think our decision must be against both propositions.

By the British North America Act the Province may exclusively make laws relating to "the incorporation of companies with provincial objects." Bearing in mind the rule that we must assign such full, large and reasonable meaning to the phrase as the language of the Act will allow, I think the true anithesis or phrase of exclusion is not "Dominion objects," or "extra-provincial objects," but "non-provincial objects," and that the phrase "provincial objects" includes both "intra-provincial" and "extra-provincial objects."

It is well known that provincial companies have for many years undertaken outside of their province of origin such contracts as that of loan and insurance, the investing of trust funds, the buying and selling of bonds and other obligations, the buying and selling of natural and manufactured products, etc., etc., and no authoritative judicial doubt, so far as I know, has ever been thrown on the validity of such contracts, which are enforced by and against the companies by the comity of the provinces, or by the comity of nations, as the case may be. What reason can be assigned why a provincial company should not have the power to buy and sell land, or to own and operate mines beyond the provincial boundaries if so authorized, and why can it not undertake extra-territorial contracts of carriage if not limited to intra-provincial contracts by its charter?

So to hold would not be necessarily to deny the Dominion similar power to create companies having similar objects: the only difference would be that a company if legally created by Dominion authority would operate in any province *ex proprio vigore,* while a company created by provincial authority would operate in any other province by the comity of the provinces, and both would operate outside of Canada by the comity of nations.

The power of the province to create a company is not, in my opinion, necessarily to be measured by the territorial test, but is at least co-extensive with, and apparently in some cases transcends the general powers of the province to deal with the given subject matter, assuming, of course, that it is capable of being dealt with by a corporation. The expression " provincial purposes, " in sub-section 2 of section 92, was considered by the Judicial Committee in *Dow* v. *Black* (1875), L.R. 6 P.C. 272, where it was held that the New Brunswick Legislature could authorize a municipality to bonus a railway which was to be built in the State of Maine to connect with a railway in New Brunswick. Can there be any doubt that it could also have created a company having as its object the procuring of the building of this railway by bonus, or otherwise? If not, then the question of territoriality is not necessarily the measure of the power to create a company.

But even if I am wrong in concluding that the province may create a company with power to undertake extra-territorial contracts of carriage, there is nothing to prevent such a company from securing the performance of the extra-territorial portion of the contracts by others. It is well settled by a long line of authorities, both in England and Canada, that a common carrier may undertake contracts of carriage to points beyond the line of his own vehicles, and that the consignor need not concern himself as to the ways or means. For instance, Watson, B., says in *Wilby* v. *West Cornwall Railway Co.* (1858), 2 H. & N. 703, at p. 711: "It would be strange if a company who undertook to carry goods from London to Paris were not liable for a loss at Boulogne because their line did not extend beyond Dover or Folkestone. The same way be said of the carriage of goods from London to Dublin, or from London to Barton, and from thence across the river Humber to Hull." And Channell, B., says, p. 712: "As to the objection that the carriage by sea was *ultra vires,* I do not at present see any distinction between carrying by sea and carrying on the line of another person." In fact, according to the leading judgment in *Doolan* v. *Midland Railway Co.* (1877), 2 App. Cas. 792, delivered by Lord Blackburn, it is useless for the company to set up a plea of *ultra vires.* He says, p. 806-7:

"I may here dispose of a point on which great reliance seems to have been placed by the pleaders and by some of the Judges below, though I think it was abandoned on the argument at your Lordships' Bar. The Midland Railway Company is not authorized by any Act of Parliament to own or work steamboats, and therefore, it is said that this company, if owning and working steamboats, would be doing so illegally, and therefore would be free from the restrictions imposed, it is said, only on those railway companies legally owning and working steamers. It is impossible to suppose that the Legislature intended those companies who were wrongfully working steamers to be in a better position than those who were rightfully working them; and the Act should not be so construed if the words permit of any other construction. And even if the words compelled this construction, I think the railway company could not set up its own wrong, against a plaintiff who contracted with the company in innocence and ignorance. Doolan and the Midland Railway Company are not *in pari delicto*. Doolan might perhaps set up against the Midland Railway Company that it was acting illegally, if it would in any way help him (which I do not think it in any way could), but it does not lie in the mouth of the railway company to set up its illegality, even if it would help it, which I do not think it would."

Moreover, Lord Blackburn's remarks lead to the conclusion that under such circumstances as exist here the plea is worse than useless as against an innocent plaintiff, because it virtually admits a tortious dealing with his property. Other cases which may be referred to in this connection are *Muschamp* v. *Lancaster and Preston Junction Railway Co.* (1841), 8 M. & W. 421; *Scothorn* v. *South Staffordshire Railway Co.* (1853), 8 Ex. 340; *Directors, &c., of the Bristol and Exeter Railway* v. *Collins* (1859), 7 H.L. Cas. 194, in which the Lords polled the opinions of the Judges before giving their decision; *Merchants' Despatch Transportation Co.* v. *Hatley* (1886), 14 S.C.R. 572; *The Grand Trunk Railway Co.* v. *McMillan* (1889), 16 S.C.R. 543; *The Northern Pacific Railway Co.* v. *Grant* (1895), 24 S.C.R. 546; *Hamilton* v. *Hudson's Bay Company* (1884), 1 B.C. (Pt. 2) 1, and in appeal at p. 176.

Another objection raised by Mr. Duff is that the judgment being by default is not final and conclusive within the meaning of that expression as applied to foreign judgments, by reason of the decision in *Nouvion* v. *Freeman* (1889), 15 App. Cas. 1, and Mr. Duff admitted that he was driven to contend that no judgment obtained by default is enforceable as a foreign judgment. This contention is, on the face of it, unreasonable, as of course all that a defendant, having no assets in the foreign jurisdiction, would have to do would be to ignore the process. I do not think that this is the effect of *Nouvion* v. *Freeman*. In that case the action was brought on a "remate" judgment, which, by the law of Spain, concludes nothing between the parties as the same, and, in fact, all questions may be agitated in another action, called a "plenary" action, in which it may happen that the "remate" judgment is for all purposes annulled, and had for nothing. Lord Herschell says, at p. 9:

"My Lords, I think that in order to establish that such a judgment has been pronounced it must be shewn that in the Court by which it was pronounced it conclusively, fi-

8

nally, and forever established the existence of the debt of which it is sought to be made conclusive evidence in this country, so as to make it *res judicata* between the parties. If it is not conclusive in the same Court which pronounced it, so that notwithstanding such a judgment the existence of the debt may between the same parties be afterwards contested in that Court, and upon proper proceedings being taken and such contest being adjudicated upon, it may be declared that there existed no obligation to pay the debt at all, then I do not think that a judgment which is of that character can be regarded as finally and conclusively evidencing the debt, and so entitling the person who has obtained the judgment to claim a decree from our Courts for the payment of that debt. "

It is true that under the system which prevails in the Yukon, as well as in our Courts, as also in England, a default judgment may be set aside either absolutely or on terms, but so long as it stands it is a final and conclusive adjudication that a debt is due by the defendant if the claim is for debt. It is also true that other expressions occur in the judgments which at first sight would seem to imply that a default judgment has not the finality necessary to make it an enforceable foreign judgment. but I think such expressions must be taken *secundum subjectam materiam*, as remarked by Lord Bramwell in *Sewell* v. *Burdick* (1884), 10 App. Cas. 74, at p. 104. For example, Lord Watson, says: " It must be final and unalterable in the Court which pronounced it. " Now, of course, this judgment is not unalterable in the wide sense. because it can be set aside by a Judge of the Yukon Court. but it is unalterable in the sense that it is conclusive while it stands, being for a fixed ascertained amount, and as Lord Bramwell says. " The judgment is of such a nature as would found an action of debt. " Again, Lord Herschell says, that " The judgment must be such as cannot thereafter be disputed. and can only be questioned in an appeal to a higher tribunal. " This also must be taken to mean so long as the judgment stands, as both the Lord Chancellor, and Lindley. L. J., in the case below, 37 Ch. D. 25-6, evidently considered that default judgments may possess the necessary degree of finality and conclusiveness, and if a default judgment taken as here by reason of the defendant not appearing at the trial (being equivalent to a judgment on the merits, according to Armour v. Bate [1891], 2 Q.B. 233) has not this quality, then it is difficult to see what kind of default judgment would have the quality required. In fact, if we were to say merely because a default judgment may be set aside by the Court in which it is taken that therefore it is of not final legal validity for the purpose of international suit, we would, in effect, be saying that the clearer the plaintiff's case the more useless his judgment would be. Take, for instance, the case of a defendant having no defence to a promissory note. Is it to be said that a plaintiff on getting a default judgment takes nothing by his judgment in the foreign jurisdiction? It seems to me that the law is, as stated by Erle, C.J., in *Vanquelin* v. *Bouard* (1863), 15 C.B.N.S. 341, cited by Mr. *Peters*, subject to the limitations as above explained laid down in *Nouvion* v. *Freeman* about the quality of the judgment, and subject to the qualification that it is not void for manifest error or for want of jurisdiction or fraud, or as being contrary to natural justice, or the like. He says, at p. 367-8, " I apprehend that every judgment of a foreign Court of competent jurisdiction is valid, and may be the foundation of an action in our Courts, though subject to the contingency, that, by adopting a certain course, the party against whom the judgment is obtained might cause it to be vacated or set aside. But, until that course has been pursued, the judgment remains in full force and capable of being sued upon. "

Another objection raised was that the defendants had not been given long enough notice of the plaintiff's intention to put in an exemplification of the Yukon proceedings. The notice was given on the 13th of February, 1902, for the trial which commenced on the 17th of March. The learned trial Judge, considering the time insufficient, granted an adjournment at the instance of the plaintiff until the 4th of April; but if the original time was insufficient, then perhaps in strictness it should have been neglected in fixing the time of the adjournment. At the same time, assuming that there was error in this, the defendants knew as early as December, 1901, that they were being sued on the Yukon judgment, and on February 5th, 1902, that the plaintiff was going to trial, and they must also have known that the proper way for the plaintiff to prove his case was by producing an exemplification of the proceedings, so that they are not in a position to say that they have been taken· by surprise. At any rate, I think the error, if there was any, is immaterial, as I am unable to see how it caused any substantial miscarriage of justice.

I think the appeal must be dismissed with costs.

Irving, J., concurred with Hunter, C. J.

Martin, J.: First, the counsel for the appellant urges that the notice of intention to produce copies of certain documents under sections 11 and 20 is not sufficient either in point of certainty or in time; to which it is answered that no notice is necessary because what was tendered is an exemplification of the record as distinguished from a copy. It is stated in Stephen's Digest of Evidence, 5th Ed., p. 85, that " An exemplification is equivalent to the original document exemplified," and an exemplification is defined to be " a copy of a record set out either under the Great Seal or under the Seal of a Court." And in Taylor on Evidence, 9th Ed., 1,534, *et seq.*, the matter is fully considered, and it is stated that " exemplifications are proved by mere production, as the Judges are bound to take judicial notice of the seals attached to them; and are deemed of higher credit than examined copies, being presumed to have undergone a more critical examination." See also to the same effect, *Tilton* v. *Mc-Kay* (1874), 24 U.C.C.P. 94; Tomlin's Law Dictionary. Vol. 1, Article, Evidence, 1; Sweet's Law Dictionary. 341. Applying the foregoing to the document now before us, which is sealed with the seal of the Territorial Court of the Yukon Territory, I am of opinion that it is an exemplification of the record and proceedings therein mentioned, and, consequently, the notice contended for was not necessary.

It appears from paragraph 1 of the statement of claim of the action commenced in this Court that " the defendants are a duly incorporated company, incorporated under the Companies' Acts of the Province of British Co-

lumbia," and it further appears from the affidavit of
Henry E. Ridley, filed in the Territorial Court of the
Yukon Territory on the 26th day of October, 1900, that
at the time of the order to amend the writ and for substitutional service thereof, obtained the same day, there was
no local manager of the defendant company residing in
the Yukon Territory. From the said affidavit of Ridley,
and from the statement of claim filed in the said Territorial Court, it further appears that the defendant company at the time of the contract sued on "operated as a
transportation company between Bennett, in the Province of British Columbia, and Dawson, in the Yukon Territory," and that the cause of action arose out of the failure of the said company to carry certain goods between
the said points of Bennett and Dawson according to a contract made in September, 1899. Though not so alleged in
the statement of claim, it appears from the examination
for discovery of Daniel Carmody that this contract was
made at Bennett, in this Province, where the defendant
company had a local manager, with another local manager at Dawson, Y.T., the head office being at Victoria. It
further appears from the evidence that before the said
order for substitutional service was made the company
had no representative in the Yukon, and had ceased to
carry on any business in that Territory, not having done
so since Daniel Carmody, who acted for it, had left in the
last of August or first of September, 1900. Under such
circumstances, the order for substitutional service has no
effect, and may be disregarded: *Sirdar Gurdyal Singh* v.
Rajah of Faridkote (1894), A.C. 670. Though no appearance was entered to the writ on behalf of the defendant company, yet a statement of defence, so-called, was
filed on the 1st of March, 1900, by a firm of advocates purporting to act for it, and who did so act in some interlocu-
tary proceedings, but not at the trial held on the 11th of
July, 1901, whereat it was not represented by counsel. The
statement of defence in effect admits the first paragraph
of the statement of claim, and the question as to whether
or not the contract sued on was *ultra vires* was not raised,
though it was and is one of importance to the shareholders
of the company. It does not appear how the said advocates came to act for the company. Carmody says he has
no recollection of giving any instructions with regard to

this suit at all, though it is likely he was served with the original writ before it was amended, and before he left the Yukon, and gave that original writ to the advocates who were also solicitors for his company in all other suits against the company then pending. But there is nothing in his evidence, or in that of the president of the company, to shew that any instructions were given in regard to the amended writ, which alone affects this action, the original writ having been defective because of the misnomer of the defendant company. Nevertheless, counsel for the appellant stated that he does not raise the point that the said advocates did not *de facto* act for the company at Dawson, but he does contend that under such circumstances there is here what is tantamount to the obtaining of judgment by consent on an *ultra vires* contract, and it is urged that this defence should have been raised, and that the consent not to raise it was illegal, and that the company should not now be debarred from setting it up in this Court.

On the facts, I can come to no other conclusion than that what was done in the Territorial Court was tantamount to obtaining a judgment by consent. What then is the effect of one so obtained against a corporation? It is argued that it was the duty of the company to defend that point, and if it does not, the judgment is not binding, and the case of *Great North-West Central Railway Co.* v. *Charlebois* [1899], A.C. 114, 124, is relied upon. It is there laid down by the Judicial Committee of the Privy Council that " such a judgment cannot be of more validity than the invalid contract on which it was founded." The views on this point of the Chancellor of Ontario, who tried the case, are given at pp. 115-116, as follows:

" A Company created by Act of Parliament has no right to spend a penny of its money except in the manner provided by the Act. The expenditure of money for a purpose unauthorized by the Act is *ultra vires* absolutely. Such an expenditure cannot be validated by promoters, directors, or shareholders for the time being, nor can it be sanctioned by the Company itself. It follows that, if the act is beyond the power of the Company to do or ratify, no judgment obtained by the consent of the Company, treating it as authorized, can remove its invalidity, for the virtue of such judgment rests merely on the agreement of the parties, and the incapacity to do the act involves the incapacity to consent that it be treated as valid. I think, therefore, that the judgment by consent obtained by the defendant Charlebois against the company (upon which depends the subsequent judgment *in invitum*) forms no obstacle to the plaintiffs if the transaction impeached is inherently *ultra vires."*

I note that in Brice on Ultra Vires (1893), 625, it is stated that, " In New Zealand, however, it has been explicitly decided that a judgment, obtained on a compromise of an action agains a corporation to enforce an *ultra vires* agreement, was void. The subject was thoroughly discussed, and the opinion of the Court is valuable."

The question then arises, is this contract *ultra vires.'* In support of the affirmative, the appellant's counsel contends that under section 92, sub-section 10 (*a.*) of the British North America Act, a provincial company such as this has no power to undertake the business of common carriers between this province and the Yukon Territory. Certain general propositions arising out of sections 91 and 92 of the British North America Act are given at p. 617 of Lefroy on Legislative Power in Canada, and the subject is discussed generally in the succeeding pages down to 644. At p. 637, it is stated " Although the provincial power to incorporate is confined to ' companies with provincial objects,' a corporation, though existing only within the limits of the sovereignty which created it, may, as a general rule, act elsewhere through agents, if the laws of other countries permit." In our Canadian Courts the point has of later years been more or less considered in the cases of *Howe Machine Co.* v. *Walker* (1874), 35 U.C.Q.B. 37; *Ulrich* v. *National Insurance Co.* (1877), 42 U.C.Q.B. 141, 158; *Clarke* v. *Union Fire Insurance Co.* (1883), 10 P.R. 313, 3 Cartw. 335; *Loranger* v. *Colonial Building and Investment Association* (1883), 3 Cartw. 133, 136; *Colonial Building and Investment Association* v. *Attorney-General of Quebec* (1883), 9 App. Cas. 157, 3 Cartw. 118; and *Canadian Pacific Railway Co.* v. *Western Union Telegraph Co.*

(1889), 17 S.C.R. 151. In the last mentioned case many earlier decisions are reviewed, and it is laid down at pp. 155-6, that " the comity of nations distinctly recognizes the right of foreign incorporated companies to carry on business and make contracts outside of the country in which they are incorporated, if consistent with the purposes of the corporation, and not prohibited by its charter, and not inconsistent with the local laws of the country in which the business was carried on, subject always to the restrictions and burthens imposed by the laws enforced therein; for there can be no doubt that a state may prohibit foreign corporations from transacting any business whatever, or it may permit them to do so upon such proper terms and conditions as it may prescribe... In the absence, as in this case, of any prohibition or restriction, no intention to exclude can be presumed." This general principle, as above stated, had already been recognized, as I understand the decision of the Judicial Committee of the Privy Council. in *Bateman* v. *Service* (1881), 6 App. Cas. 386 (though that case was not brought to the attention of the Supreme Court of Canada) wherein it was decided that a foreign company could carry on business and make contracts by its agent in Western Australia, though it had not complied with the provisions of the Joint Stock Companies' Ordinance Act, 1858, which only applied to companies incorporated within that colony. In Brice on Ultra Vires (1893), it is stated at p. 6, that

" A corporation being entirely fictitious and the creation of law, it might fairly be argued that it can exist only where the power which called it into being exists to give continued vitality to the artificial creation. Doubts have from time to time been expressed as to whether the English Courts at all, and if at all, how far, can recognize foreign corporations and their incidents. Some of these doubts may remain, but in so far as relates to legal proceedings, it is since the Judicature Acts quite settled that foreign corporations, even though not incorporated according to English law, may sue and be sued in English Courts to judgment, whether resident in England or not."

And after a consideration of certain apparent distinctions between the law of England and that of the United States. the learned author arrives at the following conclusion, p.

8 : " The views of the United States Courts so expressed and qualified, are probably substantially, if not exactly, the same as those held'in this country. "

In regard to the " undertaking " of the company within the meaning of said sub-section 10 (a.), the memorandum and articles of association are not before us, so our information on that point is confined to the material already noticed ; but we are entitled to assume that the transportation business as carried on was not inconsistent with the purposes for which the company was formed, even though, as a matter of fact, the jurisdiction and authority of the Provincial Legislature cannot extend beyond the boundaries of this province, no matter what wider powers were on paper taken or claimed by the company on incorporation.   " The true question is, not whether one state can legally grant powers of contracting, etc., in another state, but to what extent does one state recognize the acts of another? " — Lindley on Companies, 6th Ed., 1,222, wherein, it may be observed, there is a strange omission to refer to the later Canadian authorities above cited, though the earlier ones are mentioned in note (1).

I should perhaps note that it was contended at the Bar that if the defendants were so operating as a transportation company, it should be regarded as an " undertaking... extending beyond the limits of this Province " within the meaning of sub-section 10 (a.), and this contention was not, as I understand it, disputed.   It was, however, suggested that the contract, though a " through one, " should be looked at as one to act for a certain part of the route as forwarders only, and to deliver the shipment to others for transportation beyond this province.   It may be that if this were the fact that would afford an additional reason for not holding the contract to be *ultra vires,* but in my opinion the fair construction of the allegations already noticed is that the company itself undertook the carriage for the whole distance, and so I think the question should be considered on that basis, and I have come to the conclusion that to hold it to be an *ultra vires* contract would be contrary to the authorities above quoted, and others cited at Bar, which I have also consulted.

Lastly, it is urged that because under r. 256 of the Judicature Ordinance in force in the Yukon Territory, the judgment sued on may now be, it is contended, set aside despite the lapse of the prescribed time of fifteen days, according to the views expressed by the Court of Appeal in *Bradshaw* v. *Warlow* (1886), 32 Ch. D. 403, therefore it is not final and unalterable as required by *Nouvion* v. *Freeman* (1889), 15 App. Cas. 1, 13-4, but is still inconclusive and open.

A large number of cases were cited on both sides, but in my opinion the point is exactly determined by the case of *Vanquelin* v. *Bouard* (1863), 15 C.B.N.S. 341, 367-8, wherein Chief Justice Erle says, " I apprehend that every judgment of a foreign Court of competent jurisdiction is valid, and may be the foundation of an action in our Courts, though subject to the contingency, that, by adopting a certain course, the party against whom the judgment is obtained might cause it to be vacated or set aside. But until that course has been pursued, the judgment remains in full force and capable of being sued upon. "

Applying these expressions to the case at Bar the contention must fail. The appeal should be dismissed with costs.

Appeal dismissed.

Solicitors for the Appellants: Bodwell & Duff.

Solicitors for the Respondent: Tupper, Peters & Griffin.

[IN THE HIGH COURT OF JUSTICE FOR ONTARIO.]

BLACK ET AL.

v.

IMPERIAL BOOK CO., LTD., ET AL.

BEFORE STREET, J.

Copyright—Encyclopaedia—Primâ facie proof of proprietorship—Entry at Stationer's Hall—License to print and sell—Foreign reprints—Notice to Commissioners of Customs—Imperial Acts in force in Canada—Imp. 39-40 Vict. ch. 36, sec. 152—Imp. 5-6 Vict. ch. 45, secs. 17, 18, 19.

The defendants, the Imperial Book Company, imported into Canada large numbers of an American reprint of the plaintiffs' encyclopaedia, which plaintiffs maintained was an infringement of their copyright. They had registered the publication pursuant to 11th section of the Copyright Act of 1842, and produced and gave in evidence a certificate of the entry.

Held, the production of the certificate was all that was necessary to make out a *primâ facie* proprietorship in the copyright of an encyclopaedia under secs. 18 and 19.

Held, also, that sec. 152 of the Imperial Customs Law Consolidation Act, 1876, 39-40 Vict., ch. 36, which requires notice to be given to the Commissioners of Customs of copyright and of the date of its expiration, is not in force in Canada, despite that, in Part IV. of the appendix to vol. III. of the Revised Statutes of Ontario, 1897, a statement to the contrary appears.

Semble (such a notice would be invalidated by), an erroneous statement of the date of the expiration of the copyright.

The plaintiffs, in consideration of a large sum of money, by an agreement in writing, gave certain other persons the exclusive right to print and sell the publication in question for a period terminating four years before the expiration of the plaintiffs' copyright, and agreed to deliver to them the plates used in the publishing and not to publish or announce a new edition until the expiration of such period. The other parties agreed to sell only at certain prices, not to alter the text of the book, and on the expiration of the period mentioned, to deliver up any unsold copies and all the plates used in printing them. The plaintiffs expressly reserved the copyright to themselves.

Held, the agreement must be construed as a license merely and not as an assignment, and need not be registered pursuant to section 19 of 5-6 Vict. ch. 45 (Imp.).

Action by the owners of the copyright in the 9th edition of the Encyclopædia Britannica and the licensees of exclusive rights of sale, to restrain the importation and sale of an edition printed in the United States. Street, J., heard the case at the Toronto Non-Jury Sittings on September 23rd, 1902.

The facts appear in the judgment.

W. Barwick, K.C., and *J. H. Moss*, for the plaintiffs.

S. H. Blake, K.C., and *W. E. Raney*, for the defendants, the Imperial Bank Company.

A. Mills, for the defendant Hales.

January 26, 1903. STREET, J.:—The present action was begun on September 18th, 1901, and it appears that the firm of Hales & Sparrow, who had been importing into Canada an American reprint of the plaintiffs' Encyclopædia,, had, a little more than a year before the issue of the writ in the present action, formed the Imperial Book Co., Limited, who are defendants in this action, along with James Hales, and that upon the formation of that company it took over their business, and since it did so, Hales & Sparrow have not, nor has the defendant James Hales, imported the book in question. He has pleaded the 26th section of the Copyright Act, which requires actions for breaches of it to be brought within one year, and I think there is therefore nothing proved against him for which he can be held liable. He is the president of the defendant company, and anything he has done within the year has been done in that and not in his individual capacity. The Imperial Book Co., Ltd., have, however, continued to import large numbers of copies of the reprint since September 1st, 1900.

A certificate purporting to be signed by the registering officer appointed by the Stationers' Company, pursuant to the 11th section of the Copyright Act of 1842, is produced and given in evidence, setting forth a copy of an entry made in the Book of Registry of Copyrights and Assignments kept at the Hall of the Stationers' Company, pursuant to the said section, which is as follows:—

"Time of making the entry. April 5th, 1875.

"Title of book. The Encyclopædia Britannica: a dictionary of arts, sciences and general literature. Ninth edition.

"Name of publisher and place of publication. Adam & Charles Black, Edinburgh.

"Name and place of abode of the proprietor of the copyright. Adam & Charles Black, Edinburgh.

"Date of first publication. January 30th, 1875."

This certificate is given by the plaintiffs in evidence as *primâ facie* proof, under the 11th section of the Act, of their proprietorship of the copyright.

It is objected by the defendants that it is necessary for the plaintiffs to prove *dehors* this certificate that they are in fact proprietors of the copyright, because under the 18th section proprietorship in the copyright of an encyclopedia is only acquired by the proprietor of the work under the circumstances set forth in that section. I am of opinion, however, that the production of the certified copy of the entry in the Book of Registry at Stationers' Hall is all that is necessary to make out a *primâ facie* proprietorship in the copyright of an encyclopædia under secs. 18 and 19, as it is under sec. 11 to make out a *primâ facie* proprietorship in the copyright of a book: for this facility of proof is one of the benefits of the registration at Stationers' Hall referred to in the 19th section of the Act.

A number of English cases were cited by counsel for
the defendants in support of his argument that the production of a copy of the entry at Stationers' Hall did not
do away with the necessity of proving by direct evidence,
other than the copy of the entry, the facts, which, by the
18th section of the Copyright Act of 1842, Imp. 5-6 Vict.,
c. 45, are conditions precedent to the vesting of the copyright in one who is not the author. It certainly is a matter
of some surprise to find so little reference in the cases upon
the subject to the effect given by the statute to copies of
the entry at Stationers' Hall as *primâ facie* evidence of
the proprietorship of the copyright. In the case of *Sweet*
v. *Benning* (1855), 16 C.B. 459, in which copyright was
claimed in the weekly paper called *The Jurist,* under sec.
18 of the Copyright Act, Imp. 5-6 Vict., ch. 45, by the proprietors of the paper, who were not the authors of the
articles in it, it is stated by Mr. Lush, one of the counsel
for the plaintiffs, with whom was Mr. Sergeant Byles, that
the entry of the paper at Stationers' Hall was, by the 11th
section of the Act, made *primâ facie* evidence of the proprietorship of copyright, and that the question in the case,
therefore, was whether there was anything in the case to
rebut the *primâ facie* proof. This view of the statute
seems to have been accepted by the opposing counsel and
the Court, and the case turned upon the inferences to be
drawn from the admitted facts. The other cases which
were cited do not appear to contain anything inconsistent
with this statement of the plaintiff's counsel in *Sweet* v.
Benning.

The earliest case cited is *Brown* v. *Cooke,* 16 L.J.N.S.
Ch. 140, decided December 23rd, 1846, in which a motion
for an injunction was made before V.-C. Wigram by the
registered proprietor of a newspaper to restrain the pub-

lication in another newspaper of articles appearing in the plaintiff's paper. The injunction was refused upon the ground that it did not appear upon the plaintiff's affidavit that the articles copied by the defendants, which had been supplied by various writers to the editor of the plaintiff's paper, whose contract with the plaintiff required him to supply the articles himself, had been paid for by the plaintiff. There was nothing to the contrary in the affidavit, but the Vice-Chancellor thought that it was necessary upon a motion for injunction that the plaintiff should in his affidavit set out his title fully, and so he refused the injunction.

The Trade Auxiliary Company v. *Jackson*, 4 Times L.R. 130, was a case of the same sort, and was also decided upon a motion for injunction.

There the defendants had copied from an unregistered circular, published by third parties with the consent of the plaintiffs, being itself a copy of the plaintiffs' newspaper. Mr. Justice Kay, before whom the motion was made, expresses doubt as to the right of the plaintiffs to succeed under these circumstances: but he adds that there is the further objection that the plaintiffs have not upon their material brought themselves within sec. 18 of the Copyright Act, Imp. 5-6 Vict., ch. 45, and he refused the injunction.

The principles which were acted upon in refusing these two injunctions seem to be thoroughly sound: they are the same as those laid down by Lord Chancellor Cottenham in *Spottiswoode* v. *Clarke* (1846), 2 Ph. 154, 156, and are well worth repeating here. He says: "I have often expressed my opinion, that, unless a case of this kind, depending upon a legal right, is very clear, it is the duty of the Court to take care that the right be ascertained

before it exercises its jurisdiction by injunction. The first
question to be determined is as to the legal right, and if
the Court doubts about that, it may commit great injustice
by interfering until that question has been decided.''

In the two cases to which I have referred, the Judges
who refused the injunctions asked for were not satisfied
to grant injunctions upon a mere *primâ facie* case.

In *The Bishop of Hereford* v. *Griffin*, 16 Sim. 190, and
in *Trade Auxiliary Company* v. *Middlesborough and District Tradesmen's Protection Association*, 40 Ch.D. 425,
and in *Aflalo* v. *Lawrence & Bullen (Limited)*, [1902] 1
Ch. 264, and in *Coote* v. *Judd* (1883), 23 Ch.D. 727, the
actual facts upon which the claim to copyright under the
18th section was based were before the Court, and were,
of course, acted upon without reference to the *primâ facie*
case.

In *Walter* v. *Howe*, 17 Ch.D. 708, which was an action
brought on behalf of *The Times* newspaper for republication of a life of Lord Beaconsfield which appeared in its
columns, there was no registration of the newspaper at
Stationers' Hall. In *Lamb* v. *Evans*, [1892] 3 Ch. 462,
the determination was of a question not arising under the
Copyright Act. In *Collingridge* v. *Emmott*, 57 L.T.N.S.
864, the plaintiff's registration at Stationers' Hall of the
work in question was held to be defective, and so no rights
could have been claimed under a copy of it. *Richardson*
v. *Gilbert*, 1 Sim. N.S. 336, seems to have involved merely
a question as to the sufficiency of the allegations in the
Bill and not any question of proof.

In the present case the plaintiffs Adam & Charles Black
assert in their statement of claim that they are proprietors
of the copyright in the Encyclopædia Britannica: the
defendants deny it, and the plaintiffs produce a copy of

the entry in the book at Stationers' Hall as evidence of
the right they claim.   There is no evidence on either side
upon this point except this copy, and I think that is sufficient to establish the plaintiffs' right.

Their title to the copyright being therefore established,
the first objection on the part of the defendants to their
right to maintain this action is that the effect of an agreement entered into between Messrs. Adam & Charles Black
and their co-plaintiffs the Clarke Company, Limited, dated
February 21st, 1899, was to transfer the copyright to that
company: that Messrs. Adam & Charles Black cannot
maintain the action because they have assigned the copyright to the Clarke Company: and that the Clarke Company cannot maintain the action because they have not
registered the assignment at Stationers' Hall.

I have examined the agreement in question, and I am
of opinion that it is not to be treated as an assignment
but merely as a license.   In this agreement Messrs. A. & C.
Black are called the publishers, and the Clarke Company
are called the company: by the agreement the publishers
agree that until December 31st, 1912, the company shall
have the exclusive right to print and sell the 9th edition
of the Encyclopædia Britannica, and for the purpose of
enabling them to print it the publishers agree to deliver
to the company the existing plates used in its publication:
and not to publish or announce the publication of a 10th
edition of the work until after December 31st, 1912.   The
company on its part agrees not to alter the text of the work,
and that the style of paper, printing and binding shall
remain unaltered: that they will pay £40,000 to the publishers for the rights acquired under the agreement: that
they will not sell any copy of the work under £15 either
in Great Britain or America, and that they will as soon as

possible after December 31st, 1912, deliver to the publishers any unsold copies of the work and all the plates used in printing it then in their possession. The company further agrees that they will not knowingly issue any advertisement of and concerning the work of a nature likely to do injury to the publishers either in their business or as the owners of the copyright of the work. Authority is also given to the company to institute in the names of the publishers any proceedings they may deem proper in respect of any breach of copyright of the work.

The duration of the copyright was forty-two years, from January 30th, 1875, the date of first publication—that is to say, until January 30th, 1917. The rights given to the company under the agreement will therefore expire nearly four years before the expiration of the copyright, and the publishers have provided in the agreement with much care for the protection and preservation of their interest in the work by reason of any alteration by the company in its substance of form or selling value.

They have expressly reserved the copyright to themselves, and this reservation is entirely consistent, it appears to me, with the full enjoyment by the company of the rights given them. The agreement therefore must, in my opinion, be construed as a license merely and not as an assignment: *Stevens* v. *Benning* (1854), 1 K. & J. 168; *Hole* v. *Bradbury* (1879), 12 Ch.D. 886; *Cooper* v. *Stephens*, [1895] 1 Ch. 567; *Trade Auxiliary Company* v. *Middlesborough and District Tradesmen's Protection Association*, 40 Ch.D. 425, at p. 434; MacGillivray on Copyright, pp. 80, 81, 82.

It is further objected that the plaintiffs are not entitled to the relief they ask, because the edition of the Encyclopædia Britannica sold by the defendants was printed in the United States and imported into Canada:

and the plaintiffs, it is alleged, did not give notice to the
Commissioners of Customs of the existence of their copyright, and of the proper date of its expiration, as required
by sec. 152 of the Imperial Customs Laws Consolidation
Act, 39 & 40 Vict., ch. 36.

If that Act were in force in Canada, I think it would
be an answer to the plaintiffs' claim in this action, because
under sec. 152 of it, it is expressly declared that foreign
reprints of books entitled to British copyright are not
prohibited from being imported into the British possessions unless notice has been given to the Commissioners
of Customs of the existence of the copyright and the date
when it will expire. Now, it appears from the Blue Book
produced by the plaintiffs as evidence of the giving of this
notice, that the date of the expiration of the copyright is
stated as being "January 30th, 1924." Assuming that
the fact of the giving of the notice is sufficiently proved
by the production of this Blue Book, which is denied by
the defendants, the objection remains that the date given
is wrong. The first publication of the first number of the
Encyclopædia as registered at Stationers' Hall was January 30th, 1875, and the duration of the copyright is
forty-two years from that date, so that the proper date of
expiration is January 30th, 1917. An erroneous statement
of the date of the expiration of the copyright in the notice
is clearly not a compliance with the condition imposed by
sec. 152 of the Customs Act, and therefore, as I have said,
if that Act were in force in Canada, the objection would,
it seems to me, be fatal to the plaintiffs' right to recover:
because sec. 152 being an enactment *in pari materiâ* with
sec. 17 of the Copyright Act of 1842, must be read in connection with it, and as an essential part of the legislation
upon the subject.

In considering whether sec. 152 of the Customs Consolidation Act of 1876 is in force in Canada, I find at the outset that in part IV. of the appendix to vol. III. of the Revised Statutes of Ontario, 1897, headed, "Table of Imperial statutes . . . appearing to be in force in Canada *ex proprio vigore* at the end of 1901," this sec. 152 of 39 & 40 Vict., ch. 36, is included: and this expression of opinion on the part of the learned commissioners who prepared the table, although not binding upon me, and not accompanied by their reasons, has made me hesitate a good deal before arriving, as I have done, at a different conclusion.

Section 152 is as follows: "Any books wherein the copyright shall be subsisting, first composed or written or printed in the United Kingdom, and printed or reprinted in any other country, shall be and are hereby absolutely prohibited to be imported into the British Possessions abroad: provided always that no such books shall be prohibited to be imported as aforesaid, unless the proprietor of such copyright, or his agent, shall have given notice in writing to the Commissioners of Customs that such copyright subsists, and in such notice shall have stated when the copyright will expire: And the said Commissioners shall cause to be made and transmitted to the several ports in the British Possessions abroad, from time to time to be publicly exposed there, lists of books respecting which such notice shall have been duly given, and all books imported contrary thereto shall be forfeited: but nothing herein contained shall be taken to prevent Her Majesty from exercising the powers vested in her by the 10th and 11th Vict., ch. 95, intituled 'An Act to amend the law relating to the protection in the Colonies of works entitled to copyright in the United Kingdom' to suspend in certain cases such prohibition."

This section, standing by itself, no doubt extends to Canada: the previous section, however, being sec. 151, seems to me, when taken along with the interpretation clause, sec. 284, to exclude the Act from applying to Canada. In the interpretation clause the words "Customs Acts" when used in the Act are declared to "mean and include this and all or any other Acts or Act relating to the Customs" when not inconsistent with the context or subject-matter. Then by sec. 151 it is provided as follows:

"151. The Customs Acts shall extend to and be of full force and effect in the several British possessions abroad, except . . . as to any such possession as shall by local Act or ordinance have provided, or may hereafter with the sanction and approbation of Her Majesty and her successors, make entire provision for the management and regulation of the customs of any such possession, or make in like manner express provisions in lieu or variation of any of the clauses of the said Act for the purposes of such posssesion."

The late Province of Canada was brought clearly within this exception by the statute of the Province, 10 & 11 Vict., ch. 31, by which, in pursuance of the authority conferred by the Imperial statute, 9 & 10 Vict., ch. 94, the application of the Imperial customs theretofore imposed was terminated, and entire provision was made for the present and future regulation of the customs of the Province by the Provincial Legislature. It was provided by the Provincial Act, 10 & 11 Vict., ch. 31, that it should not take effect until a proclamation should be issued by Her Majesty, and this proclamation was made on 18th March, 1848, bringing the Provincial Act into force on April 5th, 1848: see *Canada Gazette* for 1848, p. 5197.

I can find no reason in the context or subject-matter

of sec. 152 of the Customs Consolidation Act requiring
me to say that it ought to be held to be in force in Canada
notwithstanding sec. 151, under the circumstances above
set forth; and I am therefore obliged to conclude that it
never was in force here, because Canada had with the
assent of Her Majesty assumed entire control of its own
customs before the Customs Consolidation Act of 1876
was passed.

The elimination of the provisions of sec. 152 of the
Customs Consolidation Act from the consideration of the
plaintiffs' rights leaves sec. 17 of the Copyright Act of
1842, Imp. 5-6 Vict., ch. 45, as governing them as against
the defendants. I leave sec. 15 of the Act out of the question, because that section applies only to books subject to
British copyright which are unlawfully printed in the
British dominions, and does not extend to books subject
to British copyright which are printed in foreign countries.

Section 17 declares "that it shall not be lawful for any
person authorized by him, to import into any part of the
United Kingdom, or into any other part of the British
dominions, for sale or hire, any printed book first composed or written or printed and published in any part of
the said United Kingdom wherein there shall be copyright,
and reprinted in any country or place whatsoever out of
the British Dominions; and if any person not being such
proprietor or person authorized as aforesaid, shall import
or bring or cause to be imported or brought, for sale or
hire, any such printed book into any part of the British
dominions, contrary to the true intent and meaning of this
Act, or shall knowingly sell, publish or expose to sale or
let to hire, or have in his possession for sale or hire any
such book" . . . under penalty of forfeiture, etc.

It has been proved beyond question in the present action that the defendants, without authority from the plaintiffs, the proprietors of the copyright in the ninth edition of the Encyclopædia Britannica, have imported into Canada for sale, and have there sold large quantities of a copy or reprint of that work which have been printed in the United States.

The defendants set up in their answers that the English Copyright Act of 1842, Imp. 5-6 Vict., ch. 45, is not in force in Canada, and that the plaintiffs can only claim such rights as are conferred by Canadian statutes upon them. This objection is, however, one which has been determined adversely to the view suggested by the defendants, and I am unable to entertain it: *Routledge* v. *Low* (1868), L.R. 3 H.L. 100; *Smiles* v. *Belford*, 1 A.R. 436; *Morang* v. *Publishers' Syndicate*, 32 O.R. 393.

The next objection taken is that the plaintiffs have disentitled themselves to recover by reason of delay amounting to acquiescence. I can find, however, in the evidence no definite statement of anything of the kind. By reason of the agreement between Messrs. A. & C. Black and their co-plaintiffs, the latter were the persons most directly concerned in enquiring into the acts of persons infringing the copyright, and we have the statement of Mr. H. E. Hooper, the managing director of the Clarke Company, that he did not know that the defendants' reprint was being sold extensively in Canada until just before the defendants were notified of the plaintiffs' intention to proceed against them. It is, of course, also to be borne in mind that the degree of delay which might stand in the way of the success of a motion for an interlocutory injunction would by no means necessarily be an answer to an action: see *Hogg* v. *Scott*, L.R. 18 Eq. 444; and here whatever delay has taken place in the part of the Blacks after they seem to have heard reports of the sale of pirated copies in Canada, are far from sufficient to establish acquiescence on their part.

I think the plaintiffs have established their right to an injunction perpetually restraining the defendants, the Imperial Book Co., Limited, their servants and agents, from importing into Canada any copies of the Encyclopædia Britannica, ninth edition, or of any parts thereof printed in any country outside the British dominions which infringe the copyright of the plaintiffs Adam & Charles Black; and ordering the said defendants, the Imperial Book Co., Limited, to deliver up for cancellation all and any copies so printed in their possession. The plaintiffs are also entitled to an account of the profits realized by the defendants, the Imperial Book Co., Limited, from the sale of any such copies within one year before the commencement of this action. This is an equitable remedy to which the plaintiffs' seem entitled under the authorities, although it is not specially given by the Act, because the importation by the defendants is declared to be unlawful, and the plaintiffs have been injured by their unlawful act: *Colburn* v. *Simms* (1843), 2 Hare 543; McLaughlin on Copyright, p. 86; Copinger on Copyright, 3rd ed., p. 301.

The defendants, the Imperial Book Co., Limited, must also pay the costs of the action to the hearing inclusive.

Should the plaintiffs require it, there will be a reference to ascertain the profits realized by the Imperial Book Co., Limited, and the costs of the reference will be reserved.

The action will be dismissed as against the defendant Hales. He has, however, made large profits out of the sale of the unlawfully imported copies of the plaintiffs' book, and escapes accounting for them by pleading the statute, and under the circumstances I think he should pay his own costs.

Editor's Note:—

An appeal to the Court of Appeal has been taken from the above judgment and is now standing for argument. Notes on the case are deferred until delivery of the judgment of the Court of Appeal.

[IN THE HIGH COURT OF JUSTICE FOR
ONTARIO.]

IN RE BERGMAN

v.

ARMSTRONG.

BEFORE FALCONBRIDGE, C.J., K.B.

Bankruptcy and insolvency—Assignments and preferences—Establishment of claim—Inferior Court—R.S.O. (1897),·ch. 147, sec. 22 (1).

An action for a declaration of the right of a creditor to rank against an insolvent estate, brought under R.S.O. (1897), ch. 147, sec. 22 (1), cannot be maintained in the Division Court.

In an action in the 1st Division Court of Middlesex the plaintiff endeavoured to establish his claim for $56.55 against the setate of one George Bergman, who had made an assignment for the benefit of creditors under the Assignments and Preferences Act, R.S.O. 1897, ch. 147.

A motion for prohibition was made on the ground that the Division Court has no jurisdiction.

W. H. Blake, K.C., for the defendant.

William Davidson, for the plaintiff.

December 6, 1902. FALCONBRIDGE, C.J.:—*Perry v. Laughlin*, decided by my brother Ferguson in July, 1901, seems to cover the very point in question.

As that judgment was not reported, and as colour seems to be lent to the plaintiff's contention by the appearance for the first time in the revision of 1897 of the words (in ch. 147, sec. 22), "or summons in case the action is brought in a Division Court," the prohibition will go without costs.

It is plain that the above words were deliberately inserted by the commissioners in pursuance of their quasi-legislative powers. I have looked up the draft with the kind assistance of Mr. J. G. Scott, K.C.

But the binding force of the judgment in *Perry* v. *Laughlin* relieves me from the necessity of considering their effect.

[IN THE COURT OF APPEAL FOR ONTARIO.]

THE GRAND HOTEL COMPANY OF CALEDONIA SPRINGS (Limited).

v.

WILSON.

THE SAME COMPANY

v.

TUNE.

Trade mark—Infringement of—" Caledonia Water "—" Water from Caledonia Springs"—"Water from New Springs at Caledonia."

The plaintiffs had been for many years the owners of certain mineral springs, the waters from which had been on the market for years and, owing entirely to the enterprise of and expenditure by the plaintiffs, had become widely used, medicinally and as a beverage. They had registered a trade mark containing, among other things, the words " Caledonia Water " and " Caledonia Mineral Water." The springs were situated on lot number 20 in the first concession of the township of Caledonia and, long ago, and before the plaintiffs acquired them, were known by the name of Caledonia Springs; about the springs a village known as " Caledonia Springs" had grown up. In 1876 the plaintiff company was incorporated, acquired the land on which the springs and a hotel known as the Caledonia Springs Hotel are situated, and has since been carrying on the hotel business and that of selling the mineral water. In 1898, L. & Co., who had acquired a property adjacent to the plaintiffs' land, discovered thereon two springs of mineral water, having medicinal qualities and composed of many of the ingredients found in the water produced by the plaintiffs' springs. This water L. & Co. supplied to their agents, Wilson and Tune & Co., who bottled and sold it, using bottles similar in size and shape to those used by the plaintiffs, and designating the water as " Caledonia Water," " Water from the New Springs at Caledonia."

Held, Moss C.J.O., dissenting, that the defendants could not be enjoined from using the word " Caledonia " in designating the water used by them.

These were appeals by the defendants from the judgment of Boyd, C., granting an injunction restraining the defendants from selling the mineral water under said labels.

The facts appear in the judgment of Boyd, C., and Maclennan, J.A.

The judgment of Boyd, C., was as follows:—

July 18, 1901. BOYD, C.:—From the evidence I think the proper conclusion is that the words "Caledonia Water" and "Water from Caledonia Springs" mean the mineral water supplied by the plaintiffs, which has been for many years on the market and widely used medicinally and as a beverage. The use by the defendants of the words "Caledonia Water" and "Water from Caledonia Springs," is calculated to mislead, and has been used so as to mislead purchasers.

One of the defendants, Lyall, admits that his object in calling his production "Caledonia Water" was "to sell as Caledonia Water in the established market," *i.e.*, to avail himself of the benefits of the large expenditure ($30,000) for advertising on the part of the plaintiffs, which has familiarized the public with this particular water from the Caledonia Springs owned by the plaintiffs and their predecessors.

The contention of the defendants is, in effect, that the description adopted by the plaintiffs is ambiguous, or open to the disadvantage of duplicity, that is, it fits the plaintiffs' product and defendants' product, because both are water of saline character, drawn from the township of Caledonia; but the observations made by Lord Macnaghten in *Reddaway* v. *Banning*. [1896] A.C. 199, pp. 218, 219, shew the fallacy and inefficiency of this method of defence.

The evidence generally shews an intention on the part of the defendants to imitate the shape and make-up of the

plaintiffs' goods, and yet to sail so close to the wind that
their right is no legal infraction. With the exception of
the temporary invasion of the trade-mark by Tune's use
of the first label, they have not actually infringed the
plaintiffs' registered trade-mark; but as to the trade names
first mentioned by me, I think the case of the plaintiffs is
established.

No doubt the township name may have originally, early
in the last century, suggested the application of it to the
water; but in course of time the township name has been
lost sight of in the particular name "Caledonia Springs,"
localized through the agency of the plaintiffs. At this point
where the three springs are situated there grew up in
course of time the Caledonia Springs village (attached to
the hotel), the Caledonia Springs post-office, and the Caledonia Springs station. A letter merely addressed to
"Caledonia" would go to that place in the township of
Haldimand. This distinctive character now and for a long
time past generally attributed to the "Caledonia Springs,"
arose from the exertions and expenditure of the plaintiffs
in making known the qualities and worth of the water
arising from their springs. The wide spread market for
this water known by this name was made entirely by the
enterprise of the plaintiffs.

Knowing this the defendants have sought to profit by
it, and not perhaps by means of perfectly accurate representations. The defendants call their product "Water
from the New Springs at Caledonia," and their labels
carry prominently the words "Springs" and "Caledonia."
Now, it is not correct to speak of the water vended by them
as "New Springs." Their water was reached by means
of boring and drilling, and it rises as from an artesian
well. The plaintiffs' water issues naturally from the earth,

and is and has long been the spontaneous outflow of mineral springs. Neither are the so-called "New Springs" of the defendants at Caledonia. They may be in Caledonia, *i.e.*, the township of that name, but the desire was to localize the new venture so that it might be confounded with the better and well-known product.

Proof was given in this case of that which was held an actionable wrong by James, L.J., in *Singer Manufacturing Co. v. Loog* (1880), 18 Ch.D. 395, at p. 412 (cited in *Reddaway* v. *Banning*): "No man is permitted to use any mark, sign or symbol, device or other means, whereby, without making a distinct false representation himself to a purchaser who purchase from him, he enables such purchaser to tell a lie, or to make a false representation to somebody else who is the ultimate customer."

Many cases were cited, but it is not necessary to dwell on the authorities at greater length. I had occasion to consider the law pretty fully in *Robinson* v. *Bogle* (1889), 18 O.R. 387; *Rose* v. *McLean Publishing Co.* (1897), 27 O.R. 330, and 24 A.R. 240.

Judgment should be entered for the plaintiffs with costs.

The appeals were argued before ARMOUR, C.J.O., OSLER, MACLENNAN, MOSS, and LISTER, JJ.A., on the 21st and 22nd November, 1901, when judgment was reserved.

J. J. Maclaren, K.C., and *W. E. Middleton*, for the appellants.

Walter Cassels, K.C., and *F. Arnoldi*, K.C., for the respondents.

Lister J.A., having died, and Armour, C.J.O., having been appointed to the Supreme Court of Canada, the appeals were re-argued on December 4th, 1902, before MOSS, C.J.O., OSLER, and MACLENNAN, JJ.A.

W. E. Middleton, for the appellants.

F. Arnoldi, K.C., for the respondents.

December 4. MOSS, C.J.O.:—I am of opinion that the judgment appealed from should be affirmed.

I see no good reason for interfering with the learned Chancellor's conclusions of fact, which are, I think, well supported by the testimony.

Many years before the defendants began the production or sale of mineral waters from the neighbourhood of the plaintiffs' springs in the township of Caledonia, the waters derived from the plaintiffs' springs had gained a reputation and acquired an established market as "Caledonia Water," not because they were so named by the early proprietors, but because they grew into favour and came to be known to dealers and consumers by that name. The name gradually became attached to and connected with the plaintiffs' waters, and was understood to designate those which the proprietors of the springs supplied to their customers. This had become so complete and certain before the defendants put any water on the market that anyone hearing the term "Caledonia Water" would instantly conclude that it referred to the plaintiffs' waters.

All this was well known to the defendants when they began making their arrangements for bringing their water before the public and placing it in the market.

The question seems to me to be largely, if not altogether, one of fact, whether the defendants have so dealt with their waters as to lead consumers to the belief that they were selling the plaintiffs' waters, which were well known to the trade and general public as "'Caledonia Water."

The only distinction between such cases as *Wotherspoon* v. *Currie* (1872), L.R. 5 H.L. 508; *Montgomery* v. *Thompson*, [1891] A.C. 217; and *Reddaway* v. *Banham*, [1896] A.C. 199, and this case, that can be suggested, is that they related to manufactured articles, whereas this case relates to a natural product. No such distinction appears to have been recognized in *Radde* v. *Norman* (1872), L.R. 14 Eq. 348, or *Appolinaris Co. (Limited)* v. *Norrish* (1875), 33 L.T.N.S. 242, in both of which *Wotherspoon* v. *Currie* was relied upon for the plaintiffs. The plaintiffs' waters are not natural products from sources available to all the world, nor found in many places within a certain district.

The defendants claim that their waters are different from the plaintiffs in chemical ingredients, and not only different but superior on account of the differences. For all that appears, the plaintiffs have the exclusive access to the sources whence are derived waters possessed of the qualities they claim for theirs. And I see no good reason why the principle of the above mentioned cases should not apply to this case. It is peculiar and special in its facts and circumstances, and may well be classed with them.

The defendants contend that, even admitting that the plaintiffs have shewn themselves entitled to the use of the words "Caledonia Water," as designating their waters, the use by the defendants of the words, "water from the new springs at Caledonia," clearly distinguishes their waters from the plaintiffs' waters.

I am unable to adopt that view. In the designation of the plaintiffs' waters, "Caledonia" is the dominating factor—the word which conveys to the consumer the idea of the waters supplied by the plaintiffs. And the question of the particular springs whence they are derived would scarcely present itself to his mind. To say that the waters are from the new springs at Caledonia is not to inform him that they are not the plaintiffs' waters. Unless he has special information as to the history of the plaintiffs' springs he will not see any distinguishing mark in the mention of the new springs, which may well suggest, or be taken to indicate, new springs of the plaintiffs' waters.

The words convey the idea of Caledonia waters, and suggest the well-known waters supplied by the plaintiffs.

It is not easy to explain why the defendants use the words "at Caledonia," unless for the purpose of gaining the advantage to be derived from the reputation of the plaintiffs' waters. The defendants' waters could just as well have been put on the market—and if they have intrinsic merit, gain popular favour—under some other name. Being, as they are, chemically different from any of the plaintiffs' waters, the word "Caledonia" suggests no special attribute or quality common to the waters from the township or locality. And, so far as the defendants' waters are concerned, there is nothing in the name "Caledonia" except an advantage from the reputation of the plaintiffs' Caledonia waters.

It is argued that the words "Caledonia Water" mean nothing more than waters obtained in the township of Caledonia, and that any person having mineral waters obtained at or in that township is entitled to use the word "Caledonia" in designating them. But that argument does not hold in view of the secondary meaning to be attached in this case to the words as denoting the plaintiffs' waters. Where the secondary meaning has been acquired, the defendants cannot justify themselves by the statement that they are telling the simple truth.

In *Reddaway* v. *Banham, supra,* Lord Herschell thus

dealt with the argument, at p. 212: "I think the fallacy lies in overlooking the fact that a word may acquire in a trade a secondary signification differing from its primary one, and that if it is used to persons in the trade who will understand it and be known and intended to understand it in its secondary sense, it will none the less be a falsehood that in its primary sense it may be true."

In the same case Lord Macnaghten said, at p. 219: "I venture to think that a statement which is literally true, but which is intended to convey a false impression, has something of a faulty ring about it."

To my mind the words employed by the defendants to designate their waters, so far from clearly distinguishing them from the plaintiffs' product, appear calculated to mislead and to induce the public to suppose that what the defendants are vending comes from the plaintiffs' springs.

I think, therefore, the plaintiffs are entitled to an injunction. But I also think that the injunction awarded is not in the form now usually accepted as the proper one in cases of this kind. It should be to restrain the defendants, their servants and agents, from selling or offering, or exposing or advertising for sale, or procuring or enabling to be sold, any mineral waters (not being of the plaintiffs' production) under or in connection with the word "Caledonia" without clearly distinguishing such waters from the plaintiffs' waters.

The precise language of the injunction may be discussed (if any question arises concerning it) at the instance of any party.

With this modification I think the judgment should be affirmed, and the appeal dismissed with costs.

Since the argument of this case two decisions have been reported which appear to assist the plaintiffs' case. I refer to *Worcester v. Locke* (1902), 14 Times L.R. 712, and *Boston Rubber Shoe Co.* v. *Boston Rubber Co. of Montreal* (1902), 32 S.C.R. 315.

MACLENNAN, J.A.:—After a very careful perusal and consideration of the oral and other evidence in this case, I have arrived at a different conclusion from that of the Chancellor.

In the beginning of last century mineral springs were discovered quite near each other in lot number twenty in the first concession of the township of Caledonia, in the county of Prescott. The waters from these springs were all found to possess medicinal qualities, though differing considerably from each other in their component elements. These springs soon became known by the name Caledonia Springs, and have ever since retained that name. They also became a place of resort by invalids, and the water therefrom has, for a long time, been a subject of merchandise by the proprietors by the name of "Caledonia Water."

As early as the year 1839, as appears by the abstract of title put in by the plaintiffs, the neighbourhood of the springs was divided into village lots, with streets and squares; there being as many as seventeen different streets mentioned in the abstract. Ever since that time the locality of the springs, as well as the springs themselves, has been called and known by the name of "Caledonia Springs."

In the year 1866 a company was incorporated called "The Caledonia Springs Hotel Co.," for the purpose of building and maintaining a hotel, and their charter declares that the company's place of operation is "the landed property in the township of Prescott, called and known as the Caledonia Springs property." That company built a hotel and carried on the hotel business; and, in the year 1876, the plaintiff company was incorporated for the purpose of acquiring the land on which the springs and the Caledonia Springs hotel are situate, and for carrying on a hotel business, and the business of selling mineral waters. The plaintiff company accordingly acquired the said property, including the hotel, and have carried on the hotel business and the business of selling mineral waters ever since.

Several years ago the plaintiff company induced a railway company to construct a line of railway to pass near the springs, affording communication by rail with Montreal and Ottawa, and the railway company has ever since maintained a station on its line at or near the springs, called "Caledonia Springs." For many years, also, a post office has been maintained at the plaintiffs' hotel by the Government of Canada, called "Caledonia Springs."

In the year 1898 the defendants Lyell, McDonell & Trenholm, whom it will be convenient to call Lyell & Co., became the owners, as tenants in common, of part of the east half of lot 21 in the township of Caledonia, which lies adjacent to the plaintiffs' land and to their hotel and springs, and by boring thereon they discovered two springs of mineral water, having medicinal qualities and composed of many of the ingredients composing the water produced by the plaintiffs' springs. These springs of the defendants, although only discovered by boring, are flowing springs like those of the plaintiffs, and the defendants Lyell & Co. have engaged in the business of selling the water therefrom for profit.

The plaintiffs commenced these actions on the 5th of February, 1901, for an injunction and damages, alleging that the defendants Lyell & Co. as principals, and the other defendants as their agents, have been, in carrying on their business, infringing the plaintiffs' trade-marks, and selling their water as the plaintiffs' water to the great injury of the plaintiffs.

The actions were consolidated, and were tried before the learned Chancellor, who decided the case in favour of the plaintiffs.

The judgment restrains the defendants: (1) From advertising or selling their water in the Province of Ontario under the name of "Caledonia Water;" (2) or as coming from the springs owned or leased by the plaintiffs; (3) or enclosed in any bottles, barrels or packages having any mark or label contrived to represent their water as coming from the plaintiffs' springs; (4) and, particularly, from using or applying in Ontario to the defendants' water the words "Caledonia Water," "water from Caledonia Springs," "water from the new springs at Caledonia;" and (5) from so using and applying in the Province of Ontario any name or title of which the word "Caledonia" forms a part, in a way calculated to deceive the public into the belief that the water sold by the defendants is mineral water from the plaintiffs' springs.

There is also a reference as to damages.

The facts appear to be as follows: The defendants Lyell & Co., finding by analysis that their water contained valuable medicinal properties opened a correspondence with the defendants Wilson, at Toronto, and the defendants Tune & Co., at London, and employed them respectively as agents for the sale of the water from their wells or springs. The defendants Wilson and Tune & Co. having received from their principals consignments of water in barrels from their springs, began the sale thereof in bottles, specimens of which, with the labels used affixed thereto, have been produced in evidence.

The plaintiffs' waters have usually been put on the market in a similar way. They supply agents in Quebec and Ontario with water in barrels. The agents bottle and sell it to the dealers. The plaintiffs' agents in Ontario are McLachlin & Co., of Toronto. The bottles used by Wilson and Tune & Co. are similar in size and shape to those used by McLachlin.

The plaintiffs claimed in their statement of claim that the defendants had infringed five different trade-marks used by them to distinguish their goods. It is proved that for a short time before, and at the time the action was commenced, the defendants Tune & Co. used a label upon their bottles which in shape and colour and several other respects resembled one of the plaintiffs' trade-marks, whereby a consumer, but I think not a dealer, might be deceived. This label had not been sanctioned by Lyell & Co., and was at once abandoned when complaint was made, and another was adopted to which no objection could be made. The defendants Wilson never used a label which could be regarded as an infringement of any of the plaintiffs' trade-marks. The learned Chancellor has, therefore, found that with the exception of what was done by Tune & Co. there was no infringement of the plaintiffs' trade-marks, and in that conclusion I agree. It was said, however, that the defendants had been selling their water as "Caledonia Water" without distinguishing it from the plaintiffs' water. The defendant Tune admits that he did sell some of the defendants' water as *Caledonia Water*, and that without any label or anything to distinguish it from the plaintiffs' water. This was just prior to the commencement of the action on the 5th of February, 1901. On the

previous day the plaintiffs' solicitors wrote to Tune & Co.,
threatening proceedings, to restrain the use of a label with
the words, "From the new springs at Caledonia, selzer
beaver brand, natural saline water," as an infringement
of plaintiffs' trade-mark, and claiming exclusive right to
use the words *Caledonia* and *Caledonia Springs* in connection with their mineral waters. The service of the writ
followed immediately, and on the 6th February, Tune &
Co. answered the solicitors' letter, saying they were ignorant of the plaintiffs' claim to the word "Caledonia," and
did not intend to imitate their trade-mark, and they offered
to cease using the label objected to, and to re-label all the
"new Caledonia springs water" with a label no one could
mistake for the plaintiffs' label. This fair and reasonable
proposal was not regarded as satisfactory, and those defendants were informed that they must submit to the relief asked for, and pay the costs, otherwise proceedings
would not be stayed.

The Wilsons do not appear to have at any time used
a label which could be regarded as an imitation of the
plaintiffs marks or any of them, or to have sold any water
merely as Caledonia Water. Their label is very different
from any of the plaintiffs' labels in colour and size and
device, and has nothing thereon of which the plaintiffs
could complain, unless it be the word Caledonia as part of
the phrase, "From the new springs at *Caledonia.*" So
far as Tune & Co. are concerned, I think their appeal fails
as to that part of the judgment which enjoins them from
selling their water as Caledonia Water. On reading the
correspondence between Tune & Co. and their principals,
Lyell & Co., and the evidence at the trial, it is quite clear
the latter are not responsible for the act of their agent in
selling their water as Caledonia Water without distinguish-

ing it from the plaintiffs' water. On the contrary, Lyell
& Co. distinctly cautioned them not to use a label which
would infringe upon any other water in the market. The
first member of the mandatory part of the judgment must,
therefore, be allowed to stand against Tune & Co. But I
think it ought not to stand against any of the other defendants. There is no evidence that they or any of them
sold, or desired or intended to sell, their water as or under
the name of *Caledonia Water*, or that any of the defendants, Tune & Co. included, intended or desired to lead
their customers to suppose that they were getting water
which came from the plaintiffs' springs. If any intention
of that kind had been shewn, it would have been proper to
make the injunction wide enough so as effectually to prevent such a fraud. But where no wrong was intended,
an injunction should be confined to the precise act committed.

For the same reason, I think the second, third and
fourth members of the mandatory part of the decree objectionable, and that they should be struck out. There is
no evidence that any of the defendants, except Tune & Co.,
as already mentioned, advertised or sold their water as
coming from the springs owned or leased by the plaintiffs;
or inclosed in any bottles, barrels or packages having any
mark or label, contrived to represent their water as coming from the plaintiffs' springs; or used or applied in
Ontario to the defendants' water the words "Caledonia
Water," or, "water from Caledonia Springs."

They have used the last phrase mentioned in the fourth
member of the injunction, namely, "water from the new
springs at Caledonia," as descriptive of their water, and
they justify their doing so; and the question is whether
they are right.

The learned Chancellor thought that it was not correct
for the defendants to speak of the water sold by them as
from "new springs," because it was reached by means of
boring and drilling, and rises from an artesian well while
the plaintiffs' water issues naturally from the earth, and
is and has long been the spontaneous outflow of mineral
springs. I am unable to take that view. As we have seen,
the defendants' wells are flowing wells. The water springs
up spontaneously from the earth through the orifices
drilled or bored by the defendants. One of the definitions
given in both the Standard and Century Dictionaries of a
well is *a spring* or *well spring*, a *spring* of water, a foun-
tain. The Century says: "A spring is a place where water
comes naturally to the surface of the ground and flows
away. A spring may be opened or struck in excavating,
but cannot be made." I confess I should have thought
the word *spring* the natural and appropriate word to use
in order to designate the flowing wells of the defendants.
I am, therefore, of opinion that the defendants do no more
than exercise their legal rights in designating and describing their wells as springs.

The learned Chancellor also finds fault with the use by
the defendants of the word *Caledonia*. The defendants
describe their water as from "the new springs at Caledonia." Their springs are within a quarter of a mile
or less from the old springs, within a stone's throw of the
village called Caledonia Springs, near a railway station
and a post office of the same name. Now, the defendants
have an undoubted right to describe their water correctly
and truthfully. It is a saline mineral water. It is derived from new springs, and those springs are in the township of Caledonia, and they are at a place called "Caledonia Springs." If the defendants' water is likely to be

more sought after and more marketable, and if the business of selling it is likely to be more profitable by reason of the situation of the springs, and their nearness to the famous old springs, the defendants are entitled to the benefit of that. They might say, in so many words, that they were situate within so many yards of the old springs, just in order to gain favour in the market. The learned Chancellor also things there is inaccuracy in saying "new springs *at* Caledonia," instead of *in* Caledonia. They might have said with perfect correctness "new springs at Caledonia Springs," for the phrase "Caledonia Springs" unquestionably means not only the springs of water, but the place, the locality, the neighbourhood where they are situate. The defendant McDougall lives and keeps a hotel there. The first question put to him by the plaintiffs' counsel on his examination for discovery, was: "You live at Caledonia Springs? Ans. Yes." If a crime were committed at or near the defendants' springs, the indictment would charge that it was committed *at* the township of Caledonia, and not *in* the township. Therefore, the defendants' description of their water as water from "the new springs at Caledonia," is, in my opinion, a perfectly true and accurate description, and not only so, but one which clearly and sufficiently distinguishes it from the plaintiffs' water. There might have been some danger of confusion if they had said "the new springs at Caledonia Springs," although that would have been a true description; but they perhaps wisely avoided that.

It was very strenuously contended that the defendants have no right to use the word *Caledonia* at all in designating their water. A similar contention was made in *Singer Manufacturing Co.* v. *Loog* (1882), 8 App. Cas. 15. At p. 27 Lord Selborne says: "For that argument no authority

was cited; and it cannot, in my opinion, be maintained on
any principle. . . If the defendant has (and it is not
denied that he has) a right to make and sell in competition
with the plaintiffs articles similar in form and construction to those made and sold by the plaintiffs, he must also
have a right to say that he does so, and to employ for that
purpose the terminology common in his trade, provided
always that he does this in a fair, distinct and unequivocal
way." And at pp. 37, 38, Lord Blackburn uses similar
language; and Lord Watson at pp. 38, 39. Therefore, the
defendants' springs being at Caledonia, they have a right
to say so, taking care to distinguish them from those of
the plaintiffs at the same place.

It was also contended that the make up of the defendants' goods was calculated to deceive the public, because
the bottles used were similar. But it was not shewn that
the plaintiffs' bottles were in any way peculiar in form or
size or colour, or different from bottles in common use for
the sale of other waters. It was said that it was common
to put such goods on ice, and that the labels then came off,
and the customer might be deceived, but it is not shewn
that the defendants did things of that kind. As to this
contention, see observations of Lords Macnaghten and
Davey in *Payton* v. *Snelling*, [1901] A.C. 308.

I am, therefore, of opinion that the whole of the fourth
member of the injunction is unwarranted.

It remains to consider the fifth element, and it follows
from what I have said, that, in my opinion, no part of it
can be maintained as against any of the defendants. None
of the defendants, except Tune & Co., have been shewn to
have done anything that is here enjoined, and that part of
the judgment which I think ought to stand against Tune
& Co. is sufficient as against them.

The result is that as to all the defendants, except Tune & Co., the appeal should be allowed with costs, and the action should be dismissed with costs. As to Tune & Co., the appeal should be allowed, except as to the first clause of the injunction; and the reference as to damages, if the plaintiffs think it worth while. As against them the action was rightly enough brought. I think, however, if the plaintiffs had asked no more than that, Tune & Co. would have contested the matter no further. I think the plaintiffs should have against Tune & Co. such costs as they would have incurred in entering up judgment against them by default for so much of the injunction as they still retain, and I think they should pay them the rest of the costs of the action and appeal, with set off.

OSLER, J.A., concurred with MACLENNAN, J.A.

[IN THE HIGH COURT OF JUSTICE FOR ONTARIO.]

DIVISIONAL COURT.

BIRNEY

v.

THE TORONTO MILK CO., LIMITED.

Company—Appointments of manager—Want of by-law—Contract under seal—Shareholders sanction for payments for services—R.S.O. 1897, ch. 191, secs. 47 and 48.

The plaintiff was named as a director and as manager of the defendant company, incorporated under the Ontario Joint Stock Companies Act, in resolutions passed at a meeting of the provisional directors. His services as manager did not result in any benefit to the company, which never went into operation. In an action for his salary,

Held, he was not entitled to recover because (1) no by-law for his appointment as manager had been passed, and (2) no contract had been made with him under the seal of the company.

This was an appeal from the judgment of Lount, J., at the trial in favor of the plaintiff for $495 and costs. The appeal was argued on the 11th September, 1902, before Street and Britton, JJ.

J. B. O'Brian, for the appellants.

J. M. Godfrey, for the respondent.

November 15, STREET, J. (stating the facts), said:—

The defendants were incorporated on the 17th May, 1901, by letters patent under the Ontario Companies Act, for the purpose of buying, selling and dealing in milk and its products, the capital stock of the company was fixed at $125,000, and six provisional directors were named in the letters patent.

On 25th May, 1901, a meeting of the provisional directors was held at which by-laws were adopted, one of which provided that the affairs of the company should be managed by a board of "not less than three nor more than nine directors."

On the same day a general meeting of the shareholders was held at which all were present or were represented by proxy. At this meeting the above by-law was adopted, but no directors seem to have been elected.

No minute book of this or any other meeting of directors or shareholders was kept; the record of the minutes of the shareholders' meeting is imperfect.

A sheet of paper was produced purporting to contain minutes of a meeting of directors held at Mr. O'Brian's office on 29th June, 1901, at which three of the provisional directors were present.

The first resolution at that meeting was that the plaintiff in the present action should be appointed a director: the second resolution was that he should be appointed manager of the company for the ensuing year, with a salary as follows:—

First nine weeks at	-	$25 per week
Second nine weeks at	-	$30 per week
Remaining weeks at	-	$40 per week

making the year's salary $1,855: subject to dismissal at the termination of any one of the above mentioned periods, with one week's salary at the discretion of the board of directors.

The plaintiff was made aware of his appointment as a director and also of his appointment as manager. He afterwards attended a meeting as a director of the company.

No president was ever appointed to the company, and it never went into operation.

The plaintiff says that, acting under his appointment as manager of the company, he endeavored to get certain persons to go on the board and to put up money to enable the company to go into operation. He failed in doing so, and as a result the company never went into operation.

The present action was brought to recover $495, being salary as manager for the first eighteen weeks.

The defendants denied any contract binding upon them.

The nominal capital of the defendants' company was fixed by the letters patent at $125,000, divided into 125,000 shares of $1 each, of which it is stated by the plaintiff that he subscribed for 12,000 shares, and each of the other six corporators for 200 shares.

No money seems to have been paid in by any one, but the plaintiff says that his $12,000 has been paid in full by commissions upon his efforts to induce a number of established milkmen to sell out their businesses to the company, and that his salary as manager has been earned by his efforts to induce certain of these milkmen to go upon the board, and to advance the money necessary to enable the company to begin the business for which it was incorporated.

None of these efforts of the plaintiff have been successful, nor has the company reaped any advantage from them, for it has never been able to go into operation.

If the plaintiff's view of his position is correct, however, the result will be that the other corporators will be liable to pay him $495 for which he has done, because his

shares he says are fully paid up by his work and theirs are
not paid up.

It is further to be remarked that his interest in the success of the company was ten times that of all the other
corporators put together, and that the only work which he
says he did as manager after his appointment seems to
have been merely a continuation of the work which he says
he was doing before his appointment.

I am of opinion that the plaintiff is not entitled to recover upon a contract with the company, because no by-law
for his appointment as manager of the company was
passed, and no contract was made with him under the seal
of the company.

The Ontario Companies Act, ch. 191, R.S.O. 1897, sec.
47, clearly contemplates that such appointments should be
made by by-law; and, apart altogether from the statute,
it is clear that whatever latitude may be allowed to trading
corporations in the manner of appointment of mere servants, or in the case of casual or temporary hirings, appointments of an important character such as that of the manager of the company, in order to be binding, must be under
seal.

Such was the holding of the late Mr. Justice Rose in
Re The Ontario Express and Transportation Company
(1894), 25 O.R. 587, and it is in accordance with numer-
ous preceding authorities: *Dunston* v. *The Imperial Gas
Light and Coke Co.* (1832), 3 B. & Ad. 125, and especially
judgment of Parke, J., at p. 132; *Church* v. *The Imperial
Gas Light and Coke Co.* (1838), 6 Ad. & El. 846, at p. 861;
Young v. *Leamington* (1883), 8 App. Cas. 517; Lindley on
Company Law, 6th ed., p. 269 *et seq.*

I think the plaintiff is further prevented from recovering by the effect of the provisions of sec. 48 of ch. 191,

R.S.O., which are as follows: "No by-law for the payment of the president or any director shall be *valid or acted upon* until the same has been confirmed at a general meeting."

There is in the first place the underlying assumption from the terms of this section that a by-law of the directors in the first place is necessary before payments can be made to them or to the president: and this is coupled with the express provision that such a by-law when passed is of no validity until it has been confirmed at a general meeting of shareholders.

It has been argued before us by the plaintiff that this section is only intended to apply to payments to the president for performing the duties of president, and to directors for performing their duties as directors, and Mr. Justice Rose in his judgment in *Re The Ontario Express and Transportation Co.*, 25 O.R. 587, appears to have expressed an opinion to that effect. The opinion so expressed, however, does not seem to have been anything beyond an *obiter dictum*, and is not technically a part of his judgment in the case, and is therefore not binding upon me.

In my opinion we should hold the section as requiring the sanction of the shareholders as a condition precedent to the validity of every payment voted by directors to any one or more of themselves whether under the guise of fees for their attendance at board meetings or for the performance of any other services for the company.

It is not conceivable that the Legislature intended to forbid the directors from voting small sums to themselves for their attendance at board meetings, without obtaining the consent of the shareholders, and at the same time, to allow them to vote large sums to themselves for doing other work, without reference at all to the shareholders. The interpretation contended for by the plaintiff would in fact render the section nugatory, for nothing would be easier than to evade it.

I think the section should be given a broad and wholesome interpretation, and that it should be held wide enough to prevent a president and board of directors from voting to themselves or to any one or more of themselves any remuneration whatever for any services rendered to the company without the authority of a general meeting of the shareholders.

The views I have expressed are such as to prevent the plaintiff from having a right to recover for the value of his work done for the company.

For these reasons, the appeal should, in my judgment, be allowed with costs, and the action should be dismissed with costs.

BRITTON, J.:—I agree that in this case the appeal should be allowed and the action dismissed.

There is no properly authorized contract under the seal of the corporation, and this is not a case in which the plaintiff can succeed upon an executed consideration. I come to this conclusion apart altogether from the effect in this case of sec. 48, ch. 191, R.S.O. 1897, upon plaintiff's rights.

The company never really went into operation; there was no payment in money by any subscriber for shares for any portion of the stock. The plaintiff was promoter, and as such, no doubt, did a good deal of preparatory work in getting ready for the business the company was authorized to do. For this the plaintiff received "paid-up" shares.

At a meeting of directors, assuming that the meeting was properly called, the plaintiff was appointed a director, and then it was resolved that the plaintiff be manager for the ensuing year. This, in my opinion, only means that

defendants in the action and an execution was at the time of the assignment in the hands of the sheriff. This assignment by the terms of R.S.O. ch. 147, sec. 11, took precedence of the judgment and of the execution except as to and subject to the lien of the plaintiffs for their costs. The plaintiffs, however, failed to observe the proper course under the circumstances, which was to have the sheriff proceed to seize and sell under the execution the property assigned for these costs, and so lost their lien under the execution. They could therefore claim for their costs as merely ordinary creditors.

It would appear that the judgment debtor can effectively stay the hand of the sheriff at any time before the actual sale by payment of the costs of the judgment creditor and the sheriff's costs. After the sale, the purchaser is completely protected, even though he be the judgment creditor himself.

Vide on this point Parker on Frauds on Creditors, at p. 293.

[IN THE SUPREME COURT OF CANADA.]

MICHAEL POWER (Defendant) Appellant

v.

J. M. GRIFFIN ET AL. (Plaintiffs) Respondents.

BEFORE SIR ELZEAR TASCHEREAU, C.J., AND SEDGEWICK, DAVIES, MILLS AND ARMOUR, JJ.

Patent of invention—Infringement—Manufacture—Expiration—Extension of time—"Obiter Dicta"—R.S.C. 1886, ch. 61, sec. 37, sub-sec. 1, as amended by 53 Vict. ch. 13, sec. 2.

A patentee's rights expire in two years from the date of the patent or at the end of any extension of time thereof, unless he has commenced and carried on, in Canada, continuously, the manufacture of the patented article so that any person desiring to use it could obtain it or cause it to be made.

A patent is not kept alive (after the two years have expired) by reason of the fact that the patentee is ready either to furnish the article himself or to license the right of using it to anyone desiring to use it if he has not commenced to manufacture in Canada. *Barter v. Smith* ((1877), 2 Ex. C.R. 455), overruled on this point.

The power of extension given to the Commissioners of Patents can only be exercised once. It is doubtful whether this power can be exercised by an Acting Deputy-Commissioner.

This was an appeal from a judgment of the Exchequer Court of Canada* in favour of the plaintiffs. The action was by the respondents against the appellant for infringement of letters-patent of invention for improvements in abrading shoes for truing up car wheels. The judgment appealed from maintained the respondents' action and restrained the appellant from using the invention in question.

* (1902) 7 Ex. C.R. 411 *sub nom. Griffin v. Toronto Railway Co.*

The questions of the merit of the patent *ab initio* and that of damages were not argued for the reasons stated in the judgment of the Chief Justice.

W. Cassels, K.C., and *Anglin*, for the appellants.
Ridout, for the respondents.

December 15, 1902. THE CHIEF JUSTICE:—This is an appeal from the judgment of the Exchequer Court upon an action by the respondents against the appellant for the infringement of certain letters-patent of invention for improvements in abrading shoes for truing up car wheels. That judgment maintains the respondents' action and restrains the appellant from using the invention in question, with a reference to ascertain the damages that the respondents may have suffered.

I am of opinion that the said restraining order should be rescinded (upon this alone we can now pass as I will state later on) for the reason that it appears upon the record that the respondents' patent has now lapsed.

The said patent bears date on the 11th of August, 1899. It therefore lapsed on the 11th of August, 1901, under sec. 37,* sub-sec. 1, of ch. 61 of the Revised Statutes of Can-

---

*Sec. 37, sub-sec. 1, of ch. 61, R.S.C. (1866) as amended by 53 Vict. ch. 13, sec. 2, reads as follows:—

Every patent granted under this Act shall be subject and be expressed to be subject to the condition that such patent and all the rights and privileges thereby granted shall cease and determine, and that the patent shall be null and void, at the end of two years from the date thereof, unless the patentee or his legal representatives or his assignee, within that period or any authorized extension thereof, commences and, after such commencement, continuously carries on in Canada the construction or manufacture of the invention patented, in such manner that any person desiring to use it may obtain it, or cause it to be made for him, at a reasonable price, at some manufactory or establishment for making or constructing it, in Canada, and that such patent shall be void if, after the expiration of twelve months from the granting thereof or any authorized extension of such period, the patentee or his legal representatives or his assignee for the

ada, as amended in 1892, by sec. 6 of 54 & 55 Vict. (D), unless the respondents, before that last date (or before the expiration of any authorized extension thereof), commenced and, after such commencement, continuously carried on in Canada the construction or manufacture of their patented invention in such a manner that any person desiring to use it could obtain it, or cause it to be made for him at a reasonable price at some manufactory or establishment for making or constructing it in Canada. The grant of the patent is expressly made subject to that statutory condition.

Now, there is no evidence that the respondents ever carried on in Canada the construction or manufacture of their invention. That the burden of proving it was on them is unquestionable. An essential allegation of their statement of claim is that their patent is in full force and valid, and that allegation is expressly put in issue by the appellant's pleas as allowed by sec. 33 of ch. 61 of the Revised Statutes of Canada, by which it is enacted that the defendant in any action for infringement the defendant

> may plead specially as a matter of defence any act or default which by this Act or by law, renders the patent void; and the Court shall take cognizance of that special pleading and of the facts connected therewith, and shall decide the case accordingly.

Upon a suggestion by the Court, during the argument at bar, that, if so desired, the case would be remitted back

whole or a part of his interest in the patent, imports, or causes to be imported into Canada, the invention for which the patent is granted; and any difference which arises as to whether a patent has or has not become null and void, under the provisions of this section may be adjudicated upon by the Exchequer Court of Canada, which court shall have jurisdiction, upon information, in the name of the Attorney-General of Canada, and at the relation of any person interested, to decide any such question; provided that this section shall not be held to take away or affect the jurisdiction which any court, other than the Exchequer Court of Canada, possess."

to the Exchequer Court in order to give the respondents
an opportunity to prove the fact, if their not doing so before was due to an oversight or a misunderstanding, their
counsel conceded that such a reference would not help
their case as he was instructed that his clients had not, at
any time, carried on in Canada the construction or manufacture of their invention.

It was argued on behalf of the respondents, that under
the decision of this Court in *Smith v. Goldie,*[*] their not
manufacturing in Canada within two years was not fatal
to their patent. But that case merely determines that,
under the statute as it then read (35 Vict., ch. 26, sec. 28),
the Deputy Commissioner's decision, as to the invalidity
of a patent for the non-manufacturing within the two
years was final. Anything that may be found in the report of that case (and of any case), that was not necessary
for the determination of the controverted points therein is
obiter and not binding as authority. And the number of
Judges who concurred in such *obiter* does not make it anything else. Then a simple concurrence is nothing more
than a concurrence in the conclusions or, at most, in the
reasons upon which exclusively the points actually determined are based. The statute is clear. There is no room
for construction. It says, in express words, that if a
patentee has not manufactured in Canada during the two
years, the patentee's rights are at an end.

It is further argued, however, on behalf of the respondents, that their patent has been kept, and is now in force
in virtue of an extension of time granted to them by the
Commissioner, under provisions of sub-sec. 2 of sec. 37 of

*(1882), 9 S.C.R. 46.

ch. 61 of the Revised Statutes of Canada, which reads as follows :—

> Whenever a patentee has been unable to carry on the construction or manufacture of his invention within the two years hereinbefore mentioned, the commissioner may, at any time not more than three months before the expiration of that term, grant to the patentee an extension of the term of two years, on his proving to the satisfaction of the commissioner that he was, for reasons beyond his control, prevented from complying with the above condition

of commencing and continuously carrying on in Canada, within the two years from the date of the patent, the construction or manufacture of his invention as enacted in sec. 1 of said sec. 37.

It is in evidence that under the said provision a "further delay of twelve months to manufacture" (from the 11th of August, 1901), was granted to the respondents on the 8th of June, 1901, by the Acting Deputy Commissioner. But these twelve months expired on the 11th of August last. Another extension, it is true, for another twelve months, up to the 11th of August next, appears to have been granted in May last by the same officer; but this last extension is absolutely unauthorized by the statute, and is an absolute nullity. Having once exercised the power given to him by the statute, the Commissioner was *functus officio*. He might have extended the delay for more than twelve months, but he could not twice exercise the same power. There is no possible room, under the wording of the statute, for the contention that the Commissioner could extend this delay from time to time, and a jurisdiction of this nature cannot be extended by construction. We therefore have to hold that this patent lapsed on the 11th of August last.

The fact of their asking for these extensions, I may here notice, imparts a clear admission by the respondents, that they had not within the two years, fulfilled the obligations required from them by the statute in order to keep their patent in force, and that admission extends to the 11th of August last, for, when they then applied for another extension up to the 11th of August next, they admitted that, without that extension, their patent was gone.

Having come to the conclusion that the respondents' patent expired on the 11th of August last, it necessarily follows that the order restraining the appellant from using it must be set aside. But that does not put an end to this appeal. The patent issued on the 11th of August, 1899. The writ on the 5th of April, 1901; the trial was in March, 1902, and the judgment of the Exchequer Court on April 21st, 1902. The patent, therefore, lapsed only since the judgment appealed from. So that we are not in a position to dispose of the whole case. The question of damages has to be disposed of. The respondents are 'entitled to the damages, if any, that they may have suffered up to the 11th of August last, from the alleged infringement by the appellant. And for determining whether or not they are entitled to any damages we will have to hear the parties upon their respective contentions as to the validity of the patent *ab initio*, up to the 11th of August last, and the alleged infringement of it by the appellant, during three years from its date. It may be that, now that their patent for the future is out of existence, as we now determine, the respondents will not think it advisable to proceed further. But that must appear of record. The case will, therefore, be postponed till the February term. The parties will, in the meantime, decide what to do; either to re-inscribe the case for hearing, upon which hearing the points we now determine will not be allowed to be re-opened, or file with the registrar the retraxit by the respondents of their claim for damages necessary to enable us to enter a final judgment in the case. We make no order as to costs for the present.

There is a point which it is expedient to allude to. The statute says that any extension of the two years' term may be granted by the Commissioner. Now the extension to the respondents in June, 1901, is granted, not by the Commissioner, not even by the Deputy Commissioner, but by an officer calling himself the Acting Deputy Commissioner. In my opinion, I would not be disposed to hold this extension void on that ground. The majority of the Court, however, think it advisable to hear the parties on that point, if the respondents proceed further in the case. On this point depends whether it is for two or three years that the respondents are entitled to damages.

The entry to be made by the Registrar will be as follows:—

The Court declares the respondents' letters-patent to have lapsed on the 11th of August last. No order to be drawn up till the final judgment in the whole case. Costs reserved. Either party at liberty to re-inscribe the case for hearing at the next term or at any time thereafter. If respondents file in the Registrar's office a retraxit of their claim as to damages, case to be re-submitted without argument. If no such retraxit is filed, case to be heard upon th respective contentions of the parties as to the validity of the patent before the 11th of August last and the alleged infringement thereof by the appellant and whether or not, if the respondents are entitled to any damages at all, these damages shall be assessed for three years or only for two years.

SEDGEWICK, J.:—I concur in the judgment for the reasons stated by His Lordship the Chief Justice.

DAVIES, J.:—I concur with the judgment of the Chief Justice. I reserve my judgment as to the power of an *Acting* Deputy Commissioner of Patents to grant an extension of the term of the patent under the statute.

MILLS, J.:—I concur in the conclusions reached by His Lordship the Chief Justice.

ARMOUR, J.:—This is an appeal from a judgment of the Exchequer Court in an action brought by the plaintiffs against the defendants for infringement of their patent by which it was declared that the defendants had infringed the plaintiffs' patent.

The plaintiffs' patent was issued on the 11th of August, 1899, and by it was granted for the period of eighteen years the exclusive right, privilege and liberty of making, constructing and using and vending to others to be used in the Dominion of Canada, certain alleged new and useful "improvements in abrading shoes for truing up car wheels," subject to adjudication before any Court of competent jurisdiction and subject to the conditions in the Patent Act, ch. 61 of the Revised Statutes of Canada, and the Acts amending the same.

The defendants pleaded that the said patent had become void by reason of non-compliance with and breach of the terms and conditions of the Patent Act and amendments thereto.

Section 37 of the Patent Act provides that every patent granted under this Act shall be subject and be expressed to be subject to the following conditions:—(*a*) That such patent and all the rights and privileges thereby granted shall cease and determine and that the patent shall be null and void at the end of two years from the date thereof, unless the patentee or his legal representatives or assigns within that period or any authorized extension thereof, commence, and after such commencement, continuously carry on in Canada the construction or manufacture of the invention patented in such a manner that any person desiring to use it may obtain it or cause it to be made for him at a reasonable price at some manufactory or establishment for making it or constructing it in Canada. And also provides that whenever a patentee has been unable to carry on the construction or manufacture of his invention within the two years hereinbefore mentioned, the Commissioner may, at any time, not more than three months before the expiration of that term, grant to the patentee an extension of the term of two years, on his proving to the satisfaction of the Commissioner that he was, for reasons beyond his control, prevented from complying with the above condition.

It was admitted on the argument before us that neither the construction nor manufacture of the invention patented had ever been commenced or carried on in Canada.

But it was contended that this was not necessary in order to satisfy the above condition, and reliance was had for this contention upon the decision of Dr. Taché, when Deputy Minister of Agriculture, in the case of *Smith* v. *Barter*, reported in 2 Exchequer Court Reports, at p. 474, and upon the reference thereto in *Smith* v. *Goldie* (3), and in the same case in this Court (4).

This decision was upon sec. 28 of the Patent Act of 1872, containing a similar provision to that contained in sec. 37 of the present Patent Act, but providing that, in case disputes should arise, as to whether a patent had or had not become void thereunder, such disputes should be

(3) (1882), 7 A.R. 628.
(4) (1882), 9 S.C.R. 46.

settled by the Minister of Agriculture or his deputy, whose decision should be final.

The purport of Dr. Taché's decision will appear from the following quotations:—

> The words "carry on in Canada, the construction or manufacture" with their context, cannot therefore mean anything else than that any citizen of the Dominion, whether residing in Prince Edward Island, in British Columbia, in Ontario, Quebec or elsewhere on Federal soil, has a right to exact from the patentee a license to use the invention patented or obtain the article patented for his use at the expiration of two years' delay, on condition of applying to the owner for it and on payment of a fair royalty.

> The real meaning of the law is that the patentee must be ready either to furnish the article himself or to license the right of using it on reasonable terms to any person desiring to use it. But again that desire on the part of a person is not intended by the law to mean a mere operation or motion of the mind or of the tongue, but, in effect, a *bona fide* serious and substantial proposal, the offer of a fair bargain accompanied with payment. As long as the patentee has been in a position to hear and acquiesce in such a demand and has not refused such a fair bargain proposed to him, he has not forfeited his rights.

thus holding, contrary to the express words of the condition, that it was not necessary that the patentee should within the period mentioned commence, and after such commencement continuously carry on, in Canada the construction or manufacture of the invention patented, and holding, without any words in the condition to warrant it, that the condition would be sufficiently satisfied by the patentee granting to any person desiring to use the invention patented, a license to use it upon applying to him for it and upon payment of a fair royalty. This decision cannot be supported by the decisions in the Court of Appeal for Ontario and in this Court in *Smith* v. *Goldie* (5), for what was said by Mr. Justice Patterson in the former Court

(5) 9 S.C.R. 46.

and by Mr. Justice Henry in this Court, was plainly *obiter*, for each of them held that the decision of Dr. Taché was final and not subject to appeal.

Reliance was also had upon the following extensions indorsed upon the plaintiffs' patent :—

A further delay of twelve months to manufacture, granted, June 8th, 1901, A. L. Jarvis, Acting Deputy Commissioner.

A further delay of twelve months to manufacture, granted, May 14th, 1902, A. L. Jarvis, Acting Deputy Commissioner.

The power of granting an extension of the term when the patentee has been unable to carry on the construction or manufacture of his invention within two years from the date of his patent, is conferred upon the Commissioner upon the patentee proving to his satisfaction that he was, for reasons beyond his control, prevented from carrying on and complying with the conditions. This power is, by the Patent Act, conferred upon the Commissioner alone, and having regard to the context and that the power so conferred is a judicial one and not a ministerial one, it is, in my opinion, doubtful whether the provisions of sec. 7 of the Interpretation Act and of its sub-sec. 40 apply so as to authorize the Deputy Commissioner or the Acting Deputy Commissioner, the Deputy Commissioner being alive, to grant the extension. But assuming, without however determining that they do so apply, the words used in granting the power authorize only one extension, and by the grant of the extension of the 8th of June, 1901, the power was exhausted.

The plaintiffs' patent, therefore, became void on the 11th of August, 1902, by reason of non-compliance with the condition.

Solicitors for the appellant: *Blake, Lash & Cassels.*

Solicitor for the respondents: *John G. Ridout.*

Notes:—

A patent right is a restriction in favour of an individual against the public and the words of the statute creating the right and imposing the conditions under which it is to be exercised are not to be given any meaning beyond their plain literal one. If the requirements of a statute which prescribes the manner in which any thing is to be done be expressed in negative language, that is to say, if the statute enact that it shall be done in such a manner and in no other manner, it has been laid down that those requirements are in all cases absolute and that neglect to attend to them will invalidate the whole proceeding.

The decision in *Barter* v. *Smith* (6) now, in part, overruled by the above judgment, proceeded on the ground that the granting of letters-patent to inventors is in the nature of a contract between the state and the discoverer, and this contract should receive a wide and lenient interpretation.

The *obiter dicta* of Mr. Justice Patterson in *Smith* v. *Goldie* (7) referred to above are, in part, as follows:—

But, if the subject (i.e. the question of manufacture) were one proper for our decision, I should be content to follow the very careful and able judgment of Dr. Taché, the Deputy Minister, which commends itself to me as a sound exposition of the principles upon which the law laid down by the section (i.e., the 37th of the Patent Act) should be administered, as well as a judicious investigation of the facts.

And Henry, J., in the same case in the Supreme Court (8), after referring to the decision of Dr. Taché as a "very logical and sound" one, said:

I think the law as laid down and explained by him in his exhaustive, and, I will add, able judgment, cannot properly be questioned.

In *Griffin* v. *Toronto Railway Co.*(9) (under which caption *Powers* v. *Griffin* appeared in the Exchequer Court) the points raised in the Supreme Court—the questions of

(6) (1877), 2 Ex. C. R. 455.
(7) (1882), 7 A.R. p. 643.
(8) (1883), 9 S.C.R. p. 68.
(9) (1902), 7 Ex. C.R. 411.

manufacture and of extension of time—were not mooted, and the decision was on the merits entirely. This decision still stands unaffected by that in the Supreme Court, the last mentioned Court having directed the argument as to the merits—the other side of the appeal—to be had in February term 1903 of this year.

There is no provision in the English Patents Act ((1888), 51-52 Vict., ch. 50) similar to sec. 37 in the Canadian Act, but the Crown imposes a condition on the grantee of every letters-patent. This condition is a proviso in the letters-patent to the effect that, if at any time during the term for which the patent is granted it be made to appear that the grant is contrary to law, or prejudicial, or inconvenient to the public in general or that the invention is not a new invention or that the patentee is not the first and true inventor, the letters-patent shall forthwith determine and be void to all intents and purposes (10).

Mr. Frost thinks that a valid patent might probably be cancelled under the above proviso, if the conduct of the patentee rendered the grant prejudicial or inconvenient to the public, *e.g.*, if the patentee refused to sell the patented article or to grant licenses on reasonable terms (11).

(10) 46 & 47 Vict., c. 57, 1st schedule Form D.

(11) Frost on Patents, 2nd ed. (1898), 390; *Universities of Oxford and Cambridge* v. *Richardson* (1802), 6 Ves. 712.

[IN THE JUDICIAL COMMITTEE OF THE PRIVY COUNCIL.]

BEFORE THE EARL OF HALSBURY, L.C., LORD MACNAGHTON, LORD DAVEY, LORD ROBERTSON, AND LORD LINDLEY.

DOMINION COTTON MILLS COMPANY, LTD., ET AL.
(Defendants) Appellants

and

GENERAL ENGINEERING COMPANY OF ONTARIO, LTD., (Plaintiffs) Respondents.

On appeal from the Supreme Court of Canada.

The Patent Act (R.S.C. ch. 61, sec. 8)—55-56 Vict. ch. 24, sec. 1—Expiration of patent—Status of a British patent under the Canadian Patent Act.

According to the proper construction of sec. 8 of ch. 61, of the R.S.C. (The Patent Act), as amended by 55-56 Vict. ch. 24, sec. 1, a Canadian patent expires upon the expiration of any foreign patent granted for the same invention and in force at any time during the existence of the Canadian patent.

A British patent is a foreign patent within the meaning of the Canadian Patent Act.

Appeal from a judgment of the Supreme Court of Canada (31 S.C.R. 75) reversing a judgment of the Exchequer Court.

The facts of the case, and the section upon the construction of which it turned, are fully set forth in the judgment.

Fletcher Moulton, K.C., and *Lochins*, for the appellants.
Edward Blake, K.C., and *J. L. Ross*, for the respondents.

In the course of the argument *Dreschel* v. *Auer Incandescent Light Manufacturing Co.* (6 Ex. Ct. Reps. and 28

S.C.R. 608), and *In re Betts' Patent* (1 Moore, N.S., 49), were referred to.

July 23, 1902. The judgment of their Lordships was delivered by

LORD LINDLEY:—The question raised by this appeal is simply what is the true construction of the last clause of sec. 8 of the Canadian Patent Act, ch. 61, of the Revised Statutes of Canada, as amended by sec. 1 of the Canadian Act 55 & 56 Vict., ch. 24. This Act came into operation on July 9, 1892, and applied to all Canadian patents granted after that date.

The section, as amended, is as follows:—

"8. Any inventor who elects to obtain a patent for his invention in a foreign country before obtaining a patent for the same invention in Canada, may obtain a patent in Canada, if the same be applied for within one year from the date of the issue of the first foreign patent for such invention; and if within three months after the date of the issue of a foreign patent, the inventor gives notice to the Commissioners of his intention to apply for a patent in Canada for such invention, then no other person having commenced to manufacture the same device in Canada during such period of one year, shall be entitled to continue the manufacture of the same after the inventor has obtained a patent therefor in Canada, without the consent or allowance of the inventor; and, under any circumstances, if a foreign patent exists, the Canadian patent shall expire at the earliest date on which any foreign patent for the same invention expires."

The material facts and dates are as follows:—

On March 1, 1892, a Mr. Jones, an American, obtained a patent in the United States for improvements in boiler and other furnaces. On the same day Mr. Jones applied in Canada for a Canadian patent and in England for a British patent for the same invention.

On July 12, 1892, the British patent was granted for fourteen years from March 1, 1892, but its duration for that period depended on the payment of the necessary fees.

On October 15, 1892, the Canadian patent was granted for eighteen years from October 15, 1892.

On March 1, 1897, the British patent expired, the fees necessary for keeping it subsisting not having been paid.

On September 1, 1898, the owners of the Canadian patent, i.e., respondents in this appeal, brought an action against the appellants for infringing that patent, and the plaintiffs were successful and obtained judgment in the action.

Afterwards the defendant, in an action obtained leave to amend their pleadings in order to plead that before the commencement of the action the Canadian patent had expired by reason of the expiration of the British patent, and also by reason of the expiration of an Italian patent, to which, however, it is unnecessary now to allude.

A new trial was directed, and took place before Burbidge, J., who had tried the action, and judgment was given for the defendants, i.e., the present appellants, on the ground that the amended defence was proved. From this decision (which is referred to as the judgment of the Exchequer Court) the plaintiffs appealed to the Supreme Court, and the judgment was reversed. Hence this appeal.

It is common ground, that their Lordships concur in the view, that a British patent is a foreign patent within the meaning of the Canadian Patent Act; and that the British patent and the Canadian patent were for the same invention, and that the former expired in March, 1897.

The whole question, therefore, turns on the meaning and legal effect of the words "under any circumstances, if a foreign patent exists, the Canadian patent shall expire at the earliest date on which any foreign patent for the same invention expires."

The words "if a foreign patent exists" invite the question—When—what time is referred to? The Supreme Court have held (by a majority) that these words refer to the date of the application for the Canadian patent; the Exchequer Court held that they referred to the date of the grant of the Canadian patent. This last construction is sufficient for the appellants in this particular case; but their counsel contended that even this construction is too narrow, and that the words refer to any time during the continuance of the Canadian patent, the duration of which is made to depend on the earliest termination of any foreign patent for the same invention. Their Lordships are of opinion that this wider construction of the words is the true one. They are unable to discover any sufficient reason for putting any more restricted meaning on the words. The language is clear and imperative. Their Lordships can only understand it as declaring that under all circumstances as soon as any foreign patent for the same invention expires the Canadian patent, if then existing, shall expire also. They can find no limit as to time except that the foreign patent must both exist and expire after the Canadian patent has been granted, and before it has ceased from any other cause. The French version of the Act is, if possible, even clearer than the English version. Both, however, express the same meaning.

The Supreme Court were naturally influenced by a prior decision of their own on sec. 8 as it stood in its original shape. In *Dreschel* v. *Auer Incandescent Light Manufac-*

turing Co. (6 Ex. Ct. Reps. 55; 28 S.C.R. 608) it was held that similar words in the original section referred to the date of the grant, and that a foreign patent obtained subsequently to the grant of a Canadian patent and expiring during its continuance did not affect its duration. Their Lordships do not think it necessary to reconsider this case; but assuming it to have been correct, having regard to sec. 8 as it then stood, they are unable to concur in the view that in sec. 8 as it now stands the date of the application has become the date to which the last clause applies.

Their Lordships will, therefore, humbly advise His Majesty to reverse the judgment of the Supreme Court, with costs to be paid by the respondents, and to restore the judgment of the Exchequer Court.

The respondents must pay the costs of this appeal.

Solicitors for the appellants: *Bompas, Bischoff, Dodgson, Cofe and Bompas.*

Solicitor for the respondents: *S. V. Blake.*

[IN THE SUPREME COURT OF NOVA SCOTIA.]

THE SHEDIAC BOOT AND SHOE COMPANY

v.

BUCHANAN.

BEFORE McDONALD C.J., RITCHIE AND TOWNSHEND, JJ., AND
GRAHAM, E.J.

*Assignments and preferences—Bill of sale—Sale by sheriff—Intent
to prefer—" Proceeding " to impeach—R.S.N.S. (1900), ch. 145,
sec. 4, sub-secs. 1 and 2.*

The defendant, a sheriff, seized and sold goods under an execution at
the suit of third parties. Plaintiffs claimed the goods sold under
a bill of sale from R., which had been given to plaintiffs when
R. was heavily indebted to them and other creditors and unable
to pay his debts in full. The seizure and sale by the sheriff took
place on the 30th day of October, 1901. the bill of sale having
been given on the 1st of that month.

Held, in an action for trespass and conversion, that the levy by the
sheriff was an " action or proceeding " taken to set aside the
transaction within the meaning of sub-section 2 of section 4 of
R.S.N.S. (1900), ch. 145, and that the bill of sale must be presumed to have been made with intent to give an unjust preference, and to be such preference and that as against the creditors
represented by the defendant, it was utterly void.

In an action by plaintiffs, an incorporated company,
with headquarters at Shediac, in the Province of New
Brunswick, against the defendant, the Sheriff of the County
of Victoria, Cape Breton, to recover the price of goods
seized and sold by defendant under execution and for
damages, judgment for the defendant was delivered by
MEAGHER, J., as follows:—

The defendant seized and sold the goods, the subject of
this action, on the 30th day of October, 1901, under an execution at the suit of the Campbell Boot and Shoe Company,
against one Robert Roberts.

The plaintiff's title depends upon a bill of sale from Roberts given on the 1st of October, 1901, which covered everything owned by him, except an equity of redemption in a small house and lot of land upon which there were encumbrances amounting to $1,130, and which was completed quite recently before the date of the bill of sale.

When he gave the bill of sale he was indebted to the plaintiff in a sum of upward of $560, all of which was overdue, and in addition he owed some trade debts aggregating, with plaintiff's debt, over $900.

The defendant sold all the boots and shoes and leather on Roberts' premises which produced $255. Beyond that, I have no proof of the value of Roberts' personal property, nor of the goods covered by the bill of sale. The sum cannot, however, be regarded as a fair criterion of their real value.

The main question is whether the bill of sale offended against the provisions of ch. 145 relating to assignments and preferences.

Roberts did a small business selling ready-made boots and shoes, and he and another man worked at boot and shoe making. In addition to this he kept a number of boarders, fifteen or thereabouts. He has been in business upwards of two years. He testified that his profits were from $75 to $100 a month from his operation. This appeared to me to be more than a rough guess on his part, and I feel confident his estimate was excessive to say the least. If his profits were so large he never would have got so far behind as he did, especially as there is no proof of any losses by him.

A few weeks before the bill of sale was given, his wife and daughter became ill with typhoid fever. His servant and boarders left, and he was obliged to absent himself from business in order to care for those who are ill. So far as profits are concerned, this, even at his own estimate, would only involve a loss of $100 or thereabouts. His sales, of course, did not go on in the meantime, and that would leave him short of money, but his stock in trade would remain unchanged. He attributes his inability to meet his liabilities to that circumstance. But if the result was to make him insolvent or unable to pay his debts in full when he gave the bill of sale, I must give effect to the law applicable to such a situation without paying any heed, whatever, to the causes which brought about that condition. If he was insolvent when he gave the bill of sale, it cannot affect the legal aspect that his insolvency was due to causes over which he had no control.

The plaintiffs took possession of the goods conveyed to them within a few hours after the bill of sale was given, and put Roberts in charge to make sales and remit the proceeds to them monthly.

Nothing was said as to whether he was to be paid for his services or not. They engaged to supply him with new goods necessary to bring the stock up to a fair assortment of sizes for sale which were to be charged to him.

The arrangement, it appears to me, was intended to enable him to continue his business rather than a realization of the plaintiff's security.

Roberts admits that when the bill of sale was given, he was not in a position to pay his debts in full, nor has he been since. He was sued by the Campbell Boot and Shoe Co. about ten days before the bill of sale was given, and was subsequently sued by several others.

None of these things which he says caused his inability to pay his debts in full occurred or were done after he gave the bill of sale, excepting perhaps the recovery of the judgment and the levying of an execution upon the judgment recovered in the action which was commenced against him ten days or so before he gave the plaintiff that document.

He thought that if he had not been interefered with by the levy he would have been able to pay his debts as they matured. As to this I am sure it was entirely too sanguine and moreover, he gave no reasons to enable me to say that his opinions were well founded. Moreover, I do not know how he could entertain that belief when he admitted that on October 1st, some days, at least, before any levy was made, he was not able to pay his debts in full.

I feel quite strongly that the facts in proof require me to find that the bill of sale was made by him at a time when he was insolvent within the meaning of ch. 145, that it was made with intent to defeat and prejudice his other creditors, and he gave the plaintiffs an unjust preference over his other creditors, and it was therefor void.

He claimed that his house and land were worth $2,000 at the date in question, but as to that I have no facts— nothing but his unsupported opinion, which I have to repeat, was, in my judgment, far too sanguine a notion of its value. The soliciter for the execution creditor was offered payment in full of the claim before the sale was made under the execution, but did not accept it, and went on with the sale. I cannot avoid saying that I find it impossible to discover any plausible excuse for such action. It operated most cruelly, to use a mild expression, upon Roberts. If I accepted the reasons for the course taken, which the witness McDonald stated were given to him, I should be obliged to conclude that such case had a feature in it more objectionable than cruelty. I need not say whether I believed that testimony or not.

The defendant will have judgment with costs.

From this judgment the plaintiffs appealed to the Supreme Court. Judgment was reserved.

January 17th, 1903. The judgment of their Lordships was delivered by RITCHIE, J. :—

This action was brought against the Sheriff of Cape Breton for the conversion of goods on which he levied in October, 1901, under executions against Robert Roberts. The plaintiff claims these goods under a bill of sale from the said Roberts dated the first day of October, 1901, which bill of sale the defendant claims to be invalid under the provisions of ch. 145 of the Revised Statutes of this Province.

These provisions are contained in sec. 4, and are as follows :—

"(4) Every transfer of property made by an insolvent person

"(a) with intent to defeat, hinder, delay or prejudice his creditors or any one or more of them, or

"(b) to or for a creditor with intent to give such creditor an unjust preference over other creditors of such insolvent person or over any one or more of such creditors, shall as against the creditor or creditors injured, delayed, prejudiced or postponed be utterly void.

"(2) If any such transfer to or for a creditor has the effect of giving such creditor a preference over the other creditors of such insolvent person, or over any one or more of them, such transfer shall

"(a) in and with respect to any action or proceeding which brought, had or taken to impeach or set aside such transfer within sixty days after the giving of the same be presumed to have been made with intent to give

such creditor an unjust preference, whether such transfer
was made voluntarily or under pressure.''

The levy was made within sixty days after the giving
of the bill of sale, and the first question that arises is,
whether or not such levy was an action or proceeding
brought, had or taken to impeach or set aside such transfer.

I think it was. Such a proceeding is, in my experience,
the most usual and effective way of testing the validity of
a bill of sale of personal property, and it would be unduly
straining the Act to hold, as the plaintiff's counsel contended, that the only mode by which a creditor could invoke
this provision was by an action to set aside the bill of sale.
Besides, this provision is made in relation to such an action
by different words—''action brought''—and in interpreting the Act some meaning must be given to—''proceeding
had or taken''—which are very comprehensive words.

It is clear that the effect of the giving of the bill of
sale was to give the plaintiff a preference over the other
creditors of the said Robert Roberts, and if the levy was,
as I think it was, an action or proceeding had or taken to
impeach it, the bill of sale by the provisions of sub-sec. 2
must be presumed to have been made with intent to give
an unjust preference and to be an unjust preference whether
such transfer was made voluntarily or under pressure. The
last words remove, I think, from our consideration all the
questions so fully discussed in Ontario and in the Supreme
Court of Canada in relation to what is known as ''pressure'' in dealing with such conveyances. When most of
these decisions were given the Ontario Act was not similar
to ours, but it has since been amended, and they are now
almost alike, the words *''primâ facie,''* which in the
Ontario Act precede the word ''presumed'' have been
omitted from ours, and the argument that the ''intent''

has been made rebuttable materially strengthened. This question came before the Court of Appeal in Ontario in *Webster* v. *Crickmore* (a), and the Court then held that under the Act now in force, evidence of pressure was not admissible to rebut the presumption of an intent to give preference.

If I am right so far, it has been established that this bill of sale was given by a person to one of his creditors with intent to give such creditor an unjust preference over the other creditors of such person.

The only thing remaining to bring this case clearly within sub-sec. (b) of sec. 4 is as regards the insolvency of Roberts.

Was Roberts insolvent when he gave the bill of sale? In my opinion he was.

The statement that he gave on the trial, of his business affairs, shewed it conclusively to my mind, and he admitted on his cross-examination that he was not able on the 1st October, 1901, to pay his debts in full, nor had been since.

The result is that this bill of sale being a transfer made by an insolvent person to a creditor with intent to give him an unjust preference over other creditors of such insolvent is, as against the creditors so delayed, prejudiced or postponed (in this case represented by the defendant) utterly void.

The appeal will be dismissed with costs.

Solicitor for plaintiff : *Charles P. Fullerton.*
Solicitor for defendant : *Finlay McDonald.*

(a) (1898), 25 A. R. 97.

Notes :—

· ''Action or proceeding.'' The attack made against the fraudulent transaction in this instance was collateral, arising as a matter of defence to an action brought the persons claiming under the transfer. The question of validity may also be decided on an interpleader proceeding (*b*). Or, in Ontario, by a summary application to the Court under Consolidated Rule 1015 (*c*).

The commoner method of attacking a fraudulent conveyance is by a substantive action at law or in equity. If the creditor sue on his own behalf merely, he must be an execution creditor with an execution in the sheriff's hands (*d*). If, however, he sue on behalf of himself and all other creditors, he may bring his action without first obtaining judgment and execution (*e*).

It is formally proper that the writ and claim should state that the plaintiff is suing on behalf of himself and all other creditors (*f*) ; but whether the action be or be not so entitled, the Court will see to it that the proper order is made for the benefit of all creditors (*g*).

Except where the action is brought by the assignee for the benefit of creditors, the debtor is a proper party to be joined (*h*). The grantor, the grantee (and all parties interested) should also be parties so that the whole matter may be disposed of at one time(*i*).

(*b*) *Cole* v. *Porteous* (1892), 19 A.R. 111; *Thomson* v. *Stone* (1902), 4 O.L.R. 333.

(*c*) See also sec. 202 of the Ontario Division Courts Act.

(*d*) *McCall* v. *McDonald* (1885), 13 S.C.R. 247.

(*e*) *Whiting* v. *Laurason* (1859), 7 Gr. 603; *Turner* v. *Smith* (1879), 26 Gr. 198; *Colver* v. *Swayze* (1879), 26 Gr. 395; *Murphy* v. *Wilson* (1879), 27 Gr. 1; *Abell* v. *Morrison* (1876), 23 Gr. 109. And see Parker's Frauds on Creditors, p. 207.

(*f*) *Soane* v. *Duckett* (1883), 3 O.R. 370; *Worraker* v. *Pryer* (1876), L.R. 2 Ch. D. 110.

(*g*) *Wooldridge* v. *Norris* (1868), L.R. 6 Eq. p. 44; *Hooper* v. *Smart* (1875), L.R. 1 Ch. D. 90.

(*h*) *Beattie* v. *Wenger* (1897), 24 A.R. 72; *Leacock* v. *Chambers* (1886), 3 Man. 645.

(*i*) *Gibbons* v. *Darvill* (1888), 12 P.R. 478.

The right of action may be lost by delay if the laches has continued long enough to bar the legal right (j). This does not mean that a deed fraudulent as to creditors is made good because it is not attacked for ten or twenty years; if it is fraudulent it remains so, although it may be secure from attack because purchasers for value without notice have come in, or because the claims of all creditors have been barred by lapse of time (k).

The right of action (under the Statute of Elizabeth) of a person defrauded may also be lost in either of the two following ways:—

(1) By the deed having become for value by a consideration arising *ex post facto* before any steps are taken to impeach it.

(2) The voluntary grantee may have divested himself of the property by a *bona fide* transfer of it for value to a *bona fide* purchaser for value without notice of fraud (l).

(j) *Trites* v. *Humphreys* (1898), 2 N.B. Eq. 2.

(k) *Boyer* v. *Garfield* (1886), 11 O.R. 571.

(l) May on Fraudulent Conveyances, 2nd ed., p. 325; *Tennant* v. *Gallow* (1894), 25 O.R. p. 61.

[IN THE SUPREME COURT OF NOVA SCOTIA.]

HARRISON ET AL.

v.

THE WESTERN ASSURANCE CO.

BEFORE McDONALD, C.J., RITCHIE AND TOWNSHEND, JJ.,
GRAHAM, E.J., AND MEAGHER, J.

*Fire Insurance—Construction of Policy—Warranties and representa-
tions—Materiality—Arbitration—Words " value of the property
insured "—Burden of proof—Joint and several interests—Right
to recover—Conditions in policies—R.S.N.S. (1900), c. 147.*

One of the conditions of a fire insurance policy, issued by the defendant company, provided that, notwithstanding anything in the
contract, the question of materiality, as to any representation in
the application, should be a question for the court.

Held, that the court were precluded by this condition from holding
statements contained in the application to be " warranties," in
the strict sense that they must be absolutely true, or absolutely
complied with.

Held, that such statements were mere representations which, if untrue, must be material order to avoid the contract.

Held, that if there was anything in the contract which placed these
statements in a different category from ordinary representations
it was contrary to the statutory conditions and inoperative, the
4th section of the Act, R.S.N.S. (1900), c. 147, with respect to
the variation of conditions by the insurer, not having been complied with.

Held, that the intention of the statute could not be defeated by putting different stipulations, generally known as conditions in the
body of the contract itself.

One of the substituted conditions provided, that, " in the event of
disagreement as to the amount of the loss, the same shall be ascertained in the following manner." Then followed a provision
for the appointment of arbitrators to estimate the loss, stating
separately sound value, damage, etc.

Held, that the arbitrators, appointed under this provision exceeded
their duty in attempting to fix the value of the property at the
time the insurance was effected, the words " value of property
insured," meaning the value at the time of the fire, and not the
value at the time the insurance was effected.

Held, with respect to the question of value, that the onus was upon
the company, relying upon overvaluation, to prove it.

One of the questions asked in connection with the application for insurance was: " 5. State fully applicant's interest in the property, whether owner, trustee, etc." This was answered "Owner."

Held, that this answer was correct, the evidence shewing that the plaintiffs were husband and wife, and that one part of the property insured was owned by the husband, and the remainder by the husband and wife jointly.

Held, that if particulars of title were required a different question would be required, and should have been asked.

The 11th and 12th questions were intended to elicit information as to whether the applicants had ever any property destroyed by fire, and if so, the date of the fire, and, if insured, the name of the company interested. The applicants replied in the affirmative to the first question, and, in reply to the second question, said " 1892. National, and London and Lancashire."

Held, that these questions were correctly answered, the evidence shewing that the applicants had a house destroyed by fire in June, 1892, and a barn in September of the same year, and that the company last named were the insurers of the house and barn, and the company first named the insurers of the furniture in the house.

Held, that the questions were not material to the risk, and that, if further information was desired, more definite enquiries should have been made.

Defendants claimed that plaintiffs, in their proofs of loss, falsely stated the value of the property insured, and that this, under the statutory conditions, was a false and fraudulent statement which vitiated the claim.

Held, that the words of the condition meant a statement false to the knowledge of the person making it, and not a statement of the value in excess of that fixed by arbitrators, this being a matter in respect to which there was room for diversity of opinion.

Held, that as soon as plaintiffs proved the policy, the fire, and the submission and award, their case was complete and the onus then rested upon defendants.

Held, that the action was one in which the plaintiffs were entitled to sue jointly and recover, notwithstanding the fact that they had separate interests in the property covered by the insurance.

This was an appeal from the judgment of WEATHERBE, J., in favor of plaintiffs in an action to recover the amount of loss by fire to property insured in the defendant company. The facts appear sufficiently in the judgment of the Court per Ritchie, J.

In the argument the following cases were referred to: *North British Ins. Co.* v. *McLennan*(1); *Hambrough* v.

(1) (1892), 21 S.C.R. 293.

Mutual Life Ins. Co.(2) ; *Anderson* v. *Fitzgerald*(3) ; *Tate*
v. *Hyslop*(4) ; *Ionides* v. *Pender*(5) ; *Moore* v. *Ins. Co.*(6) ;
London Ins. Co. v. *Mansel*(7) ; *Findley* v. *Fire Ins. Co.*(8) ;
London Ass. Co. v. *Great Northern Transit Co.*(9) ; *Wilson*
v. *Standard Fire Ins. Co.*(10) ; *Butler* v. *Standard Ins.
Co.*(11).

W. E. Roscoe, K.C., for the appellants.

A. Drysdale, K.C., for the respondents.

Jany. 17th, 1903.—Ritchie, J., delivered the judgment
of the Court:—

In consequence of the stringent and inequitable conditions inserted in their policies by many fire insurance companies doing business in this Province, the Legislature, in
1899 (R.S.N.S. 1900, ch. 147), enacted that certain statutory conditions set forth in a schedule to the Act should, as
against any insurer be deemed to be a part of every contract of fire insurance, and no stipulation to the contrary,
or providing for any variation addition or omission should
be binding on the assured unless evidenced in the manner
prescribed in that behalf.   The Act also contained the following provisions:—

(2) 1895), 72 L.T. 140.
(3) (1853), 4 H.L.C. 484.
(4) (1885), 15 Q.B.D. 368.
(5) (1874), L.R. 9 Q.B. 531.
(6) (1888), 14 A.R. 597.
(7) (1879), 11 Ch. D. 367.
(8) (1895), 25 O.R. 515.
(9) (1879), 26 Gr. 345.
(10) (1878), 29 C.P. 308.
(11) (1879), 4 A.R. 391.

4. If the insurer desires to vary the said conditions, or to omit any of them or to add new conditions, there shall be added on the instrument of contract containing the printed statutory conditions words to the effect set out in the second schedule, printed in conspicuous type and in ink of a different colour and with the heading " Variations in conditions."

5. No such variation, addition or omission shall, unless the same is distinctly indicated and set forth in the manner hereinbefore mentioned, or to the like effect, be valid and binding on the assured; and no question shall be considered as to whether any such variation, addition or omission is, under the circumstances, just and reasonable, but, on the contrary, the policy shall, as against the insurer, be subject to the statutory conditions only, unless the variations, additions or omissions are distinctly indicated and set forth in the manner or to the effect aforesaid.

6. Where a policy is entered into or renewed containing or including any condition other than or different from the conditions set forth in the first schedule to this chapter, if the condition so contained or included is held by the Court or Judge before whom a question relating thereto is tried, to be not just and reasonable such condition shall be null and void.

In July, 1900, the defendant Company issued a policy to plaintiffs insuring them against loss or damage by fire on certain personal property described in the policy, and situate at Cambridge, Nova Scotia. The statutory conditions are printed in the policy, but they are not numbered in the same way as in the statute. I have cited them from the statute.

Beyond all doubt the personal property so insured was injured by the perils insured against, while the policy was in force, and the damage occasioned by the fire was ascertained by arbitrators chosen as provided by the terms of the policy, who awarded the sum of $660.45 as the amount of the damage caused by the fire.

The defendant company refused to pay the amount so awarded, and relies upon certain legal objections, which it is alleged, afford the company a defence to this action brought on said policy. This cause was tried without a jury and judgment given for the plaintiffs for $660.45. From this judgment the defendant company has appealed on several grounds which I shall now consider.

The first ground was that by the terms of the contract the statements contained in the application for the insurance were made "warranties" and were, therefore, conditions precedent and as they were not strictly correct the policy never attached.

In an insurance contract, the difference between a "warranty" and a "representation" seems to be that a warranty must be strictly complied with, and if it is not, or is untrue, the policy is avoided, it being of no consequence, whether it is material to the risk or not, while a representation, if untrue, will not avoid the policy unless it is material to the risk.

There is nothing in this contract which in terms makes the statements in the application warranties, and the fourth statutory condition precludes, I think, this Court from so holding. This condition is as follows: —

> Notwithstanding anything in the contract between the assured and the insurer, the question of materiality as to any representation in the application shall be a question for the court, provided, however, that such question shall be decided by the Judge or Judges trying or hearing the cause and not by the jury.

If the trial Judge is required to pass upon the question of the materiality of the statements in the application, they cannot be "warranties" in the strict sense that they must be absolutely true or absolutely complied with, but are mere "representations" which, if untrue, must be material in order to avoid the contract. If there be anything in the contract which places these statements in a different category from ordinary representations, they are contrary to the statutory conditions and are inoperative, the 4th section of the Act above cited not having been complied with.

A further contention was made that these statements were not conditions but part of the contract but this position is, I think, untenable because, if that should prevail, the statute would be useless and could be avoided and its intention defeated by putting the different stipulations which are generally known in such contracts as "conditions" in the body of the contract itself, which would not be tolerated.

Another point was that the statements were misrepresentations and material to the risk.

The statements as to which objections are made are those relating to the value of the property insured and the answers given to the fifth, twelfth and thirteenth questions in the application. As regards the value at the time of the insurance, counsel for the defendant company contended that the plaintiffs were bound by the award made by the arbitrators. I think they are not for the following reasons :—

The seventeenth statutory condition provides that

> If any difference arises as to the value of the property insured, of the property saved or of the amount of the loss, such value and amount and the proportion thereof (if any) to be paid by the insurer, shall, whether the right to recover on the policy is disputed or not, and independently of all other questions, be submitted to arbitration, etc., etc.

The defendant company has, in accordance with the provision in the statute varied this condition by substituting another, and I cannot say that the variation in this respect is not just and reasonable as it imposes no additional burthen on the assured. The substituted condition is :—

> In the event of disagreement as to the amount of the loss, the same shall, whether the right to recover on this policy is disputed or not, be ascertained in the manner following. The insured and this company shall each select one competent and disinterested appraiser, who shall, together estimate and appraise the loss to detail, stating separately sound value and damage, and their award, in writing, etc., etc.

It will be seen that the words in the statutory condition "if any difference arises as to the value of the property insured" have been omitted, and there is no authority in this policy for referring such a matter to arbitration so as to bind the plaintiffs to accept any award as to the true value when the insurance was effected, when the question arises as to whether the value given in the application was true or false. Besides this it was not referred by the submission which is in these terms :—

> It is hereby agreed that the value of the property insured and the value of the property salved and the amount of the loss sustained by etc., etc., be and the same is hereby referred, etc., etc.

These words taken with those of the substituted condition I have quoted "stating separately sound value and damage" clearly indicate to my mind that the words in the submission "the value of the property insured" meant the value at the time of the fire and not the value at the time the insurance was effected. If the latter was meant it should have been clearly stated so that the plaintiffs would have notice that evidence was required on that point. It is manifest, I think, that the only question intended to be referred and ascertained was the amount of the loss and not any other question which might materially affect the position of plaintiffs and defeat any action on the policy. The arbitrators, in my opinion, exceed their authority when they attempted to fix the value of the property at the time the policy was effected. It is not good evidence and binds no one.

There are four different lots of goods included in the policy (1) goods in the barn; (2) dyes and chemicals in a wooden building; (3) household furniture; (4) piano.

It must be remembered that, under the first statutory condition, concealment and misrepresentation of material facts by the assured only affect the insurance on the property in respect of which the concealment and misrepresentation took place and, in this case, overvaluation is claimed in respect of only two of the four different lots insured, viz., the dyes and chemicals and the household furniture.

If the defendant company be relying upon the fact that the property was overvalued in the application, the onus is on the company to prove it and this, I think, has not been done. For the reasons already given, I exclude from my consideration any evidence that may be afforded by the award. The same remarks apply to the furniture. The defendant company did not attempt to shew that it was not of the value of $1,000 at the time it was insured.

Now as regards the answers to the questions: The 5th is: "State fully applicant's interest in the property, whether owners, trustee, etc. Answer. Owners."

The facts in evidence are that the plaintiffs being husband and wife were the applicants. The dyes and chemicals were owned by the husband and the other property by the husband and wife jointly. The contention on the part of defendant company was that the plaintiffs should in answer to this question state the nature of their title and the respective interest of each of them.

The object of the question as I understand it is to ascertain the nature of the interest required to be insured, and the words "whether owners, trustees, etc.," shew this. A great many persons besides owners have insurable interests, such as mortgagees, agents, bailees, etc., and it might be important to the insurers to know what was the nature of the interest of the applicants in the property. If they wished to know the particulars of the title a different question would be required, and I assume it would be asked. The answer given was a correct one.

The 11th and 12th questions are:—

Q.—Have you, or if a firm, has any member of it ever had any property destroyed by fire?

A.—Yes.

Q.—Give the date of the fire and if insured name of company interested?

A.—1892. National and London and Lancashire.

These questions are, I think, not material to the risk. They might possibly be so limited as to make them to some extent material but this has not been done. I fail to see how it can be material to a company insuring property in Nova Scotia to know whether or not the applicant has had property destroyed by fire, perhaps years ago, in some other part of the world. If the company wished to enquire into the moral character of the applicants it might be material to know if they had committed arson, but nothing of that sort was suggested by the counsel for the company, and I never heard of any such inquiries being made by a fire insurance company in the application. The answers, however, are, I think, correctly given. The evidence is that the applicants had a house burnt in June, 1892, and a barn in September of the same year, both of which they rebuilt. The London & Lancashire Insurance Company was the insurer of the house and barn on both occasions and the National Insurance Company the insurer of the furniture in the house in June. If any further information was required the question should have been differently framed and the inquiries more definite. Besides this there was no actual concealment. McMasters, the local agent of the defendant company, when he forwarded and recommended the application for this insurance was fully aware of the fires in June and September, 1892.

The defendant company further claimed that the plaintiffs, in their proofs of loss, falsely stated the value of the property destroyed.

The 16th statutory condition is, "Any fraud or false statement in a statutory declaration in relation to any of the above particulars shall vitiate the claim."

This, I think, means a statement false to the knowledge of the person making it, in other words, a false statement for which he could be indicted. The onus of proving this is also on defendant company. The plaintiffs declared that the amount of their loss was $1,481.00 and a magistrate in the vicinity certified under his hand that he verily believed they had sustained a loss by the fire to that amount. Now what evidence has the defendant company given to prove that this statement was incorrect and that the plaintiffs knew it was? Absolutely nothing but the award. That is certainly conclusive as to the amount for which the defendant company is liable but it is not evidence given under oath and would not be sufficient to convict the plaintiffs or to justify anyone in holding that, when they made the declaration, they knew that their loss did not amount to $1,481.00. The discrepancy is principally in relation to the dyes and chemicals and the furniture, and there is plenty of room for the existence of a great diversity of opinion, for, after all, it is not a fact but a mere matter of opinion. Persons would naturally value their own furniture at a higher price that strangers would and make a larger estimate of the damage done to it. As regards the dyes which were manufactured one person might value them at their selling price while another person might think that the value of the chemicals of which they were composed was all the insurance company ought to pay. In my opinion this defence has not been proven.

The defendant company also objected to the reception of the testimony of the plaintiff, Cuthbert Harrison, in relation to the amount of the damage sustained. But such evidence was immaterial and the plaintiffs' case was complete without it. As soon as they proved the policy, the fire, the submission and award their case was complete and the onus was then on defendant company to substantiate any defence the company had and this, I think, has not been done.

The appeal will be dismissed with costs.

McDONALD, C.J., TOWNSHEND and GRAHAM, E.J., concurred.

MEAGHER, J.—I agree in the conclusions reached. I say this because of some expressions in the judgment just read to which I do not wish to commit myself. For a time I had some doubt as to the right of these parties to sue jointly on a policy in which they had separate interests, but I find in May on Insurance, sec. 35, that an action may be brought on such a policy, and that the parties may recover.

Appeal dismissed with costs.

Solicitor for (plaintiffs) respondents: *E. B. Cogswell.*
Solicitor for (defendants) appellants: *A. E. Dunlop.*

Notes:—

The fourth statutory condition under R.S.N.S. (1900), ch. 147, reads as follows: "Notwithstanding anything in the contract between the assured and insurer, the question of the materiality of any representation in the application shall be a question for the Court and not for the jury." This condition, which leans to the advantage of the assured, is not to be found in the statutes of any other Province.

On the contrary the sixteenth statutory condition of the Nova Scotia Statute, or the gist of it, is to be found in the statutory conditions in force in all the Provinces. The Nova Scotia Act is worded as follows: "Any fraud or false statement in a statutory declaration in relation to any of the above particulars (of proofs of loss) shall vitiate the claim." The Courts have always been very strict in construing the various statutory requirements respecting proof of loss. Anything that has the appearance of fraud is frowned upon and non-compliance with the conditions is generally fatal.

Where proofs of loss were, by the terms of the policy, to be delivered "as soon after the loss as possible" and were delayed without reason for eight months, the policy was avoided(a); and in the same case where it was required to state the actual value of the property at the time of the loss but a statement was given shewing the cost a year previous to the placing of the insurance, it was held that this was not a compliance with the policy and condition(b). In *Camwell* v. *Beaver and Toronto Mutual*(c), it was held that the words "as soon after as possible" do not apply to the magistrate's certificate, which is required to be produced only within a reasonable time.

The plaintiff having insured the contents of her house and having suffered loss, stated in her statutory declaration that her loss was over $1,500 whereas the contents were proved to be worth only $150. This mis-statement, it was

(a) *Cameron* v. *Canada Fire, etc., Co.* (1884), 6 O.R. 392.

(b) *Ibid.*

(c) (1876), 39 U.C.R. 1.

held, vitiated the whole claim and not merely the claim in respect to the particular property as to which it was made(d).

An assured was required to produce a certificate of two magistrates most contiguous to the place of the fire. Failing in this on their refusal, he finally obtained such certificate from two magistrates residing at a distance from the fire. This was held by a strong Court not to be a compliance with the condition, and the assured was precluded from recovering on the policy(e). See also on this point *Shannon* v. *Hastings* (*f*) and *Platt* v. *Gore* (*g*).

A coroner is a magistrate, who may give a certificate(h).

Where the certificate did not state, as required by the policy, that the magistrate had enquired into the truth of the matter set out nor that the loss was sustained on the subject matter insured, it was held clearly insufficient(i).

The condition as to arbitration in case of difference of opinion as to the value of the property and the loss is substantially the same in all provinces. Proceedings under such a clause were held to be in the nature of an arbitration and not of a valuation merely(j).

Where the reference to arbitration was taken after an action commenced and the arbitrators awarded the assured $1,700 on a valuation at $2,500, while the jury at the trial found that the assured had truly represented the property as having been worth $3,500 and estimated his loss at that amount, it was held that the assured was entitled to judgment for the amount of the award(k).

(d) *Harris* v. *Waterloo Fire Ins. Co.* (1886), 10 O.R. 718.

(e) *Logan* v. *The Commercial Union* (1886), 13 S.C.R. 271.

(f) (1869), 26 C.P. 380.

(g) (1860), 9 C.P. 405..

(h) *Kerr* v. *Brit. Am. Ass. Co.* (1872), 32 U.C.R. 569.

(i) *Mason* v. *Andes Ins. Co.* (1873), 23 C.P. 37.

(j) *Vineberg* v. *Guardian, etc., Co.* (1892), 19 A.R. 293.

(k) *Smith* v. *City of London Ins. Co.* (1887), 14 A.R. 328; affirmed 15 S.C.R. 69.

Mis-statements and misrepresentations as to title: vide *Naughter* v. *Ottawa Agricultural*(*l*),; *Walroth* v. *St. Lawrence*(*m*); *Brogan* v. *Manufacturers*(*n*); *Sherbonneau* v. *Beaver Mutual*(*o*); *Mason* v. *Agricultural*(*p*); *Graham* v. *Ontario Mutual*(*q*); In *Sinclair* v. *Canadian Mutual*(*r*); it was *quaered* whether a false statement or concealment must be fraudulent in order to avoid the policy.

The general rule is that any fraud, concealment or misrepresentation by the applicant of a matter material to be known by the insurer, will avoid the policy(*s*). Thus to conceal one's knowledge that there is danger of incendearism is fraudulent and will avoid the policy(*t*). But questions as to former fires are immaterial to the risk and incorrect answers will not vitiate the policy(*u*). Where questions remain unanswered and the omissions are made in good faith, then, unless the company gives notice that such answers are indispensable to the validity of the contract, the policy will not be avoided by the failure to answer(*v*). And omissions to state immaterial facts will not be fatal(*w*).

(*l*) (1878), 43 U.C.R. 121.

(*m*) (1853), 10 U.C.R. 525.

(*n*) (1878), 29 C.P. 414.

(*o*) (1870), 30 U.C.R. 472.

(*p*) (1868), 18 C.P. 19.

(*q*) (1887), 14 O.R. 358.

(*r*) (1876), 40 U.C.R. 206.

(*s*) *Kniseley* v. *Brit. Am. Ass. Co.* (1900), 32 O.R. 376; *McFaul* v. *Montreal* (1845), 2 U.C.R. 59; *Greet* v. *Citizens* (1879), 27 Gr. 121; May on Insurance, 4th ed., 1900, p. 399, etc.

(*t*) *Herbert* v. *Mercantile* (1878), 43 U.C.R. 384; *Kinseley* v. *British America* (1900), 32 O.R. 376; *Campbell* v. *Victoria Mutual* (1881), 45 U.C.R. 412; *Greet* v. *Citizens* (*supra*); *Bufe* v. *Turner* (1815), 6 Taunt. 338; *Uzielli* v. *Commercial, etc. Ins. Co.* (1885), 15 Q.B.D. 11; May on Insurance, 4th ed., 1900, pp. 412 and 422.

(*u*) *Stott* v. *London & Lancashire Fire Ins. Co.* (1892), 21 O.R. 312.

(*v*) *Rowe* v. *London & Lancashire* (1866), 12 Gr. 311; *Laidlaw* v. *Liverpool & London* (1867), 13 Gr. 377.

(*w*) *Naughter* v. *Ottawa Agricultural Ins. Co.* (1878), 43 U.C.R. 121.

On the other hand ''an equivocal or evasive answer where all the facts are known to the applicant so that he can answer unequivocally is just as fatal as a false one''(*x*).

If an authorized agent of the applicant conceals or misrepresents any material fact, the fraud will be visited upon the principal whether he participates or not(*y*).

It has been long settled that any variation of the statutory conditions have to be reasonable and just. The companies cannot by the means of added stipulations impose on the insured terms more stringent or onerous or complicated than those attached by the statute to the contract. The standard is that which the statute itself affords(*z*). Any variation of the statutory conditions is *primâ facie* unjust and unreasonable(*a*). If variations are inserted but without being so designated they are to be treated as nullities and the policy will be read as containing only the statutory conditions(*b*). The reasonableness of variations is to be tested with relation to the circumstances at the time the policy was issued(*c*).

Thus in *Smith* v. *City of London Ins. Co.*(*d*) an added stipulation that no action should be brought until the expiry of sixty days after proof of loss was held to be unjust and unreasonable. So a condition that a policy shall be void if the title to the property insured shall be disputed in a proceeding at law or in equity(*e*); making any mis-

---

(*x*) May on Insurance, 4th ed., 1900, p. 417; *Cazenove* v. *British Equit. Ass. Co.* (1859), 6 C.B. N.S. 437; *Monson* v. *Muspratt* (1827), 4 Bing. 60; *Huckman* v. *Fernie* (1838), 3 M. & W. 505; *London Ass. Soc.* v. *Mansel* (1879), 48 L.J. Ch. 331.

(*y*) *Shannon* v. *Gore District Mutual* (1875), 37 U.C.R. 380; May, *ibid.* p. 418.

(*z*) *May* v. *Standard* (1880), 5 A.R. 622; *Bellagh* v. *Royal* (1880), 5 A.R. 107; *Butler* v. *Standard* (1879), 4 A.R. 395.

(*a*) *Smith* v. *City of London Ins. Co.* (1886), 11 O.R. 38.

(*b*) *Findley* v. *Fire Ins. Co.* (1895), 25 O.R. 515; *Parsons* v. *Citizens Ins. Co.* (1879), 4 A.R. 96; 7 Ap. Cas. 96.

(*c*) *McKay* v. *Norwich Union* (1895), 17 O.R. 251.

(*d*) *Supra.*

(*e*) *May* v. *Standard, supra; Sands* v. *Standard* (1868), 27 Gr. 167.

· representation a cause of forfeiture was held to be unreasonable in *Butler* v, *Standard*(*f*). Where houses insured were seven in number and likely to be occupied by
tenants for short periods, a stipulation that the policy
would not cover vacant houses unless the company by endorsement allowed the insurance to be continued, was dis-
allowed(*g*).

(*f*) *Supra.*
(*g*) *McKay* v. *Norwich Union* (1895), 17 O.R. 251.

[IN THE SUPREME COURT OF NOVA SCOTIA.]

GEORGE ARMSTRONG

v.

WILLIAM BUCHANAN.

BEFORE McDONALD, C.J., RITCHIE AND TOWNSHEND, JJ., AND
GRAHAM, E.J.

*Bank Act—Warehouse receipt—Title—Sale by pledgee—Waiver of
formalities—53 Vict. (D.), ch. 31, sections 73 and 78 as amended
by 63-64 Vict., chs. 26 and 27.*

A trader being indebted to a bank gave as security two documents,
one a warehouse receipt under the Bank Act, and the other a
sort of bill of sale. On the bank attempting to remove the goods
covered by these documents, the trader resisted and the bank resorted to replevin actions and so obtained the goods. Subsequently an agreement was come to between the parties whereby
the goods were to become the property of the bank and it was
authorized to sell the goods at private sale and to apply the proceeds to the trader's debt, while the trader waived the necessity
of notice and public sale. The right of the creditors under
whom the defendant justified did not then exist. The bank then
sold the goods to the plaintiff and, later, the defendant, a sheriff,
levied on them under executions.

Held, in an action to recover back the goods, that whatever may have
been the irregularities in respect to the Bank Act, the title of the
bank was complete by the compromise made between the bank
and the trader, and that, even if the security held by the bank
was void under the provisions of the Bank Act, not being a present advance but for a past debt, the bank had acquired title by
the subsequent transaction by which the bank became the actual
purchaser of the goods.

This was an appeal from the following judgment of
MEAGHER, J., in which the facts are fully stated: —

The plaintiff purchased the goods in question from the
Commercial Bank of Windsor on the 14th of November,
1901, received delivery of them and put them in his store
forthwith.

On the 10th day of January, 1902, the defendant, the
Sheriff of Cape Breton County, levied upon them an execution of Laing Packing Co. against John H. Bertram and
one at the suit of G. J. Hamilton & Sons.

The goods were orginially the property of John H. Bertram & Co,, who was largely indebted to the above named
bank on and before the 20th of December, 1900, and thence-
forth until after the events occured which gave rise to this
suit.

On the 20th of December, 1900, Bertram & Co. gave the
bank two documents, one purporting to be a warehouse
receipt under the Banking Act, and the other a sort of
general transfer or Bill of Sale. These were given in substitution of other documents which the bank held from
Bertram at that time. What these were for, what shape
they were in or what facts existed when they were given
has not been shewn.

On the 12th of June, 1901, a demand was made by the
bank upon Bertram to cover certain indebtedness with
which he did not comply. Soon afterwards the manager
of the bank at Sydney, and one of his assistants, went to
Bertram's where some, at least, of the goods were which
the documents referred to were intended or purported to
cover. They inspected and marked with an identifying
mark of their own all the goods just referred to which they
could find. They did that with a view to their removal by
the bank and so informed Bertram.

On the following day the bank removed a quantity of
the goods which it had marked, and while this was being
done one of Bertram's clerks forbade further removal. The
bank thereupon ceased removing the goods and resorted to
two replevin actions and through them they obtained possession of a quantity of the goods they claimed including

these now in controversy and all of which purported to be covered by the documents of the 20th of December above referred to.

An appearance was entered by Bertram in these suits by his solicitor and they remained undisposed of until the 13th of September, 1901, when both were settled by the solicitors of the parties thereto.

By the terms of that settlement, which was, as to the suits, verbal, each party was to bear and pay his own costs and the goods were to cease to be Bertram's and to become the property of the bank, which was to sell them and thus ascertain their value and thereby determine the amount Bertram was to receive credit for with the bank in respect thereto. The settlement was made subject to a further term which was to be put in writing. It was afterwards prepared and was signed by Bertram. Its effect was to authorize the bank to sell the goods at private sale and to waive the necessity of notice and public sale either under the Banking Act or the documents on the 20th of December.

It has not been shewn that at the date of that settlement Bertram had any creditors other than the bank. It was he who sought and proposed the settlement.

My attention was not directed to any provision in the Banking Act which prevented the bank making a compromise with Bertram of the replevin suits and of the disputes which gave rise to them. Their debt was then overdue, and so far as I am aware, Bertram had no creditors to be injured or delayed by the settlement he made.

Bertram for a good consideration and in compromise of disputed rights between him and the bank divested himself of whatever title he had to the goods, abandoned all right to the possession thereof and authorized the bank to sell them and apply the proceeds to his indebtedness.

Assuming in this connection, that the documents of title, on which the bank relied, were invalid, it cannot in my judgment, affect the transaction. A dispute as to ownership or possession—strictly speaking as to both existed in the pending suits each party claimed the property, and that controversy was ended by a compromise by which Bertram conceded the bank's right to hold and dispose of the goods and the bank conceded his right to the benefit of the net proceeds in account with it when sold. They were accordingly sold in pursuance of that authority and an innocent party became the purchaser in good faith.

The right of the creditors under whom the defendant justifies did not, I assume, then exist.

The bank's right to possession and its power for sale, was, at the time of the sale to the plaintiff undoubted.

Bertram could never be permitted to dispute these and neither do I think the defendant can.

The plaintiff is entitled to judgment. I do not know whether the plaintiff obtained an order of replevin or not in this action nor whether the goods were sold by defendant nor whether a return bond was given. No evidence was offered and nothing was said on any of these aspects. There was no evidence given of value or of damages and therefore it appears to me that all I can do is to declare the plaintiff's title to the goods and that he is entitled to a judgment.

If a claim is made for damages I shall direct a reference, if need be, to ascertain the amount, and now adjourn further consideration to meet the exigencies of the case.

The plaintiff will have his costs.

From this judgment the defendant appealed.

Jan. 17th, 1903. TOWNSHEND, J., read the judgment of the Court.

It is hardly necessary to say anything more than the learned trial Judge has very clearly pointed out that whatever may have been the irregularities in respect to the Banking Act, the title of the bank to the goods in question was complete by the compromise made between the bank and Bertram & Co. The bank having become owners, as well as possessors of the goods, sold them to the plaintiff, and after the sale while in plaintiff's possession, the defendant levied upon, and took them out of plaintiff's possession under an execution against Bertram. The only possible justification for such an act would be that they were still the property of Bertram. How is this claim asserted? It was contended that the security on the goods held by the bank was void under the provisions of the Banking Act not being for a present advance but for a past due debt. Assume this contention to be correct in law that by reason of the nature of the loan, the bank were not entitled to hold the security against creditors of Bertram, is it not plain that the bank is not obliged to rest its title on that document, nor would its defects, if any, affect the consequent transaction by which the bank became the actual purchaser of the goods and dealt with them as its property.

I am unable to understand on what grounds the defence of this action was justifiable, still less, why an appeal should have been asserted.

The appeal will be dismissed with costs.

Solicitor for plaintiff : *Charles P. Fullerton.*
Solicitor for defendant : *Finlay McDonald.*

Notes:—

The decision in this case turned on the agreement or settlement made between the Commercial Bank and Bertram by which the bank acquired its title and became a purchaser for value of the goods in question. It was, therefore, unnecessary to decide what effect the non-compliance with the provisions of section 78 of the Bank Act requiring notice to the pledgee and the sale to be by auction would have had on the rights of the parties.

Section 78 made the Common Law of England applicable to the Dominion, it having been well settled at common law that a pledgee, upon default, may sell at public auction goods or chattels that are pledged without judicial process upon giving the pledgor reasonable notice to redeem(a).

Sub-sections 2 and 3, of section 78, which contain the stipulations as to the notice necessary before sale and as to the sale being by auction are expressed in negative words, i.e., the statute enacts that sale is to be made in such a manner and not otherwise. It would, therefore, appear that unless these stipulations be strictly complied with the sale will be void, as being unauthorized by either common law or statute (b).

The word "negotiated" is used in section 75 as referring only to the purchase or discount of a bill or note by the bank and does include the renewal which is treated as something apart in the concluding words of the section(c). Where money realized from the discount of notes and placed to the credit of the customer were really controlled by the bank, it was held this was not a negotiation of the notes within this section(d).

(a) MacLaren's Banks and Banking, 2nd ed., 176; *Tucker v. Wilson* (1714), 1 P. Wms. 261; *Kempt v. Westbrook* (1749), 1 Ves. Sr., 278; *Pigot v. Cubley* (1864), 15 C.B.N.S. 701.

(b) MacLaren, *ibid.*, p. 177; *R. v. Leicester* (1827), 7 B. & C. 6; *R. v. All Saints' Wigan* (1876), 1 App. Cas. 629.

(c) MacLaren, *ibid.*, 167; *Iommenjog Coondoo v. Watson* (1884), 9 A.C. 561; *Bank of Hamilton v. Shepard* (1894), 21 A.R. 156.

(d) *Bank of Hamilton v. Halstead* (1897), 28 O.R. 235.

The obligation contracted at the time cannot be made to cover past indebtedness, though it may extend to future advances (e). But where as security for drafts, warehouse receipts were given as collateral security and the debtor agreed that if the proceeds of the goods were more than sufficient to pay these drafts, the surplus should go to pay an old debt, the agreement was held void as to the latter(f).

(e) *Robertson* v. *Lajoie* (1878), 22 L.C.J. 169.

(f) *Perkins* v. *Ross* (1880), 6 O.L.R. 65.

DIGEST.

AGENCY.

See CONTRACT, 3—COMPANY, 4—INSURANCE (Fire), 4, 5, 7.

ARBITRATION.

See FIRE INSURANCE, 8.

ASSIGNMENT.

For Benefit of Creditors.]—*See* INSOLVENCY.

AVAL.

See PROMISSORY NOTES, 3.

BANKING.

1. *Partnership—Two Accounts Charging Personal Account With Partnership Overdraft.*]—R. and R. had a partnership account in a certain bank, and when the firm was dissolved the ledger-keeper gave it credit for a balance, for which the partners wrote cheques. About the same time one of the partners opened a personal account at the same bank, and when it was discovered that, through an error, the partnership account had been credited with about $200 too much, the bank, after notice, charged the partnership overdraft which had resulted from this mistake to the personal account of the partner above referred to.

Held, that the bank had no legal right to so charge such overdraft.

Richards v. *The Bank of B.N.A.* (B.C.) 198.

2. *Advances by Bank—Goods Hypothecated—The Bank Act —Insolvent Estate.*] — Sub-section 2 of section 74 of the Bank Act (53 Vict. ch. 31, as amended), which authorizes banks to "lend money to any wholesale purchaser or shipper of or dealer in products of agriculture, the forest," etc., upon the security of such products, does not apply so as to cover an advance made by a bank upon the security of lumber which, at the date of such advance, has been through the saw mill—the lumber, when converted into logs, being no longer the product of the forest within the meaning of that section.

Judgment of the Superior Court affirmed.

The Molsons Bank v. *Beaudry et al.* (P.E.) 201.

3. *Execution — Money Paid Out by Bank Teller—Passing of Property Therein.*]—H., a superannuated civil service employee, handed his superannuation declaration to the teller of the bank which was authorized to pay the superannuation allowance. The teller counted the money due under the certificate, and placed the bank-notes upon the ledge in the wicket between the teller's box and the outer office where H. was standing; but before H. touched the notes they were seized by a bailiff under an execution against H. which had been placed in the hands of the sheriff.

Held, that the property in the bank-notes passed to H. as soon as they were placed on the ledge, and that, therefore, the seizure on behalf of the executioner creditor was legal.

Hall v. *Hatch, Bank of Montreal* v. *Hatch,* (Ont.) 235.

4. The fact that a bank charges more than seven per cent. interest does not render the transaction in question void—though the bank might be unable to recover such interest under section 80 of the Bank Act.

Adams & Burns v. *The Bank of Montreal et al.* (B.C.) 248.

5. *Bank Act—Warehouse Receipt—Title—Sale by Pledgee— Waiver of Formalities — 53 Vict. (D.), ch. 31, sections 73 and 78 as amended by 63-64 Vict. chs. 26 and 27.*]—A trader being indebted to a bank gave as security two documents. one a warehouse receipt under the Bank Act, and the other a sort of bill of sale. On the bank attempting to remove the goods covered by these documents. the trader resisted and the bank resorted to replevin actions, and so obtained the goods. Subsequently an agreement was come to between the parties whereby the goods were to become the property of the bank. and it was authorized to sell the goods at private sale and to apply the proceeds to the trader's debt. while the trader waived the necessity of notice and public sale. The right of the creditors. under whom the defendant justified, did not then exist. The bank then sold the goods to the plaintiff. and, later. the defendant, a sheriff, levied on them under executions.

Held, in an action to recover back the goods, that whatever may have been the irregularities in respect to the Bank Act. the title of the bank was complete by the compromise made between the bank and the trader, and that, even if the security held by the bank was void under the provisions of the Bank Act, not being a present advance but for a past debt, the bank had acquired title by the subsequent transaction by which the bank became the actual purchaser of the goods.

Armstrong v. Buchanan, 506.

BILL OF LADING.

Carriers—Time Limited for Notice of Loss—Implied Warranty of Seaworthiness.]—A bill of lading contained certain provisions limiting the liability of the carriers, and concluded with a clause to the effect that the owners would not be liable for any loss or damage to merchandise shipped on the vessel in question, unless the claim on account of the same was made within one month from the date of the bill of lading. D.'s goods were damaged, the injury being occasioned by the unseaworthiness of the vessel, but the demand for compensation was not made within the stipulated period.

Held, that the condition as to time in the bill of lading only referred to the other matters and exceptions referred therein; and that, as the implied warranty of seaworthiness was both outside and antecedent to the bill of lading, a claim for damages for breach of that warranty was not affected by the provision in the bill of lading that all claims should be made within one month.

Tattersall v. *National Steamship Co.* (1884), 12 Q.B.D. 297, and *Maori King* v. *Hughes* (1895), 65 L.J.Q.B. 168, followed.

Drysdale v. *The Union Steamship Co.* (B.C.), 156.

Reversed on appeal to the Supreme Court of Canada, which *held* (Mills, J., dissenting), that the contract between the parties was such as to cover all the time from the hour of the delivery of the goods by the shipper to the shipowner, irrespective of the time when the goods were actually loaded on the vessel; that the implied warranty of seaworthiness was, therefore, not antecedent to the bill of lading, and that consequently the conditions contained in that instrument applied, and the claim for compensation should have been made within one month.

The Union Steamship Co. v. *Drysdale* (S.C.), 341.

BILL OF SALE.

See INSOLVENCY, 4.

BOND.

See COMPANY, 5—WINDING-UP, 2.

BOOK DEBTS.

See COMPANIES, 6.

BURDEN OF PROOF.

See FIRE INSURANCE, 8.

CARRIERS.

See BILL OF LADING.

CHATTEL MORTGAGE.

*Promissory Note—Liability of Stranger Endorsing—Bills of Exchange Act, 1890 (45-46 Vict. ch. 61), sec. 56—"Aval"—Chattel Mortgage—Consideration—R.S.O. (1897), ch. 148, secs. 2, 4, 5, 8 and 38.]—*W. M. requested G. M. to endorse his (W. M.'s) note, which G. M. did, being given as security for such endorsement a chattel mortgage on W. M.'s stock in trade. The note was signed by W. M. and was made payable to the order of the Molson's bank; G. M. then endorsed it, and W. M. got it discounted at the Molsons Bank, at whose instance it was subsequently protested for non-payment. A few days after protest G. M. paid the amount due on the note, and took possession under his mortgage, and about two weeks later W. M. assigned for the general benefit of his creditors. Upon action being brought by the assignee to set aside the chattel mortgage as fraudulent and void, it was contended, *inter alia,* that G. M. had never incurred any liability by endorsing the note in question because it was not made payable to him, but to the Molsons Bank, and was never endorsed by the payee.

Held, that the requirement of R.S.O. (1897), ch. 148, sec. 8, that a chattel mortgage shall set forth the consideration, had been sufficiently satisfied by setting out therein the note itself, and declaring that the endorsement thereof was the consideration—it not being necessary to state in the mortgage the legal effect of the facts set out.

Robinson v. Mann (S.C.), 128.

See also COMPANIES, 6.

COLLUSION.

See COMPANY, 6.

COMMERCIAL CONTRACT.

See CONTRACT, 2—SALE OF GOODS—MISE EN DEMEURE.

COMPANY.

1. *Petition for Winding-up Order—Service of Demand for Payment.*]—The demand for payment of a debt due, the neglect to comply with which is proof of insolvency, under R.S. C., ch. 129 (The Winding-up Act), sec. 6, is a formal demand in writing, duly served on the company. The service of a specially endorsed writ of summons does not meet these requirements, not being a "demand," but only a notice that certain proceedings will be taken if the amount thereby claimed is not paid within eight days.

It is a condition essential to the making of a winding-up order that the company shall have had the four days' notice of the application given by R.S.C., ch. 129, sec. 8.

Re Abbott-Mitchell Iron & Steel Co. (Ont.), 23.

2. *Managing Director Conducting all Business—Liability of Company for Notes Made by Him.*]—When the directors of an incorporated company leave the conduct of the general business in the hands of a managing director or secretary, who accepts or makes or endorses such bills or notes as he sees fit, recording such transactions in the books of the company which are examined by its auditors, it will be inferred (even when there is a by-law to the effect that promissory notes shall be signed by the president and the secretary or managing director), that such secretary or managing director was duly authorized to make promissory notes on behalf of the company; and any such notes so made and used by him in the ordinary course of business will bind the company.

The Imperial Bank v. *Farmers' Trading Co.* (Man.), 26.

3. *Management of Company—Power of Majority to Accumulate Profits as Reserve Funds—Sale by Director to Company—Salary of Director.*]—The majority of the shareholders of an incorporated joint stock company have the power, even against the wishes of the minority, to set aside as a reserve fund whatever proportion they deem fit of the annual profits to the company, and there is no jurisdiction in the court to compel such company, so long as it is a going concern, to divide the whole of these profits amongst

its shareholders. The question as to what proportion should be so divided is entirely a matter of internal management, which the shareholders must decide for themselves, the court having no jurisdiction to control the decision so arrived at, or to say what is a "fair" or "reasonable" sum to retain undivided. And since the company thus has power to retain a balance of undivided profits, it follows that it may invest the moneys so retained in such securities as the directors may select, subject to the control of a general meeting of the shareholders.

The president of an incorporated joint stock company bought the plant of an insolvent concern, which he shortly afterwards sold to the company of which he was president, at a considerable profit. There was no evidence that the president was authorized by his own company to purchase these assets, or that he was in any way a trustee for his company of the property so bought.

Held, that though, u p o n these facts, the c o m p a n y might, perhaps, have at one time obtained a decree of rescission of the contract, yet the court had no power to compel the vendor to accept another contract whereby he would be disposing of the assets at a less price.

Burland et al. v. *Earle et al.* (P.C.), 93.

4. *Company Promoting — Fraud in Obtaining Stock Subscriptions—Liability of Directors for Acts Done by Agent for their Benefit.*]—H., who was managing director of an incorporated company, was authorized by his board to secure the services of McK. to solicit stock subscriptions for the company. H. subsequently interviewed W. for that purpose, gave him a prospectus of the company and stated that he himself, as well as each of the various directors, had subscribed and actually paid for a large amount of stock. McK. also made similar statements to W., who subsequently gave his cheque, $1,000, in payment for certain shares. This cheque, endorsed by H. as managing director and by E. as president of the company, was then deposited to the credit of the company, and the proceeds eventually used to pay certain salaries which had been voted by the directors to certain of the promoters as officials of the company. W. having become aware that nothing had ever actually been paid in, brought action to recover the money he had thus paid, on the ground that he had been induced to subscribe by false representations regarding the financial standing of the company.

Held, that since E. and the other directors had authorized H. and McK. to act for them in obtaining W.'s subscription, and had derived a profit from the fraud practised upon him, they were liable for the acts of H. and McK.

Hotchkiss et al. v. *Wilson et al.* (S.C.), **144.**

5. *Winding-up—Assignee Becoming Liquidator—Bond for Performance of Duties—Liability Thereunder.*]—H. was the assignee of the estate of an incorporated company under an assignment made by virtue of the Assignments and Preferences Act (Ontario). Winding-up proceedings were subsequently taken, and H. was then appointed liquidator, and the appellants in this case entered into a bond conditioned on the due performance by H. of his duties of liquidator. H. misappropriated certain monies which were in his hands as assignee at the date of the winding-up order, and which, by the terms of such order, he should have paid over to the liquidator.

Held, that those executing the bond were liable for such monies.

Held, further, that the appellants could not now object to the jurisdiction of the court to make the various orders in the winding-up proceedings (which were recited in the bond itself) or to question the validity of the appointment of H. as liquidator.

Held, further, that the appellants were entitled to bring this appeal from the order of the Master, fixing the amount of their liability under the bond.

In re Army & Navy Clothing Co. (Ont.), **149.**

6. *Debtor and Creditor—Preference — Collusion — Pressure —R.S.B.C., 1897, chs. 86 and 87 —Bank Act, sec. 80—Mortgage by Directors—Ratification by Shareholders — The Companies Act and Amendments.*]—Where there is good consideration, a mortgage comprising the whole of a debtor's property will not be set aside even though the mortgagor is in insolvent circumstances to the knowledge of the mortgagee and the effect of the mortgage is to defeat, delay and prejudice the creditors, if pressure is proved.

A mortgage made by the directors of a company prior to the consent of its shareholders, without which consent there was no power to borrow, may be ratified by the shareholders.

Adams & Burns v. *Bank of Montreal et al.* (B.C.), 248.

7. *Appointment of Manager —Want of By-law — Contract Under Seal—Shareholders Sanction for Payments for Services— R.S.O. 1897, ch. 191, secs. 47 and 48.]*—The plaintiff was named as a director and as manager of the defendant company, incorporated under the Ontario Joint Stock Companies Act, in resolutions passed at a meeting of the provisional directors. IIis services as manager did not result in any benefit to the company, which never went into operation. In an action for his salary,

Held, he was not entitled to recover because (1) no by-law for his appointment as manager had been passed, and (2) no contract had been made with him under the seal of the company.

Birney v. *Toronto Milk Co.,* 452.

8. *Extra-territorial Contract of Company—B.N.A. Act, sections 91 and 92.]*—The Province of British Columbia has the right to incorporate a company with power to enter into extra-territorial contracts of carriage, and it is therefore not *ultra vires* of a company which has been granted a charter by that province to carry goods from British Columbia to the Yukon Territory.

The Victoria Yukon Trading Co. v. *Boyle* (B.C.), 399.

CONDITIONS IN POLICY.

See FIRE INSURANCE, 8.

CONSTITUTIONAL LAW.

See COMPANY, 7.

CONSTRUCTION OF POLICY.

See FIRE INSURANCE, 8.

CONTRACT.

1. *Vis Major—Quantum Meruit.]*—When a tug contracts to tow a stranded vessel, but is prevented from actually doing so by stress of weather and by ice, nothing will be allowed for the work done in attempting to reach the vessel, when the evidence shows that by the exercise of due diligence the master of the tug might have informed himself that it would be impossible to effect a passage by the route attempted.

The Donnelly Salvage and Wrecking Co. v. *Turner* (Ont.), 32.

2. *Sale of Goods — Implied Cancellation of First Agreement —Mise en demeure.*] — Where a contract for the sale of goods stipulated that on one part the delivery thereof, and on the other the payment therefor, should be made at certain specified dates, and it appeared that the vendor had not been ready to deliver at the time agreed upon, that the vendee had then taken no action, but had subsequently demanded and received delivery of smaller orders, and that the vendor had treated this, in his books, as a cancellation of the original contract, it was held on the evidence (there being no allegation that the vendee had tendered, or even that he had been able to pay the amount due on the first contract at the time named) that the contract had been rescinded by the conduct and acts of the parties.

The fact that a contract is of a commercial nature only avoids the necessity for a *mise en demeure* (i.e., the making of a demand for the fulfillment of the obligation) when the date for the doing of the act in question is stated in the contract. Moreover, since, where a *mise en demeure* is necessary, damages only run from the time that the same is given, the mere bringing of an action for damages for the non-delivery of goods some time previous thereto is not such a *mise en demeure* as will entitle the vendee to damages, as, in such a case, whatever loss there may have been has been suffered before the date of the *mise en demeure.*

Goldberg v. *The Dominion Woollen Co.* (Que.), 45.

3. *Sale of Goods by Sample— Warranty—Warehouse Receipts —Agency.*]—A bank advanced money upon the promissory notes of a cold storage firm, endorsed by M., one of the members of the firm, warehouse receipts for goods deposited by M. with his firm being taken as security for his endorsations. The cold storage company bought eggs with the monies so obtained, and warehoused them in the name of M., receipts being issued to him. The firm becoming financially embarrassed, the manager of the bank checked over the goods then in the warehouse, and instructed O'R., the other partner, to sell them and to pay the proceeds of such sales into the bank, which was duly done. One of the purchasers having brought an action for damages caused by breach of warranty regarding the condition of the eggs, the bank contended that it had not been the vendor.

Held, that since the bank had, in fact, had the control over the goods, their title not being disputed, it was immaterial whether or not the warehouse receipts upon which the title was based were such as would have proved good against all comers.

Held, further, that the arrangement between the local manager of the bank and O'R. virtually constituted the latter the agent of the bank for the sale of the goods, no ratification by the head office being necessary; and that, therefore, the bank was liable for the breach of the implied warranty, which, it appeared, was given by O'R., so acting as its agent.

Saunders v. *The Ontario Bank* (Ont.), 56.

4. *By Correspondence—Mailing Letter of Acceptance—Place Where Contract Made—Indication of Place of Payment—Jurisdiction — Declinatory Exception—Waiver — Procedure — C. P.Q. Articles 85, 94, 129, 1164, 1173, 1175, 1176—C.C.P.Q. Articles 85-86.*—An offer was made by the plaintiff by letter dated and posted at Quebec, and was accepted by defendant by a letter dated and posted at Toronto. An action having been brought upon the contract in the Superior Court for the District of Quebec, the defendant, who had been served substitutionally petitioned in revocation of a judgment which had been entered by default, first taking exception to the jurisdiction of the court, and then constituting himself incidental plaintiff, and, as such, making a cross-demand for damages to be set off against the plaintiff's claim.

Held, that in the Province of Quebec, as in the rest of Canada, in negotiations carried on by correspondence, it is not necessary for the completion of the contract that the letter accepting an offer should have actually reached the party making it, but the mailing in the general post-office of such letter completes the contract. (*Underwood* v. *Maguire.* R.J.Q., 6 Q.B. 237, overruled.)

Article 85 of the Civil Code, as amended by 52 Vict. ch. 48 (P.Q.), providing that the indication of a place of payment in any note or writing should be equivalent to election of domicile at the place so indicated, requires that such place should be actually designated in the contract.

In forming an opposition or petition in revocation of judgment the defendant, in order to comply with Art. 1164 C.P., P. Q., is obliged to include therein any cross-demand he may have by way of set-off or in compensation of the plaintiff's claim, and, unless he does so, he cannot afterwards file it as of right.

A cross-demand so filed with a petition for revocation of judgment is not a waiver of a declinatory exception previously pleaded, nor an acceptance of jurisdiction of the court.

In order to take advantage of waiver of a preliminary exception to the competence of the tribunal over the cause of action on account of subsequent incompatible pleadings, the plaintiff must invoke the alleged waiver of the objection in his answers.

Magann v. *Auger* (S.C.), 71.
Magann v. *Auger* (S.C.), 92.

5. *Construction of Apparently Contradictory Clauses—Principle of Giving Effect, if Possible, to Every Stipulation.*]—Plaintiffs agreed to light a certain hotel leased by defendant, and the latter agreed to pay for the light so supplied. · The written contract between the parties contained the two following clauses:—"This contract is to continue in force for not less than thirty six months from the date of first burning, and thereafter until cancelled in writing by one of the parties thereto"; and—"This contract to remain in force after the expiration of the said thirty-six months for the term that the party of the second part renews his lease for the Russell House . . . ." The defendant's lease having expired at the end of the thirty-six months he renewed it for a period of five years.

Held, that he could not, during that time, cancel the contract by a notice in writing, as, if so, the second clause above quoted would be nugatory.

Judgment of the Court of Appeal for Ontario reversed, Girouard, J., dissenting.

The Ottawa Electric Co. v. *St. Jacques* (Ont.), 140.

6. *Fire Insurance—Agent delegating His Authority—Lex loci and Lex Fori.*]—The local agent of a fire insurance company was empowered to make interim insurances by means of receipts countersigned by himself, provided that in all such cases the premiums for the insurances thus effected were paid in cash. The agent employed a canvasser, who assumed to make a contract of insurance for the company— giving an interim receipt countersigned by himself as agent of the company, and taking in payment of the premium a promissory note payable to his own order three months from date.

Held, that the *lex loci* of a contract must be presumed to be that of the *lex fori*, unless the former law is proved to be different.

The Canadian Fire Ins. Co. v. *Robinson et al.* (S.C.), 205.

7. *Completion of.*]—*See* IN-SURANCE (Life), 4.

8. *Gaming.*]—*See* GAMING.

9. *Induced by False State-ment.*]—*See* INSURANCE (Life), 5.

10. *Under Seal.*]—*See* COM-PANY, 7.

────────

COPYRIGHT.

Encyclopaedia — Primâ facie Proof of Proprietorship—Entry At Stationer's Hall—License to Print and Sell—Foreign Re-prints—Notice to Commissioners of Customs—Imperial Acts in Force in Canada—Imp. 39-40 Vict. ch. 36, sec, 152—Imp. 5-6 Vict. ch. 45, secs. 17, 18, 19.]— The defendants, the Imperial Book Company, imported into Canada large numbers of an Am-erican reprint of the plaintiff's encyclopaedia, which plaintiffs maintained was an infringe-ment of their copyright. They had registered the publication pursuant to 11th section of the Copyright Act of 1842, and gave

in evidence a certificate of the entry.

Held, the production of the certificate was all that was neces-sary to make out a *primâ facie* proprietorship in the copyright of an encyclopaedia under secs. 18 and 19.

Held, also, that sec. 152 of the Imperial Customs Law Consoli-dation Act, 1876, 39-40 Vict. ch. 36, which requires notice to be given to the Commissioners of Customs of copyright and of the date of its expiration, is not in force in Canada, despite that, in Part IV. of the appendix to Vol. III. of the Revised Statutes of Ontario, 1897, a statement to the contrary appears.

Semble such a notice would be invalidated by an erroneous statement of the date of the ex-piration of the copyright.

The plaintiffs, in consideration of a large sum of money, by an agreement in writing, gave cer-tain other persons the exclusive right to print and sell the pub-lication in question for a period terminating four years before the expiration of the plaintiffs' copyright, and agreed to deliver to them the plates used in the publishing and not to publish or announce a new edition until the expiration of such period. The other parties agreed to sell only at certain prices, not to alter the text of the book, and on the expiration of the period mentioned, to deliver up any unsold copies and all the plates used in printing them. The plaintiffs expressly reserved the copyright to themselves.

Held, the agreement must be construed as a license merely and not as an assignment, and need not be registered pursuant to section 19 of 5-6 Vict. ch. 45 (Imp.).

Black v. *Imperial Book Co.*, 417. ·

CORPORATE NAME.

See TRADE MARK, 2.

CORRESPONDENCE.

See CONTRACT, 4.

CURATOR.

See PROTEST — PROMISSORY NOTE, 6.

DAMAGE.

See RAILWAY COMPANY.

DEBTOR AND CREDITOR.

Preference—Collusion —Pressure—R.S.B.C. 1897, chs. 86 and 87—Bank Act, sec. 80—Company—Mortgage by Directors—Ratification by Shareholders—The Companies Act and Amendments.]—Where there is good consideration a mortgage comprising the whole of a debtor's property will not be set aside, even though the mortgagor is in insolvent circumstances to the knowledge of the mortgagee, and the effect of the mortgage is to defeat, delay and prejudice the creditors, if pressure is proved.

A mortgage made by the directors of a company prior to the consent of its shareholders without which consent there was no power to borrow, may be ratified by the shareholders.

Adams & Burns v. *Bank of Montreal et al.* (B.C.), 248.

See also EXECUTION — COMPANY, 6.

DECEPTION..

Proof of.]—*See* TRADE NAME, 2—TRADE MARK, 2.

DECLINATORY EXCEPTION.

See CONTRACT, 4.

DEFAULT.

Putting in.]—*See* MISE EN DEMEURE—CONTRACT, 2—SALE OF GOODS.

DESCRIPTIVE LETTERS.

See TRADE MARK, 1.

DIRECTOR.

1. *Salary of.*]—*See* COMPANY, 3.

2. *Sale by to Company.*]—*See* COMPANY, 3.

3. The president of an incorporated joint stock company bought the plant of an insolvent concern, which he shortly afterwards sold to the company of which he was president at a considerable profit. There was no evidence that the president was authorized by his own company to purchase these assets, or that he was in any way a trustee for his company of the property so bought.

Held, that though, upon these facts, the company might, perhaps, have at one time obtained a decree of rescission of the contract, yet the court had no power to compel the vendor to accept another contract whereby he would be disposing of the assets at a less price.

Burland et al. v. *Earle et al.* (P.C.), 93.

4. *Liability of.*]—*See* COMPANY, 4.

5. *Mortgage Made By.*]—A mortgage made by the directors of a company prior to the consent of its shareholders, without which consent there was no power to borrow, may be ratified by the shareholders.

Adams & Burns v. *The Bank of Montreal et al.* (B.C.). 248.

DISHONOUR.

Notice of.]—*See* PROMISSORY NOTE, 4.

ENCYCLOPAEDIA.

See COPYRIGHT.

ENDORSEMENT.

Liability for.]—*See* PROMISSORY NOTES.

EXECUTION.

Money Paid Out by Bank Teller—Passing of Property Therein.]—H., a superannuated civil service employee, handed his superannuation declaration to the teller of the bank which was authorized to pay the superannuation allowance. The teller counted the money due under the certificate, and placed the bank-notes upon the ledge in the wicket between the teller's box and the outer office where H. was standing; but before H. touched the notes they were seized by a bailiff under an execution against H., which had been placed in the hands of the sheriff.

Held, that the property in the bank-notes passed to H. as soon as they were placed on the ledge, and that, therefore, the seizure on behalf of the execution creditor was legal.

Hall v. *Hatch, Bank of Montreal* v. *Hatch,* (Ont.), 235.

EXEMPLIFICATION.

· *See* Foreign Judgment.

EXTENSION OF TIME.

See Patent, 4.

FIRE INSURANCE.

See Insurance (Fire).

FOREIGN JUDGMENT.

Exemplification — Right to Question Judgment Founded on Void Contract—Extra-territorial Contract of Company—B.N.A. Act, sections 91 and 92.]—The Province of British· Columbia has the right to incorporate a company with power to enter into extra-territorial. contracts of carriage, and it is therefore not *ultra vires* of a company which has been granted a charter by that province to contract to carry goods from British Columbia to the Yukon Territory.

In an action upon a foreign · judgment the defendant may question the validity of such judgment on the ground that it is manifestly erroneous, as for instance, being founded on a contract void from its inception. ·

Although a foreign judgment obtained by default is liable to be set aside, yet so long as it stands it is "final and conclusive" within the meaning of that expression as applied to foreign judgments, and consequently an action may be brought upon it in another jurisdiction.

Per Martin, J.:—Exemplification of judgment under the seal of the Court by which the judgment was pronounced is equivalent to the original judgment exemplified, and notice under the Evidence Act of an intention to produce it in evidence is unnecessary.

The Victoria Yukon Trading Co. v. *Boyle* (B.C.), 399.

FOREIGN REPRINTS.

See Copyright.

FORMALITIES.

Waiver of.]—*See* BANKING, 8.

FRAUD.

See TRADE MARK, 1, 2—COM-PANY. 4—TRADE NAME, 2—IN-SURANCE (Life), 5.

GAMING.

Contract—Dealing in Differences—Illegality of the Transaction.]—In an action brought by brokers against a customer to recover money alleged to have been paid to satisfy the latter's liability on an order given to the brokers to sell a number of shares of a certain stock, it appeared in evidence that no scrip of shares ever passed, and that the brokers, according to their own admissions, would have closed the transaction at any time upon the payment of the difference in the price of the stock at that time and when they were directed to sell the same.

Held, that the contract was illegal, and that the court would, therefore, leave the parties to it in the position they then were.

The British Columbia Stock Exchange, Limited, v. Irving (B.C.), 134.

GUARANTEE INSURANCE.

See INSURANCE (GUARANTEE).

HUSBAND AND WIFE.

See PROMISSORY NOTE, 4.

INFRINGEMENT.

See PATENT—TRADE MARK—TRADE NAME.

INSOLVENCY.

1. *Assignment for Benefit of Creditors—Effect of Provisions in the Deed.*]—A deed of assignment for the benefit of creditors provided that after the satisfaction of certain specified liabilities, the creditors who signed the deed within sixty days from the date thereof should be paid *pari passu*, and without any preference; and that the residue of the estate should then go towards the payment, *pari passu* and without preference, of the claims of such creditors as did not become parties to the deed within sixty days.

Held, that the creditors who executed the deed after the sixty days, but before any dividend had been paid, were entitled to rank *pari passu* with those who had executed it within that period; and that those who executed it after the payment of the first, but before the payment of the second dividend, were entitled to share equally with those who had executed before, except that they could not participate in the first dividend.

Whitmore v. *Turquand*, 3 De G. F. & J. 107; *Haliburton* v. *de Wolfe*, 1 N.S.D. 12, and *Douglas* v. *Sanson*, 1 N.B. Eq. 137, followed.

Capstick et al. v. *Hendry et al.* (N.S.), 224.

2. *Assignments and Preferences—Establishment of Claim —Inferior Court—R.S.O.* (1897) *ch.* 147, *sec.* 22 (1).]—An action for the declaration of the right of a creditor to rank against an insolvent estate, under R.S.O. (1897), ch. 147, sec. 22 (1), cannot be maintained in the Division Court.

Bergman, In re, v. *Armstrong,* 432.

3. *Assignments and preferences —Sale under prior execution— Sale under assignment—Priority—Sheriff.*

A sheriff acting under a writ of *fieri facias* seized and advertised for sale the defendant's lands, the sale to take place on the 27th of February, 1899. On the 24th February, 1899, the defendant made an assignment for the benefit of creditors under R. S.O. 1897, ch. 147. The assignee wrote to the sheriff notifying him of the assignment and asking for a memo. of costs. There was no tender of any costs nor any undertaking that the costs would be paid. The sheriff went on with the sale and the plaintiff bought the lands. Later the assignee, notwithstanding this sale, sold and conveyed to a third party.

Held, that the assignment did not stand in the way of the sheriff's right to sell under execution, that the sale by the assignee was therefore of no effect, and that the plaintiff was entitled to possession of the land.

Gillard v. *Milligan* (1897), 28 O.R. 645, followed.

Elliott v. *Hamilton,* 459.

4. *Assignments and preferences—Bill of sale—Sale by sheriff—Intent to prefer—"Proceeding" to impeach—R.S.N.S.* (1900), *ch.* 145, *sec.* 4, *sub-secs.* 1 and 2.

The defendant, a sheriff, seized and sold goods under an execution at the suit of third parties. Plaintiffs claimed the goods sold under a bill of sale from R., which had been given to plaintiffs when R. was heavily indebted to them and other creditors and unable to pay his debts in full. The seizure and sale by the sheriff took place on the 30th day of October, 1901, the bill of sale having been given on the 1st of that month.

Held, in an action for trespass and conversion, that the levy by the sheriff was an "action or proceeding" taken to set aside the transaction within the meaning of sub-section 2 of section 4 of R.S.N.S. (1900), ch. 145, and that the bill of sale must be presumed to have been made with intent to give an unjust preference, and to be such preference that as against the creditors represented by the defendant, it was utterly void.

Shediac v. *Buchanan,* 481.

INSOLVENT ESTATE.

See BANKING, 2—COMPANIES, 6.

INSURABLE INTEREST.

See INSURANCE (LIFE), 1, 2 —INSURANCE (FIRE), 1.

INSURANCE (FIRE.)

1. *Insurable Interest—Unpaid Vendor.*]—An unpaid vendor, who by agreement with his vendee has insured the property sold, may recover its full value in case of loss, though his interest may be limited, if when he effected the insurance he intended to protect the interest of the vendee as well as his own.

The fact that the vendor is not the sole owner need not be stated in the policy, nor disclosed to the insurer.

Keefer v. *Phoenix Insurance Co.* (S.C.) 1.

2. *Transfer of Rights Under Policy—Signification—Art.* 1571 *Quebec Civil Code—Interprovincial Rights of Fire Insurance Companies.*]—The stock of a commercial firm, which was insured, having been destroyed by fire, the firm transferred by private writing all its rights under the policy to a bank. The solicitors of the bank then wrote the insurance company that such transfer had been made ; and subsequently the solicitors of the bank at Montreal again notified the insurance company of this transfer by a letter, the bearer of which also handed the agent of the company a copy of such transfer, the original being open to inspection at the office of the solicitors.

Held, (Hall and Wurtele, J.J., dissenting) that this signification of the sale or transfer was not sufficient to satisfy Article 1571 of the Civil Code, and that the signification should have been made by a ministerial officer (i.e., in notarial form) in order that the insurance company might have been fully assured that it should pay to the bank the moneys due under the policy.

Held, further, (by the full Court), that a fire insurance company, incorporated by the Legislature of the Province of Quebec to carry on business therein, might effect in the Province of Quebec an insurance on goods or premises situated in another Province.

The Bank of Toronto v. *The St. Lawrence Fire Insurance Co.* (P.E.) 104.

(N.B.—The dissenting judgment is the one reported. On appeal to the Judicial Committee of the Privy Council the judgment. of the majority of the Court was reversed.)

3. *Effect of Renewal of Contract—Non-disclosure of Prior Insurance—Rights of Mortgagees.*]—The "renewal" of a contract of fire insurance is really the formation of. a new contract between the parties, and therefore, the fact that there was prior insurance not disclosed at the date of the making of the original contract, does not affect the validity of the subsequent contract (known as the "renewal"), when no such prior insurance is then in force.

A mortgagee who, by the terms of the policy, is entitled to payment according to his interest, may sue the insurers in his own name for the amount thus due him.

The Agricultural Savings & Loan Co. v. *The Liverpool, London & Globe Insurance Co.* (Ont.) 187.

4. *Agent Delegating his Authority—Lex loci and lex fori.*]—The local agent of a fire insurance company was empowered to make interim insurances by means of receipts countersigned by himself, provided that in all such cases the premiums for the insurances thus effected were paid in cash. The agent employed a canvasser, who assumed to make a contract of insurance for the company,— giving an interim receipt countersigned by himself as agent of the company, and taking in payment of the premium a promissory note payable to his own order three months from date.

Held, that the action of the person employed as canvasser did not bind the company, as he had assumed to make a contract of such a nature as the agent himself had no authority to make.

Held, further, that in any event the agent could not act through a sub-agent, the authority given to an agent of an insurance company invested with such powers as the one in question, being such as involved and implied trust and confidence in the very person so chosen as original agent.

Summers v. *The Commercial Union Insurance Co.,* 6 S.CR., 19, followed.

Held, further, that the *lex loci* of a contract must be presumed to be that of the *lex fori,* unless the former law is proved to be different.

The Canadian Life Insurance Co. v. *Robinson et al.* (S.C.) 205.

5. *Abandonment of Prior Policy—Interim Receipt—Authority of Agent—Acceptance of Note in Payment of Premium.*]—B. wrote to the agent of the defendant company, stating that he had a policy of insurance in another company which he was going to abandon and that he wished to obtain a policy from the defendant company. The agent, without B.'s knowledge, filled out the usual form of application for insurance on B.'s behalf, and for-

warded the same to his head office : in answer to the question "What other insurance have you on the property now to be insured ?" he wrote "None." The company issued a policy on this application and sent the same to the agent ; the latter, who had previously given B. an interim receipt, and who had received from B. and had credited the company with the amount due on the first premium, kept the policy, and did not notify B. of its receipt. Subsequently and before the maturity of a note which had been given in part payment of the premium, B.'s premises and property were destroyed by fire. He had not then abandoned the prior insurance. He paid the note when it fell due, put in his proof of loss, and his assignees subsequently sued the defendant company.

Held, that the interim receipt only constituted an executory contract, it being a condition thereof that the prior insurance should be abandoned.

Held, further, that the fact that B. had not paid the note given for the premium before the date of the loss would not have constituted a good defence to the action, since before that time the agent of the defendant company had negotiated the note, and had credited the company with the amount so realized and had accounted for the same. *Whitla* v. *The Royal Insurance Co.* (Man.) 271.

6. *Policy—Conditions Regarding Subsequent Insurance.*]— The plaintiff, as assignee of B., sued the defendant company on a policy issued by it to B. One of the conditions indorsed upon the policy was as follows : "The Company is not liable for loss . . . . . if any subsequent insurance is effected in any other company unless or until the Company assents hereto," etc., and the defence was based solely upon this clause. The other facts were the same as those in the preceding case of *Whitla* v. *The Royal Insurance Co.*

Held, that as B. and the Royal Insurance Co. had never entered into a contract for insurance to run concurrently with that effected by the prior contract with the present defendant, the condition above set forth had no application, and plaintiff was entitled to recover on the policy. *Whitla* v. *The Manitoba Assurance Co.* (Man.) 285.

7. *Fire Insurance Company— Agent of — Tax — Fire Companies Aid Ordinance* 1869 (*No.* 121), (B.C.) and *Fire Companies Aid Amendment Act,* 1871 (*No.* 154), (B.C.)]—In an action against defendant company under the Fire Companies' Aid Amendment Act of 1871, which applies only to city of Victoria, for taxes due by it as a company issuing policies within the city limits, it was held at the trial, that the plaintiff had failed to establish an agency.

Held, by the Full Court, dismissing plaintiff's appeal, that the action was misconceived ; that the tax sought to be recovered was not on the company directly, but in respect of a special form of agency described in the statute ; and that the evidence negatived the existence of such an agency.

Dower v. *The Union Assurance Society of London* (B.C.) 306.

8. *Construction of Policy— Warranties and Representations — Materiality — Arbitration — —Words "Value of the Property Insured" — Burden of Proof—Joint and Several Interests—Right to Recover—Conditions in Policies—R. S. N. S.* (1900,) *ch.* 147.]—One of the conditions of a fire insurance policy, issued by the defendant company, provided that, notwithstanding anything in the contract, the question of materiality, as to any representa-

tion in the application, should be a question for the Court.

Held, that the Court were precluded by this condition from holding statements contained in the application to be "warranties," in the strict sense that they must be absolutely true, or absolutely complied with.

Held, that such statements were mere representations, which if untrue, must be material order to avoid the contract.

Held, that if there was anything in the contract which placed these statements in a different category from ordinary representations it was contrary to the statutory conditions and inoperative, the 4th section of the Act, R.S.N.S. (1900) c. 147, with respect to the variation of conditions by the insurer, not having been complied with.

Held, that the intention of the statute could not be defeated by putting different stipulations, generally known as conditions in the body of the contract itself.

One of the substituted conditions provided, that. "in the event of disagreement as to the amount of the loss, the same shall be ascertained in the following manner." Then followed a provision for the appointment of arbitrators to estimate the loss, stating separately sound value, damage, etc.

Held, that the arbitrators, appointed under this provision exceeded their duty in attempting to fix the value of the property at the time the insurance was effected, the words "value of property insured," meaning the value at the time of the fire. and not the value at the time the insurance was effected.

Held, with respect to the question of value, that the onus was upon the company, relying upon overvaluation, to prove it.

One of the questions asked in connection with the application for insurance was : "5. State fully applicant's interest in the property, whether owner, trustee, etc." This was answered "Owner."

Held, that this answer was correct, the evidence showing that the plaintiffs were husband and wife, and that one part of the property insured was owned by the husband, and the remainder by the husband and wife jointly.

Held, that if particulars of title were required a different question would be required., and should have been asked.

The 11th and 12th questions were intended to elicit information as to whether the applicants had ever any property destroyed by fire, and if so, the date of the fire, and, if insured, the name of the company interested. The applicants replied in the affirmative to the first question, and, in reply to the second question, said "1892. National, and London and Lancashire."

Held, that these questions were correctly answered, the evidence showing that the applicants had a house destroyed by fire in June, 1892, and a barn in September of the same year, and that the company last named were the insurers of the house and barn, and the company first named the insurers of the furniture in the house.

Held, that the questions were not material to the risk, and that, if further information was desired, more definite enquiries should have been made.

Defendants claimed the plaintiffs, in their proofs of loss, falsely stated the value of the property insured, and that this, under the statutory conditions, was a false and fraudulent statement which vitiated the claim.

Held, that the words of the condition meant a statement false to the knowledge of the person making it, and not a statement of the value in excess of that fixed by arbitrators, this being a matter in respect to which there was room for diversity of opinion.

Held, that as soon as plaintiffs proved the policy, the fire, and the submission and award, their case was complete and the onus then rested upon defendants.

Held, that the action was one in which the plaintiffs were entitled to sue jointly and recover notwithstanding the fact that they had separate interests in the property covered by the insurance.

Harrison v. *Western Assurance Co.* 490.

INSURANCE (GUARANTEE.)

Policy of Guarantee Insurance — Condition that Insured Should Furnish Proof of Loss Satisfactory to Insurer — Expense of Insured — Employer Prosecuting Employee at Request of Insurer.]—Where a condition in a policy of guarantee insurance required the employers to give the insurers immediate notice in writing of the discovery of any fraud on the part of the employee, and the employer did immediately communicate such information to the insurers, but did not give any formal notice of same, and the insurers then took steps themselves to find out the exact facts, it was *held* that the insurers had thereby waived their right to the strict performance of this condition.

Held, further, that a condition requiring the furnishing of ·proof of loss to the satisfaction of the insurers did not compel the employers to establish to the satisfaction of the insurers themselves, their absolute liability under the policy.

Where in the application for the policy the insured had stated that the pass-books and bank-books in which the employee made entries would be. checked by the head office every month, it was *held* that the insurers had a right to rely upon such statements, and that if the course thus indicated was not in fact followed, the insurers would, on equitable grounds, thereby be discharged from liability,— apart altogether from the question whether or not the incorporation of the application in the policy effected a warranty that the employers would have such examination made.

When the informal communication of loss was made, the insurers, under a term in the policy, required the employers to prosecute the employee. The employee was convicted for various offences ; some of which were committed after the first communication by the insured to the insurers,

Held, that independently of the condition in the policy, the insurers were bound to reimburse the employers for all reasonable expenses incurred in connection with the prosecution of the employee for fraudulent acts done prior to the date when the insured first gave the insurers information of the loss.

The Globe Savings & Loan Co. v. *The Employers Liability Insurance Corporation* (Man.) 167.

INSURANCE (LIFE.)

1. *Action to Recover Premiums Paid—Insurable Interest of the Insurer in the Life of the Insured—14 Geo. III, cap. 48.*]— When an insurance is effected on the life of C. by his wife (who is named as the beneficiary), the mere fact that the premiums are subsequently paid by H. (a person not having an insurable interest in the life of C.) will not of itself render the policy void as being in contravention of 14 Geo. III, cap. 48, unless it is also proved that the real transaction was the insurance by H. of the life of C. for her own (H.'s) benefit.

Harding et al. v. *The Metropolitan Life Insurance Co.* (Ont.) 54.

2. *Lack of Insurable Interest 14 Geo. III, cap. 48—Form of Decree.*]—A policy of insurance

was issued by an insurance company upon the life of C., the premiums being paid by B., who, at the same time, bought from the same company an annuity, the entire proceeds of which were to be and were devoted to that purpose, and the whole transaction being made with the intention of benefiting B., to whom the policy was subsequently assigned by C. The latter, having died, the company brought an action for the cancellation and delivery of the policy.

Held, that the policy was void as being in contravention of 14 Geo. III. cap. 48, the defendant B. not having any insurable interest in the life of C.

Held. further, that, the trial judge having determined that the company had no knowledge of the true nature of the transactions, the latter was entitled to ask for the cancellation of the policy, but that in so seeking the intervention of the Court the company itself was bound to do equity, and should therefore return the defendant B. the balance of the total amount of all premiums paid on the policy, with interest, after having set off against this sum the costs of the action.

Brophy v. *North American Life Insurance Co.* (Ont.) 79.

On appeal to the Supreme Court of Canada, held (reversing the second finding of the above judgment,—Davies and Mills, J.J., dissenting) that a return by the company of the premiums paid would not be made a condition of the cancellation.

Brophy v. *North American Insurance Co.* (S.C.) 357.

3. *Policy—Delivery—Premium —Conditional Receipt.*]—

Held, (1.) That the mailing by a company at New York, to its Montreal superintendent, of a policy containing a condition that the company assumed no obligation until the policy was delivered and the premium paid when the proposed life was alive and in good health, did not constitute a delivery to the assured.

(2.) That although the application containing the above mentioned conditions had been signed on February 24th, 1900 ; the applicant had been medically examined on the 28th of February, 1900 ; the policy had been approved of by the defendant's chief medical examiner, at New York, on March 5th ; a policy had been prepared and signed on the 8th of March, and mailed at New York on the 9th, addressed to defendant's Montreal superintendent, where it arrived on the 10th of March, 1900, and although deceased had paid $4.00 as an advanced premium, receiving a receipt containing the condition that "no insurance is to be in force upon the application unless and until the policy be issued thereon and delivered in accordance with the terms of the application," yet as proposed life had become dangerously ill on the 8th March, 1900, and had died on the 10th of March, 1900, before the policy had arrived in Montreal ready to be delivered conditionally on his being alive and in good health, and his paying balance of premium, no obligation was incurred by the company.

Girard v. *The Metropolitan Life Insurance Co.* (P.Q.) 229.

4. *Initialling of Application—Completion of Contract—Due Dates of Premiums.*]—The mere initialling by the officers of an insurance company of an application for a policy of insurance, although it may show that the company intend to issue the policy applied for therein, does not of itself constitute any contract with the applicant. But if a policy is subsequently made out and the applicant is told that it is ready for him, there will then be an acceptance of the original application, and the policy may be antedated to correspond with the date of the application.

When there is a provision in the policy that the same shall not go into effect until the first premium is paid, and the dates upon which the premiums are payable are also set forth in the policy, the fact that the first premium is paid to and accepted by the company after the date specified in the policy will not affect the time of payment of subsequent premiums, which will fall due on the dates stated in the policy.

Per BOYD, C. :—"The receipt of the policy after the first payment, accompanied by the silence implying the satisfaction of the applicant and the consequent payment of the second premium according to the terms of the policy, is cogent and. indeed. after his death conclusive, evidence of his assent to the contract as expressed by the company in this policy."

Armstrong v. *The Provident Savings Life Assurance Society.* (Ont.) 288.

5. *Contracts Induced by False Statements—Article 1049. Civil Code of Lower Canada.*]—In an action for resiliation of two contracts made with a mutual life

insurance company, and for the recovery of the moneys paid thereunder, it was proved to the satisfaction of the Court, that the insured had entered into the contracts in question relying on the truth of certain false statements made by the company in circulars and through its agents, the same including a table of the alleged minimum and maximum rates of premiums which would ever be charged ; that such statements were false to the knowledge of the officials of the company ; that the insured paid certain premiums greater than the alleged maximum rate so long as the same were covered by bonds placed to his credit by the company as part profits,—but that, upon the rates being again raised considerably he paid one premium under written protest (so as not to be without any insurance whatever) and then brought action.

Held, that there had been no acquiesence on the part of the insured, who had acted in good faith throughout the transaction ; and that (in accordance with article 1049 of the Civil Code), he was entitled to recover all moneys paid under the contracts, with interest from the date, of payment.

Angers v. *The Mutual Reserve Fund Life Association* (P.E.) 370.

INSURANCE (MARINE.)

Policy of Re-Insurance — Meaning of "Special Charges" —Effect of Payment by First Insurer as for a Total Loss.]— Plaintiff insured a cargo, and re-insured part of the risk with defendant, the policy stating that the latter was to be liable for "special charges." The vessel carrying the cargo was wrecked, but some cattle were saved. and were taken to Halifax and elsewhere. It being found impossible to obtain another ship to take them to their destination they were finally sold, and the first insurer (the plaintiff) paid the principals who then abandoned, as for a total constructive loss. Plaintiff then claimed from the defendant its proportion of the moneys spent for salvage of the cattle, for keeping them, and for the expenses in connection with their sale.

Held, that these expenses came within the meaning of the term "special charges."

Held, further, that the so-called abandonment did not affect defendant's liability, as all the charges had then been incurred,—it being immaterial in the result whether the principals took the proceeds of the sale and were paid the balance due them by the first insurer, or whether the latter paid them in full, and then took the proceeds of the sale himself.

Western Assurance Company v. Baden Marine Insurance Co. (P.E.) 381.

INTENT TO PREFER.

See INSOLVENCY, 4.

INVENTION.

See PATENT.

LEX LOCI.

See INSURANCE (FIRE), 4—CONTRACT, 6.

LEX FORI.

See INSURANCE (FIRE), 4—CONTRACT, 6.

LICENSE.

See COPYRIGHT.

MANAGER.

Appointment of.]—*See* COMPANY, 7.

MISE EN DEMEURE.

The fact that a contract is of a commercial nature only avoids the necessity for a *mise en demeure* (i.e., the making of a demand for the fulfillment of the obligation) when the date for the doing of the act in question is stated in the contract. Moreover, since, where a *mise en demeure* is necessary, damages only run from the time that the same is given, the mere bringing of an action for damages for the non-delivery of goods some time previous thereto is not such a *mise en demeure* as will entitle the vendee to damages, as, in such a case, whatever loss there may have been has been suffered before the date of the *mise en demeure.*

Goldberg v. *The Dominion Woollen Co.* (Que.) 45.

MORTGAGES.

Rights of.]—*See* INSURANCE (FIRE), 3—COMPANIES, 6.

NON-DISCLOSURE.

Effect of.]—*See* INSURANCE (FIRE), 3.

NOTICE.

See COPYRIGHT.

OBITER DICTA.

See PATENT, 4.

PARTNERSHIP.

1. When judgment has been taken against partners in their firm name subsequent judgments may be taken against them individually on a promissory note which they gave as collateral security for the same debt.

Arnoldi v. *La Banque Provinciale.* (Ont.) 121.

· 2. *Bank—Partnership — Two Accounts — Charging Personal Account with Partnership Overdraft.*]—R. and R. had a partnership account in a certain bank, and when the firm was dissolved the ledger-keeper gave it credit for a balance, for which the partners wrote cheques. About the same time one of the partners opened a personal account at the same bank, and when it was discovered that, through an error, the partnership account had been credited with about $200 too much, the bank, after notice, charged the parnership overdraft which had resulted from this mistake to the personal account of the partner above referred to.

Held, that the bank had no legal right to so charge such overdraft.

Richards v. *The Bank of B.N. A.* (B.C.) 198.

PATENT.

1. *For a Combination—Rules of Construction—No Infringement Unless all the Elements are Used.*]—A patent is a contract between the government granting the same, or the public, and the, patentee, and must be construed like all other contracts ; but when there is any doubt as to the true meaning of the patent, which expresses the intentions of the parties to the contract, it must be interpreted against the patentee, as the latter is the stipulator.

Where a patentee, in one of his claims, describes the working of a locking and unlocking device, without any specific mention of a hinge joint (referred to in the other claims) which, in the opinion of the court, is one of the elements co-operating in that process, and contributing to the firmness of the locking, such hinge joint will be held to form part of the locking device, and to be included in the claim of the same.

The true rule, both in Canada and England, regarding the infringement of a patent for a combination is the same as that which has been firmly established in the United States, namely, that the patent is not infringed unless all the elements which go to make up the combination are used. In such cases it is impracticable to declare that there has been an infringement by the taking of the "pith and marrow," or "the substance and essence" of the patent, as it is generally impossible to arrive at the exact meaning of these terms with reference to a particular patent.

Came v. *Consolidated Car Heating Co.* (Que.), 12.

2. *Infringement of—Assignee Selling Article after Reassignment to Patentee—R.S.C. ch. 61, secs.* 28 *and* 31.]—The words "puts in practice any invention" as used in R.S.C. ch. 61, sec. 28 (which defines the acts which give a right of action for the infringement of a patent), should be construed so as to include the act of selling "the subject matter of the patent," authority to restrain which by injunction is conferred by sec. 31; and, in any event, the court has always power under such latter section to restrain the sale of a patented article by one who has no legal right to sell it.

B., having obtained a patent for a certain invention, assigned the same to W. for the term of four months, with the option of purchasing the same at the end of that period. At the expiration of the time so fixed, W. elected not to buy the patent, and reassigned the same to B.; but he continued to sell the patented articles which he had manufactured during the four months in which he had been the assignee of the patent. B. having brought action to restrain such sales, it was held that, while the making of the articles in question during the four months was a lawful act on the part of W., yet the latter, on and by the reassignment of the patent to B., had divested himself as to the future of all rights (including the right to sell the patented articles then manufactured) which he had acquired under the previous assignment, and that these rights were thereby again exclusively vested in B.

Bennett v. *Wortman*, (Ont.), 51.

3. *Of Invention—Effect of Importation and Non-manufacture—Section* 37 *of the Patent Act as Applied to a Process.*]—The patentee of any invention is only in default for the non-manufacture of his invention when there is a demand for the same which he has not met, or when any person wishing to use the

same has been unable to get it at a reasonable price.

Where the invention is a process the patentee complies with the requirements of the Patent Act if he is prepared to permit the same to be used by anyone for a reasonable compensation.

In the case of an article made according to the patent process being imported, section 37 of the Patent Act only renders the patent void as regards the interest of the person so importing the article or causing it to be imported: and importation by a licensee will not affect the interest of the owner.

Hambly v. *Albright & Wilson,* (Ex. Ct.), 347.

4. *Of Invention — Infringement — Manufacture — Expiration—Extension of Time—"Obiter Dicta"—R.S.C. 1886, ch. 61, sec. 37, sub-sec. 1, as Amended by 53 Vict. ch. 13, sec. 2.]*—A patentee's rights expire in two years from the date of the patent or at the end of any extension of time thereof, unless he has commenced and carried on, in Canada, continuously, the manufacture of the patented article so that any person desiring to use it could obtain it or cause it to be made.

A patent is not kept alive (after two years have expired) by reason of the fact that the patentee is ready either to furnish the article himself or to license the right of using it to anyone desiring to use it if he has not commenced to manufacture in Canada, *Barter* v. *Smith* ((1877), 2 Ex. C.R. 455), overruled on this point.

The power of extension given to the Commissioners of Patents can only be exercised once. It is doubtful whether this power can be exercised by an Acting Deputy-Commissioner.

Power v. *Griffin,* 463.

5. *The Patent Act (R.S.C. ch. 61, sec. 8)—55-56 Vict. ch. 24, sec. 1—Expiration of Patent—Status of a British Patent Under the Canadian Patent Act.]*—According to the proper construction of sec. 8 of ch. 61 of the R.S.C. (The Patent Act), as amended by 55-56 Vict. ch 24, sec. 1, a Canadian patent expires upon the expiration of any foreign patent granted for the same invention and in force at any time during the existence of the Canadian patent.

A British patent is a foreign patent within the meaning of the Canadian Patent Act.

Dominion, etc., Co. v. *General Engineering Co.,* 476.

PRACTICE AND PROCEDURE.

PREFERENCE.

PRESSURE.

PRINCIPAL AND SURETY.

PRIORITY.

"PROCEEDING" TO IMPEACH.

PROCESS.

PROMISSORY NOTES.

1. *Liability of Incorporated Company for Notes Made by Managing Director.*]—When the directors of an incorporated company leave the conduct of the general business in the hands of a managing director or secretary, who accepts or makes or endorses such bills or notes as he sees fit, recording such transactions in the books of the company which are examined by its auditors, it will be inferred (even when there is a by-law to the effect that promissory notes shall be signed by the president and the secretary or managing director) that such secretary or managing director was duly authorized to make promissory notes on behalf of the company; and any such notes so made and used by him in the ordinary course of business will bind the company.

The Imperial Bank v. *The Farmers Trading Co.* (Man.), 27.

2. *Material Alteration by Holder — Subsequent Cancellation Thereof—Effect on Renewal Note — Sureties.*]—When the holder of a promissory note (some of the makers of which are sureties for the others) inserts the words "jointly and severally," in order to establish a liability of that nature, such addition is a material alteration which avoids the note: And the fact that the holder subsequently strikes out the words so inserted will not render the note enforceable against the makers, even though they did not know of the

addition until after the same had been struck out.

A note given in renewal of one which has been dealt with as above mentioned cannot be enforced, since, as the original note is avoided, there is no consideration for the one given in renewal thereof.

When the holder of a promissory note is aware that some of the makers thereof are sureties for the others, his acceptance of a renewal note not signed by one of the sureties discharges the other sureties.

When judgment has been taken against partners in their firm name, subsequent judgments may be taken against them individually on a promissory note which they gave as collateral security for the same debt.

Arnoldi et al. v. *La Banque Provinciale* (Ont.), 121.

3. *Liability of Stranger Endorsing—Bills of Exchange Act, 1890 (45-46 Vict. ch. 61), sec. 56 —"Aval"—Chattel Mortgage— Consideration—R.S.O. (1897), ch. 148, secs. 2, 4, 5, 8 and 38.]—* W.M. requested G.M. to endorse his (W.M.'s) note, which G.M. did, being given as security for such endorsement a chattel mortgage on W.M.'s stock in trade. The note was signed by W.M., and was made payable to the order of the Molsons Bank; G.M. then endorsed it, and W.M. got it discounted at the Molsons Bank, at whose instance it was subsequently protested for non-payment. A few days after protest G.M. paid the amount due on the note, and took possession under his mortgage, and about two weeks later W.M. assigned for the general benefit of his creditors. Upon action being brought by the assignee to set aside the chattel mortgage as fraudulent and void, it was contended, *inter alia,* that G.M. had never incurred any liability by endorsing the note in question because it was not made payable to him but to the Molsons Bank, and was never endorsed by the payee.

Held, that G.M. was liable on the note as an endorser by virtue of the Bills of Exchange Act, 1890 (45-61 Vict. ch. 46), sec. 56.

Held, further, that the requirement of R.S.O. (1897), ch. 148. sec. 8, that a chattel mortgage shall set forth the consideration, had been sufficiently satisfied by setting out therein the note itself, and declaring that the endorsement thereof was the consideration—it not being necessary to state in the mortgage the legal effect of the facts set out.

Robinson v. *Mann* (S.C.), 128.

4. *Notice of Dishonour—Sufficiency of—Husband and Wife.*]—On the day after a promissory note fell due, notice was sent to one of the endorsers thereof in the following terms:—"Dear Sir: I beg to advise you that Mr. T. C. L.'s note for $3,500 in your favour and endorsed by yourself and wife, and held by our estate, was due yesterday. As I have not received renewal, will you kindly see that same is forwarded with cheque for discount, as there is no surplus on hand." *Held*, that this letter was a sufficient notice of dishonour both to the endorser to whom it was addressed, and also to his wife, as the evidence showed that he was her agent in the transaction.

Counsell v. *Livingston et al.* (Ont.), 244.

5. *Principal and Surety—Effect of Giving Time—King's Bench Act (Man.,* 58-59 *Vict. ch.* 6), *sec.* 39, *sub-sec.* 14.]—Defendant and G.H.C. made a promissory note for $3,500, payable to the order of D.M.B., by whom it was endorsed over to the plaintiffs, who discounted the same at their bank, and gave the proceeds to D.M.B., who used them as agreed. It had been arranged between defendant, G.H.C., and D.M.B., that each should pay one-third of the amount of the note, but this was unknown to plaintiffs until shortly before the note fell due. Defendant then paid one-third by accepting a draft for that amount drawn on him by plaintiffs, who had refused to accept his cheque for the same sum marked "in full of note $3,500." At the same time, D.M.B. gave plaintiff his note for $2,000, and money sufficient (with what defendant had paid) to retire the original note. D.M.B.'s note for $2,000 was renewed several times, and was finally paid by plaintiffs, who subsequently sued defendant for the balance due on his note for $3,-500, which they had kept. Defendant set up the defence that he was only a surety, and that he was released by the fact that the plaintiffs had given time to G.H. C. and D.M.B.

Held, that even if defendant was a surety he would only be released from liability on the note upon proving that he had been prejudiced by the giving of time, and this he had failed to do.

The prejudice required to satisfy the King's Bench Act (Man. 58-59 Vict. ch. 6), sec. 39, subsec. 14, must be such pecuniary loss or damage as is the reasonably direct and natural result of the creditor having given the extension of time. The fact that defendant, relying upon D.M.

B.'s statement that he had paid
the note paid him certain sums
of money which he might otherwise have withheld, did not bring
him within this rule.

Blackwood v. *Percival* (Man.),
332.

6. *Insolvency of Endorser—
Right of Curator to Waive Protest.*]—An endorser of a promissory note who, before the maturity of the same becomes insolvent. is nevertheless entitled to
protest as required by section 51
of the Bills of Exchange Act,
1890, and the curator to the insolvent estate has no power to
waive protest, that being a right
attaching to the insolvent personally. If, therefore, the curator undertakes to waive protest
of his own accord, the holder of
the note will lose his recourse
against the endorser.

Dunenberg et al. v. *Mendelsohn et al.* (P.E.), 353.

PROMOTING.

See COMPANY, 4.

PROOF.

See TRADE NAME, 2—TRADE
MARK, 2.

PROOF OF LOSS.

See INSURANCE (GUARANTEE).

PROPERTY.

Passing of.]—*See* EXECUTION;
BANKING, 3.

PROTEST.

*Right of Curator to Waive—
Promissory Note—Insolvency of
Endorser.*]—An endorser of a
promissory note who, before the
maturity of same becomes insolvent, is nevertheless entitled to
protest as required by section 51
of the Bills of Exchange Act,
1890, and the curator to the insolvent estate has no power to
waive protest, that being a right
attaching to the insolvent personally. If, therefore, the curator undertakes to waive protest
of his own accord, the holder of
the note will lose his recourse
against the endorser.

Dunenberg et al. v. *Mendelsohn et al.* (P.Q.), 353.

QUANTUM MERUIT.

See CONTRACT, 1.

RAILWAY COMPANY.

*Railway Company—Sparks
From Locomotive—Liability for
Damage.*]—A railway company,
authorized by statute to run locomotive engines along its line, is
not, in the absence of proof of

negligence, responsible for damage caused by sparks emitted from one of its locomotives which is properly managed and equipped, and is being used in the ordinary manner.

Judgment of the Court of Queen's Bench for Lower Canada (Appeal Side) reversed.

The C. P. R. Ry. Co. v. *Roy* (P.C.), 210.

RECEIPT.

Conditional.]—*See* INSURANCE (Life), 3.

Interim.] — *See* INSURANCE (Fire), 5.

RE-INSURANCE.

Policy of.]—*See* INSURANCE (MARINE).

SALE BY PLEDGEE.

See BANKING, 5.

SALE UNDER EXECUTION.

See INSOLVENCY, 3.

SALE OF GOODS.

1. *Commercial Contract—Implied Cancellation of First Agreement—Mise en Demeure.*] —Where a contract for the sale of goods stipulated that on one part the delivery thereof, and on the other the payment therefor, should be made at certain specified dates, and it appeared that the vendor had not been ready to deliver at the time agreed upon, that the vendee had then taken no action, but had subsequently demanded and received delivery of smaller orders, and that the vendor had treated this, in his books, as a cancellation of the original contract, it was held on the evidence (there being no allegation that the vendee had tendered, or even that he had been able to pay the amount due on the first contract at the time named) that the contract had been rescinded by the conduct and acts of the parties.

The fact that a contract is of a commercial nature only avoids the necessity for a *mise en demeure* (i.e., the making of a demand for the fulfillment of the obligation) when the date for the doing of the act in question is stated in the contract. Moreover, since, where a *mise en demeure* is necessary, damages only run from the time that the same is given, the mere bringing of an action for damages for the nondelivery of goods sometime previous thereto is not such a *mise en demeure* as will entitle the vendee to damages, as, in such a case, whatever loss there may have been has been suffered before the date of the *mise en demeure.*

Goldberg. v. *The .Dominion Woollen Co.* (Que.), 45.

2. *Contract—Sale of Goods by Sample — Warranty — Warehouse Receipts—Agency.*]—A bank advanced money upon the promissory notes of a cold storage firm, endorsed by M., one of the members of the firm, warehouse receipts for goods deposited by M. with his firm being taken as security for his endorsations. The cold storage company bought eggs with the monies so obtained, and warehoused them in the name of M., receipts being issued to him. The firm becoming financially embarrassed, the manager of the bank checked over the goods then in the warehouse, and instructed O'R., the other partner, to sell them and to pay the proceeds of such sales into the bank, which was duly done. One of the purchasers having brought an action for damages caused by breach of warranty regarding the condition of the eggs, the bank contended that it had not been the vendor. *Held,* that since the bank had, in fact, had the control over the goods, their title not being disputed, it was immaterial whether or not the warehouse receipts upon which the title was based were such as would have proved good against all comers.

Held, further, that the arrangement between the local manager of the bank and O'R. virtually constituted the latter the agent of the bank for the sale of the goods, no ratification by the head office being necessary; and that, therefore, the bank was liable for the breach of the implied warranty which, it appeared, was given by O'R., so acting as its agent.

Saunders v. *The Ontario Bank* (Ont.), 56.

SAMPLE.

Sale of Goods by.]—*See* SALE OF GOODS, 2.

SEAWORTHINESS.

Implied Warranty of.]—*See* CARRIERS—BILL OF LADING.

SHAREHOLDERS.

Satisfaction by.]—*See* COMPANY, 6.

Sanction for payments.]—*See* COMPANY, 7.

SHERIFF.

See INSOLVENCY, 3.

SPECIAL CHARGES.

See INSURANCE (MARINE).

STATUTES.

STATUS OF BRITISH PATENT.

See PATENT, 5.

SURETIES.

See PROMISSORY NOTES, 2, 5.

TIME.

Effect of Giving.]—*See* PRO-
MISSORY NOTE, 5.

TAX.

See INSURANCE (Fire), 7.

TOWING CONTRACT.

See CONTRACT.

TRADEMARK.

1. *Descriptive Letters—Registration—Secondary Meaning—Proof of Acquisition—Fraud—Deception.*]—The letters C.A.P., standing for the words "cream acid phosphates," being descriptive merely, are not the proper subject of a trademark, and registration of them as a trademark, under the Trade Mark and Design Act, will not give a right to the conclusive use of them.

Partlo v. Todd (1888), 17 S.C. R. 196, followed.

Words or letters which are primarily merely descriptive may come to have in the trade a secondary meaning signifying to persons dealing in the articles described that when branded with such words or letters the articles are of the manufacture of a particular person.

But where the plaintiffs used the letters C.A.P., standing for "cream acid phosphates," in connection with acid phosphates manufactured by them, and the defendants used the same letters, signifying "calcium acid phosphates," in connection with acid phosphates manufactured by them, and prominently stated thereon to be manufactured by them and the evidence did not show that there was on the part of the defendants any fraud, or any intention of appropriating any part of the plaintiff's trade, or that any purchaser or person invited to purchase was deceived or misled, or that the letters have come to mean in the trade, acid phosphates of the' plaintiffs manufacture:—

Held, that the plaintiffs could not complain of the use of the letters by the defendants.

Reddaway v. Banham (1896), A.C. 199, applied.

Provident Chemical Works v. *Canada Chemical Manufacturing Co.* (Ont.), 63.

N.B.—The above decision was reversed by the Court of Appeal.

2. *Infringement—Use of Corporate Name—Proof of Intent.*]—"The Boston Rubber Shoe Company" registered its name as a trade mark in Canada about a year after "The Boston Rubber Company of Montreal, Ltd.," had obtained incorporation as such. In an action brought by the former company to restrain the latter from using what was, in effect, its corporate name upon its goods (which were of the same nature as those manufactured and sold by the plaintiff company), it was *held* that

no such injunction could be granted, and that there was no infringement unless the evidence satisfied the court that such name had been chosen by the defendant company for the purpose of using it in order to obtain some advantage from the reputation which the plaintiff company's goods had acquired under a somewhat similar name, or that, subsequently, defendant company had used its corporate name fraudulently or in bad faith in connection with the sale of its goods.

The Boston Rubber Shoe Co. v. The Boston Rubber Co. of Montreal (Ex. Ct.), 217.

On appeal to the Supreme Court of Canada this judgment was reversed, it being held that the use made by defendant company of its corporate name was an infringement of plaintiff company's registered trade mark and was such as would lead purchasers of defendant's goods to believe that they were buying those made by plaintiffs, and that plaintiff company was therefore entitled to the injunction demanded.

The Boston Rubber Shoe Co. v. The Boston Rubber Co. of Montreal (S.C.), 317.

3. *Infringement of*—"*Caledonia Water*"—"*Water from New Springs at Caledonia.*"] — The plaintiffs had been for many years the owners of certain mineral springs, the waters from which had been on the market for years, and, owing entirely to the enterprise of and expenditure by the plaintiffs, had become widely used, medicianally and as a beverage. They had registered a trademark containing, among other things, the words "Caledonia Water" and "Caledonia Mineral Water." The springs were situated on lot number 20 in the first concession of the township of Caledonia, and, long ago, and before the plaintiffs acquired them, were known by the name of Caledonia Springs; about the springs a village known as "Caledonia Springs" had grown up. In 1876 the plaintiff company was incorporated, acquired the land on which the springs and a hotel known as the Caledonia Springs Hotel are situated, and has since been carrying on the hotel business and that of selling the mineral water. In 1898, L. & Co., who had acquired a property adjoining to the plaintiffs' land, discovered thereon two springs of mineral water, having medicinal qualities, and composed of many of the ingredients found in the water produced by

the plaintiffs' springs. This water L. & Co. supplied to their agents, Wilson and Tune & Co., who bottled and sold it, using bottles similar in size and shape to those used by the plaintiffs, and designating the water as "Caledonia Water," "Water from the New Springs at Caledonia."

Held, (Moss C.J.O., dissenting), that the defendants could not be enjoined from using the word "Caledonia" in designating the water used by them.

Grand Hotel Co. v. *Wilson*, 434.

TRADE NAME.

1. *Place of Manufacture—Common Law Right*.]—A manufacturer, whose goods are generally known to the public by a certain name, has a common law right, apart from the Trade Mark Act, for protection against a competitor who uses the same or some similar name in such a manner that the ordinary purchaser is liable to think that his goods are made by the manufacturer to whose goods the word or words composing the name originally applied.

This right extends to the use of the name of the place where the goods are made when the same has always been used in connection with them. The beer manufactured by the plaintiff company was always known as "Milwaukee" beer, and an injunction was therefore granted restraining the defendants from advertising their beer (which was made elsewhere) as "Milwaukee" beer.

The Pabst Brewing Co. v. *H. A. Ekers and the Canadian Breweries, Limited.* (Que.), 38.

2. But, on appeal, it was held by the Court of Review (reversing the above judgment given at the trial) that a manufacturer, whose goods are generally known to the public by a certain name, has a common law right to protection against a competitor using the same or some similar name only upon making proof either of fraud or deception as regards such use, and of prejudice resulting therefrom.

And where the alleged infringement has extended over a number of years, the fact that there is no proof of anyone having been deceived during that period is very material.

The Pabst Brewing Co. v. *H. A. Ekers and the Canadian Breweries, Limited* (Que.), 295.

TRANSFER OF RIGHTS.

Under Fire Insurance Policy—Signification of.]—See INSURANCE (Fire), 2.

VIS MAJOR.

Towing Contract—Quantum Meruit.]—When a tug contracts to tow a stranded vessel, but is prevented from actually doing so by stress of weather and by ice, nothing will be allowed for the work done in attempting to reach the vessel, when the evidence shows that by the exercise of due diligence the master of the tug might have informed himself that it would be impossible to effect a passage by the route attempted.

The Donnelly Salvage and Wrecking Co. v. *Turner* (Ont.), 32.

WAREHOUSE RECEIPTS.

1. *Contract—Sale of Goods by Sample — Warranty — Warehouse Receipts — Agency.*]—A bank advanced money upon the promissory notes of a cold storage firm, endorsed by M., one of the members of the firm, warehouse receipts for goods deposited by M. with his firm being taken as security for his endorsations. The cold storage company bought eggs with the monies so obtained, and warehoused them in the name of M., receipts being issued to him. The firm becoming financially embarrassed, the manager of the bank checked over the goods then in the warehouse, and instructed O'R., the other partner, to sell them and to pay the proceeds of such sales into the bank, which was duly done. One of the purchasers having brought an action for damages caused by breach of warranty regarding the condition of the eggs, the bank contended that it had not been the vendor.

Held, that since the bank had, in fact, had the control over the goods, their title not being disputed, it was immaterial whether or not the warehouse receipts upon which the title was based were such as would have proved good against all comers.

Held, further,. that the arrangement between the local manager of the bank and O'R. virtually constituted the latter the agent of the bank for the sale of the goods, no ratification by the head office being necessary; and that, therefore, the bank was liable for the breach of the implied warranty which, it appeared, was given by O'R., so acting as its agent.

Saunders v. *The Ontario Bank* (Ont.), 56.

2. *See* BANKING, 5.

WARRANTY.

Implied.]—*See* CONTRACT, 3—SALE OF GOODS, 2.

WARRANTIES AND REPRESENTATIONS.

See FIRE INSURANCE, 8.

WINDING-UP.

1. *Company — Petition for Winding-up Order—Service of Demand for Payment.*]—The demand for payment of a debt due, the neglect to comply with which is proof of insolvency, under R.S.C. ch. 129 (The Winding-up Act), sec. 6, is a formal demand in writing, duly served on the company. The service of a specially endorsed writ of summons does not meet these requirements, not being a demand, but only a notice that certain proceedings will be taken if the amount thereby claimed is not paid within eight days.

It is a condition essential to the making of a winding-up order that the company shall have had the four days' notice of the application given by R.S.C., ch. 129, sec. 8.

Re Abbott-Mitchell Iron & Steel Co. (Ont.), 23.

2. *Assignee Becoming Liquidator—Bond for Performance of Duties—Liability Thereunder.*]—H. was the assignee of the estate of an incorporated company under an assignment made by virtue of the Assignments and Preferences Act (Ontario). Winding-up proceedings were subsequently taken, and H. was then appointed liquidator, and the appellants in this case entered into a bond conditioned on the due performance by H. of his duties of liquidator. H. misappropriated certain monies which were in his hands as assignee at the date of the winding-up order, and which, by the terms of such order, he should have paid over to the liquidator. *Held,* that those executing the bond were liable for such monies.

Held, further, that the appellants could not now object to the jurisdiction of the court to make the various orders in the winding-up proceedings (which were recited in the bond itself), or to question the validity of the appointment of H. as liquidator.

Held, further, that the appellants were entitled to bring this appeal from the order of the Master, fixing the amount of their liability under the bond.

In re Army & Navy Clothing Co. (Ont.), 149.

WORDS AND PHRASES.

"*Caledonia Water.*"]—*See* TRADE MARK, 3.

"*Value of the Property Insured.*"]—*See* FIRE INSURANCE, 8.

Lightning Source UK Ltd.
Milton Keynes UK
26 September 2010

160371UK00004B/27/P